INLAND & MARITIME WATERWAYS & PORTS

Design - Construction - Operation

VOIES NAVIGABLES ET PORTS INTERIEURS ET MARITIMES

Conception - Construction - Exploitation

PROCEEDINGS OF THE TECHNICAL SESSIONS
COMPTE RENDU DES SESSIONS TECHNIQUES

(11 Volumes)

XXV INTERNATIONAL NAVIGATION CONGRESS

Edinburgh 10-16th May 1981

XXV CONGRES INTERNATIONAL DE NAVIGATION

Other Pergamon Titles of Interest

ANGEL	A Voyage of Discovery
COLLINS et al	Industrialised Embayments and Their Environmental Problems
GORSHKOV	World Ocean Atlas
ICID	Application of Systems Analysis to Problems of Irrigation, Drainage and Flood Control
MCCORMICK	Anchoring Systems
MCCORMICK	Port and Ocean Engineering in Arctic Conditions
RAUDKIVI	Loose Boundary Hydraulics, 2nd Edition
SCHACH	Rock Bolting
TCHERNIA	Descriptive Regional Oceanography
YALIN	Mechanics of Sediment Transport, 2nd Edition

Pergamon Related Journals *(Free specimen copy gladly sent on request)*

DEEP-SEA RESEARCH

INTERNATIONAL JOURNAL OF ENGINEERING SCIENCES

INTERNATIONAL JOURNAL OF MECHANICAL SCIENCES

INTERNATIONAL JOURNAL OF ROCK MECHANICS AND MINING SCIENCES & GEOMECHANICS ABSTRACTS

MARINE POLLUTION BULLETIN

OCEAN ENGINEERING

PROGRESS IN OCEANOGRAPHY

TRANSPORTATION RESEARCH

INLAND & MARITIME WATERWAYS & PORTS

Design – Construction – Operation

VOIES NAVIGABLES ET PORTS INTERIEURS ET MARITIMES

Conception – Construction – Exploitation

Published for the

PERMANENT INTERNATIONAL ASSOCIATION OF NAVIGATION CONGRESSES

by

PERGAMON PRESS

OXFORD · NEW YORK · TORONTO · SYDNEY · PARIS · FRANKFURT

U.K.	Pergamon Press Ltd., Headington Hill Hall, Oxford OX3 0BW, England
U.S.A.	Pergamon Press Inc., Maxwell House, Fairview Park, Elmsford, New York 10523, U.S.A.
CANADA	Pergamon Press Canada Ltd., Suite 104, 150 Consumers Rd., Willowdale, Ontario M2J 1P9, Canada
AUSTRALIA	Pergamon Press (Aust.) Pty. Ltd., P.O. Box 544, Potts Point, N.S.W. 2011, Australia
FRANCE	Pergamon Press SARL, 24 rue des Ecoles, 75240 Paris, Cedex 05, France
FEDERAL REPUBLIC OF GERMANY	Pergamon Press GmbH, 6242 Kronberg-Taunus, Hammerweg 6, Federal Republic of Germany

First edition 1982

British Library Cataloguing in Publication Data
Inland and maritime waterways and ports =
Voies navigables et ports interieurs et
maritimes.
1. Shipping - Congresses
I. Permanent International Association
of Navigation
387 HE562 80-42105

ISBN 0 08 026732 7
ISBN 0 08 026750 5 (11 vol. set)

In order to make this volume available as economically and as rapidly as possible the typescripts have been reproduced in their original form. This method unfortunately has its typographical limitations but it is hoped that they in no way distract the reader.

Printed in Great Britain by A. Wheaton & Co. Ltd., Exeter

Officials of the XXVth Congress
Personalités officielles du XXVe Congrès

PATRON

His Royal Highness Prince Philip Duke of Edinburgh
Son Altesse Royale Le Prince Philippe Duc d'Edimbourg

PRESIDENT

Sir William Harris

DEPUTY PRESIDENT / SUPPLÉANT

J H H Gillespie

HONORARY VICE PRESIDENTS OF THE CONGRESS
VICE PRESIDENTS HONORAIRES DU CONGRÈS

Rt. Hon. Michael R D Heseltine MP Secretary of State for the Environment
Rt. Hon. George Younger MP Secretary of State for Scotland
Rt. Hon. Norman Fowler MP Secretary of State for Transport
Sir Humphrey Browne, Chairman, British Transport Docks Board
P A Cox, President, Institution of Civil Engineers
Councillor John A Crichton, Convenor, Lothian Regional Council
J P Davidson, Chairman, British Ports Association
G A Hepburn, Chairman, Forth Ports Authority
Rt. Hon. Tom Morgan, Lord Provost, Edinburgh
Sir Arthur Peterson, Chairman, National Ports Council
Sir Frank Price, Chairman, British Waterways Board
A C Swire, President, General Council of British Shipping

ORGANISING COMMITTEE
COMITÉ D'ORGANISATION

Chairman / Président J H H Gillespie
Deputy Chairman / Suppléant N N B Ordman

D P Bertlin
D C Coode
Capt. A F Dickson
R P Gibbs
Mrs E S Gillespie
F Irwin Childs
D Jones
W J Leaman
N N B Ordman

Secretary General / Secretaire Général John T Williams
Assistant / Adjoint C I Gazzard
Secretary / Secrétaire Miss Yvonne Brooks
Deputy Secretary / Suppléant Mrs Barbara O'Donoghue
Conference Assistants/Receptionists – Alison Shattock
Vivien Hopkirk
Lizzie Dickins

FOREWORD

The XXVth Congress was held in Edinburgh, May 10-16, 1981, under the distinguished Patronage of His Royal Highness The Prince Philip, Duke of Edinburgh, K.G., K.T., who addressed the following message to the participants:

BUCKINGHAM PALACE

It is easy to dismiss international conferences as nothing more than social gatherings and talking shops. However I am quite convinced that they perform an extremely important function. Much information is exchanged during the formal sessions but equally, if not more important, are the opportunities for contacts and discussions between individuals concerned with similar problems and the lasting personal friendships that can develop from them.

The subject matter of the P.I.A.N.C. Congresses is inevitably technical and I suspect that in the early days it was generally believed that all problems could be solved and all progress achieved by technical means. It is true that since the last time I was Patron of the Congress in London in 1957 there have been dramatic improvements, particularly in cargo-handling techniques, but these have not been achieved without major difficulties in management and human relations. Also in the early days the primary consideration was the improvement of navigation and trade. Today many other factors such as pollution, the conservation of nature and the special problems of the less prosperous nations have to be taken into account as well.

In the 96 years of the Association this is the first Congress to be held in Scotland and I know that all delegates will receive a very warm welcome in the capital city. The ports and inland waterways of Scotland should provide a great deal of interest. Facing both the Atlantic and the North Sea, handling all sorts of trade as well as deep sea fishing, the oil industry, ship building and yachting interests, there should be something for every taste.

When it is all over I hope that all delegates will look back on the experience with pleasure and that it will help you look forward with greater confidence and determination.

1981

AVANT-PROPOS

Le 25ème Congrès a eu lieu à Edimbourg, 10-16 Mai 1981, sous le patronage distingué de son Altesse Royale Le Prince Philippe, Duc d'Edimbourg, K.G., K.T., qui a adressé le message suivant aux participants:

Ou a tendance à traiter les congrès internationaux comme n'ayant guère plus d'importance que des réunions sociales et des discussions d'affaires. Je suis cependant convaincu qu'ils jouent un rôle extrêmement important. Teut un échange d'idées se fait au cours des séances organisées mais également, voire même plus importantes, sont les occasions de contacts et de discussions entre les personnes concernées par des problèmes semblables, et les solides liens d'amitié personnelle qui peuvent s'y établir;

Les sujets traités aux Congrès de l'A.I.P.C.N. sont inévitablement techniques, et il me semble qu'à l'origine l'impression générale était que tous problèmes pouvaient se résoudre et tout progrès s'accomplir par des moyens techniques. Il est vrai que depuis le dernier Congrès de Londres tenu sous mon patronage en 1957 des progrès dramatiques se sont réalisés, en particulier dans les techniques de la manutention des cargaisons, mais ceux-ci n'ont pas été accomplis sans difficultés majeures au niveau de la direction et des rapports humains. Aussi au début la considération primordiale était l'amélioration de la navigation et du commerce. Aujourd'hui bien d'autres éléments tels que la pollution, la préservation de la nature et les problèmes speciaux des nations moins prospères doivent également être pris en considération.

Dans les 96 années de l'Association c'est le premier Congrès qui a lieu en Ecosse et je sais que tous les délégués recevront un accueil très chaleureux dans la capitale de l'Ecosse. Les ports et voies navigables de l'Ecosse devraient être d'un grand interêt. Faisant face à la fois a l'Océan Atlantique et àl a Mer du Nord, gérant toutes sortes de commerce en même temps que la pêche des grands fonds, l'industrie pétrolière, les chantiers navals et la navigation de plaisance, tout ceci devrait fournir quelque chose pour tous les goûts.

Une fois le Congrès terminé, j'espère que tous les délégués conserveront un agréable souvenir de cette rencontre et qu'elle vous aidera à affronter l'avenir avec plus de confiance et de détermination.

INTRODUCTION

This was the first time that a PIANC Congress had been held in Scotland. Previous Congresses held in the UK were: IV in Manchester 1890 (Inland Navigation only), XIII in London 1923 and XIX in London 1957.

The number of papers presented at the 25th Congress by members from 26 countries totalled 125, 60 of them for Section I, Inland Waterways and Ports and 65 for Section II, Maritime Ports and Seaways. The substance of the technical discussions of the papers is given in this volume.

The text of the lecture "Shipping and Port Futures" given by T. L. Beagley, C.B., F.C.I.T. on 15th May 1981, was published in the P.I.A.N.C. Bulletin No. 38, together with accounts of the technical commission meetings held during the 25th Congress.

Reports of the Ladies' programme and other events associated with the 25th Congress will also be published in the Bulletin.

We should like to express our gratitude to all those organisations and individuals whose support helped to ensure the success of the Edinburgh Congress.

J. T. WILLIAMS

Secretary General
25th Congress, P.I.A.N.C.

INTRODUCTION

C'était la première fois qu'un Congrès de AIPCN avait eu lieu en Ecosse. Des Congrès tenus dans le Royaume Uni étaient: IV à Manchester en 1890 (Navigation Intérieure seulement), XIII à Londres en 1923 et XIX à Londres en 1957.

Le nombre de rapports présentées au 25ème Congrès par des membres résidant dans 26 pays s'élevait jusqu'à 125 dont 60 étaient pour la Section I, Voies Navigables et Ports de Navigation Intérieure, et 65 pour la Section II, Ports et Accès Maritimes. L'essentiel des discussions techniques sur les rapports est présenté dans ce volume.

Le texte du discours "Perspectives D'avenir pour la Navigation et des Ports" par T. L. Beagley, C.B., F.C.I.T. le 15 Mai 1981 a été publié dans le Bulletin No. 38 de AIPCN avec des compte-rendus des réunions des commissions techniques qui ont eu lieu pendant le 25ème Congrès.

Des rapports sur le programme des dames et sur d'autres événements associés au 25ème Congrès seront également publiés dans le Bulletin.

Nous voudrions exprimer notre gratitude à toutes personnes et organismes dont l'appui a assuré le succès du Congrès d'Edinbourg.

J. T. WILLIAMS

Sécrétaire Général
25ème Congrès, A.I.C.P.N.

CONTENTS—TABLE DES MATIERES

INLAND WATERWAYS AND PORTS

SECTION I — SUBJECT 1

New means for the protection of banks and bottom of waterways against the attack by currents and waves, including those generated by ships

Monday 11 May 1981

Chairman:	*J CHAPON (France)* *Ingénieur Générale des Ponts et Chaussées* *Vice-Président du Conseil Générale des Ponts et Chaussées* *Ministère de l'Environnement et du Cadre de Vie, Paris*
Vice Chairman:	*Prof C E D'ALMEIDA (Brazil)* *Departamento de Hidraulica, Sao Paulo*
Reporter General:	*J THEUNS (Belgium)* *Inspector General of the Maritime Services of the River Scheldt* *Ministry of Public Works*
Secretary:	*C COCOZZA (France)* *Ingénieur des Ponts et Chaussées* *Directeur de l'Exploitation du Port Autonome de Paris*
Asst. Secretary:	*A E C HOMASSEL (France)* *Secrétaire Adjoint, Section Française*

All page numbers cited in these discussions refer to Inland Waterways and Ports, Volumes 1-5, Proceedings of the XXV Congress of the Permanent International Association of Navigation Congresses (PIANC) Edinburgh, 1981, ISBN 0 08 026753 X Pergamon Press, 1981

Speakers

M HAGER (FRG), R TENAUD (France), A J WOESTENENK (The Netherlands), C EVANS (UK), C H GAUM (USA), R AGOSTINI (Italy), D MUSKATIROVIC (Yugoslavia), Y ZECH (Belgium), P BROUNS (Belgium), J D WINDERS (UK), T SAVILLE Jr. (USA), G DELMAS (France), R DE PAEPE (Belgium), H OEBIUS (FRG), W MELLEMA (USA), G GLAZIK (GDR), J De KONING (The Netherlands), P R LISLE (UK)

JAN THEUNS (BELGIUM) REPORTER GENERAL

Nearly all the papers point to the reasons why the protection of banks and bottom of waterways has commanded increasing attention in recent decades. These reasons are: the growth in the number of self-propelled vessels, the higher-powered engines installed in the vessels, the introduction of pushed convoys and the increased speed of vessels.

It should further be noted that bank revetment represents quite a large percentage in the investment cost of a new canal and especially for the modernisation works on existing canals.

Several papers mention the fact that environment and ecology are playing an increasingly important role in projects for the defence of waterway banks.

For the above reasons, renewed attention is being devoted in all countries to bank defence projects. The ultimate aim is to arrive at a project offering adequate protection against erosion resulting from hydraulic actions, a project with the lowest possible sum of investment and maintenance costs, and a project harmonising with the environment and permitting the preservation of flora and fauna.

Some papers draw special attention to the protection of banks and bottom of a waterway at the places where manoeuvres and berthing occur. The reason for erosion in these places is the more frequent utilisation of landing-stages and the fact that ships are less and less assisted by tugs, as they have their own means of manoeuvring (bow-thrusters).

The causes of erosion of banks and bottom of waterways are well-known. The principal causes on canals are the hydraulic phenomena resulting from navigation. In the case of free-flowing and canalised rivers, there are additionally the hydraulic phenomena due to flow and more particularly to the evacuation of flood waters. For example, the rapid fall of the water level after a spate is one reason for the erosion of banks.

Defence of the banks of a waterway therefore differs as between a canal and a river. In the case of a canal, the water level generally varies little and the defence can be limited to a relatively modest height. The defence in the case of a river is much more extensive; we may distinguish a defence project at the low water level (ship wave zone) against the hydraulic effects of navigation; above that is a defence which must be stable for frequent floods (e.g. annual); and at a still higher level, the bank must be protected against the hydraulic actions of extreme floods.

Although the hydraulic phenomena due to navigation are already well-known, certain papers deal as well with some particular aspects, such as the return current, the critical speed of the vessel and the lowering of the water level.

Several papers stress the research carried out on the propeller current. The theory applied in this research work is the theory of an immersed jet. The theoretical results are checked and supplemented by field tests and scale-model tests. Some papers emphasise a special aspect of hyraulic action, i.e. the pressure variations in the banks and bottom of the canal. These variations are of a dynamic and cyclical nature.

The bank protection processes from the object of the largest number of papers. Indeed, protection of banks is most frequent on waterways, whereas bottom protection is in general met with only near the landing-stages and in the bends of a canal, or else in order to obtain a watertight basin.

The bank revetments most widely used at the present time are: rock fillings on a filter, concrete slabs, sheet piling in concrete and steel, gabions and revetments in asphalt concrete.

It emerges from the papers, however, that a simple rock filling with or without penetration (cement concrete, asphalt concrete) or incorporated in the gabions, is the most common revetment. A primary requirement for this revetment is an adequate filter. There has been an important development in the design of filters as a result of the introduction of synthetic fabrics based on artificial fibres. These filters are used in a number of countries and several authors deal with the characteristics required of synthetic fabrics.

The use of a synthetic filter combined with artificial elements (concrete blocks, rolls filled with gravel) forms a new revetment. Some authors mention the use of this revetment in their countries. Its utilisation and development will certainly continue.

Several authors recommend, for the construction of revetments, the greatest possible use of materials available on the spot or nearby and of residual products (e.g. slag, breeze, old tyres, lopped wood, concrete scrap, etc.). It may be wondered, however, whether a revetment with old tyres harmonises with the landscape.

One paper describes a revetment formed entirely by vegetation. This is a most interesting revetment from the environmental point of view.

Lastly, we should mention that one paper describes the use of submerged groynes as a means of regularising a bend in a river; another paper determines the dredging depth in cases where megaripples form in a maritime fairway.

The papers do not mention any entirely new revetments. Several countries are carrying out research with a view to obtaining less expensive revetments harmonising with the environment. However, these research efforts are mainly in the direction of improving conventional revetments.

The general conclusion is therefore that the present methods which have already won their spurs are preferable for the design of a bank defence revetment.

The use of materials available <u>in situ</u> or nearby is advisable so as to diminish the cost of construction.

The structure must be able to resist the effects of the most frequent hydrodynamic actions in order to reduce the cost of maintenance and the resulting drawbacks. Special attention should be paid to making the structure harmonise with the environment and avoiding harmful consequences for the fauna and flora.

We propose the following points for discussion:

1. the importance of the impact of a bank revetment on the environment, and the question of when and to what extent the protection design should take account of the environment.

2. For vegetation, should preference be given to monoculture or the promotion of new cultures?

3. the use of synthetic filters: characteristics, tests, etc.

4. philosophy of the project: deterministic or probabilistic: the pros and cons of the two methods.

5. the dimensions of a cross section as a function of the hydraulic data:
   - sloping section, either combined with a berm or not
   - section with vertical walls with or without submerged berm.

We propose the following conclusions:

1. Continue the theoretical research and the tests, both scale-model and <u>in situ</u>, with a view to going more deeply into the hydraulic phenomena due to navigation, both during sailing and during manoeuvring of ships. Special attention should be paid to fluctuations of water pressures in the embankments.

2. Improve the existing revetment processes with the results of the research referred to in (1)

3. It is advisable, when a new project is being examined, to obtain the co-operation of experts so as to incorporate the structure in the landscape and to conserve the ecosyster

4. Study and encourage the use of materials available <u>in situ</u> or nearby, and of residual products.

5. Continue research to determine the criteria which will make it possible to implement an economically justified project in relation to the extent of the damage caused by hydraulic actions.

I wish to thank all the authors who have submitted papers on the subject we are discussing this morning.

The majority of the papers relate strictly to the subject as formulated. There are two papers which stray a little from the subject, but which are nevertheless of great technical value. I therefore thank the authors of these two papers, i.e. Japan and Yugoslavia.

Before proceeding to the discussion, I should like to clarify some terms used in my general report.

<u>Kellner Jacks</u>:

This is a form of protection used on large rivers in the United States. A Kellner Jack is an element consisting of three rectilinear frames assembled at their central point in such a way that each frame is perpendicular to the other. The French term is: "chevaux de frise".

<u>"Bouture de bois"</u>:

The English paper refers to "timber hedge" (p. 149). In the French summary of the English paper the term "bouture de bois" is used. I think that this is the correct term, since the text refers to formation of roots. The appropriate English term is "wattle work".

Some other points call for discussion.

1. Some papers (FR Germany, Netherlands) mention pressure variations in the banks and (or) the bottom of the canal due to currents provoked by shipping. As it is a question of scale-model and on-site tests, I presume that there are no general formulae expressing these variations. I think it is necessary to continue these tests so as to find out more about these pressure variations.

2. The French paper describes an entirely vegetal revetment. How does this revetment behave in the course of time?

3. The Swedish paper gives a formula for the critical driving speed. The units are not specified. I presume that v is expressed in m/s and d in m?

4. The paper from the German Democratic Republic gives a similar formula, but taking account of the position of the rudder and the propeller (the latter may be free or fitted in a tube) and applying to the propellar current.

   Sweden: $v = 5\sqrt{d}$

   German Democratic Republic:

   $v = 3.62\sqrt{d}$ no central rudder and propeller in a tube

   $v = 5.02\sqrt{d}$ in the case of a central rudder.

5. The Soviet paper shows that "the passage of the movement of a ship towards the critical regime occurs in an interval of time or rather in an interval of speed". It would be interesting to know the physical significance.

6. In my opinion, Kellner Jacks are used solely for the protection of banks of free-flowing rivers with a great variation of the water surface. Is this indeed so?

7. The French paper recommends using, on the same canal, different types of protection so as to attenuate the impact on environment and ecology.

8. The papers from Sweden, the Federal Republic of Germany and the German Democratic Republic give an expression for the speed of the propeller jet. There are some discrepancies between the formulae, more particularly as regards the diameter used in them. Furthermore, the thrust coefficient K_T is constant according to one paper, whereas in actual fact it varies.

   I propose that the different authors form a small working party to examine this problem.

9. Is there a preference as between the gabions used in France and Italy (respectively welded lattice work and metal grid with hexagonal double-twist mesh)?

10. For the different propeller jet zones, it is recommended to use uniform terms. This could be incorporated in the working party proposed above.

11. I would ask the authors of the Soviet paper to provide us with explanations about a rock filling formed by the action of the waves.

12. The Netherlands paper suggests some simple formulae for determining cross sections. Do these formulae meet with a general consensus? In addition, there is an error in Figure 6 page 118 -H is used twice. The slope of the banks is variable from one paper to another. A good average seems to be 1/3. The important thing is never to exceed the natural angle. Furthermore, this slope depends on the revetment used. For the points to be discussed in the course of the session, I would refer you to my general report. That is, I propose that we discuss the following points:

   1) The importance of the impact of a bank revetment on the environment.

   2) Vegetation: monoculture or promotion of new crops.

   3) Synthetic filters. On this point, I should mention that in the Netherlands, for the protection of the bottom of the Eastern Scheldt, the Rijkswaterstaat required the polypropylene fabrics to have a life of 200 years. A special committee developed a new short-term testing technique so as to obtain data on the long-term behaviour of polypropylene in sea water. This led to the use of special additives. The new fabric, obtained with the additives, was tested and the result is that the 200-year guarantee demanded is possible.

   4) Probabilistic or deterministic philosophy.

   5) The dimensions of the cross section for a new canal.

DISCUSSION

M HAGER (FRG)

May I add two short notes to the German paper regarding new methods for the protection of banks and the bottom of waterways.

1. The protection of artificial canals is necessary mainly due to the influence of ships. Our experience has shown that special attention must be given to the flows of ground water and seepage especially in dams. Piping effects inside the embankments and the effects of internal erosion are well known. But not so well known are the effects on the canal bank revetment.

   We know that the power of the channel flows resulting from craft passage can alter ground conditions and cavities can arise which are dangerous to the protection works. Protection works made of asphalt can resist such effects for only a limited time. The problems are more difficult for small embankments which often exist in artificial waterways, if the bottom has nearly the same level as the ground surface in this area. In this case the seepage usually cannot be recognised in time, therefore it is necessary to broaden the embankment and to provide indicators on the outer face.

   Crossing elements should not be allowed, to avoid formation of cavities.

We must take into account the above mentioned phenomena of Soil Mechanics in considering the type of bank protection.

2. Reference is made to supplying a natural river with reclaimed material to prevent the erosion of the alluvial bottom. This method is useful if the normal sediment transport is interrupted because the upper part is canalised. The required material – dredged beside the river – will be brought into the site by dumping barges and the material distributed evenly. Experience has shown, that this method is easier than other solutions and attracts no kind of environmental problem. The gravel material can be placed during the highest water levels giving time for the natural balance to be recreated each season. In the case of the Rhine only 170000 m^3 of material is required each year which is less than any other solution. Also dredging, regulation structures, and so on – disturb the equilibrium of the river but our method supports it. The method is most appropriate in the special situation of the Rhine River. Another similar situation is on the Danube where the upper part and the part downstream of the German border is canalised.

R TENAUD (FRANCE)

As regards protection of banks by vegetation, experiments carried out on the Moselle have shown that vegetation alone, even with precultivated coverings, is very quickly destroyed in the ship wave zone corresponding to the normal water level.

Above this, the results vary with the nature of the soil of the embankment. On very gravelly zones and when no vegetable soil has been brought in, the roots do not take well. On the other hand, on more clayey soils, the result is good.

With a revetment in honeycombed concrete slabs, the vegetation develops very well in the gaps between the slabs, thus rendering the slabs almost invisible. Moreover, this revetment is very effective against ship waves.

As regards the calculation of stability of the bank defence sheet-pile curtains, we indicated in the paper that it would be advantageous to use a small computer programme to determine the pressure at each level of the curtain.

We have developed this programme and we have used it to perfect the method described in the paper.

The programme uses Coulomb's theory which is correct when the angle of friction between the earth and the curtain is zero.

At each point of the curtain where we wish to determine the pressure, the programme calculates the horizontal force on the curtain necessary to determine the equilibrium of the wedge of earth corresponding to several planes of rupture obtained by progressive variation of the angle α. The minimum value thus obtained is the pressure sought.

The same type of programme applies for the calculation of the pressure, taking the maximum instead of the minimum.

This programme makes it possible to calculate very rapidly the pressure or the thrust with any solid configuration whatever; it can take into account several (horizontal) layers of soil with different characteristics, as well as vertical forces uniformly distributed over any length and punctual forces.

By means of the results obtained with this programme, we have sought to improve the manual method of determining the pressure, when there is a slope with or without berm in front of the curtain.

We proceed in the following way with a berm.

The points A', B,C,D are determined as indicated in Figure 1.

The angle α is the angle of the plane of rupture corresponding to a slope with inclination β, and is given in the table included in the paper.

- Between A and B we take the unit pressure Ka_1 corresponding to a horizontal terrain (angle of rupture $\frac{\pi}{4} + \frac{\varphi}{2}$), and we obtain the point 1.
- We determine the unit pressure in C (point 2) by taking on the basis of A' the coefficient Ka_2 corresponding to a slope of inclination β (value given in the table in the paper).
- Between C and D, we take the unit pressure corresponding to $1/2\ (Ka_1 + Ka_2)$ and we obtain the point 3.
- Below D, we take the coefficient Ka_1.

This method is more exact than that indicated in the paper and gives results very close to those obtained by the computer programme (example in Figures 2 and 3).

It is very simple and entirely sufficient for the calculation of bank defence curtains.

A J WOESTENENK (NETHERLANDS)

I would like to mention the Suez Canal Revetments, both in the trials and the final works at Port Said Bypass. I understand that the Suez Canal Authority found that only two protection models resisted against the severe conditions:

- the trial of Bitumarin
- the trial of Maccaferri Gabions with sand mastic or artificial fabric mattresses.

This experience appears to contradict what is said in the Italian paper about other types of mattress. The paper states that in September 1979 the Suez Canal Authority, after inviting tenders selected the mastic grouted Maccaferri Reno Mattresses for berm protection for a 24 km length of the new West Bank of the Bypass Canal, and the East Bank of the Suez Canal. A peculiar detail in this respect is that the sandasphalt filter layer, which is queried in the paper as being suspect, is retained in the finally executed design.

C EVANS (UK)

I would like to describe a system of bank protection that has recently been developed and has not been decribed in the published

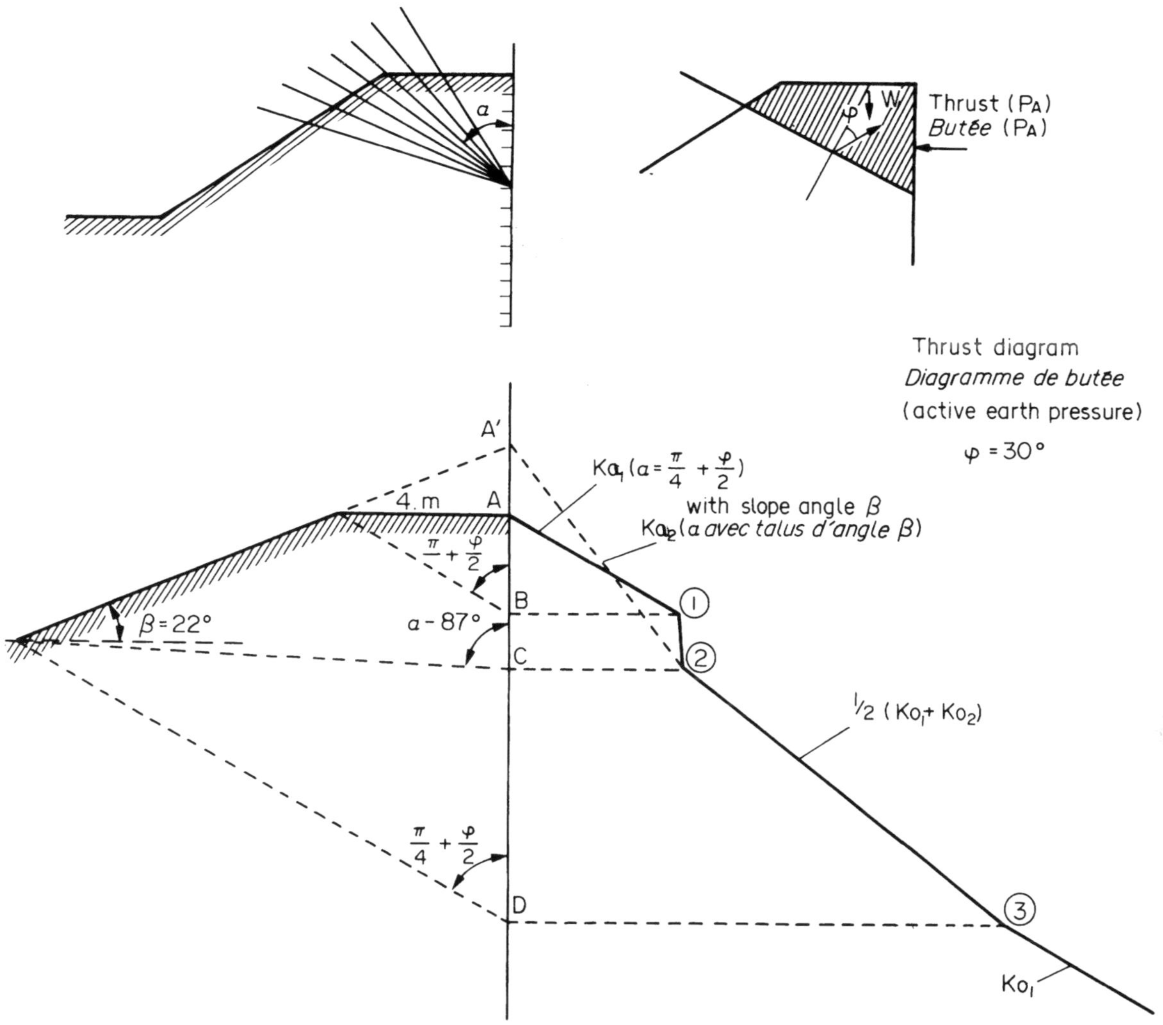

Fig. 1

papers but which is, I believe, of technical interest.

The system was initially developed as an impermeable canal lining both to prevent loss of water through seepage and also to prevent bank erosion and in this form consists of a three layered membrane — a Terram filter membrane, Butyl sheeting and Paraweb — a thermo-plastic interwoven membrane which acts as protection to the butyl sheeting. The membrane is fixed by means of plastic anchor stakes driven into the soil, the spacing and length being dependent on soil conditions.

The main advantage of the system compared to conventional methods is that it can be laid and fixed under water and does not require a canal to be dewatered.

Where seepage is not a problem the butyl layer can be omitted so that a permeable membrane is provided which prevents unequal water pressure occurring behind the membrane and it can thus cater for rapid changes in water level due to ship work and thus prevent bank erosion. If seepage and wash are both important the butyl layer can be omitted above low water level so that it is impermeable below water level and permeable in the wash zone, so that both effects are catered for.

Other advantages are that the Paraweb is ultra-violet resistant, and is very strong so that it can resist damage from rocks falling on it or from a tracked vehicle, and being flexible can accommodate small movements in the soil without affecting its efficiency. It can also be used to improve soil properties of the banks.

It has been used on the Ismaili Canal in Egypt and I am confident has a role in the future.

C H GAUM (USA)

An additional point to consider in the prevention of bank erosion is over land flow and the related changes in infiltration and ground water discharge. Prevention of a problem may be less costly than bank protection after slumping and

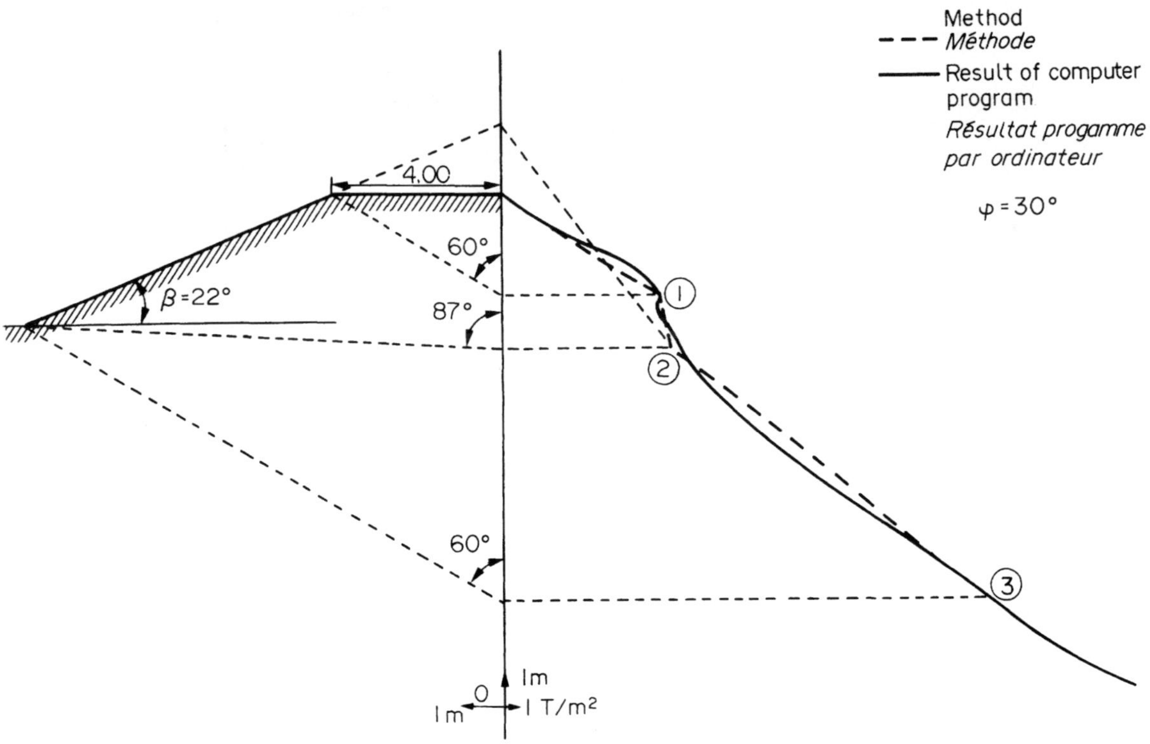
Method
Méthode
Result of computer program
Résultat progamme par ordinateur
φ = 30°
4.00
60°
β = 22°
87°
60°
1
2
3
1m
0
1m
1 T/m²

Fig. 2.

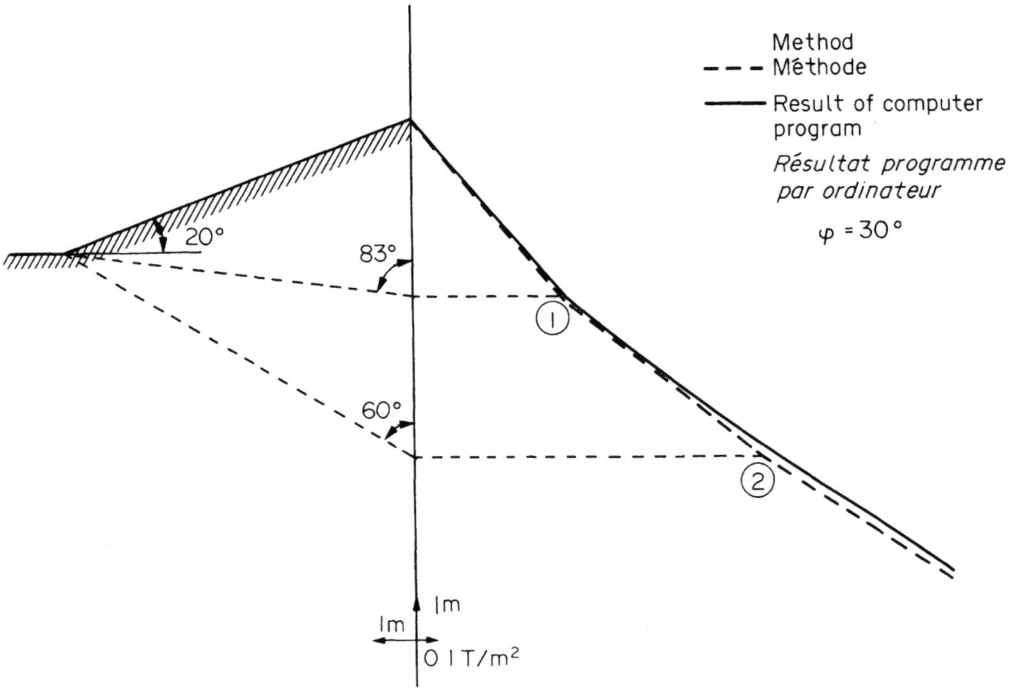
Method
Méthode
Result of computer program
Résultat programme par ordinateur
φ = 30°
20°
83°
60°
1
2
1m
1m
0 1 T/m²

Fig. 3.

associated erosion and undercutting by the stream flow. Prevention of bank failure by engineering methods maintains the natural vegetation, protects the animals and keeps sediment out of the stream, all environmentally desirable.

New highway construction, housing or industrial development changes the run-off and if not properly collected can increase the surface run-off over a bank and cause severe erosion. Increased infiltration can change the ground water level and pressure. If this is expected to cause bank slumps then underground drains should be installed to intercept the flow and keep the ground water level close to its natural conditions. Periodic inspection of the banks and the review of aerial photos can show where expected problems may occur, caused by change in run-off. Also local authorities and developers should be made aware of the drainage control problem and inform the proper authority for co-ordination of drainage designs.

In the USA the anticipated stream bank is studied during the planning stage of a waterway and the design considers bank protection where necessary. The US Army Corps of Engineers is responsible for most waterways in the United States and hence bank erosion is taken into account in design, and it is the unusual cases that need attention. Towboats operate at slow speed in the centre of the stream and in wide streams are not a major problem.

As regards fluctuating levels of the stream on bank erosion, again design of the waterway attempts to keep receding flood flows similar to natural conditions, and except in those cases where you have large multipurpose storage reservoirs, major unnatural drawdown fluctuation does not occur. There may be, in very rare instances, a case of gate failure at a lock and dam which can cause a rapid stream drawdown. Since these instances are caused by accidental ramming by a barge under unusual conditions, combined with a high flood it is not considered reasonable to provide bank protection for these isolated cases, which are very infrequent, but do happen.

R AGOSTINI (ITALY)

We agree with the conlusions of the Reporter General. As regards economic problems, it is a fact that the basic components of the final cost have greatly changed in relative weight.

The increased costs of transport, manpower and certain materials (bitumen, in particular) have determined the conditions for the development of the use of thin revetments which are possible thanks to the utilization of metal gratings. These revetments have very good technical characteristics, as confirmed by their recent use for the protection of pipelines on the bed of the Mediterranean. Moreover, they utilize materials available locally and entail very low maintenance costs.

As regards the ecological problem, it must be said that in Italy it has not been given the attention it deserves. The quality of the new canals, from the point of view of harmonization in the environment, is not good, whereas the old canals represent an enrichment of the landscape.

D MUSKATIROVIC (YUGOSLAVIA)

Hitherto, river training structures on the Yugoslav part of the Danube, have been built with so called "classical" materials: brush, brush works, brush mattress, sand, gravel, stone etc.

In the last few years, a great effort has been made in Yugoslavia to avoid hard manual labour, and to find more economical methods in the field of river training works.

Special efforts were made in construction of the most used structures in the training works on the Danube, as: spur dikes, bottom sills and training dikes.

The principal ideas were:

- Mechanisation of works
- Using of river sediment from the site
- Better qualities of river training works
- Less costs per unit length of structures

Having in mind all these principles, different solutions were examined in detail, and as a result of these wide investigations it was concluded that the plastic bags filled with river sand represent the most convenient solution. The bags are filled by hydrocyclone, in which the water is released from the mixture of sand and water. The weight of bags is approximately 5 kN. A few stretches of the Danube were regulated by using the plastic bags as elements of different types of river structures: system of spur dikes (at Backa Palanka stretch), bottom sills (downstream from the Apatin stretch) and a combination of spur dikes and bottom sills (at Dalj stretch). The experience obtained during construction of these structures, and observation of effects during and after finalising these works, confirmed the proposed solution.

The main conclusions are as follows:

The spur dikes are efficient in causing siltation over their entire length although the form of cross section is adopted by the use of sand bags. It is not necessary to revet the slopes of the spur dikes.

Revetment downstream from the spur dike was necessary. The bottom sills (5-10 m below the navigation levels) can be constructed with upstream slope 1:1.50 and downstream 1:12. The bottom sills constructed from the sand bags show impressive stability which is very important with regard to their role. The relative savings depend on structure height and compared with costs of corresponding river structures built from classical materials, vary between 15 to 65%.

The time saving is also appreciable – by using the new technique, the period of realisation of structures of sand bags is shortened by 25-30%.

Y ZECH (BELGIUM)

Several Belgian universities have undertaken a study, on reduced model and on site, of the stability of canal banks, under the coordination of a working group animated by the President of PIANC, Professor Willems.

Within this framework, and by way of comparison with subsequent tests, the University of Louvain has carried out a series of experiments on a canal bank in sand, without revetment, submitted to the sole action of a ground wave, reproducing the variation in the water level by the passage of a European-type vessel of 1 350 tons. The return current and the ship wave, which are of less importance in the bank destruction mechanism, are not reproduced. The pressures inside the bank are measured.

A 16 mm colour film has been made with shots controlled by the same computer which pilots the fluctuations of the water level, so as to obtain an image accelerated 1 200 (2 images per 100-second cycle) or 2 400 times (1 image per cycle).

The film presented contains the following parts:

1. Diagram of the installation: the ground wave causing fluctuation of the water level, which necessitates enormous variations of flow, is achieved by exchange of the quantity of movement in nozzle ejectors.

2. Fluctuation imposed on the water level: cycles of 100 seconds, with simulation of the bow wave, the depression at right angles to the ship (40 seconds) and the wake waves.

3. Accelerated views of the deterioration of the bank:

- creation of a new equilibrium slope in the soiled zone;
- creep upstream of this zone and creation of a sort of cliff;
- microchannels on the foreshore and the appearance of buckling zones at the foot of these microchannels;
- slips in the upstream cliff, continuously adding to the movement of the grains.

P BROUNS (BELGIUM)

Permeable protection systems, installed on site, using cohesive materials (see also classification in the Netherlands paper, p. 119), have been executed in Belgium in recent years.

The cohesive material utilized is a bituminous mixture consisting of a putty (20%) and crushed stone (80%).

By the actual mixing process and by the choice of grain size, a stable product is obtained which, after cooling retains about 20% of the voids, thus ensuring the permeable character of the protection. Because of this high percentage of voids it is obviously necessary to use a filter between the body of the embankment, or the banks, and the bituminous mixture.

This filter may vary depending on the nature of the materials of the banks themselves. Thus, a polypropylene fabric may be used because the bituminous protection is laid at a temperature of about 110°C, or a filter composed of a non-woven and a polypropylene fabric and a layer of asphalt sand.

Up to the present, revetments of this kind have been executed in Belgium on canal banks solely on polypropylene fabrics.

The LYS avoiding canal was given a revetment 15 cm thick. The bank was nearly 16 m wide, with a slope of 2/1 in the upper part and 2.5/1 in the lower part. The length of the bank was 1 000 m, the area to be covered — 17 000 m^2 — was executed in only 15 working days. The equipment consisted of two hydraulic cranes.

In the Zeebrugge inner harbour, a thickness of 20 cm was selected. The execution of some 25 000 m^2 is now under way.

Referring on the one hand to the different papers dealing with the problem of hydraulic pressures in the banks and on the other hand, to the summary of the Reporter General recalling the recommendations of many authors about using materials to be found locally (in this case, sand, crushed stone and a small quantity (4%) of a residual product: bitumen), it may be said that this revetment, which is open and continuous and therefore applicable in a thin layer, thereby giving an economical facing, can meet in many cases the requirements of a good revetment.

J D WINDERS (UK)

I would like to correct the impression gained by the Reporter General that in our paper consideration of the environment is not given importance. This impression has been gained from the French precis. In the full version it is clear, in the embankment situation, that in order to protect the surrounding ground the lining must be sensibly watertight to prevent structural failure and the revetment is only seen from the towpath or vessels on the canal. In the channel situation the environment is most important — the hard revetment must be restricted to the critical toe zone. The importance of the protection of the toe zone was shown in the previous film.

I agree with the Chairman and Reporter General that few new methods are described and here I think that the use of local by-products which otherwise would be waste, should be used whenever possible. Use of minimum energy concepts, not in the hydraulic sense — but real energy input. Here the use of natural vegetation is a prime example and in our paper the timber hedge, as opposed to wattle, which will provide stability through a new root system is strongly recommended where bankside maintenance is not of high importance.

T SAVILLE Jr. (USA)

The papers have dealt primarily with channels and canals in fresh water. However, in the US there are a large number of channels and canals in our bays, sounds, estuaries which are in saline water. Many of these are of shallow depth, but some, as the channel to Baltimore, a major deep water port, are of considerable depth. The Intra Coastal Waterway, for example, stretches for thousands of miles along our Atlantic and Gulf coasts. Most of these have shallow gently sloping shelves between the channels and the actual banks. They are thus different from the steeply sloped banks of most inland waterways, and vegetation can be quite effective against damage and erosion from wave wash. Vegetation can grow quite thickly, and both absorb the wave energy and promote rapid settling of such sediment particles as do get stirred up. The grasses do have to be planted, but can become quite thick in one to two years. They are particularly effective in areas where marsh grasses exist naturally. There are definite environmental advantages. The natural habitat is preserved or even enhanced; ecological balance is maintained, and aesthetics are preserved. In some cases vegetative protection provides new and additional habitat for both water and bird life.

Research is underway on types of grasses, use of fertilisers, times and methods of planting; also in different environmental conditions (water and air temperature, salinity, soils etc.).

In summer, while vegetation may be difficult to use as a protective device on the steep banks associated with most inland waterways, it can be, and has been, exceedingly effective along our channels and waterways in saline water where the side shelves and banks are gently sloping.

G DELMAS (FRANCE)

I should like to comment on the German paper as regards the dumping of gravel to combat the erosion of the bed of the Rhine.

Reading this paper might lead one to think that the canalization of the Rhine was solely responsible for the erosion of the riverbed downstream from Iffezheim.

In fact, the erosion is a very long-standing phenomenon which developed on the Rhine with the natural current long before any canalization, owing to the fact that the river's longitudinal section did not correspond to a section in equilibrium.

This phenomenon was considerably accentuated by the rectification of the riverbed between Bale and Mannheim from 1840 to 1860: by concentrating the flow of the Rhine's mean waters in a single bed, whereas previously they spread among several arms, the rectification of the Rhine has shortened the river's main course, thus increasing the slope and the current; erosion then attained substantial proportions and the lowering of the water level reached 7.00 m at Chalempe, 30 km downstream from Bale and led to the fall of the level of the ground water in the whole of this area.

Canalization put an end to this phenomenon in the canalized sector, but carried the erosion downstream from the last fall, which is at present the Iffezheim fall.

Consequently, the Federal Republic of Germany and France had, by the terms of a Convention signed in 1975, decided on the joint construction of a new fall downstream from Iffezheim. Since then, however, the Federal Republic of Germany has sought, by experimenting with the process of dumping gravel, a solution making it possible to avoid the construction of this fall.

Unlike this fall, however, the gravel dumping process does not settle the other problems arising on the Franco-German sector of the Rhine: improvement of the navigation conditions; and the absolute necessity for restoring the flood protection level to at least the equivalent of that existing before canalization upstream.

Foregoing comments, of course, in no way detract from the great interest of the gravel dumping process when the only problem to be coped with, on a river like the Rhine, is that of erosion.

The gravel to be dumped in the Rhine has to be extracted from the zones along the banks of the Rhine in the flood area, zones which are essentially covered by a Rhine forest of very great interest from the ecological point of view. It is precisely the anxiety to preserve this forest which was one of the reasons that led the Federal Republic of Germany to seek a solution making it possible to avoid the fall and its substantial encroachments.

But what is the average surface that has to be cleared of trees each year to extract the gravel to be dumped in the Rhine, without limitation in time? In the long run, does this not involve the risk of excessive encroachments on this forest which it was precisely the aim to preserve?

R DE PAEPE (BELGIUM)

In reply to the specific question by the Reporter General as to when and to what extent the project for the protection of banks should take account of the environment, I should like to say: always!

Furthermore, the ecological study which should lead to protection of the environment should meet the following conditions:-

1. It should relate to all aspects of the environment, i.e. problems concerning fauna and flora as well as problems of pollution, integration in the environment, etc.

2. It should be made not only by experts but more precisely by ecologists.

H OEBIUS (FRG)

I feel that one of the authors should answer the Reporter General's questions regarding the propeller jet reaction on the channel bottom. The differences in the given formulae reflect the complexity of the propeller jet problem.

The paper of the FRG for example gives the basic hydrodynamic conditions in a free running locally fixed screw propeller, working in a continuum, i.e. without influence from the ship itself, the water surface or restriction in the water body. The contributions of the GDR, Sweden and Russia, however, more or less neglect the local velocity distribution in a propeller jet by calculating a mean velocity from the total thrust of the propulsion device. This enables a relatively easy approach to the effects of the influence on a propeller jet like the shape of the stern of the ship, the flow, the rudder, the water surface, side walls and the bottom of the water, and there should not be great differences in the results gained under similar conditions as is stated by the development of a critical bottom velocity for ships with centrally installed rudders, mentioned in the report of the GDR and Sweden.

The sum total of influencing parameters is not quite known yet and not even their grade of effect, but the number mentioned above already demonstrate the complexity of the problem which is to be faced. Dealing with erosions caused by propellers this means that not only even slight changes in the set-up of any scaled model may cause remarkable differences in the results, but also that the erosion problem caused by ships, sailing at manoeuvring speed (propeller jet influences) or normal speed (displacement current influence) is not yet well understood.

For the future work I would recommend firstly moves to define the grade of effects of those different influence parameters hydrodynamically based upon the velocity distribution in a propeller jet and to determine a critical bottom speed, valid universally, and able to be correlated to the various well known sediment transportation or shear stress formulae.

W MELLEMA (USA)

The US paper introduces a programme recently started in our country which offers us a means to evaluate and compare the effectiveness of various means and methods of bank protection. Since writing the paper and the beginning of the programme, a total of nearly 80 streambank and river control demonstration projects have been built throughout the United States, reflecting a large variety of streams and causes of erosion. All of these projects are being closely monitored to determine their advantages and disadvantages. In addition, nearly 40 previously existing projects have been selected to be evaluated and reported upon, and model tests have also been conducted.

One of the underlying goals of the programme is to attempt to develop low-cost environmentally acceptable methods to control erosion on our nation's waterways. The programme offers a unique opportunity to compare both traditional methods and new methods. Most of the projects have now been built, are being evaluated, and the results I am sure, will be reported upon in future sessions.

M HAGER (FRG)

I refer to the interesting contribution by Mr. Delmas. It is also necessary to take into account the demands of the shipping and flood protection. It is necessary to balance all the elements in the plan. The environmental aspects are some of the most important points in this plan. We only need in one hundred years an area of 1 km^2 for the extraction of gravels, that is less than 1.5% of the gravels dredged for commercial purposes. For our barrage we would require only about 3 km^2. Another calculation is that we would need for the dams about 14M. m^3 of material but with these erosion would begin downstream.

G GLAZIK (GDR)

I will try to clarify with some additional remarks, the questions by the Reporter General concerning the propeller jet, especially the formulae for the critical bottom velocity in the case of erosion and the comparison of these formula given in the reports from Sweden and the German Democratic Republic.

The work described was done in the Department of our Institute (FAS) headed by myself. I will not go into the details of the complex velocity field of the propeller jet. They are indicated in the paper. Because none of the authors of the paper from the GDR is present, I will give some explanatory remarks.

In equation (16) of our Paper the value of the factor "B" is eminent. This value was interpreted as a result of experimental investigations. Among others it depends on the Reynolds number. This is a case similar to Fig. 19 for wave attack. There we extrapolated the coefficient for greater Reynolds numbers from the results of model tests with smaller grain diameters. Actually we prepare tests in situ to prove these results. Compared with other published data the values of B given in our paper on p. 39 seem correct. In this context the agreement with the expression in the Swedish Paper is not surprising. The Swedish authors refer also to research results of our Institute previously published by Romisch. As already stated by the Reporter General and in the discussion the details of the velocity field of the propeller jet are dependent on the form and position of propeller and rudder. These influences are reflected in the value of the factor B as mentioned above. The differences of the values for different types of ships as for instances given on page 39 of our paper, emphasises the important effect of these influences.

Finally, I want to thank the Reporter General for his report and especially for his remarks which emphasise the importance of understanding hydraulic phenomena in designing waterways. On principle we agree with his general conclusions. In the introductory remarks it is recalled that this subject has already been dealt with at several preceding congresses. This fact I think, emphasises its importance. I am glad that our work in this field interested experts in several countries. We think that the determination of relevant hydraulic criteria is very important for developing construction methods and, as stated in the conclusions of the general report, and by the Section Chairman, therefore adequate research must continue. PIANC activities have already promoted such work and the interchange of worldwide experience.

J de KONING (THE NETHERLANDS)

I refer to the contribution of the USA, page 158 Figure 4 and page 161 photo 1. Additionally I would like to mention the film shown by M. Zech. Both relate to bank erosion phenomena of rivers and canal banks. The formation and the shape of the erosion cavities have a strong resemblance with erosion craters formed while dredging with sand winning suction dredgers with plan suction pipes in sand pits. My proposal is that the engineers and scientists studying these phenomena co-operate and exchange experience with engineers and scientists from the dredging world. The same physical phenomena could occur in both cases.

P R LISLE (UK)

Many of the Papers submitted recognise that bank protection is an expensive element in waterways structural work whether in new canal construction or in improving existing waterways. Cost is an important factor which needs careful attention. Much of the original bank protection may still exist but may require strengthening or modification to meet new conditions. These changes can include instances where the frequency of use has increased and an increase also taken place in the size of ships, tugs, push-tows and other craft using it so that the erosion effect will have increased correspondingly. As a result the channel section may be inadequate for to-day's needs and the bank protection insufficient for the erosion effects now being experienced. We need to re-establish the right conditions for the avoidance of erosion by achieving a blockage factor which reduces the need for bank protection and its cost. A ratio of immersed area of ship to channel cross-section of at least 1:5 will assist. Thus if less than this ratio applies one solution is to withdraw or dismantle the existing bank protection on one side, widen the channel to the extent needed and either re-use the existing material or construct a new revetment. At least this has the advantage that the cost of new material can be eliminated or reduced in finding a satisfactory solution. This method is being used successfully on canals in the United Kingdom especially the Aire and Calder Navigation and Sheffield and South Yorkshire Navigation which connect with the Humber estuary. It depends on having available or being able to acquire the land needed. This is often easily arranged in rural areas but less simple in urban areas. However if land can be bought for channel widening, it will often provide an economic solution compared with the cost of new bank protection. Careful planning can provide valuable cost savings.

A further point relates to the environmental impact of bank protection work. There is a growing awareness and insistence on the part of the public that engineering work of all kinds shall blend in with the environment in an acceptable form and that the benefit of public works shall be available to them in a pleasing manner. Construction of new waterways and the modification of older waterways are major works which have an obvious effect on the environment. Advice is needed on visual treatment and on such points as how wildlife can gain access from water to land and the probable effect of extensive unrelieved bank protection on the vegetation and habitat needed for fish life. The effects will be obvious for many generations to come and we shall be blessed or otherwise according to what we have achieved or failed to achieve in this field.

J THEUNS (BELGIUM) REPORTER GENERAL

I am grateful to all the speakers who contributed to the discussion of this Subject. Once again I notice that bank protection is a problem which preoccupies a considerable number of countries. Furthermore, as already mentioned in the papers, the discussion clearly stresses that the impact of a bank protection on the environment plays an important role in the projects for new protections.

The speakers' remarks also gave the proof that research should be pursued, e.g. for the calculation of the propeller backwash.

The use of materials available on the spot or in the vicinity and of residual products must be encouraged.

Another thing made clear by the discussions is that for bank protection it is preferable to resort to a supple revetment able to adapt itself to the bank's deformations.

I believe that the conclusions I proposed in my General Report remain valid as the outcome of this session and I would suggest they be retained with maybe a few changes to the wording.

CONCLUSIONS

1. Artificial and natural waterways are an essential element in the present environment. It follows that any important new works or modification to existing works, must be the object of an environmental impact study. This study must take into account all aspects of the effect of the proposed works on both the human and natural environment; included in this study must be ecological and hydrological effects and possible further nuisances. It is recommended that this study should be carried out with the help of experts in every pertinent discipline.

2. Capital and maintenance costs of a waterway are greatly affected by the proportion of revetment works. It is therefore advisable to limit the works both in plan and cross section to those reaches which are most likely to suffer damage, e.g. the outside of bends, areas where ships manoeuvre and where current or wave attack are most severe.

   It is recommended that, so as to develop the most cost effective systems, locally occurring or waste material should be used where possible. In addition, the planting of suitable vegetation may further reduce costs and provide an environmentally acceptable solution.

3. Particular importance must be given to the effects of fluctuating water pressures, e.g. the free water surface in the waterway due to navigational processes or changes in discharge and in the water table elevation in the particular soil type adjacent to the waterway, on the stability of the banks and bed of that waterway.

   Where leakage to or from a waterway is not a hydraulic constraint it is essential to consider protection systems which include an efficient filter. This filter must allow the passage of clear water and prevent the loss of material from the bed and banks due to internal erosion.

4. It is recommended that the design of new revetment systems, including the so called rigid systems, shall include sufficient flexibility so as to allow for predicted long term movements in the surrounding soils.

5. It is suggested to PIANC that the Permanent Technical Committee I should carry out a study into whether significant savings in the overall cost of bank protection works

can be made by applying probabilistic methods in the design state.

This involves the acceptance of a calculated risk of damage to certain elements of the revetment system.

INLAND WATERWAYS AND PORTS

SECTION I — SUBJECT 2

Methods of increasing the capacity and safety of waterways by: improved operation; the use of icebreakers, etc.; navigation by night

Wednesday 13 May 1981

Chairman:	*J CHAPON (France)* *Ingénieur Générale des Ponts et Chaussées* *Vice-Président du Conseil Générale des Ponts et Chaussées* *Ministère de l'Environnement et du Cadre de Vie, Paris*
Vice Chairman:	*Prof V DEGTIAREV (USSR)* *Rector, Novosibirsk Institute of Water Transport Engineers*
Reporter General:	*Capt W R RIEDEL (USA)* *Chief, Ports and Waterways Planning Staff* *U.S. Coast Guard H/Q, Washington*
Secretary:	*C COCOZZA (France)* *Ingénieur des Ponts et Chaussées* *Directeur de l'Exploitation du Port Autonome de Paris*
Asst. Secretary:	*A E C HOMASSEL (France)* *Secrétaire Adjoint, Section Française*

Speakers

C H GAUM (USA), R H Le ASHBURNER (UK), A B HOCHSTEIN (USA), E J VAN DE KAA (The Netherlands), J D METTAM (UK), F DROUIN (France), J MARCHAL (Belgium), J AUBERT (France), A A RUDIN (Sweden), L MOINEAU (France), K K GOGOI (India), I M WALKER (UK), A J M HARRISON (UK), W F BLAIR (Canada), J DUBOIS (Central Commission for the Navigation of the Rhine), R H SMITH (Canada), G CERUTTI (Italy)

CAPT. W. R. RIEDEL (USA) REPORTER GENERAL

A total of fourteen papers were presented on this general subject. Although four of these papers used deep draft navigation to illustrate the identified issues, the discussions presented are relevant to the inland navigation section. The other ten papers presented discussions directly applicable to both general and specific problem areas found in inland navigation.

Authors in each of the papers identify certain problems relating to the general topic and, by use of specific examples within their own countries, indicate how they have approached the problems. Nearly all of the papers illustrate one or more of the following measures to generally improve navigation:

- systems approach
- traffic management
- full scale trials
- model basin and hydraulic modelling
- ship simulation
- improving aids to navigation
- tug and "shunter" assistance
- night navigation
- icebreaking and ice management.

Both model basin and mathematical simulation using computers have played an important part in the results.

1. Clearly the major conclusion to be derived from the series of papers on this topic is that the use of waterways for cargo movement is increasing in every country.

2. In a similar manner, both through modest means and dramatically, the capacity of our waterways is being increased.

3. Continual research in all sectors of the waterway systems is required to keep pace with the increasing demand. Improvements must meet the "eeesp" test — "be economical, be environmentally sound, be energy efficient, be safe, and be politically acceptable".

DISCUSSION

C H GAUM (USA)

The Reporter General had mentioned the importance of human factors in considering the subject. However in improving the capacity and continued safety on inland waterways only limited attention has been given to the human factors in tow operations. To illustrate this the captain of a large tow (365 metres long x 33 metres wide) operating in the Ohio River had said that equipment continues to improve and become more complicated and that this resulted in the need for specialised training. A further point was that as the older and more experienced captains retire insufficient young people are coming forward to take over because they are not willing to stay on the water for long periods away from families and friends. The knowledge of the older captains had been gained over many years during the period that the waterway itself and its equipment had evolved to their present state of efficiency. New captains however were faced with all the problems far more quickly and training programmes are needed to help them to learn about the hazards more quickly and develop a proper response to them.

Structural measures are still needed to increase capacity and safety but the replacement of locks and dams is expensive, often costing hundreds of millions of U.S. dollars. Although the lockage time of a tow is fixed, the approach time may be up to one hour or more for large tows and this engages the lock for this period. A reduction of this operating time in a safe manner would allow more lockages per day to take place. For this purpose training of new captains by the use of real time visual simulators, which show the relevant lock approach conditions, can be helpful. Ways must be found to train operators more quickly. The simulators can reflect fog, rain, night, currents and wind effects in the visual computer, so giving the pilot a real time relationship to his operation of rudder and engines. Obviously a life-time of experience cannot quickly be replaced but at least the new pilot can gain some advance idea of action necessary during the high hazard periods. Although these are rare events, the pilot will, through training, at least have a head start when the critical event confronts him. In the meantime the training can speed up lockages during normal river conditions. Accidents usually occur in fog, ice, flood or other adverse conditions. Even one accident is one too many and should be avoided since it is costly, closes the waterway and can result in serious environmental harm. To summarise, the human factor is increasing in importance as vessels and waterways become more complex and it deserves greater attention than it usually receives.

R H Le ASHBURNER (UK)

Comments made related to points arising on the Egyptian paper and the Japanese paper and also drew attention to the present position on the Suez Canal.

Referring first to the Egyptian paper, following enlargement of the cross-section and opening in December 1980 the channel can accommodate vessels up to 16.2 m (53 ft.) draught and 150,000 DWT and 350,000 DWT in ballast. This sectional area (Fig. 1) is twelve times the original and twice the previous cross-section in 1966. The last increase was substantial and the Suez Canal Authority wisely increased the permissible draught in stages. The fist stage allows 12.5 m (41 ft.) against the former 11.6 m (38 ft). At present the demand by large vessels is not great because of the depressed market. This is helpful in enabling the Authority to gain experience and to gather equipment and trained men gradually and at a steady pace.

At present ships over 100,000 DWT are escorted by tugs to assist in an emergency with lines or bridles by countering the tendency of the ship to shear off the axis of the canal. The Canal Authority is understandably proceeding cautiously in introducing VLCC's.

Important points arise on the function of the tug. Thus if the ship alone used continuous astern power it would soon take a shear and run aground. The function of the tug is to counteract this tendency and to pull or push sideways to maintain the course. In reasonable weather the ship could stop alone with use of astern power only and bursts of ahead to correct the alignment, but the stopping distance would be much extended. Tugs generally contributed about 25% of the total power used during stopping, though only a small proportion of this would have been applied in the ship's astern direction.

Fig. 2 shows a ship in difficulty and illustrating the need for the second ship to stay short of the point of difficulty. The stopping distance had been estimated using results of work on a ship simulator, but increased by a factor of 1.8 to allow for a real situation. Only the ship immediately behind a disaster has to stop in the minimum distance. Others have twice the space. The separation intervals are being constantly studied and will be adjusted as experience is gained. It will be interesting to observe future developments.

Referring next to the Japanese paper, this was an interesting contribution on a subject of great importance in making the best possible use of a restricted waterway. In particular

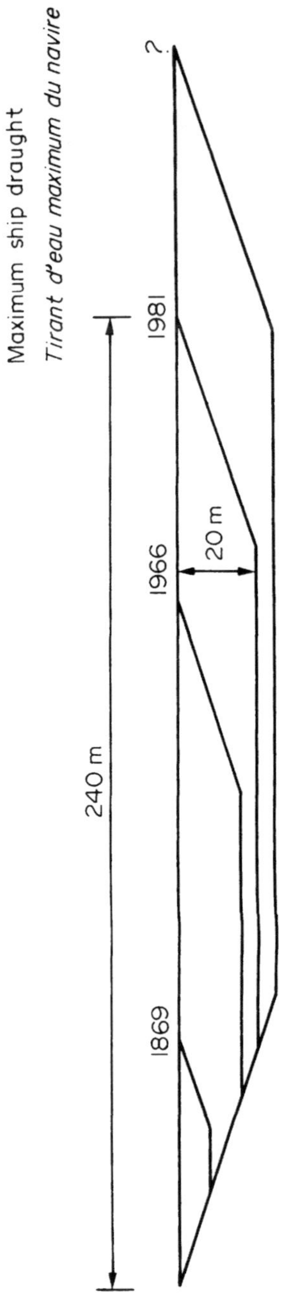

Fig. 1: Development of the Suez Canal
Développement du Canal de Suez

mention is made of a possible extension of the operational cycle time of the Suez Canal. As part of a feasibility study for the development of of the Suez Canal, carried out in 1976 by Maunsell Consultants Ltd., much attention was given to capacity, both from a theoretical standpoint and by use of mathematical simulation. Considerable work has been done by Dr. Griffiths of the University of Wales. Fig. 3 illustrates the result of theoretical analysis and demonstrated the effect on capacity, of cycle time based on 1, 2 or 3 convoy operation. Permanently increased or variable cycle times have

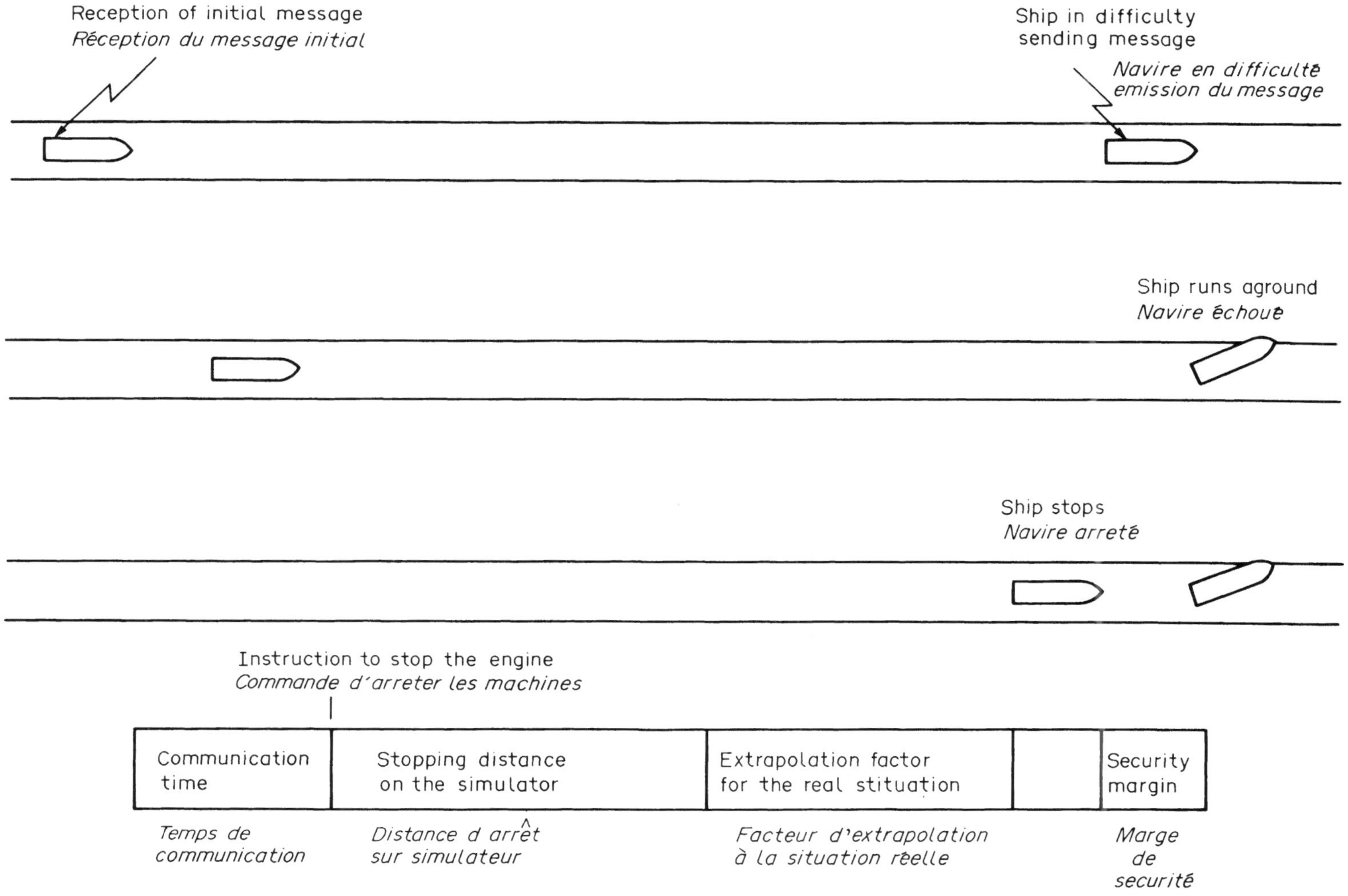
Reception of initial message
Réception du message initial
Ship in difficulty sending message
Navire en difficulté emission du message
Ship runs aground
Navire échoué
Ship stops
Navire arreté
Instruction to stop the engine
Commande d'arreter les machines
Communication time
Stopping distance on the simulator
Extrapolation factor for the real stituation
Security margin
Temps de communication
Distance d arrêt sur simulateur
Facteur d'extrapolation à la situation réelle
Marge de securité

Fig. 2

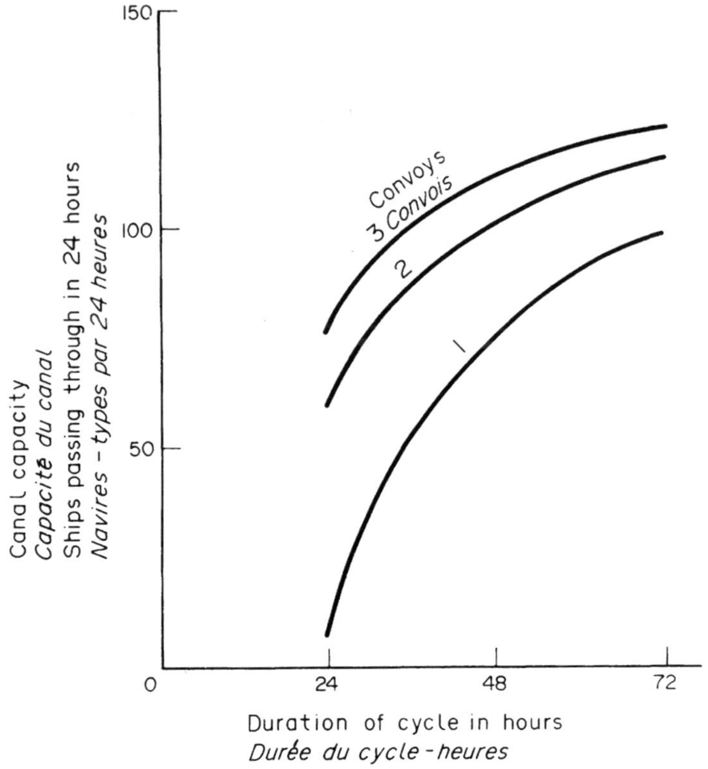

Fig. 3: Suez Canal - Capacity variation in relation to the duration of the cycle

Canal de Suez - Variation de la capacitié en raison de la durée du cycle

disadvantages but they are useful as a temporary measure at times of heavy demand or to clear ships following interruption by bad weather or from other cause. Further by-passes can be built as demand increases but as the maximum capacity is approached it will be necessary to duplicate the channel to continue the present level of service. A master plan could be formulated so that all interim development would then be consistent with the plan, and represent a logical progression towards its achievement.

A B HOCHSTEIN (USA)

The subject is a broad one, covering canals, rivers and locks. The term capacity, however, has different and sometimes not even comparable meanings, depending on the type of operation concerned, and there is a need to define these differences. Thus locks present a physical restraint to increasing capacity which can usually be measured in tonnage throughput. In contrast, the capacity on canalised or free-flowing rivers is almost limitless. Even on rivers with numerous one-way reaches the capacity usually exceeds that of the locks and in the United States it is generally much higher than foreseeable traffic density. These factors obviously affect the economic position on particular waterways.

Channel capacity or capability should not therefore be measured in tonnage throughput. It is the channel navigation conditions which are the main factors, i.e. the vessel size possible and the travel time, which eventually determine the waterway transportation cost.

In a canal certain engineering standards apply and capability is a function of depth, width and cross-sectional area. In natural or canalised rivers, restricted reaches are always followed by wider segments and there are no abrupt cut-off points of channel dimensions which preclude use of a waterway by vessels of a certain size. Instead the maximum size of vessel for a given waterway is determined by an operational decision which balances the economies of large vessels against the increased travel time, delays, risk and crew stress associated with navigation in a more restricted waterway. There is at present a need for a more sophisticated analysis to evaluate and optimise the vessel size on a river system, taking into account not only the engineering standards but also the other factors mentioned.

A study had recently been completed of the non-structural and minor structural measures needed to increase the capacity of the locks in the Upper Mississippi River system. It was found that up to 30% additional capacity can be achieved by measures such as lockage scheduling, extension of guide walls, employing 'helper' boats, improving design deficiencies, re-alignment of approaches, introducing de-icing and trash cleansing devices. A new measure consisted of a self-propelled unit installed on rails along the lock chamber and guide walls which pulls unpowered strings of barges into and out of the lock. The increase in capacity can be very significant but further tests and experience of the design and performance of the equipment is needed.

Hitherto there has been a trend towards increasing the power of tow-boats. Indications are that this trend is over, due, among other factors, to the rising cost of fuel. To offset this the use of bow-thrusters is increasing, though their use on the U.S. waterways is still experimental and designs are still being developed. If successful however these designs can serve a double purpose of assisting tow movement in the restricted reaches and also during lockage operations. They could have an important influence on the size of vessels accommodated by a given channel and on the capacity of locks as a factor in waterway capacity.

E J VAN DE KAA (THE NETHERLANDS)

In investigating safety standards the analysis of accidents is important to enable the main risk factors to be determined. An understanding of these factors is necessary to decide the most effective measures to improve the capacity and safety of waterways. For example many accidents are caused by human factors, namely errors of judgement and misunderstandings. Such accidents mainly occur at places where shipping lanes are crossing and at anchorages and mooring areas. A system of traffic regulation may be effective in reducing accidents.

Analysis of accidents in Holland showed that human factors contribute to 50% of all accidents. Technical failures increased from 10% in 1966 to 20% in 1977, but in the same period a reduction took place in the percentage attributable to human failures. Standards of visibility were a factor in 15% of accidents.

In the Papers and General Report on the subject more attention seems to have been paid to increasing the capacity of waterways than to increasing their safety. The emphasis is on allowing the passage of larger ships. This causes a decrease in safety and this effect has to be countered by improving the steering qualities of the ships, systems of traffic regulation and improved navigational aids. At low traffic densities one-way traffic with convoys of ships may be effective, without increase in risk. Deepening of an old canal in the eastern part of the Netherlands on the canal axis proved to be very advantageous compared with two-way traffic, whether with or without deepening of the channel. This was largely because in the one-way traffic solution, reconstruction or modification of bank protection was not necessary.

More and more dangerous goods are being carried on the waterways of Western Europe. This trend gives rise to greater risks for the densely populated areas alongside the waterways, but again the provision of better navigational aids assists. There is a need to avoid excessive risk and to decide what is an acceptable level.

In order to recognise the situation the conclusions should include a recommendation that particular attention should be paid to assessing internationally acceptable criteria for appropriate safety levels for inland waterways.

J D METTAM (UK)

In the United Kingdom paper, when referring to improvements to locking systems, the advantages of 'Delta' sector gates for speeding up locking operations, and possibly also for the automatic operation of unmanned locks, were mentioned. It should be stressed that from the safety standpoint the forces acting on these gates while closing with a flow of water through the lock tends always to assist closure. It is further suggested that where the risk of vandalism or possible electrical failure exists safety can be ensured by adding an independent hydraulic/mechanical system to initiate closure. This closure would be initiated by the head of water caused by the water flow arising from leaving both gates open or from accidental cause.

Research on this subject was recommended to overcome the objections to unmanned lock operations referred to by the Reporter General.

F DROUIN (FRANCE)

The attention of delegates was drawn to two safety developments in France. The first relates to an improvement in signalling, and especially day and night beaconing, by luminous buoys, which also assists under flood conditions or in conditions of poor visibility. Features of the system are that it is economical, reliable and easily carried. The buoys are formed of reinforced polyester with an aluminium alloy cap. The range of visibility of the light is up to 2 km and a light flash is displayed every second. The buoys have the advantages of being easily carried by boat, are light in weight and are battery-operated.

Another type of buoy developed since the last Congress was also referred to. In this case the buoy was specially shaped to have the minimum drag. This is easily secured and, although considerable maintenance is required, it also assists in reducing accidents.

The next point dealt with increasing the traffic capacity of a waterway network and the difference between the physical and the achievable traffic carrying capacity of such a network. The difference is due to the natural features of the waterways in the network. In the particular instance referred to a number of traffic clearance sub-networks were formed to overcome the traffic demand peaks. When unbalanced demand occurs the solution is to re-arrange the take-up of capacity through an established central chartering clearance centre. This enables flexibility to be achieved between the peaks of traffic demand on particular waterways and the capacity available from time to time with the various carriers to meet the need.

J MARCHAL (BELGIUM)

The proper dimensioning of a waterway adapted to the traffic of large convoys should be a major concern in research work.

After very thorough research carried out at the Hydraulics Structures Laboratory of the University of Liege between 1970 and 1975, based on a very large number of tests on scale models, I had defined the optimum section adapted to the navigation of tows of 9 000 tons composed of four barges: this dimensioning was based on the notion of practical speed limit, i.e., that from which any doubling of the power does not increase the speed by more than 5%. In this way, I arrived at a ratio for canal wet sections/ship of 14, which although badly received at the time I am glad to have maintained.

I also made a point of seeking the necessary optimum depth, which I defined at 6 metres and which was recently adopted in Rumania.

Finally, this dimensioning led to a section having a strict minimum of 100 metres width at water level and 6 metres depth for inland navigation. In Belgium, I was reproached at the time for having exaggerated the depth but I persist in thinking that this depth has a preponderant influence, especially as it must be clearly realized that, in the cost of building a waterway, the additional cost necessary for deepening is very far from proportional to the volume of additional spoil.

Moreover, this deepening diminishes the maintenance cost of the waterway.

With this dimensioning, the navigational safety is fully ensured.

I should now like to make a comment on the German paper which refers to the manoeuvrability of large push-tows in the bends of canals.

As regards this problem, I wish to stress that the extreme case to be taken into consideration is the crossing of two push-tows in ballast, for in this case the influence of side winds is of prime importance. Has this factor been taken into account? And, in the case of a waterway with a current, has attention been paid to the big decrease of manoeuvrability in the direction of the current?

The width of the canal is linked to the concept of practical speed limit. I think that the dimension which it is important to define in a bend is its radius of curvature.

J AUBERT (FRANCE)

This Subject relates to the study of different methods that can be used to increase the capacity of waterways.

As these methods are numerous, the papers submitted deal with different subjects.

The Canadian paper tells us about shunters. Designed as floating propulsion units which are fitted on ships of large tonnage, these shunters are an interesting innovation.

Independent tugs have been used for a long time for moving large ships, but the linking of two floating units by a cable is naturally less effective than a rigid link.

This method of shunters may be compared to that of the "thrusters", used exceptionally on the Rhine. These are propellers fixed to the upstream end of a self-propelling vessel or a tow, which make it possible to move this end sideways. The action of the rudder is thus amplified.

The emergence of shunters leads us to reflect on the methods available for moving a vessel.

Figure 1 shows a vessel, in diagram form, and the forces that can be exerted on it.

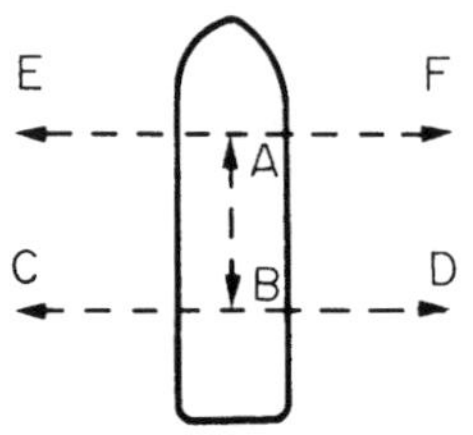

Fig. 1

The propeller makes it possible to exert forces directly such as A or B in the direction of the axis of the vessel. The action of the rudder enables the stern of the vessel to be moved in the direction of the arrows C or D, but there is no possibility of exerting actions in the directions E or F.

Such lateral actions are made possible by the shunter concept.

<u>Typical sideways movement</u>. In the vicinity of the very many locks throughout the world, the situation shown in Figure 2 frequently arises. Ship A has just left the lock, at which ship B, was waiting at the tying-up place, and has to enter by following the path shown by the dotted line.

It does so without difficulty, but takes rather a long time, and the problem facing us is precisely how to reduce this time.

The sideways movement of the ship corresponds to a certain amount of work. If the process occurs very slowly, this work is slight, but the resistance of the water to the movement of a solid body is in rapidly ascending proportion to the speed of this movement.

If, therefore, it is desired to proceed more quickly, the work to be performed becomes greater. The power that has to be utilized increases, firstly, because of the increased work and secondly because of the shortening of the time in which this work is performed.

Installing a considerable power which would be used only for a very small fraction of the time would entail inadmissible expense.

The obvious solution is to seek to implement a process of continuous accumulation of energy

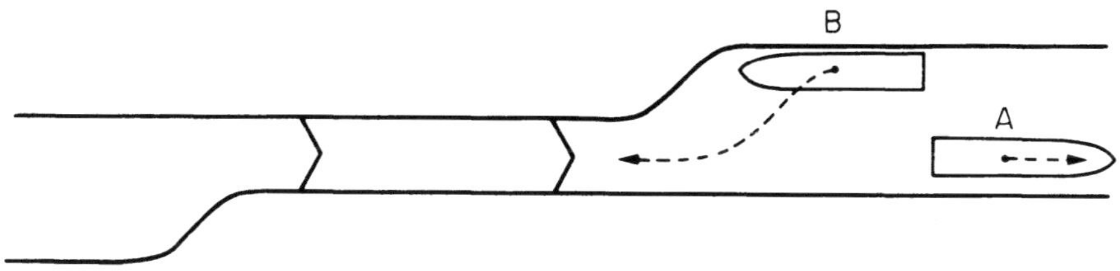

Fig. 2

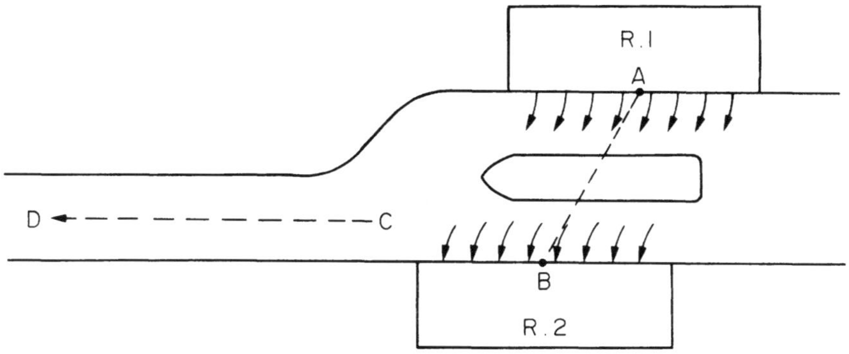

Fig. 3

which is then suddenly released from time to time.

This is the process which has been tested at the Chatou laboratory.

Figure 3 shows an upper reservoir R1 and a lower reservoir R2.

To effect the required movement, the sluices of the two reservoirs are opened and the vessel, drawn by the current, follows the dotted line AB. A low-powered pump, in action for the entire duration of the cycle, then makes it possible to re-establish the initial difference in level between the two reservoirs.

Two other reservoirs R3 and R4, not shown in Figure 3, then make possible subsequently (or at the same time) the movement CD.

This method of reservoirs would possibly enable the postponement of the time when a lock has to be duplicated but, to our knowledge, it has not yet been used.

The typical movement shown in Figure 2 also has to be effected at the upstream head of a water gradient.

In this case, it is necessary to proceed with great speed, because it is the aim, in the case of a water gradient some fifty metres in height, to obtain a duration of cycle similar to that of a lock with a fall of ten metres.

The power of the driving shield of a water gradient represents five to ten times that of the actual propulsion system of the vessels or tows using this water gradient. It so happens that this power is unused precisely during the interval between the upgoing vessel A and vessel B which is preparing to descend the gradient. It was quite obvious to think of using this power to facilitate the exchange of vessels A and B. Both the plan and the cross section show in diagram form the mask of the driving shield which, in order to accelerate the exit of the upgoing vessel A, has continued its advance almost until contact with the swing gate which retains the water of the upper reach.

On Figure 4, this mask draws back and, due to the closure of a second gate, known as the flap gate, discharges the water into the lateral branch shown on the plan.

This branch ends in a widening similar to a spray cone.

Discharging the water by one of its faces and drawing it in by the other, the mask creates a kind of liquid roundabout, a fraction of which corresponds exactly to the path that has to be followed by vessel B.

As soon as the latter has entered the level stretch, the flap gate is lowered and the gates

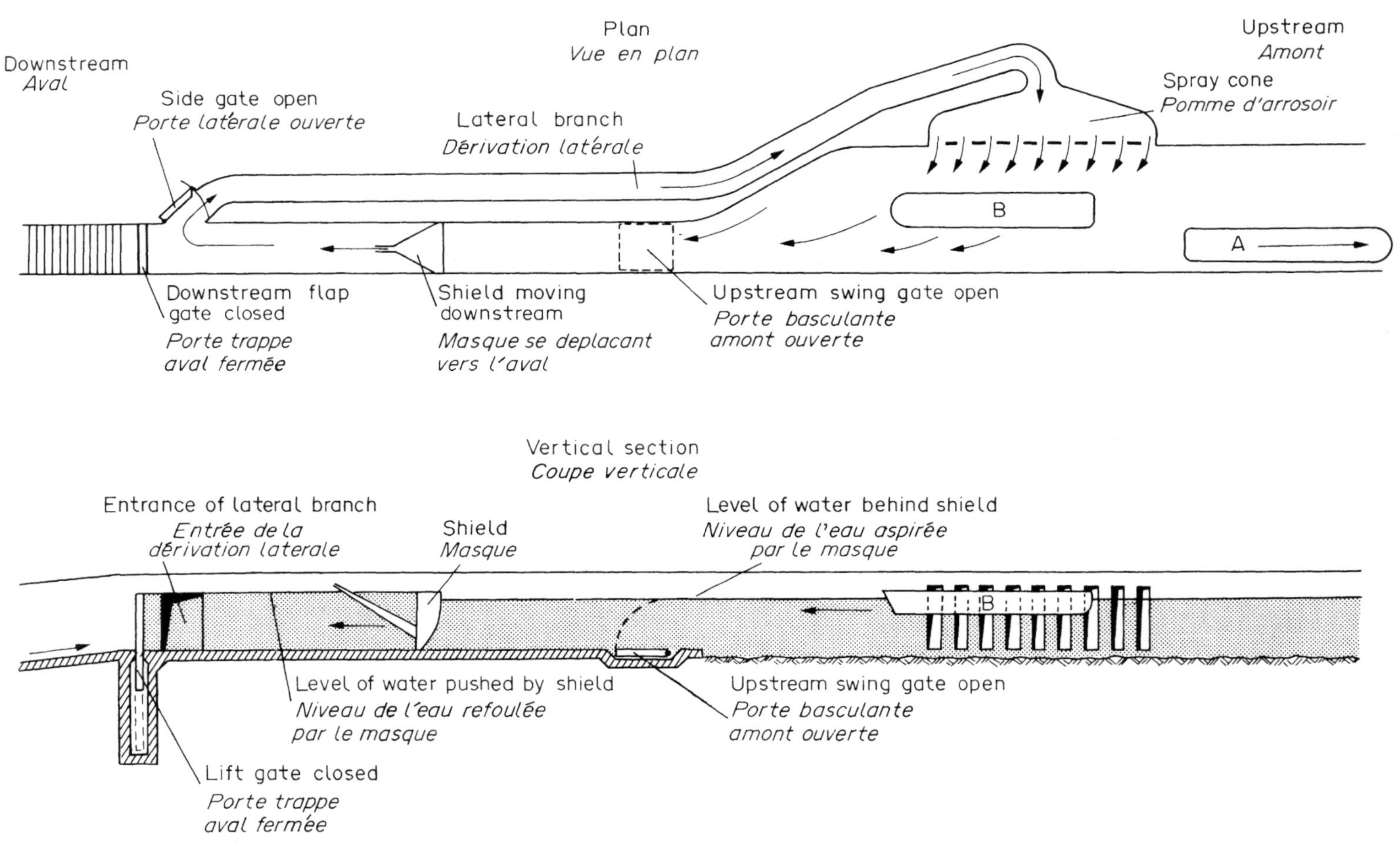

Plan
Vue en plan
Downstream
Aval
Upstream
Amont
Side gate open
Porte latérale ouverte
Lateral branch
Dérivation latérale
Spray cone
Pomme d'arrosoir
B
A
Downstream flap gate closed
Porte trappe aval fermée
Shield moving downstream
Masque se deplacant vers l'aval
Upstream swing gate open
Porte basculante amont ouverte
Vertical section
Coupe verticale
Entrance of lateral branch
Entrée de la dérivation laterale
Shield
Masque
Level of water behind shield
Niveau de l'eau aspirée par le masque
Level of water pushed by shield
Niveau de l'eau refoulée par le masque
Upstream swing gate open
Porte basculante amont ouverte
Lift gate closed
Porte trappe aval fermée

Fig. 4

of the lateral branch are closed. The mask will then continue its movement in the inclined channel.

At the end of its climbing movement, the mask will have pushed the upgoing ship into the upper reach and, at the start of its return movement, will draw the vessel B into the triangle of water which will descend downstream.

As regards the duration of the cycle, there is therefore no need to count an exchange time at the upstream head of a water gradient between the two ships A and B. As we have seen, this exchange is indeed the consequence of the movements of the mask, now upstream and now downstream.

We have shown that the sideways movement necessary for the very rapid restarting-up of a ship standing in a tying-up place could be effected:-

1. In the case of a lock, by the use of reservoirs specially designed for this purpose.

2. In the case of a water gradient, by the simple utilization of its driving gear.

A A RUDIN (SWEDEN)

With the assistance of some slides I wish to add some further comments to my Paper on the Improvement of Navigation through the Trollhätte Canal and in Lake Vänern and Mälar, with special reference to ice conditions. On the Gothenburg Canal the waterway has now been kept open throughout the year for six seasons. The slides illustrate certain aspects of this achievement.

The first slide shows a thickness of 60-70 cm of ice on the lake. On the canal the shipping and power plants co-operate in keeping the waterway open. Further slides show the position in February 1980 following a period of three weeks at -25° C., the ice-breaker on the lake, a high air-draft ship moving in the ice, the growth of ice in the locks and the use of hot water sprays in the locksides to deal with this problem, and a system of ice removal by crane. The final slide shows the beauty of the canal under summer conditions, to contrast with the severe winter conditions shown on the earlier slides.

L MOINEAU (FRANCE)

Several speakers have referred in a most interesting way to the dispatching arrangements adopted to increase the capacity and safety of waterways. I should like to tell you about two details suggested to us by our experience of traffic regulation, more particularly on the Seine and the Moselle, where we were faced with problems of saturation and of navigation by night in difficult conditions.

1. Our experience shows that the regulation of traffic to increase capacity is advisable when the traffic attains 75% of saturation and well before having reached this proportion when the aim is to speed up the traffic and not only to increase capacity.

2. The regulation of night traffic practised with advantage on the Seine and the Moselle is necessary as soon as this traffic appears on waterways with relatively numerous locks, so as to make it possible to provide, without prohibitive cost, for each lock and at the approximate time of passage announced beforehand, the means necessary to ensure passage in optimum conditions as regards time and labour saving.

K K GOGOI (INDIA)

In terms of peak period discharge the River Brahmaputra in India is the third largest river in the world after the Rivers Amazon and Congo. It experiences a heavy rainfall period of up to six months annually.

Navigation by night on the waterways of the River Brahmaputra for inland waterway transportation, where the annual traffic is nearly one million tonnes, is mainly guided by pintail lights. This method can be used wherever the situation is similar, as perhaps in certain developing countries. The Brahmaputra is alluvial with considerable bed movement and movement of suspended silt due to heavy bottom scouring. This causes the fixing of navigation lights in the navigable channel to be very difficult. This is particularly the case as the river frequently shifts its main channel, forming a number of braided secondary channels which do not maintain their navigable depth. In these conditions the use of conventional buoys was not practicable. In hard ground and rocky areas the permanent fixing of lights was arranged but in the middle of the channel, where bed movement takes place and the movement of submerged logs is experienced, the fixing of navigational aids is done using telescopic and collapsible tripod stands of weight about 20 kg. The light and the battery body are bolted together on a normal tripod stand. The total assembly is considerably cheaper than the cost of a buoy. The tripod length is about 5 metres overall, of which 1 metre is driven into the channel, with a 3 metre depth of water and 1 metre above the water line. The body of the light is made of fibreglass instead of steel because of the damp climate of the region. The movement and setting of the lights and stands are readily achieved by three men from a suitable boat.

I M WALKER (UK)

In response to the Chairman's request for clarification of the United Kingdom paper in its reference to the automation of locks and bridges when compared with the United Kingdom paper to the 1977 Congress in Leningrad, I wish to explain that the system described in 1977 depended on the remote detection of barges when approaching and on leaving a lock or bridge by the use of underwater sonic beams. It had been found later that problems arose with this method of detection in attaining the high degree of accuracy needed under the more extreme climatic conditions and in flows carrying suspended solids. It was for this reason that the suggestion is now made to use radio controls to initiate the automatic remote system of operation. As the United Kingdom commercial waterways also carry significant pleasure traffic, recent operational experience also shows that it can be unwise to remove all manual attendance from major operational points during normal daylight hours. However out of normal hours the procedure of automatic operation with remote surveillance as suggested in 1977 will be used but initiated instead as now described in the United Kingdom paper. Similarly on the Gloucester and Sharpness Canal in South West England consideration is currently being given to the improvement of the waterway. In order to limit costs it is likely that a single width channel will be provided with passing places. A close control of traffic will be required to minimise delays to shipping and principles of telemetered surveillance will be used. This could also be used to provide information to road traffic control systems in the urban areas of Gloucester so as to minimise road traffic congestion when lift-bridges are operated for the passage of ships.

A J M HARRISON (UK)

One method of improving the capacity of waterways has not been mentioned in the papers presented. This is the improvement in the capacity of large rivers to accept larger vessels, which could be achieved by better prediction or forecasting of water levels. I refer to the British Paper on Subject 3, by Colyer and Thorn, which dealt with improvements to the River Paraguay in South America.

Considerable development has taken place in the past 10 to 15 years of deterministic numerical models for analysing flows in large rivers. Given adequate data input of flows in the headwaters of a river system it may be possible to forecast water levels quite precisely up to several weeks in advance. When physical improvements to rivers to take larger vessels are under discussion I suggest that the alternative of better forecasting of water levels should be seriously considered.

W F BLAIR (CANADA)

The use of specially designed tugs on the Welland Canal was considered to be the best means of improving the capacity of the canal where capacity problems were expected by 1985. An experimental programme to prove the concept was started in 1979 and continued into 1980, based on specially designed tugs and thrusters. During the experiment both medium size and maximum size vessels were used to obtain data, so that a full evaluation could be conducted under actual operating conditions. Ratchet type connecting links were used between the shunter and the bow of the vessel.

The experimentation and evaluation of data indicates that the capacity of the canal could be increased from around 30 lockages per day as existing up to 39-40 lockages per day, which is an increase of some 33%.

When embarking on the project the cost of a fleet of shunters was estimated at approximately 100 million Canadian dollars. Since completion of the programme and of the necessary later design information a more realistic cost assessment has been made at some 200 million Canadian dollars. This, when combined with annual operating costs of some 30 million Canadian dollars, leads to the conclusion that the shunter system does not show significant benefit over conventional improvements to increase capacity. These improvements include such projects as additional widening in areas of restricted channel where at present vessels are not permitted to meet, removal of bridges and improvements to lock wall layouts.

In spite of the economic evaluation, however, research was carried out to ensure that the problem of shunter attachment could be overcome. In fact after following through design proposals from consultants it was clear that sufficient information was available to proceed with further detailed design of the attachments. During the investigation process it was also discovered that an operational suction cup attachment had been developed in Japan. Examination of this equipment indicated that it would be possible to develop a practical shunter design. It was also understood that shunters are being considered for use in the Suez Canal and that a Japanese shipyard has been licensed to produce such equipment.

J DUBOIS (Central Commission for the Navigation of the Rhine)

Concerning the paper of the Federal Republic of Germany on the regulation of traffic and regulations on navigational aids, I shall confine myself to the Rhenish field. By reason of the technical features of the Rhine and the density of the traffic using it, Rhenish experience may indeed be of general interest.

1. As regards regulation of traffic, I shall merely refer to the utilization of the departure area system (known in German as "Startplatzsystem"). This method, used in Germany and more especially on the Rhine, to encourage an optimum utilization of locks, is also practised on the canalized Rhine and the Grand Canal d'Alsace with a view to preventing or reducing bottlenecks when one of the two locks of a fall is out of action because of closure or breakdown. Experience has shown that, with simple and inexpensive organizational measures, this method gives good results.

2. In the field of navigational aids, the experience acquired in the use of radar has led to an important development in data and ideas since the last major revision of the Police Regulations for the Navigation of the Rhine, completed in 1970 on the basis of the European Inland Waterways Code (CEVNI).

Considered at the outset as an auxiliary means which could be "taken into account" when navigating with reduced visibility, radar has become an essential safety factor.

This evolution is taken into consideration in the work in progress for revision of the Police Regulations for the Navigation of the Rhine and will be reflected in the provisions.

It is only natural that the increased use of radar entails, by way of counterpart, corresponding guarantees of reliability.

Firstly in the field of equipment, the radar installations and gyration indicators used on the Rhine already have to be of a type approved for Rhenish navigation.

Secondly in the field of personnel, the use of

radar requires the presence on board of a person holding the radar officer's certificate issued in accordance with the relevant regulations adopted by the Central Commission.

The generalization of improved techniques is bound to involve the need for supervisory measures. Indeed, navigational aids do not eliminate the difficulties and the resulting danger, but merely make it possible to overcome them in conditions of safety that are maintained and if possible improved. It is the price of progress.

R H SMITH (CANADA)

In referring to the Belgian and United States Papers comment can be made about Canada's thinking on the use of electronic radio aids to improve marine navigation in confined situations.

On the St. Lawrence Seaway, and at the request of Canada's Dominion Marine Association, tests were made of the Precise Radar Navigation System (PRANS). Their operational requirement was stated to be ± 3 metres accuracy. It is believed that this degree of accuracy can be relaxed and this can be proved by simulation. Further, with better ship monitoring and a change in operating procedures, the possible worst case situations would not arise.

PRANS uses the ship's radar to range on passive radar reflectors whose positions have been surveyed to a very close tolerance. These readings are entered into a microprocessor and a chart of the waterway is stored on cassette or hard memory showing the channel limits and the centre-line. When the vessel enters the system the programme is started and it then shows the master or pilot how far the vessel is from the centre-line, the distance to the next waypoint, the attitude of the vessel and its speed.

PRANS trials were completed during the summer and fall of 1980. Although in the static mode the desired accuracy and performance were achieved, in the dynamic mode while underway accuracies dropped off and it was impossible always to acquire the radar reflectors or once acquired to continue to track them. Because of these difficulties the project has been deferred indefinitely.

The next step is to evaluate differential Loran-C. The short baseline, low powered mini-Loran-C chain has been evaluated by USCG in the St. Mary's River over a number of years. The conclusion is that the regular chain can be utilised if monitoring and error transmitting sites are established at a number of points where accuracy is critical. More study and field trials are required.

Racons (linear swept, stepped swept, fixed frequency, frequency agile) are being looked at very closely to be used either as an input to a microprocessor for very accurate range information or for visual radar guidance by the master or pilot.

An increasing operational requirement is for improved guidance for passage under bridges. Racons either marking the channel centre-line or bridge piers seem to be the present trend, although Canada is installing underwater lighting for evaluation at the Second Narrows railway bridge in Vancouver Harbour.

Finally to give further emphasis and support to the significance of the human factor in navigation it had been reported in the earlier Section II discussions that a summary of vessel casualties and accidents reported to the Canadian Coast Guard in 1979 showed that operational mistakes, i.e. the human factor, was the identified cause in approximately 38% of the cases, which was more than twice the percentage of any of the various other causes identified.

G CERUTTI (ITALY)

My comments concern the Italian experience of the use of radar reflectors for giving warning of the presence of bridge piers on the River Po. Navigation in the River Po is continuous without interruption throughout the 24 hours each day and during long periods of fog. Experience over 15 years has been that radar reflectors placed on tubes fixed to bridge piers had given very satisfactory results. The installation must be completed by the provision of lights on the line of the channel course.

CONCLUSIONS

1. The use of waterways for cargo movement is increasing in every country. Although the capacity of waterways is being increased through both modest means and dramatically, it is concluded that additional improvements in capacity and safety are required.

2. It is concluded that a system approach for managing the operation of a river or a network should be used to improve both capacity and safety. Improvements must meet the "eeesp" test — be economical, be environmentally sound, be energy efficient, be safe, and be politically acceptable.

3. To enhance capacity,

   a) measures should be taken to improve the non-structural parts of the waterways system and lock equipment including: aids to navigation for all types, communications such as traffic information exchange and directions, ice control, and lighting. Computerized data processing and its immediate transmission should be employed where practical.

   b) measures should be taken on board to improve vessel/boat capabilities including communication and navigational equipment as well as manoeuvrability.

   c) where necessary, measures should be taken to improve external assistance to vessels/boats by providing pilots, tugs, shunters, towboats, icebreakers, and shoreside winches.

   d) measures should be taken to improve crew training in new techniques and assure proper consideration of all aspects of human factors.

   e) measures should be taken to give due consideration to the movement of hazardous goods on the waterways.

4. When considering structural improvements, it is concluded that:

   a) priority should be given to identification and to elimination of "black spots" and "bottlenecks";

   b) to minimize waiting time appropriate distance between locks should be provided;

   c) to improve safety and to facilitate passage through locks, proper chamber dimensioning, approach and alignment configuration of lock entrances, and lock operating equipment should be provided along with precautionary measures concerning "surges" in smaller waterways.

5. In utilizing the systems approach consideration should be taken of all externalities affecting the system including, namely:

- rerouting of traffic to minimize congestion when possible;
- simplification of lock procedures;
- traffic regulations;
- minimizing empty transport by exchange of cargo information.

6. Continual research in all sectors of the waterway systems is required to keep pace with the increasing demand.

   Referral of research effort to the PTC should prevent duplication and assure appropriate publication of noteworthy completed research projects in the PIANC Bulletin and other similar publication.

INLAND WATERWAYS AND PORTS

SECTION I — SUBJECT 3

Reducing sedimentation, improving and maintaining navigable depths in alluvial channels by control of flows and proper geometry

Thursday 14 May 1981

Chairman:	*J CHAPON (France)* *Ingénieur Générale des Ponts et Chaussées* *Vice-Président du Conseil Générale des Ponts et Chaussées* *Ministère de l'Environnement et du Cadre de Vie, Paris*
Vice Chairman:	*Dr W MAGIERA (Poland)* *Ministère des Transports par Voies Navigables, Warsaw*
Reporter General:	*W H JACKSON (UK)* *Director of Research* *British Transport Docks Board*
Secretary:	*C COCOZZA (France)* *Ingénieur des Ponts et Chaussées* *Directeur de l'Exploitation du Port Autonome de Paris*
Asst. Secretary:	*A E C HOMASSEL (France)* *Secrétaire Adjoint, Section Française*

Speakers

P SAVEY (France), C RICARD (France), M F THORN (UK), D M McDOWELL (UK), K K GOGOI (India), D MUSKATIROVIC (Yugoslavia), H C FRIJLINK (The Netherlands), D DREYFOUS-DUCAS (France), J MARCHAL (Belgium), G THUES (Belgium), M HAGER (FRG), A J M HARRISON (UK), P LAGROU (Belgium), S MONTEJO (Colombia)

W. H. JACKSON (UK) (GENERAL REPORTER)

The provision and maintenance of required depths and the safe navigation in waterways, although made more difficult in recent times because of the increasing size of ships, has been a subject of concern for many centuries. A number of training works have been built in the past, some of which have been successful, others have solved the problem for which they were designed only to create further problems elsewhere and some have been unsuccessful. Knowledge of failures is just as important as knowledge of successful works and the papers in this section give attention to both.

Where the river training is considered to be the right answer, the detailed design must clearly depend on local conditions but the basic method of approach and type of structures used in different countries show considerable similarity. These are briefly summarised in the conclusions.

Generally, in river navigation, the main problem is one of accretion of sand and gravel but if the main river is by-passed and separate navigation canals are built then the sedimentation of fine material becomes a problem in the backwater areas. The authors of the French paper give specific examples of these sedimentation processes.

Two interesting and original ways of dealing with specific problems are:-

1. The egg-shaped basins at the crossing of the Amsterdam-Rhine Canal and River Lek which give the necessary area for safe navigation without unduly altering the main river flow conditions.

2. An example of the use of vanes on the bed of the River Rhône to induce secondary currents and cause scour.

With the arrival of automation a large increase in the intensity of sounding data becomes practical and specially equipped launches to achieve this are described in the German and French papers. Both use several transducers to record simultaneously the depths at a number of points in the cross-section.

Economic considerations are also covered in these papers and these include:-

1. An assessment and comparison of relative costs of regular maintenance dredging and river training.

2. A study of whether by stockpiling or using partly laden ships it is necessary to maintain full channel depths at times of low flows.

A mathematical model designed to estimate the economic penalty of limiting the channel depth is described in the contributions from the Netherlands.

The papers present such a large amount of practical information on the difficulties which arise in trying to maintain the necessary depths for safe navigation as well as details of many types of training structures that it is difficult to do justice to them in a brief summary. I have therefore restricted my summary to recommend methods of approach over which there is a fair consensus of opinion.

i) There should be a clear specification of the objective of any proposed training works in which basic parameters such as minimum depth, minimum radius of bends etc. are set down.

ii) Before considering in detail the training of a river, a careful analysis of historical data should be made so that the natural regime and any natural changes to this regime can be ascertained.

iii) A considerable amount of field data needs to be collected of which water levels, bed surveys, velocities and sediment transport for normal and extreme freshwater flows are the most important.

iv) Model techniques, hydraulic and mathematical, are extensively used to predict the effects of training works to be built in the river.

v) Training structures include reinforcement of banks (usually the first stage) spur groynes to encourage accretion on certain banks and hence concentrate flow elsewhere, longitudinal groynes, and groynes designed to discourage and prevent secondary channels from forming. Dredging is often an essential part of the initial training.

vi) A step by step approach with careful monitoring is recommended by several of the authors.

Sand and gravel winning can be an ideal way of maintenance dredging provided the material is removed from the right place in the correct quantities but frequently overdredging takes place which can result in loss of depth elsewhere due to reduced water levels. Loss in water levels can also result from subsidence due to mining operations.

Eleven papers were submitted on the subject of ways of reducing sedimentation, improving and maintaining navigable depths in alluvium channels by control of flows and proper geometry. These papers were submitted by authors from Czechoslovakia, France, the German Democratic Republic, the German Federal Republic, the Netherlands, Poland, Spain, the United Kingdom, the United States of America, the Union of the Soviet Socialists Republic and Yugoslavia.

These papers generally describe works carried out in their particular country and although there are areas of similarity there are marked differences between the different schemes described, even in the same country. Much depends on site conditions.

Some of the difficulties are man made either by previous unsuccessful or only partially successful attempts at river training, overdredging for the winning of sand and gravel, subsidence caused by mining, the building of structures in the river and in a number of other ways.

The philosophy of river training is usually to encourage the river to do what you want it to do. I purposely choose the word encourage for as many engineers have found to their cost, a river can be very stubborn and very devious in its response to interference by man. It is most useful to read in the papers of the less successful enterprises as it prevents others repeating in the future the mistakes already made in the past.

There is, however, much common ground and I have summarised in the conclusions a relatively standard form of training suitable for many conditions. The first stage is usually to reinforce the banks which become most vulnerable to attack, then to build spur groynes to have the effect of building out a bank encouraging accretion of the bank, and faster flow elsewhere, longitudinal groynes to guide the flow along the channel and the building of additional works, if necessary, to prevent secondary channels from forming. Capital dredging is often an essential part of the scheme.

Despite similarities, the design detail varies considerably. However, the Russian authors suggest some quantitative relationships between various dimensions such as the height and length of groynes for convex and concave bends as well as for straight sections. It would be interesting to hear whether other engineers use similar relationships to assist in their designs.

Where I found the greatest agreement between the various authors was in the basic approach to the problems and I would now like to review briefly the stages leading up to the final design.

Before embarking on an expensive programme of river training aimed at improving navigation either by allowing larger vessels to navigate in the river or existing vessels less restrictive use, some cost benefit needs to be carried out. Particular stress is laid on this aspect in two of the papers. The United Kingdom Contribution describes a study made of the Parana River which takes into account the seasonal nature of much of the traffic and considers how the limitations caused by depth restriction can be minimised by stock piling. The Netherlands paper describes a method of assessing the long term economic effects of deeper and shallower fairways which includes the use of a mathematical model. Such detailed investigations into the economic gains from deepening channels is a very important field of study.

A further development made possible by the rapid advances in electronics and computing in recent years is the feasibility of taking much more sounding data than would have been practical until quite recently. Two such advanced sounding techniques are described in the papers submitted by France and by the German Federal Republic. In both cases the depths at many points across the width of the channel (there are 41 in the case of the German Survey Launch) can be recorded and plotted as the vessel moves along the channel. Such a detailed study should allow less underkeel clearance to be acceptable and therefore it may be possible to slightly reduce the mean depth in the channel.

When decisions have been taken to increase the navigable depth in a particular river or part of a river, it is generally agreed that the first stage must be a clear statement of the aims and requirements in specific terms, for example minimum depth and width of channel and minimum radius of bends need to be specified.

The building of training works is not necessarily the correct solution for in some cases it may be cheaper to increase the dredging effort. This was found to be so in part of the Danube river and is described in the Czechoslovakian paper. The longer term solution here as in other places is to combine navigational interests with power generation in which case the ships navigate in special channels thus bypassing the river.

Most of the authors recommend that a detailed study of historical changes which have taken place either by natural processes or by interference to the regime by man through previous training, channel deepening, gravel winning etc.

Extensive field studies then need to be undertaken and these should include detailed soundings, distribution of velocities and sediment transport so as to allow relationships to be obtained which will, with other information, enable the settlement and redistribution of the sediment caused by the future works to be predicted. This data is essential for as the author of the French papers point out, the generalised formulae which have been produced to quantify the transport of coarse materials by currents cannot be applied with confidence despite the large amount of work that has been done. My personal, though limited, experience is that the prediction from such formulae can be grossly wrong when current velocities are high.

Having achieved some understanding of the mechanism of sediment movement and the present regime of the river it is generally agreed that some modelling is necessary if one is to predict with any degree of confidence the effect that a proposed scheme will have on the river. Both physical and mathematical techniques are used and the general opinion is that both are required. It is considered that the mathematical model supplements the physical model rather than replaces it. There is an admirable summary of the pros and cons of models in the Netherlands paper.

Even when all this has been done there are still doubts in some of the engineers' minds as to whether the actual length and number of groynes etc. is exactly right and therefore to be on the safe side they recommend the building of such works in stages so that the quantitative effect on the river can be monitored. I am not sure how far this cautious approach is common practice.

To summarise my conclusions

1. There is considerable agreement as to the general approach to river training.
2. There should be a clear specification of the basic parameters.
3. A careful analysis should be made of historical data.
4. There is need for extensive field measurements.
5. Both mathematical and hydraulic model studies are usually required.
6. There is a similarity in the types of structure used in many river training schemes but there are some interesting and unique designs.

I have suggested the following items for discussion and these are problems associated with river training.

1. How accurate and useful are the generalised formulae for calculating sediment transport in such river training problems?
2. What are the relative merits and limitations of hydraulic and mathematical models? The checking of predictions against what has actually happened when structures have been built is most important. This may be too big a subject to discuss here.
3. How important is it to take into account the natural meander length of the river? Should these meander lengths be maintained as far as possible?
4. I have also set down as an item for discussion, further views on intensive sounding techniques.
5. Sedimention resulting from piled structures either at the structures or downstream of them is another field where much has yet to be learnt.

I look forward with great interest, Mr. Chairman, to hearing the views of subsequent speakers on the conclusions in the general report and other aspects of this complex subject.

DISCUSSION

P SAVEY (FRANCE)

Attention has been drawn to the difference between the hydrographic ships on the Seine and the Rhone. The general conditions differ very greatly on the two rivers: width of water surface, speed of current, present volume of shipping. It is therefore hardly surprising that the hydrographic ships are different.

It would be interesting to compare the two techniques, but there can be no a priori conclusion about the superiority of one or other of the two systems.

Bottom panels were used on the Lower Rhone for three reasons.

1. They do not reduce the flow, which is an important point in an agricultural area near the sea, where salt water moves upriver at low water; indeed, the roughness of the bottom panels is much less pronounced than that of the groins and does not exert an effect on the distribution of the deposits between the two arms of the river.
2. They involve less cost, for the delta in question is far away from quarries which could provide rubble in economical conditions.
3. They exert a less violent effect on the bottom, which is important for a narrow river.

The bottom panels technique is not universal, but it can render valuable service in certain cases, more particularly in estuary zones with fine sediments.

Nearly all the papers refer to the management of natural channels combining dredging and submerged dikes. It would be interesting to know the limits of this process.

Examples of successful works include the upper Mississippi, lower Rhine, and certain reaches of the Danube, which never seem to exceed depths of 2.5 m - 3 m.

It would be particularly important for modern shipping to obtain a somewhat greater depth, 4 m for example, with a view to competing effectively with other forms of transport..

To obtain this result, or even to make modern navigation possible in certain difficult cases which are also common (the Vistula, for instance, or the Danube in certain reaches), the only convenient method is that of canalization by dams and locks. The drawback of this process is its cost. In this connection, account should be taken of the evolution of the energy market which has made viable a large number of low-fall hydraulic developments which had been abandoned prior to 1973.

For certain waterways, we may therefore hope to find a repetition of the favourable conditions existing on the Rhone where, for example, electricity production has covered 95% of the development cost. This is an opportunity to be seized for river navigation.

The other comment relates to intermittent transport associated with variations of hydrology.

While inevitable in cold countries where the rivers are frozen over in winter, it is not desirable in industrialized countries where the shipowners have made very big investments in inland waterway vessels, so that it is an economic necessity for them to be able to use this equipment throughout the year. On the other hand, this type of navigation may be envisaged in developing countries and more particularly in the tropical countries having a very pronounced seasonal cycle, where navigation at low water is almost impossible, whereas it is easy in the rainy season.

As regards the question of the opportunity for theoretical work, bearing in mind the importance of the coefficients used in river hydraulics, the reply seems to us to be in the affirmative. Indeed, great efforts have yet to be made with respect to solid discharge as well as on diffusion (thermal pollution) and on the balance of dissolved oxygen.

As for the comparison between mathematical and physical models, the former must be credited with the advantage of being economical and able to include important variables. On the other hand, they have the drawback of reducing the cross section of the river to a single dimension and they cannot yet take into account the effects of curvature of the channel, which has an important bearing on solid transport. Lastly, to a much greater degree than physical models, they are vulnerable to the errors caused by an insufficient data base.

The optimum solution to our problems will therefore be found by a harmonious combination of theoretical research, physical models and mathematical models.

C RICARD (FRANCE)

1. Control works on the Rhône, from Lyon to the Mediterranean Sea, entrusted to the Compagnie Nationale du Rhône, were completed in 1980 by commissioning the last of 12 locks at Vaugris, 35 km downstream of Lyon. The navigable channel, open to the passage of push-tows, is 310 km long and was opened 33 years ago. The minimum width for navigation is 60 m and the least depth of water, at low tide, is 3 m. In addition there are branches serving ports with a total length of 20 km.

2. Development and maintenance of this waterway is the responsibility of CNR. At present, to meet its obligations CNR has at its disposal vessels equipped with hydrographic sounding and plotting equipment capable of automatically producing profiles along and across the channel; but not by automatic means, charts of the bed. Although the canalisation of the Rhône has almost eliminated the problems posed by sands and gravels, there is instead a real problem due to fine sediments accentuated by the requirements of ship owners who want to maximise the potential profit from the waterway where, consequently, the least obstacle represents a danger. In order to meet these problems it has been necessary to increase the number of vessels and also the specialist crew and supporting personnel on land. And all this is to obtain, in the end, fragmentary information after a more or less long delay which is hardly compatible with the needs of modern navigation. CNR has therefore decided to fit out, at the request of other navigation services, a hydrological boat capable of making continuous surveys of the bed.

3. The vital characteristics of this boat which are mentioned in the French paper. Her length is 33.5 m, width 8.8 m, draught 1.1 m. She carries two arms each 15 m long, stowed along the hull at some 50 cm above the water surface. These arms can be manoeuvered together or individually in 18 seconds by means of an hydraulic control. When open, the boat sweeps a width of 38 m. Normal cruising speed is 20 km/h and when working the speed is between 2 and 8 km/h relative to the water. These characteristics were necessary to allow the boat to complete its mission properly; in effect, it is convenient if the channel can be covered in two passages of the boat. In addition it has been designed to navigate and eventually to work in the sea under calm conditions.

4. Hydrographic equipment of the boat. This consists, in one part, of sounding equipment and in the other part, of equipment designed to find the bearings of the boat, the whole coordinated by a system particularly useful for the missions for which it is intended. The sounding equipment consists of an array of transverse sounders and an array of longitudinal sounders which can function separately or together. The transverse system consists of 50 transducers spaced 0.80 m apart on the arms. They are commanded and managed by one minicomputer. They thus provide a cross-section consisting of 50 points which can be spaced at will, either by means of a program or by altering the speed of the boat. The computer holds in its memory the reference level of the water surface and corrects the measurements automatically taking count of the indications of the inclinometer in the case of heeling or rolling. The longitudinal system consists of 4 transducers. Two are situated under the keel, one at the bow and the other (in line with) the arms and the other two at the ends of the arms. They can particularly provide longitudinal profiles but also an indication of depth for the pilot of the boat. The sounders of the two systems can operate with two different frequencies to allow sounding on mud beds as well as levels on an alluvial bed. The results obtained by these two systems are made visible:

- firstly on a cathode-ray screen, where each sounding made is displayed independently or else on a printer, where, thanks to an advance of the paper combined with and linked to the speed of the boat, a chart of the bottom is displayed.

- secondly, on another printer where two longitudinal profiles from the four possible ones can be automatically recorded graphically.

The equipment of location of the boat consists of two independent systems:

- the first operates by interrogating two radio beacons placed ashore, at precisely located points which enable the centre of the boat to be found to an accuracy of some tens of centimeters.

- the second position of the vessel is found by measuring the longitudinal and transversal displacements or speeds from the point of commencement of the voyage, with the aid of an apparatus operating on the DOPPLER-FIZEAU principle. Angles are measured by gyro-compass.

While the first system gives absolute measurements immediately, the second requires periodical recalibrations of the telemetric measurements which are done using laser apparatus, on leading-mark panels of known coordinates.

- The ensemble of two sets of apparatus just described is coordinated and controlled by a computer. This serves particularly, (by taking count of the output of the gyro-compass which is automatically provided):

1. To plot the route followed by the boat, in real time, on a curve plotter 28 cm wide.
2. To plot a chart of depths of curves of level, at different times, on a curve plotter 56 cm wide.
3. To programme a route to be followed by the boat and to indicate eventually the corrections made in the course of the passage of the boat.
4. To store the data and the results of the mission on cassettes.
5. To correct the deviations due to the different drifts in the measurement when the system of positioning is the second system described by summing up systematically the recalibrations of laser telemeter.
6. To make all the calculations and usual manipulations done by a computer of this size.

But the MOSEL carries different equipment, which has the arms but not the system of location, for the time being. All this equipment is sited in a sufficiently large cabin to house also the helmsman's post where analog or digital screens provide a certain number of indications needed for pilotage of the boat. This cabin also holds a drawing table and a bureau.

5. Other equipment of the boat. The boat is also equipped to carry out other current missions concerning surveillance and maintenance of the navigable way. In particular, it carries tackle for raising and placing channel marker buoys. Given the length of the Rhône, the boat can be required to undertake missions of long durations so it carries all that is necessary for life on board, consisting of a team of hydrographers, surveying technicians, electrical and electronic technicians, pilot and crew. The boat has, in consequence, 5 cabins, a galley, a meeting room able to receive up to 70 people.

6. Possibilities of the boat. The hydrographic boat of the Rhône has entered service and for the time being it is making trial voyages — one expects that it could do the complete survey of channel over a length of 25 to 30 km in a single day. Planned initially for work along the length of the Rhône between Lyon and the Mediterranean Sea, this boat could be arranged to broaden its field of action. In fact, the French government decided to make a link between the Rhine and the Saône by a deep-draught canal and to entrust, when the link is completed, the management and improvement of the 750 km of navigable way which joins the Rhine to the Mediterranean, to the Compagnie Nationale du Rhône. It is therefore possible that the FREDERIC MISTRAL would be able, occasionally, to begin work in the north, on the Saône and the canal from the Saône to the Rhine where the channels join the Rhône, to the Mediterranean ports (Fos, Sete, La Nouvell ...) and its equipment allows this.

M F THORN (UK)

There is a typographical correction to UK paper: (p. 515 § iv). "The total dominant discharge in the river system (Q_D) increases from 23,400 m^3/s at Km 1208 to 27,800 m^3/s at Km 128, and.."

The UK paper considered to what extent navigation in a long navigable river could be improved without embarking upon a massive programme of capital works. I see this concern also expressed in the papers from the USSR and Yugoslavia. The USSR paper asks the direct question "What are the technical limits of the depth increase on free rivers with movable bed?

The UK paper suggests 2 possible approaches to this question:

- Try to make use of the predictable cyclic variations in water level to synchronise and optimise the movement of cargo on the river.

- Apply hydraulic regime theory analysis to the river to determine its natural limitations on navigable depth. The General Reporter says there is a weakness in the approach in that it can predict only average depths. Although this is true of the computation presented in the paper, I believe the principle is right, and that it can be refined to take account of asymmetry of the channel cross-section e.g. by analysing the relationship between the mean depth, and minimum depths at cross-overs and maximum depths in bends.

The central issue is this: there comes a point when, in order to increase navigable depth, it is necessary to move from a managed river (in which depths are achieved by control of the discharge within the natural banks) to a trained river (in which increased depth is obtained by artificially narrowing the river channel by capital training works). In heavily used rivers of industrialised countries, such as the Rhine or the Mississippi, training may be economically justifiable and practically possible and in any case it is now too late to go back.

But I would not lightly encourage any country with a long, less intensively used waterway to start trying to improve navigable depth by training the river or by intensive maintenance dredging. Rather, I would say to them "Find out how far navigable depth can be increased by management of both the navigation and the river (including some minor maintenance dredging in difficult spots) and set your sights on that.

D M McDOWELL (UK)

At first sight, the effect of a piled jetty in a waterway might not appear to be a means of reducing sedimentation. However, jetties are an unavoidable part of a navigable river and their effect must be taken into account. Moreover, it is desirable to optimise their design to minimise drag. The contribution by Dr. Ball is one result of an extensive study of the interaction of flow with structures and vessels. The work has led to some interesting results concerning the handling of ships in the vicinity of piled structures and possible patterns of sedimentation. In the past, it has been difficult to determine the effect of structures on river behaviour, even by use of physical models. The purpose of this research has been to obtain a better understanding of this problem. It would be useful if the author could receive any information regarding the effect of piled structures in practice, on patterns of flow, on sedimentation or on ship behaviour.

K K GOGOI (INDIA)

The river Brahmaputra in Assam, India, is an alluvial river which carries an enormous amount of fine silt due to bank erosion and influx from tributaries. We use bandalling for river training for navigation; lines of bamboo piles are driven into the silt at 45° to the secondary channel to induce deposition in it and to reduce deposition in the main channel. This causes the current to shift more and more to the main channel thereby increasing the navigable depth. The number of bandals depends on width of the secondary channel. They are placed in rows one after the other in about 2 m depth with bamboo woven mats as surface panels. The bandals are shifted periodically following improvement or deterioration of the main channel. Maintenance is done by a team of about 12 persons per boat with two work boats. This method was started in India almost a century ago and has stood the test of time. It is very effective and avoids the need for costly dredging.

About a decade ago, two Frenchmen, M. Ramallieux and M. Russlloms introduced a new system of bottom panelling on the main Brahmaputra to close secondary channels. One large secondary channel named Mooskhowa near Gauhati was closed in two months by such bottom panels. One difference from bandals is that the bamboos are driven deeper and the panels are plain or corrugated iron sheets. Other differences are that the panels are placed in the opposite direction, i.e. at 45° to the main channel, and the panels are allowed to rest on the bottom — hence the name. (Fig. 1)

The current in the secondary channel must be between 0.5 and 2ft/sec for effective bandalling. Detailed hydrographic surveys should be conducted before and after placing of bandals before the rise and fall of water levels — say February/March and October/November in North India.

D MUSKATIROVIC (YUGOSLAVIA)

Planning of river training works is a creative, responsible and usually complex problem. I will present a brief description of the philosophy of solving this problem, based on Yugoslavian experience gained from extensive training work for navigation on the Danube. The main approach may be explained by a simple scheme:

FIELD INVESTIGATIONS

- Hydraulic measurements
- River Geometry
- Sediment measurements

MORPHOLOGIC ANALYSES

- Correlations
- Distributions and frequency curves of geometric characteristics of river channel

HYDRAULIC ANALYSES

- Water levels
- Average velocities
- Sediment transport
- River bed deformation
- Disposition of river training structures

ECONOMIC ANALYSES

- Costs (Materials, mechanisation, execution, transport

ECOLOGICAL ANALYSES

DIFFERENT VARIANTS

OPTIMUM SOLUTION

As can be seen from this scheme, numerous aspects of planning river training works for navigational improvements are involved and, being equally important, must be equally treated. It is our opinion that wide, creative and concrete investigations, instead of an empirical approach, represents the right way to plan such works.

H C FRIJLINK (THE NETHERLANDS)

In view of the importance of maintenance dredging as a means of improving the navigability of rivers, in particular for developing countries, it is suggested that two earlier statements by the Reporter-General be included in the Conclusions.

"An assessment and comparison of relative costs

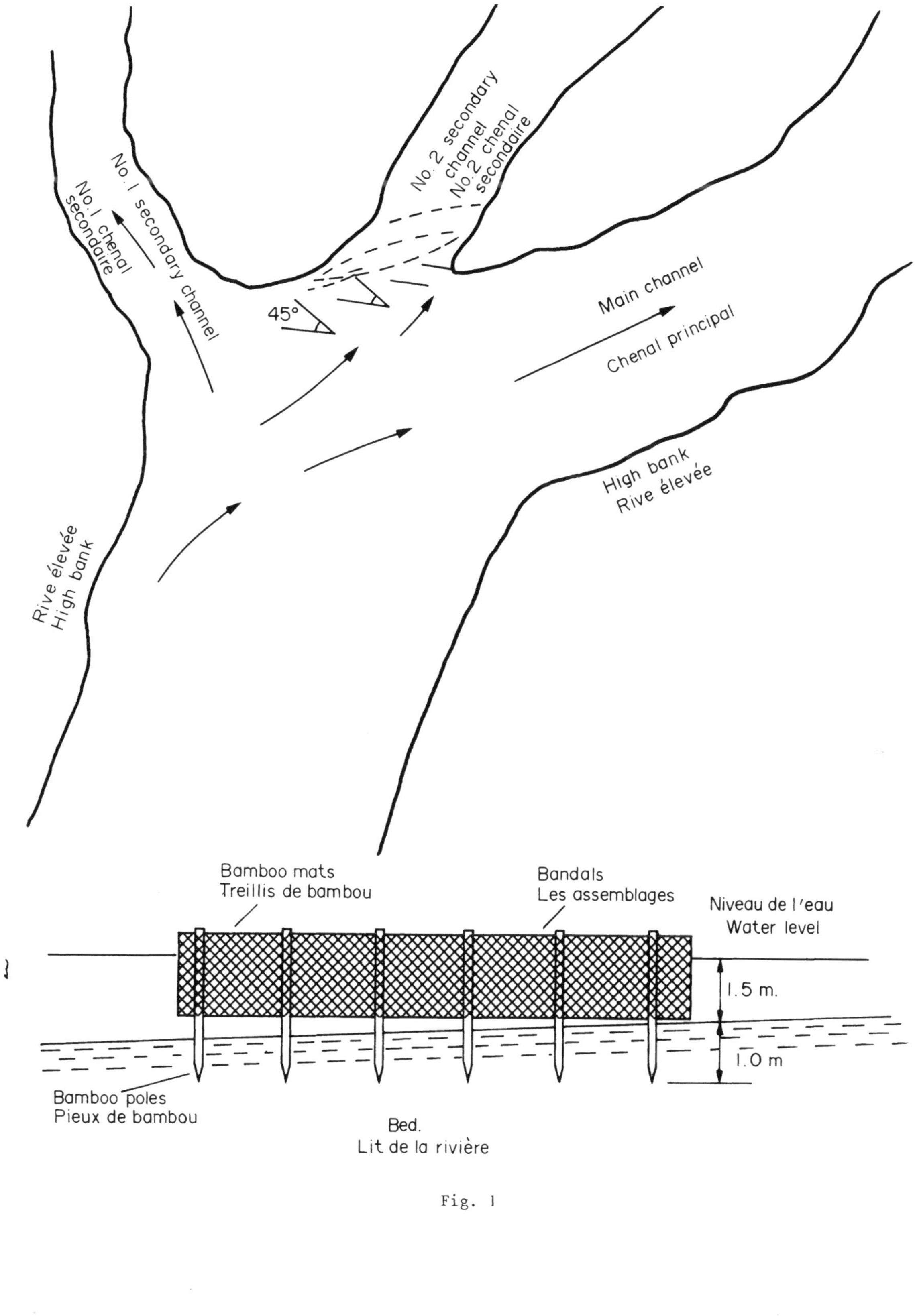
No. 2 secondary channel
No. 2 chenal secondaire
No. 1 secondary channel
No. 1 chenal secondaire
45°
Main channel
Chenal principal
High bank
Rive élevée
Rive élevée
High bank
Bamboo mats
Treillis de bambou
Bandals
Les assemblages
Niveau de l'eau
Water level
1.5 m.
1.0 m
Bamboo poles
Pieux de bambou
Bed.
Lit de la rivière

Fig. 1

of regular maintenance dredging and river training should be made"; and "A study should be done of whether by stockpiling or using partly laden ships it is necessary to maintain full channel depths at time of low flows".

The relevance of regular dredging is exemplified by recent dredging along a 500 km long stretch of the Niger River in West Africa.

D DREYFOUS-DUCAS (FRANCE)

1. On the communication of M. Savey and concerning the use of bottom panels: I think that the method of construction of the panels, their upkeep and their installation makes their principle of use very limited to the exceptional case of very muddy bottom where the use of spurs on submerged foundations is not possible.

2. On the contribution of M. Ricard and that of M. Savey relative to the survey vessel "Frederic Mistral", I think that the use of lateral arms has two drawbacks; considerable interference with navigation, and vulnerability in the case of collision. I also think that the equipment of this boat is very expensive and that the comparison of quality/price between this type of boat and the "Ecoranda", which progresses sidways, is to the advantage of the "Ecoranda".

One can also ask if the analysis of the surveys would not be done better and more cheaply in an office (displacement of people etc.) It would be interesting to ask the two departments to compare the cost of a hydrographic chart of the same length and covering the same distance.

J MARCHAL (BELGIUM)

I wish to make an important suggestion to the committee of PIANC in support of the contribution which was made by M. SAVEY.

Many studies have been made to try to define as functions of technical-economic criteria, the optimum depths sufficient for navigable ways which can be guaranteed at any price. Debates have already taken place in the past on this subject. I wish to suggest that PIANC continues to make it possible in future to debate this fundamental and complex problem in more detail. In such debates, technicians and water transport economists should be present simultaneously, so that the relevant criteria which should be adapted to navigational conditions cannot be overlooked.

I wish also to offer my opinion on the question posed as point 1 of the conclusions to know if the weighty theoretical work done on the movement of coarse sediments is really justified when one knows that the engineers generally have recourse to field measurements and to empirical formulae to determine the anticipated values. I think that one must be extremely sceptical, when answers given by empirical formulae are as numerous as authors interested in the problem, formulae apparently sophisticated, to obtain which there are for the most part large numbers in play, but unhappily which have attributed to them equally empirical coefficients which I would define as coefficients of ignorance! To solve a particular problem, I have already computed the results obtained by different formulae; the extreme results obtained differed by a factor of 10! My advice is that the route to follow is that of using an hydraulic model calibrated by a limited number of full-scale measurements with which a mathematical model is linked, allowing investigations to be made in parallel with much flexibility.

I thus endorse totally the opinion given on this subject in the report of the German Democratic Republic which mentions that progress would be particularly fruitful when the results of the two methods are compared with each other. One should not dissociate these two approaches.

G THUES (BELGIUM)

Antwerp, an inland situated seaport, along the ridal river Scheldt, at a distance of 80 km from the North Sea, is separated from the river by 5 locks. However, the Port Authority has to cope with a maintenance dredging of 2.5 x $10^6 m^3$ per year. Two topics have been discussed during this Congress which can be related to the experience of Antwerp.

1. The maintenance dredging is done by the Port Authority with its own equipment, consisting mainly of 3 bucket-dredgers, 10 vessels of $650 m^3$ capacity for transport of dredged material, a floating grab crane (for removing harder material such as iron ore and all kinds of objects and for precision dredging), and very soon a new split-hopper, trailing suction dredger of $1500 m^3$ capacity, more specially to be used in and near to the locks. All maintenance dredging has to be done while giving priority to the normal ship traffic, and therefore has to be interrupted very often. The productivity is therefore lower than construction-dredging and the overall cost is about 3 US$ per m^3, which is lower than the price obtained from hiring a time-charter from a privately owned dredging group working in the same conditions.

2. In order to keep up with the constant flow of sediment into the port area, accurate and easily understandable charts of the state of the bottom in the docks are needed in a short production time. The concept of "nautical depth" is also to be incorporated. Investigation of the sedimentation layers gave insight into the relationship between this concept and particular sonar recordings.

   A specialised craft has been built giving x, y and z coordinates of the deck bottom by means of radio bearings on land and a sonar on board with an accuracy of about 0.5 m for x and y, and 10 cm for z. The information is put on magnetic tape, taken on land and there, after treatment in a small computer, fed into a plotter giving results 2 or 3 hours after leaving the ship, in the form of a map with dock contours and points of reference on land for the pilots. The dock bottom situation is represented by isobaths (lines of equal depth) for the pilots. An adapted map will be produced for use by the dredger masters, enhancing information about areas to be dredged.

M HAGER (FRG)

In the first session of Section I, I reported about the possibility of maintaining the sediment flow of the stream in equilibrium in order to guarantee the proper geometry.

The other possibility to prevent the bed erosion and the deepening of the cross section is the use of a special sort of movable groins. These groins are constructed with synthetic sheets and can be inflated by filling with water and emptying. The purpose is to concentrate the stream flow in the main-bed and to maintain the necessary navigable depth. They will be filled and be brought into action at the time of low water level, and they are emptied when the stream flow becomes stronger and the water level high. These special groins are now being studied scientifically and by practical investigation. This is one of several ideas for investigation of special problems of the lower Rhine. The whole region lowers because of the coal mining in the Rhur basin and also this part of the Rhine river. The newest experiment is that the experience filling and emptying must be changed. In our report we have shown a sophisticated idea to fill and empty the groin with a self pumping construction using the effect of a Venturi nozzle, but now it will be practical to use a normal pump, situated on the bank.

A J M HARRISON (UK)

Mr. Harrison drew attention to the General Reporter's comments on theoretical work on sediment transport, formulae. Although he did not agree totally with the General Reporter,s view he thought the comments revealed the two major problems in this field.

a) the difficulty of accurately measuring sediment transport, particularly bed load, in the full scale situation

b) the difficulty of extending sediment transport formulae based on flume data to the full scale situation

For several years, research at the Hydraulics Research Station, Wallingford, has centred around these two problems. Mr. Harrison described the development of the Ackers-White transport formula, its testing against independent flume and full scale measurements and its favourable comparison with other sediment transport formulae. The formula is theoretically based with empirical coefficients. Further developments, on the same theoretical basis, had been successfully made of a resistance relationship, a morphological model and of regime relationships.

HRS had also developed a bed-frame which enabled accurate profiles of sediment concentration to be measured, even at low concentrations, using a pump-sampling technique. This equipment would be used in July 1981 to measure sediment transport in the River Nile. The data would be compared with the predictions of the Ackers-White sediment transport formula and be used in a morphological model study of degradation at barrages.

P LAGROU (BELGIUM)

The Office de la Navigation which is responsible for the development of the Albert Canal — an important waterway which connects the Port of Liege with the Port of Antwerp with traffic of order 40 million tonnes and through which operation by push-tow of 9000 tonnes is now in course of execution — has recently converted a pontoon to a sounding-boat. This boat, equipped with two Voith-Schneider propellers, has been provided with measuring instruments enabling immediate interpretation on board of the output of 60 echo sounders which can then provide drawn cross-sections. This choice was made with a view to detecting during the same voyage profiles which can be irregular and to return to them as needed. The objective followed was, among others, the control of bank slopes under water and the study of zones of erosion of these banks. We chose the sytem with lateral arms 5 m long on each side of the boat allowing continuous sounding over a width of 30 m from the piles — here including the under-water slope — while maintaining sufficient distance from the under-water slopes to avoid danger of erosion due to the propellors.

S MONTEJO (COLUMBIA)

The hydraulic laboratory of Bogota, which is a dependency of the Ministry of Public Works, has been working on the subject presented in the paper of the D.R. Germany. During our work we have had some problems with selection of the relationship between Δx and Δt, because a wrong selection leads to an unstable solution of the model. Some troubles have also arisen with transport formulae.

Two questions must therefore be put to the authors of the paper from D.R. Germany:

1. How are Δx and Δt chosen, how was the mathematical model stabilised?

2. What are the dimensions of the parameters involved in the expression in (p. 440 § 13).

W. H. JACKSON (UK) (REPORTER GENERAL)

The many speakers have given us a most interesting and enjoyable session and I will not attempt to summarise at this stage all the comments that have been made, but will draw attention to two particular aspects.

Firstly there were several contributions on the subject of advanced sounding techniques which showed personal preferences and the need to adapt the techniques to local conditions and justifiable cost.

Attention was drawn to the lack of any reference to environmental effects in my summary which was clearly an oversight. This subject will be given particular consideration by the editing committee with a view to making reference to it in the final conclusions.

CONCLUSIONS

1. There should be a clear specification of the

objectives of any proposed navigation improvement in which basic parameters such as minimum depth, channel width, minimum radius of bends, maximum velocity and water level, etc. are set down.

2. Before considering in detail the navigation improvement of a river, a careful analysis of historical data should be made so that the natural regime and any natural changes to their regime can be ascertained.

3. A considerable amount of field data needs to be collected including water levels, bed surveys, velocities, sediment transport and ecological data, for normal and extreme flows.

4. Physical or mathematical models or both are usually needed to predict the effects of navigational improvement.

5. Training structures include reinforcement of banks (usually the first stage), spur groynes to encourage accretion on certain banks and hence concentrate flow elsewhere, longitudinal groynes, and groynes designed to discourage and prevent secondary channels from forming. Light training works such as bottom or surface pannels and "bandals" may be used to correct undesirable bad configurations in rivers with gentle slopes and fine sand and silt beds.

6. A step by step approach, with careful monitoring is recommended especially when there are doubts as to the magnitude of the effects of the improvement. Sand and gravel winning can be a way of maintenance dredging, provided the material is removed from the right place in the correct quantities: it is recommended to avoid overdredging which can result in loss of depth elsewhere, and other physical and ecological damage due to reduced water levels.

7. There is a limit to the increase in depth that can be achieved by river training; if this is to be exceeded, canalisation works, i.e. weirs and locks, are required.

8. A wide range of navigation improvement systems is available. Careful analysis of all relevant benefits and costs, including social and ecological effects, must be made for each feasible solution. This should include:

   - an assessment and comparison of relative costs of regular maintenance dredging and river training.

   - a study of whether by stockpiling or using partly laden ships it is necessary to maintain full channel depths at time of low flows.

9. It is important to make both technical and economical studies to determine the optimum depth for navigation.

INLAND WATERWAYS AND PORTS

SECTION I — SUBJECT 4

Integration of ocean-coastal-inland navigation

Friday 15 May 1981

Chairman:	*J CHAPON (France)* *Ingénieur Générale des Ponts et Chaussées* *Vice-Président du Conseil Générale des Ponts et Chaussées* *Ministère de l'Environnement et du Cadre de Vie, Paris*
Vice Chairman:	*C J L LAWRIE (Canada)* *Head, Waterways Program* *Department of Transport, Ottawa*
Reporter General:	*Prof Dr-Ing H H HEUSER (FRG)* *Versuchsanstalt fur Binnen-Schiffbau eV, Duisburg*
Secretary:	*C COCOZZA (France)* *Ingénieur des Ponts et Chaussées* *Directeur de l'Exploitation du Port Autonome de Paris*
Asst. Secretary:	*A E C HOMASSEL (France)* *Secrétaire Adjoint, Section Française*

Speakers

P R LISLE (UK), M BALDWIN (UK), Y MENDELEEV (USSR), D A BARENDSEN (The Netherlands), K K GOGOI (India), J C AILLERET (France), M DEPLAIX (ESCAP), N N B ORDMAN (UK), F DROUIN (France), E R HEIBERG (USA), M HAGER (FRG), D DREYFOUS-DUCAS (France), N OSWALT (USA), H L REVELL (UK)

H. HEUSER (GERMANY F.R) REPORTER GENERAL

Indication of those aspects of the subject which should with most profit be discussed at the session meeting.

a) Integration from the view of the vessels

b) Integration from the view of the ports

1. Waterborne traffic with transhipment of goods:

- Particularly adaptable and economic transport systems.
- Improvements of transhipment facilities in maritime ports.

Waterborne traffic without transhipment of goods:

- Inland port — to inland port traffic across waters with unlimited seaway conditions:

  barges (lighters) and barge carrying vessels (BCV)

  efforts for standardization

- Inland port to inland port traffic across waters with limited seaway conditions:

  coasters, also suitable for inland navigation

  inland waterways' ships also suitable for service in coastal waters.

  Provisions to be taken for reasons of safety and economy in connection with aspect 1.

2. Special measures to be provided for seaport areas where integration of traffic comprizing ocean-coastal and inland vessels is a necessity.

DISTILLATION OF IMPORTANT INFORMATION AND OPINIONS TO THE SUBJECT

1. Containerization plays a still increasing role in transport modes of sea-going, coastal and even inland water ships. A favourable method of transhipment from land to waterborne transport and vice-versa seems to become more and more the RO-RO system instead of the conventional methods.

   There are several successful attempts with special RO-RO arrangements even on large inland water ships.

   Sea ports as well as inland terminals round the world make efforts to improve their facilities for storage and transfer of containers. Ramps for easier RO-RO service with containers and very heavy bulky goods as well are under construction or in preparation.

2. BCV-systems for waterborne traffic without transhipment make rapid progress. Having started with LASH, SEABEE or, more recently, BACAT and INTERLIGHTER the tendency is changing more and more from LO-LO to FO-FO systems.

   Limits to the utilization of FO-FO ships are set by the necessary water depth. Very recent designs for inland water BCV's are narrowed even more by those limits. On the other hand it is a good possibility to overcome shallow water sectors, especially in non-regulated rivers, if only the area of loading resp. unloading has sufficient water depth for floating the barges on and off the river-BCV.

   The future tendency with FO-FO systems is going to larger barges, even to those of normal dimensions for inland service in push tows.

   It would be very desirable to make progress to a world-wide unification of barges and lighters, which enables them to suit inland water service in push tows and for BCV-purposes as well.

   Standardization of those multi-purpose units should be based on a modular system, derived from a standard river barge.

3. A total integration of coastal-river navigation is possible either by inland-going sea ships, especially low draught coasters, or by inland water ships, qualified for service in waters with limited seaway conditions.

A lot of experience was gained already in this field but development work is still in progress especially to improve the behaviour of river-sea ships in waves of larger heights by optimizing the ship's form, keeping very high block coefficients. At the same time type and arrangement of propulsion devices should be specifically adapted to this service.

4. For economic reasons the integration of ocean-coastal-river navigation will become a necessity in long-distance freight traffic.

   Discovering the most cost-saving method for the different trade connections and sorts of transport goods should be achieved within the years to come.

   A very important task will be to reduce time and costs by improving the traffic without transhipment of goods as far as this is possible.

5. Aspects of traffic safety are to be considered in particular when river sea ships are increasingly utilized for coastal and restricted sea-going service. In the first line a safe network of sea routes for these vessels should be laid down. Certain ports of refuge or sheltered anchorages for the case of rapid change of weather conditions must be provided.

   Moreover an improved forecast of wind and sea state is necessary and is e.g. in the North Sea area already in progress. Last but not least a harmonization of navigational marks both for inland waterways and for coastal and maritime waters should be achieved as valuable assumption regarding safety and ease for vessels in throughgoing traffic.

6. Mixed navigation areas as big sea ports are meeting points for two different nautical worlds, as far as regulations and shipping route signals are concerned. Therefore and because of the different sizes and manoeuvring qualities of the ships it is necessary to take particular precautions to keep a high level of traffic safety. The measures comprize e.g.

   - advanced RADAR control and VHF communication
   - utilization of a determined language,
   - compulsory instructions to keep certain navigation routes.

7. Integration of ocean-coastal-inland shipping, in general being a desirable aim for the future, is in most of the large seaport areas at all times a reality. The density of today's harbour traffic and the shipment of dangerous goods have generated new problems of safety and economic dispatching. Solving these problems is a precondition for success in the other fields of integration.

Contributions from 12 countries all over the world show the great interest in the questions and answers connected with this subject. As a matter of fact the INTEGRATION OF OCEAN-COASTAL-INLAND-NAVIGATION is a fascinating subject, not least because it comprises a return to ancient practices of shipping on a modern level. The problems involved are, of course, emphasized and treated by the numerous authors in a different way. A general division into two parts is evident.

The integration seen on the one hand from the viewpoint of the vessels and waterways and on the other hand from the viewpoint of the ports and cargo-handling methods.

In addition, some important aspects of safety for sea-going inland water ships are demonstrated.

Most of the contributions are predominantly dealing with aspect 1, their focal point being the integration as far as vessels and waterways are concerned.

Our discussion on this topic is suggested to go along the following lines:-

1. Waterborne traffic with transhipment of goods,
2. Waterborne traffic without transhipment of goods.

The first point comprises all aspects of modern transport systems for inland waterways' and sea-going traffic, for example: push-towing, tug-barge-systems or ocean-going barges.

In this field INTEGRATION in the first line means to achieve the most economic methods of transhipment — avoiding or at least reducing storage time in seaport areas — especially as far as containerized goods are concerned.

The second point could be divided into 3 special aspects:-

1) Throughgoing traffic across waters with unlimited seaway conditions, referring mainly to BARGES or LIGHTERS and the different methods of loading and unloading them into or from BARGE CARRYING VESSELS.

2) Throughgoing traffic across waters with limited conditions of wind and waves, e.g. coasters, also suitable for inland navigation or, on the other hand, inland ships, also suitable for service on sea.

3) Measures necessary for safety on sea for inland vessels, for example harmonization of navigational marks, reliable forecast of sea-waves, prescription of shipping routes and providing ports of refuge.

A minority of contributions set up their priority on the aspect of economy and safety with cargo-handling methods and on special measures to be provided for the safety in coastal areas and the integration of simultaneous ocean-coastal-inland shipping in the big seaport areas and their approach sections.

RECOMMENDATIONS FOR FUTURE ACTION BY THE CONGRESS

1. Further development of BCV systems including river BCV's should be carefully observed and supported.

2. Standardization of barges for river and BCV-transport based on a modular system should be promoted. The constitution of a special study group is recommended.

3. Active support should be given to all research activities to improve the prediction of wind and sea state not only for deep sea but particularly for areas with limited depths of water. Encouraging potential authors to publish their appropriate reflections or results in the PIANC-BULLETIN could be a valuable step in this direction.

DISCUSSION

P R LISLE (UK)

In commenting on a number of points arising from the British paper, I wish to draw attention to certain factors which may help to draw conclusions in this important subject. They represent difficulties experienced, opportunities which exist and symptoms which may be observed in guiding thought on the integration of coastal and inland navigation.

The first point is that in the U.K. commercial activity is mainly confined to river navigations and canalised rivers penetrating inland from the four main estuaries. Although serving particular areas only, they are important elements in the economy of those regions and are being developed to secure greater penetration by larger ships and craft. A further point is to observe changes in the pattern of trade such as have occurred in the U.K. with mainland Europe and to use them as opportunities for increased coastal/inland navigation activities. A consequence of this is a requirement for faster turn-round of vessels and the development of more inland terminals for freight handling inland for the established ports. Recent studies in ship design have revealed a trend towards increased beam, shallower craft and greater length for a given capacity. Although overside loading is decreasing for economic reasons, penetration to inland terminals is increasing and perhaps this is a typical symptom elsewhere. There is a need for standardised barges in particular areas to provide flexibilities and interchangeabilities in use between navigation systems and particularly in unitised craft systems. It is important to relate craft design and channel improvements because of the greater cost and life of channel work than those of the craft which use them. It is therefore essential to study these factors carefully and optimise the solution. Other opportunities which arise relate to estuarial/inland traffic where oil, grain and other movements arise to inland countries. There is a danger that some of the BCV systems being developed will be too large for inland penetration and there is a need for standardisation in this field. There is also a need for the development of standards for low-profile coasters to ensure that infrastructure development in the form of new bridges does not prevent navigation inland by craft of this kind. It is important to study the possible improvement of existing waterways to make the best use of what is already available to limit capital cost.

The allocation of costs to navigation in a multiple use waterway is a difficult matter which, it is hoped, will be covered in the deliberation of a working party of Permanent Technical Committee I.

Although containers have been carried on inland craft in the U.K. their use has emphasised the need for a suitable craft module to be developed to meet the requirements of standard container dimensions.

Finally, reference was made to the recent development of ½ lash craft as a suitable and narrower standard craft for use on the smaller commercial waterways.

M BALDWIN (UK)

I would like to take this opportunity to develop a few of the ideas contained in the U.K. paper.

1. On page 678, it is suggested that lack of suitable traffics and economic factors have led to a decline of transhipment to barges. Although such a decline has undeniably occurred in the U.K. I don't believe that the reasons for it are so simple as the paper supposes. This belief is based partly on observations of traffic developments elsewhere, and partly on the results of a study published by a firm of British Naval Architects in 1978. This study analysed the costs of transport of industrial bulk materials from an inland site in England to an inland site in Germany. Neither origin nor destination was accessible by navigable waterway. Seven different routes were assessed; three maximised the use of water, two maximised the use of rail, and two maximised the use of road. Despite the need for transhipment, all three water routes provided cheaper transport than any of the road or rail routes.

   It is therefore probable that other factors besides those mentioned by the authors are in fact operating to reduce this type of traffic in the U.K. These other factors are, I would suggest, firstly insufficient investment in enlargement and development of the inland waterway routes to allow economically-sized craft to penetrate suitable distances and, secondly, that many potential users of the waterways for this type of traffic are unaware of the extent of those waterway services which currently do exist. Both these regrettable factors are symptomatic of the way in which this mode of transport has been neglected in the U.K. in recent years.

2. On page 681, river-going ships are mentioned. Some examples may be of interest to the delegates. Typical amongst U.K. ships of this type are:

   LADY SANDRA - 380 tonne capacity, freshwater draft 2.5m. Air draft 5m.

HULL MILLER - 470 tonne capacity, freshwater draft 2.5m. Air draft 4.3m.

UNION GEM - 715 tonne capacity, freshwater draft 2.5m. Air draft 5.5m.

URGENCE - 1824 tonne capacity, freshwater draft 3.3m. Air draft 6.5m.

One of the UNION GEM'S particularly impressive journeys was from Goole England to Basle, Switzerland, with a cargo of 600 tonnes of coke. This demonstrates the excellent door-to-door transport that this type of vessel can achieve.

Another example of their successful use is shown by the revival of the river Port of Fosdyke Bridge on the River Welland, England. After some ten years without any ships, this was re-opened in 1979 and is now a rapidly expanding port, using river-going ships to import fertilisers from manufacturers in the Netherlands and Belgium, and to export cereals. Although the ships are only small, typically of 500 tonnes capacity, they provide economical door-to-door transport by eliminating transhipment to road at larger sea-board ports.

3. Although U.K. waterways are neither as large nor as extensive as many of those in the countries from which many of our colleagues come, they are interesting in that they are used by many different systems which provide integration between inland and deep-sea shipping. Thus we have coasters, river-going ships, towed off-shore barges (mostly for North Sea Oil and gas work), and BCVs of various types, including LASH, SPLASH, FLASH, SEABEE and BACO. Indeed, I would commend Sheerness as a port to visit as it handles four of these systems, and is thus U.K's most important BCV port.

In Conclusion. Although some nations are only using river-going ships for internal use, many nations are using both these and BCVs in their international trade. The future use of such vessels would be enhanced by dimensional standardisation of the waterways upon which they travel. Perhaps this might be included amongst the recommendations which will be made by this Session.

Y MENDELEEV (USSR)

I would like to discuss some special aspects of the construction of Soviet river-sea navigation vessels. These differ from those of other countries in one major respect, namely that our vessels are designed with hulls of optimum strength in regard to the weather conditions and areas of operation.

The rules of the Soviet ship classification societies (in particular the USSR Register of Shipping and the River Register of Shipping of the Russian Federation) provide for various classes of river-sea vessels. One of these requires the ability to navigate safely in waves produced by winds up to Force 5 on the Beaufort Scale, and limits the range of operation to within 50 nautical miles of a possible port of shelter in closed seas such as the Baltic and Black Seas. Another, the "II — SP" class, is designed for waves produced by winds up to Force 6, and allows operation up to 100 nautical miles from port of shelter in closed seas and up to 50 nautical miles in open seas such as the North Sea.

The analysis of the rules of ship classification societies in Europe shows that, for vessels of this type, the design standards require hull strengths suitable to resist the effect of the worst possible wind and wave regimes of the particular seas. The natural result of these different approaches is that ships designed to meet Russian classification rules have smaller drafts for a given capacity than do ships designed to meet European rules.

Twenty years successful operating experience with "M — SP" and "II — SP" Class vessels has proved the correctness of the Russian approach. Experimental trials of "M — SP" class vessels in the Caspian and Aegean Seas shows that they have sufficient hull strength for use in these waters, and the extension of the operating areas of these vessel types will increase their overall usefulness and further reduce the need for transhipment of cargoes.

The other way to improve the utility of river-sea vessels is to increase their cargo capacity. Design work is now nearly complete on a 5000 cwt vessel with a fresh water draft of 7 metres, the first of which should come into operation next year. Under our conditions, we think this is the correct way to develop river-sea navigation.

D A BARENDSEN (NETHERLANDS)

The development in the USSR with regard to integration of ocean and inland navigation as set forth in the USSR paper and in Mr. Mendeleev's remarks, has been possible thanks to the presence of a vast and large-scale navigation system in the USSR. In particular, the canalized Volga and the system of canals between the upper course of this river and the Baltic Sea are equipped for quite large vessels.

Participants at the 24th Congress of PIANC had the opportunity to see a great deal of this inland waterway network and the numerous types of ships using it.

The inland waterway craft of the "Baltistres" type (referred to as MSP in the USSR paper) sometimes make the trip from Leningrad to the port of Den Helder in the Netherlands, to the north of Amsterdam, provided that conditions in the North Sea permit.

Photographs taken at the 24th Congress and during the boat trip on the Volga after the Congress were projected as slides.

They show the types of rivercraft met with in the seaport of Leningrad and at several places on the Volga, and some locks on the Volga and the Volga-Don Canal.

These photographs give an idea of the large dimensions of these two waterways.

K K GOGOI (INDIA)

The current shortage of funds for investment in

the development of inland and coastal waterways in the developing countries, such as India, precludes the possibility of harmonising these modes with those of the developed countries of Western Europe and North America. Thus for the foreseeable future, the river and coastal transport systems of Asia, Africa and some parts of South America can not be brought into line with the standards prevailing in the North American Gulf Ports, Great Lakes, inland and intracoastal waterways or in the European river systems. Thus the expansion of the use of LASH and SEABEE systems will have to wait until the developing countries can afford to improve their waterways to accept these standard modules. In many cases, the problem arises because, on attaining their independence, the developing countries had to give priority to investing in their road and rail transport systems, and had insufficient resources to make comparable investments in their port and waterway facilities.

Container handling can be harmonised in the foreseeable future provided that the West is prepared to accept the 20' x 8' x 8' container rather than the 40' x 8' x 8' unit, because the roads in developing countries are not yet able to match those in developed countries. In fact, in some parts of the developing countries there are, as yet, no roads at all. In such areas, LASH or float-on/float-off systems may provide the answer.

So any harmonisation of waterways on a world-wide basis must make due allowance for the characteristics of the waterways in the developing countries of Asia, Africa and South America.

J C AILLERET (FRANCE)

In the papers, much interest has been shown in eliminating or improving bulk-breaking operations between ocean-going vessels and inland waterway craft (lighter-aboard-ship, standardized barges).

The container has the same end in view and it is moreover applicable to types of goods which are being increasingly transported.

I am surprised, therefore, that greater interest is not shown in containers in the inland waterway world and that, in any case, this type of traffic has been very little developed.

Indeed, the river transport of containers raises very few technical problems:

- There is no need for specialized barges, as any ship can transport containers; it requires no chute or stowing.
- There is no problem in the seaports, since the inland waterway vessels act in the same way as feeders vis-à-vis the port operators.
- In the river ports, the equipment required is inexpensive (with small gauge and low frequency) and can be polyvalent.
- The minimum volume for this traffic on a given link is quite amall: 60 TEU/week, or 3 000 TEU/year and per direction, i.e. about 30,000 T/year and per direction.

Moreover, the advantage as to transport cost may be substantial if the distance is not too short.

The objection is often made that the transport takes a long time, but the difference is not considerable (less than 48 h to cover 700 km between Strasbourg and Rotterdam by the Rhine); the problem of departure frequencies is doubtless more real, but the shippers are often more concerned about regularity and reliability than about speed.

I am convinced that container traffic by inland waterways has a future and I am surprised that except for the Rhine (approx. 100 000 TEU in 1980), this type of traffic has been so little developed.

I think that, for once, we should lay stress on an awareness of the present possibilities rather than on the need for making new investments.

M DEPLAIX (United Nations Economic and Social Commission for Asia and the Pacific {ESCAP})

There are certain peculiarities of waterways in Asia with regard to standardization of the dimensions of ships, coastal navigation and the transport of pallets on inland waterway vessels.

However, it should be stressed that inland transport, in particular by rail, is not more rapid than by waterways in the countries of Asia and sometimes in Europe as well, and that the traditional references to the slowness of waterway transport are far from being justified in all cases.

N N B ORDMAN (UK)

The recent dramatic increase in energy costs, and factors such as road congestion costs argue the case for increased use of inland waterways and integrated ocean/inland waterway systems. It is to be expected that there will be a consequential increase in investments, and this implies the need for an acceptable means of determining the system costs. Classically, in transportation systems, the costs are categorised as those related to:

- vessels and vehicles
- ports
- cargo-handling, including trans-shipment
- track (in this case, the inland waterway)

There are well-established methods for dealing with the first three categories. However, there are some serious difficulties in determining the true costs of inland waterways related to their use for transport because river and canal systems have multiple uses which may include drainage and sewage disposal, water supply, hydro power and recreation. Has this problem been studied and resolved?

F DROUIN (FRANCE)

Is there a future for barge-carrying vessels? There is little sign of it; they are not developing. Much is said about them in the papers. What is precisely the situation?

The Permanent Technical Committee I at its second session, admitted that they were not a problem and that there was no need to devote much research to them.

Do they point a way to the future, or is it a blind alley?

E R HEIBERG (USA)

I refer to the remarks on cost allocation made by Mr. Ordman, Mr. Lisle and M. Dreyfous.

The US has studied this over the last year, looking specifically at three short river segments. We looked at those items nominally oriented to navigation use, to include locks, channels and certain contributing reservoirs. In these specific examples, we found that 60% to 90% appeared to be the range of costs attributed to navigation. The rest supports hydropower, flood control, recreation, and other uses.

There has been a huge growth in inland transport in recent years, particularly on the lower Mississippi River, the Ohio River, the western section of the Gulf Intercoastal (coastal) Waterway, and on the Columbia River. That growth has been accelerated by energy considerations and the growth of coal and grain movements.

On the other hand, cost allocation has come into national focus, and takes the form of what we call the "User Charge" question. Rather than Federal funding of most inland waterway and coastal port construction, operation and maintenance, the discussion today is to find a fair way for the user to meet more of those costs.

But this remains difficult. We spend millions of dollars annually for example, to hold the Lower Mississippi River in its banks. Not only, however, does that effort provide safe navigation, but just as important, it ensures flood control for millions of people, industrial and city fresh water for the estuary segment of the river and, incidentally, recreation opportunities. It is most difficult to decide the percentages of cost allocation.

We look forward to the work of PTCI to help us in our efforts to divide costs fairly.

M HAGER (FRG)

To follow General Heiberg's remarks, and in answer to Mr. Ordman's question, I can say that in West Germany we have developed a method for the analysis of all the benefits of a waterway project, be this a redevelopment of an existing waterway or a totally new route. The method evaluates all the effects, including those on the environment, changes of land use, etc. This analysis is now carried out during the planning stage of all projects.

We reported on this form of cost-benefit analysis in a recent PIANC Bulletin. We will be happy to bring this to the attention of the relevant PIANC Working Group.

D DREYFOUS-DUCAS (FRANCE)

The delay in developing the use of the container on inland waterways is partly due, in countries such as France, to the rigidity of the transport systems and the habits of transport auxiliaries and dockers.

Proof of this is afforded by the development of small ports in the United Kingdom and of integrated shipping line systems.

Previous studies, more particularly by the Transport Research Institute (I.R.T.), did not yield results because anything that could not be calculated was neglected. Another path is possible, i.e. to calculate the costs that would remain if the waterway were to be closed to commercial shipping and pleasure craft. The survey which I made three years ago showed that, for the maintenance of the waterway, the cost to be apportioned to transport is of the order of 50 to 60% according to the importance and character of the waterway; for investment, the share to be apportioned to transport is 70% on rivers and of the order of 75 to 80% on certain canals.

N OSWALT (USA)

It was suggested in Section I, Subject I that the blockage ratio be set at a factor of 5. I must express a concern for this change in relation to inland confined waterways with berms. A recent model study by the US, on the Sacramento Deep Water Ship Channel indicated that where excessive speeds occur, a ratio greater than 5 is necessary to preserve the stability of the banks.

H L REVELL (UK)

Waterways may have other uses which perhaps should be recognised and maybe a corresponding contribution towards total costs should be provided by the community, but if so, there is a real danger that this could be seen as a special subsidy to this transport mode. Other transport modes have effective lobbies and will be quick to use this for propaganda.

Waterway traffic needs to be specific and have long-term potential. Traditionally, marine equipment has been depreciated over 20 to 25 years whereas road equipment is usually depreciated over a much shorter term, and furthermore can easily be converted to other uses. Therefore, to encourage investment in waterway facilities is that much more difficult.

CONCLUSIONS

The present world economic situation provides motivation for reducing transport costs. In the field of energy inland waterways will be increasingly used because of their low transport energy cost. With respect to integrated ocean-coastal-inland navigation the reduction of transhipment costs will be very important.

This appreciation of the situation has many implications of the following categories:

- technical measures
- regulations
- socio-economics

1. It is necessary to encourage unit load systems which in respect of general cargo include palettization, containerization, RO-RO and barges-on-board ships.

A total integration of coastal-river navigation is possible either by inland-going sea ships, especially low air draught coasters, or by inland water ships, qualified for service in waters with limited seaway conditions.

With very long waterways, systems transhipment into special river vessels may still be economic, but each case must be studied separately.

Safety considerations will require the provision of:

- a safe network of sea routes
- ports of refuge
- forecast of wind and sea states.

With respect to dimensions of vessels and the consequential structures, the modular concept is appropriate.

These are subjects which we recommend to the Association for study.

2. Harmonization of ocean and inland systems will be very important with regards to buoyage and lighting (regarding which considerable progress has been made by IALA) and also in the regulation of navigation. A degree of conformity in navigation aids is also desirable.

   Measures to ensure safety in harbours and their approaches are very important and special arrangements must be developed.

3. Important strategic planning considerations must be understood and resolved. For instance, opportunities have been and will continue to be created for the siting alongside the waterways of industrial development areas and associated urbanization away from present established industrial concentrations.

   Inland waterways have many functions. The proportion of cost attributed to the navigation function should be fair and realistic so as not to give rise to tariff levels which would deter integration of ocean-coastal-inland navigation.

INLAND WATERWAYS AND PORTS

SECTION I — SUBJECT 5

The exchange of planning and engineering technologies with developing countries and its relationship to improving maritime ports and inland terminals

Saturday 16 May 1981

Chairman:	*J CHAPON (France)* *Ingénieur Générale des Ponts et Chaussées* *Vice-Président du Conseil Générale des Ponts et Chaussées* *Ministère de l'Environnement et du Cadre de Vie, Paris*
Vice Chairman:	*O P NARULA (India)* *Development Adviser* *Ministry of Shipping and Transport, New Delhi*
Reporter General:	*T P STEEN (Norway)* *Norconsult A S Consulting Engineers, Hovik*
Secretary:	*C COCOZZA (France)* *Ingénieur des Ponts et Chaussées* *Directeur de l'Exploitation du Port Autonome de Paris*
Asst. Secretary:	*A E C HOMASSEL (France)* *Secrétaire Adjoint, Section Française*

Speakers

T TAKEUCHI (Japan), H C FRIJLINK (Netherlands), J D METTAM (UK), C Van EERDENBRUGH (Belgium), J AUBERT (France), O P NARULA (India), A FUGLUM (Norway), J M DEPLAIX (ESCAP), L K TERHO (Finland), J W MORRIS (USA), P SIREYJOL (France), N N B ORDMAN (UK)

T P STEEN (REPORTER GENERAL)

The many interesting papers submitted on this subject are an indicative of the considerable attention given to the developing countries and their problems by industrialised countries. The authors represent world wide experience from the exchange of planning and engineering technologies which take place to an increasing extent between the two types of countries.

Unfortunately, there were no papers from developing countries. It would have been of great value to hear also the opinions of people involved on that side. They could have corrected possible misunderstandings and clarified questions occurring in industrialised countries and contributed to our better insight into this most important and challenging subject. In this connection, let us point out, like many of the authors, that the phrase "developing country" covers a wide range, from the countries emerging from relatively backward conditions to those which are already advanced in knowledge and application. Still, lack of adequate capital and a surplus of unskilled labour are symptoms which we associate with most developing countries.

The ports are meeting-places for international exchange of goods and thus excellent examples of industrialised undertakings where exchange of technologies takes place on a global scale. However, developing countries have been granted relatively short time in which to develop their ports to modern standards and are therefore dependent on a close co-operation with industrialised countries. Many authors have underlined that this co-operation should not take the form of an uncritical copying but be based on policies laid down by the country in question, taking into account its individual characteristics and needs. Thus the phrase "exchange of technology" implies that a two-way process shall take place.

The great majority of the papers emphasise the influence of the human factor upon all important matters related to this subject. A proper manpower policy is called for, making the port personnel, its capabilities and needs the centre of attention. The papers give a series of advice regarding training of personnel at all levels to secure satisfactory execution of all necessary maintenance, operation and management in the ports. It is stated that the motivation for top achievement is sometimes missing, partly because low pay encourages the taking of second jobs and reluctance to take time for training. Two papers give detailed project descriptions of great interest from an engineering point of view. Although no comments are made in these papers on the co-operation with local personnel, the projects have certainly involved a fruitful exchange of technologies.

Some authors make reference to the activities of PIANC's Permanent Committee for Developing Countries. We take this opportunity to mention that this committee plans to arrange, in co-operation with the British Organising Committee an informal meeting during the congress in Edinburgh. The intention is to present the programme of the committee to representatives from developing countries and other congress participants interested in this subject.

The papers include a number of comments and proposals aiming at promoting exchange of technologies with a view to improvement of ports and terminals, their technical standards, operation and management. Among the many aspects calling for attention we presume that the following could be discussed with particular profit at the session meeting:

INTERNATIONAL STANDARDISATION

It is a common view that developing countries should, in their own interest, make their ports more efficient to cope with international shipping and contribute to the industrialisation of the regions they serve. In industrialised countries the answer to similar challenges have usually been the introduction of more sophisticated and capital-intensive techniques. Is this the answer also in developing countries? Should international standardisation at the highest level be encouraged, or should technologies be governed by local conditions? On the one hand, regard should be paid to unemployment and lack of capital, on the other hand there is the wish to transfer human efforts from unnecessary tasks to those benefitting the basic economy.

STATUS OF PORTS WITHIN INDUSTRY

The status of the ports within the industry of a country is viewed differently. Some authors maintain that, as the ports serve primarily as infrastructural elements, their economy should not be based on profitability criteria. Due regard must be paid to the indirect benefits derived in their hinterlands, which are usually of greatest importance, but difficult to quantify. Others emphasise the challenges involved when ports are run like industrial enterprises in a competitive market and considered as such also as far as financing is concerned. Are we obliged to resort to a compromise in this political question? How to appraise the indirect benefits with some degree of reliability?

DYNAMIC OR STATIC PLANNING?

In some papers attention is drawn to the advantages that may be derived from dynamic development planning. This approach implies a phased development that will satisfy immediate needs at moderate costs, while further developments will be effected first when precise indications of additional needs are available. A static planning implies that the initially constructed facilities are dimensioned to cover also possible future demands. Thus a large initial capital investment is required and the facilities will be underemployed during at least a part of their lives. Why is then the static approach the more usual, also in developing countries?

MAINTENANCE

Many authors point out that all port facilities and equipment should be designed in such a way that a minimum of maintenance will be required. This emphasis reflects the general experience that maintenance is very often neglected by port authorities in developing countries. It would be interesting to hear about possible examples contradicting this view, so as to learn what concrete measures could be taken to improve the situation.

TRAINING

Training of port personnel is the subject most frequently referred to in the papers — as an area where exchange of technology can give a good yield. The personnel is divided into three categories: graduate professionals (top-management), intermediate staff (middle-management, sub-professionals, technicians) and workers. It is recommended, inter alia, that emphasis should now be given to training and strengthening of the middle-management. This would have a positive effect on the continuous planning that ought to be carried out by the port's own personnel, as well as on the continuous follow-up on cargo handling and maintenance that is too often neglected. Will also the port authorities support the idea of placing middle-management in focus? How should the training be carried out to achieve the best possible results?

FORMS OF CO-OPERATION

It is generally recognised that local personnel should participate to the fullest extent possible in technical assistance programmes. In the paper from U.S.A. two methods of organising an exchange of technology according to this principle are presented. One method consists of the pooling of local talent within regional organisations, which would be associated with existing international organisations in this field. The other method is to establish a direct contact between the port authority of a developing country and that of a port with similar characteristics in an industrialised country. Further information on practical applications of these forms of co-operation would be of great interest.

WHAT CAN BE DONE TO SPEED UP TECHNOLOGY EXCHANGE?

This highly relevant question has been raised in the paper from the United Kingdom. Developing countries are concerned about the comparatively slow speed with which technology is being exchanged. It is felt that changes of approach are needed in all sectors. In the paper, several points are put forward for consideration by governments and aid agencies in industrialised countries and for consideration by the developing countries themselves. Further comments to these points could lead to a useful discussion. Are there also other points that should be taken into account?

The papers received allow us to draw the following preliminary conclusions:

1. Developing countries have been granted a relatively short time to develop their maritime ports and inland terminals to modern standards and are therefore dependent on a close co-operation with industrialised countries. It is in the interest of the developing countries that this co-operation does not take the form of an uncritical copying, but should be based on policies laid down by the developing country in question, taking into account its individual characteristics and needs.

2. In most developing countries lack of adequate capital and a surplus of unskilled labour are important factors to be considered in the planning of industrial developments. Thus high employment of local labour and local materials should be emphasised, likewise less sophisticated service installations and equipment which require relatively simple methods of operation and a minimum of maintenance. In many regions, running of port facilities must take place without assistance from an industrialised environment. However, the facilities should be planned in such a way that future modifications for a higher degree of mechanisation are facilitated.

3. Operation, maintenance and management are activities of indefinite duration and, although they might initially be undertaken by expatriates, they should as soon as possible pass to local personnel. Therefore, this personnel should participate actively

in all phases of the development planning and implementation so as to become familiar with the facilities "from the inside". Furthermore, special training of personnel at all levels is in many cases a prerequisite to making possible a successful running of the facilities.

4. It is an international responsibility to assist developing countries to meet the demands that are made upon them in connection with the application of modern technology. This responsibility is recognised by PIANC and other international organisations. Sharing of experiences in the exchange of technology should form part of the steady flow of information which such bodies should be able to provide.

   PIANC's activities in this field should be channelled through its Permanent Committee for Developing Countries (PCDC) which is available to provide advice and guidance on a wide range of marine transportation problems. It is suggested that PCDC, in addition to its already planned activities, should initiate the setting up of a working group of representatives for PIANC, IAPH, UNCTAD and IBRD to discuss and formulate a joint programme in the field of training of port personnel. It should also be made more commonly known that PCDC is prepared to assist in establishing regional organisations in developing countries, alternatively direct port-to-port contacts, with a view to promoting exchange of technology.

The subject to be discussed this morning is not only technical. Exchange of technology between the developing and the industrialised countries depends largely on political decisions. However, engineers can pave the way for the politicians by establishing international collaboration based on science and engineering practice, acceptable to everybody.

A great number of engineers are involved in the exchange of planning and engineering technologies throughout the world, and the eleven papers submitted on this subject are an indication of the great attention that is focussed on it. The authors represent wide experience, and their contributions are of a high standard.

The authors have approached the subject in two different ways. The papers from Belgium and the Soviet Union relate to particular port projects known to the authors from their involvement in the planning of the facilities described. Extensive exchange of technology has no doubt taken place in connection with these projects in Tanzania, Syria and Yemen, and it would be interesting to have some comments from the authors also on their experience from collaboration with local personnel.

The other nine papers reflect the authors' general experiences from their assignments in developing countries. They all emphasise the importance of involving lcoal personnel to the fullest extent possible in each phase of a project, keeping in mind that local personnel will sooner or later take over full responsibility for operation and maintenance of the facilities.

It would therefore have been of greatest interest if papers had been submitted also by developing countries. They could have corrected possible misunderstandings and contributed to our better insight into the subject. However, we hope that representatives of developing countries will compensate for this in the discussion this morning and, indeed, later on as members of our organisation.

The papers draw attention to a great many aspects out of which I have found the following to be of particular interest for discussion as previously mentioned:

- International standardisation of port facilities
- Economic status of ports
- Dynamic, versus static planning
- Maintenance of port facilities
- Training of port personnel

I shall comment briefly on the underlying questions raised in the papers:

In ports of industrialised countries the answer to challenges from international shipping and industry has usually been the introduction of more sophisticated and capital-intensive techniques. However, is this the right answer also in developing countries?, or should technologies be governed primarily by local conditions? On one hand, regard should be paid to unemployment and lack of capital, which are characteristics of most developing countries. On the other hand, there is the wish to transfer human efforts from unnecessary tasks to those benefitting the basic economy.

The economic status of the ports is viewed differently. Some authors maintain that the economy of the ports should not be based on narrow profitability criteria, but that due regard should be paid to all indirect benefits. Others emphasise the challenges involved when ports are run like industrial enterprises. Of course, this is primarily a political question. Nevertheless, the economic status of a port will also affect the technical aspects of the port planning, for instance, in connection with feasibility studies.

Some authors draw attention to the advantages that may be derived from dynamic development planning, which implies a phased development that will satisfy immediate needs at moderate costs, while further developments will be effected only when precise indications of additional needs, are available.

However, the static approach seems to be more usual. This implies that the initially constructed facilities are dimensioned to serve both present and possible future demands. Thus a large initial investment is required and the facilities will be underemployed during at least a part of their lives. Here again, we are confronted with a political/economic question rather than a technical one. But, the technical planning will normally be greatly affected by the policy chosen in this respect.

Proper and regular maintenance of the port

facilities is a matter emphasised in many papers. This reflects the general experience that maintenance is often a neglected field. However, this matter has been dealt with already in this Congress at the meeting arranged by PIANC's Permanent Committee for Developing Countries. Still, it would be interesting to hear about possible examples of well organised maintenance, so as to learn what measures could be taken to improve the situation in general.

Training of port personnel on all levels is the matter most frequently referred to in the papers. It is suggested, inter alia, that emphasis should now be placed on the training of middle-management, since this would normally be the most effective way of achieving a continuous planning and development in the ports.

The Swedish authors recommend that our Permanent Committee for Developing Countries should initiate the setting up of a working group of representatives for PIANC, AIPH, UNCTAD and the World Bank to formulate a joint programme for training of port personnel.

The paper from the United States presents two methods of organising exchange of technology according to the principle that local personnel should participate to the fullest extent possible in technical assistance programs. One method takes advantage of the pooling of local talent within regional organisations, the other method is to establish direct contact between the port of a developing country and a port with similar characteristics in an industrialised country.

Last, but not least, I would like to draw attention to the highly appropriate question raised in the paper from the United Kingdom, namely "What can be done to speed up technology exchange?" The authors suggest that consideration should be given by governments and aid agencies to:

- reducing the time for getting decisions
- appointing consultants and contractors to carry through a whole project
- giving more emphasis to follow-up training and advice, and to maintenance of the projects
- giving more support to intensive training of sub-professional and technician grades

Developing countries should on their part be prepared to:

- obviate time-consuming bureaucratic processes
- minimise delays in customs
- accept a reasonable balance of expatriate inputs at all levels
- accept a reasonably high degree of initial expatriate management.

Further comments to these suggestions could lead to a useful discussion.

In the General Report preliminary conclusions are drawn up in four paragraphs. The first three paragraphs give a summary of certain general recommendations, about which there seems to be consensus of opinion among the authors, namely that:

- it is in the interest of developing countries that their co-operation with industrialised countries does not take the form of an uncritical copying, but be based on policies laid down in the developing country in question.
- high employment of local labour and local material should be emphasised, likewise less sophisticated service installations and equipment which require relatively simple methods of operation and a minimum of maintenance.
- local personnel should participate actively in all phases of the development planning and implementation, and training of personnel at all levels should be given highest priority.

The last paragraph of the suggested conclusions points to the international responsibility that is recognised by PIANC, as well as by other organisations, to assist developing countries. It is recommended that PIANC's activities in this field be channelled through its Permanent Committee for Developing Countries.

DISCUSSION

T TAKEUCHI (JAPAN)

Japan's port construction techniques have been developed over more than 100 years, modelled on the advanced technology of European countries, and today there are more than 1,000 ports in active operation. Japan is now fully capable of using its own technology although the background underlining the present port policy, the strategy of port development or the method of port planning developed in Japan may well be applicable to port development in Developing countries. However, the economic appraisal of port projects, especially that of its indirect benefits, involves difficult problems. Ports should not be considered just as junctions between inland communications and the sea but as centres for industry. They should not be judged just on their own profitability. It is therefore suggested that Developing countries should judge ports on the same basis, and PIANC should continue its efforts to try to find reasonable criteria for the economic appraisal of projects.

H C FRIJLINK (NETHERLANDS)

There is no specific technology for Developing countries, all subjects dealt with in PIANC Congresses are relevant. Developing countries wish to belong to PIANC to have professional contacts with their colleagues from industrialised countries. PIANC must encourage "the South" to participate in its Congresses and PIANC itself must "go South".

The second paragraph of the proposed Conclusion 4 should be redrafted:-

"PIANC's activities in this field should be channelled through its Permanent Committee for Developing Countries (PCDC) which should:-

1) Formulate policies to obtain greater participation in PIANC Congresses by delegates from Developing countries;

2) Liaise with PIANC's Executive Committee and the Permanent Technical Committees (PTC's) in recommending subjects relevant both to Developing and Industrial countries;

3) Recommend formats and venues for conferences to be held in Developing countries on subjects that have a world-wide relevance, and

4) Liaise with IAPH, UNCTAD IBRD, on activities that relate also to these other organisations.

The Chairman in thanking Mr. Frijlink for his remarks pointed out that Conferences are expensive to run and make a great deal of work. He suggested that they should be by invitation.

J D METTAM (UK)

It is suggested that the use of the expression "Navigation" in an archaic sense may inhibit engineers from Developing countries coming to our Congresses, and that the role of National Committees in preparing papers may prevent presentation of papers from Developing countries. Attendance would be very valuable in developing skilled engineers, and encouraging such participation is the most important contribution PIANC can make.

The training of operatives and maintenance staff requires the establishment of training schools in the countries concerned. The General Report does not sufficiently emphasise the shortage of skilled engineers and ways of correcting this.

There are serious disadvantages in trying to build up local consultants specialising in port design where there is insufficient port work to employ them fully. The speaker's firm prefers to combine two ways of helping to build up skilled engineers in Developing countries: 1) to take engineers on secondment in the U.K. office for training, and 2) to open a local office headed by an expatriate (or local) employee of the U.K. firm, employing local staff working with expatriates.

A difficult and important element in port planning is the drafting of terms of reference for planning studies. In the absence of a thoroughly experienced donor like the World Bank, it is suggested that the best method of getting the optimum depth and breadth of study may be to employ an experienced consulting engineer (or more than one) to prepare terms of reference upon which proposals can later be invited.

C Van EERDENBRUGH (BELGIUM)

Two papers (Russian and Belgian) deal with specific technical topics; most papers deal with the philosophy of approach in the exchange of planning and engineering technologies. Some details on the topic of the Belgian paper could be useful for the discussion.

International standardisation of Containers. At the moment a small number of containers are transhipped from train to barge and vice-versa by means of a man driven crane. The trend, however, shows an increase of this type of transport, so that appropriate equipment is becoming essential. It is not wise to stop these trends, customers of the transport systems are interested in them — if only for the good protection that containers provide for the cargo on long voyages.

Dynamic or static planning. The Kigoma Masterplan can be executed in steps, and probably will be executed in that way. Some port projects however do not allow step-by-step development due to their nature — for example sea ports requiring breakwaters. The choice between dynamic or static planning is not only a political question but also technical aspects are involved.

Status of Ports within Industry. Cost-benefit analyses of the investment of the works proposed in the Kigoma Masterplan showed, in fixed prices, an internal rate of return of 0%, but by incorporating indirect gains a substantial rate of return is obtained.

I think that in port investment gains should come mainly from indirect positive effects, while an internal rate of return of 0% by calculating direct income, results in no extra cost for the community in the long term.

J AUBERT (FRANCE)

The authors of the papers have rightly laid stress on the idea that the methods to be used to create new waterways in the developing countries must make full allowance for the local circumstances which naturally vary from one country to another.

I wholeheartedly endorse this first idea, but I think it should be supplemented by a second which seems to me just as important.

Because of the fact that the developing countries have only limited financial resources at their disposal, it would be deplorable to encourage them to execute waterways which might be termed second-rate.

We must be careful not to foist on foreign countries our past ideas which have culminated in the creation of certain existing waterways that we now consider to be out-of-date.

In exchange of technology, our correspondents are entitled to receive the very best — in other words, our present ideas. I would go even further and say that we should export our future ideas.

You will perhaps feel inclined to accuse me of wanting to squander money uselessly. It is easy for me to reply to this allegation: quite the contrary, I am advocating a reduction of expenditure. Indeed, to my mind, progress can only be real if it entails a saving. To attain a specific goal, the engineer's duty is to make use of techniques that are more and more simple and less and less expensive. If progress is made along the lines I have indicated, we may assert that it is within everyone's reach.

It is time that I illustrated my argument by examples.

I should first like to refer to the evolution of ideas concerning the establishment of the longitudinal section of a new artificial waterway. I will show you what we did 150 years ago and what we should do today.

The diagram shown relates to a section of the waterway linking Paris to the Rhine (Fig. 1).

The present canal corresponds to the southern course. The much shorter alignment is the one which would be adopted today. The old course comprises 54 locks and a 5 km tunnel. The new alignment has only two engineering works: two water gradients, the respective heights of which are 125 and 65 metres (Fig. 2). The time taken to cover the new route would be 7 or 8 times shorter than on the existing canal. Its cost would be much less.

As the second example of a modern and economical project, I shall take the case of the big Cabora-Bassa dam on the Zambesi, in Mozambique.

Shortly before they left Mozambique, the Portuguese engineers came to examine with us the question of crossing the dam by a water gradient.

The Zambesi is navigable downstream and the building of a single structure would have sufficed to create a navigable waterway of 500 km upstream.

I have no time left to tell you of a third example of economical structure. This is the last dam built on the Seine downstream from Paris. It was inaugurated six months ago at Denouval. The saving made, by comparison with the traditional solutions, was 30 to 40%.

Several brochures about new techniques are available in the exhibition on the ground floor. Further information can be obtained from

Mme N. Martin, Tour Anjou,
33 Quai de Dion Bouton,
92814 Puteaux, Cedex, France.

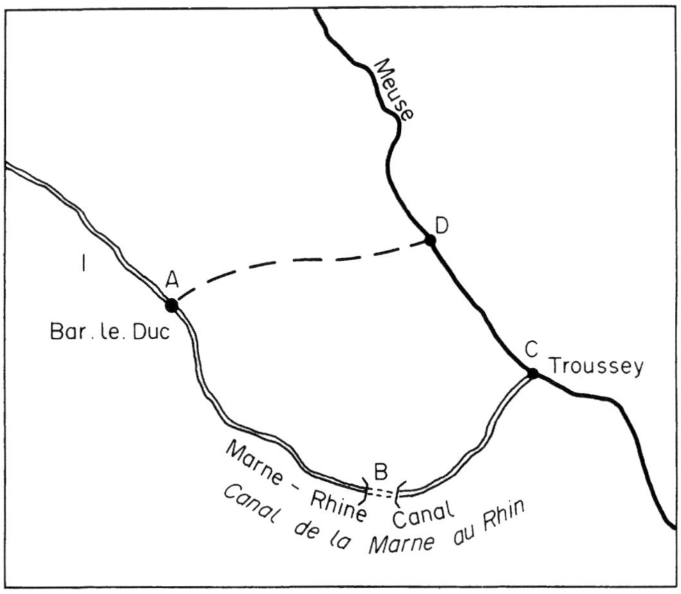

Fig. 1

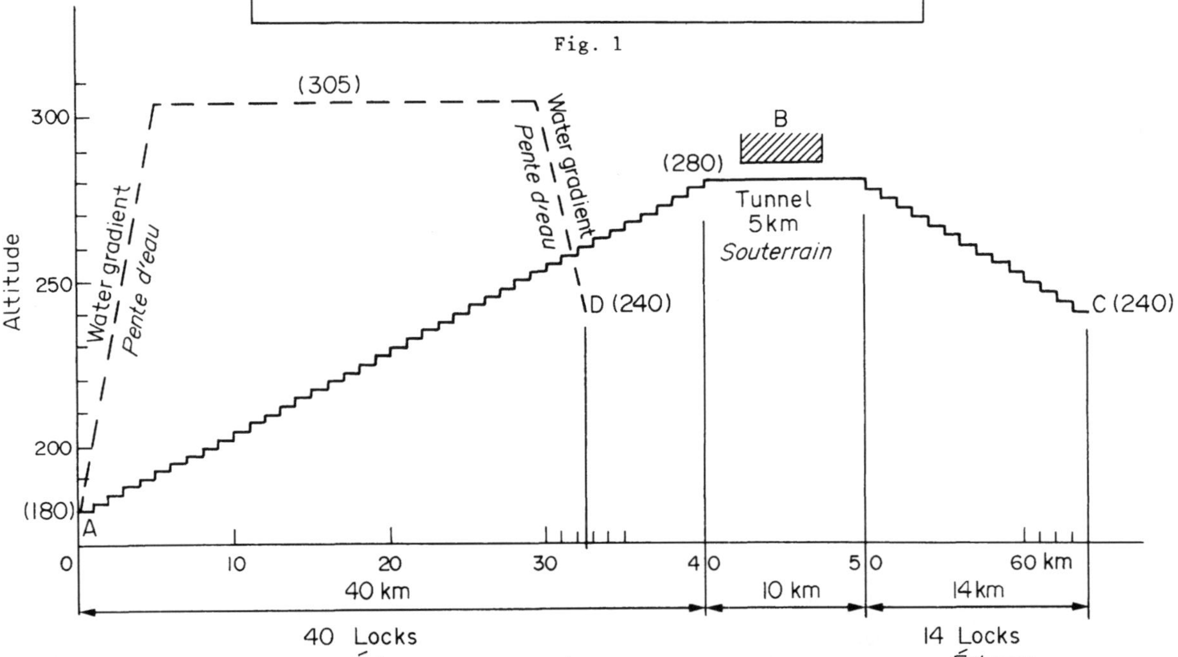

Fig. 2

O P NARULA (INDIA)

The problem of Developing countries is the imbalance of trade flowing in and out, most of exports being raw materials and imports finished goods. Also empty containers in large numbers. This imbalance makes planning difficult.

On standardisation, there must be an appropriate technology which meets the requirements of international shipping whilst at the same time continues to provide employment for a large number of workers. Ports development must take both into consideration.

Hinterland development will take place through the port acting as a catalytic agent. Techno-economic considerations have to be taken into account.

As regards Dynamic/static planning, a synthesis of the two is useful — long range planning for basic facilities like protective works, quays etc., and meeting the immediate needs of handling equipment which can be progressively added to.

The main problem on Maintenance is the planning of procurement and stocking of spares.

As regards Consulting engineers, those from Developed countries should operate along with similar engineers from the Developing country. There is a problem of "Brain Drain", namely loss of technical manpower to the more affluent and developed countries.

A FUGLUM (NORWAY)

There must not only be an 'either-or' as regards highly advanced techniques or less sophisticated solutions, when developing ports in Developing countries. It could be a combination to cope both with foreign trade and local transport.

The question of economic justification of a project should be viewed as part of the infrastructure of a new industrial development, as regards the initial costs of a port construction, so as not to have the operational costs running the port out of competition.

To improve the understanding of maintenance it is not only necessary to convince port people of it but, even more, to convince politicians and other people concerned with decisions on where to place the funds, of the economic consequences of <u>not</u> carrying out proper maintenance.

As far as the training programme is concerned there is a need for gathering and co-ordinating present training and advisory programmes on a joint venture basis in order ultimately to get improved training programmes agreed.

J M DEPLAIX (UNITED NATIONS/ESCAP)

I represent the United Nations Economic and Social Commission for Asia and the Pacific (ESCAP), which your Association has kindly invited to attend this 25th Congress.

On behalf of the Secretary-General of ESCAP and the Head of the Maritime Transport, Ports and Waterways Division, I thank you for this opportunity to make known the problems of the Asian countries and to hear about the latest technical developments.

I shall now deal in succession with some of the points of interest raised this morning.

As regards the standardization of barge dimensions proposed by the Czechoslovak paper on Subject 4, this problem is also a source of concern to us at ESCAP. It is a very complex field and the Czechoslovak attempt is most interesting from many points of view, particularly in the calculation of an optimum for an intercontinental barge, i.e., a barge that would navigate on the waterways of several continents. But in ASIA, the problems are different. The locks are few in number and often of 6 m or 20 feet (6.05 m). When they are large gauge, they do not measure 12 m, like the European waterways, but 14 m to 18 m, and even more in China Except for small barges 5.70 m wide for the canals, there does not seem to be an "Asian" gauge, so that very often one has to attempt to optimize the dimensions of barges on the basis of the network which they are to use. In Thailand, the dimension chosen was, I think, 6.79 m by 45 m, with a superbarge measuring 13.50 m by 70 m. The other networks will soon be defining their standards and ESCAP hopes on that occasion to arrive at a system of compatible dimensions.

Reverting to a point raised by Mr. Ailleret concerning the slowness, alleged or real, of inland waterway transport, I am not even sure that this is true of Europe since, some time ago, it was quicker to go from Le Havre to Paris by waterway than by rail. This is certainly not the case in ASIA, as the average speed of trains in Pakistan, India or Bangladesh is of the order of 15 km/h, including the time spent in the marshalling-yards. I have therefore had the opportunity to say in these different countries that those who tell them about the slowness of waterways are mistaken and deceive them, and moreover do not act in favour of a development of this type of transport.

As regards integration between inland, coastal and ocean-going shipping, the majority of the Asian countries continue to implement this integration, which was traditional for them, in the form of ligher-based handling.

I should simply like to mention two quite new examples of coastal navigation in Thailand: the first consists of a floating terminal for the transhipment of tapioca, which is able to handle ships of over 100,000 T and which is entirely fed by inland waterway barges. It is located at about 40 km from the river mouth in a natural roadstead and the barges are towed to it from Bangkok, where a first transhipment has occurred, or else directly from the factories when they are situated near a large-gauge waterway.

The second example is the service of the Port of Sattahip, developed with World Bank loans and located at over 100 km from the mouth of the Chao Phaya.

At present, there is no rail service, but the World Bank has just agreed to finance it. Barge trains are towed along the coast to this port, a route which is however very exposed to the full sea swell over several kilometres. This transport is effected by the same barges as before which, although sturdy, are not fluvio-maritime. If they are used permanently, they could call in question the breakdown of traffic among the different types of transport, as planned in the preliminary studies.

These two examples show the vitality of inland navigation in Asia, when natural conditions permit. I should now like to give another example concerning pallet transport, referred to in the French paper, and more particularly the use of superpallets adapted to river transport. I think it would be interesting to mention the existence in Asia of a transport network for soft drinks, using this method. The distance covered is about thirty km, from the bottling plant which had to move outside the conurbation for ground water reasons, to the central depot from which urban deliveries take place. The loading unit represents the equivalent of 8 classic-type pallets and is handled by crane. The deck barges, two in number, are towed, thus ensuring a regular turn-round. This system was devised as the result of restrictions on the movement of trucks which formerly supplied the depot from the plant. They were allowed on the road only a limited number of hours each day, obliging the firm to overdimension the flows during the periods when the trucks could be used and creating very expensive peak-hour problems. In this case, a single 120 HP tug suffices, whereas otherwise some forty trucks of the same horse power would have been necessary.

The French paper concluded that industrialists hesitate to take the plunge into the unknown. This example from a less developed country might help them to go ahead.

L K TERHO (FINLAND)

I had the pleasure of being a member of a working group of the United Nations (UNCTAD) whose aim it was to plan a model port for the Developing countries. This was in 1974, in Geneva.

The basis of the planning was the multi-purpose port which could be used for all kinds of dry cargo traffic. The multi-purpose idea was expressed as follows:-

1. The time factor
   - for today's traffic needs
   - for tomorrow — more unitisation
   - for later needs — fully unitised cargo.

2. The different traffic methods
   - conventional
   - roll-on/roll-off
   - lift-on/lift-off

3. In order to minimise the initial outlay the extensive use of ship's gear was planned for unitised cargoes.

4. This condition cannot be fulfilled otherwise than in good co-operation with shipping companies.

5. It was thought very important to provide different berths for ocean going traffic and river traffic (if any).

Other important factors. New ports should be built away from the big cities, where they are not viable. Therefore such sites should be sought and reserved for port purposes. On the other hand the new ports must not be built too far from the existing ports as new infrastructure would then be needed. Of extreme importance is:

- simple solutions
- enough space
- sufficient land communications.

The report of the working group was published in 1976-1977 and there were naturally other factors included, such as financing, economics, operations, training, paperwork, customs procedures etc. Although the Report is some years old its thoughts and findings are still, for the greater part, relevant today.

J W MORRIS (USA)

PIANC has undertaken a noble task in assisting Developing countries. As engineers we may become guilty, or at least victims, of applying our logic as the primary basis for assisting these cases. Rarely, if ever, does the tidy rationalisation of the engineer control the decision process or the implementation thereof. While our approach may be the correct one, "what is to be done" and "how to do it" are most often the product of more complex and sometimes conflicting matters. Among these are:

Political - What are the national objectives of the developing countries and how do these relate to the nations providing assistance?

- Are there nation to nation agreements? Laws?

Customs - Communications always are difficult, yet a developed nation's approach may be socially offensive and thus doomed.

Funding - Where is the source of the funds - are they the developing nation's or the developed nation's or both?

Objective of the assistance - In a real world of national interests — what are the priorities of "peace" or "Extension of Power" — is long term resource growth a worthy goal versus immediate returns — is the specific task really as important as the training of local people?

My key point to PIANC is to be patient — understand all the issues impacting the decisions to develop, counterbalance with the sure knowledge that funding, political and social conditions pass to a degree and in the long run the quality of our work will stand alone for judgement. That means we must provide a quality product which has a real chance to serve the purpose, and finally serve the future of the developing countries by training indigenous personnel and by preserving for generations to come the resources of the developing countries. The ingredients of success are five in number — understanding and patience, with honesty, integrity and technical excellence sharing the remaining part.

P SIREYJOL (FRANCE)

As regards the design and construction of ports, transfers of technology are greatly facilitated by the participation of a Consulting Engineer or a Contractor from a developed country whenever an important task is involved.

The situation is different for tasks which are normally performed by the local port authority:

- maintenance work, straightforward but of daily occurrence, requiring a high degree of continuity;
- operational management functions, which are the very last to be delegated.

In fact, all those among us who are at all familiar with the ports in developing countries know that it is in these two fields that the functioning of these ports leaves most to be desired.

This situation is not unknown to the World Bank, and it might have been expected that, along the lines of the action it took in the field of road maintenance, it would have engaged in a large number of operations in favour of the developing countries in the field of organization, maintenance, operation and training, with a view to improving their functioning in this field. Although some operations of this kind have indeed been embarked upon, it seems that there is still much to be done.

N N B ORDMAN (UK)

Having listened to the stimulating and constructive discussion, my impressions can be briefly summed up as follows: Technology comprises ideas and information. These reside in the minds of men. Hence technology transfer amount to communication. Thus PIANC is in the communications business and that is the purpose of our Congresses and our documentation. As Mr. Frijlink has said, we must make great efforts to reach and contact the developing countries. "If the mountain will not come to Mahomet, Mahomet must try to go to the mountain". Finally, as a consulting engineer, I would remind my colleagues that, although we may be of assistance to developing countries we must not fall into the trap of sometimes thinking that Developing countries exist for the benefit of consulting engineers!

T P STEEN (REPORTER GENERAL)

The discussion has brought forth many important and interesting aspects and I feel certain that it will now be possible for the Editing Committee to draw up conclusions that reflect adequately the views of the Congress. I shall sum up very briefly the points made by the twelve speakers.

Mr. Takeuchi referred to the successful Japanese port policy, under which the ports are developed as parts of the national infrastructure, not as individual economic enterprises. He recommended a similar approach for developing countries. The indirect benefits of a port must be taken into account but we lack reasonable criteria for evaluating such benefits. Maybe PIANC could help in this matter?

Mr. Frijlink commented on the much debated term "appropriate technology" by underlining that the appropriate approach would be to make maximum use of available production factors and minimum use of scarce production factors. The most important task of the PCDC should be to arrange for "The South to come to PIANC" and vice versa. The General Reporter has been too optimistic in his suggested conclusions, point 4, second paragraph, as regards PCDC's possibilities of providing advice and guidance.

The Reporter thanks Mr. Frijlink for his comments and is sure that the Editing Committee will consider very seriously the revised text he has suggested.

Mr. Mettam considered that PCDC's best contribution would be to confer individuals from developing countries with PIANC membership. Lack of skilled personnel is the developing countries' greatest handicap, and training should preferably be carried out in the respective developing countries. In his opinion it is not to be recommended to build up local consultants since there are numerous qualified foreign consultants ready to cover the demands. The Reporter does not feel that everybody will agree with Mr. Mettam in this. Reference is made to, inter alia, regulations of international financing institutions prescribing association with local consultants on all projects.

With reference to his paper on the development of the Port of Kigoma in Tanzania Mr. Eerdenbrugh gave interesting additional information about the handling of increasing numbers of containers in this inland port, and the great indirect benefits to the entire transportation sector that will be derived from its modernisation. As regards dynamic or static planning, he mentioned that the choice could depend also on technical factors. For instance, a stepwise building of breakwaters and other infrastructural elements might be difficult in many cases.

Mr. Aubert illustrated by examples how modern techniques and thorough planning can lead to economic savings. He emphasized that there is no better way of assisting developing countries than by seeking the most economic solutions in each case.

Mr. Narula called attention to the imbalance that exists in the trade of most developing countries, which also affects port planning: outgoing raw materials in bulk, versus incoming piece goods. However, forecasting of port traffic is normally very difficult, and so is the evaluation of indirect benefits, although such benefits have often been the decisive factor for the development of a port. As regards the question of international standardisation the most appropriate technology should be the answer in each case.

Mr. Narula further mentioned that for maintenance dredging, over-capacity is a well-known feature in many areas. The Reporter should like to add that for most other types of maintenance, under-capacity is unfortunately the norm. Mr. Narula also stressed that foreign consultants and local organisations are now working together on the understanding that the latter shall take over full responsibility in the future.

Mr. Fuglum maintained that the question as to whether one should introduce advanced equipment or not, could hardly be answered by simple yes or no. The optimal solution should be sought in each case. The economic justification for port developments lies very often in infrastructural benefits, a fact that should be closely considered by financing institutions. The economic consequences of neglected port maintenance should obviously be better explained to politicians and financing authorities.

Mr. Deplaix gave interesting information on the work of ESCAP (Economic and Social Commission for Asia and the Pacific), its assistance programs for more efficient operation of ports and waterways, and its information services, etc. He also pointed out that the existence of PIANC is not at all well known among port people in developing countries.

Mr. Terho called attention to the UNCTAD report of 1976-77 which describes a model port or multipurpose terminal and emphasizes the need for cooperation between shipowners and port authorities. The problem of finding new sites for old ports encircled by built-up areas is well known and the report recommends that new ports be constructed initially as simply as possible but allotted very spacious areas for future developments.

General Morris referred to his experience from service in developing countries as head of a big semi-military organisation. He emphasized that PIANC should also consider the political sides of the subject we are discussing and go more deeply into the question: What is the objective of the assistance? In any case, we must see to it that PIANC's work is always of high standard.

Mr. Sireyol emphasized that the main problem lies in maintenance, which is a task that has to be attended to permanently in the ports. It is right therefore that our PCDC is now concentrating on this matter. Another important field for PCDC activities could be port management. Mr. Sireyol also maintained that the advantages of self-supporting status in ports in industrialised countries are not so obvious in developing countries where high initial investments tend to dominate the picture.

Finally, Mr. Ordman gave a brief conclusive statement:

- The purpose of PIANC congresses and documentation is transfer of technology at high level.
- We must make great efforts to reach the developing countries, and not yet expect them to take the initiative.
- Developing countries do not exist for our benefit.

I believe, Mr. Chairman, that we may now safely leave to the Editing Committee what remains to be done in formulating our Conclusions.

CONCLUSIONS

1. It is an international responsibility falling upon developed countries to assist developing countries to meet the demands that are made upon them in connection with the application of modern technology. This responsibility is recognized by PIANC and accepted as a central factor in the determination of its activities. Central to this effort must be much more effective and extensive communication to ensure that all countries and especially developing countries are aware of the Association and what it offers.

   The PCDC will doubtless be the major PIANC organ working in the context. But in addition the Association must seek ways to secure the greater participation of developing countries.

2. Developing countries have been granted a relatively short time to develop their maritime ports and inland terminals to modern standards and are therefore dependent on close cooperation with industrialised countries. It is in the interest of the developing countries that this cooperation does not take the form of an uncritical copying, but should be based on policies laid down by the developing country in question, taking into account its individual characteristics and needs.

3. In most developing countries high employment of local labour and local materials should be emphasized, likewise service installations and equipment which require relatively simple methods of operation and minimum of maintenance.

   In some regions, ports must be planned against a background of comparatively low levels of industrialisation. However they should be planned in such a way that higher degrees of mechanization in the future are made possible.

4. Personnel from developing countries should participate actively in all phases of the development planning and implementation so as to become familiar with the facilities "from the inside".

   Furthermore, special training of personnel at all levels is in many cases a prerequisite to making possible a successful running of the facilities, which should be as far as possible done by local personnel.

VOIES NAVIGABLES ET PORTS DE NAVIGATION INTERIEURE

SECTION I — SUJET 1

Nouveaux moyens de protection des rives et du fond des voies navigables contre les effets des courants et des vagues, y compris celles engendrées par les bateaux

Lundi 11 mai 1981

Président: *J CHAPON (France)*
Ingénieur Générale des Ponts et Chaussées
Vice-Président du Conseil Générale des Ponts et Chaussées
Ministère de l'Environnement et du Cadre de Vie, Paris

Vice Président: *Prof C E D'ALMEIDA (Brézil)*
Departamento de Hidraulica, Sao Paulo

Rapporteur Général: *J THEUNS (Belgique)*
Inspector General of the Maritime Services of the River Scheldt
Ministry of Public Works

Secrétaire: *C COCOZZA (France)*
Ingénieur des Ponts et Chaussées
Directeur de l'Exploitation du Port Autonome de Paris

Secrétaire Adjoint: *A E C HOMASSEL (France)*
Secrétaire Adjoint, Section Française

All page numbers cited in these discussions refer to Inland Waterways and Ports, Volumes 1-5, Proceedings of the XXV Congress of the Permanent International Association of Navigation Congresses (PIANC) Edinburgh, 1981, ISBN 0 08 026753 X Pergamon Press, 1981

Orateurs

M HAGER (RFA), R TENAUD (France), A J WOESTENENK (Pays-Bas), C EVANS (GB), C H GAUM (Etats-Unis), R AGOSTINI (Italie), D MUSKATIROVIC (Yougoslavie), Y ZECH (Belgique), P BROUNS (Belgique), J D WINDERS (GB), T SAVILLE Jr. (Etats-Unis), G DELMAS (France), R DE PAEPE (Belgique), H OEBIUS (RFA), W MELLEMA (Etats-Unis), G GLAZIK (RDA), J De KONING (Pays-Bas), P R LISLE (GB)

JAN THEUNS (BELGIQUE) (RAPPORTEUR GENERAL)

Presque tous les rapports indiquent les raisons pour lesquelles la protection des berges et du fond des voies navigables exige dans les dernières décennies une attention accrue. Ces raisons sont: l'accroissement du nombre de bateaux automoteurs, l'augmentation de la puissance installée dans les bateaux, l'introduction des convois poussés, la vitesse plus grande des bateaux.

Il faut encore remarquer que dans les frais d'investissement d'un nouveau canal et surtout pour les travaux de modernisation des canaux anciens, le revêtement des berges intervient pour un assez grand pourcentage.

Plusieurs rapports mentionnent que l'environnement et l'écologie jouent un rôle de plus en plus important dans le projet d'une défense des berges.

Ces raisons font que, dans tous les pays, une attention renouvelée est donnée aux projets de défense des berges. Le but est finalement d'aboutir à un projet qui offre une protection suffisante contre l'érosion se produisant sous les actions hydrauliques, un projet dont la somme des frais d'investissement et d'entretien est minimale, un projet qui s'harmonise avec l'environnement et qui permet la préservation de la flore et de la faune.

Quelques rapports attirent spécialement l'attention sur la protection des berges et du fond d'une voie navigable aux endroits de manoeuvre et d'accostage. La raison de l'érosion à ces endroits est l'utilisation plus fréquente des débarcadères et le fait que les navires sont de moins en moins assistés par des remorqueurs car ils possèdent leurs propres moyens de manoeuvre (bow-thrusters).

Les causes de l'érosion du fond et des berges d'une voie navigable sont bien connues. Ce sont les phénomènes hydrauliques engendrés par la navigation qui en sont les causes principales sur les canaux. Pour les rivières à écoulement libre et pour les rivières canalisées s'ajoutent les phénomènes hydrauliques dus à l'écoulement des eaux et en particulier à l'évacuation des crues. L'abaissement rapide du plan d'eau après une crue est p.ex. une raison de l'érosion des rives.

Une défense des berges d'une voie navigable est donc différent pour un canal ou une rivière. Dans le cas d'un canal, le plan d'eau en général varie peu, et la défense peut se limiter à une hauteur relativement restreinte. La défense dans le cas d'une rivière est beaucoup plus étendue; elle comprend une défense aux environs du plan d'eau d'étiage (zone du batillage) devant résister aux actions hydrauliques de la navigation; au dessus se trouve une défense qui doit être stable pour les crues fréquentes (p.ex. annuelles); plus haut la berge doit être protégée pour les actions hydrauliques des crues extrêmes.

Quoique les phénomènes hydrauliques dus à la navigation soient déjà bien connus, certains rapports traitent encore de quelques aspects particuliers, notamment le courant de retour, la vitesse critique du bateau, l'abaissement du plan d'eau.

Plusieurs rapports mettent l'accent sur le courant d'hélice. La théorie appliquée dans cette recherche est la théorie d'un jet immergé. Les résultats théoriques sont controlés et complétés par des essais <u>in situ</u> et sur modèle réduit. Quelques rapports soulignent un aspect spécial de l'action hydraulique, c.a.d. les variations des pressions dans les berges ou dans le fond du canal. Ces variations ont un caractère dynamique et cyclique.

Ce sont les procédés de protection des berges qui font l'objet du plus grand nombre de rapports. En effet, la protection des berges est la plus fréquente sur les voies navigables tandis qu'une protection du fond ne s'applique en général que près des débarcadères et dans les coudes d'un canal, ou bien pour obtenir une cuvette étanche.

Actuellement les revêtements des berges les plus utilisés sont: les enrochements sur un filtre, les dalles en béton, les palplanches en béton et en acier, les gabions, les revêtements avec du béton d'asphalte.

Cependant il ressort des rapports qu'un enrochement simple avec ou sans pénétration (béton de ciment, béton d'asphalte) ou incorporé dans les gabions, est le revêtement le plus employé.

Une exigence primordiale pour ce revêtement est un filtre adéquat. Un développement important est intervenu dans la construction des filtres par l'introduction de toiles synthétiques à base de fibres artificielles. Ces filtres s'appliquent dans divers pays et plusieurs auteurs traitent des caractéristiques auxquelles les toiles synthétiques doivent répondre.

L'emploi d'un filtre synthétique combiné avec des éléments artificiels (des blocs en béton, des rouleaux remplis de gravier) forme un nouveau revêtement. Quelques auteurs mentionnent l'emploi d'un tel revêtement dans leur pays. Il est certain que l'utilisation et le développement de ce revêtement se poursuivra.

Plusieurs auteurs recommandent pour la construction de revêtements d'employer le plus possible des matériaux disponibles sur place ou à proximité et des produits résiduaires (p.e. scories, fraisil, pneus usés, bois ébranché, déchet de béton, etc.). On peut se demander toutefois si un revêtement avec des pneus usés s'harmonise avec le paysage.

Un rapport décrit un revêtement formé entièrement par la végétation. C'est un revêtement fort intéressant du point de vue environnement et milieu.

Pour terminer nous signalons qu'un rapport décrit l'emploi d'épis immergés comme moyen de régularisation d'un coude dans une rivière; un autre rapport détermine la profondeur de dragage dans le cas où des mégaripples se forment dans un chenal de navigation maritime.

Les rapports ne mentionnent pas des revêtements totalement nouveaux. Divers pays font des recherches afin d'obtenir des revêtements moins coûteux et qui s'harmonisent avec l'environnement. Ces recherches sont cependant surtout orientées vers l'amélioration des revêtements conventionnels.

La conclusion générale est donc que, pour le projet d'un revêtement de défense des berges, les méthodes actuelles éprouvées sont préférables.

L'emploi de matériaux disponibles sur place ou à proximité est à conseiller pour diminuer le coût de la construction.

La construction doit pouvoir résister aux effets des actions hydrodynamiques les plus fréquentes afin de diminuer les frais d'entretien et les inconvénients qui en découlent.

Une attention spéciale doit être réservée pour faire harmoniser la construction avec l'environnement et pour éviter les conséquences nuisibles à la faune et à la flore.

Pour la discussion à la séance nous proposons les points suivants:

1. l'importance de l'impact d'un revêtement de rive sur l'environnement, et quand et dans quelle mesure le projet de protection doit tenir compte de l'environnement;
2. pour la végétation doit-on donner la préférence à une monoculture ou la promotion de nouvelles cultures?
3. l'emploi de filtres synthétiques: caractéristiques, essais, etc.;
4. la philosophie du projet: déterministe ou probabiliste: le pour et le contre des deux méthodes;
5. les dimensions d'un profil en travers en fonction des données hydrauliques:
   - profil à talus combiné (oui ou non) avec un risberme
   - profil à parois verticales avec ou sans berme immergée.

Nous proposons les conclusions suivantes:

1. Continuer les recherches théoriques et les essais tant en modèle réduit qu'en nature en vue d'approfondir les phénomènes hydrauliques dues à la navigation, aussi bien pendant la marche que pendant les manoeuvres des bateaux. Une attention spéciale est à réserver aux fluctuations des pressions d'eau dans les digues.
2. Améliorer les procédés de revêtement existants avec les résultats des recherches mentionnées sous 1)
3. Il est à conseiller lors de l'étude d'un nouveau projet, de faire appel au concours de spécialistes afin d'incorporer la construction dans le paysage et de conserver le système écologique.
4. Etudier et encourager l'emploi de matériaux disponibles sur place ou à proximité et de produits résiduaires.
5. Continuer la recherche pour déterminer les critères qui permettront de réaliser un projet économiquement justifié, par rapport à l'importance des dégâts causés par les actions hydrauliques.

Je remercie tous les auteurs qui ont présentés des rapports sur le sujet que nous discutons ce matin.

La plus part des rapports a strictement trait au sujet comme il a été formulé. Il y a deux rapports qui dévient un peu du sujet, mais qui ont tout de même une grande valeur technique. Je remercie donc les auteurs de ces deux rapports, notamment du Japon et de la Yougoslavie.

Avant de passer à la discussion je voudrais éclaircir quelques termes employés dans mon rapport général.

Kellner Jacks:

C'est une protection employée aux Etats-Unis

d'Amerique pour les grandes rivières. Un Kellner Jack est un élément de trois membrures rectilignes, assemblées à leur point central, tel que chaque membrure est perpendiculaire sur l'autre. En français on emploie le mot: chevaux de frise.

Bouture de bois:

Le rapport anglais parle de "timber hedge" (p. 149). Dans le résumé du rapport anglais on emploie le mot "bouture de bois". Je crois que c'est le terme correct, puisque on parle dans le texte de formation de racines. Le terme anglais approprié est "wattle work".

D'autres points exigent des discussions.

1. Quelques rapports (R.F.A., Pays-Bas) évoquent les variations de pression dans les berges et (ou) le fond du canal dues aux courants provoqués par la navigation. Puisqu'il s'agit d'essais en modèle et en nature, je suppose qu'il n'y a pas de formules générales exprimant ces variations. Je crois qu'il est nécessaire de poursuivre ces essais en vue de voir plus clair dans ces variations de pressions.

2. Un rapport (France) décrit un revêtement entièrement végétal. Comment se comporte ce revêtement dans le temps?

3. Le rapport suédois donne une formule pour la vitesse critique d'entrainement. Les unités ne sont pas précisées. Je suppose que v est exprimée en m/s et d en m?

4. Le rapport du R.D.A. donne une formule analogue, mais celle-ci tient compte de la position du gouvernail et de hélice (celle-ci peut être libre ou montée dans un tube) et s'applique au courant de l'hélice.

   Suède: $v = 5\sqrt{d}$

   R.D.A.: $v = 3{,}62\sqrt{d}$ pas de gouvernail central et hélice dans un tube

   $v = 5{,}02\sqrt{d}$ pour le cas d'un gouvernail central

5. Le rapport soviétique montre que "le passage du mouvement d'un bateau vers le régime critique se fait dans un interval de temps ou plutôt dans un interval de vitesse" (p. 173). Il serait intéressant de connaître la signification physique.

6. Les chevaux de frise sont, à mon avis, uniquement utilisés pour la protection des berges des rivières à écoulement libre et avec une grande variation du plan d'eau. Est-ce vrai?

7. Un rapport (France) recommande d'utiliser sur un même canal différents types de protection pour atténuer l'impact sur l'environnement et l'écologie.

8. Les rapports de la Suède, du R.F.A. et du R.D.A. donnent une expression pour la vitesse du jet d'hélice. Il y a quelques divergences entre les formules, notamment en ce qui concerne le diamètre qui intervient dans les formules.

   En plus le coëfficient de poussée K_T est suivant un rapport constant, tandis qu'il varie en réalité.

   Je propose que les divers auteurs forment un petit groupe de travail pour étudier ce problème.

9. Est-ce qu'il y a une préférence entre les gabions utilisés en France et en Italie (resp. treillis soudé et grillage métallique à maille hexagonale avec fil d'acier à double torsion?)

10. Pour les différents zones du jet d'hélice il est recommandé d'employer des termes uniformes. Ceci peut être incorporé dans le groupe de travail proposé sous le point 8.

11. Je demande aux auteurs du rapport soviétiques de nous fournir des explications sur un enrochement formé par l'action des vagues (p. 170).

12. Le rapport néerlandais suggére des formules simples pour la détermination des profils en travers. Ces formules recueillent-elles l'assentiment général? En plus il y a une faute sur la figure 6 p. 118: on utilise deux fois le H. L'inclinaison des talus est variable d'un rapport à l'autre. Une bonne moyenne semble 1/3. Ce qui est important de ne jamais dépasser l'angle naturel. En plus cette inclinaison dépend du revêtement employé.

Pour les points à discuter au cours de la session je vous renvois à mon rapport général. C'est à dire je propose de discuter sur:

1. L'importance de l'impact d'un revêtement de rive sur l'environnement.

2. La végétation: monoculture ou promotion de nouvelles cultures.

3. Les filtres synthétiques. Pour ce point je vous signale qu'au Pays-Bas, pour la protection du fond de l'Escaut Orientale, le Rijkswaterstaat exigeait que le tissus en polypropène devait avoir une durée de vie de 200 années. Une commission spéciale a mis au point une nouvelle technique d'essai à courte durée pour obtenir des données sur le comportement à long terme du polypropène en eau de mer. Ceci conduisait à l'emploi d'additifs spéciaux. Le nouveau tissu, obtenu avec les additifs, a été essayé et le résultat est que la garantie de 200 années demandées est possible.

4. La philosophie probabiliste ou déterministe.

5. Les dimensions du profil en travers pour un nouveau canal.

LES DEBATS

M HAGER (R.F.A)

Je souhaite ajouter deux brèves remarques au rapport allemand sur les nouvelles méthodes de protection des berges et du lit des voies d'eau:

1. La protection des canaux artificiels est rendue nécessaire essentiellement par l'action des bateaux. Notre expérience nous

a enseigné qu'une attention particulière doit être réservée au courant de l'eau souterraine et à la percolation, surtout dans le cas de barrages. Les remards qui se forment dans les talus et les effets de cette érosion interne sont bien connus. Nous savons ainsi aujourd'hui que la puissance du courant peut modifier le sol et les conditions de sol à tel point que peuvent se former des trous extrêmement dangereux pour les ouvrages de protection. En particulier, ces ouvrages de protection réalisés en asphalte ne résistent que pendant un temps limité à ces influences. Tout dépend, en outre, de la température. Mais les problèmes se compliquent encore pour les petits barrages, fréquents sur les voies d'eau artificielle, lorsque le niveau du fond est proche de celui de la surface du sol de la région. Dans ce cas, il est difficile d'identifier la percolation à temps. Il est dès lors nécessaire d'élargir le barrage et de l'équiper à l'extérieur d'indicateurs. Les éléments croisés ne devraient pas pouvoir éviter la formation de trous. Je pense que, dans le domaine de la protection des berges, nous ne pouvons ignorer les phénomènes de mécanique des sols mentionnés ci-dessus.

2. La deuxième remarque porte sur la possibilité d'apport de sédiments dans une voie d'eau naturelle dans le but d'éviter l'érosion du lit alluvial. Cette méthode est utile si le transport alluvial est interrompu parce que la section amont est canalisée. Les matériaux nécessaires — dragués à côté de la voie fluviale — sont déposés au fond de celle-ci par des barges à clapet, de sorte que le matériau est réparti de manière uniforme. L'expérience montre que cette méthode, plus simple que les autres solutions, n'entraîne aucun trouble du point de vue de l'environnement. Les graviers peuvent être déposés au cours des périodes des plus hautes eaux, de sorte que l'équilibre naturel peut être respecté en tout moment. Dans le cas du Rhin, il suffit de 170.000 m^3 par an, ce qui est inférieur à ce qu'exigent toutes les autres solutions.

   Il faut en outre savoir que celles-ci, qu'il s'agisse par exemple, du dragage ou des ouvrages de régulation, perturbent l'équilibre de la voie d'eau tandis que notre méthode renforce celui-ci. Cette méthode est appliquée dans les conditions particulières au Rhin, où la profondeur d'eau en aval des barrages est moindre qu'en amont. On peut mentionner les conditions différentes du Danube, dont la section supérieure et la section en aval de la frontière allemande sont canalisées. C'est pourquoi des ouvrages hydrauliques sont en cours de construction dans la partie restante, et notamment les écluses et barrages à proximité de Geisling et Straubing.

R TENAUD (FRANCE)

Au sujet de la protection des berges par la végétation, les expériences faites sur la MOSELLE ont montré que la végétation seule, même avec des tapis précultivés, est très rapidement détruite dans la zone de batillage correspondante au niveau normal des eaux.

Au-dessus, les résultats sont variables avec la nature des terres du talus. Dans les zones très graveleuses et lorsqu'il n'y a eu d'apport de terre végétale, la fixation des racine se fait mal. Par contre, sur des terrains plus argileux, le résultat est bon.

Avec un revêtement en pavés de béton alvéolés, la végétation se développe très bien dans les orifices entre les pavés, et les pavés deviennent presque invisibles. De plus, ce revêtement est très efficace contre le batillage.

Au sujet du calcul de stabilité des rideaux de défenses de berge en palplanches, nous avions indiqué dans le rapport qu'il y aurait intérêt à utiliser un petit programme informatique pour déterminer la butée à chaque niveau du rideau.

Nous avons mis au point ce programme et nous l'avons utilisé pour perfectionner la méthode décrite dans le rapport.

Le programme utilise la théorie de Coulomb qui est exacte lorsque l'angle de frottement entre les terres et le rideau est nul.

A chaque point du rideau où on veut determiner la la butée, le programme calcule la force horizontale sur le rideau nécessaire pour réaliser l'équilibre du coint de terre correspondant à plusieurs plans de rupture obtenus par variation progressive de l'angle α. La valeur minimale ainsi obtenue est la valeur cherchée de la butée.

Le même type de programme s'applique pour le calcul de la poussée en prenant le maximum au lieu du minimum.

Ce programme permet de calculer très rapidement la butée ou la poussée avec une configuration quelconque du terrain; il peut prendre en compte plusieurs couches de terrain (horizontales) avec des caractéristiques différentes, ainsi que des forces verticales uniformément réparties sur une longueur quelconque et des forces ponctuelles.

A l'aide des résultats obtenues avec ce programme, nous avons cherché à améliorer la méthode manuelle de détermination de la butée, lorsqu'il y a devant le rideau un talus avec ou sans risberme.

On procède ainsi avec une risberme.

Les points A',B,C,D, sont déterminés comme indiqué sur le croquis No 1. (page 7)

L'angle α est l'angle du plan de rupture correspondant à un talus d'inclinaison B, il est donné dans la table incluse dans le rapport.

- Entre A et B on prend la butée unitaire Ka_1 correspondant à un terrain horizontal (angle de rupture $\frac{\pi}{4} + \frac{\varphi}{2}$), on obtient le point 1.

- On détermine la butée unitaire en C (point 2) en prenant à partir de A' le coefficient Ka_2 correspondant à un talus d'inclinaison β (valeur donnée dans la table du rapport).

- Entre C et D on prend la butée unitaire correspondant à $1/2\ (Ka_1 + Ka_2)$, on obtient le point 3.

  Au dessous de D on prend le coefficient Ka_1.

Cette méthode est plus précise que celle indiquée dans le rapport, elle donne des résultats très voisins de ceux obtenus par le programme informatique (exemple croquis Nos 2 et 3). (page 8)

Elle est très simple et bien suffisante pour le calcul des rideaux de défense de berge.

A J WOESTENENK (PAYS-BAS)

J'aimerais mentionner les revêtements du Canal de Suez, tant au niveau des essais que des ouvrages définitifs de la dérivation de Port Saïd. On m'a donné à comprendre que l'Autorité du Canal de Suez a constaté que les deux seuls modes de protection résistant aux conditions sévères sont:

- l'essai de Bitumarin
- l'essai de Gabions Maccaferri utilisant du mastic de sable ou des matelas en tissu artificiel.

Cette expérience semble être en contradiction directe avec ce qui est dit dans le rapport italien au sujet d'autres types de matelas.

Le rapport affirme qu'en septembre 1979, l'Autorité du Canal de Suez, après mise en adjudication, a choisi les matelas Maccaferri Reno avec coulis de mastic pour la protection des bermes sur une étendue de 24 km de la nouvelle rive occidentale du canal de dérivation et la rive orientale du Canal de Suez.

Il est piquant de constater à cet égard que la couche de filtre en sable enrobé à chaud, qui est décrite comme suspecte dans le rapport, a été retenue dans la conception qui a été finalement réalisée.

C EVANS (GB)

Je voudrais décrire un système de protection de rives récemment mis au point et qui n'a pas été décrit dans les rapports publiés, bien que son intérêt me semble certain du point de vue technique.

Au départ, le système consistait en un revêtement imperméable de canal destiné à éviter à la fois les pertes d'eau par infiltration et l'érosion des berges. Sous cette forme, il comporte une membrane à trois couches, à savoir une membrane de filtre Terram, une épaisseur de Butyl et un Paraweb, c'est-à-dire une membrane entrelacée de thermo-plastique, qui agit comme protection de l'épaisseur du Butyl. La membrane est fixée au moyen de pitons d'ancrage en plastique enfoncés dans le sol, leur longueur et leur espacement dépendant des conditions-mêmes de ce sol.

Le principal avantage du système, par rapport aux méthodes conventionnelles est qu'il peut être mis en place et ajusté sous eau, donc sans besoin de canal de mise à sec.

Lorsqu'il n'y a pas de problème d'infiltrations, la couche de Butyl peut être omise, ce qui donne lieu à une membrane perméable qui empêche l'apparition derrière cette membrane d'une pression d'eau inégale et qui s'adapte donc rapidement aux modifications du niveau d'eau, empêchant ainsi l'érosion des berges. En cas de délavage et d'infiltration importants, il est possible de ne pas mettre de Butyl au-dessus du niveau d'eau basse, de manière à rendre la membrane imperméable sous ce niveau et perméable dans la zone de délavage, de manière à tenir compte des deux phénomènes.

Un autre avantage est donné par le fait que le Paraweb, outre qu'il n'est pas sensible aux rayons ultra-violets, résiste parfaitement aux chutes de débris de roche et aux attaques des véhicules à chenilles, tandis que son élasticité lui permet d'absorber de petits mouvements du sol sans que son efficacité en soit affectée.

On l'a utilisé sur le canal d'Ismaili en Egypte et je suis sûr qu'il aura un rôle à jouer à l'avenir.

C H GAUM (USA)

Les conclusions proposées sont pertinentes. Néanmoins, un élément supplémentaire demande attention. Il s'agit de la prévention de l'érosion des rives due à l'écoulement de terres et aux modifications subséquentes du niveau de l'infiltration et de l'évacuation des eaux phréatiques. Prévenir ces problèmes peut s'avérer moins coûteux que les travaux de protection des rives intervenant après affaissement, érosion associée et affouillement par l'écoulement du cours d'eau. La prévention de désordres au niveau des rives basée sur des méthodes de génie civil respecte la végétation naturelle, protège la faune et écarte la sédimentation, autant d'éléments souhaitables du point de vue de l'environnement.

La construction d'autoroutes nouvelles, de zones résidentielles et industrielles modifie l'écoulement et si ces eaux ne sont pas adéquatement collectées, il peut en résulter un accroissement de l'écoulement de la nappe sur les rives et une grave érosion. L'infiltration accrue peut modifier le niveau et la pression de la nappe phréatique. Si on peut en attendre un affaissement des rives, il faut installer des drains souterrains pour intercepter l'écoulement et maintenir la nappe phréatique à un niveau proche de ses conditions naturelles. Une inspection régulière des rives et une étude de photos aériennes permettront de détecter les endroits où peuvent survenir des problèmes en raison de la modification de l'écoulement. Les autorités et les responsables de l'aménagement du territoire locaux devraient également être rendus attentifs aux problèmes posés par la surveillance du drainage, afin d'informer les organes compétents de la nécessité de coordonner la conception des systèmes de drainage.

Aux Etats-Unis, l'érosion attendue des berges est analysée au cours de la phase de planification d'une voie d'eau et la conception prend en considération la protection des berges chaque fois que c'est nécessaire. Le Corps d'Ingénieurs de l'Armée des Etats-Unis est chargé de la plupart des voies d'eau aux Etats-Unis et donc l'érosion des berges est intégrée dans la conception et les cas spéciaux se voient réserver une attention particulière. Les remorqueurs travaillent à faible vitesse au centre de la voie d'eau et n'entraînent pas de problèmes dans les voies les plus larges.

En ce qui concerne l'impact de la fluctuation du niveau de la voie d'eau sur l'érosion des rives, ici aussi, la conception de la voie d'eau s'efforce de maintenir les débits de crue décroissants à des niveaux proches des conditions naturelles. Sauf dans les cas de grands barrages-réservoirs réservés à plusieurs fins, il n'y a pas de fluctuations importantes vers le bas.

En de très rares circonstances, une déficience des portes d'écluse ou de barrages peut entraîner une évacuation rapide des eaux, dans la mesure où ces incidents sont provoqués par l'éperonnage d'une barge survenant dans des circonstances exceptionnelles à un moment où le niveau d'eau est élevé. Il n'est pas considéré comme raissonnable de prévoir une protection des berges pour ces cas isolés, très rares, mais qui se produisent néanmoins.

R AGOSTINI (ITALIE)

Nous marquons notre accord avec les conclusions du Rapporteur Général. Au regard des problèmes économiques, on enregistre le donné que les composants élémentaires du coût final ont fort changé leurs poids relatifs.

L'augmentation des coûts des transports, de la main-d'oeuvre et de certains matériaux (le bitume en particulier) ont déterminé les conditions pour le développement de l'emploi de revêtements minces, qui sont possibles grâce à l'utilisation de grillages métalliques. Ces revêtements ont des caractéristiques techniques très bonnes, comme a été confirmé par leur récente application à la protection des pipelines sur le fond de la Mer MEDITERRANEE, utilisent les matériaux disponibles sur place et présentent des frais d'entretien très réduits.

Au regard du problème écologique, on doit dire que, en ITALIE, il n'a pas encore l'attention qu'il mérite. La qualité des canaux nouveaux, au point de vue de l'harmonisation dans l'environnement n'est pas bonne, tandis que les canaux anciens représentent un enrichissement du paysage.

D MUSKATIROVIC (YOUGOSLAVIE)

Dans le passé, et jusqu'à présent, les ouvrages directeurs fluviaux de la partie yougoslave du Danube ont été construits à l'aide de matériaux dits "classiques": brousailles, assemblages de broussailles, matelas de broussailles, sable, gravier, pierre, etc.

Depuis quelques années, de grands efforts sont réalisés en Yougoslavie en vue d'éviter les travaux manuels pénibles et de trouver des moyens plus économiques de réaliser les ouvrages directeurs fluviaux. Une attention particulière en ce sens a été réservée à la construction des ouvrages les plus utilisés des aménagements directeurs sur le Danube, tels que: épis, seuils, digues directrices, etc.

Les grands principes de départ retenus par les experts sont:

- mécanisation des travaux
- utilisation des sédiments fluviaux locaux
- qualité accrue des ouvrages directeurs
- coût moindre par unité de longueur d'ouvrage.

A partir de ces principes, plusieurs solutions ont été examinées de manière approfondie et ces recherches de grande ampleur ont débouché sur la conclusion que les bacs en plastique remplis de sable de rivière constitueraient la solution la plus adéquate en tant qu'éléments d'ouvrages directeurs.

Ces sacs sont remplis par hydrocyclone, opération pendant laquelle l'eau est séparée du sable. Chaque sac pèse environ 5 KN. Ces sacs ont été utilisés en tant qu'éléments d'une série d'ouvrages différents dans quelques sections du Danube: système d'épis (à Backa Palanka), seuils de fond (en aval de la section d'Apatin) et combinaison des deux (section de Dalj).

L'expérience acquise lors de la construction de ces ouvrages aussi bien que l'observation de leur comportement depuis lors, confirment que la solution proposée était justifiée.

Les principales conclusions sont les suivantes:

- les épis provoquent suffisamment de sédimentation sur la totalité de leur longueur, même si la forme de la coupe transversale est adaptée en vue de l'utilisation des sacs de sable;

- les flancs en aval des épis ne doivent pas nécessairement être revêtus;

- le revêtement en aval des digues transversales s'est avéré nécessaire;

- les seuils de fond (5 à 10 m sous les niveaux de navigation) peuvent être construits avec une pente amont de 1: 1,50 et une inclinaison aval de 1: 2; les seuils de fond construits en sacs de sable se révèlent être d'une remarquable stabilité – ce qui, vu leur rôle, est très important;

- l'économie réalisée dépend de la hauteur de l'ouvrage, mais, par rapport aux ouvrages similaires construits avec des matériaux classiques, elle varie entre 15 et 65%;

- l'économie de temps n'est pas non plus négligeable, puisque la nouvelle technique permet de réduire de 25 à 30% la durée de construction des ouvrages au moyen de sacs de sable.

Y ZECH (BELGIQUE)

Plusieurs université belges ont entrepris une étude, sur modèle réduit et en nature, de la stabilité des berges de canaux de navigation intérieure, ceci sous la coordination d'un groupe de travail d'ailleurs animé par le Président de l'A.I.P.C.N., le Professeur WILLEMS.

Dans ce cadre, et à titre de comparaison avec des essais ultérieurs, l'Université de LOUVAIN a réalisé une série d'expériences sur une berge en sable, non revêtue, soumise à la seule action d'une onde de masse, reproduisant la variation du niveau du plan d'eau lors du passage d'un bateau de 1 350 tonnes de type européen. Le courant de retour et le batillage, qui sont de moindre importance dans le mécanisme de destruction de la berge, ne sont pas reproduits. Les pressions à l'intérieur de la berge sont mesurées.

Un film 16 mm-couleurs a été réalisé avec prises de vue commandées par le même ordinateur qui pilote les fluctuations du plan d'eau, afin d'obtenir une image accélérée 1 200 (2 images par cycle de 100 secondes) ou 2 400 fois (1 image par cycle).

Le film présenté contient les parties suivantes:

1. Schéma de l'installation: l'onde de masse de fluctuation du niveau d'eau, qui nécessite d'énormes variations de débit, est réalisée par échange de quantité de mouvement dans des éjecteurs à tuyère.

2. Fluctuation imposée au plan d'eau: cycles de 100 secondes, avec simulation de l'onde d'étrave, de la dépression au droit du bateau (40 secondes), et des ondes de sillage.

3. Vues accélérées de la dégradation de la berge:

- naissance d'une nouvelle pente d'équilibre dans la zone de marnage;
- fluage à l'amont de cette zone et création d'une sorte de falaise;
- microchenaux sur l'estran et apparition de cones de déjection au pied de ceux-ci;
- éboulements dans la falaise amont, alimentant le mouvement des grains de manière continue.

P BROUNS (BELGIQUE)

Des protections "permeables mises en place <u>in situ</u>, par des "matériaux cohésifs" (voir aussi classification dans le rapport des Pays-bas p. 119) ont été éxécutées en Belgique ces dernières années.

Le matériel cohésif utilisé est un mélange bitumineux constitué par un mastic (20%) et un concassé (80%).

Pour le procédé du mélange même et par le choix de la granulométrie on obtient un produit stable qui après refroidissement (on le place en effet à chaud) garde encore environ 20% de vides assurant ainsi le caractère perméable de la protection. En raison de ce grand pourcentage de vides, il est évidemment nécessaire d'utiliser un filtre entre le corps de la digue ou des berges et le mélange bitumineux.

Ce filtre peut varier selon la nature des matériaux des berges mêmes. Ainsi on peut utiliser un tissu polypropylène parce que la protection bitumineuse est posée à une température de quelques 110 degrés centigrades, ou un filtre composé d'un non "woven" et d'un tissu polypropylène et d'une couche de sable asphaltique.

Jusqu'à présent on a exécuté en Belgique des revêtements de ce genre sur les berges des canaux sur le tissu polypropylène uniquement.

Le canal de dérivation de la Lys a reçu un revêtement épais de 15 cm. La berge avait presque 16 m de largeur et avait en partie haute une pente de 2/1 et sur sa partie basse une pente de 2,5/1. La longueur de la rive était de 1 100 m, la superficie à couvrir de 17 000 m^2 fut exécutée en 15 jours ouvrables seulement. L'équipement consistait en deux grues hydrauliques.

Dans l'arrière port de Zeebrugge, une épaisseur de 20 cm a été retenue. L'exécution de quelques 26 000 m^2 est à ce moment en cours.

Me référant d'un côté aux différents rapports traitant du problème des pressions hydrauliques dans les berges et de l'autre au sommaire du Rapporteur Général rappelant les recommandations de beaucoup d'auteurs sur l'utilisation des matériaux trouvés sur place (dans ce cas du sable, du concassé et une faible quantité (4%) d'un produit résiduaire: le bitume) on peut dire que ce revêtement, ouvert, cohérent et de ce fait applicable en une couche de faible épaisseur, d'où un revêtement économique, peut répondre, à maintes reprises, aux exigences auxquelles un bon revêtement doit répondre.

J D WINDERS (GB)

Je voudrais corriger l'impression qu'a eue le Rapporteur Général lorsqu'il pense que l'environnement n'est pas suffisamment pris en considération dans notre rapport. C'est le résumé en français qui est à l'origine de cette impression. Dans la version complète, il est indiqué à propos du remblai qu'afin de protéger les terrains adjacents, le revêtement doit en être raisonnablement étanche, si l'on veut éviter les déficiences structurales, ce revêtement n'étant visible que du chemin de halage ou des bateaux utilisant le canal. Du point de vue du chenal, l'environnement revêt une importance toute particulière, le revêtement en dur devant être limité aux zones critiques des pieds de talus. Le film qui a précédé a montré toute l'importance de la protection de ces zones.

Je suis d'accord avec le Président et le Rapporteur Général pour dire que peu de nouvelles méthodes ont été décrites. A cet égard, je voudrais recommander chaque fois que possible l'utilisation de sous-produits locaux qui seraient de toute manière destinés au rebut. Utiliser, aussi, le concept d'énergie minimum, non au sens hydraulique du terme, mais au sens de l'input réel d'énergie. Ici, un exemple évident est l'utilisation de la végétation naturelle, et notre rapport recommande à cet égard le recours à la haie d'arbres plutôt qu'au clayonnage, le nouveau système de racines des premiers assurant la stabilité des rives dont l'entretien n'est pas de première importance.

T SAVILLE Jr. (USA)

Les rapports ont essentiellement traité des chenaux et canaux en eau douce. Aux Etats-Unis, cependant, nous comptons de nombreux chenaux et canaux dans nos baies, goulets & estuaires, qui sont en eau salée. Beaucoup d'entre eux sont de faible profondeur, mais certains, comme le chenal vers Baltimore, un grand port en eau profonde, ont une profondeur très grande. La Voie d'Eau Intracôtière, par exemple, s'étend sur des milliers de miles le long de nos côtes de l'Atlantique et du Golfe. La plupart du temps, une bande d'eau peu profonde et de faible inclinaison sépare les chenaux des rives. Il s'agit donc d'une situation différente des rives à forte inclinaison des voies d'eau intérieures, et la végétation peut dans ces conditions s'avérer très efficace contre les dégâts et l'érosion dûs aux vagues. La végétation, qui peut être très dense, absorbe l'énergie des lames et favorise une fixation rapide des particules sédimentaires en mouvement. Les herbacées doivent être semées, mais deviennent très touffues en un an ou deux. Elles sont particulièrement efficaces dans les zones où existe une végétation de marais spontanée. Les avantages pour l'environnement sont certains. L'habitat naturel est préservé, voire amélioré; l'équilibre écologique est maintenu, de même que les qualités esthétiques. Dans certains, cette protection par la végétation suscite un habitat nouveau et supplémentaire pour la vie aquatique aussi bien que pour les oiseaux.

Des recherches se poursuivent en vue de déterminer les meilleurs types de végétation, les engrais à utiliser, les périodes et les méthodes de plantation les plus efficaces selon les différents types d'environnement (température de l'eau et de l'air, salinité, sols, etc.)

En résumé, si la végétation constitue un mode de protection d'utilisation difficile sur les rives escarpées de la plupart des voies d'eau intérieures, elle peut être et s'est effectivement avérée extrêmement efficace le long de nos chenaux et voies d'eau en eau salée lorsque les plateformes latérales et les rives sont en pente douce.

G DELMAS (FRANCE)

Si M. HAGER le permet, observation sur le rapport allemand à propos du déversement de graviers pour lutter contre l'érosion du lit du Rhin.

La lecture de ce rapport pourrait laisser penser que la canalisation du Rhin est seule responsable de l'érosion du lit du Rhin à l'aval d'Iffezheim.

Or l'érosion est un phénomène très ancien qui s'est développé sur le Rhin à courant libre bien avant toute canalisation, du fait que le profil en long du fleuve ne correspondait pas à un profil d'équilibre.

Ce phénomène a été considérablement accentué par la correction du lit du Rhin exécutée entre Bale et Mannheim de 1840 à 1860: en concentrant l'écoulement des eaux moyennes du Rhin dans un lit unique, alors qu'elles se répandaient auparavant entre de nombreux bras, la correction du Rhin a raccourci le cours principal du fleuve, donc augmenté la pente et le courant; l'érosion a alors atteint des proportions considérables, et l'abaissement du plan d'eau d'étiage a atteint 7,00 m à Chalempe, à 30 km à l'aval de Bale, et entraîné l'effondrement du niveau de la nappe phréatique dans toute cette région.

La canalisation a mis un terme à ce phénomène dans le secteur canalisé, mais a reporté l'érosion à l'aval de la dernière chute, aujourd'hui celle d'Iffezheim.

La RFA et la France avaient par conséquent, au terme d'une Convention signée en 1975, décidé la construction en commun entre les deux pays d'une nouvelle chute à l'aval d'Iffezheim — Mais la RFA a recherché depuis, en expérimentant le procédé de déversement de gravier, une solution permettant d'éviter la construction de cette chute.

Cependant, contrairement à cette chute, le procédé de déversement de gravier ne régle pas les autres problèmes qui se posent sur le secteur franco-allemand du Rhin:

- amélioration des conditions de navigation;
- nécessité absolue de rétablir le niveau de protection contre les crues à un niveau au moins équivalent à celui qui existait avant canalisation à l'amont.
- Ce qui précède n'enlève bien entendu rien au grand intérêt du procédé de déversement de gravier lorsqu'on a à faire face sur un fleuve comme le Rhin au seul problème de l'érosion.
- Questions — Les graviers à déverser dans le Rhin doivent être extraits des zones riveraines du Rhin dans le champ d'inondation, zones qui sont pour l'essentiel couvertes par une forêt rhénane d'un très grand intérêt sur le plan de l'écologie — C'est précisément le souci de préserver cette forêt qui a entre autres poussé la RFA à rechercher une solution permettant d'éviter la chute, et ses emprises importantes.

  Mais quelle est la surface qu'il faut, en moyenne, déboiser chaque année pour y extraire les graviers à déverser dans le Rhin, et ce, sans limitation dans le temps? Cela ne risque-t-il pas de conduire à la longue à des emprises excessives sur cette forêt qu'il s'agissait précisément de préserver?

R DE PAEPE (BELGIQUE)

A la question concrète de M. le Rapporteur Général de savoir quand et dans quelle mesure le projet de protection des berges doit tenir compte de l'environnement, je voudrais répondre: toujours!

En plus, l'étude écologique qui doit conduire à la protection de l'environnement doit satisfaire aux conditions suivantes:

1. cette étude doit porter sur tous les aspects de l'environnement, c'est-à-dire aussi bien les problèmes qui concernent la faune et la flore que les problèmes de pollution, d'intégration dans l'environnement, etc ...

2. cette étude doit être faite non seulement par des spécialistes, mais plus précisément par des écologistes.

H OEBIUS (RFA)

J'ai le sentiment que l'un ou l'autre des auteurs présents devrait répondre aux questions posées par le Rapporteur Général sur l'interaction hélices-fond.

Les différences dans les formules proposées traduisent la difficulté du problème des projections dues aux hélices. Le rapport de la R.F.A., par exemple, donne les conditions hydrodynamiques de base relatives à une hélice à axe fixe en course libre fonctionnant dans un continuum, c'est-à-dire en-dehors de l'influence du navire lui-même, de la surface de l'eau ou de la limitation du volume d'eau. Les contributions de la R.D.A., de la Suède et de l'U.R.S.S., par contre, négligent plus ou moins la distribution locale de la vitesse de la projection de l'hélice et calculent une vitesse moyenne à partir de la poussée totale de l'organe de propulsion. Ceci engendre une approche relativement simple de l'influence sur une projection d'hélice d'éléments tels que la forme de l'arrière du navire, le brassage de l'hélice, le gouvernail, la surface de l'eau, les murs latéraux ou le fond du chenal. Il ne devrait pas y avoir de grandes différences dans les résultats obtenus dans des conditions semblables au départ de cette méthode, comme l'indique l'émergence d'une vitesse critique au fond pour les navires équipés d'un empennage central, signalée par les rapports de la R.D.A. et de la Suède.

Néanmoins, la résultante cumulée globale des divers paramètres qui interviennent n'est pas encore bien connue, pas plus que ne l'est l'intensité de l'action de chacun d'entre eux, mais le chiffre mentionné ci-dessus suffit à prouver la complexité du problème de l'érosion due aux hélices. Ceci veut dire que, non seulement, la moindre modification d'une des conditions d'expérimentation modélisée peut entraîner des différences significatives au niveau des résultats, mais aussi que le problème de l'érosion due aux navires se déplaçant à vitesse de manoeuvre (influence de la projection d'hélice) ou à vitesse normale (influence du courant de déplacement) n'est pas encore bien appréhendé.

Pour l'orientation des travaux futurs, je me permets de recommander tout d'abord de définir l'intensité des effets dûs aux différents paramètres pertinents en fonction du point de vue hydrodynamique, de la distribution de vitesse au sein d'une projection d'hélice, et ensuite de déterminer une vitesse critique au fond universellement applicable et qui puisse être corrélée avec les diverses formules bien connues de transport de sédiments et d'effort de cisaillement.

W MELLEMA (USA)

Le rapport des Etats-Unis vous présente un programme lancé récemment dans notre pays, programme qui nous donne un moyen d'évaluer et de comparer l'efficacité de divers procédés et méthodes de protection des berges. Depuis la rédaction du rapport et le début du programme, environ 80 projets expérimentaux de lutte contre l'érosion des berges ont été réalisés à travers tout le pays, couvrant une large gamme de voies d'eau et de causes d'érosion. Tous ces projets sont suivis de très près en vue de déterminer leurs avantages et désavantages respectifs. En outre, environ 40 projets antérieurs ont été choisis en vue de leur évaluation, qui fera l'objet d'un rapport. Enfin, des essais sur modèles ont également été effectués.

L'un des objectifs sous-jacents du programme est de tenter de mettre au point des méthodes relativement peu coûteuses et respectueuses de l'environnement pour lutter contre l'érosion de nos voies d'eau. Le programme en cours offre une possibilité unique de comparer les méthodes tant anciennes que nouvelles. La plupart des ouvrages sont à présent construits. Ils sont en cours d'évaluation et je suis convaincu qu'il sera possible de faire état des résultats au cours des sessions à venir.

M HAGER (FRG)

Je suis reconnaissant à M. Delmas de sa très intéressante contribution. Il est également nécessaire de tenir compte des exigences de la navigation et du bassin de protection contre les crues. Le plan doit réaliser un équilibre entre tous ces éléments et les divers critères et exigences peuvent être rencontrès. Les aspects relatifs à l'environnement sont les plus importants dans le cas qui nous occupe, à savoir:

En un siècle, nous n'avons besoin que d'une surface de 1 km^2 pour extraire le gravier, c'est-à-dire moins de 1,5% du volume de graviers dragué à des fins commerciales. Pour un seul barrage, il nous faudrait au contraire une surface d'environ 3 km^2, sans compter les quelque 14 mill. m^3 de matériaux nécessaires pour les barrages, mais la conséquence n'en resterait pas moins que l'érosion en aval commencerait à partir de ceux-ci.

G GLAZIK (RDA)

Je voudrais tenter, par quelques commentaires, de jeter quelque lumière sur les questions posées par le Rapporteur Général sur les jets d'hélices, et en particulier sur les formules relatives à la vitesse critique au fond en cas d'érosion et sur la comparaison des formules fournies par les rapports de la Suède et de la République Démocratique d'Allemagne. Les expressions sont dérivées d'un point de départ identique: l'étude du jet submergé. Je ne vais pas entrer ici dans les détails du champ de vitesse complexe du jet d'hélice. Ils sont indiqués dans le rapport. Cependant, comme aucun des auteurs du rapport de la RDA n'est présent, je vais tenter de fournir quelques éléments d'explications. Le travail présenté a en effet été réalisé au sein du département que je dirige dans notre Institut (FAS).

Dans l'équation (16) de notre rapport, il faut souligner la valeur du facteur "B". Cette valeur a en effet été interprétée sur la base de nos recherches expérimentales. Elle dépend entre autres du facteur de Reynolds. Il s'agit d'un cas semblable à celui de la Fig. 19 pour l'attaque des vagues. Ici nous avons extrapolé le coefficient relatif à des facteurs de Reynolds supérieurs à partir de résultats d'essais modélisés portant sur des éléments de granulation inférieure. A l'heure actuelle, nous préparons des essais sur le terrain pour consolider les résultats. Quand on la compare à divers énoncés de la littérature, les valeurs de "B" que l'on trouve à la page 39 de notre rapport semble acceptable. A cet égard, la correspondance avec l'expression du rapport suédois n'est donc pas surprenante. Les auteurs suédois font également mention des résultats de recherche de notre Institut, publiés auparavant par Römisch. Comme l'a déjà dit le Rapporteur Général et comme cela a été souligné dans la discussion, les détails du champ de vitesse du jet d'hélice dépendent de la forme et de la position de l'hélice et de l'empennage. Ces facteurs réflètent, comme on l'a dit plus haut, dans la valeur du facteur "B". Les différences des valeurs relatives aux différents types de Bateaux qui sont, par exemple, indiquées à la page 39 de notre rapport, sont représentatives de l'importante influence de ces paramètres.

Pour terminer, je voudrais remercier le Rapporteur Général pour l'ensemble de son rapport et en particulier pour les commentaires où il soligne l'importance des phénomènes hydrauliques dans la conception des voies d'eau. En principe, nous approuvons ses conclusions générales. Ses remarques introductives rappellent que ce sujet a été traité déjà par plusieurs Congrès antérieurs. Cela suffit à en souligner l'importance. Je suis par conséquent heureux que nos travaux en ce domaine aient retenu l'attention d'experts de plusieurs pays. Nous pensons qu'il est extrêmement important de préciser les critères hydrauliques pertinents en vue de la mise au point des méthodes de construction. En outre, comme le mentionnent les conclusions du rapport général et comme l'a rappelé le Président de session, les recherches en ce domaine doivent se poursuivre. Les activités de l'A.I.P.C.N. ont en fait déjà promu ce type de recherches aussi bien que l'échange d'expériences en ce domaine au niveau international.

J de KONING (PAYS-BAS)

Monsieur le Président, je voudrais faire référence à la contribution des Etats-Unis, page 158, Fig. 4 et page 161, photo 1. J'aimerais aussi mentionner le film de l'Université de Leuven présenté ce matin. Dans les deux cas, il s'agit des phénomènes d'érosion des berges des voies fluviales et canalisées.

La constitution et la forme des cavités d'érosion présentent de grandes similitudes avec les cratères d'érosion qui apparaissent au cours de dragages à l'aide de dragues aspirantes utilisant de simples tuyaux d'aspiration dans les sablières.

Je propose donc que les ingénieurs et les scientifiques qui se penchent sur ces problèmes collaborent et échangent leurs expériences avec leurs collègues du monde du dragage. Les mêmes phénomènes physiques peuvent en effet se produire dans les deux univers.

P R LISLE (GB)

Nombreux sont les rapports présentés qui reconnaissent que la protection des berges est un élément coûteux parmi les ouvrages d'aménagement des voies d'eau, qu'il s'agisse de la construction d'un nouveau canal ou de l'amélioration d'une voie existante. Il se peut en effet que la majeure partie de la protection des berges originales subsiste, mais doive être renforcée ou modifiée pour répondre à des conditions nouvelles. Ces modifications des conditions incluent un accroissement de la fréquence d'utilisation de la voie d'eau, avec, éventuellement, augmentation de la taille des bateaux, des remorqueurs, des convois poussés et des autres embarcations qui l'utilisent. Le résultat peut en être une érosion également accrue, qui rend la section concernée du chenal inadéquate face aux besoins actuels et la protection des rives insuffisante par rapport aux nouveaux phénomènes d'érosion. Il peut donc recréer les conditions susceptibles d'éviter l'érosion en mettant en place un facteur de blocage réduisant les besoins en protection des berges et donc le coût de celle-ci. Un rapport d'au moins 1:5 entre la partie immergée des bateaux et la section transversale du chenal est un facteur favorable à cet égard. Si ce rapport n'est pas atteint, une solution consiste à démanteler la protection de berges existant d'un côté, élargir le chenal autant que nécessaire et, soit ré-utiliser les matériaux de l'ancienne protection, soit construire un nouveau revêtement. Cette solution permet au moins d'éviter ou de réduire le coût de nouveaux matériaux tout en assurant une situation satisfaisante. Cette méthode est utilisée avec succès sur les canaux de Grande-Bretagne et en particulier pour les navigations d'Aire et Calder, ainsi que de Sheffield et South Yorkshire, qui sont reliés à l'estuaire de l'Humber. Tout dépend de la possibilité de disposer de ou d'acquérir le terrain nécessaire. Dans les régions rurales, ceci ne pose généralement pas de problème, au contraire des zones urbaines. Toutefois, chaque fois qu'il est possible d'acheter du terrain pour élargir la voie d'eau, le coût en est souvent inférieur à celui d'une nouvelle protection des rives. Une planification sérieuse peut donc contribuer à substantiellement réduire les coûts.

J'ai une autre remarque quant à l'impact sur l'environnement des ouvrages de protection des berges. L'opinion publique est de plus en plus consciente de la nécessité pour les ouvrages de génie civil de s'intégrer de manière acceptable dans l'environnement existant, de sorte que le coût esthétique de ces ouvrages ne vienne pas en tempérer les avantages directs. La construction de nouvelles voies d'eau et l'aménagement de celles qui existent sont des travaux de grande envergure qui ont un impact évident sur l'environnement. Il faut donc pour les réaliser prendre conseil quant à leur impact esthétique et à leurs conséquences sur la faune, et notamment en ce qui concerne l'accès de celle-ci à la terre et à l'effet d'une protection ininterrompue des berges sur une grande distance sur les conditions de végétation et d'habitat des poissons. Les conséquences, en effet, seront ressenties par de nombreuses générations à venir et celles-ci nous seront ou non reconnaissantes selon ce que nous avons réalisé ou négligé de réaliser à cet égard.

J THEUNS (BELGIQUE) RAPPORTEUR GENERAL

Je remercie tous les participants qui ont contribué à la discussion sur ce sujet. Je constate une fois de plus que le problème de la protection des berges préoccupe un grand nombre de pays. En plus comme déjà mentionné dans les rapports, il ressort clairement des discussions que l'impact sur l'environnement d'une protection des berges joue un rôle important pour le projet de nouvelles protections.

Les interventions ont aussi prouvé que les recherches doivent être poursuivies, p.ex. pour les sollicitations dûes au jet d'hélice.

L'emploi de matériaux disponibles sur place ou à proximité et de produits résiduaires doit être encouragé.

Il ressort aussi des discussions que pour la protection des berges on doit, de préférence, faire appel à un revêtement souple qui puisse suivre les déformations de la digue.

Je crois que les conclusions que j'ai proposées dans mon rapport général restent valables après cette séance et je vous propose de les maintenir avec peut-être une rédaction modifiée.

CONCLUSIONS

1. Les voies d'eau artificielles et naturelles sont aujourd'hui un élément essentiel de l'environnement. En conséquence toutes créations ou modifications importantes doivent faire l'objet d'une étude d'impact sur l'environnement.

   Cette étude doit prendre en compte tous les aspects nécessaires à une bonne insertion de l'opération dans l'environnement naturel et humain, notamment les effets écologiques et hydrologiques et les nuisances éventuelles.

   Il est recommandé de réaliser cette étude avec le concours d'experts de chaque discipline.

2. La protection des rives constitue un élément généralement important du coût d'une voie d'eau, tant en investissement qu'en entretien.

   Il est donc souhaitable de limiter la réalisation des revêtements aux sections de la voie et aux parties du profil en travers qui sont les plus exposées aux risques de dommages: par exemple les concavités des courbes, les zones de manoeuvre des bateaux, les parties exposées aux forts courants et au batillage.

   Pour constituer des systèmes de protection économiques, il est recommandé de développer l'utilisation des matériaux locaux ou des produits résiduaires. En outre, le recours à des plantations peut, à la condition de choisir des espèces appropriées, constituer un moyen encore plus économique pour protéger les berges contre les érosions et permet d'améliorer l'insertion dans l'environnement.

3. Une attention particulière doit être apportée aux fluctuations de la pression de l'eau dans les berges, le sol et le sous sol sous l'effet combiné de la navigation, du régime hydraulique de la voie et de la nappe phréatique, en tenant compte des caractéristiques du sol. Lorsqu'il n'est pas nécessaire d'assurer l'étanchéité de la voie d'eau, un filtre efficace permettant un bon écoulement de l'eau et empêchant les pertes de matériaux solides doit être réalisé afin de réduire le coût de la protection des berges.

4. Il est recommandé que la conception des revêtements, même s'ils sont constitués d'éléments rigides, leur donne une souplesse suffisante pour suivre les déformations qui se produisent toujours à long terme dans les sols.

5. Il est proposé à l'AIPCN que le Comité Technique Permanent I étudie si des économies appréciables peuvent être réalisées sur le coût global des protections de rives en prenant en compte le caractère aléatoire de certains éléments qui conditionnent le projet — ce qui suppose que soit accepté un risque calculé de dégradation des ouvrages.

VOIES NAVIGABLES ET PORTS DE NAVIGATION INTERIEURE

SECTION I — SUJET 2

Méthodes pour accroître la capacité et la sécurité des voies navigables par: l'amélioration de l'exploitation; l'utilisation de brise-glaces, etc.; la navigation de nuit

Mercredi 13 mai 1981

Président:	*J CHAPON (France)* *Ingénieur Générale des Ponts et Chaussées* *Vice-Président du Conseil Générale des Ponts et Chaussées* *Ministère de l'Environnement et du Cadre de Vie, Paris*
Vice Président:	*Prof V DEGTIAREV (URSS)* *Rector, Novosibirsk Institute of Water Transport Engineers*
Rapporteur Général:	*Capt W R RIEDEL (Etats-Unis)* *Chief, Ports and Waterways Planning Staff* *U.S. Coast Guard H/Q, Washington*
Secrétaire:	*C COCOZZA (France)* *Ingénieur des Ponts et Chaussées* *Directeur de l'Exploitation du Port Autonome de Paris*
Secrétaire Adjoint:	*A E C HOMASSEL (France)* *Secrétaire Adjoint, Section Française*

Orateurs

C H GAUM (Etats-Unis), R H Le ASHBURNER (GB), A B HOCHSTEIN (Etats-Unis), E J VAN DE KAA (Pays-Bas), J D METTAM (GB), F DROUIN (France), J MARCHAL (Belgique), J AUBERT (France), A A RUDIN (Suede), L MOINEAU (France), K K GOGOI (Inde), I M WALKER (GB), A J M HARRISON (GB), W F BLAIR (Canada), J DUBOIS (Commission Centrale pour la Navigation du Rhin), R H SMITH (Canada), G CERUTTI (Italie)

CAPT. W. R. RIEDEL (USA) RAPORTEUR GENERAL

Quatorze rapports ont été soumis dans le cadre de ce sujet. Si quatre d'entre eux utilisent la navigation en eau profonde à titre d'illustration des divers problèmes traités, les thèmes soulevés se rapportent bien à la navigation intérieure. Les dix autres rapports traitent quant à eux d'aspects directement liés aux problèmes tant généraux que spécifiques rencontrés par la navigation intérieure.

Les auteurs des différents rapports s'attachent à identifier un certain nombre de problèmes soulevés dans le cadre général du sujet et, à l'aide d'exemples spécifiques, à indiquer comment ceux-ci ont été rencontrés dans leurs différents pays. Il semble utile de préciser que pratiquement tous les rapports illustrent une ou plusieurs des mesures d'amélioration de la navigation reprises ci-dessous:

- approche systémique
- gestion du trafic
- essais à échelle réelle
- bassins pour essais sur modèles hydrauliques
- simulation navale
- amélioration des aides à la navigation
- recours aux remorqueurs et aux engins de manoeuvre
- navigation de nuit
- brise-glaces et gestion de la glace.

Les résultats ont été obtenus aussi bien à partir d'essais sur modèles en bassin que de simulations mathématiques sur ordinateur.

1. La conclusion majeure qui se dégage clairement des divers rapports présentés en liaison avec ce sujet est que l'utilisation de la voie d'eau pour le transport de marchandises est en plein essor dans tous les pays.

2. Parallèlement, la capacité des voies d'eau intérieures est sans cesse accrue autant par des moyens modestes que par des aménagements fondamentaux.

3. Des recherches incessantes dans tous les secteurs des systèmes de navigation intérieure sont indispensables pour faire front à la demande croissante. Les améliorations qu'elles peuvent apporter doivent cependant passer avec succès le test du "ééésp": elles doivent être "économiquement utiles, écologiquement non agressives, énergétiquement efficaces, sûres et politiquement acceptables".

LES DEBATS

C H GAUM (USA)

On n'a accordé que peu d'attention au facteur humain dans les opérations de remorquage en vue de l'accroissement de la capacité et de la sécurité continue des voies d'eau intérieures. Un capitaine de remorqueur d'un grand convoi (33 mètres de large et 365 mètres de long) sur l'Ohio a déclaré:

"a) L'équipement ne cesse de s'améliorer, mais à mesure qu'il se complique s'accroît l'importance d'une formation spécialisée.

b) Les capitaines ayant l'expérience la plus grande prennent leur pension alors qu'est insuffisant pour les remplacer le nombre des jeunes qui acceptent de naviguer pendant des semaines, loin de leur famille et/ou de leurs amis.

c) Les capitaines plus âgés ont acquis leur expérience au cours de nombreuses années, pendant lesquelles les voies d'eau et l'équipement évoluaient vers leur état d'efficacité actuel.

d) Des programmes de formation sont nécessaires afin de permettre aux nouveaux capitaines d'apprendre plus vite les situations qui peuvent survenir et les réactions qu'elles appellent."

Bien sûr, il faut encore de nouveaux ouvrages pour accroître la capacité et la sécurité des voies d'eau, mais la construction de barrages et d'écluses nouveaux où de remplacement coûte cher, atteignant souvent l'ordre des centaines de millions de U.S. dollars. Le temps d'éclusage réel, c'est-à-dire le temps nécessaire au remplissage ou à la vidange de l'écluse et le temps de manoeuvre des portes, est déterminé. Cependant, l'opération d'approche, qui peut prendre une heure ou davantage pour les grands convois, immobilise l'écluse pendant tout ce temps. La réduction de ce temps de manoeuvre dans de bonnes conditions de sécurité est susceptible de permettre d'accroître le nombre d'éclusages par jour. A cet égard, il peut être utile d'avoir recours à des simulateurs visuels en temps réel pour former les nouveaux capitaines aux conditions pertinentes d'approche des écluses. Ces simulateurs peuvent recréer les conditions de brume, de pluie, de nuit, de courants et de vents par l'ordinateur visuel et donc offrir au pilote une relation en temps réel avec son gouvernail et ses moteurs. Une expérience s'étalant sur une carrière professionnelle entière reste irremplaçable, mais au moins ces nouveaux moyens donnent-ils au nouveau pilote une idée des initiatives à prendre au cours des périodes à risque élevé. Il s'agit là de circonstances exceptionnelles: la formation proposée devrait empêcher que le pilote soit pris totalement au dépourvu lorsqu'il sera confronté à ces situations. De toute manière, elle est susceptible d'accélérer les éclusages dans des conditions de navigation normales. Les accidents surviennent généralement en présence de brume, de glace, d'inondation ou d'autres circonstances défavorables. Cependant, un accident, c'est déjà trop, si l'on tient compte non seulement du coût qu'il entraîne, mais aussi de la fermeture de la voie d'eau qu'il provoque et des conséquences néfastes qu'il peut avoir pour l'environnement. Le facteur humain devient de plus en plus important à mesure que s'accroît la complexité des voies d'eau et des bateaux qui les empruntent. Aussi mérite-t-il une attention redoublée.

R H Le ASHBURNER (GB)

COMMENTAIRES RELATIFS AU RAPPORT SUEZ — Section I, Sujet 1, p. 251

A. Aggrandissement supplémentaire de la section transversale mis en service en décembre 1980.

Tirant d'eau max. 16.2 m (53 pieds) peut recevoir 150 000 TPM en charge et 350 000 TPM en lège. (page 18, Fig. 1).

Superficie de la section actuelle: à présent 12 x l'originale et 2 x l'antérieure.

Maintenant première étape permet 12,5 m (41 pieds) — auparavant 11,6 m (38 pieds).

La demande de grands navires est à l'heure actuelle limitée en raison dépression marché des pétroliers. Même si cela peut paraître malheureux à première vue, c'est en fait très utile pour permettre progressivement à l'ACS d'acquérir l'expérience nécessaire et de rassembler les équipements et le personnel qualifié.

Les réglementations de transit sont constamment révisées en fonction de l'expérience acquise.

A l'heure actuelle, tous les navires de plus de 100 000 TPM doivent être escortés d'un remorqueur libre à l'arrière les navires prévoyant des câbles de remorqueur susceptibles d'être accrochés en cas de besoin, un cable de chaque côté de l'avant du pont de la dunette de sorte qu'ils puissent servir de lignes de quart ou de patte-d'oie. Le Canal de Suez est unique au point de vue de la dimension des navires l'utilisant régulièrement en convois dans une voie d'eau restreinte. C'est pourquoi il est normal que l'ACS fasse preuve de prudence dans l'introduction des très grands navires qui peuvent désormais être reçus. Il sera intéressant de suivre l'expérience, particulièrement lorsque les grands navires en charge emprunteront le canal.

B. Un problème important qui se pose est celui de la fonction principale des remorqueurs.

Si un navire seul utilisait continuellement sa force motrice arrière, il ne tarderait pas à faire une forte embardée et à échouer.

La fonction du remorqueur est de contrebalancer la tendance du navire propulsé par l'arrière à faire une embardée en tirant ou poussant latéralement pour maintenir le navire dans l'axe du canal.

Par temps convenable, le navire pourrait s'arrêter par ses propres moyens en n'utilisant que partiellement sa propulsion arrière combinée avec des touches de propulsion avant pour corriger son alignement, mais la distance nécessaire serait bien entendu beaucoup plus longue.

La puissance du remorqueur est modeste par comparaison à celle du navire et je souligne que l'intention n'est pas que le remorqueur freine le navire mais plutôt qu'il le pilote pour permettre au navire d'utiliser la puissance considérable dont il dispose à l'arrière.

On a déterminé que les remorqueurs apportent généralement environ 25% de la puissance totale déployée pendant une opération d'arrêt, mais qu'une faible proportion seulement en est appliquée en direction de l'arrière du navire.

C. Une section (page 19, Fig. 2) traite de l'évaluation de la distance de sécurité entre les navires d'un convoi. Ceci peut être illustré.

Prenons le cas d'un navire ayant des problèmes, par exemple, de perte de puissance et de gouverne par mauvais temps, ensuite d'échouage résultant en un blocage du canal.

Le navire qui le suit doit s'arrêter dans de bonnes conditions de sécurité avant d'arriver au navire échoué.

L'intervalle total représenté entre navires comprend la marge de sécurité, la longueur du navire, la distance d'arrêt effective et le temps de réaction/communication.

La distance d'arrêt a été estimée sur la base des résultats obtenus sur simulateur, multipliés par un facteur de 1,8 pour l'extrapolation à la situation réelle, car:

- sur simulateur, le pilote est parfaitement préparé et expérimenté. Dans la réalité, les pilotes ne sont pas aussi expérimentés.

A l'avenir, l'utilisation du simulateur dans la formation pourrait améliorer cette situation.

- sur simulateur, le navire démarre sur et parallèlement à la ligne médiane du canal. Dans la réalité, le navire pourrait devoir se réaligner avant de commencer la manoeuvre d'arrêt.
- dans des conditions atmosphériques réelles, comportant éventuellement une mauvaise visibilité, le pilote pourrait agir avec plus de précautions que sur simulateur.

On voit tout de suite que seul le navire placé immédiatement derrière l'incident doit s'arrêter sur une distance minimale. Celle-ci est double pour les autres navires.

On peut espérer que le navire en difficulté réussira à éviter l'échouage pendant un certain temps, laissant donc une plus grande distance pour celui qui le suit.

En tout cas, il semble que le facteur de 1,8 donne une tolérance suffisante à ce stade sans entraîner des espacements si grands qu'ils en seraient non économiques pour l'ACS ou pour les sociétés pétrolières.

Ces espacements seront bien entendu adaptés à mesure qu'on disposera d'une plus grande expérience et je répète qu'il sera intéressant de suivre l'évolution de cet énorme et fascinant projet.

COMMENTAIRES RELATIFS AU RAPPORT DU JAPON — Section I, Sujet 2, p. 297

Les auteurs ont présenté un intéressant rapport sur un sujet de grande importance en vue de l'utilisation la meilleure d'une voie d'eau confinée. Ils y mentionnent une extension éventuelle du temps du cycle d'exploitation du Canal de Suez.

Dans le cadre d'une étude de faisabilité relative au développement du Canal de Suez et exécutée par Maunsell Consultants Ltd en 1976, une attention particulière fut consacrée au problème de la capacité, tant d'un point de vue théorique qu'au moyen de la simulation mathématique. L'UWIST apporta sa collaboration à ce travail et on peut citer à titre de référence à cet égard un article du Dr. Griffiths.

La figure montre les résultats d'une analyse théorique portant sur l'impact de la durée du cycle sur la capacité, mesurée ici en termes de navires-types conceptuels.

On voit les droites pour des exploitations à 1, 2 et 3 convois et les références sont indiquées quant aux figures du rapport qui illustrent ces systèmes (page 20, Fig. 3).

Comme tous les systèmes sont asymptotiques à la même capacité maximale absolue, les marges se rétrécissent à mesure que croît la complexité des systèmes.

Une exploitation permanente sur la base de durées de cycles accrues ou variables comporte plusieurs désavantages, encore que l'accroissement obtenu soit utile en tant que mesure provisoire en période de forte demande ou à la suite d'une fermeture temporaire du Canal en raison de mauvaises conditions météorologiques, lorsqu'il faut faire passer un grand nombre de navires aussi rapidement que possible.

A mesure que croît la demande, il est possible de construire des chenaux de dérivation supplémentaires, mais lorsque l'on approche de la capacité maximale, il devient nécessaire de dédoubler le canal lui-même, si l'on veut maintenir le même niveau de service.

Dans son rapport à l'A.C.S., Maunsell Consultants attire l'attention sur l'éventuelle nécessité d'envisager un deuxième canal. Un maître-plan de développement pourrait être conçu de telle sorte que tous les développements intermédiaires soient cohérents par rapport à cet objectif ultime, en constituant des stages logiques dans la réalisation de celui-ci.

A B HOCHSTEIN (USA)

Le sujet de notre session est particulièrement vaste puisqu'il embrasse les voies d'eau, les écluses, les canaux, etc. Cependant le concept de "capacité" revêt des significations différentes et parfois non compatibles, selon le type d'opération auquel il est appliqué. Une écluse constitue une barrière physique à laquelle se heurte une demande croissante: sa capacité peut généralement être évaluée en tonnes de transit. Au contraire, la capacité d'un chenal en termes de tonnage de trafic est rarement un facteur limitatif. Même dans le cas de voies d'eau comportant de fréquents biefs à voie de navigation unique, l'ordre de grandeur est supérieur à celui des écluses et, aux Etats-Unis du moins, généralement bien supérieur à la densité de trafic prévisible. C'est pourquoi la capacité — ou, plus proprement, la capacité potentielle — d'un chenal ne doit pas être mesurée en termes de tonnage de transit. Les conditions de navigation d'un chenal déterminent en effet d'autres paramètres importants, tels que la dimension des navires qu'il peut recevoir, le temps de navigation et en dernier ressort le coût du transport.

Dans le cas d'un canal, la dimension des convois qui peuvent l'emprunter peut être spécifiée sur la base de critères de génie civil, essentiellement en fonction de la profondeur, de la largeur et de la surface de la section transversale. Dans les voies d'eau naturelles ou canalisées, où les biefs confinés sont toujours suivis de sections plus larges, il n'existe pas de limite précise de dimension de chenal excluant l'utilisation du chenal par des navires d'une dimension donnée. Au contraire, la dimension maximale des navires qui peuvent emprunter le chenal dépend d'une décision d'exploitation mettant en balance d'une part le moindre coût du transport par grands navires et d'autre part le temps de navigation accru, les retards, les risques et la tension nerveuse des équipages, autant d'éléments associés à la navigation dans les biefs confinés. Une analyse plus approfondie semble s'imposer aujourd'hui afin d'estimer les dimensions des navires pouvant emprunter les diverses sections du système de voies d'eau intérieures, non seulement en fonction de critères de génie civil, mais aussi en tenant compte des facteurs mentionnés ci-dessus.

Trés récemment, nous avons mis le point final à l'inventaire et à l'évaluation d'une série de mesures non structurales ou structurales mineures susceptibles d'accroître la capacité des écluses existantes sur le réseau des voies navigables du Haut Mississippi. De manière générale, il a été constaté qu'il était possible d'accroître cette capacité dans une mesure allant jusqu'à 30% au moyen d'initiatives telles que la programmation des éclusages, l'extension des murs de guidage, l'assistance de remorqueurs, l'amélioration de la conception, le réalignement des approches, l'installation de systèmes de lutte contre la glace et les détritus, etc. Parmi les mesures les plus originales, le système dit du "taquet mobile" retint une attention toute particulière. Il s'agit d'une unité automotrice posée sur un rail longeant le sas et les murs de guidage, qui tire un train de barges non moteur à l'intérieur et en-dehors de l'écluse. Bien que la conception et l'opérationnalité de cet engin posent encore de nombreuses questions, il permet dans certains cas d'accroître significativement la capacité. On peut donc recommander la poursuite de l'évaluation de l'applicabilité de ce "taquet mobile".

La tendance prédominante dans le passé a été d'accroître la puissance des remorqueurs. Pour plusieurs raisons, parmi lesquelles le coût accru du carburant, il semble aujourd'hui que cette tendance soit dépassée. Une technologie semble avoir pris le relai sous la forme des boutoirs de proue. Certains types conventionnels de ces boutoirs de proue sont déjà en service sur les voies navigables des Etats-Unis. Néanmoins, à ce-jour, leur utilisation peut être considérée comme une expérience menée par l'industrie du remorquage. Plusieurs prototypes pourront assister le mouvement des convois à la fois dans les biefs confinés et en cours d'éclusage. Leur utilisation peut avoir un impact fondamental sur les dimensions des navires compatibles avec ceux des divers chenaux ainsi que sur la capacité des voies navigables (écluses).

E J VAN DE KAA (PAYS-BAS)

L'analyse des accidents est importante pour déterminer les principaux facteurs de risques. La compréhension de ces facteurs est indispensable pour identifier les mesures les plus susceptibles d'accroître la capacité et la sécurité. C'est ainsi que beaucoup d'accidents sont provoqués par des erreurs d'appréciation et des malentendus. Ces accidents surviennent souvent aux endroits où les bateaux se croisent et dans les zones d'ancrage et d'amarrage. C'est pourquoi la régulation du trafic peut être un facteur déterminant dans ces circonstances.

Les rapports aussi bien que le rapport général accordent une importance plus grande à l'accroissement de la capacité plutôt qu'au renforcement de la sécurité. Permettre le passage de navires plus grands semble en conséquence être efficace. Mais ceci entraîne un affaiblissement de la sécurité qui doit être compensé par une manoeuvrabilité accrue de ces grands bateaux, un contrôle du trafic, une intensification des aides à la navigation, etc. Lorsque la densité du trafic est faible, le passage en sens unique des convois peut s'avérer efficace. Ainsi, l'approfondissement d'un ancien canal dans la région orientale des Pays-Bas uniquement dans la zone de l'axe du canal s'est avéré extrêmement rentable par comparaison au trafic à deux voies avec ou sans approfondissement. Ceci s'explique pour une large part par le fait que les protections des berges ne devaient pas être reconstruites dans le cas du trafic à une seule voie.

Des quantités sans cesse croissantes de substances dangereuses sont transportées sur les voies navigables d'Europe occidentale. Ceci entraîne des risques accrus pour les régions à forte densité de population riveraine des voies navigables. Je suggère d'ajouter au projet de conclusions une recommandation visant à accorder une attention particulière à l'évaluation de critères internationalement acceptés régissant les niveaux tolérables de risques pour les voies de navigation intérieures.

J D METTAM (GB)

Dans le rapport britannique sur "L'Amélioration des Systèmes d'Eclusage", il est fait mention des avantages des portes-secteurs du type "Delta" en vue de l'accélération des opérations d'éclusage et éventuellement de l'automatisation des écluses sans personnel. Du point de vue de la sécurité, il faut faire remarquer que les forces agissant sur ces portes au cours de leur fermeture, alors qu'un courant traverse l'écluse, vont toujours dans le sens de la fermeture des portes. En cas de vandalisme ou de panne d'électricité, il est suggéré que la sécurité pourrait être maintenue grâce à l'addition d'un système hydraulique/mécanique indépendant permettant de déclencher la fermeture en utilisant la chute d'eau due à l'écoulement des eaux créée par exemple en laissant les portes ouvertes — ou par accident.

On recommande l'étude de ce sujet en vue de dépasser les objections relatives au fonctionnement totalement automatisé des écluses soulevées par le Rapporteur Général.

F DROUIN (FRANCE)

RESUME DE L'EXPOSE

Présentation de deux réalisations:

- l'une qui accroît la sécurité des voies navigables: (bouées lumineuses);
- l'autre qui accroît la capacité d'un réseau: le multiplex.

J MARCHAL (BELGIQUE)

Je voudrais, par cette brève intervention, rappeler qu'un bon dimensionnement d'une voie navigable adaptée au trafic des grands convois doit être une préoccupation importante des études.

Après une recherche très poussée réalisée au Laboratoire des Constructions Hydrauliques de l'Université de LIEGE entre 1970 et 1975, basée sur un très grand nombre d'essais sur modèles, j'avais défini la section optimum adaptée à la navigation des convois de 9 000 Tonnes composés de quatre barges: ce dimensionnement était basé sur le concept de vitesse limite pratique qui est celle à partir de laquelle toute augmentation double de la puissance n'augmente pas la vitesse de plus de 5%. J'arrivais ainsi à un rapport des sections mouillées canal/bateau de 14 qui avait été mal accueilli à l'époque et que je me réjouis d'avoir maintenu.

Je m'étais également attaché à chercher la profondeur optimum nécessaire que j'avais définie à 6 mètres et qui fut récemment adoptée en ROUMANIE.

Finalement ce dimensionnement a conduit à une section ayant un strict minimum de 100 mètres de largeur au plan d'eau et de 6 mètres de profondeur pour la navigation intérieure. En BELGIQUE, le reproche m'avait été fait à l'époque d'exagérer la profondeur: je persiste à penser que cette profondeur a une influence prépondérante d'autant plus qu'il faut bien se rendre compte que, dans le coût de construction d'une voie navigable le supplément de coût nécessaire à l'approfondissement est très loin d'être proportionnel au volume de déblais supplémentaires.

De plus cet approfondissement diminue le coût d'entretien de la voie navigable.

Avec un tel dimensionnement la sécurité de navigation est entièrement assurée.

Je me permets à présent de faire une remarque sur le rapport allemand qui parle de manoeuvrabilité des grands convois poussés dans les courbes des canaux.

Je voudrais souligner qu'en ce qui concerne ce problème, le cas extrême à prendre en considération est le croisement de deux convois poussés navigant à vide car dans ce cas l'influence considérable des vents latéraux est primordiale. Ce facteur a-t-il été pris en compte? Et, dans le cas d'une voie d'eau à courant, s'est-on préoccupé de la forte diminution de la manoeuvrabilité dans le sens du courant?

La largeur du canal est liée au concept de vitesse limite pratique: je crois que la grandeur importante à définir dans une courbe est son rayon de courbure.

Quelle est l'opinion de mes collègues allemands à ce sujet?

Merci de votre bonne attention.

J AUBERT (FRANCE)

Le sujet No 2 comporte l'étude des divers moyens que l'on peut utiliser pour augmenter la capacité d'une voie navigable.

Ces moyens sont nombreux, de sorte que les rapports présentés traitent de sujets différents.

Le rapport canadien nous parle des "shunters". Conçus comme des unités de propulsion flottantes, que l'on fixe à des navires de tonnage important, ces shunters constituent une nouveauté intéressante.

Il y a longtemps que l'on utilise, pour le déplacement des gros navires, des remorqueurs indépendants, mais la liaison de deux unités flottantes par un câble est forcément moins efficace qu'une liaison rigide.

On peut rapprocher ce procédé des shunters du système des bouteurs, que l'on a utilisé exceptionnellement sur le Rhin. Il s'agit d'hélices qui sont fixées à l'extrémité amont d'un automoteur ou d'un convoi, et qui permettent de déplacer latéralement cette extrêmité. L'action du gouvernail est ainsi amplifée.

L'apparition des shunters conduit à réfléchir sur les moyens d'action dont on dispose pour déplacer un bateau.

Sur la figure 1 (page 22) on a représenté schématiquement un bateau, ainsi que les forces que l'on peut excercer sur lui.

L'hélice permet d'excercer directement des efforts tels que A ou B dirigés dans l'axe du bateau. L'action du gouvernail permet de déplacer l'arrière du bateau en direction des flèches C ou D, mais la possibilité n'existe pas d'exercer des actions dirigées dans les sens E ou F.

De telles actions latérales sont permises par le "shunter concept".

Déplacement latéral type. Aux abords des très nombreuses écluses du monde, on se trouve fréquemment dans la situation représentée sur la figure 2 (page 23). La bateau A vient de quitter l'écluse, dans laquelle le bateau B, qui était en attente au garage, doit pénétrer, en suivant le tracé figuré par le trait interrompu.

Il l'effectue sans difficulté, mais en y consacrant un temps assez long, et le problème qui nous occupe est précisémment de réduire ce temps.

Le déplacement latéral du bateau correspond à un certain travail. Si l'on procède très lentement, ce travail est faible, mais la résistance opposée par l'eau au déplacement d'un corps solide est une fonction rapidement croissante de la vitesse de ce déplacement.

Si donc on veut procéder de plus en plus vite, le travail à effectuer est de plus en plus important. La puissance qu'il faut mettre en jeu augmente, une première fois, en raison de la croissance du travail et, une deuxième fois, en raison de la réduction du temps pendant lequel ce travail est effectué.

L'installation d'une puissance considérable, destinée à n'être utilisée que pendant une très petite fraction du temps, correspondrait à une dépense inadmissible.

Il est donc normal de chercher à mettre en oeuvre un procédé d'accumulation continue d'une énergie, que l'on déclenche brusquement de temps à autre.

C'est ce processus qui a été essayé au laboratoire de Chatou.

Sur la figure 3 (page 23) on voit un réservoir supérieur R1 et un réservoir inférieur R2.

Pour effectuer le déplacement souhaité, on ouvre les vannes des deux réservoirs, le bateau, entraîné par le courant, parcourant alors la ligne interrompue AB. Une pompe de faible puissance, agissant pendant toute la durée d'un cycle, permet ensuite de rétablir la dénivellation initiale entre les deux réservoirs.

Deux autres réservoirs R3 et R4, non représentés sur la figure 3, permettent d'effectuer ensuite (ou en même temps) le déplacement CD.

Ce procédé des réservoirs permettrait éventuellement de retarder l'époque du doublement d'une écluse mais, à notre connaissance, il n'a encore jamais été utilisé.

Le déplacement type représenté sur la figure 2, doit également être effectué à la tête amont d'une pente d'eau.

Il est, dans ce cas, nécessaire de procéder avec une grande rapidité, parce que l'on se propose, dans le cas d'une pente d'eau de quelques cinquante mètres de hauteur, d'obtenir une durée de cycle voisine de celle d'une écluse de dix mètres de chute.

La puissance du bouclier-moteur d'une pente d'eau représente cinq à dix fois celle du système de propulsion propre des bateaux ou des convois qui utilisent cette pente d'eau. Or cette puissance se trouve précisémment être inutilisée pendant l'échouage entre le bateau A montant et le bateau B, qui se prépare à descendre la pente. Il était normal de penser à utiliser cette puissance pour faciliter l'échange des bateaux A et B.

Sur le plan, comme sur la coupe verticale, on a représenté schématiquement le masque du bouclier-moteur, qui, pour accélérer la sortie du bateau montant A, a poursuivi sa course presque jusqu'au contact de la porte basculante, qui retient l'eau du bief amont.

Sur la figure 4 (page 24) ce masque recule et, grâce à la fermeture d'une deuxième porte, dite porte-trappe, il refoule l'eau dans la dérivation latérale représentée sur le plan.

Cette dérivation se termine par un élargissement, analogue à une pomme d'arrosoir.

Refoulant l'eau par une de ses faces et l'aspirant par l'autre, le masque crée une sorte de manège liquide, dont une fraction correspond exactement au parcours que doit suivre le bateau B.

Dès que celui-ci sera engagé sur le palier, on abaissera la porte-trappe et on fermera les portes de la dérivation latérale. Le masque poursuivra ensuite son mouvement dans la rigole inclinée.

A la fin de sa montée, le masque aura donc poussé le bateau montant dans le bief amont et, au début de son mouvement de retour, il aspirera le bateau B dans le triangle d'eau qui va descendre vers l'aval.

En ce qui concerne la durée du cycle, il n'y a donc pas lieu de compter un temps d'échange à la tête amont d'une pente d'eau, entre les deux bateaux A et B. Comme on vient de le voir, cet échange est en effet la conséquence des déplacements du masque tantôt vers l'amont et tantôt vers l'aval.

Nous avons montré que le déplacement latéral nécessaire à la remise en route très rapide d'un bateau stationnant dans un garage pouvait s'effectuer:

- dans le cas d'une écluse, par l'emploi de réservoirs spécialement conçus à cet effet,

- dans le cas d'une pente d'eau, par la simple utilisation de son engin moteur.

A A RUDIN (SUEDE)

En montrant 10 diapositives, l'orateur ajoute quelques remarques à sa contribution intitulée "Amélioration de la Navigation sur le Canal Trollhätte et le Lac Vänern".

L MOINEAU (FRANCE)

Plusieurs orateurs ont évoqué de façon fort intéressante les dispositions adoptées en matière de "dispatching" pour augmenter la capacité et la sécurité des voies navigables.

Je voudrais faire part en quelques mots de deux précisions que nous a suggéré notre expérience de la régulation du trafic, notamment sur la Seine et sur la Moselle, où nous avons été confrontés à des problèmes de saturation et de navigation de nuit dans des conditions difficiles.

1. D'après notre expérience, la régulation du trafic, pour augmenter la capacité, est de règle lorsque le trafic atteint les 3/4 de la saturation et largement avant d'avoir atteint cette proportion lorsque l'on a en vue l'accélération du trafic et non plus seulement l'augmentation de la capacité.

2. La régulation du trafic de nuit pratiquée avec avantage sur la Seine et sur la Moselle s'impose dès que ce trafic apparaît sur les voies d'eau à écluses relativement nombreuses, de manière à permettre à faire face, sans dépenses prohibitives, pour chaque écluse et à l'heure approximative de passage annoncé à l'avance, aux moyens nécessaires pour assurer le passage dans les meilleures conditions de temps et d'économie de personnel.

K K GOGOI (INDE)

Le Brahmaputra est le troisième fleuve en importance du monde, après l'Amazone et le Congo, selon le critère du débit en période de pointe. Il s'agit d'une région du pluie intensive — 200 à 300 pouces en moyenne — pendant une période de six mois par an.

La navigation de nuit sur les voies navigables du Brahmaputra, en Inde, en matière de navigation intérieure — soit un trafic d'environ 1 million de tonnes — s'effectue essentiellement à l'aide de signaux lumineux Pintail. Cette méthode peut être utilisée par les pays en développement qui connaissent des situations similaires. Le fleuve est alluvial et comporte des mouvements de sédiments en suspension et de lit dûs à un important affouillement du fond, ce qui rend très difficile la fixation des signaux de navigation dans le chenal navigable. Le problème est d'autant plus aigu que le fleuve modifie fréquemment son chenal principal en constituant une série de chenaux secondaires sinueux ne conservant pas la profondeur souhaitable.

Sur sols durs et rochers, la fixation des signaux est permanente et les bouées conventionnelles peuvent être utilisées dans ce cas, mais au milieu du chenal, lieu du mouvement de lit et de réception de billes de bois submergées, la fixation est effectuée au moyen de tripodes téléscopiques et rétractables (environ 20 kgs). Les supports sont identiques aux tripodes habituels avec signal et corps de batterie boulonnés. Le coût est inférieur à celui d'une bouée. La longeur des tripodes est de 5 m. Le corps des signaux est fait de F.R.P. plutôt que d'acier en raison du climat humide de la région. Le déplacement des signaux sur tripodes est effectué par trois hommes sur un bateau.

I M WALKER (GB)

En réponse à la demande de clarification du Président quant à la référence faite par le rapport de la Grande-Bretagne à la contribution britannique au Congrès de Léningrad en 1977 sur l'automatisation des Ecluses et des Ponts.

Le système décrit en 1977 était fonction de la détection à distance des barges approchant et quittant une écluse ou un pont au moyen de rayons ultrasoniques immergés. Il s'est avéré difficile, dans des conditions climatiques extrêmes et en présence de matières en suspension, d'atteindre un niveau élevé de précision avec cette méthode. C'est pourquoi il est à présent suggéré d'avoir recours aux contrôles radiophoniques pour déclencher les systèmes automatiques ou télécommandés. Etant donné que les voies d'eau commerciales britanniques sont utilisées par un volume important de trafic de plaisance et en raison de l'expérience d'exploitation récente, il est à présent déconseillé d'abolir le service manuel aux principaux postes d'exploitation pendant les heures de travail diurnes normales.

Néanmoins, en-dehors de ces périodes, la procédure automatisée avec télésurveillance décrite en 1977 est utilisée, le déclenchement étant réalisé comme l'a indiqué M. Pyrah.

On étudie actuellement, dans le sud-ouest de l'Angleterre, l'amélioration du Canal Gloucester-Sharpness. Pour limiter les coûts, ce canal sera à voie unique avec zones de dépassement. Il faudra un système de contrôle de trafic élaboré pour minimiser les retards de navigation et on aura recours au télécontrôle, non seulement pour la navigation, mais aussi pour la circulation urbaine, afin de limiter les embouteillages occasionnés par les passages des bateaux sous les ponts levants de Gloucester.

A J M HARRISON (GB)

M. Harrison souligne une méthode d'accroissement de la capacité qui n'a pas été mentionnée dans les rapports présentés. Il s'agit de l'accroissement de la capacité des grands fleuves en vue du passage de plus grands navires au moyen d'une meilleur prévision ou estimation des niveaux de l'eau. Il se réfère à cet égard à la contribution britannique au Sujet 3, par Colyer et Thorn, sur l'amélioration du Fleuve Paraguay en Amérique du Sud.

Au cours des 10 à 15 dernières années, les modèles numériques déterministes d'analyse du débit des grands fleuves se sont considérablement développés. Si l'on dispose de données d'input valables sur les eaux d'amont d'un système de voies fluviales, il est possible de prévoir plusieurs semaines à l'avance et avec grande précision les niveaux d'eau en aval.

M. Harrison suggère que, dans l'analyse des améliorations physiques à apporter aux systèmes fluviaux en vue de la réception de plus grands bateaux, la possibilité d'une meilleure prévision des niveaux d'eau soit sérieusement envisagée.

W BLAIR (CANADA)

"Utilisation de remorqueurs de conception spéciale en vue de l'accroissement de la capacité du Canal Welland".

Il est apparu que l'utilisation de remorqueurs de conception spéciale était le meilleur moyen d'accroître la capacité du canal Welland et un programme expérimental a été lancé en 1979 et poursuivi en 1980 pour tester ce concept. Au cours de la phase d'essai, des navires de dimension moyenne et maximale ont été utilisés pour recueillir des données permettant une évaluation complète dans des conditions d'exploitation réelles.

L'expérimentation et l'évaluation des données ont indiqué que la capacité du canal pouvait être accrue des quelque 30 éclusages par jour actuels à environ 39-40 éclusages par jour, soit une augmentation de 33%.

Au début du programme, le coût d'une flotte de remorqueurs était estimé à environ Can. $100 millions. La réalisation du programme et l'élaboration des données de conception pertinentes ont conduit à une estimation plus réaliste de Can. $200 millions. Si on y ajoute le coût d'exploitation annuel, le système des remorqueurs ne présente aucun avantage déterminant par rapport aux méthodes conventionnelles d'accroissement de la capacité, telles que l'élargissement des biefs confinés interdisant le croisement des navires, la suppression des ponts et l'amélioration des murs d'écluse.

En dépit de cette évaluation économique, nous avons poursuivi les recherches visant à résoudre le problème de la fixation. Les réponses à un appel d'offre de conception auprès des bureaux d'ingénieurie indiquent qu'il est possible d'aller de l'avant dans la solution de ce problème. Entretemps, une fixation par rotule aspirante a été mise au point au Japon et une étude de cet équipement indique qu'un système de remorqueur automatisé est réalisable.

Nous apprenons que ce système est envisagé pour le Canal de Suez et qu'un chantier naval japonais a été chargé de fabriquer l'équipement nécessaire.

J DUBOIS (Commission Centrale pour la Navigation du Rhin)

Concernant deux aspects soulevés dans le rapport de la République Fédérale Allemande, la régulation du trafic et la réglementation concernant les aides à la Navigation, je me limiterai au domaine rhénan. En raison des caractéristiques techniques du Rhin et de la densité du trafic qui l'utilise, l'expérience rhénane peut, en effet, présenter un intérêt général.

1. Sur le plan de la régulation du trafic, je me borne à signaler l'utilisation du système des aires de départ (en allemand "Starplatz-system"). Cette méthode, appliqée en Allemagne, notamment sur le Main pour favoriser une utilisation optimale des écluses, est également pratiquée sur le Rhin Canalisé et le Grand Canal d'Alsace en vue de prévenir ou de réduire les encombrements aux ouvrages lorsqu'une des deux écluses d'une chute est hors service lors d'un chômage ou par suite d'une avarie. L'expérience a montré que moyennant des mesures d'organisation simples et peu coûteuses, cette méthode donne de bons résultats.

2. Dans le domaine des aides à la Navigation, l'expérience acquise dans l'utilisation du radar a conduit à une importante évolution des faits et des idées depuis la dernière grande révision du Réglement de police pour la Navigation du Rhin (R.P.N.R.), achevée en 1970 sur la base du Code européen des voies de Navigation intérieure (C.E.V.N.I.).

Considéré au départ comme un moyen auxiliaire dont on pourrait "tenir compte" pour naviguer par visibilité réduite, le radar est devenu un élément essentiel de la sécurité.

Cette évolution est prise en consédération dans les travaux en cours pour la révision du R.P.N.R. et trouvera sa traduction dans les prescriptions.

Il est naturel que l'utilisation accrue du radar entraîne en contrepartie des garanties correspondantes de fiabilité:

- d'une part, sur le plan de l'équipement:

  actuellement déjà les installations de radar et les indications de giration utilisées sur le Rhin doivent être d'un type agéé pour la Navigation rhénane;

- d'autre part, sur le plan du personnel:

  l'utilisation du radar postule la présence à bord d'une personne, titulaire du diplôme de Conducteur au radar délivré conformément aux prescriptions adoptées à ce sujet par la Commission Centrale.

Il est normal que la généralisation de techniques perfectionnées entraîne la nécessité de mesures de contrôle. En effet, les aides à la Navigation ne suppriment pas les difficultés et le danger qui en résulte, elles permettent de les surmonter dans des conditions de sécurité maintenues et, si possible, améliorées. C'est le prix du progrés.

R H SMITH (CANADA)

Notre Département Aides à la Navigation nous indique que nous pouvons mettre en liaison avec le rapport belge, à partir de la page 183, et le rapport des U.S.A., page 389, l'approche canadienne en matière d'utilisation des aides radio-électroniques visant à améliorer la navigation maritime en eaux confinées.

Pour la voie maritime du St Laurent, la Canada Dominion Marine Association nous demande de tester le PRANS (Precise Radar Navigation System). Une précision de $\pm$ 3 m était exigée. Nous pensions alors et continuons de penser qui cette précision peut être tempérée et ceci peut être prouvé par simulation. En outre, une meilleure surveillance de la navigation, assortie d'une modification des procédures d'exploitation, permettrait d'éviter les situations extrêmes dont on parle tant.

Le PRANS utilise le radar de bord pour balayer des réflecteurs radar passifs dont les positions ont été repérées avec une très faible tolérance. Les données ainsi recueillies alimentent un micro-processeur et une carte de la voie navigable est stockée sur cassette ou mémoire montrant les limites et la ligne médiane du chenal. Quand le navire est intégré dans le système, le programme se déclenche et dès lors indique au capitaine ou au pilote sa distance par rapport à la ligne médiane et par rapport au prochain cap, ainsi que le comportement du navire et sa vitesse.

Les essais PRANS furent réalisés au cours de l'été et de l'automne derniers. Si, en mode statique, la précision et la performance souhaitées furent obtenues, en cours de route ou en mode dynamique, les degrés de précision s'effondrèrent et il s'avéra impossible d'atteindre dans tous les cas les réflecteurs ou, une fois ceci fait, d'en garder la trace. En raison de ces difficultés, le projet a été mis indéfiniment en suspens.

La prochaine étape consistera à évaluer le Loran-C différentiel. La mini-chaîne Loran à base rapprochée et faible puissance a été testée par l'U.S.C.G. pendant plusieurs années sur le fleuve St Mary. La conclusion a été que la chaîne régulière peut être utilisée pourvu que des centres de surveillance et de transmission d'erreurs soient implantés en une série d'endroits où la précision est cruciale. Des recherches théoriques et sur le terrain restent nécessaires.

Les systèmes radar de navigation (balayage linéraire et différentiel, fréquence fixe et variable) sont étudiés de très près en vue de les utiliser soit en tant que fournisseurs d'inputs pour microprocesseur dans le cas d'informations de très haute précision, soit en tant qu'assistance radar visuelle pour le capitaine ou le pilote.

Une exigence d'exploitation de plus en plus aiguë consiste en une meilleure assistance au pilotage pour le passage sous les ponts. La tendance actuelle semble favoriser les systèmes radar indiquant la ligne médiane ou les piles de pont. Le Canada, cependant, installe actuellement en vue de son évaluation un système d'éclairage sous l'eau au pont de chemin de fer de Second Narrows dans le port de Vancouver.

Enfin, il convient d'accorder plus d'importance au facteur humain en matière de navigation. Ainsi, j'ai indiqué à la Section II, lundi dernier, qu'un rapport sur les accidents de navigation et leurs victimes présenté à la Garde Côtière canadienne en 1979 démontrait que les erreurs d'exploitation, c'est-à-dire le facteur humain, consitituaient la cause identifiée du sinistre dans environ 38% des cas, soit plus du double de chacune des diverses autres causes identifiées.

G CERUTTI (ITALIE)

Monsieur Cerutti Giancarlo fait part des résultats de l'emploi de réflecteurs radar pour la signalisation des piles de ponts sur le fleuve PO.

La navigation est exploitée 24 heures sur 24, sans interruption même pendant les longues et fréquentes périodes de brouillard.

Après quinze années de mise en service, les réflecteurs radar mis en place sur tubes fixés sur les piliers des ponts ont donné des résultats très satisfaisants.

CONCLUSIONS

1. L'utilisation des voies d'eau pour les transports de marchandises s'accroît dans tous les pays. Bien que la capacité de voies d'eau croisse grâce à la mise en oeuvre de moyens à la fois modestes et importants, des améliorations supplémentaires doivent être apportées tant en ce qui concerne la capacité que la sécurité.

2. Il est conclu également qu'une approche globale de l'exploitation d'une rivière ou d'un réseau doit être utilisée pour améliorer à la fois la capacité et la sécurité. Les améliorations doivent respecter le "test eeesp", c'est-à-dire être économiques, respecter l'environnement, être efficaces sur le plan de l'énergie, être sûres et politiquement acceptables.

3. Pour accroître la capacité, il faut:

   a) améliorer les équipements des voies navigables et des écluses: aides à la navigation de tous types, communications telles que l'échange d'informations sur la circulation des marchandises et la transmission d'instructions, contrôle des glaces et éclairage.

   Le traitement informatique des données et sa diffusion instantanée doivent être utilisées partout où c'est possible.

   b) améliorer les caractéristiques des bateaux en y incluant aussi bien les communications que les équipements pour la navigation et la manoeuvrabilité.

   c) partout où cela est nécessaire améliorer l'assistance extérieure aux bateaux en mettant à la disposition des usagers de pilotes, des remorqueurs, des pousseurs, des propulseurs amovibles ("shunters"), des brise glace et des treuils de rive.

   d) améliorer la formation des équipages aux nouvelles techniques et prendre en considération tous les facteurs humains.

   e) porter l'attention qu'ils méritent aux transports de matières dangereuses par voie navigable.

4. En ce qui concerne les améliorations de l'infrastructure, les conclusions suivantes sont retenues:

   a) priorité doit être donnée à l'identification et à la suppression des "points noirs" et des "goulots d'étranglement".

   b) afin de diminuer les temps d'attente, les écluses doivent être séparées par des biefs de longueur convenable.

   c) pour accroître la sécurité de la navigation et faciliter le passage des écluses, les ouvrages doivent avoir des dimensions adéquates et doivent présenter un alignement correct des entrées, ainsi que l'équipement nécessaire à leur exploitation; il convient également de prendre les mesures nécessaires pour limiter les effets des ondes d'éclusées dans les voies de petites dimensions.

5. Dans une vision globale du problème, il convient de prendre en considération les facteurs externes, en particulier:

   - le détournement du trafic pour diminuer les congestions chaque fois que possible;
   - la simplification des procédures propres à l'éclusage;
   - la régulation du trafic;
   - la réduction des transports à vide par l'échange d'informations sur les frets.

6. Une recherche permanente dans tous les domaines relatifs aux voies navigables est nécessaire afin de répondre à la croissance de la demande. La transmission aux CTP des thèmes de recherches éviterait les doubles emplois et permettrait d'assurer une diffusion convenable des travaux dignes d'intérêt par le Bulletin de l'AIPCN ou pour d'autres publications similaires.

VOIES NAVIGABLES ET PORTS DE NAVIGATION INTERIEURE

SECTION I — SUJET 3

Réduction de la sédimentation, amélioration et entretien des profondeurs navigables dans les chenaux alluvionnaires par la maîtrise des débits et des travaux de normalisation

Jeudi 14 mai 1981

Président: *J CHAPON (France)*
Ingénieur Générale des Ponts et Chaussées
Vice-Président du Conseil Générale des Ponts et Chaussées
Ministère de l'Environnement et du Cadre de Vie, Paris

Vice Président: *Dr W MAGIERA (Pologne)*
Ministère des Transports par Voies Navigables, Warsaw

Rapporteur Général: *W H JACKSON (GB)*
Director of Research
British Transport Docks Board

Secrétaire: *C COCOZZA (France)*
Ingénieur des Ponts et Chaussées
Directeur de l'Exploitation du Port Autonome de Paris

Secrétaire Adjoint: *A E C HOMASSEL (France)*
Secrétaire Adjoint, Section Française

Orateurs

P SAVEY (France), C RICARD (France), M F THORN (GB), D M McDOWELL (GB), K K GOGOI (Inde), D MUSKATIROVIC (Yougoslavie), H C FRIJLINK (Pays-Bas), D DREYFOUS-DUCAS (France), J MARCHAL (Belgique), G THUES (Belgique), M HAGER (RFA), A J M HARRISON (GB), P LAGROU (Belgique), S MONTEJO (Colombia)

W. H. JACKSON (GB) RAPPORTEUR GENERAL

La création et le maintien de profondeurs suffisantes et des conditions de sécurité de la navigation sur les voies d'eau intérieures, bien que rendus plus difficiles à mesure que croissaient les dimensions des navires, ont fait l'objet de préoccupations constantes depuis de nombreux siècles. De nombreux ouvrages directeurs ont été construits à cette fin au cours du temps, dont certains ont rempli leur objectif, d'autres n'ont résolu le problème pour lequel ils avaient été créés que pour en engendrer de nouveaux ailleurs et d'autres encore ont été des échecs. La connaissance de ces échecs est tout aussi importante que celle des ouvrages réussis et c'est pourquoi les rapports présentés par cette Section traitent des deux.

Lorsque la construction d'un ouvrage directeur semble susceptible de résoudre le problème, sa conception spécifique doit bien entendu être adaptée aux conditions locales. Il n'en reste pas moins que les méthodes de base et les types d'ouvrages sont très semblables d'un pays à l'autre. On en donnera d'ailleurs une description sommaire dans les conclusions.

En navigation fluviale, le problème majeur consiste souvent en une réduction du mouillage par dépôts de sable et de graviers. Cependant, dans le cas de dérivation de la navigation du fleuve lui-même vers des canaux de navigation distincts, on se heurte à un problème de sédimentation de matériaux fins dans les chenaux latéraux. Les auteurs du rapport français donnent plusieurs exemples précis de ces processus de sédimentation.

Deux méthodes intéressantes et originales utilisées pour traiter ce genre de problème sont:

1. Les bassins ovoïdes à l'intersection du canal Amsterdam-Rhin et du Lek, qui permettent de disposer d'une zone suffisamment grande pour assurer la sécurité de la navigation sans pour autant modifier exagérément les conditions d'écoulement du cours principal.

2. Un exemple d'utilisation d'ailettes sur le lit du Rhône dans le but d'induire des courants secondaires et de provoquer une érosion.

L'automatisation a permis un recours accru aux sondages et les rapports allemand et français décrivent plusieurs types de chaloupes spécialement équipées à cette fin. Dans les deux cas, des capteurs sont utilisés pour enregistrer simultanément les profondeurs en plusieurs points de la section transversale de la voie d'eau.

Ces deux rapports envisagent également les implications économiques de ces méthodes et notamment:

1. une évaluation et une comparaison des coûts relatifs d'un dragage d'entretien régulier ou d'ouvrages directeurs;

2. une étude visant à déterminer si le recours au stockage et au chargement partiel des bateaux permet d'éviter l'entretien du mouillage complet de la voie d'eau pendant les périodes d'étiage.

Un modèle mathématique destiné à évaluer le coût économique de la limitation de la profondeur des chenaux est par ailleurs décrit dans le rapport des Pays-Bas.

Les rapports fournissent une telle richesse d'informations concrètes sur les difficultés associées à l'entretien des profondeurs nécessaires pour assurer la sécurité de la navigation ainsi que sur les types d'ouvrages directeurs utilisés à cette fin qu'il est malaisé d'en refléter toute la valeur en un bref résumé. C'est pourquoi j'ai limité celui-ci à quelques recommandations d'ordre méthodologique sur lesquelles un large accord s'est dessiné.

i) Les objectifs de tout programme envisagé en matière d'entretien des profondeurs de chenal doivent être clairement spécifiés sur la base de paramètres tels que profondeur minimale, rayon minimum de courbure, etc.

ii) Avant d'aborder l'étude détaillée de ces travaux, une analyse approfondie des données historiques doit être réalisée en vue de cerner le régime naturel du fleuve concerné ainsi que toute modification naturelle de celui-ci.

iii) Un nombre considérable de données doivent être relevées sur le terrain, parmi lesquelles les plus importantes semblent avoir trait aux niveau d'eau, au comportement du lit, aux vitesses et aux transports de sédiment dans des conditions d'écoulement normales et extrêmes.

iv) Les techniques faisant appel aux modèles soit hydrauliques soit mathématiques sont très généralement utilisées pour prévoir l'incidence des travaux directeurs envisagés.

v) Parmi les ouvrages directeurs, on citera le renforcement des berges (généralement dans une première étape), les épis d'agitation favorisant les dépôts sur certaines rives et donc la concentration de l'écoulement ailleurs, les épis longitudinaux et les épis destinés à contrecarrer et éviter la formation de chenaux secondaires.

vi) Une approche étape par étape avec suivi continu de l'incidence des travaux est recommandée par plusieurs auteurs.

L'extraction du sable et du gravier peut constituer une manière idéale de réaliser un dragage d'entretien pourvu que les matériaux soient prélevés aux bons endroits et en quantités adéquates. Elle donne cependant souvent lieu à un sur-dragage qui peut entraîner des pertes de profondeur en d'autres endroits en raison de l'abaissement des niveaux d'eau. De tels phénomènes peuvent également être la conséquence d'affaissements entraînés par l'exploitation minière.

Onze rapports ont été remis sur le sujet de la "réduction de la sédimentation, amélioration et entretien des profondeurs navigables dans les chenaux alluvionnaires. Ceux-ci ont été présentés par les rapporteurs de Tchécoslovaquie, de France, de la République Démocratique Allemande, de la République Fédérale Allemande, des Pays-Bas, de Pologne, d'Espagne, du Royaume-Uni, des Etats-Unis d'Amérique, de l'U.R.S.S. et de Yougoslavie.

En général, ces rapports décrivent des travaux entrepris dans chaque pays concerné et malgré des simiItudes, il existe des différences marquées entre les projets décrits, même pour un même pays. Cela provient en grande partie des conditions locales.

Certaines des difficultés ont été créées par l'homme qu'il s'agisse de tentatives préalables et infructueuses ou partiellement fructueuses de canalisation de rivière, d'excès de dragage pour obtenir du sable ou du gravier, d'affaissements dus à des travaux de mine, de constructions dans la rivière ou d'autres causes.

La philosophie de la canalisation d'une rivière c'est généralement d'amener celle-ci à faire ce que l'on désire qu'elle fasse. J'ai choisi à dessein le mot amener parce que beaucoup d'ingénieurs ont appris à leurs dépens qu'une rivière peut manquer de souplesse et être très capricieuse dans ses réactions suite à l'intervention de l'homme. Il est très utile de lire les rapports des entreprises qui ont le moins bien réussi pour éviter de répéter les erreurs du passé.

Il y a cependant beaucoup de points communs et j'ai résumé dans les conclusions un modèle de canalisation pratiquement classique et qui convient dans beaucoup de cas. Le premier stade consiste généralement à renforcer les rives qui sont devenues très vulnérables à l'érosion, puis on construit des arêtes en éperon qui ont le même effet que la construction d'une rive et favorisent les apports le long de la rive et augmentent ailleurs la vitesse du courant, des arêtes longitudinales pour guider le courant dans le chenal et éventuellement on construit d'autres ouvrages pour éviter que ne se forment des chenaux secondaires. Un dragage minutieux est en général la partie essentielle de l'entreprise.

Malgré des points communs, les détails du projet varient considérablement. Cependant, les auteurs russes suggérent des relations quantitatives entre différentes dimensions comme la hauteur et la largeur des arêtes tant pour des courbes concaves et convexes que pour des sections rectilignes. Il serait intéressant de savoir si d'autres ingénieurs emploient les mêmes relations pour en tirer parti dans leurs projets.

C'est dans l'approche des problèmes de base que j'ai trouvé le plus de points d'accord entre les différents auteurs et j'aimerais passer brièvement en revue les différents stades qui conduisent au projet final.

Avant d'entamer un programme coûteux d'aménagement d'une rivière tendant à améliorer la navigation soit en permettant à de plus grands bâtiments existants une meilleure utilisation, il faut se livrer à une étude de la relation bénéfice-coût. Deux des rapports insistent particulièrement sur cet aspect. La contribution du Royaume-Uni décrit une étude effectuée sur la Rivière Parana qui tient compte de l'aspect saisonnier de la plus grande partie du trafic et examine comment les limitations causées par la réduction de la profondeur peuvent être minimisées par l'augmentation des stocks. L'étude néerlandaise décrit un moyen d'évaluer les effets économiques à long terme de voies navigables plus ou moins profondes ce qui implique l'utilisation d'un modèle mathématique. Des investigations aussi détaillées en ce qui concerne le profit économique à retirer de l'approfondissement des chenaux constituent un terrain d'étude très important.

Une autre ouverture rendue possible par les progrès rapides de l'électronique et de la science des ordinateurs ces dernières années est le fait de pouvoir utiliser un plus grand nombre de données résultant de sondages qu'on n'aurait pu le faire jusqu'il y a peu.

Deux de ces techniques de pointe pour le sondage sont décrites dans les communications soumises par la France et la République Fédérale d'allemagne. Dans les deux cas, les profondeurs sont prises à de nombreux points sur la largeur du chenal (41 dans le cas de l'Etude allemande) et sont enregistrées et notées pendant la marche du bateau. Une étude aussi détaillée devrait permettre d'accepter un espace libre sous la quille plus faible et pourrait donc rendre possible une légère réduction de la profondeur moyenne du chenal.

Lorsqu'on a pris la décision d'augmenter la profondeur navigable d'une rivière ou d'une partie de rivière, on admet généralement que le premier stade doit spécifier clairement les buts et les exigences en termes spécifiques, par exemple, la profondeur et la largeur minimum du chenal ainsi que le rayon minimum des courbes.

La construction d'aménagements n'est pas nécessairement la meilleure solution et dans certains cas, il peut être plus avantageux d'augmenter l'effort de dragage. C'est le cas qui s'est présenté dans une section du Danube et qui est décrit dans la contribution Tchécoslovaque. La solution à plus long terme, ici comme dans d'autres cas, est de combiner les intérêts de la navigation avec la production d'énergie. Dans ce cas, les bâtiments empruntent des chenaux spéciaux et "court-circuitent" la rivière.

La plupart des auteurs recommandent une étude détaillée des modifications historiques du régime soit en raison des processus naturels soit par suite des interventions humaines comme des aménagements antérieurs, l'approfondissement d'un chenal, le prélèvement de graviers, etc. Des études intensives sur le terrain doivent alors être entreprises. Elles doivent comprendre des sondages détaillés, le calcul de la distribution des vitesses et du transport des sédiments pour en arriver à obtenir un dossier qui, avec d'autres informations, permettront de prévoir quels seront, à la suite des travaux à entreprendre, le dépôt et la redistribution des sédiments. Ces renseignements sont essentiels car, comme l'indique l'auteur du rapport français, les formules générales qu'on a obtenues pour exprimer en termes quantitatifs le transport de matériaux bruts par les courants, ne peuvent s'appliquer, sans réserves, malgré le soin mis à l'étude. Mon expérience personnelle, bien que limitée, me permet d'indiquer que les prévisions à partir de ces formules peuvent être largement erronées là où les vitesses du courant sont élevées.

Lorsqu'on est arrivé à une certaine compréhension du mécanisme de mouvements de sédimentation et du régime existant de la rivière, on convient généralement qu'il est nécessaire de faire des études sur maquette si l'on veut prévoir d'une manière fiable l'effet d'un projet sur la rivière. On peut utiliser des techniques physiques ou mathématiques et, de l'opinion générale, les deux sont nécessaires. On considère que le modèle mathématique constitue un supplément au modèle physique plutôt qu'un substitut. On trouve dans le rapport néerlandais un résumé admirable des avantages et des inconvénients des modèles.

Quand tout cela a été réalisé, il subsiste encore dans l'esprit de certains ingénieurs des doutes concernant la longueur et le nombre des arêtes. Par mesure de sécurité, ils recommandent que les travaux seront effectués par paliers pour permettre de surveiller les effets quantitatifs sur la rivière. Je ne peux pas garantir que cette approche prudente soit de pratique généralisée.

Pour résumer mes conclusions:

1. Il y a accord quant à l'approche générale dans le cas d'aménagement d'une rivière.

2. Il faudrait spécifier clairement les paramètres de base.

3. On devrait établir une analyse minutieuse des données historiques.

4. Il faut procéder de manière intensive à des mesurages sur place.

5. Il faut en général à la fois des études sur modèle mathématique et hydraulique.

6. Il existe une similitude dans les types de structures utilisés dans beaucoup de projets d'aménagement de rivière mais certains programmes sont intéressants et originaux.

J'ai suggéré d'étudier les points suivants qui représentent des problèmes liés à l'aménagement de rivière:

1. Peut-on considérer comme exactes et utiles les formules générales pour le calcul du transport des sédiments dans les problèmes d'aménagement de rivière?

2. Quels sont les mérites et limites relatifs des modèles mathématiques et hydrauliques? Il est important de comparer les prévisions avec ce qui s'est réellement passé lors de la construction des aménagements. Le sujet est trop complexe pour être discuté ici.

3. Est-il important de tenir compte de la longueur d'un méandre naturel de la rivière? Faut-il autant que possible respecter les longueurs des méandres?

4. J'ai aussi indiqué comme sujet de discussion un échange de vues sur les techniques de sondage intensif.

5. Un domaine où il reste beaucoup à apprendre est celui de la sédimentation résultant des ouvrages sur pieux, soit au droit de ceux-ci, soit en aval.

J'attends avec intérêt, Monsieur le Président, les exposés des autres orateurs sur les conclusions du rapport général et les autres aspects de ce sujet complexe.

LES DEBATS

P SAVEY (FRANCE)

1. Réponses à des questions. L'attention a été attirée sur la différence entre les bateaux hydrographiques de la SEINE et du RHONE. Les

conditions générales sont très différentes sur les deux fleuves: largeur du plan d'eau, vitesse du courant, importance actuelle de la navigation. Il n'est donc pas surprenant que les bateaux hydrographiques soient différents.

Il sera intéressant de confronter les deux techniques, mais on ne peut conclure a priori de la supériorité de l'un ou de l'autre des deux systèmes.

Les panneaux de fond ont été utilisés sur le Petit-RHONE pour trois raisons:

- non réduction du débit, importante dans une région agricole proche de la mer, où l'eau salée remonte le fleuve à l'étiage; en effet la rugosité des panneaux de fond est beaucoup plus faible que celle des épis et n'a pas d'incidences sur la distribution des dépôts entre les deux bras du fleuve;

- moindre coût, car l'on se trouve dans un delta loin des carrières pouvant fournir des enrochements dans des conditions économiques;

- effet moins brutal sur les fonds, ce qui est important pour une rivière étroite.

La technique des panneaux de fond n'est pas universelle, mais peut rendre de grands services dans certains cas, notamment dans les zones d'estuaires à sédiments fins.

2. Observations générales sur les divers rapports. Presque tous se réfèrent à des aménagements à courant libre, considérant les dragages et les digues submersibles. Il serait intéressant de connaître les limites de ce procédé.

Les exemples d'ouvrages réussis: MISSISSIPI supérieur, RHIN inférieur, certains secteurs du DANUBE, ne semblent jamais dépasser l'enfoncement de 2,5 m - 3 m.

Or il serait particulièrement important pour la navigation moderne d'obtenir un tel enfoncement ou même plus: 4 m par exemple, afin de lui permettre de lutter efficacement avec la concurrence des autres modes de transport.

Pour obtenir un tel résultat, ou même pour rendre simplement possible la navigation moderne dans certains cas difficiles, qui sont aussi fréquents (la VISTULE par exemple ou le DANUBE dans certains secteurs) le seul procédé convenable est celui de la canalisation par barrages et écluses. On reproche à ce procédé d'être coûteux. Il faut tenir compte de l'évolution du marché de l'énergie qui a rendu rentables un grand nombre d'aménagements hydrauliques de basse chute abandonnés avant 1973.

On peut espérer ainsi retrouver, pour certaines voies navigables, les conditions favorables du RHONE, où par exemple, la production d'énergie électrique a couvert 95% de la dépense d'aménagement. Il y a là une chance à saisir pour la navigation fluviale.

L'autre remarque est relative au transport intermittent, associé aux variations de l'hydrologie.

Inévitable dans les pays froids où les rivières sont prises par les glaces en hiver, il n'est pas souhaitable dans les pays industrialisés où les armements ont consenti de très lourds investissements en matériel fluvial et il leur est indispensable de l'utiliser toute l'année pour obtenir un amortissement convenable de ce matériel.

Par contre, ce type de navigation peut s'envisager dans des pays en voie de développement et notamment dans les pays tropicaux qui comportent un cycle saisonnier très marqué et où la navigation à l'étiage est quasiment impossible, tandis qu'elle est facile en saison humide.

3. Réponses à deux questions posées par le Rapporteur Général. Concernant la question de l'opportunité du travail théorique, compte tenu de l'importance des coefficients utilisés en hydraulique fluviale, la réponse nous paraît devoir être positive. En effet, d'importants efforts sont encore à faire en matière de débit solide ainsi qu'en matière de diffusion (tâche thermique) et de bilan d'oxygène dissous.

Quant à la comparaison entre les modèles mathématiques et physiques, on doit porter au crédit des premiers d'être économiques et de pouvoir couvrir des secteurs importants. Par contre, ils présentent l'inconvénient de réduire le profil en travers de la rivière à une seule dimension, et ne prennent pas en compte les effets de courbure du chenal, pourtant très importants pour le transport solide. Enfin, ils sont beaucoup plus que les modèles physiques, vulnérables aux erreurs et aux insuffisances des données de base.

C'est donc par une combinaison harmonieuse de la recherche théorique des modèles physiques et des modèles mathématiques que l'on trouvera la meilleure solution à nos problèmes.

C RICARD (FRANCE)

Monsieur le Président, Mesdames, Messieurs, je vous remercie de me permettre d'exposer brièvement les caractéristiques du bateau hydrographique qui vient d'être mis en service sur le Rhône et qui constitue un peu une synthèse de ses prédécesseurs en tenant compte des conditions particulières du Rhône.

1. Les travaux d'aménagement du Rhône confiés à la Compagnie Nationale du Rhône ont ouvert à la circulation des convois poussés, une voie navigable longue de 310 km, réalisée en 33 ans où la largeur minimale du chenal est de 60 mètres, et le tirant d'eau minimal, à l'étiage, de 3 mètres.

L'exploitation et l'entretien de cette voie d'eau sont à la charge de la C.N.R. qui dispose de vedettes capables de fournir, de manière automatique, des profils en long et en travers, mais pas de cartes des fonds. Or, comme le souligne le rapport français du présent Sujet 3, et bien que la canalisation du Rhône ait éliminé, en grande partie, les problèmes posés par les sables et graviers charriés sur le fond du cours d'eau, il subsiste un réel problème dû aux sédiments fins, accentué par les exigences des armateurs qui souhaitent profiter au maximum des possibilités de la voie d'eau.

La C.N.R. et le personnel ont donc décidé de s'équiper d'un bateau hydrographique capable d'effectuer des levés de fond de manière continue.

Ce bateau a une longueur de 33,50 m, sa largeur est de 8,80 m, et son tirant d'eau de 1,10 m. Il comporte deux bras de 15 m, repliables le long de la coque. Ces bras peuvent être manoeuvrés ensemble ou séparément. Bras ouverts, le bateau a une "envergure" de 38 m, ce qui lui permet de couvrir la largeur du chenal en 2 passages.

La vitesse normale de croisière est de 20 km/h par rapport à l'eau. En mission, il peut se déplacer à une vitesse comprise entre 2 et 8 km/h par rapport à l'eau.

Enfin, il a été conçu pour naviguer et effectuer des missions en mer calme.

2. Equipement hydrographique du bateau. Il comprend un équipement de sondage et un équipement de repérage du bateau coordonnés par un calculateur.

L'équipement de sondage se compose d'un ensemble de sondeurs transversaux et d'un ensemble de sondeurs longitudinaux pouvant fonctionner séparément ou simultanément.

Le système de sondage transversal comporte 50 transducteurs espacés de 0,80 m portés par les bras commandés et gérés par un ordinateur.

Celui-ci possède en mémoire les niveaux de référence du plan d'eau et corrige automatiquement les mesures, en tenant compte des indications fournies par un inclinomètre, en cas de gîte ou de roulis.

Le système longitudinal comporte 4 transducteurs: deux sous la quille, à l'avant et à hauteur des bras, et les deux autres aux extrémités des bras. Ils peuvent fournir des profils en long, mais aussi une indication de la profondeur pour le pilote du bateau.

Les sondeurs des deux systèmes peuvent fonctionner avec deux fréquences différentes pour permettre les levés sur fond vaseux aussi bien que les levés sur fond alluvionnaire.

Les résultats fournis par ces deux systèmes apparaissent:

- pour le premier, sur un écran cathodique où chaque levé transversal est visualisé, et sur une imprimante où par défilement continu du papier, apparaît une carte des fonds;
- pour le second, sur une deuxième imprimante où deux profils en long parmi les quatre possibles peuvent être automatiquement reportés graphiquement.
- l'équipement de repérage du bateau se compose de deux systèmes indépendants:
  - le premier opère par interrogation de 2 balises radio situées à terre, en des points rigoureusement coordonnés;
  - le second positionne le navire par mesure des vitesses ou déplacements longitudinaux et transversaux à partir du point de départ du trajet, à l'aide d'un appareil dont le principe est fondé sur l'effet DOPPLER-FIZEAU.

Ce dernier nécessite un recalage périodique par des mesures télémétriques qui sont effectuées au moyen d'appareils à Laser.

L'ensemble est coordonné et exploité par un ordinateur. Celui-ci permet notamment, en tenant compte des données du gyrocompas:

- de tracer la route suivie par le bateau, en temps réel,
- de tracer une carte des fonds en courbes de niveau, en temps différé,
- de programmer une route et d'indiquer les corrections à effectuer,
- de stocket données et résultats sur cassettes,
- de corriger les écarts dus aux dérives,
- d'effectuer tous calculs et traitements habituels réalisés par un ordinateur.

Ce matériel est placé dans une vaste salle où se trouve le poste de pilotage qui reçoit directement un certain nombre d'indications intéressant le pilotage du bateau.

3. Le bateau peut assurer d'autres missions courantes concernant la surveillance et l'entretien de la voie navigable (bouées de balisage).

Le bateau peut être amené à effectuer des missions de longue durée. Il dispose donc de tout ce qui est nécessaire à la vie à bord de 5 hommes composant l'équipage; cabines, cuisine, bar et une salle de réunion permettent d'accueillir 70 personnes.

4. Possibilités du bateau. Ce bateau vient d'entrer en service. Il pourra faire le levé complet du chenal sur 25 à 30 km en une seule journée. Prévu initialement pour travailler le long du RHONE, entre LYON et la Mer MEDITERRANEE, ce bateau pourrait être amené, suite à la décision du Gouvernement Français, de réaliser la liaison entre le RHIN et la SAONE par un canal à grand gabarit, et occasionnellement à entrer en action vers le Nord, sur la SAONE et le Canal de la SAONE au RHIN ou sur les voies de raccordement du RHONE aux ports méditerranéens (FOS, SETE, La NOUVELLE ...) et son équipement le lui permet.

M F THORN (GB)

1. Correction typographique au rapport britannique: (p. 515 § iv). "Le débit total dominant dans le système fluvial (Q_D) augmente de 23.400 m^3/s <u>au km 1208 à 27.800 m^3/s au km 128, et ...</u>"

2. Le rapport britannique étudie la mesure dans laquelle la navigation sur un long fleuve navigable peut être améliorée en l'absence d'un programme massif d'investissement en capital. La même préoccupation apparaît dans les rapports de l'U.R.S.S. et de la Yougoslavie. Le rapport soviétique pose très directement la question: "Quelles sont les limites techniques à l'approfondissement des fleuves non canalisés à lit mouvant?"

Le rapport britannique suggère deux approches possibles de ce problème:

a) Tenter de tirer parti des variations cycliques prévisibles du niveau de l'eau de l'eau en vue de synchroniser et d'optimiser le trafic sur le fleuve.

b) Appliquer l'analyse de la théorie du régime hydraulique au fleuve concerné afin de déterminer ses limites naturelles en matière de profondeur de navigation. Selon le Rapporteur Général, cette approche souffre du fait qu'elle ne permet de prévoir que des profondeurs moyennes. C'est effectivement le cas des calculs présentés dans le Rapport. Je crois, cependant, que le principe reste correct et qu'il peut être affiné pour tenir compte des asymétries de la coupe transversale du fleuve, par exemple en étudiant la relation entre la profondeur moyenne, les profondeurs minimales aux points de dépassement et les profondeurs maximales dans les courbes.

Le problème de base est le suivant: à un certain moment, pour accroître la profondeur de navigation, il est nécessaire de passer d'un fleuve <u>régulé</u> (dans lequel les profondeurs sont obtenues en contrôlant le débit à l'intérieur des berges naturelles) à un fleuve <u>dirigé</u> (dans lequel l'accroissement des profondeurs résulte du rétrécissement artificiel du chenal au moyen d'ouvrages guides). Sur les fleuves à trafic intensif des pays industrialisés, tels que le Rhin ou le Mississippi, ces ouvrages peuvent se justifier économiquement et être concrètement possibles. De toute manière, il est trop tard pour faire marche arrière.

Néanmoins, je n'encouragerais pas volontiers un pays disposant d'une voie d'eau longue à moindre taux d'utilisation à se lancer dans une tentative d'accroissement des profondeurs de navigation au moyen d'ouvrages guides et de dragages d'entretien intensifs. Je dirais plutôt dans ce cas: "Essayez de savoir jusqu'où la profondeur de navigation peut être accrue par une gestion à la fois du trafic et de la voie navigable (y compris quelques dragages d'entretien limités aux endroits les plus difficiles) et concentrez-vous sur cela".

D M McDOWELL (GB)

A première vue, il n'est pas évident que l'effet d'une jetée sur pieux dans une voie d'eau puisse contribuer à réduire la sédimentation. Les jetées sont pourtant un élément indissociable d'une voie d'eau navigable et leur impact doit être pris en considération. En outre, il est souhaitable d'optimaliser leur conception en vue de réduire au minimum l'effet de traînée.

La contribution du Dr. Ball est un des résultats d'une étude approfondie de l'interaction entre le courant d'une part et les ouvrages et bateaux de l'autre. Ce travail a conduit à certaines conclusions intéressantes en ce qui concerne la conduite des bateaux à proximité d'ouvrages sur pieux en présence de courants, de même qu'en matière de traînée provoquée par ces ouvrages et des configurations de sédimentation possibles. On sait que, même en ayant recours à des modèles physiques, il s'est toujours avéré difficile de préciser l'impact des ouvrages sur le comportement de la voie navigable. L'objet de l'étude en question était précisément de conduire à une meilleure compréhension de ce problème. Il serait utile que l'auteur puisse recevoir des informations sur les effets dans la réalité des ouvrages sur pieux, sur les configurations de débits, sur la sédimentation ou sur le comportement des bateaux.

K K GOGOI (INDE)

Sur le fleuve Brahmaputra en Assam, Inde, cours d'eau alluvial qui transporte d'énormes quantités de sédiments (30 pieds) provenant de l'érosion des rives et des affluents, nous réalisons des ouvrages directeurs pour la navigation sous forme, par exemple, de rangées de pieux de bambou enfoncés dans les sédiments à un angle de 45% par rapport au chenal secondaire afin d'y favoriser les dépôts et ainsi de réduire la sédimentation dans le chenal principal. Les dépôts provoquent une déviation croissante du courant principal vers le chenal principal, ce qui accroît la profondeur de navigation dans celui-ci. Le nombre d'assemblages dépend de la largeur du chenal secondaire: ils sont placés en lignes les uns derrière les autres dans une profondeur d'environ 2 mètres, les plaques de recouvrement étant constituées de treillis de bambou. Les assemblages doivent être déplacés périodiquement, en fonction de l'amélioration ou de la détérioration de la situation du chenal principal. L'entretien en est assuré par des équipes de 12 personnes par bateau utilisant deux ensembles de bateaux. Il s'agit d'une méthode ancestrale utilisée en Inde depuis presque un siècle et qui a résisté à l'épreuve du temps: elle est très efficace et évite le coût du dragage d'entretien par dragues mécaniques.

Il y a environ dix ans, deux Français, ont introduit un nouveau système consistant en un cloisonnement au fond du fleuve Brahmaputra en vue de fermer les chenaux secondaires. Ce système a permis de fermer en deux mois seulement un grand chenal secondaire appelé Mooskhowa. La différence par rapport au système précédent est que les bambous sont enfoncés plus profondément et que les panneaux sont constitués de plaques simples ou C.J. En outre, les panneaux sont placés en sens inverse, à savoir à 45° par rapport au chenal principal et ils sont déposés sur le fond d'où le nom de cloisonnement au fond. Pour que ce système soit efficace, il faut que le courant du chenal secondaire soit de l'ordre de 0,5 à 2 pieds par seconde. Une étude hydrographique détaillée doit être réalisée avant et après le placement des panneaux de fond. Ceux-ci sont mis en place par eaux montantes ou descendantes, soit en octobre-novembre ou en février-mars. Un dragage coûteux s'est révélé inutile, de sorte que les dépôts de sédiments des dragues à désagrégateurs sont plus qu'éliminés.

D MUSKATIROVIC (YOUGOSLAVIE)

La planification des ouvrages guides fluviaux est une tâche créative, responsable et très complexe. Je voudrais brièvement décrire l'approche de la solution de ce problème retenue en Yougoslavie à la faveur de l'expérience acquise à travers de grands ouvrages guides effectués pour les besoins de la navigation sur le Danube.

Je le ferai dans les grandes lignes au moyen d'un schéma très simple:

ETUDE DU TERRAIN

- mesures hydrom.
- géométrie de la voie d'eau
- mesures de sédimentation

ANALYSES MORPHOLOGIQUES

- corrélations
- courbes de distribution et de fréquence des caractéristiques géométriques du chenal fluvial

ANALYSES HYDRAULIQUES

- niveaux d'eau
- vitesses moyennes
- transport de sédiments
- déformations du lit
- disposition des ouvrages guides

ANALYSES ECONOMIQUES

- coûts (matériaux, mécanisation, exécution, transport)

ANALYSES DE L'ENVIRONNEMENT

→ VARIANTES → SOLUTION OPTIMALE

Ce schéma indique clairement que la planification des ouvrages guides d'amélioration des voies navigables fait intervenir de nombreux aspects dont il ne faut pas oublier qu'ils sont d'importance égale et méritent tous d'être pris en considération. A notre avis, des recherches ouvertes, créatives et concrètes sont préférables aux approches empiriques pour obtenir une bonne planification des ouvrages guides susceptibles d'améliorer la navigation.

H C FRIJLINK (PAYS-BAS)

En raison de l'importance du dragage d'entretien en tant que moyen d'améliorer les conditions de la navigation fluviale, en particulier dans les pays en voie de développement, il est suggéré d'inclure deux remarques antérieures du Rapporteur Général dans les conclusions.

"Une évaluation et une comparaison des coûts relatifs d'un dragage d'entretien régulier et d'un système d'ouvrages directeurs doivent être effectuées"; et

"Il convient d'entreprendre une étude visant à déterminer si la constitution de stocks ou l'utilisation de bateaux partiellement chargés ne pourraient éviter l'entretien de la totalité de la profondeur de chenal en période de basses eaux".

La pertinence d'un dragage régulier est illustrée par un dragage récemment effectué sur une distance de 500 kms sur le Niger en Afrique occidentale.

D DREYFOUS-DUCAS (FRANCE)

1. Sur la communication de M. SAVEY et concernant l'utilisation de panneaux de fond.

   Je pense que le coût de main-d'oeuvre pour la pose délicate des panneaux, leur entretien, et leurs déplacements, rend leur principe d'utilisation très limité au cas exceptionnel de fonds très vaseux où l'utilisation d'épis en enrochements n'est pas possible.

2. Sur l'intervention de M. RICAUD et la communication de M. SAVEY relative au bateau sondeur Frédéric MISTRAL.

   Je pense que l'utilisation de bras latéraux a deux inconvénients: gêne pour la navigation commerciale, et fragilité en cas d'avarie.

   Je pense également que l'équipement de ce bateau est très coûteux et que le rapport qualité/prix entre ce type de bateau et l'ECORANDA qui progresse en crabe est à l'avantage de l'ECORANDA.

On peut se demander aussi si l'exploitation des relevés n'est pas plus aisée à terre dans un bureau et moins coûteuse (déplacement du personnel, etc.)

Il serait souhaitable de demander aux 2 Services de comparer le coût d'une carte hydrographique de même longueur et sur une même longueur.

J MARCHAL (BELGIQUE)

Je voudrais par cette brève intervention à chaud faire d'abord une première suggestion au Comité de l'A.I.P.C.N. renforcée d'ailleurs par l'intervention que vient de faire M. SAVEY.

Beaucoup d'études ont été réalisées pour essayer de définir en fonction de critères technico-économiques, la profondeur optimum suffisante des voies navigables qu'il faut à tout prix garantir. Des débats ont déjà eu lieu dans le passé à ce sujet: je voudrais suggérer que l'A.I.P.C.N. continue à donner la possibilité dans le futur de débattre plus en détail encore de ce problème fondamental et complexe. Dans de tels débats des techniciens et des économistes du transport fluvial doivent être présents simultanément, faute de quoi aucuns critères valables qui doivent être adaptés aux conditions de navigation ne pourront être dégagés.

Je voudrais également apporter mon opinion quant à la question posée au point 1 des conclusions, à savoir si le travail théorique important réalisé sur le mouvement des sédiments grossiers se justifie encore lorsque l'on sait que les ingénieurs ont généralement recours à des mesures sur le terrain et à des formules empiriques pour déterminer les valeurs prévues?

Je pense qu'il faut rester extrêmement sceptique quant aux résultats issus de formules empiriques aussi nombreuses qu'il y a d'auteurs intéressés par le problème, formules apparemment sophistiquées, obtenues en essayant d'y introduire la plupart des grandeurs en jeu, mais malheureusement qui se voient attribuer des coefficients tout aussi empiriques, coefficients que je définirai plutôt comme étant des coefficients d'ignorance: pour un problème déterminé, je me suis déjà intéressé à comparer les résultats obtenus par différentes formules: les résultats extrêmes obtenus étaient différents entre eux d'un facteur 10!

A mon avis, la voie à suivre est celle de l'emploi d'un modèle hydraulique calibré sur un nombre limité de mesures en vraie grandeur sur lequel ensuite est étalonné un modèle mathématique permettant de poursuivre ensuite les investigations plus souplement.

Je rejoins donc totalement l'opinion émise à ce sujet, notamment par le rapport de la République démocratique d'ALLEMAGNE qui mentionne que les progrès deviennent particulièrement féconds lorsque sont mis en relation mutuelle les résultats des deux approches. Il ne faut donc pas dissocier les deux approches.

G THUES (BELGIQUE)

Anvers, port maritime situé à l'intérieur des terres, sur le fleuve à marées Escaut, à quelque 80 kms de la mer du nord, est séparé du fleuve par 5 écluses. Pourtant, l'Autorité portuaire est confrontée à un dragage d'entretien de 2,5. $10^6 m^3$ par an. Il y a deux thèmes qui ont été abordés au cours de ce Congrès et qui ne sont pas sans liens avec l'expérience d'Anvers.

1. Le dragage d'entretien est effectué par l'Autorité portuaire au moyen de son propre équipement, soit essentiellement 3 dragues à godets, 10 vaisseaux de $650 m^3$ de capacité affectées au transport des matériaux de dragage, une grue flottante à benne preneuse (pour l'enlèvement des matériaux plus durs tels que minerais de fer et toutes sortes d'objets ainsi que pour le dragage de précision) et, bientôt, une drague suceuse porteuse traînante fendable d'une capacité de $1500 m^3$, qui sera plus spécifiquement utilisée à proximité des écluses. Tout le dragage d'entretien doit s'effectuer tout en accordant la priorité au passage des navires, ce qui entraîne de fréquentes interruptions. La productivité en est par conséquent inférieure à celle du dragage d'approfondissement, et le coût global s'élève à 3 $US par m^3, ce qui reste inférieur au coût de location d'une équipe de dragage privée travaillant dans les mêmes conditions.

2. Afin de suivre les apports constants de sédiments dans la zone du port, des cartes précises et aisément compréhensibles de la situation des fonds des bassins doivent être disponibles à brève échéance. Le concept de "profondeur nautique" doit également être pris en considération. L'étude des couches de sédimentation a permis de se rendre compte de la liaison entre ce concept et certains enregistrements par sonar.

   On a construit un bateau spécial, qui donne les coordonnées x, y et z du fond du bassin au moyen de radio-phares à terre et du sonar de bord, et ceci avec une précision d'environ 0,5 m pour x et y et de 10 cm pour z. L'information est enregistrée sur bande magnétique, ramenée à terre où elle est introduite dans un petit ordinateur dont la table traçante fournit les résultats graphiques 2 à 3 heures après avoir quitté le navire, sous la forme d'une carte dessinant la configuration des bassins et les points de référence à terre pour les pilotes. A l'usage de ceux-ci également, la situation du fond des bassins est représentée au moyen d'isobathes (lignes d'égale profondeur). Une carte plus détaillée des zones à draguer est préparée à l'intention des responsables des opérations de dragage.

M HAGER (RFA)

Au cours de la première session de la Section I, j'ai fait rapport sur la possibilité de maintenir équilibré l'apport de sédiments du cours d'eau en vue d'en garantir une géométrie adéquate.

Une autre manière d'éviter l'érosion du lit et l'approfondissement de la coupe transversale consiste à utiliser un type particulier d'épis mobiles. Ces épis sont constitués de feuilles en matière synthétique et pouvant être gonflés en les remplissant d'eau, puis vidés de celle-ci. L'objectif est de concentrer le débit du cours d'eau dans le lit principal afin d'y maintenir la profondeur de navigation voulue. Ils sont remplis et utilisés en périodes de basses eaux. Ils sont vidés à mesure que le flot grossit et que le niveau d'eau s'élève. Ces épis spéciaux en sont à l'heure actuelle au stade de la recherche scientifique et de l'expérimentation pratique. Il s'agit d'une des approches qui sont à l'étude pour résoudre les problèmes du Rhin inférieur. La totalité de cette région, y compris cette portion du Rhin, s'affaise en raison de l'exploitation minière du Bassin de la Ruhr. Aux dernières nouvelles, l'équipement de remplissage et de vidange des épis doit être modifié. Dans notre rapport, nous avons présenté une manière sophistiquée de remplir et de vider les épis utilisant une installation auto-pompante équipée d'une buse spéciale. Il semble à présent plus réaliste d'utiliser une pompe normale située à terre.

A J M HARRISON (GB)

M. Harrison attire l'attention sur les commentaires du Rapporteur Général relatifs aux travaux théoriques portant sur les formules de transport de sédiments. Bien que ne partageant pas totalement l'opinion du Rapporteur Général a cet égard, M. Harrison y voit la mise en évidence de deux grands problèmes qui se posent en ce domaine;

a) la difficulté d'une mesure précise, à échelle réelle, du transport de sédiments et en particulier du transport au fond,

b) la difficulté de l'extrapolation des formules de transport de sédiment basées sur les données de bassins d'essai à la situation réelle.

Depuis plusieurs années, les chercheurs du Centre de Recherche Hydraulique de Wallingford se penchent sur ces deux problèmes. M. Harrison rappelle la mise au point de la formule de transport de Ackers-White, la manière dont elle a été testée par comparaison entre données en bassins d'essai et mesures à échelle réelle et les bons résultats qu'elle donne par rapport à d'autres formules de transport de sédiments. La formule est théoriquement fondée sur des coefficients empiriques. Sur la même base théorique, une relation de résistance, un modèle morphologique et des relations de régime ont été testés avec succès.

Le Centre de Wallingford a également mis au point un modèle de lit qui permet de mesurer avec précision même pour de faibles taux la concentrations de sédiments, au moyen d'une technique de prélèvement d'échantillons par pompage. Cet équipement doit étre utilisé en juillet 1981 pour mesurer le transport de sédiments sur le Nil. Les données ainsi recueillies seront comparées aux résultats obtenus au moyen de la formule de transport de sédiments de Ackers-White et seront utilisées dans une étude sur modèle morphologique de la dégradation des barrages.

P LAGROU (BELGIQUE)

L'Office de la Navigation qui assure l'exploitation du Canal Albert, voie d'eau importante qui relie le Port de Liège au Port d'Anvers avec un trafic de l'ordre de 40 millions de tonnes et dont l'aménagement pour les convois poussés de 9 000 tonnes est actuellement en cours d'exécution, a récemment transformé un ponton en bateau de sondage.

Ce bateau équipé de deux propulseurs Vorth-Schneider a été pourvu des instruments nécessaires permettant l'interprétation immédiate à bord des données de 60 "echo-sounders" dont il est muni, allant jusqu'au dessin des profils en travers. Ce choix a été fait afin de pouvoir détecter pendant le trajet même les profils paraissant anormaux et y revenir au besoin.

Le but poursuivi était entre autres, le contrôle des talus des berges sous eau et la recherche des zones d'érosion de ces talus. On a opté pour le système avec bras latéraux de 5 mètres de chaque côté du bateau permettant le sondage continu d'une bande de 30 mètres de largeur depuis les palplanches – y compris la zone de la risberme sous eau – tout en maintenant le bateau à une distance suffisante des talus sous eau afin d'éviter le danger d'érosion de ce talus sous l'effet des propulseurs.

S MONTEJO (COLUMBIA)

Le laboratoire hydraulique des Travaux Publics de Colombie, à Bogota n'est occupé du sujet présenté par le rapport d'Allemagne (R.D.). Au cours des études nous avons eu quelques difficultés, principalement dans le choix du rapport entre Δx et Δt, parce que une solution déséquilibrée vient d'une sélection inexacte.

Aussi il faudrait demander deux questions aux auteurs:

1. Pourqoi ont-ils choisis Δx et Δt? et pourqoi stabilisé le modèle mathématique?

2. Quelles sont les dimensions des paramètres dans l'expression § 13, p. 440?

CONCLUSIONS

1. Les objectifs de tout projet d'amélioration de voies navigables doivent être clairement spécifiés et doivent définir les paramètres de base tels que: mouillage minimal, largeur du chenal, rayon de courbure minimal, vitesse maximale et côte de l'eau, etc...

2. Avant d'étudier en détail l'aménagement d'une rivière pour la navigation, une analyse soigneuse des données historiques doit être faite de façon à bien maîtriser la connaissance du régime naturel et de ses variations.

3. Une quantité considérable de données doit être recueillie sur le terrain: niveau d'eau, étude du fond, vitesses, transport solide et données écologiques, pour les débits normaux et extrêmes.

4. Des modèles physiques et/ou mathématiques sont en général nécessaires pour prévoir les effets des projets d'amélioration pour la navigation.

5. Les structures utilisées pour le calibrage comprennent:

- les défenses de berge qui en constituent en général la première étape;

- les épis, qui provoquent les dépôts sur certaines rivières et par suite devient le courant;

- les digues submersibles longitudinales et les seuils conçus pour empêcher la formation de bras secondaires ou les supprimer.

Des ouvrages légers de calibrage tels que les panneaux de fonds ou de surface et des "bandals" peuvent être utilisés pour corriger la géométrie de rivières à pente faible et à lit de sable fin ou de vase.

6. Une approche progressive, assortie d'un contrôle soigneux, est recommandée spécialement lorsqu'existent des doutes quant à l'importance des effets de l'aménagement projeté. Les extractions de sable et graviers peuvent éventuellement tenir lieu de dragages d'entretien, à la condition que les matériaux soient extraits aux endroits et en quantités appropriés: il est recommandé d'éviter les dragages excessifs qui peuvent provoquer une diminution du mouillage en d'autres points de la voie et causer, par suite de l'abaissement du plan d'eau, des dommages physiques et écologiques.

7. Il existe une limite à l'accroissement du mouillage par l'aménagement d'une rivière à courant libre. Pour aller au-délà, une canalisation est nécessaire.

8. L'amélioration des conditions de navigation peut être réalisée par des moyens variés. C'est pourquoi il faut effectuer, pour chaque solution possible, une étude de rentabilité appropriée, incluant les facteurs sociaux et écologiques.

Cette étude doit comprendre notamment:

- une évaluation et une comparaison des coûts respectifs de dragages d'entretien réguliers ou d'un aménagement de la rivière à courant libre;

- une comparaison pour la période d'étiage entre, d'une part, l'utilisation d'un stockage des marchandises ou le chargement à enfoncement réduit des bateaux, d'autre part le maintien systématique des profondeurs normales.

9. La détermination du mouillage optimal doit procéder d'études à la fois techniques et économiques.

VOIES NAVIGABLES ET PORTS DE NAVIGATION INTERIEURE

SECTION I — SUJET 4

Navigation maritime, navigation côtière, navigation intérieure, intégrées

Vendredi 15 mai 1981

Président:	*J CHAPON (France)* *Ingénieur Générale des Ponts et Chaussées* *Vice-Président du Conseil Générale des Ponts et Chaussées* *Ministère de l'Environnement et du Cadre de Vie, Paris*
Vice Président:	*C J L LAWRIE (Canada)* *Head, Waterways Program* *Department of Transport, Ottawa*
Rapporteur Général:	*Prof Dr-Ing H H HEUSER (RFA)* *Versuchsanstalt fur Binnen-Schiffbau eV, Duisburg*
Secrétaire:	*C COCOZZA (France)* *Ingénieur des Ponts et Chaussées* *Directeur de l'Exploitation du Port Autonome de Paris*
Secrétaire Adjoint:	*A E C HOMASSEL (France)* *Secrétaire Adjoint, Section Française*

Orateurs

P R LISLE (GB), M BALDWIN (GB), Y MENDELEEV (URSS), D A BARENDSEN (Pays-Bas), K K GOGOI (Inde), J C AILLERET (France), M DEPLAIX (CESAP), N N B ORDMAN (GB), F DROUIN (France), E R HEIBERG (Etats-Unis), M HAGER (RFA), D DREYFOUS-DUCAS (France), N OSWALT (Etats-Unis), H L REVELL (GB)

H. HEUSER (RAPPORTEUR GENERAL)

Indication des aspects du thème les plus susceptibles de discussion fructueuse en session.

a) Intégration à partir des bateaux

b) Intégration à partir des ports

1. Trafic par eau avec transbordement de marchandises:

- Systèmes de transport particulièrement souples et économiques.
- Amélioration des installations de transbordement dans les ports maritimes.

Trafic par eau sans transbordement de marchandises:

- Trafic port intérieur à port intérieur par eau avec conditions maritimes illimitées:

  barges (allèges) et navires porte-barges;

  efforts de normalisation;

- Trafic port intérieur à port intérieur par eau avec conditions maritimes limitées:

  navires côtiers convenant également pour la navigation intérieure;

  bateaux de navigation intérieure convenant également pour le service en eaux côtières.

Mesures de sécurité et d'économie liées au point 1.

2. Mesures spéciales à prendre dans les ports maritimes où l'intégration des navigations intérieure, côtière et maritime s'avère nécessaire.

SYNTHESE DES INFORMATIONS ET AVIS IMPORTANTS SUR LE SUJET

1. La conteneurisation joue un rôle sans cesse croissant en tant que modalité du transport de la navigation maritime, côtière et même intérieure. Le système roulier semble de plus en plus prendre le pas sur les autres systèmes conventionnels de transbordement de marchandises de la terre vers l'eau et inversément. Plusieurs tentatives de dispositifs rouliers spéciaux adaptés même aux grands bateaux de navigation intérieure se sont révélées fructueuses.

   A l'heure actuelle, les ports maritimes et les terminaux intérieurs un peu partout dans le monde s'efforcent d'améliorer leurs installations d'entreposage et de transfert de conteneurs. Ils étudient en outre ou ont déjà commencé l'installation de rampes facilitant le service roulier des conteneurs et des marchandises très lourdes et encombrantes.

2. Les systèmes de navires porte-barges permettant le transport par eau sans transbordement connaissent un développement rapide. Après les systèmes LASH, SEABEE ou, plus récemment, BACAT et INTERLIGHTER, la tendance actuelle favorise les systèmes FO-FO (float-on/float-off) au détriment des systèmes LO-LO (load-on/load-off). La profondeur d'eau qu'ils exigent limite l'utilisation des navires FO-FO. Cette contrainte pèse encore plus lourdement sur les dernières conceptions de navires porte-barges. Ceux-ci constituent cependant une excellente solution pour traverser les sections d'eau peu profonde, particulièrement sur les fleuves non canalisés, pourvu toutefois que les zones de chargement et de déchargement aient une profondeur d'eau suffisante pour mettre les barges à flot à partir de porte-barges fluviaux ou au contraire les charger sur ceux-ci. La tendance qui se dessine pour les systèmes FO-FO va vers l'accroissement des dimensions des barges, même pour celles qui sont destinées au service intérier dans des convois poussés. Il devient donc souhaitable de réaliser une harmonisation à l'échelle mondiale des barges et des allèges afin de pouvoir les utiliser aussi bien en service intérieur en convois poussés qu'en service porte-barges. La normalisation de ces unités multi-fonctionnelles doit se réaliser à partir d'un système modulaire modelé sur une barge fluviale type.

3. L'intégration totale de la navigation côtière/intérieure peut être envisagée à partir de navires mer-intérieur, particulièrement des navires côtiers à faible tirant d'eau, ou à

partir de bateaux de navigation intérieure pouvant être exploités dans les eaux dotées de conditions maritimes limitées. Bien qu'une substantielle expérience ait déjà été acquise en ce domaine, le travail de dévélop-pement se poursuit dans le but notamment d'améliorer le comportement des bateaux de navigation intérieure aux lames de hauteur supérieure par une optimalisation des formes de ces bateaux leur conservant leur coef-ficient de bloc élevé. Ce service exige en outre une adaptation spécifique des types et des dispositifs de propulsion.

4. Pour des raisons économiques, l'intégration des navigations intérieure, côtière et mari-time deviendra de plus en plus nécessaire dans le cadre du trafic de frêt long courrier. L'objectif pour les années à venir est d'identifier les méthodes les plus économiques correspondant aux diverses liaisons commerciales ainsi qu'aux différ-ents types de marchandises transportées. En particulier, il s'avérera très important de réduire les temps et les coûts de transport en favorisant dans la mesure du possible les trafics sans transbordement des marchandises.

5. Les éléments de sécurité prennent toute leur importance lorsque les bateaux de navigation intérieure sont utilisés de plus en plus fréquemment en service côtier et maritime limité. Tout d'abord, il convient d'établir un réseau sûr de lignes maritimes réservé à ces bateaux. Ces itinéraires doivent être dotés de ports-abris ou de mouillages de sécurité rapidement acces-sibles en cas de détérioration des con-ditions météorologiques. En outre, il faudra améliorer la prévision des conditions de mer et de vent, notamment dans la mer du Nord, où certains progrès en ce sens ont du reste déjà été réalisés. Une autre con-dition nécessaire à la sécurité et à la facilité du trafic de transit est l'améliora-tion de la signalisation, aussi bien dans les eaux intérieures ou côtières qu'en pleine mer.

6. Les zones de navigation mixte tels que les grands ports maritimes constituent des points de rencontre pour deux mondes naut-iques différents tant en matière de réglementation qu'au point de vue de la signalisation. Les dimensions et les possibilités de manoeuvre différentes des navires concernés exigent qu'un certain nombre de précautions soient prises pour sauvegarder la sécurité du trafic. Ces mesures peuvent notamment consister en:

   - contrôle radar et système de communication VHF modernes
   - utilisation d'un langage harmonisé
   - instructions impératives de suivre certaines routes maritimes.

7. Si l'intégration des navigation intérieure, côtière et maritime est un objectif souhait-able dans l'avenir, elle est de tout temps une réalité dans la plupart des grands ports maritimes. La densité du trafic portuaire et le transport de marchandises dangereuses a suscité de nouveaux problèmes de sécurité et de distribution économique. La solution de ces problèmes est une condition préalable à la réalisation des objectifs fixés dans les autres domaines de l'intégration.

Les contributions émanant de 12 pays dans le monde entier montrent le grand intérêt suscité par les questions et les résponses relatives à ce sujet. En fait, L'INTEGRATION DES NAVIGATIONS MARITIME-COTIERE-INTERIEURE constitue un sujet fascinant, dont le moindre mérite n'est pas de traduire en moyens modernes des pratiques de navigation déjà anciennes. Les auteurs ont, bien extendu, dans le cadre du sujet traité, adopté des angles d'approche et des accents très différents. Il ne se dégage pas moins de l'ensemble des contributions une distinction générale en deux grands aspects:

L'intégration est considérée, d'une part, du point de vue des vaisseaux et des voies d'eau et, d'autre part, du point de vue des ports et des méthodes de manutention des marchandises. S'y ajoutent certains éléments importants de la sécurité des bateaux de navigation intérieure navigant en mer. La plupart des contributions traitent essentiellement du premier aspect, leur point d'impact étant l'intégration dans le domaine des bateaux et des voies d'eau.

Je suggère que notre discussion de ce problème suive le schéma suivant:

1. Trafic par eau avec transbordement de marchandises,

2. Trafic par eau sans transbordement de marchandises.

Le premier point couvre tous les aspects des systèmes modernes de transport concernant le trafic par voie d'eau intérieure et par mer, par exemple, trains de barges poussés, systèmes barges-remorqueurs et barges maritimes. En ce domaine, l'INTEGRATION signifie tout d'abord la mise en oeuvre des méthodes de transbordement les plus économiques — évitant ou du moins mini-misant les temps de stockage dans les zones portuaires — particulièrement en ce qui concerne les marchandises en conteneurs.

Le deuxième point pourrait être organisé en 3 aspects particuliers.

1) Trafic traversant les eaux à caractère maritime illimité, concernant essentiellement les BARGES et CHALANDS ainsi que les diverses méthodes de chargement et de déchargement de ceux-ci sur et hors des NAVIRES PORTE-BARGES.

2) Trafic traversant des eaux à conditions limitées de vent et de lames, par exemple dans le cas de caboteurs également aptes à la navigation intérieure ou, au contraire, de bateaux de navigation intérieure capables de service maritime.

3) Mesures nécessaires à la sécurité en mer

des bateaux de navigation intérieure, telles que l'harmonisation de la signalisation de la navigation, la prévision fiable des lames, l'imposition de routes maritimes et l'implantation de ports-abris.

Une minorité de contributions mettent l'accent sur les aspects de sécurité et d'économie des méthodes de manutention des marchandises et sur les mesures spéciales qui doivent être prises pour assurer la sécurité dans les zones côtières et l'intégration de la navigation simultanée maritime-côtière-intérieure dans les grandes zones portuaires maritimes et leurs sections d'approche.

RECOMMANDATIONS D'ACTION FUTURE DU CONGRES

1. La poursuite du développement des systèmes de navires porte-barges, y compris de navigation intérieure, doit être suivie de près et encouragée.

2. L'harmonisation des barges pour le transport fluvial et par navires porte-barges doit être stimulée. La constitution d'un groupe d'étude spécial est recommandée à cet égard.

3. Un soutien actif doit être apporté à toutes les activités de recherche visant à améliorer la prévision des conditions de vent et de mer, non seulement pour la haute mer, mais surtout pour les zones à profondeur d'eau limitée. Encourager les auteurs potentiels à publier leurs réflexions ou résultats en ce domaine dans le BULLETIN de l'A.I.P.C.N. pourrait constituer une étape utile dans cette voie.

Monsieur le Président, Mesdames, Messieurs, je vous remercie de votre attention.

LES DEBATS

P R LISLE (GB)

Dans mes commentaires d'une série de points soulevés par le rapport britannique, je voudrais attirer votre attention sur certains facteurs permettant de formuler des conclusions dans cet important domaine. Elles reflètent des difficultés rencontrées, des possibilités qui existent et des symptômes qui peuvent être observés pour orienter la réflexion en matière d'intégration de la navigation côtière et intérieure.

La première remarque est que l'activité commerciale britannique est essentiellement concentrée sur la navigation sur fleuves et fleuves canalisés pénétrant à l'intérieur des terres à partir des quatre grands estuaires. Bien qu'ils ne desservent que des régions limitées, ces trafics constituent des facteurs importants dans l'économie de ces régions et sont développés en vue d'une pénétration accrue des navires et embarcations de plus grandes dimensions.

Je voudrais aussi souligner les modifications intervenues dans la configuration du trafic entre la Grande-Bretagne et le continent européen et les utiliser en vue du renforcement de la navigation côtière/intérieure. Une des conséquences en est la nécessité d'une rotation accrue des navires et de la construction d'un plus grand nombre de terminaux intérieurs pouvant recevoir davantage de navires en provenance des ports traditionnels. Les études récentes en matière de conception des navires ont révélé une tendance vers de plus grandes largeurs, des tirants d'eau réduits et une longueur accrue pour une capacité donnée. Malgré la réduction, pour des raisons économiques, de l'importance du transbordement, la pénétration vers les terminaux intérieurs se développe. Ceci est peut-être un symptôme typique en d'autres régions. Pour chaque zone d'exploitation, il faut standardiser les barges afin d'accroître la souplesse et l'interchangeabilité dans l'utilisation des systèmes de navigation et en particulier des systèmes unitarisés. Il est important à cet égard de mettre en liaison la conception des bateaux et celle des améliorations des voies d'eau, en tenant compte du coût et de la durée de vie supérieurs de celles-ci par rapport aux embarcations qui les empruntent. Il est donc essentiel d'étudier ces facteurs et d'optimaliser la solution. D'autres possibilités se présentent au niveau du trafic estuaire/intérieur, au sein duquel se développe le transport de pétrole, de céréales et d'autres marchandises vers les centres intérieurs. Il peut s'avérer que certains des systèmes porte-barges qui sont mis au point soient trop grands pour la pénétration à l'intérieur des terres. Ceci appelle aussi une standardisation. Il faut également préciser les normes relatives aux caboteurs à profil bas si l'on veut éviter que le développement de l'infrastructure sous forme de nouveaux ponts fasse obstacle à l'utilisation de ces embarcations pour la navigation intérieure. Afin de limiter les dépenses de capital, il faut enfin étudier la meilleure utilisation possible de ce qui existe.

L'allocation des coûts de navigation sur une voie navigable multifonctionnelle pose de difficiles problèmes qui, espère-t-on, seront étudiés lors d'une prochaine réunion du Comité Technique Permanent I.

Si le trafic de conteneurs s'est développé en Grande-Bretagne sur les voies d'eau intérieures, il n'en appelle pas moins la mise au point d'un module de bateau porteur approprié aux dimensions standard des conteneurs.

Enfin, l'orateur mentionne le développement récent du LASH en tant qu'embarcation plus étroite mieux adaptée aux petites voies d'eau commerciales.

M BALDWIN (GB)

Je voudrais saisir cette occasion pour commenter quelque peu les idées présentées par le rapport britannique.

1. A la page 678, il est suggéré que l'absence de trafics adaptés, combinée à des facteurs économiques, a contribué au déclin du transbordement sur barges. S'il est indéniable qu'on a assisté à un tel déclin en Grande-Bretagne, je ne crois pas que les raisons en sont aussi simples que le suggère le rapport. Cette conviction s'inspire pour une parte de l'observation de l'évolution du trafic en

d'autres régions et pour l'autre part des résultats d'une étude publiée en 1978 par une firme d'architecture navale britannique. Cette étude analysait les coûts du transport de marchandises industrielles en vrac d'une localisation intérieure en Grande-Bretagne vers une localisation intérieure en Allemagne. Ni l'endroit de départ, ni le lieu d'arrivée n'étaient accessibles par navigation intérieure. Sept itinéraires différents ont été estimés: trois d'entre eux maximisaient l'utilisation de l'eau, deux maximisaient l'utilisation du rail et deux celle de la route. En dépit du besoin de transbordement, les trois itinéraires privilégiant l'eau fournissaient un transport moins cher que chacun des itinéraires privilégiant la route et le rail.

Il est donc probable que d'autres facteurs que ceux que mentionnent les auteurs ont contribué à réduire l'importance de ce mode de trafic en Grande-Bretagne. Je suggère que ces facteurs pourraient comprendre, tout d'abord, un investissement insuffisant en vue de l'élargissement et du développement du réseau de voies navigables intérieures, permettant à des embarcations de dimensions économiquement adaptées de pénétrer suffisamment à l'intérieur des terres. Deuxièmement, beaucoup d'utilisateurs potentiels des voies d'eau intérieures selon ce mode de transport ne sont tout simplement pas conscients de l'ampleur des services actuellement disponibles par eau. Ces deux facteurs regrettables indiquent combien ce mode de transport a été négligé en Grande-Bretagne au cours des dernières années.

2. A la page 681, on mentionne les navires capables de navigation intérieure. Les délégués seront peut-être intéressés par quelques exemples, représentatifs des navires britanniques de ce type:

   LADY SANDRA - capacité 380 tonnes, tirant d'eau douce 2,5 m, tirage 5 m.

   HULL MILLER - capacité 470 tonnes, tirant d'eau douce 2,5 m, tirage 4,3 m.

   UNION GEM - capacité 715 tonnes, tirant d'eau douce 2,5 m, tirage 5,5 m.

   URGENCE - capacité 1824 tonnes, tirant d'eau douce 3,3 m, tirage 6,5 m.

   L'un des voyages particulièrement impressionnants de l'UNION GEM l'a conduit de Goole, Angleterre, à Bâle, Suisse, avec un chargement de 600 tonnes de coke. Ceci démontre l'excellence du service porte-à-porte que peut assurer ce type de navires.

   Un autre exemple du succès de leur utilisation est fourni par la renaissance du port fluvial de Fosdyke Bridge, sur le Welland, Angleterre. Au terme d'environ 10 ans pendant lesquels il n'avait reçu aucun bateau, il a été réouvert en 1979 et connaît actuellement une expansion rapide grâce aux navires fluviaux qui importent des engrais en provenance des Pays-Bas et de Belgique et qui exportent des céréales. Malgré leur taille réduite, offrant essentiellement une capacité de 500 tonnes, ces bateaux assurent économiquement un transport du type porte-à-porte, en éliminant le besoin de transbordement vers la route dans des ports côtiers plus grands.

3. Bien que le réseau de navigation intérieure britannique ne soit ni si grand ni si développé que ceux de certains pays que représentent ici de nombreux délégués, son intérêt réside dans la multiplicité des systèmes de transport qu'il accueille pour assurer l'intégration entre navigation intérieure et navigation maritime. Nous avons des caboteurs, des bateaux fluviaux, des barges de mer remorquées (surtout pour le pétrole et le gaz de la mer du nord), ainsi que des navires porte-barges de différents types, parmi lesquels le LASH, le SPLASH, le FLASH, le SEABEE et le BACO. En fait, je recommande la visite du port de Sheerness, qui traite quatre de ces systèmes et s'inscrit donc en première ligne comme port pour navires porte-barges britannique.

<u>En conclusion</u>, je dirai que si certains pays n'utilisent les bateaux fluviaux que pour la navigation intérieure, de nombreux autres pays les utilisent, de même que les navires porte-barges, dans leur trafic international. L'utilisation future de ces bateaux se verrait encouragée par l'harmonisation des dimensions des voies navigables qu'ils empruntent. Peut-être ceci pourrait-il faire l'objet d'une des Recommandations de notre Session.

Y MENDELEEV (URSS)

Je voudrais commenter certains aspects particuliers de la construction des navires de navigation maritime/fluviale soviétiques.

En Union Soviétique, les navires de navigation maritime/fluviale diffèrent de ceux des autres pays à un égard important. Nos navires sont en effet conçus avec des coques de résistance optimale par rapport aux conditions météorologiques et à la région de leur mise en exploitation.

Les Règles des sociétés de classification des navires soviétiques et en particulier le Registre de la Navigation et le Registre de la Navigation Intérieure de la Fédération Russe comprennent les conditions suivantes: Tout d'abord, en matière de lames: lames allant jusque la force 5 sur l'échelle de Beaufort. Ensuite, en matière de navigabilité: d'un port-refuge éventuel jusqu'à 50 miles nautiques en mer fermée telle que la Baltique ou la Mer Noire.

Les bateaux de la classe "II — SP" dans le Registre de la Navigation de l'U.R.S.S. doivent pouvoir affronter des lames allant jusque force 6 et aller des ports-refuges jusqu'à 50 miles nautiques dans les mers ouvertes telles que la Mer du Nord et jusqu'à 100 miles en mers fermées.

L'analyse des règles des sociétés de classification des navires en Europe pour les bateaux de ce type montre qu'elles déterminent une résistance de coque standard qui doit permettre aux navires d'affronter les vents et les lames les plus forts dans les mers concernées. Il s'ensuit que, pour une capacité de chargement donnée, les navires conçus selon les critères des sociétés de classification soviétiques ont des tirants d'eau considérablement inférieurs à ceux des navires similaires conçus selon les critères des sociétés de classification européennes.

Vingt années d'utilisation harmonieuse des navires des classes "M-SP" et "II-SP" ont montré l'opportunité du choix des critères de conception rappelés ci-dessus, particulièrement en matière de limites imposées à la construction des bateaux de navigation maritime/fluviale.

L'utilisation expérimentale de la classe "M-SP" dans la Mer Caspienne et dans la Mer Egée confirme que la résistance de leur coque est suffisante pour la navigation dans ces eaux. L'extension des aires de navigation maritime de ces bateaux contribuera à accroître leur efficacité dans le trafic maritime/intérieur et à éviter le transbordement des marchandises.

L'accroissement de la capacité des navires de navigation maritime/intérieure constitue une autre possibilité d'améliorer leurs caractéristiques économiques en réduisant les coûts de transport.

Nous sommes à l'heure actuelle près de terminer des travaux de conception d'un navire de 5 000 tpm et d'un tirant d'eau de 4 mètres en eau douce. Ce navire pourrait être opérationnel dès l'année prochaine. Dans les circonstances de notre navigation, nous pensons qu'il s'agit là d'une manière satisfaisante d'accroître la navigation maritime/intérieure.

D A BARENDSEN (PAYS-BAS)

Le développement en U.R.S.S. dans l'intégration de la navigation maritime et la navigation intérieure, comme exposée dans le rapport de l'U.R.S.S. et l'exposé de M. Mendeleev, a été possible grâce à la présence d'un réseau de navigation en U.R.S.S. qui est vaste et qui a des grandes dimensions. Surtout le fleuve Volga canalisé et le système des canaux entre le cours supérieur de ce fleuve et la Mer Baltique sont aménagés pour les bateaux assez grands.

Plusieurs participants du XXIVe Congrès de l'A.I.P.C.N. ont eu l'occasion de voir une grande partie de ce réseau fluvial, et les nombreux types de bateaux qui utilisent cette voie d'eau.

Les bateaux fluviaux du type "Baltistres" (dit MSP dans le rapport de l'U.R.S.S.) quelquefois font le voyage au large de Leningrad vers le Port de Den Helder aux Pays-Bas, au nord d'Amsterdam, pourvu que les conditions en mer du Nord permettent un tel voyage.

Des photos, qui ont été prises pendant le XXIVe Congrès et pendant le voyage en bateau sur la Volga après le Congrès, sont montrées en diapositives.

Elles montrent dans le Port maritime de Leningrad et en plusieurs endroits sur la Volga les types de bateaux fluviaux rencontrès, et quelques écluses dans la Volga et le Canal Volga-Don.

Ces photos donnent une idée des grandes dimensions de ces deux voies d'eau.

K K GOGOI (INDE)

En raison d'investissements insuffisants, ou de pénurie de moyens de financement pour développer les voies navigables intérieures et côtières dans des pays en voie de développement comme l'Inde, l'harmonisation de ces modes de transport n'est pas envisageable, du moins dans un avenir prévisible, dans une mesure suffisante pour assurer l'intégration avec le trafic des pays industrialisés d'Europe occidentale et d'Amérique du Nord.

Les systèmes de navigation en usage dans les ports du Golfe, sur les Grands Lacs et sur les voies intérieures d'Amérique du Nord, les systèmes inter-côtiers du Golfe et les systèmes fluviaux européens ne peuvent à l'heure actuelle être harmonisés avec les systèmes d'Asie, d'Afrique et sans doute avec certains ports d'Amérique du Sud. C'est pourquoi l'harmonisation des systèmes LASH et SEABEE devra attendre le jour où les pays en voie de développement auront pu suffisamment développer leurs voies navigables pour répondre aux normes des pays occidentaux. Le seul autre système disponible, le trafic par conteneurs, pourra quant à lui être harmonisé dans un avenir prévisible, à la condition toutefois que l'occident accepte les conteneurs 20' x 8' x 8' ft au lieu des conteneurs 40' x 8' x 8' ft, car le système routier des pays en voie de développement n'est pas comparable à celui des pays industrialisés. En fait, dans certaines régions des pays en voie de développement, il n'y a pas de route du tout. Dans ces cas, les systèmes LASH ou FLOAT-ON/FLOAT-OFF offrent une réponse adéquate. Mais comme, au lendemain de leur indépendance, les pays en voie de développement ont dû donner la priorité aux routes et au rail, ils n'ont pu en même temps développer les réseaux de navigation intérieure et côtière dans la même mesure que les pays industrialisés.

L'harmonisation à l'échelle mondiale de certains modes de transport ne peut se faire sans tenir compte des caractéristiques des voies navigables des pays en voie de développement d'Asie, d'Afrique et d'Amérique du Sud.

J C AILLERET (FRANCE)

On s'est beaucoup intéressé dans les rapports à la suppression ou à l'amélioration des ruptures de charge entre navires de mer et bateaux fluviaux (navire porte-barges, barges normalisées ...)

Le conteneur a le même objet; il s'applique à des types de marchandies qui sont de plus en plus transportées.

Je suis donc surpris que dans le monde des Voies Navigables on ne s'intéresse pas plus aux conteneurs et en tous cas que ce type de trafic soit très peu développé.

En fait le transport fluvial des conteneurs pose très peu de problèmes techniques:

- Il n'y a pas besoin de barges spécialisées, tout bateau peut transporter des conteneurs; il ne faut pas de glissière et il n'a pas besoin d'arrimage.

- Pas de problème dans les ports maritimes, les bateaux fluviaux se comportent vis-à-vis des exploitants portuaires comme les caboteurs (feeders).
- Dans les ports fluviaux, il faut des équipements peu onéreux (gabarit, cadence faible) et qui peuvent être polyvalents.
- Le volume minimum pour un tel trafic sur une liaison donnée est assez faible: 60 TEU/ semaine, soit 3 000 TEU/an et par sens, soit 30 000 T/an/sens environ.

Par ailleurs l'avantage du coût de transport peut être important, si la distance n'est pas trop faible.

On objecte souvent la durée du transport; la différence n'est pas considérable (moins de 48 h de trajet fluvial, soit 700 km entre Strasbourg et Rotterdam par le Rhin); le problème des fréquences de départ est sans doute plus réel mais les chargeurs sont souvent plus sensibles à la régularité et à la fiabilité qu'à la rapidité.

Je suis persuadé que le trafic des conteneurs par voie fluviale a de l'avenir et surpris que sauf sur le Rhin (environ 100 000 TEU en 1980) ce type de trafic soit si peu développé.

Je pense que pour une fois, c'est plus sur une prise de conscience des possibilités actuelles que sur la réalité de réaliser des investis sements nouveaux que nous devrions mettre l'accent.

M DEPLAIX (UNITED NATIONS - ESCAP/CESAP)

Remercie l'A.I.P.C.N. pour l'invitation faite à la CESAP;

Présente certaines particularités des voies d'eau d'ASIE en matière de standardisation des dimensions des bateaux, la navigation côtière et le transport de palettes sur des bateaux de navigation intérieure;

Souligne que les transports intérieurs, en particulier le rail, ne sont pas plus rapides que la voie d'eau dans les pays d'ASIE et parfois aussi en EUROPE, et que les traditionnelles références à la lenteur de la voie d'eau sont loin d'être toujours justifiées.

N N B ORDMAN (GB)

L'augmentation récente et spectaculaire du prix de l'énergie, alliée à des facteurs tels les coûts de congestion du trafic routier, milite en faveur d'une utilisation accrue des voies de navigation intérieure et des systèmes combinés de navigation maritime/intérieure. Il faut s'attendre à ce que cette évolution appelle un accroissement des investissements en ce domaine. Il convient donc de définir les modes d'évaluation des coûts des systèmes mis en oeuvre. Conventionnellement, pour les systèmes de transports, les coûts sont répartis en fonction de

- navire et véhicule
- ports
- manutention des marchandises, y compris transbordement
- voie (dans ce cas: voie navigable intérieure)

Les trois premières catégories peuvent être appréhendées par des méthodes bien connues. Au contraire, de sérieux problèmes se posent lorsqu'il faut évaluer le coût réel des voies d'eau intérieures pouvant servir à des fins de transport, en raison des utilisations diverses des réseaux fluviaux et de canaux, qui peuvent aller de l'évacuation des matériaux de dragage et des eaux usées, à la fourniture d'eau, en passant par l'énergie hydraulique et les loisirs.

M. Ordman demande si ce problème a été étudié et, éventuellement résolu.

F DROUIN (FRANCE)

Les navires porte-barges ont-ils de l'avenir? On en voit peu; ils ne se développent pas. On en parle beaucoup dans les rapports. Qu'en est-il exactement?

Le C.T.P.I., dans sa séance n° 2, avait admis qu'ils ne constituaient pas un problème et qu'il n'y avait pas lieu d'y consacrer beaucoup de recherches.

Est-ce une voie d'avenir; est-ce périmé?

E R HEIBERG (USA)

Je voudrais revenir sur les commentaires de Messieurs Ordman, Lisle et Drayfous relatifs à l'allocation des coûts. Les Etats-Unis se penchent sur ce problème depuis un an, en particulier à partir d'une analyse portant sur trois petits segments de fleuves. Nous étudions les éléments concernant explicitement l'usage "navigation" y compris les écluses, les chenaux et certains réservoirs d'appoint. Dans ces trois cas d'espèce, 60 à 90% des coûts semblent attribuables à la navigation. Le solde est imputable à l'énergie hydraulique, au contrôle de débit, aux loisirs et autres usages.

Le transport intérieur s'est considérablement développé au cours des dernières années, en particulier sur le Mississippi inférieur, l'Ohio, la section occidentale du réseau intercôtier (côtier) du Golfe et sur le Columbia. Les explications de cette expansion résident dans des considérations d'ordre énergétique et dans l'extension du trafic de charbon et de céréales par barges.

Par ailleurs, le problème de l'allocation des coûts est posé, au niveau national, dans le cadre de ce que nous appelons "contribution de l'usager". Il s'agit, plutôt que de financer par des fonds fédéraux la majeure partie des frais de construction, d'exploitation et d'entretien des voies de navigation intérieure et des ports côtiers, de trouver des modes raisonnables d'une prise en charge accrue de ces coûts par les usagers.

Les difficultés restent grandes. Nous dépensons des millions de dollars chaque année, par exemple, pour maintenir le Mississippi inférieur entre ses rives. Cet effort ne vise pas seulement à garantir la sécurité de la navigation, mais, et c'est tout aussi important, il assure une protection contre les crues dont profitent des millions de personnes, il permet de fournir l'eau dont ont besoin les industries aussi bien que les municipalités et, accessoirement, il permet le développement d'activités de loisirs. L'allocation des coûts à ces divers usages se révèle donc particulièrement épineuse.

Nous attendons beaucoup des travaux du C.T.P.I. pour nous aider à progresser vers une imputation équitable des coûts.

F HAGER (RFA)

En réponse à la question de M. Ordman, et compte tenu des remarques du Gén. Heiberg, je puis dire qu'en République Fédérale d'Allemagne, nous avons mis au point une méthode d'analyse de tous les bénéfices résultant de travaux hydrauliques, qu'il s'agisse d'un nouvel ouvrage ou d'une nouvelle voie, ou du développement d'une installation existante. Cette méthode incorpore tous les éléments et conditions pertinents, y compris l'impact sur l'environnement et les effets de l'aménagement du territoire sur l'industrialisation de la zone concernée.

Cette méthode d'analyse est à présent utilisée pour éclairer toutes les décisions préalables au début des travaux.

Nous en avons rendu compte dans un article récemment publié par le Bulletin de l'A.I.P.C.N. (n° 34). Nous sommes prêts à l'introduire dans notre contribution aux travaux du nouveau groupe de travail constitué par l'A.I.P.C.N. sur ce sujet.

D DREYFOUS-DUCAS (FRANCE)

1. Conteneur et voie d'eau. Le retard dans le développement de l'emploi du conteneur sur les voies navigables provient en partie dans des pays comme la FRANCE de la rigidité des chaînes de transport et des habitudes des auxiliaires de transport et des dockers.

Le développement des petits ports en Grande-Bretagne et des chaînes intégrées des lignes de navigation en constitue une preuve.

2. Polyvalence de la voie d'eau. Les études antérieures notamment d'Institut de Recherche des Transports, ne donnaient pas de résultat car on comptait pour 0 ce qu'on ne savait pas calculer. Un autre cheminement est possible. Faire calculer les coûts qui subsisteraient si on fermait la voie au trafic de la navigation commerciale et de plaisance. L'enquête à laquelle j'ai procédé il y a 3 ans a montré que pour l'entretien de la voie, la coût à imputer au transport est de l'ordre de 50 à 60% selon l'importance de la voie et son caractère; pour les investissements, la part à imputer au transport est de 70% sur les rivières et de l'ordre de 75 à 80% sur certains canaux.

N A OSWALT (USA)

Il a été suggéré dans la Section I — Sujet 1 que le rapport entre la section du canal et la section du bateau soit établi à 5.

Cette modification me pose problème en ce qui concerne les voies navigables intérieures restreintes avec bermes. Une étude sur modèle récemment effectuée aux Etats-Unis pour le chenal navigable en eau profonde de Sacramento a indiqué qu'un rapport supérieur à 5 est nécessaire à la stabilité des rives en cas de vitesse excessive.

H L REVELL (GB)

Les voies navigables peuvent avoir d'autres usages qui devraient sans doute être reconnus et donc justifier une contribution aux coûts de la part de la collectivité concernée. Le danger existe cependant que ceci soit considéré comme un avantage particulier réservé à ce mode de transport. Les autres modes de transport sont défendus par des groupes de pression très efficaces, qui ne tarderont pas à se saisir de cette circonstance dans leur propagande.

Le trafic par voies navigables doit être spécifique et se voir reconnaître des potentialités à long terme. Conventionnellement, l'équipement maritime fait l'objet d'un amortissement de longue durée (20 à 25 ans), alors que l'équipement routier est amorti en beaucoup moins de temps et peut, en outre, être aisément reconverti vers d'autres usages. La promotion de l'investissement dans les voies navigables en est d'autant plus difficile.

CONCLUSIONS

La situation économique mondiale actuelle fournit de nouveaux motifs de reduire les coûts de transport. L'usage du transport par voie d'eau augmentera en raison de son faible cout énergétique et la réduction du coût des ruptures de charge conditionnera le developpement de l'integration des navigations maritime et fluviale.

Cette appréciation de la situation a des implications d'ordre:

- technique
- réglementaire
- socio-économique.

1. Il faut encourager les sytèmes de charges unitaires qui, pour les marchandises générales, utilisent la palettisation, la conteneurisation, ainsi que les navires rouliers et porte-barges.

   Une intégration complète des navigations maritime et intérieure peut être réalisée soit par l'utilisation de navires remontant les voies intérieures — en particulier des caboteurs à faible tirant d'air — soit par l'utilisation de bateaux de rivière effectuant des parcours maritimes, au moins pour certaines conditions de mer.

   Lorsque les voies navigables ont une très grande longueur, le transbordement de marchandises entre navires et bateaux de navigation intérieure peut rester économique, mais chaque cas doit faire l'objet d'une étude particulière.

   Pour assurer la sécurité de la navigation, il faut:

   - un réseau sûr de voies maritimes
   - des ports-abris
   - des prévisions correctes du vent et de l'état de la mer.

   Le système modulaire est particulièrement approprié pour réaliser une certaine harmonisation du dimensionnement des navires et des bateaux et par conséquent des ouvrages.

Les considérations qui précèdent constituent des sujets d'étude recommandés à l'Association.

2. L'harmonisation de la signalisation entre les systèmes maritimes et de voies intérieures (pour laquelle des progrès considérables ont déjà été réalisés grâce à l'Association Internationale de Signalisation Maritime) sera très importante. Pour ce qui est des règles de route et de manoeuvre, il est également souhaitable de réaliser une certaine uniformisation des aides à la navigation.

Il est important de prendre les mesures nécessaires pour assurer la sécurité dans les ports et leurs accès.

3. L'intégration des navigations maritime et intérieure pose des problèmes d'aménagement du territoire qui doivent être analysés et résolus. Par exemple, elle favorise la

localisation le long des voies d'eau de zones industrielles et urbaines, en dehors des concentrations industrielles existantes.

Etant donné la multiplicité des fonctions des voies d'eau, la part des coûts imputée à la fonction "transport" doit conduire à l'établissement de justes tarifs qui ne dissuadent pas l'intégration des deux modes de navigation.

VOIES NAVIGABLES ET PORTS DE NAVIGATION INTERIEURE

SECTION I — SUJET 5

Echange de technologies sur la programmation et l'ingénierie avec les pays en voie de développement et ce qu'il implique pour l'amélioration des ports maritimes et des terminaux de navigation intérieure

Samedi 16 mai 1981

Président:	*J CHAPON (France)* *Ingénieur Générale des Ponts et Chaussées* *Vice-Président du Conseil Générale des Ponts et Chaussées* *Ministère de l'Environnement et du Cadre de Vie, Paris*
Vice Président:	*O P NARULA (Inde)* *Development Adviser* *Ministry of Shipping and Transport, New Delhi*
Rapporteur Général:	*T P STEEN (Norvege)* *Norconsult A S Consulting Engineers, Hovik*
Secrétaire:	*C COCOZZA (France)* *Ingénieur des Ponts et Chaussées* *Directeur de l'Exploitation du Port Autonome de Paris*
Secrétaire Adjoint:	*A E C HOMASSEL (France)* *Secrétaire Adjoint, Section Française*

Orateurs

T TAKEUCHI (Japon), H C FRIJLINK (Pays-Bas), J D METTAM (GB), C Van EERDENBRUGH (Belgique), J AUBERT (France), O P NARULA (Inde), A FUGLUM (Norvege), J M DEPLAIX (CESAP), L K TERHO (Finlande), J W MORRIS (Etats-Unis), P SIREYJOL (France), N N B ORDMAN (GB)

T P STEEN (RAPPORTEUR GENERAL)

Les nombreux et intéressants rapports soumis dans le cadre de ce sujet reflètent bien l'attention considérable qui est portée par les pays industrialisés aux pays en voie de développement et à leurs problèmes. Les auteurs traduisent une expérience acquise dans le monde entier dans le domaine de l'échange des technologies de programmation et d'ingénierie qui se développent de plus en plus entre les deux groupes de pays.

Malheureusement, aucun document n'a été présenté par les pays en voie de développement eux-mêmes. Il eût été extrêmement intéressant pourtant de voir refléter les opinions prévalant au sein de ce second groupe de pays. Ils auraient pu redresser certains malentendus éventuels et répondre aux questions que se posent les pays industrialisés, nous aidant ainsi à mieux comprendre tous les aspects de ce sujet si important et si stimulant pour nous. Nous voudrions, comme de nombreux auteurs, faire remarquer à cet égard que l'expression "pays en voie de développement" couvre toute une série de pays dont les conditions varient du premier stade de développement à un stade déjà nettement plus avancé en matière d'acquisition et d'application de connaissances. Le manque de capitaux et l'excédent de main d'oeuvre non qualifiée restent cependant deux caractéristiques associées à la plupart des pays en voie de développement.

Les ports constituent des carrefours pour les échanges internationaux de marchandises et fournissent à ce titre d'excellents exemples d'entreprises industrialisées où l'échange de technologie se déroule à l'échelon global. Cependant les pays en voie de développement n'ont eu que peu de temps pour faire évoluer leurs ports vers les normes modernes et dépendent encore pour cette raison d'une collaboration étroite avec les pays industrialisés. De nombreux auteurs ont souligné que cette collaboration ne devrait pas consister en un simple transfert imitatif, mais être basée sur les politiques définies par les pays concernés eux-mêmes en tenant compte de leurs caractéristiques et de leurs besoins spécifiques. L'expression "échange de technologie" implique donc bien un processus réciproque.

La plupart des rapports insistent sur l'influence des facteurs humains dans tous les domaines couverts par ce sujet. Une politique de la main d'oeuvre adéquate est nécessaire, et doit mettre au centre des préoccupations le personnel du port, sa formation et ses besoins. Les rapports fournissent un ensemble de conseils en ce qui concerne la formation du personnel à tous les niveaux, formation qui doit permettre une réalisation satisfaisante de toutes les tâches nécessaires d'entretien, d'exploitation et de gestion dans les ports. On remarque parfois une certaine absence de motivation pour réaliser le meilleur travail possible, absence qui est sans doute partiellement due au fait que les bas salaires encouragent la pratique des deuxièmes occupations et découragent les gens de consacrer une partie de leur temps à leur formation personnelle. Deux des rapports fournissent en outre des descriptions détaillées de projets extrêmement intéressantes au point de vue de l'ingénierie. Bien que ces projets ne mentionnent pas explicitement la coopération avec le personnel local, la nature même des projets concernés a certainement nécessité de fructueux échanges de technologie.

Certains auteurs mentionnent les activités de la Commission permanente pour les Pays en voie de développement de l'AIPCN. Nous saisissons cette occasion pour rappeler que cette commission a prévu, en collaboration avec le comité d'organisation britannique, une session informelle au cours du Congrès d'Edimbourg. Son intention est d'y présenter son programme de travail aux délégués des pays en voie de développement et aux autres participants intéressés par ce sujet.

Les rapports formulent un certain nombre de commentaires et de propositions visant à promouvoir l'échange de technologie dans le but d'améliorer les ports et les terminaux, leur niveau technique, leur exploitation et leur gestion. Parmi les nombreux aspects qui sollicitent notre attention à cet égard, nous supposons que les suivants pourraient avec fruit faire l'objet de discussions en sessions:

NORMALISATION INTERNATIONALE

Il est généralement accepté que les pays en voie de développement devraient, dans leur propre intérêt, rendre leurs ports mieux à même de recevoir le trafic international et contribuer ainsi à l'industrialisation des régions qu'ils desservent. Les pays industrialisés ont généralement réagi à ce même genre de défi en introduisant des techniques plus sophistiquées et plus importantes en capital. Cette solution est-elle bien adaptée aux pays en voie de développement? La normalisation internationale doit-elle être encouragée au plus haut niveau d'exigence ou faut-il adapter les technologies aux conditions locales? Si d'une part il faut tenir compte du chômage et du manque de capitaux, on ne peut oublier d'autre part le souhait de transférer le travail humain des tâches non indispensables vers celles qui sont le plus utiles à l'économie.

STATUT ECONOMIQUE DES PORTS

Le statut des ports au sein de l'organisation économique d'un pays fait l'objet d'appréciations différentes. Selon certains auteurs, puisque les ports sont essentiellement des composantes de l'infrastructure du pays, leur efficacité ne peut être évaluée sur la seule base des critères de rentabilité, mais il faut tenir compte des avantages indirects auxquels ils donnent lieu pour leurs hinterlands, avantages qui pour être extrêmement importants ne sont que difficilement quantifiables. D'autres auteurs, au contraire, soulignent les défis qu'il faut relever lorsque les ports sont dirigés comme des entreprises industrielles sur un marché concurrentiel et qu'ils sont considérés comme tels en matière de financement également. Devons-nous arriver à un compromis pour répondre à cette question politique? Comment pouvons-nous apprécier de manière raisonnablement fiable les avantages indirects dont il est question?

PROGRAMMATION DYNAMIQUE OU STATIQUE

Certains rapports attirent notre attention sur l'intérêt d'une programmation dynamique du développement. Cette approche propose un développement gradué répondant aux besoins immédiats à faible coût et n'envisageant les extensions ultérieures qu'à mesure qu'apparaissent de manière précise les nouveaux besoins. Une programmation statique, au contraire, exige un dimensionnement initial des installations prévu pour répondre à tous les besoins futurs, ce qui entraîne nécessairement une depense en capital initiale plus grande et une sous-utilisation des installations pendant au moins une partie de leur durée de vie. Pourquoi dans ce cas l'approche statique est-elle plus répandue, y compris dans les pays en voie de développement?

ENTRETIEN

Beaucoup d'auteurs recommandent que les installations et l'équipement des ports soient conçus de manière à réduire au minimum leur charge d'entretien. Ce souhait reflète une expérience générale selon laquelle l'entretien est souvent négligé par les autorités portuaires des pays en voie de développement. Il serait intéressant à cet égard d'entendre des opinions reflétant des expériences contredisant cette constatation, de manière à apprendre quelles mesures concrètes pourraient être prises pour améliorer cette situation.

FORMATION

La formation du personnel portuaire est sans conteste le sujet le plus fréquemment mentionné dans les rapports, où il est considéré comme un des domaines où l'échange de technologie peut être le plus profitable. Ce personnel est réparti en trois catégories: direction supérieure, encadrement intermédiaire (contremaîtres, cadres intermédiaires, techniciens) et travailleurs. Il est recommandé entre autres choses que l'accent soit maintenant mis sur la formation et la consolidation de l'encadrement intermédiaire, dans la mesure où ceci aurait un impact positif sur la programmation continue qui doit être assurée par le personnel du port lui-même, de même que sur les tâches de manutention et d'entretien qui sont trop souvent négligées. Est-il pensable que les autorités portuaires acceptent cette idée de mettre en avant l'encadrement intermédiaire? Quelles doivent être les modalités de la formation si l'on veut obtenir les meilleurs résultats possibles?

FORMES DE COOPERATION

On considère généralement que le personnel local devrait prendre la plus large part possible dans les programmes d'assistance technique. Le rapport des Etats-Unis propose deux méthodes d'organisation de l'échange de technologie fondées sur ce principe. L'une consiste à regrouper les ressources humaines locales au sein d'organisations régionales qui pourraient collaborer avec les autres organisations internationales présentes dans ce domaine. La deuxième méthode consiste à favoriser les contacts personnels entre les autorités portuaires d'un pays en voie de développement et les responsables d'un port présentant des caractéristiques similaires dans un pays industrialisé. De plus amples informations sur des applications concrètes de ces deux modalités de coopération seraient les bienvenues.

QUE FAIRE POUR ACCELERER L'ECHANGE DE TECHNOLOGIE?

C'est le rapport britannique qui pose cette question du plus haut intérêt. En effet, les pays développés sont préoccupés par la lenteur relative qui caractérise actuellement cet échange. Il semble que des modifications d'approche doivent intervenir dans tous les secteurs. Le rapport soumet plusieurs recommandations en ce sens à l'attention des gouvernements et des organismes d'aide dans les pays industrialisés aussi bien que des pays en voie de développement. Ces orientations pourraient servir de base à une discussion très fructueuse. Quels autres points devraient par ailleurs être pris en considération?

Qu'il nous soit permis, sur la base des rapports présentés, de tirer les conclusions préliminaires qui suivent:

1. Les pays en voie de développement n'ont eu

qu'un temps relativement bref pour adapter leurs ports maritimes et leurs terminaux de navigation intérieure aux normes modernes et dépendent donc à cet égard d'une collaboration étroite avec les pays industrialisés. Dans leur propre intérêt, ces pays doivent éviter que cette collaboration ne se limite à un simple transfert imitatif et veiller au contraire à ce qu'elle se fonde sur leur propre politique et tienne compte de leurs caractéristiques et de leurs besoins spécifiques.

2. Dans la plupart des pays en voie de développement, le manque de capitaux et l'excédent de main d'oeuvre non qualifiée sont deux éléments importants qui doivent être intégrés dans la programmation des projets de développement industriel. Ceci implique qu'un recours aussi large que possible soit fait à la main d'oeuvre et aux matières premières locales, ainsi qu'à des installations et à des équipements moins sophistiqués auxquels sont associées des méthodes d'exploitation plus simples et un minimum d'entretien. Dans de nombreuses régions en effet, la gestion des installations portuaires doit se faire sans recours possible aux services d'un environnement industrialisé. Toutefois, les installations doivent être programmées de manière à permettre sans grande perturbation leur adaptation à une mécanisation plus poussée à l'avenir.

3. L'exploitation, l'entretien et la gestion sont des activités permanentes. C'est pourquoi même si au départ elles sont assurées par des étrangers elles doivent aussi tôt que possible être remises entre les mains du personnel local. Pour que cela soit possible, il faut que ce personnel participe activement à toutes les phases de la programmation et de la réalisation du développement considéré, de manière à en acquérir une connaissance vécue de l'intérieur. En outre, une formation spéciale du personnel à tous les niveaux est, dans de nombreux cas, une condition de succès indispensable dans l'exploitation des installations.

4. Il incombe comme un devoir à la communauté internationale d'aider les pays en voie de développement à satisfaire les exigences qui leur sont imposées en liaison avec l'introduction des technologies modernes. Cette responsabilité est acceptée par l'AIPCN et d'autres organisations internationales. C'est pourquoi le partage d'expériences dans le domaine de l'échange de technologie devrait être partie intégrante du flux permanent d'informations que de tels organismes devraient être à même d'assurer.

Les activités de l'AIPCN en ce domaine devraient être canalisées par la Commission permanente pour les Pays en voie de développement (CPPD), qui est prête à fournir conseils et orientations pour une large gamme de problèmes de transport maritime. Il est suggéré que cette commission ajoute à son programme actuel d'activités la mise sur pied d'un groupe de travail réunissant des représentants de l'AIPCN, de l'AIPH, de la CNUCED et de la BIRD, afin de discuter et de formuler un programme conjoint dans le domaine de la formation du personnel portuaire. Il faudrait également veiller à ce qu'il soit connu de manière plus générale que la CPPD est prête à apporter sa contribution à la création d'organisations régionales dans les pays en voie de développement ainsi qu'à l'établissement de relations directes entre ports dans le but de promouvoir l'échange de technologie.

Le sujet soumis à nos débats de ce matin n'est pas uniquement de nature technique. L'échange de technologie entre pays en voie de développement et pays industrialisés dépend en effet étroitement de décisions politiques. Néanmoins, les ingénieurs peuvent en ce domaine préparer le terrain pour les hommes politiques en mettant sur pied de leur côté une collaboration internationale centrée sur la science et le génie civil, deux domaines accessibles à tous.

De nombreux ingénieurs sont impliqués dans l'échange des technologies de planification et de génie civil dans le monde entier et les onze rapports soumis dans le cadre de ce sujet reflètent bien l'intérêt que ce sujet suscite. Leurs auteurs sont porteurs d'une expérience très large, et on ne s'étonnera donc point du niveau élevé de leurs contributions.

Deux approches du sujet peuvent être distinguées dans les rapports. En URSS et en Belgique, les auteurs s'attachent à décrire des projets portuaires spécifiques dans lesquels ils sont personnellement impliqués au niveau de la planification des installations concernées. Il ne fait pas de doute que ces projets ont donné lieu à un échange intensif de technologie en Tanzanie, en Syrie et au Yémen, et il serait intéressant d'entendre les auteurs nous parler de leur expérience en matière de collaboration avec le personnel local.

Les neuf autres rapports reflètent l'expérience générale acquise par leurs auteurs au cours de leurs diverses missions dans les pays en voie de développement. Tous insistent sur l'importance que revêt l'implication la plus large possible du personnel local dans chaque phase des projets. Dans la mesure où celui-ci sera tôt ou tard appelé à assumer la totale responsabilité de l'exploitation et de l'entretien des installations.

On comprend dès lors l'intérêt qu'aurait revêtu la présentation des rapports par les pays en voie de développement eux-mêmes. C'eût été l'occasion de redresser d'éventuels malentendus et de nous faire mieux voir les problèmes. En l'absence de tels rapports, nous espérons que les représentants des pays en voie de développement ne manqueront pas d'intervenir dans les discussions de ce matin et, plus tard, de faire entendre leur voix ent tant que membres de notre Association.

Parmi les très nombreux aspects sur lesquels les rapports attirent l'attention, il m'a paru opportun de soumettre plus particulièrement ceux qui suivent à la discussion:

- normalisation internationale des installations portuaires
- statut économique des ports
- planification dynamique ou planification statique
- entretien des installations portuaires
- formation du personnel portuaire.

Je vous livre à présent quelques commentaires sur les problèmes de base abordés dans les rapports.

Dans les ports des pays industrialisés, la réaction au défi posé par la navigation internationale et par l'expansion industrielle a généralement revêtu la forme de techniques modernes intensives en capital. On peut cependant se demander si elle constitue la bonne solution pour les pays en voie de développement et si les conditions locales ne devraient pas peser d'un plus grand poids dans le choix des technologies retenues. D'une part, on ne peut oublier que la sous utilisation de la main d'oeuvre disponible et la pénurie de capital sont caractéristiques de la plupart des pays en voie de développement. D'autre part, il est toujours souhaitable de faire porter l'effort de l'homme sur les tâches réellement utiles pour l'économie de base plutôt que sur des activités non nécessaires.

Plusieurs approches du statut économique des ports ont été présentées. Plusieurs auteurs défendent la thèse selon laquelle l'économie portuaire ne peut être abordée en termes de stricte rentabilité immédiate, mais qu'au contraire tous les avantages indirects doivent être pris en considération.

D'autres soulignent les défis qu'implique la gestion des ports en tant qu'entreprises industrielles à part entière. Il s'agit bien entendu d'une question de nature essentiellement politique. Il n'en reste pas moins que le statut économique assigné aux ports affecte les aspects techniques de la planification portuaire, notamment au stade des études de faisabilité.

Certains auteurs attirent l'attention sur les avantages associés à une planification dynamique du développement portuaire, impliquant une progression par étapes successives visant à rencontrer au moindre coût les besoins immédiats, chaque étape n'étant entamée que sur la base d'indications concrètes révélant des besoins nouveaux.

L'approche statique semble cependant demeurer la plus usuelle. Elle implique que les dimensions des installations originales soient calculées en fonction, notamment, des besoins actuels mais aussi de leur évolution future. Elle exige en conséquence un important investissement de départ, qui ne pourra être rentabilisé que progressivement. Il s'agit de nouveau ici d'un problème politico-économique plutôt que technique au sens strict. Néanmoins, une fois encore, la politique adoptée en ce domaine affecte considérablement la planification purement technique des installations.

De nombreux rapports insistent sur la nécessité d'un entretien régulier et correct des installations portuaires. Les auteurs ont en effet constaté une tendance très fréquente à négliger l'entretien. Ce sujet a du reste déjà fait l'objet, au cours de ce même Congrès, d'une discussion au cours de la réunion spéciale organisée par la Commission Permanente de l'AIPCN pour les pays en voie de développement. Il serait néanmoins intéressant de tenter d'identifier les mesures générales qui peuvent être prises pour améliorer la situation à cet égard, peut-être à partir de la description d'exemples éventuels d'entretiens bien organisés.

La formation des hommes à tous les niveaux est sans conteste le problème le plus souvent soulevé par les rapports. Ceux-ci suggèrent, entre autres choses, de favoriser maintenant à cet égard l'encadrement intermédiaire, en tant que moyen le plus efficace pour réaliser une planification et un développement portuaires harmonieux dans le temps.

Les auteurs suédois suggèrent que notre Commission Permanente pour les Pays en voie de Développement pourrait être à la base de la création d'un groupe de travail réunissant des représentants de l'AIPCN, de l'AIPH, de la CNUCED et de la Banque Mondiale en vue de formuler un programme conjoint de formation du personnel portuaire.

Le rapport nord-américain décrit deux méthodes d'organisation de l'échange de technologie s'inspirant du principe selon lequel le personnel local devrait prendre la plus large part possible aux programmes d'assistance technique. Tandis qu'une méthode concentre les efforts sur la mise en commun des capacités locales au sein d'organismes régionaux, l'autre méthode met l'accent sur les contacts directs entre les ports des pays en voie de développement et les ports des pays industrialisés présentant des caractéristiques semblables.

Enfin, mais ceci est tout aussi important, je voudrais rappeler la question extrêmement pertinente posée par le rapport britannique: "Que peut-on faire pour accélérer l'échange de technologie?". Selon ces auteurs, les gouvernements et les organismes d'aide devraient à cet égard s'efforcer de:

- réduire le temps des procédures de décision
- donner mission aux consultants et aux entrepreneurs retenus de réaliser la totalité des projets concernés
- accorder plus d'importance au suivi de la formation et de l'encadrement, ainsi qu'à l'entretien des installations
- intensifier la formation aux niveaux intermédiaires et techniques.

De leur côté, les pays en voie de développement devraient accepter de:

- raccourcir les circuits administratifs
- réduire les temps d'attente aux douanes
- admettre une proportion raisonnable d'apports étrangers à tous les niveaux
- admettre une proportion initiale relativement élevée d'experts étrangers.

Ces suggestions sont sans aucun doute de nature à susciter une discussion fructueuse.

Les conclusions préliminaires du Rapport Général sont présentées en quatre points. Les trois premiers s'efforcent de synthétiser un certain nombre de recommandations générales qui semblent faire l'objet d'un accord général parmi les auteurs, à savoir:

- il est de l'intérêt des pays en voie de développement que leur collaboration avec les pays industrialisés ne revête pas la forme d'une reproduction inconditionnelle de ce que font ceux-ci, mais qu'elle s'inspire de politiques définies par les pays en voie de développement eux-mêmes;

- l'utilisation intensive de la main d'oeuvre et des matériaux locaux doit être favorisée, de même que les equipements et les installations auxiliaires moins sophistiqués faisant appel à des méthodes relativement simples d'exploitation et à un entretien minimum;

- le personnel local doit participer activement à toutes les étapes de la planification et de la réalisation du projet de développement et la priorité doit être accordée à la formation à tous les niveaux de ce personnel.

Le dernier paragraphe des conclusions suggérées rappelle l'acceptation par l'AIPCN et par d'autres organisations internationales de leur responsabilité dans le domaine de l'aide aux pays en voie de développement. Il est recommandé que les activités de l'AIPCN en ce domaine empruntent le canal de la Commission Permanente pour les Pays en voie de développement.

LES DEBATS

T TAKEUCHI (JAPAN)

Les techniques de construction portuaire japonaises se sont développées à l'image de la technologie des pays européens. Plus de cent années se sont ainsi écoulées et, aujourd'hui, plus de 1.000 ports sont en exploitation au Japon.

Je voudrais rappeler le contexte dans lequel s'inscrit la politique portuaire actuelle du Japon et plus particulièrement la stratégie du développement portuaire ou des méthodes de planification portuaire qui se sont élaborées au fil des ans au Japon.

Les technologies de planification portuaire mise au point au Japon pourraient s'avérer applicables au développement portuaire des pays en voie de développement. Cependant, l'évolution économique des projets portuaires et surtout de leurs avantages indirects suscite de sérieux problèmes.

Les ports sont considérés être non seulement des jonctions entre les communications intérieures et la mer, mais aussi des centres pour l'industrie. Ils ne doivent pas être jugés sur la seule base de leur rentabilité.

Il est donc suggéré que l'A.I.P.C.N. poursuive ses efforts en vue de définir des critères raisonnables pour une telle évaluation.

H C FRIJLINK (PAYS-BAS)

Il n'existe pas de technologie spécifique pour les pays en voie de développement; tous les sujets traités par les congrès de l'A.I.P.C.N. sont pertinents pour ces pays.

Les pays en voie de développement souhaitent adhérer à l'A.I.P.C.N., avoir des contacts professionnels avec leurs collègues des pays industrialisés.

L'A.I.P.C.N. doit encourager le Sud à participer à ses congrès et l'A.I.P.C.N. elle-même doit "se tourner vers le Sud".

La conclusion 4, partie 2, doit être reformulée: "Les activités de l'A.I.P.C.N. en ce domaine seront canalisées par le C.P.V.D.,* auquel il est demandé:

1. De définir des politiques visant à accroître la participation de délégués des pays en voie de développement aux congrès de l'A.I.P.C.N.

2. D'assurer la liaison avec le Bureau Exécutif et les C.T.P. de l'A.I.P.C.N. en vue de recommander des sujets d'intérêt commun pour les pays en voie de développement et les pays industrialisés.

3. De faire des propositions tant de modalités que de lieux de conférences à organiser dans les pays en voie de développement dans des domaines d'intérît universel.

4. D'assurer la liaison avec l'A.I.P.H., la C.N.U.C.E.D. et la B.I.R.D., etc. dans les domaines dont s'occupent également ces autres organisations."

Le President, tout en remerciant Monsieur Frijlink pour ses informations, fait remarquer qu'organiser des Conférences coûte cher et entraîne énormément de travail. Il suggère que ces Conférences ne se tiennent que sur invitation.

J D METTAM (GB)

Il est suggéré que l'utilisation du terme "navigation" dans un sens archaïque pourrait dissuader les ingénieurs des pays en voie de développement de participer à nos congrès et que l'intervention des sections nationales dans la préparation des rapports pourrait constituer un obstacle à la présentation de contributions par les pays en voie de développement. La participation aux congrès de représentants des pays en voie de développement pourrait cependant constituer un apport très intéressant à la formation d'ingénieurs compétents de ces pays. Encourager cette participation constitue donc une tâche prioritaire pour l'A.I.P.C.N. en ce domaine.

La formation du personnel d'exploitation et d'entretien requiert la création de centres de formation dans les pays concernés.

Le Rapport Général ne souligne pas assez la pénurie d'ingénieurs compétents et les remèdes à apporter à cette situation.

Il existe de graves inconvénients à tenter de

*Comité Permanent pour les Pays en Voie de Développement.

susciter des vocations de consultants locaux spécialisés dans la conception portuaire là où les travaux portuaires sont insuffisants pour les employer complètement. La société de l'orateur préfère combiner deux modes de contribution à la formation d'ingénieurs compétents dans les pays en voie de développement: i) les faire participer à des stages de formation dans ses services en Grande-Bretagne et ii) ouvrir une agence locale dirigée par un cadre étranger (ou local) de la firme britannique et employant du personnel local encadré par des étrangers.

Un élément tout aussi difficile qu'important de la planification portuaire est la rédaction du cahier des charges des études de planification. En l'absence d'un donneur parfaitement expérimenté comme la Banque Mondiale, il est suggéré que la meilleure méthode pour obtenir une étude sérieuse et solide serait de faire appel à un (ou plusieurs) ingénieur(s)-conseil(s) expérimenté(s) pour la rédaction de ces cahiers des charges qui serviront ensuite aux appels d'offres.

C Van EERDENBRUGH (BELGIQUE)

Deux rapports (U.R.S.S. et Belgique) traitent de sujets techniques spécifiques. La plupart des contributions s'attachent à la philosophie de l'approche des problèmes d'échange de technologies de planification et d'exécution.

Certains aspects du rapport belge pourraient éclairer la discussion.

Normalisation internationale — conteneurs. A l'heure actuelle, peu de conteneurs sont transbordés de train à barge ou inversément au moyen d'une force motrice. Ce type de transport tend cependant à se développer, de sorte qu'un équipement approprié devient de plus en plus indispensable.

Il n'est pas sage de tenter de s'opposer à ces tendances. Les clients de ces systèmes de transport y voient un intérêt, ne fût-ce que du point de vue de la bonne protection qu'assurent les conteneurs à la marchandise sur les longs parcours.

Planification dynamique ou statique. Le maître-plan de Kigoma peut être réalisé par étapes et le sera sans doute. Certains projets portuaires, cependant, ne permettent pas une telle approche graduée, en raison de leur nature, comme c'est le cas par exemple des ports en mer exigeant des brise-lames. Le choix d'une planification dynamique ou statique n'est passeulement une affaire de politique générale, mais aussi de technique.

Statut des ports au sein de l'industrie. Les analyses coûtes-bénéfices de l'investissement nécessaire pour les travaux proposés par le maître-plan de Kigoma ont conclu, en prix constants, à un taux de rendement interne nul. L'incorporation des bénéfices indirects permet cependant d'obtenir un taux de rendement appréciable.

Je pense qu'en matière d'investissements portuaires, les bénéfices proviennent essentiellement des effets positifs indirects. Par ailleurs, un taux de rendement interne nul, ne tenant compte que des revenus directs, n'entraîne aucun coût supplémentaire à long terme pour la collectivité.

J AUBERT (FRANCE)

Les auteurs des rapports ont insisté, à juste titre, sur l'idée que les méthodes à appliquer pour créer des voies navigables nouvelles dans les pays en voie de développement doivent tenir un grand compte des circonstances locales, circonstances, qui varient d'un pays à l'autre.

J'adhère pleinement à cette première idée, mais je crois nécessaire de la compléter par une deuxième, qui me paraît tout aussi importante.

En partant du fait que les pays en voie de développement ne disposent que de ressources financières limitées, il serait fâcheux de les orienter vers la réalisation de voies navigables que l'on pourrait qualifier de voies de deuxième qualité.

Il faut se garder d'apporter à l'étranger nos idées d'hier qui ont abouti à la création de certaines voies que nous possédons, mais que nous considérons comme vétustes.

Dans les échanges de technologie, nos correspondants ont le droit de recevoir ce qu'il y a de meilleur, c'est-à-dire nos idées d'aujourd'hui. J'irai plus loin envore en disant qu'il convient d'exporter nos idées de demain.

Vous allez peut-être m'accuser de vouloir vider inutilement les caisses.

Il m'est facile de répondre que, bien au contraire, je préconise une réduction des dépenses. Pour moi, en effet, le progrès n'est réel que s'il correspond à une économie.

Pour atteindre un but bien défini, l'ingénieur a le devoir de mettre en oeuvre des techniques de plus en plus simples et de moins en moins coûteuses.

Si le progrès s'effectue dans le sens que je viens d'indiquer, on peut affirmer qu'il est à la portée de toutes les bourses.

Il est temps d'illustrer ma thèse par des exemples.

Je vous parlerai d'abord de l'évolution des idées en matière d'établissement du profil en long d'une nouvelle voie navigable artificielle. Je vais vous montrer ce que nous avons fait il y a 150 ans et ce que nous ferions aujourd'hui.

Le plan schématique qui vous est montré concerne un tronçon de la voie navigable qui relie Paris au Rhin. (page 58, Fig. 1).

Le canal actuel, correspond au tracé sud. Le tracé beaucoup plus court, est celui que l'on adopterait maintenant.

L'ancien tracé comporte 54 écluses et un souterrain de 5 Km. Le nouveau tracé ne comporte que deux ouvrages: des pentes d'eau, dont les hauteurs respectives sont de 125 et de 65 mètres. (page 58, Fig. 2).

Le temps de parcours du nouveau tracé envisagé serait 7 ou 8 fois plus court que celui du canal existant. Son prix serait bien moindre.

Les deux clichés qui viennent de vous être projetés illustrent bien le progrès qui a été réalisé en 150 ans. Je dispose de quelques exemplaires des deux dessins correspondants et je pourrais les remettre à ceux qui me les demanderaient.

Comme deuxième exemple de projet moderne et économique, je considererai le cas du grand barrage de Cabora-Bassa sur le fleuve Zambèze, au Mozambique.

Peu de temps avant leur départ, les ingénieurs portugais étaient venus nous trouver pour étudier avec nous le franchissement du barrage par une pente d'eau.

On navigue sur le Zambèze en aval et la construction d'un seul ouvrage aurait suffi pour créer en amont une voie navigable de 500 Km.

Le temps me fait défaut pour vous parler d'un troisième exemple d'ouvrage économique. Il s'agit du dernier barrage construit sur la Seine en aval de Paris. Il a été inauguré à Denouval il y a six mois. L'économie réalisée, par rapport aux solutions traditionnelles, a été de 30 à 40%.

Quelques brochures relatives aux nouvelles techniques dont il vient d'être question sont encore disponibles à l'exposition du rez-de-chaussée. Pour en obtenir d'autres, on peut écrire à: Mme N. Martin, Tour Anjou, 33 Quai de Dion Bouton, 92814 Puteaux, Cedex, France.

O P NARULA (INDIA)

L'équilibre entre trafic entrant et sortant pose des problèmes de planification. La majorité des exportations sont des matières premières alors que les importations sont des produits finis.

En ce qui concerne la normalisation, une technologie appropriée doit répondre aux critères de la navigation internationale tout en continuant de fournir un emploi à un grand nombre de travailleurs. Le développement portuaire doit tenir compte de ces deux facteurs. Le port agit comme agent catalyseur dans le développement de l'hinterland. Des considérations d'ordre technico-économique doivent être prises en considération.

En matière de planification statique/dynamique, une synthèse des deux est utile — la planification à long terme pour les ouvrages de base comme les installations de protection, les quais, etc. Il faut aussi répondre aux besoins immédiats par un équipement de manutention qui peut être progressivement étoffé.

Pour l'entretien, les principaux problèmes sont la planification, l'acquisition et le stockage des pièces de rechange.

Quant aux bureaux d'ingénieurs-conseils, ceux des pays industrialisés devraient travailler en collaboration avec les organismes similaires dans les pays en voie de développement.

Il existe un problème de "fuite des cerveaux", c'est-à-dire la perte de compétence technique en faveur des pays plus riches et plus développés.

A FUGLUM (NORVEGE)

Le choix entre techniques hautement développées et techniques moins sophistiquées en vue du développement portuaire des pays en voie de développement ne doit pas rester une alternative seulement. La combinaison des deux peut s'avérer capable de rencontrer les besoins du trafic international aussi bien que des transports locaux.

La justification économique d'un projet doit être considérée dans le contexte global de l'infrastructure d'un nouveau développement industriel pour ce qui concerne les coûts initiaux de construction portuaire, de manière à ce que les coûts d'exploitation ne rendent pas le port non compétitif.

L'amélioration de la compréhension des problèmes d'entretien exige non seulement de convaincre les responsables du port de l'importance de l'entretien, mais également, et davantage encore, de convaincre les hommes politiques et tous les responsables de l'allocation des ressources des conséquences économiques d'un entretien défectueux.

En matière de programme de formation, il convient de faire le point des programmes actuels de formation et d'encadrement et de les coordonner sur une base associative en vue de leur amélioration, qui constitue l'objectif ultime.

J M DEPLAIX (NATIONS UNIES - ESCAP/CESAP)

Je représente ici la CESAP, Commission Economique et Sociale des NATIONS-UNIES pour l'ASIE et le Pacifique, ESCAP en anglais, que votre Association a eu l'amabilité d'inviter à assister à votre 25e Congrès.

Au nom du Secrétaire exécutif de la CESAP et du Chef de la Division des Transports maritimes, des Ports et des Voies navigables, je vous remercie de cette occasion qui nous est donnée de faire connaître les problèmes des Pays d'ASIE, ainsi que d'entendre les derniers développements de la technique.

Je vais aborder en succession certains des points d'intérêt de ce matin.

En ce qui concerne la standardisation des dimensions des bateaux proposée par le rapport (SI-4) Tchecoslovaque, ce problème nous préoccupe également beaucoup à la CESAP. C'est un domaine très complexe et la tentative tchécoslovaque est très intéressante sur beaucoup d'aspects, en particulier dans le calcul d'un optimum pour une barge pluricontinentale, c'est-à-dire devant naviguer sur les voies d'eau de plusieurs continents. Mais en ASIE, les problèmes sont différents. Les écluses sont peu nombreuses et souvent de 6 m ou de 20 pieds (6,09 m). Lorsqu'elles sont à grand gabarit, elles n'ont pas les 12 m des voies d'eau européennes, mais plus: de 14 m à 18 m, et même davantage en CHINE. A l'exception de petites barges de 5,70 m de large pour les canaux, il ne semble pas qu'un gabarit "asiatique" se dégage, et l'on se trouve le plus souvent conduit à essayer d'optimiser les dimensions des barges en fonction du réseau qu'elles doivent fréquenter. En THAILANDE, la dimension choisie a été de 6,79 m par 45 m, je crois, avec une super barge de 13,50 m par 70 m. Les autres réseaux définissent bientôt leurs standards et la CESAP espère à cette occasion arriver à un système de dimensions compatibles.

Pour revenir sur un point soulevé par M. AILLERET en ce qui concerne la lenteur supposée ou réelle des transports par voie navigable, je ne suis même pas sûr que sela soit vrai en EUROPE puisque, il y a quelque temps, il était plus rapide d'aller du HAVRE à PARIS par voie d'eau que par fer. Cela n'est certainement pas vrai en ASIE, puisque la vitesse moyenne des trains au PAKISTAN, en INDE, au BANGLADESH est de l'ordre de 15 km/h, y inclus la durée du passage dans les triages. J'ai donc eu l'occasion de dire dans ces différents pays que leur parlent de la lenteur des voies navigables se trompent et les trompent, et n'agissent pas dans le sens d'un développement de ce mode de transport.

En ce qui concerne l'intégration entre la navigation intérieure, la navigation côtière et la navigation maritime, la plupart des pays d'ASIE continuent à réaliser cette intégration, qui leur était traditionnelle, sous forme de manutention à partir d'allèges.

Je voudrais simplement indiquer deux exemples assez nouveaux en THAILANDE de navigation côtière: le premier consiste en un terminal flottant pour le transbordement du tapioca, qui est en mesure de traiter des navires de plus de 100 000 T;, et qui est entièrement alimenté par des barges de navigation intérieure. Il est placé à 40 kilomètres environ de l'embouchure dans une rade naturelle, et les barges sont remorquées vers lui depuis BANGKOK, où un premier transbordement a eu lieu, ou bien directement depuis les usines lorsqu'elles sont situées près d'une voie d'eau à grand gabarit.

Le deuxième exemple est la desserte du Port de SATTAHIP, développé avec des crédits de la Banque mondiale, et qui se trouve à plus de 100 km de l'embouchure de La CHAO PHAYA.

Actuellement, il n'y a pas de desserte ferroviaire, la Banque mondiale vient d'accepter de la financer, et l'on peut voir des trains de barges remorquées le long de la côte jusqu'à ce port, trajet qui est pourtant très exposé pendant quelques kilomètres à la pleine houle du large. Ces transports sont réalisés par les mêmes barges que précédemment qui sont solides mais pas fluvio-maritimes. S'ils se perpétuent, ils pourraient remettre en question la répartition du trafic entre les différents modes telle qu'elle était prévue par les études préliminaires.

Ces 2 exemples montrent la vitalité de la navigation fluviale en ASIE, lorsque les conditions naturelles le permettent. Je vais en donner tout de suite un autre exemple, qui concerne le transport par palettes évoqué par le rapport français, et en particulier l'utilisation de super-palettes adaptées au transport fluvial; il me paraît interessant de signaler l'existence en ASIE d'un trafic de boissons gazeuses de soft drinks utilisant ce concept. Il s'agit d'un transport sur une trentaine de kilomètres entre l'usine d'embouteillage, repoussée hors de l'agglomération pour des raisons de nappe phréatique, et le dépôt central d'où sont assurées les livraisons urbaines. L'unité de charge représente l'équivalent de 8 palettes classiques et est manutentionné à la grue. La barge est chargée en pontée, c'est ce que les Anglo-Saxons appellent une deck barge. Il y a 2 barges remorquées qui assurent une rotation régulière. Ce système a été imaginé par suite des restrictions de circulation des camions qui alimentaient le dépôt à partir de l'usine. Ils ne disposaient plus que d'un nombre réduit d'heures pendant la journée pour circuler, ce qui obligeait à un surdimensionnement des flux pendant les périodes utilisables et créait des problèmes de pointes très coûteux. Ici un seul remorqueur de 180 CV suffit là où une quarantaine de camions de même puissance auraient été nécessaires.

Le rapport français concluait que les industriels hésitent à se lancer dans l'inconnu. Cet exemple venant d'un pays moins développé pourrait les aider à franchir le pas.

L TERHO (FINLANDE)

J'ai eu le plaisir d'être membre d'un groupe de travail des Nations-Unies (C.N.U.C.E.D.) dont le but était de planifier un "modèle de port" pour les pays en voie de développement. C'était en 1974 à Genève.

La base de la planification était le port multifonctionnel utilisable pour tous les types de trafic de marchandises sèches.

La multi-fonctionalité était définie comme suit:

1. Facteur temps:
   - besoins actuels du trafic
   - demain: unitarisation accrue
   - ensuite: chargements totalement unitarisés.

2. Modes de trafic:
   - conventionnel
   - roulier (ro-ro)
   - transbordement (lo-lo)

3. En vue de réduire au minimum les dépenses initiales, on prévoyait l'utilisation extensive d'équipements de manutention à bord des navires pour les chargements unitarisés.

4. Ceci ne pouvait être totalement réalisé que grâce à une excellente collaboration avec les sociétés propriétaires des navires.

5. Il semblait important de prévoir des accostages différents pour le trafic maritime et le trafic fluvial (s'il existait).

Autres facteurs importants. Les nouveaux ports doivent doivent être construits à distance suffisante des grandes cités, où ils ne sont pas viables.

Les sites appropriés doivent donc être recherchés et réservés à des fins portuaires. Par ailleurs, les nouveaux ports ne doivent pas être construits trop loin des ports existants pour éviter de nouvelles infrastructures.

Il est extrêmement important d'avoir:

- des solutions simples
- assez d'espace
- de bonnes communications terrestres.

Le rapport du groupe de travail a été publié en 1976-1977. Il abordait évidemment nombre d'autres aspects, tels que: financement, économie, exploitation, formation, administration, procédures douanières, etc.

Bien que ce rapport date de quelques années déjà, la plupart des considérations et conclusions qu'il propose restent tout-à-fait d'actualité.

J W MORRIS (USA)

L'A.I.P.C.N. a entrepris une tâche noble et essentielle en offrant son aide aux pays en voie de développement. En tant qu'ingénieurs, nous pouvons nous rendre coupables, ou au moins devenir victimes, d'une application de notre propre logique en tant que source première d'assistance à ces pays. Pourtant, il est rare, si cela existe même, que les rationalisations bien nettes de l'ingénieur inspirent les processus de décision et de réalisation. Si notre approche est sans doute correcte, "ce qui doit être fait" et "comment le faire" résultent le plus souvent de processus plus complexes et parfois contradictoires. On peut citer parmi ceux-ci:

Politique - Quels sont les objectifs nationaux des pays en voie de développement et comment sont-ils perçus des pays offrant leur assitance?

Coutumes - La communication est toujours difficile, mais l'approche d'un pays industrialisé peut s'avérer socialement offensante pour le pays en voie de développement, et donc, vouée à l'échec.

Financement - Qui assure le financement? Le pays industrialisé, le pays en voie de développement ou les deux?

Objectif de l'assitance - Dans un monde réel d'intérêts nationaux, quels sont les rôles respectifs de la "PAIX" et de l' "Extension du pouvoir"? La croissance à long terme des ressources est-elle un objectif valable par rapport au rendement immédiat? Le travail spécifique à réaliser est-il vraiment aussi important que la formation des autochtones?

La principale recommandation à l'A.I.P.C.N. serait de se montrer patiente — comprendre toutes les influences s'exerçant sur les décisions de développement, garder son calme grâce à la ferme conviction que les conditions de financement, politiques et sociales s'oublient dans une certaine mesure et qu'à long terme nous serons jugés sur la seule qualité de notre travail. Cela veut dire que nous devons fournir un produit de qualité qui a de sérieuses chances de répondre aux besoins et en définitive surtout contribuer à assurer l'avenir des pays en voie de développement en formant le personnel local et en transmettant aux générations à venir les ressources des pays en voie de développement. Les ingrédients du succès comprennent 5 éléments: compréhension et patience, pour motié, honnêteté, intégrité et compétence technique pour l'autre moitié.

P SIREYJOL (FRANCE)

En matière de conception et de construction de ports, les transferts de technologie sont grandement facilités par la participation d'un Ingénieur-Conseil ou d'un Entrepreneur venu de pays développés, chaque fois qu'il s'agit d'une tâche importante.

La situation est différente pour les tâches qui sont normalement assurées par l'Autorité portuaire locale:

- les tâches d'entretien réputées simples mais quotidiennes et qui demandent une grande continuité dans l'action;
- les fonctions de manègement et de direction de l'exploitation qui sont les dernières à pouvoir être déléguées.

De fait, tous ceux d'entre nous qui connaissent un peu les ports des pays en voie de développement savent que c'est dans ces deux domaines que le fonctionnement de ces ports laisse le plus à désirer.

Cette situation n'est pas ignorée de la Banque Mondiale et l'on aurait pu s'attendre à ce que, à l'image de l'action qu'elle avait menée dans le domaine de l'entretien routier, elle aurait engagé, en faveur des ports des pays en voie de développement un nombre important d'opérations d'opérations d'organisation — entretien — exploitation — formation, en vue d'améliorer leur fonctionnement dans ce domaine. Si un certain nombre de telles opérations a bien été engagé, il semble qu'il y ait encore beaucoup à faire.

N N B ORDMAN (GB)

Après avoir suivi cette discussion stimulante et constructive, je pourrais résumer mes sentiments comme suit:

La technologie comprend les idées et l'information. Celles-ci sont logées dans l'esprit des gens. Le transfert de technologie suppose donc la communication. L'A.I.P.C.N. est donc agent de cette communication, à travers ses congrès et ses publications.

Comme M. Frijlink l'a dit, nous devons déployer de grands efforts pour toucher et intéresser les pays en voie de développement. "Si la montagne ne vient pas à Mahomed, Mahomed doit tenter d'aller à la montagne".

Enfin, en tant qu'ingénieur-conseil, je voudrais rappeler à mes collègues que si nous pouvons assister les pays en voie de développement, nous devons nous garger de parfois penser que les pays en voie de développement existent pour le seul bénéfice des ingénieurs-conseils!

T P STEEN (NORVEGE) RAPPORTEUR GENERAL

La discussion a mis en avant de nombreux et très intéressants aspects et il me semble qu'il sera à présent possible pour le Comité de Rédaction de formuler des conclusions reflétant les avis du Congrès. Je vais résumer brièvement les contributions des douze orateurs.

M. Takeuchi a fait mention de la fructueuse politique portuaire japonaise, dans le cadre de laquelle les ports sont développés en tant qu'éléments de l'infrastructure nationale et non en tant qu'entreprises économiques individuelles. C'est l'approche qu'il recommande pour les pays en voie de développement. Les avantages indirects d'un port doivent être pris en considération, mais nous ne disposons pas de critères suffisants pour évaluer ces avantages. Peut-être l'AIPCN pourrait-elle faire quelque-chose à cet égard.

M. Frijlink discute le concept tant controversé de "technologie appropriée" et il souligne qu'il conviendrait de tirer le plus grand parti possible des facteurs de production disponibles sur place, en minimisant le recours aux ressources rares. La mission la plus importante du C.P.V.D. devrait consister à faire en sorte que "le Sud vienne vers l'AIPCN" et réciproquement le Rapporteur Général s'est montré optimiste dans ses suggestions de conclusions, point 4, paragraphe 2, en ce qui concerne les possibilités pour le C.P.V.D. de fournir conseils et consultance à cet égard.

Le Rapporteur remercie M. Frijlink pour ses commentaires et se montre convaincu que le Comité de Rédaction prendra soin de tenir compte du texte révisé qu'il a soumis.

M. Mettam considère que la meilleure contribution du C.P.V.D. pourrait consister à amener des individus dans les pays en voie de développement à devenir membres de l'AIPCN. Le plus grand handicap de ces pays est en effet la pénurie de personnel qualifié et la formation devrait de préférence être réalisée dans les pays en voie de développement eux-mêmes.

Il ne lui semble pas recommandé de constituer une réserve locale de consultants, dans la mesure où de nombreux consultants étrangers tout à fait compétents sont prêts à répondre aux besoins.

Le Rapporteur n'a pas l'impression que ce dernier avis de M. Mettam est partagé par tout le monde. On peut mentionner, entre autres, à cet égard, les règles des institutions internationales de financement, qui exigent pour tous les projets l'association avec des consultants locaux.

Faisant référence à son rapport sur le développement du port de Kigoma, en Tanzanie, M. Eerdenbrugh donne d'intéressantes informations supplémentaires sur la manutention d'un nombre croissant de conteneurs par ce port intérieur. Il souligne l'intérêt considérable que représente la modernisation de ce port pour l'ensemble du secteur du transport. Il ajoute que le choix entre l'approche statique et l'approche dynamique du développement portuaire dépend également de facteurs technologiques. Ainsi, une construction par étapes de brise-lames ou d'autres ouvrages d'infrastructure peut s'avérer difficile dans certains cas.

M. Aubert illustre au moyen de plusieurs exemples exemples la manière dont les techniques modernes et une planification attentive peuvent s'avérer économiquement rentables. Il insiste sur le fait que la meilleurs manière d'aider les pays en voie de développement consiste toujours à trouver la solution la plus économique dans chaque cas particulier.

M. Narula attire l'attention sur le déséquilibre qui caractérise les échanges de la plupart des pays en voie de développement, et qui affecte également la planification portuaire: expédition de matières premières en vrac et entrée de marchandises unitaires. Néanmoins, la prévision du trafic portuaire est généralement très difficile, de même que l'évaluation des avantages indirects, même si ceux-ci constitutent souvent un facteur décisif dans le développement des ports. En ce qui concerne le problème de la normalisation internationale, il doit se résoudre dans chaque cas par le choix de la technologie la plus appropriée.

M. Narula indique encore que la sur-capacité est la règle dans de nombreuses régions en matière de dragage d'entretien. Le Rapporteur se doit d'ajouter immédiatement que pour la plupart des autres types de dragage c'est hélàs plutôt la sous-capacité qui est de règle.

M. Narula rappelle enfin que les consultants étrangers et les organismes locaux collaborent dorénavant en tenant compte du fait qu'il incombera à ces derniers d'assumer à l'avenir la totale responsabilité des projets.

M. Fuglum ne pense pas qu'il soit possible de répondre simplement par oui ou par non à la question de savoir s'il faut introduire de la technologie avancée. Il faut chercher la solution optimale pour chaque cas particulier. La justification économique des projets portuaires se trouve généralement au niveau du développement de l'infrastructure, et ceci devrait être étudié de près par les organismes de financement. Les conséquences économiques de négligences au niveau de l'entretien des ports devraient de toute évidence être mieux expliquées aux responsables politiques et aux organismes de financement.

M. Deplaix fournit d'intéressantes informations sur les travaux de la Commission Economique et Sociale pour l'Asie et le Pacifique (CESAP) et notamment sur ses programmes d'assistance visant une exploitation plus efficace des ports et des voies d'eau, sur ses services d'information, etc. Il indique aussi que l'existence de l'AIPCN n'est pas du tout suffisamment connue parmi les milieux portuaires dans les pays en voie de développement.

M. Terho attire l'attention sur le Rapport 1976-1977 de la CNUCED qui décrit un port ou un terminal multifonctionnel modèle et souligne la nécessité d'une collaboration entre propriétaires des navires et autorités portuaires. Le problème des zones d'extension nouvelle des ports existants insérés dans des concentrations est bien connu, et le rapport recommande que les nouveaux ports soient construits au départ dans une forme aussi simple que possible, mais avec suffisamment de réserve de terrain pour tout développement futur.

Le Général Morris rappelle son expérience dans les pays en voie de développement en tant que responsable d'une importante organisation semi-militaire. Il insiste pour que l'AIPCN envisage aussi les aspects politiques du sujet dont nous discutons et qu'elle approfondisse la question de l'objectif même poursuivi par l'assistance. En tout cas, il faut faire en sorte que le travail de l'AIPCN soit toujours de haut niveau.

M. Sireyol indique que le principal problème est posé par l'entretien, qui doit être une tâche permanente dans les ports. Il est donc bon que notre CPVD s'en occupe actuellement. La question des ports constitue un autre domaine d'intérêt pour la CPVD. M. Sireyol ajoute que les avantages pour certains ports des pays industrialisés de leur statut indépendant ne sont pas immédiatement transposables dans les pays en voie de développement, en raisen de l'importance primordiale qu'y prennent les investissements initiaux.

Enfin, M. Ordman conclut brièvement:

- L'objectif du Congrès et du travail de documentation de l'AIPCN est le transfert de technologie à un niveau élevé.
- Nous devons déployer de grands efforts pour aller vers les pays en voie de développement, en n'attendant pas encore d'eux qu'ils prennent l'initiative à cet égard.
- Les pays en voie de développement ne sont pas là pour servir nos intérêts.

Je crois, Monsieur le Président, que nous pouvons maintenant nous en remettre au Comité de Rédaction pour la formulation de conclusions.

CONCLUSIONS

1. L'aide apportée par les pays industrialisés aux pays en voie de développement pour qu'ils puissent accéder aux techniques modernes est une responsabilité internationale. L'AIPCN accepte cette responsabilité et la reconnaît comme l'un des facteurs déterminants de son activité.

   L'effort principal doit porter sur une information plus efficace et plus complète afin de garantir que tous les pays, en particulier les pays en voie de développement, connaissent l'Association et ce qu'elle peut leur apporter: le CPVD sera un moyen essentiel de cette action.

   En outre, l'Association doit rechercher les moyens nécessaires pour faire davantage participer les pays en voie de développement à ses activités.

2. Les pays en voie de développement n'ont disposé que d'un délai relativement court pour moderniser leurs ports maritimes et leurs voies navigables; ils ont, à cet égard, besoin de coopérer étroitement avec les pays industrialisés. Les pays en voie de développement ont intérêt à ce que cette coopération ne consiste pas à copier sans esprit critique mais doivent élaborer leur politique en fonction de leurs caractéristiques et de leurs besoins propres.

3. Dans la plupart des pays en voie de développement, il convient d'encourager un recours aussi large que possible aux moyens humains et aux produits locaux; ils ont également intérêt à utiliser des équipements qui nécessitent des méthodes d'exploitation relativement simples et n'ont besoin que d'un minimum d'entretien.

   Dans certaines régions, les ports doivent être conçus dans un contexte de relativement faible industrialisation. Leur conception doit cependant permettre une mécanisation plus poussée dans le futur.

4. Le personnel des pays en voie de développement doit participer activement à toutes les phases de conception et d'exécution des projets afin de se familiariser directement avec les techniques employées.

   Enfin, une formation adaptée du personnel est, dans la plupart des cas, un préalable nécessaire au succès des projets d'équipement qui doivent être réalisés en utilisant aussi largement que possible les moyens humains locaux.

MARITIME PORTS AND SEAWAYS

SECTION II — SUBJECT 1

Developments in the construction of ships, navigational aids, waterways and harbours, traffic management and installations, with particular regard to risk analysis and safety criteria regarding transportation, unloading and storage of liquefied natural and petroleum gases

Monday 11 May 1981

Chairman:	*N N B ORDMAN (UK)* *Noel Ordman and Associates Ltd*
Vice Chairman:	*ENRIQUEZ FRANCISCO (Spain)* *D Ing Caminos, Canales y Puertos, Madrid*
Reporter General:	*G B M OLIVER (UK)* *Assistant Director, Technical Services,* *National Ports Council, London*
Secretary:	*P LACEY (UK)* *Ove Arup and Partners Ltd, London*
Asst. Secretary:	*Miss M-M DANEELS (Belgium)* *Secrétaire AIPCN Secrétariat Générale, Brussels*

All page numbers cited in these discussions refer to Maritime Ports and Seaways, Volumes 1-5, Proceedings of the XXV Congress of the Permanent International Association of Navigation Congresses (PIANC) Edinburgh 1981, ISBN 0 08 027278 9 Pergamon Press, 1981

Speakers

A FUGLUM (Norway), R H SMITH (Canada), V BRATIANU (USA), W H R LAWRENCE (UK), G P KOSTYLEW (IMCO), M SUZUO DAN (Japan), J A ZWAMBORN (South Africa), A L MOSS-MORRIS (South Africa), N F MATTHEWS (IALA), L R DUMAS (France)

G. B. M. OLIVER (U.K) REPORTER GENERAL

The use of natural and petroleum gases as an energy source has increased dramatically in recent years and this growth is forecast to continue. Several papers – for example those from the Netherlands, Finland and Japan – bear witness to this phenomenon. Relevant also is the fact that, whereas in 1966 there existed world-wide some 150 liquid gas carriers with a total capacity of some 500,000 cubic metres, by 1979 there were – operating or on order – just over 600 such vessels with a total capacity of 14 million cubic metres. It is evident from these figures that, simultaneously with the growth in total traffic, the average size of ship has increased by a factor of 7.

In preparing the report it has seemed appropriate to have regard to the following topics, to assess the extent to which the various papers add to the state of knowledge on each and hence to indicate areas to which attention could profitably be directed in the future:

- The potential hazard scenario
- Risk analysis
- Gas carrier design and construction
- Gas carrier safety record
- Regulation of shipping movements
- Terminal site selection, design and operations
- Security and sabotage

Most of these topics could be said to fall under the heading "safety criteria" in the subject title. This provides, perhaps, some rough and ready measure of the very considerable area to which attention needs to be directed if the level of public risk attendant upon the carriage of liquefied gases by sea is to be reduced to a minimum.

The common theme throughout the various papers is that regulation of shipping movements in congested areas is now accepted as a positive contribution toward ship safety, provided that the system is tailored to local conditions and requirements.

While there can be no disputing this statement as a general principle, concern must nevertheless be expressed regarding the tendency of individual ports or indeed individual countries to develop their own traffic schemes in isolation, without considering the operating procedures and practices of other systems. There already exists considerable disparity in standards and procedures, both within the same country and between different countries. This can lead to doubt and confusion on the part of ship masters and, possibly, to the development of a potentially dangerous situation.

Although not referred to within the papers submitted for this Subject, it is worth mentioning the work in hand within the EEC through the European Co-operation in the field of Scientific and Technical Research (COST) projects. This work is aimed at harmonisation and rationalisation of shore-based marine traffic systems, such that basic procedures and practices will be similar throughout ports in EEC member countries.

DISCUSSION

A FUGLUM (NORWAY)

The Norwegian paper on this subject high-lights two major problems of safe navigation of L.P.G carriers along the access route and in the harbour area.

Their solution required:

1. A risk analysis covering the possibilities of accidents and their effect on the public and on the environment;

   and

2. a physical model test of a narrow part of the access route with a view to effecting improvements on site.

Mr. Oliver, the Reporter General, has already stressed the essential elements of our paper, but I should like to add some points on matters raised in the General Report.

When the results of the risk analysis described in my paper were published, they provoked a lively discussion. The probability of a member of the public being killed through an accident involving a cargo of L.P.G was estimated at 1×10^{-7}, which is about the same as the risk of being killed by lightning. However, lightning does not cause fatal accidents everywhere, and in many areas that risk would be non-existent.

It is important to present the results of a risk analysis so that they can be readily understood. The Reporter General has also referred to the acceptance by the public of certain risk levels for various types of accident. However, fatal accidents resulting from the transportation of certain types of cargo covered by official regulations would certainly be less acceptable than accidents caused by individuals.

There is a real problem in having to set an acceptable level of risk before one has sufficient experience to evaluate all the factors — and the result may therefore be unjustified and uneconomic. However, an under-estimate of the level of risk is likely to lead to public criticism and possibly the loss of one's job!

Other important points mentioned in the Norwegian paper and by the Reporter General refer to human factors as causes of accidents, as well as mechanical failures in ships navigating in narrow channels or passages.

There are several known instances of ships suffering propulsion failures in the narrow ship passage at the bridge crossing the Brevik River where the channel forms an S bend. The reasons have been difficult to establish, but the use of tugs has since been made compulsory.

It was also decided to carry out surveys and model tests which established an economic method of improving the channel despite the need for blasting the solid Norwegian bed-rock. We are also concerned to establish safety zones in the harbour area and to separate ships carrying and handling hazardous goods from other activities in the port; The need for safety zones is accepted in Norway and other countries, but there is a lack of scientific data on which decisions should be based.

I am in general agreement with the recommendations for further action by The Reporter General, but would ask that consideration be given also to the following questions.

1. To what extent are the degree of risk and the probability of accidents determined by the design and construction of ships? and

2. To what extent do access routes, siting of terminals and control (or lack of control) of ship movements pose hazards to ships?

I should like to see the following items incorporated in the general conclusions for further action:-

1. Recommendations that the design and construction of ships be improved to cover special external constraints.

2. Adoption of a common international standard regarding the type of risk to be analysed in connection with the maritime transport of LNG and LPG.

3. Suggestions for international guidelines regarding the definition of normal risk levels and their presentation in a way which will be clearly understood by the public.

4. Consideration of physical precautions to be taken along access routes for optimal safe navigation.

5. Collection and presentation of traffic control regulations on a world-wide scale.

6. Recommendations for safety zones and physical barriers in the harbour area.

The papers which have been presented on this subject, together with the comments of the Reporter General, show that this is one of the most important subjects taken up by PIANC. I consider that further action is urgently required and would suggest that the matter be referred to the Working Group under Section II which has already been established.

R H SMITH (CANADA)

Based on the experience of the Casualty Investigations unit of the Canadian Coast Guard, I would comment as follows:-

1. A statistical presentation of casualties and accidents aboard ship as reported to the Canadian Coast Guard during the year 1979 shows the following:

Cause	% of Total
Operational Mistakes	38
Equipment/Structural Failure	17
Environmental Conditions	15
Other — including Vessel Condition, Aids, etc.	17
Unknown	13

   This brief summary supports the authors' preliminary conclusion of the importance of the human factor in vessel casualties.

2. Unless there is a public inquiry it is normally not possible for us to state the cause of an identifiable casualty, i.e. it is not possible to blame Captain X or Pilot Y unless they have an opportunity for public defence. We can carry out good studies of major casualties because a Preliminary Inquiry is complete and we are able to state what we reasonably believe in the report as it is confidential to us. The analysis can be presented in an anonymous way. For these reasons filling in a questionnaire is, in our opinion, an inadequate way to carry out a survey, and we sympathize with the authors' plea for extensive, reliable and uniform data.

3. We also have problems with the number of movements (density/frequency) but the introduction of VTM has helped us considerably and will improve as computer programs improve.

4. In summary, unless all casualty inquries are public, and thus all details available or the analysing agency is given direct access to full confidential reports, it is virtually impossible to carry out a complete meaningful compilation.

5. Finally, then, on the basis of our experience in Canada, we would support the Reporter General's recommendation concerning "the

creation of an international shipping accident data bank such that better statistical data would ultimately become available for the purposes of risk assessment and detection of trends in accident rates" perhaps only suggesting in a general way at this time, the addition of the phrase – "and that each country be encouraged to take appropriate action accordingly".

V BRATIANU (USA)

I wish to mention briefly some model tests on the behaviour of large LNG carriers, and to refer to some available information on marine loading arms, a critical link of the system.

The behaviour of large LNG carriers moored at piers is highly sensitive to wave period. Model tests on 125,000 cu.m. LNG vessels have shown that the pier is inoperable for such carriers in broadside wave trains with periods in excess of 10 seconds, even at significant wave heights of 0.50 -0.75 metres. For planning purposes it is important to have the proper equipment which will record also long period waves.

The Oil Companies International Marine Forum (OCIMF) has published a comprehensive guide for the design and construction of marine loading arms.

Marine arms at recent LPG and LNG terminals are equipped with emergency release systems as mentioned in many of the papers. Whether these systems are to be released automatically in case of loading arm overreach needs careful study, especially at discharge terminals handling non-dedicated carriers (surge problem).

Most industry terminals have discarded the use of electrical bond wires between ship and pier. To prevent a potential sparking due to stray currents loading arms are equipped with insulating flanges at the outboard end.

W H R LAWRENCE (UK)

I would first like to congratulate Mr. Oliver. His report is an excellent summary of the content of papers submitted on this subject, bearing in mind its complexity and the many and varied details included in the papers. To have achieved such a concise and informative report is no mean effort.

However, I would take issue with that part of the report dealing with specific hazards resulting from a spill of liquefied gas, as I believe these to be misleading without further explanation.

The report defines a major spill as being 1,000 tonnes or more resulting from a shipping accident giving rise to the penetration of the ship's containment system. That definition is as good as any for a major spill. I suggest it is the wrong one to use when discussing specific hazards which could affect local population (Paragraph 9). The thrust of all the papers presented in this section is directed in differing ways towards the design and operational procedures adopted to avoid occurrence of a major spill. I suggest therefore it is more appropriate that the hazards which could possibly affect local populations will result from a maximum credible spill during cargo operations. As is explained in the papers, for design purposes is is now customary to assume a maximum spill to be around 15 cu.m. and a lot less in most situations.

The definition of the hazards in Paragraph 9 specifically relating to a 1,000 tonne spill is therefore misleading.

I would also like to comment on the terminology used. A fire ball is an emotive description of something which is more correctly referred to as a pool fire. It results from the burning of a concentrated pool of material where, because of relatively small mixing of the vapours with air, the resulting fire, if the pool is ignited, burns with a high lazy flame and, in the case of propane, a very sooty one as well. There would certainly be radiation from such a fire, but of course if the quantity involved is small and the duration of the fire is short, it would be relatively easy to obtain protection from the effects of this radiation, as Mr. Oliver mentions.

The possibility of explosion is mentioned also, but I suggest that experimental work carried out to date on unconfined spills indicates that detonation does not take place with the quantities under discussion, and probably not with very much larger quantities. The flame acceleration speeds that have been measured are too slow to give rise to detonation and therefore quoting any figures of distances from the centre of a spill in which injuries and damage could occur as a result of explosion is misleading. I should add that I am of course referring to LNG and LPG in an unconfined spill situation.

The drift of flammable vapour clouds has been the subject of considerable investigation and, as a result of that, mathematical models to predict the drift have been developed. The drift, of course, is a function of the quantity spilt. 10km. is mentioned by Mr. Oliver but for such a drift a spill of some 25,000 cu.m. would be necessary. For the figures I have mentioned as being probable, i.e. 15 cu.m., a drift before the cloud disperses harmlessly would be in the region of 100/200 metres.

I would like to take this opportunity to support the remarks made on the need for regulation of shipping movements. Although I do not subscribe to the view that we should slavishly follow everything which has been done elsewhere, I do believe that each situation should be considered carefully and should take maximum advantage of all the natural protection that any site or harbour offers. This, together with sensible and practical control, should lead to very safe operation.

Finally, I would like to support the recommendation that a future and fruitful source of PIANC investigation could be a study to facilitate greater understanding of the criteria affecting the siting of marine terminals for the handling of liquefied gases.

G. P. KOSTYLEW (IMCO)

We in the Inter-Governmental Maritime Consultative Organization (IMCO) are most interested in the activities of PIANC as navigation forms a very important part of the work of our Organization. Our endeavours are to constantly improve the efficiency and safety of navigation and in this connection IMCO has introduced effective measures.

It would be appropriate at this stage to recount briefly the history of IMCO and the events which led to its formation. When the establishment of IMCO as the specialized agency of the United Nations concerned solely with maritime affairs was mooted, the main concern was to evolve international machinery to improve safety at sea. This was understandable for two main reasons. In the first place seafaring has always been a dangerous occupation. In the second place, because of the international nature of the shipping industry, it had long been recognized that action to improve safety in shipping operations would be more effective if carried out at an international level rather than by individual countries acting unilaterally and without co-ordination with others. Although a number of important international agreements had already been adopted, many States agreed that there was a need for a permanent body which would be able to co-ordinate and promote further measures on a continuing basis.

It was against this background that the United Nations Maritime Conference of 1948 adopted the Convention establishing IMCO as the first international body devoted exclusively to maritime matters. During the decade preceding the Convention, other problems related to safety, but requiring slightly different emphasis, had attracted international attention. One of the most important of these was the threat of maritime pollution from ships, particularly pollution by oil carried in tankers. An international convention on this subject was adopted in 1954, four years before IMCO came into existence. The responsibility for administering and promoting this Convention was one of the first tasks undertaken by IMCO at its inception in January 1959. Thus from the very beginning the improvement of maritime safety and the prevention of marine pollution have been the two cardinal objectives of IMCO.

Allow me now to mention briefly the structure of IMCO. Its principal bodies are the Assembly and the Council. The Assembly, which is the supreme governing body, consists of representatives from all Member States; it decides on the work programme of the Organization, approves proposals remitted to it, votes the budget to which all Member States contribute on an agreed scale and elects the IMCO Council. The Assembly normally meets in London every two years. The Council consists of representatives of 24 Member States elected by the Assembly for a term of two years; it normally meets twice a year and is IMCO's governing body between Assembly sessions. At the beginning of March 1981, IMCO had 120 Members and one Associate Member.

The Organization's technical work is carried out by a number of Committees, the most important of which are the Maritime Safety Committee and the Marine Environment Protection Committee. The Maritime Safety Committee has a number of Sub-Committees dealing with such matters as navigation, radio communications, life-saving appliances, training, search and rescue, ship design and equipment, fire protection, sub division, stability and load lines, fishing vessels, containers and cargoes, dangerous goods and bulk chemicals. The latter is also a Sub-Committee of the Marine Environment Protection Committee, which handles IMCO's anti-pollution activities, while other Committees are the Legal Committee, the Committee on Technical Co-operation and the Facilitation Committee.

In order to achieve its objectives IMCO has, in the last twenty-one years, promoted the adoption of 31 Conventions, and prepared a large number of Codes and Recommendations on various matters relating to maritime safety and prevention of pollution. The initial work on a Convention is normally done by a Committee or Sub-Committee; a draft instrument is then produced and agreed upon in the relevant committee before it is submitted with the approval of the Council and the Assembly to a Diplomatic Conference to which delegations from all States within the United Nations system — including States which may not be IMCO Members — are invited. The Conferences, if successful, will adopt a final text, which is submitted to Governments for ratification, accession or acceptance.

The two primary objectives of the Organization are the adoption of the highest practicable standards of maritime safety and the prevention and control of pollution from ships. The most important contributory factor in achieving these two objectives is maritime training, and therefore IMCO's activities have extended to this vital area which has been given the highest priority in recent years.

The human factor and its involvement in all types of maritime operations has necessitated the prescribing of minimum professional standards for seafarers commensurate with maritime safety. These standards are contained in the International Convention on Standards of Training, Certification and Watchkeeping for Seafarers, 1978.

In this connection, I wish to refer to the comprehensive and pragmatic programme developed by IMCO for providing technical assistance to developing countries, particularly in the field of maritime training.

IMCO is the first United Nations Specialized Agency to institutionalize a Technical Co-operation Committee. This in effect means that technical co-operation is now a regular part of IMCO's work, and that the Technical Co-operation Committee has been placed on a regular footing and on a par with the others, such as the Maritime Safety Committee, and Marine Environment Protection Committee.

The technical co-operation programme of IMCO has as its backbone the Advisory Services provided to developing countries. This programme of Advisory Services is financed mainly by the UNDP, but some advisors are also being financed by donor governments. As well as the consultants and advisors in maritime safety legislation, training, prevention of marine pollution, etc., consultants are also available in the field of port technical operations.

The port consultants have already travelled to quite a number of developing countries and have provided advice on port technical operations. Some of the matters on which advice was rendered are shown below.

1. Cargo handling equipment, cranes, vehicles, etc., and improvement in productivity by the introduction of modern equipment and employment of better techniques.

2. Stowage of cargoes.

3. Incorporation of the IMDG Code in port regulations.

4. Improvement in harbour communications, terminal operations and security, fire-fighting and cleaning of oil spillage.

5. Navigational aids, buoyage systems, their modernization, operation and maintenance.

6. Guidance in respect of manpower development of technical personnel and perspective planning.

7. Training of dock personnel in various trades.

8. Advice on acquisition of harbour craft, tugs, etc. training of pilots.

This is a very brief description of the broad outlines of IMCO's work and responsibilities.

S DAN (JAPAN)

The Port of Himeji is situated to the west of the densely populated region called Kinki, with a population of 20 million. The Port lies within the "Setonaikai" – the inland sea which is famous for its scenic beauty as well as a large coastal industrial area. Easy access and a major fishing industry makes Himeji a very busy Port.

In 1969 we presented a plan to import LNG – a clean fuel – to secure our long term needs for town gas and electricity without destroying the beautiful environment of the inland sea. We arranged meetings with the public and the fishermen on the subject of the safe operation of the gas terminal and the LNG carrier. At the same time local government made its assessment of the safety and environmental effects. Finally all the people concerned agreed to go ahead. Construction of the LNG terminal started in November 1976 and was completed in December 1978. Gas carrier operation at the terminal started in February 1979 and by April 1981 53 LNG carriers had discharged their Indonesian cargo without any accident. From our research and experience I should like to offer some comments on the potential hazard scenario:-

1. Fireballs are mostly caused by the sudden release of pressurised liquified gas. LNG is transported and stored under low temperature at atmospheric pressure. Should it leak and ignite, the possibility of fireballs is very small. This is proved by the fact that no fireballs were observed in any LNG ignition tests carried out throughout the world.

2. It is said that an explosion of an unconfined LNG vapour cloud does not occur under normal conditions. Should there be an explosion of, say, 1,000 tons of liquified gas, the danger range is assumed to be around 250 m.

3. According to the U.S. Coast Guard report an instantaneous spillage of 1,000 tons of LNG into the sea would result in a dispersion range of flammable gas of around 1.5 km.

In conclusion, I am convinced that LNG is the safest of clean fuels.

J A ZWAMBORN (SOUTH AFRICA)

Our General Reporter, mentioned some aspects of terminal design and referred to the possibility of sabotage.

I fully support his proposals that a data bank on accidents should be created; the traffic system should be harmonised and a better understanding is required of the criteria affecting the siting of gas terminals. Although these are, no doubt, the main aspects of our subject under discussion, I suggest that inter alia risks involved in berthing ships and touching the bottom of the approach or harbour channel should also be discussed.

Berthing problems are dealt with in the papers from Australia (flexibility of mooring dolphins relative to the ship's flexibility), Canada (stand-off forces for terminals in strong currents), Japan (berthing velocities) and the USSR (berthing loads).

The possibilities of grounding, with the associated risks, are briefly mentioned in the papers from Finland (95% of all accidents with LPG's occurred in the narrow sounds, not necessarily during bad visibility), France, Germany (10% under keel clearance in the Jade), Norway and the USA. (Mr. Bratianu has stressed the importance of wave-induced ship motions). In the paper from the Netherlands the dimensioning of entrance channels is covered in considerable detail and the possible causes for grounding are given as poor visibility, high wind velocities, strong currents and swell. It is mentioned that, because of the high risk value of LPG's, a relatively large under keel clearance must be allowed to reduce the danger of hitting the bottom of the fairway. I believe that 35% of the draught is used instead of 20% in the case of other vessels. Although squat also contributes to the sinkage of ships, the sinkage of a ship in the fairway is due to long-period waves (>12s) or swell. In the paper, an example is given of the calculated maximum heave amplitude, that is, Z_{max} (heave)=1.25 H where H is the wave height.

For the South African paper details are given for the recording of vertical ship motions at Richards Bay. The approach channel of this harbour was given the unusual depth of the maximum ship draught plus 40%, compared with the recommended 20% given in the Supplement to PIANC Bulletin No. 35. This depth was based on physical model tests which showed a maximum sinkage of about 5 m. for 2.5 m. high quartering sea swells of about 12s period. Prototype measurements described in the paper include a recorded maximum sinkage in the Richards Bay entrance channel of 4.5 m for a 3 m. high significant wave, that is, Z_{max} = 1.5 Hs. This means that at least 30% over-depth is needed at Richards Bay, but the most critical wave directions have not yet occurred during monitoring and it appears that the 40% allowed for is not excessive.

There seems to be little doubt that ship motions due to swell can, under certain conditions, be much larger than those given in the Supplement to PIANC Bulletin NO. 35, as preliminary design values. Taking into account that many ports around the world experience swells and considering that some of the main sea straits are very shallow relative to the draught of the large ships of today, including LPG carriers which may require higher safety standards (Dover Channel is 24 m, Singapore Strait is 23 m and the Baltic Approaches are 17 m deep) it is suggested that this meeting adopts the following recommendation.

"The further studying of vertical ship motions due to long period waves or swell with respect to the risk of touching the sea/fairway bottom."

A L MOSS-MORRIS (SOUTH AFRICA)

The comprehensive survey made by the General Reporter of the risk analysis and safety criteria for the transport, unloading and storage of liquified gases, did not refer to the obvious advantage in siting the LNG and LPG plants close to the entrance of the port or harbour. If this is done, then these vessels carrying hazardous cargoes are segregated as soon as possible after entering the confined fairways leading to the port, from the other numerous vessels, thus reducing the risk of collision. It is also obviously necessary to locate the terminal on a suitably large site which should also be segregated from other handling and storage facilities by a "safe" distance. I believe this Congress should endeavour to state what such safe distance may be, when considering the maximum credible accident. If the Congress has not the necessary data available, then I believe this is a suitable subject for study. The phrase "maximum credible accident" is one in use in the nuclear power industry and clearly it is the incident to be considered when a siting of the plant is under consideration.

Some countries such as Australia, are fortunate in having a vast undeveloped coastline available for the siting of loading and storage facilities and two LPG plants are currently being planned in isolated locations, which also enables separation of the shipping when in confined waters.

This fortunate situation does not obtain in the industrialized countries which are importers of LPG AND LNG such as Japan and Europe. It is obvious that public acceptance of the risks inherent in the transport and storage of large quantities of these volatile and highly combustible fluids will be greatly facilitated by isolation of the terminals, and thus also the removal of these carriers from narrow and crowded waterways. This can best be achieved by locating the storage facilities as close to the ocean as possible, even if this should require the building of wave protecting structures such as moles or breakwaters.

In conclusion I will repeat that I believe this Congress should set up a committee to lay down guidelines about the separation of storage facilities and jetties from other harbour installations.

N MATTHEWS (IALA)

Members here may not be consciously aware that in almost every country where there is a significant marine traffic system in use, the organisation of the facility is the responsibility of the organisation that is also the National Lighthouse Service.

The outstanding exception to this rule is the UK where each port apparently runs its own service independently.

These Lighthouse Services are all members of IALA, and as VTS Systems are usually completely interlinked with other aids to navigation, it was decided at our IALA Conference last November to set up a Committee with terms of reference almost exactly the same as those porposed by Mr. Oliver in his opening remarks.

The IALA Executive Committee meets in Paris next week, and they will have before them for approval a list of IALA members intending to take part in the Committee, and the name of the proposed Chairman.

We would therefore expect to have our first meeting around September/October of this year. On completion of our work, we would expect to submit the recommendations after approval by the Executive to our members for adoption, and to IMCO for its support.

There is a standing arrangement between the Secretaries General of IALA, PIANC, and IAPH by which we keep each other informed of what we are doing, to avoid unnecessary overlap.

Following next week's Executive Committee Meeting, and in accordance with this arrangement, full information about the Committee will be passed to the Secretaries General of PIANC and IAPA, together with an invitation for these organisations to make a contribution to our work. Thus we will welcome the contribution that PIANC can make, and I am particularly pleased that this matter has been brought up during this Conference.

With regard to Captain Lawrence's remarks, I would stress that our intention is to harmonise procedures, routines and manning questions and perhaps touch on language. We are not seeking to harmonise the hardware of systems.

Finally, I would like to make a personal remark. As stated by Mr. Oliver, the EEC is contemplating setting up a study group to deal with this VTS question. As a full-time employee of an International organisation, I welcome any international co-operation. However, for some years I have been closely associated with the IALA buoyage system to which Mr. Oliver referred.

From my experience in this field, I am very wary about forming just a European view. Shipping is truly world-wide, and I would prefer a "global view" to be formed first, prior to the formulation of more local views.

L DUMAS (FRANCE)

Mr. N. Matthews of the IALA has already expressed part of what I intended to say.

Last week, the symposium led to the emergence of a certain consensus between engineers and mariners as regards the maritime traffic services.

These services are under examination in many international bodies – the IAPH, the IALA which has set up a specialized technical committee, the Commission of the European Communities, etc. — as well as in numerous national organizations. A distinction must be made between the port services, where the nations generally apply national regulations with some local variants, and the services concerning international waters such as the Straits of Dover, where only the IMCO can legislate.

The need for an overall international harmonization, at the level of procedures, seems to be generally admitted.

The IALA technical committee would appear to be best-placed to draw up relevant proposals. However, the EEC scientific and technical subcommittee COST 301 would also make it possible to compare the European views and to facilitate the work of the IALA.

Lastly, close co-operation in this field between the authorities, the pilots and the ship's masters is essential.

CONCLUSIONS

The growth in the carriage by sea of liquified gases is a relatively recent phenomenon. PIANC, through its various organs, is exceptionally well placed to act as a continuing international forum wherein views could be exchanged on the experience of countries involved in this activity.

1. The decision by PIANC to establish a Working Group to study the problems of shipping and handling of dangerous goods is welcome and Section II consider that many aspects of shipping and handling of liquid gases should form part of the considerations of the Working Group. The Association should promote, in association with other relevant bodies the greater understanding of criteria affecting the siting of marine terminals for the handling of liquified gases and in particular the even greater interchange of views and information between all parts of the industry and associated bodies.

2. Effective traffic management is an important contribution to safety. International harmonization of maritime traffic service procedures as a basis for local arrangements should be fostered.

3. It is noted that there is already considerable activity directed towards the definition and collation of data required for risk analysis and other judgement exercises relating to the design of ships, the siting of terminals and the planning of approach channels. The Association should concern itself with this activity through the Working Group or in any other way that would be helpful, bearing in mind the long term desirability of attaining effective levels of standardization and consistency internationally.

MARITIME PORTS AND SEAWAYS

SECTION II — SUBJECT 2

Optimization of the economics of the whole dredging cycle in relation to the benefits achieved

Tuesday 12 May 1981

Chairman:	*N N B ORDMAN (UK)* *Noel Ordman and Associates Ltd*
Vice Chairman:	*E ALMAGIA (Italy)* *Chairman SIDER SpA, Rome*
Reporter General:	*M VAN DEN DOEL (The Netherlands)* *Rotterdam Port Authority*
Vice Reporter General:	*H MOLENAAR (The Netherlands)*
Secretary:	*P LACEY (UK)* *Ove Arup and Partners Ltd, London*
Asst. Secretary:	*Miss M-M DANEELS (Belgium)* *Secrétaire AIPCN Secrétariat Générale, Brussels*

Speakers

C C CABLE (USA), J B HERBICH (USA), L NEDERLOF (The Netherlands), M F C THORN (UK), D M McDOWELL (UK), A GENEVOIS (France), Y KREPS-HEYNDRIKX (Belgium), A FUGLUM (Norway), J CHAPON (France), P SIREYJOL (France), V V DEGTYAREV (USSR), E LESPINE (France), D JONES (UK), J J C M VAN DOOREMALEN (The Netherlands), G B M OLIVER (UK), J De KONING (The Netherlands), A H C STIRLING (UK), R B DAVENPORT (UK)

M. VAN DEN DOEL (THE NETHERLANDS)
REPORTER GENERAL

Maintaining proper depths in access channels and basins is an essential factor among all the activities executed in ports all over the world to function properly as locations where ships can load and unload their cargoes. In some case cases it is a relatively important cost factor but, fortunately, it can be kept under control, technically, commercially and financially. Therefore optimization of dredging activities can can be considered both important and feasible. The papers presented reflect, both in number and in their contents, this approach.

Aspects recommended to be discussed.

1. Cost benefit relations in dredging as an instrument for dredging decisions.
2. Process and handling control and the automation on trailing hoppers.
3. Programmed dredging.
4. Research needs for dredging equipment and operations.
5. Dredging in relation to nautical requirements.
6. Harbour entrance and channel lay out in relation to dredging qualities.
7. The influence of the quality of the dredged material on disposing possibilities.
8. Developments in rockblasting and dredging.
9. Experience on the use of the dipper dredge.

DISCUSSION

C C CABLE (USA)

I would like to supplement the USA paper with information on additional beach nourishment work accomplished in the State of Florida.

The Jacksonville District, US Army Corps of Engineers, has utilized dredged material as beach nourishment for a number of years. A recent job at Fernandia Harbor, Florida, optimized the harbor improvement project dredging by placing dredged material on a badly eroded beach. The dredging involved the deepening of the entrance channel to 40 feet (12.2 m) for the Naval Submarine Support Base, Kings Bay, completed in June 1979. Deepening of the exposed entrance channel was performed by the Hopper Dredge McFARLAND with assistance from the Hopper Dredge GOETHALS. Of a total of approximately 2.3 million cubic yards (1.76 million m^3) removed by both dredges in the deepening project for the U.S. Navy, approximately 500,000 cubic yards (382,277 m^3) of suitable material was placed by means of a direct pump-out system on the ocean beach south of the entrance channel at Fernandia, Florida. The operational methods employed were to obtain a load of material in the hoppers and then tie up to a mooring barge located just outside the channel near the south jetty and pump the dredged material through a submerged pipeline and shoreline down the beach approximately 6,000 feet (1829 m) to the start of the beach fill area. With the addition of two booster pumps in the line at this point in the beach, the beach fill area extended south another 7,000 feet (2134 m) for a total pumping distance from the dredge of approximately 13,000 feet (3962 m). Due to the existing irregular shore alignment the width of the beach fill area varied from 60 (18m) to 600 feet (183m) so as to provide a relatively continuous shore alignment with a berm elevation of +11 feet M.L.W. (3.4 m).

While the placement of material from the channel deepening project on the eroded beach was more costly ($6.68/cu yd, $8.74/$m^3$) than disposal at sea ($2.64/cu yd, $3.45/$m^3$); alternative source of beach fill would now cost considerably more ($5.68/cu yd, $7.43/$m^3$). The management decision to use this method of beach nourishment enables reuse of valuable sand as well as saving $1.64/cu yd ($2.15/m^3).

Another vital beach nourishment project is the Dade County erosion and hurricane (tidal flooding) protection project. For this sand was obtained from suitable sources offshore and pumped on the beach at Miami Beach, Florida.

The project provides for an initial placement of 14.2 million cubic yards (10 million m^3) of material to form a beach and protection dune for 10.5 miles (16.7 km) of shore at Miami Beach.

The plan provides for a dune 20 feet (6.1 m) wide at an elevation of 11.5 feet (3.5 m) above mean low water. Seaward of the dune a berm at an elevation of 9.0 feet (2.7 m) above mean low water extends for 50 feet, (15.2 m) thence a natural slope extends to the water. The beach will be nourished periodically as needed to compensate for erosion losses.

The present estimated project costs, including a 10 year beach nourishment, are about $56 million. The Federal share would be about $31,000,000 and non-Federal about $25,000,000.

Material for these projects are from areas 6 (1.83 km) to 12 thousand feet (3.6 km) offshore.

Most of this work was performed by Hydraulic Cutter Head Dredges. The dredges are powered by 7200 HP on their pumps and 1600 HP on their cutterheads. The suction is 34 inches (0.9 m) and the pump and discharge pipe is 27 inches (0.7 m) in diameter. The ILLINOIS moved material through an average of 12,000 feet (3.6 km) of pipeline, of which 9,700 feet (2.9 km) was submerged. The ALASKA used an average of 11,000 feet (3.3 km) of which 7,900 feet (2408 m) was submerged. A jack-up booster platform was used to assist the dredges. One problem detected early-on was oversized material being placed on the beach. Provision was made in the contracts for all material greater than 1" (2.5 cm) in diameter to be crushed until it met this criteria.

In addition to enhancing the recreational opportunities along Florida's beaches, these beach nourishment projects provide protection against tidal flooding.

J B HERBICH (USA)

I wish to make some additional comments regarding sizing of confined disposal areas and dewatering of dredged material:-

I. Correct sizing of confined disposal area is obviously very important in deciding on the size of the area and the height of the dikes required. For that reason we developed a laboratory method for determining the bulking factor for materials to be dredged. The bulking factor is defined as

$$B = \frac{Vc}{Vi}$$

where Vc = volume in containment area

Vi = volume in situ

or $$B = \frac{\gamma di}{\gamma dc}$$

where γdi = dry density in situ

γdc = dry density in containment area

or $$B = \frac{Wc\ Gs + 100}{Wi\ Gs + 100}$$

where Wc = water content in the containment area

Wi = water content in situ

(The last equation is valid only for a soil under saturated conditions)

A detailed procedure to determine the bulking factor in the laboratory is given in reference Di George III, F.P. and J.B. Herbich, "Laboratory Determination of Bulking Factors for Texas Coastal Fine-grained Materials", Texas A & M University Report No. 218, August 1978.

LABORATORY PROCEDURES — BULKING FACTOR

The following is a step by step chronological presentation of the bulking factor laboratory tests:-

1.) The wax was trimmed from the undisturbed samples as each was prepared for testing. The sample itself was then trimmed into a uniform cylindrical shape through the use of a knife and a small carpenter's square.

2.) The sample was carefully measured with a triangular metric scale, and its volume in cubic centimeters calculated from the measurements. This volume was later used in bulking factor calculations.

3.) The weight of the sample to the nearest decigram was obtained through the use of a metric balance and its specific volume obtained by dividing the volume from step 2 by this weight.

4.) The sample was then chopped and mixed into a homogeneous mass using a knife and a glass cutting plate.

5.) For those samples tested in fresh water, 13.1 $^o/oo$ salt water, and 28.6 $^o/oo$ salt water, three 200 gram portions were taken from the sample and placed aside in separate, covered 1000 ml beakers. For those samples subjected to sedimentation tests only in 28.6% $^o/oo$ salt water, a single 200 gram portion was placed aside in a covered 1000 ml beaker. Portions of each sample were resealed in parrafin and retained for Atterberg limit and sieve analysis testing.

6.) The in situ volume of each 200 gram sample was calculated by multiplying its weight by the specific volume obtained in step 3.

7.) The portions of each sample were then allowed to slake in their separate breakers with 500 ml of the water in which they were to be tested. This slaking continued for a period of approximately 24 hours.

8.) After slaking, a variable-speed mixer and a special four-bladed plastic impeller-shaped blade were used to mix the soil particles and water into a homogeneous slurry. Water was added during the mixing process, increasing the slurry volume to about 975 ml. A slurry density of 1200 grams per litre by weight was desired to simulate that density typically found in dredge slurries. The impeller blade provided a strong vortex within the beaker and served to raise the soil particles into suspension. By observing through the walls of the beaker, it was easily determined that a mixing time of five to six minutes was required to ensure all soil particles were in suspension.

9.) The slurry was then poured into a 1000 ml graduated cylinder. About 25 ml of the proper salinity water was used to rinse the adhering soil particles from the impeller blade and beaker into the graduated cylinder, raising the volume within the cylinder to exactly 1000 ml. This procedure reduced the loss of soil particles through the mixing process to a negligible amount.

10.) The slurry was then allowed to stand undisturbed while the soil particles settled out of suspension. The level of the interface between the suspended material and the supernatant liquid was observed and recorded one-half hour after beginning the test, and hourly thereafter until the rate of settlement had decreased to 10 ml per hour or less. The level of suspended material was recorded thereafter at 24 hour intervals from the start of the test until the amount of settlement was undetectable for a forty-eight hour period.

11.) When the sedimentation test for a particular sample was completed, the supernatant liquid was drawn off and its salinity determined through the use of the "Hydrolab" conductivity meter shown in Fig. 10. The sample and cylinder were weighed together, then placed in an oven to dry at 140° F.

12.) The cylinders were removed from the oven and weighed at 24 hour intervals until two consecutive weights were the same. By compensating for the weight of the small amount of salt water left in the cylinder prior to placement in the oven, and dried salt on top of the soil after removal from the oven, and the cylinder weight, the dry weight of the sample and moisture content of the sedimented material were determined. This moisture content was later used to calculate the void ratio of the sedimented material. Applicability of the employed test procedures to field conditions is based on the following assumptions:

(a)- The 200 gram portion selected for testing from each sample was representative of the total sample.

(b)- The artificial sea water of 28.6 ^{o}/oo salinity was a reasonable approximation of field conditions.

(c)- The blending process employed to mix the slurry was a reasonable approximation of the dredging process. In most cases, the vortex motion of the slurry within the beaker caused small portions of the sample to roll on the bottom, forming clay balls of 1/16 inch to 1/4 inch in diameter. No attempt was made to break these spheres down and force them into suspension. Doing so would have resulted in larger sizing factors, and it was felt that their formation was an indicator of reasonably accurate simulation of the dredging process. The clay balls, immediately settled to the bottom when the slurry was poured into a cylinder.

(d)- The loss of soil particles through adhesion to laboratory mixing apparatus was negligible.

(e)- The effects of compaction due to placement of successive lifts of dredged material was not simulated.

(f)- The effects of surface drying through mechanical dewatering and natural evaporation were not simulated.

(g)- The effects of long-term settlement and subgrade consolidation were not simulated, nor were the projected effects of shrinkage from these causes reflected in the plotted bulking factor.

II. The second item is the need to dewater the disposal site as soon as possible so that the additional volume in the containment area is made available for future disposal, for example where it is to be used for industrial or other purposes. The dewatering methods are fully described in the Dredged Material Research Program of the Corps of Engineer's Waterways Experiment Station in Vicksburg, Mississippi. Several vehicles, or towed devices can be used to construct trenches in the confined disposal area to facilitate drainage. One of such vehicles is a RUC (Riverine Utility Craft).

III. Finally in open-water disposal, particularly in shallow water, waves and currents can cause a fairly rapid erosion of islands built by cutterhead dredges. A laboratory study was conducted at Texas A & M University (Reference Vyas, Y.K. and J.B. Herbich "Erosion of Dredged Material Islands due to Waves and Currents", Proceedings, Hydraulics in the Coastal Zone Conference, American Society of Civil Engineers, 1977) to evaluate the erosion rates. The model scale was determined by comparing the model island with a prototype island which experienced appreciable erosion during a 13-year period.

L NEDERLOF (THE NETHERLANDS)

The latest experience has led to conclusions that especially in fluid mud areas the whole range of small agitation-dredging-systems could be highly effective. Based on the Rotterdam experience we believe that these tools are of extreme importance for small budget ports in developing countries.

The second item to be highlighted is the "nautical bed" and "nautical depth" in areas with a muddy bottom-material. Normally there is first water with floating silt, then a layer with loose silt and finally consolidated silt, with densities respectively 1.00 to 1.10 t/m3, 1.10 to 1.20 t/m3 and 1.20 to 1.35 t/m3.

Until recently the depth was measured with an echo-sounder which records the upper-layer of the silty bottom (about 1.03 t/m3.

Nowadays the bottom-density in the Rotterdam area is measured with a radioactive density-meter.

Also, the river authority and the City of Rotterdam harbour authority carried out model and practical tests with large ships to get more information about the safe manoeuvrebility of ships above muddy bottoms; a major point was whether a body of water containing loose silt could be included in a vessel's keel-clearance.

The tests showed:-

1. A higher resistance; to maintain speed the propellers have to make more revolutions,

2. Reduced stopping distance,

3. Less subject to squat and trim,

4. Increased rudder effectiveness: the reason is that there is a higher resistance.

The conclusion is that the presence of silt in low densities within the keel-clearance margin is causing changes in the behaviour of vessels in motion, but entails no risks of dangerous situations.

In the Rotterdam area the 1.20 t/m3-density-layer is for safety reasons chosen as the "nautical bottom"; that means that the "nautical depth" reaches from the water-surface to the 1.20 t/m3-density-layer. The "nautical depth" includes the ships' draught and the normal keel-clearance used for the area.

By using the "nautical depth" for muddy areas it is concluded that there is a better definition of the bottom level and also the bottom-materials with lower densities than 1.20 t/m3 need not be dredged (that contains 90% water and 10% solid matter).

For more information see the May 1981-issue of "Dock and Harbour Authority".

M F C THORN (UK)

In my view and experience, there is too little understanding of the processes that make up the dredging cycle. If the processes are not properly measured or properly understood, optimisation of the dredging cycle may be a nonsense. I am disappointed that the role of research is not more greatly emphasised in the papers of this session.

The Dutch contribution on "nautical depth" defined by a criterion of density rather than the bounce of an echo is a good example of how a little basic research to understand the process produces large benefits.

The following are examples of how scientific investigation and measurement of dredging processes can help in the optimisation and increase of effective output.

1. Measurements of the load density in a trailing-suction hopper dredger showed that overspilling reduced the hopper load and hence the output of the cycle. The most productive cycle was that in which the hopper was filled in the shortest time: the load was greater and the number of cycles per shift was greater.

2. Radioactive tracer measurements to compare the effectiveness of the hopper-dumping and sidecasting modes of dredging showed that although the efficiency of spoil removal/load was much higher for hopper dumping, because of the time lost in sailing and dumping, the effective output/shift was twice as high for sidecasting.

3. Radioactive tracer investigation of the dispersion of spoil discharged at a designated spoil ground showed that very little material was in fact retained within the designated area, and over 80% was totally dispersed. The concept of transporting spoil to be discharged within a designated area was quite wrong.

D M McDOWELL (UK)

It was agreed in Brussels that the subject of dredging technique and equipment was well covered for example through WODCON. The role of PIANC was seen to be wider, its membership including port engineers and managers and government representatives. The subject was intended to cover the economics of the whole dredging operation and to include the wider aspects of dredging and spoil disposal, which can prove to be very expensive.

Dredging can be likened to a game; deadly serious for the participants, who nevertheless preserve a sense of humour. Unlike most other games, this one is played by several teams simultaneously. Each team has its own rules which are seldom revealed to others. One of the secrets for success is to know the rules of the other teams. The teams include politicians, civil servants, dredging contractors and clients. In the lowest division is the dredging master, whose objective is the same as that of everyone else: to do a good job according to his rules. Of course, in reality the aim of many players is to seem to do the job for which they are paid, while the objective of others is to ensure that they actually do it.

Unlike other games, the final whistle is only blown for some participants; the contractor will eventually reach agreement and, we hope, be paid. For most other players, the game goes on and on. We have many examples of this. The earliest known to this contributor is the case of the Manchester Ship Canal. For over eighty years the proprietors have had to dispose of dredging spoil ashore. This requirement was determined by Act of Parliament for reasons which seemed good at the time. This has now become a difficult and expensive operation as suitable land for spoil disposal has been used up. We do not know precisely what benefits have been achieved or whether it is appropriate to continue removal of fine silt indefinitely.

Other examples are the classic case of spoil disposal ashore from the Delaware estuary in the United States and, more recently, the thorough study leading to disposal ashore from the Thames estuary in the United Kingdom. What are the long-term effects, now that some decades have elapsed? Other cases are the Rotterdam Waterway in which deepening has led to increased saline penetration which has had to be countered by deposition of a gravel bed that can resist erosion. We have learnt from all these cases, but there are contemporary cases, for example of dredging in tropical deltas which must lead to short-term effects which can be foreseen, but also to long-term effects which cannot.

I would like to suggest additions to the draft conclusions for this subject by adding the economic consequences of the long-term effects of dredging and spoil disposal.

A GENEVOIS (FRANCE)

The French paper dealt in detail with 3 practical instances and I should like to examine some of their results and essential lessons.

1. Regulation and maintenance of an estuary with strong tides and very fine sand – the Seine

estuary, leading to the port of Rouen.

Until about 1960, the estuary's navigable channel was erratic in course and could take vessels of maximum 8,000 dwt when fully laden. The first major stage of the works, completed in 1962, already made it possible to gain 2.50 m in draught (ships of 25,000 dwt):

- regulating by a partially submersed embankment, so as to guide the action of the currents and self-dredge the channel;
- after studies on a sedimention model, which were complete and refined, thanks to the presence of numerous data and historical tests.

A second stage based on the same principle is now in course of completion. It will enable the channel to take vessels of 35,000 dwt, by means of an improved regulation by a submersed and economical north embankment (making due allowance for environmental problems encountered).

In all: a gain of over 4 m in draught

- vessels of 8,000 t → 35,000 dwt fully laden
- but volume of maintenance unchanged: 5 million m3

2. Maintenance and mud dredging policy in the Gironde. The paper is a sequel to the one submitted at Leningrad in 1977. It shows how, in the meantime, a decrease of about 20% in maintenance charges, other things being equal, has been made possible by the installation of an automated and efficient sounding system, improved knowledge of mud sedimentation mechanism and of mud dredging (exploitation of data — physiochemical studies); and gradual transition to a preventive maintenance policy. I draw the following conclusion from these two practical instances, reinforced by others:

1) Maintenance dredging is doubtless a necessary evil, but it must be combated by all means, reverting to the dilemma "to dredge or not to dredge" and calling in question generally-held ideas.

2) A maintenance problem, especially in an estuary, must never be considered as solved. Quite the contrary, solutions can always be improved.

3) Numerous means of improvement exist: regular rather than large-scale dredgings, positioning and sounding systems, regrouping of resources, etc. The reports refer to them at some length.

4) A particularly effective method, which seems to us not always to be sufficiently made use of, is to obtain a better knowledge of the physical data of the problem, the mechanisms and functioning of the estuary: it is all very well to gain a few percent by optimizing the dredging cycle in the strict sense of the term, but it is necessary beforehand to ask questions about the choice of dumping zones, the material recycling phenomena between these zones and the channel, so as to make a complete economic calculation. Mr. Thorn has quoted some examples of this. They are indeed numerous.

Every estuary or maintenance problem has its own peculiar features and its own evolutions.

It is also a very important recommendation for a port authority to invest so as to improve constantly the data and their interpretation, and to work towards this goal simultaneously with specialized hydraulics laboratories and with estuary regulating and dredging experts, but also to show proof of imagination and flair. This recommendation is valid in the industrialized countries and in the developing countries. It is a source of progress and constant savings.

Y KREPS-HEYNDRIKX (BELGIUM)

I would like to provide some additional information concerning the dredging of the Ghent-Terneuzen Ship Canal — dumping silts in a shaft.

1. The watertight screen. A thorough examination of the subsoil was made. 25 depth penetration tests of 25 to 36 m over the entire course of the wall, 3 soundings by the Ackerman technique as far as into the clay seam — results: The watertight wall was executed in zones of differing depths (1 m in the clay seam).

Experience has shown that the geotechnical tests must be carried out with great care and in large numbers so as to ascertain precisely the levels of the watertight strata (clay). Otherwise, zones which are more or less permeable would be left, which would be detrimental to the goal pursued, i.e., construction of a watertight tank.

Execution of the wall: mud-lined walls in bentonite cement. Results of permeability tests on 6 samples:

$K = 1.57 \times 10^{-8}$ cm/sec (5×10^{-8} cm/sec was laid down)

Method: piles 3.60 m wide are drilled, overlapping by 0.90 m.

During the work, the ground water level falls.

The bentonite-cement mixture was produced on site, with a capacity of 100 m3/hour.

2. Execution of shaft. The shaft was executed by dredging the sand by means of a sectional dredge-cutter.

Some technical features:

- ∅ of pipes: 700 mm
- power: 6000 h.p.
- outlet pressure: 12 to 13 kg/cm2
- velocity in the pipes: 4 to 5 m/sec
- concentration: 1.4 t/m3 to 1.8 t/m3
- production: 1,700 m33h to 2,800 m3/h

The sand was conveyed to a distance of 9 km and it will be used for the construction of embankments of a drinking water reservoir.

3. Programme for checking the quality of the ground water. (see Fig. 1) Tubes for taking samples of ground water were drilled on 3 axes. Samples were taken at depths of 9 m and 15 m, at the sites 1, 2, 3, 4, 5 and 6.

For each site:

- index A: inside the watertight wall
- no index: outside the wall
- index B: at 50 m from the watertight wall.

At three sites, tubes were drilled in the sand layer below the clay seam. The samples of water were analysed on 27 parameters. Initial situation = zero situation, i.e., before dumping the mud in the shaft.

In tubes 5 and 6, it may be admitted that the water is drinkable (according to EEC standards).

Tubes 1, 2, 3 and 4 show a certain degree of pollution, probably due to the presence of a gypsum deposit in the vicinity.

4. Programme for checking quality of ground water after dumping of dredging mud:

a) Checking samples of water in the tubes, 3 months, 6 months, 9 months and 12 months — and then 2 years and 3 years after dumping.

b) Study by simulation model:

- to give an estimate of the nature, evolution in time and definition of the zone susceptible to pollution.
- to provide the bases for research into the sequels of pollution and to give remedial solutions in extreme cases of pollution of the ground water which could, for example, be due to a malformation of the shaft or a sudden change in the water regime in the vicinity of the shaft.

Calculations were made by computer. A concrete calculation has shown that with an overpressure of 1 m in the shaft, a permeability of the watertight wall 100 times greater than planned and a charge of 110 mg of fluorides per litre of water, it would take 5 years for the fluorides to poison a zone of 10 m around the shaft. It may also be concluded that heavy metals will remain in the shaft.

The simulation model also shows the positive influence of the ditch around the embankment of the shaft (takes 98.5% of the current lines). Meanwhile, the work of filling with dredging silts has started and the problem with which we shall soon have to cope is to find an adequate method of consolidating the mud at a depth of 18 m.

A FUGLUM (NORWAY)

I wish to point out the importance of long-term planning on an international scale to collect the predicted data on the volume of dredged materials for years ahead. This would enable the dredging industry to make long-term investment plans for the numbers and types of dredges to be constructed.

I suggest that present standard methods for identifying and classifying dredged materials (PIANC Bulletin 1972) should be reviewed and updated using mathematical figures rather than a written description. Previous experience has proved that descriptive terms are interpreted in different ways in different countries and may lead to confusion about what kind of dredges to put on the job. I refer to the seismical refraction sounding system, as described in my paper on the subject, as one method to identify and classify dredged materials in a more precise manner.

I would like to challenge the industry to develop simple electronic devices to search for high and shallow spots after initial dredging, which could be used for control purposes before the dredging equipment has been withdrawn from the dredging site.

J CHAPON (FRANCE)

My remarks concern the desirability of sharing dredging operations between the public sector and private enterprise, to which the Reporter General referred in his summary of the papers.

I do not claim to offer a solution that is universal and of absolute value, but should merely like to evoke the French position on the question.

For this purpose, I consider the public sector as embracing the State resources and the means available for port activities which, in France, are public activities.

1. The dredging potential available to the public sector must be such as to guarantee that the ports fulfil their mission of rendering service to users and that they will always be able to safeguard the depths of channels and docks.

   To this end the public sector must be capable of coping with three categories of operations and to do so with its own resources.

   a) Safety operations caused, for example, by sudden accretions brought about by a flood or storm, there is no time for an invitation to tender.

   b) Operations the quantities of which it is practically impossible to measure, for example, accretions fluctuating rapidly in volume and location, in the channel of an estuary. Even if this work is entrusted to a contractor the latter will have to be paid on the basis of time spent and not of quantities dredged, since they can hardly be measured.

   c) Lastly, operations which, by reason of the economic situation, run the risk of falling into the clutches of a private sector monopoly — for in that case, the public authorities can no longer check or contain expenditure.

2. However, the will to provide a public service should not mean renouncing the principle of a sound economy: the authorities must show concern for the profitability aspect, in the interests of the community.

   The resources of the public sector should, therefore, be of such a volume as to ensure full employment of the personnel and equipment.

   They also need to be managed with the same strictness as private resources, and in particular, their cost should be analysed and known with the same degree of accuracy.

3. In France, this has led to the calculation of the volume of public resources according

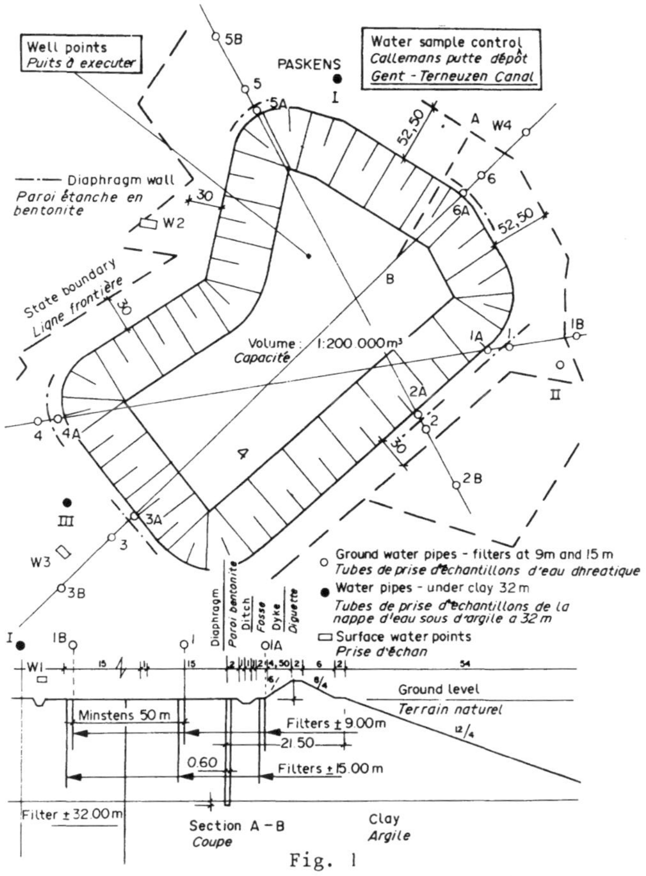

Fig. 1

to the volume of the current maintenance dredgings in the ports: the requirements over and above current maintenance must be met by calling on the private sector.

This does not mean that the administrative rules forbid a public dredger to take part in investment works, any more than they would prevent a private dredger from being used on a maintenance site. It is simply a question of aligning the potential of public resources with the maintenance volume; but this leaves the greatest degree of flexibility – and even the greatest freedom – for the use of the equipment of each sector on maintenance sites or on new works. A structure has even been created to make possible an improved combined utilization of French dredgers from the public sector and those from the domestic private sector.

P SIREYJOL (FRANCE)

I was most interested by the analysis made by our Reporter General, leading to the definition of a dredging policy based on technical considerations, on the one hand, and market considerations, on the other.

The market aspect of the problems is very well-known to the port authorities in developed countries, although doubtless less so in the developing countries.

In the latter countries, indeed, a preponderant condition for carrying out a major dredging project is to assemble the funds necessary to pay for the work. This in turn involves the assumption that an external financing institution has been persuaded to show an interest in it.

Once this condition has been met, the authorities concerned deal with the technical organization of the invitation to tender, without paying much attention to the market conditions. If the latter are unfavourable when the invitations to tender are issued, the result may be that the contract is awarded at a very high price.

It is desirable for the port authorities of the developing countries to take the necessary steps to ensure a certain financial awareness at all times. Once they have achieved this result, it is possible for them, by keeping themselves informed about the dredging market, or more precisely about the availability of dredges in the area, to negotiate in optimum conditions the dredging works they need, whether it be maintenance dredging or new work on a limited scale.

V V DEGTYAREV (USSR)

The river fleet plays an important part in the unified transport system of the USSR. In the northern regions of Siberia the river vessels are the only means of transporting bulk cargoes.

The possibilities of the development of waterways in the USSR are great. More than 100,000 rivers with the total length of almost 4 million kilometers flow on the vast territory of our country. Technical and economical analysis has shown that more than 500,000 kilometers of rivers and lakes can be developed for shipping. At present about 146,000 kilometers of waterways are already used for transportation of cargoes and passengers.

Due to the uninterrupted growth of our country's national economy the artificial waterways are used more intensively from year to year. Their channel dimensions are being increased, i.e. depths, widths and radii of turn.

The main ways of increasing ship channel dimensions on rivers in natural conditions in the USSR are dredging and construction of regulation works. The volumes of maintenance dredging come to 50-60 thousand cubic meters per 10 km stretch of a navigable river. For rivers with variable beds the volumes of maintenance dredging are still greater and amount to 100,000 cubic meters (the Northern Dvina River) and even to 340,000 cubic meters (the Ob river).

The volumes of dredging works being great, it is economically reasonable to use dredgers of high output and with low draft. For rivers with intense bed processes the short time of dredging work contributes to greater stability of a waterway in addition to the direct economical benefit. In some cases, e.g. when cutting straight through a waterway bend during the flood, the high output of dredgers appears to be decisive for the efficiency of works being carried out. Of paramount importance is the output of dredgers working in the Far North where big dredging volumes must be done within the navigation season of 2-3 months. In particular, special dredgers with the output of 5,000 cubic meters per hour are being designed to dredge ship channels in the mouths of the Siberian rivers.

Dredging works in the inland waterways are carried out without shipping interruption. This excludes the use of dredgers with spud arrangements.

Research conducted and experience gained have led to the developments which can contribute to the efficiency of dredging technology, including: dredging through a river stretch by "successive cuts from upstream to downstream"; use of wide dustpan suction heads decreasing the overdredging of cuts and reducing the volumes of dredging material; use of orientation systems for the automatic dredger positioning while working; use of specialized auxiliary craft equipped with necessary mechanisms and remote control systems to shift the dredging anchors; dredger operation on the basis of process charts.

On the rivers with intense bed processes and especially under insufficient water discharge the efficiency of dredging will greatly increase provided it is carried out simultaneously with the construction of regulation works. The regulation works on the rivers of the USSR are mainly built of earth. Such earth works proved to be the most economical in practice and allow the building process to be fully mechanized.

As a rule, dredging and erecting regulation works are aimed not only at increasing ship channel dimensions but also at improving the safety of navigation and decreasing the adverse effect of transport on the environment. On the basis of investigations of long standing the recommendations have been worked out for projecting dredging works taking into account that the dredging technology, and planned location of underwater "canals" should not seriously damage water quality and basin ecology.

Analytical calculation methods have been developed for estimating water turbidity changes in the river due to dredging.

Dredgers like other river vessels are equipped with self-contained units for collection and treatment of oil-polluted waters.

E LESPINE (FRANCE)

I think that we may tackle the optimization problems that arise when it comes to defining the number of dredges necessary to meet particular dredging requirements. I should like to say how we tackle this problem in France, along the lines of what Mr. Jean CHAPON told us.

In 1979, the Seaports Directorate deemed fit to pool all the dredging facilities previously managed almost autonomously by each of the 14 public departments responsible for maintenance of the access channels in French ports.

A private company known as "DRAGAGES-PORTS", of which I am in charge, was created for this purpose. Full ownership of the 140 dredgers and dredging appliances belonging to the French government was transferred to it. "DRAGAGES-PORTS" leases its dredgers, on a hull-only basis, to the 14 public departments which operate them with their own personnel.

What are the essential functions of "DRAGAGES-PORTS"?

1. To renew its equipment and to deploy dredging appliances which, although few in number, are efficient.

2. To see to it constantly, in liaison with its members, that all the dredging appliances available are utilized in the best possible way.

Thanks to the introduction of this pool of dredging appliances and thanks to its coordinated operation, we look forward to a considerable diminution in the cost of maintenance dredging at the French ports, despite the substantial depreciations and financial charges resulting from the investments.

So as to reduce these costs, we must ensure that the appliances necessary for maintenance dredging are fully utilized. This is why the public services can entrust deepening dredging operations to the "DRAGAGES-PORTS" appliances. Conversely, as Mr. Jean CHAPON told us, if maintenance dredgings occur at too irregular intervals and do not justify deployment by "DRAGAGES-PORTS" of permanent dredging facilities, the ports are entirely free to call on the services of other private firms.

We may therefore forecast a bright future in France for cooperation between "DRAGAGES-PORTS" and the other dredging companies, both French and foreign.

Another consequence of the creation of "DRAGAGES-

PORTS" is that France now has an organization grouping all the 'know-how' acquired over the years by French dredging experts. It is therefore an organization which, relying on the resources of the Autonomous Ports and Marine Departments and in liaison with the other French engineering companies, is in a position to give assistance to foreign countries, not only for the development of port projects involving major dredging works, but also for the follow-up of work on dredging sites.

D JONES (UK)

It has been my experience that nothing turns a profitable port into a loss making port quicker than dredging.

Port revenue is not easy to obtain and in times of recession it is very difficult to improve it. Costs must be rigorously contained and since maintenance dredging is generally a heavy cost it must come under close scrutiny. If dredging costs can be contained the loss making port can often move back into profit.

The British Transport Docks Board manages 19 ports in the United Kingdom. They all require dredging and to do this, a fleet of dredgers is owned and operated by the Authority. Even so we regularly need to get assistance from the private sector of dredging to meet variable and uncertain demands.

Research is a most important element and we maintain a constant effort in this area. We live, however, in an imperfect world. Because research facilities are available it does not follow that they are always properly used or even used at all. Yet the penalties for inadequate research can be very costly and we must make certain that those who make important investment decisions understand this.

I am glad to find that ports' pride of ownership in dredgers is giving way to the more rational approach of sharing. Time was when individual ports insisted on complete control of their own dredgers even though this was not cost effective. But dredgers get old and the cost of their replacement is frighteningly high and ports, especially those in a group under single ownership, look for other ports to share the burden. Expensive dredgers must be shared.

Then there is the question of the men who crew the dredgers. In the UK it has been traditional for most ports to own dredgers and dredge for themselves. Very often the conditions of service of the crew were established in the former days of bucket dredgers and are quite unsuitable for modern dredgers. The dredging cycle cannot be optimised however modern the equipment, if dredgers spend a large part of their time moored in their berths. Any port authority which cannot negotiate production agreements with its dredgemen should abandon dredging by direct labour.

Finally, there will always be a need for the private sector of dredging and it is against this that Port Authorities should judge their efficiency. There is no better test than that of the market place.

J J C M VAN DOOREMALEN (THE NETHERLANDS)

Automation of dredging equipment is a must due to the very complex nature of the dredging process and the number of parameters involved. One should realise that the decision to install automated systems is not solely a one-time purchase decision. It involves the necessity of having adequate staff available for operating and maintaining the equipment. This in general means additional training for the future crew of the vessel. Furthermore, the owner should realise that installing automation does not mean that a lower quality of the crew can be accepted; on the contrary, as automation processes always work by setting maxima and minima (operating limits) of the parameter involved and as circumstances change continuously during the dredging cycle, an expert dredgemaster and crew should be available to set these limits.

It should also be understood that the automation is only as good as the quality of its input signals. It is my opinion that our efforts in the near future should be directed to improving the quality of the sensors giving the input signals.

Automation will pay when complex processes have to be controlled; but even when processes are relatively simple automation should be considered because of the following aspects:

- an automate never gets tired; it works 24 hours a day;
- an automate is "honest";
- when results are being recorded it provides you with valuable data which could be the basis for further research;
- it never gets irritated.

In conclusion, I would like to propose that PIANC considers advising future and existing owners of complicated automated dredgers to pay a great deal of attention to the education and training of their staffs. In my opinion not enough capacity to give the training is available.

G B M OLIVER (UK)

Further to Mr Nederlof's previous remarks I should like to point out that the benefit which Rotterdam now gains from the nautical depth concept arises very largely from the work of Dr. Kirby and Dr. Parker of the Institute of Oceanographic Sciences, Taunton and the design, development and manufacture in Britain of a radio-active density meter.

It has been explained that it has now been accepted in Rotterdam that mud up to a specific gravity of 1.2 can be included in the underkeel clearance without harmful effects. This is a very considerable advance but 1.2 is still scarcely little more than dirty water. The question I would like to ask, therefore, is whether Mr. Nederlof and his colleagues have any plans for going even further – perhaps to the stage where the keel of the vessel is actually passing through mud of specific gravity 1.1 or 1.2?

Mr. Jones referred to some work we did a few years ago in the National Ports Council on the concept of sharing dredgers between ports and other speakers have referred also to this idea. The work involved a very large computer simulation on which the total British port maintenance dredging activity was modelled and it demonstrated that there were very considerable financial benefits to be won from dredger-sharing. I agree with Mr. Jones that the days have now gone when individual ports could own their own individual dredging plant (except perhaps in a few very special cases). But it is first and foremost, if not entirely, an organisational problem. This is why the British Transport Docks Board, managing 19 ports in Britain, can implement dredger-sharing whereas other ports in Britain have shown little or no interest in the idea. The benefits are there to be won by those who are able to win them but it is an organisational problem.

J de KONING (THE NETHERLANDS)

I would like to draw your attention to the Canadian contribution.* In Section II Volume 2 p. 224 in Table 2 under (b) it reads that the average dredging tolerance is 0,15 m for all channel sections. Under (b) it is remarked that "Dredging tolerance (± 0,15 m) indicates the accuracy with which a modern hopper dredger can achieve a specified depth".

From Table 4 on page 255 it can be learned that the channel length covers:

River 00 - 17	silt and sandy silt
River mouth 17 - 21	silt and bay mud
Inner bay 21 - 23	bay mud
Horse shoe 23 - 24	medium fine sand
Outer area 24 - 28	fine sand
(exposed to waves)	

I am afraid that a very old and persistent mistake is traced here once again. People think that something that is printed is a reflection of reality. A tolerance of one foot is stated in many dredging tenders and contracts. How dangerous that can be is clear from this paper.

Real dredging tolerances of a trailing section hopper dredger of the middle class under the circumstances mentioned will be about 0,50 to 0,75 m plus or minus from the actual average dredged depth.

May I suggest that a committee is formed to investigate and establish for publication a dredging tolerance list. Possibly the committee on "Classification of Soils to be Dredged" could serve in this respect.

May I also suggest that co-operation is sollicited with WODA, the "World Organisation of Dredging Associations".

A H C STIRLING (UK)

I would like to comment on the paper on two major dredging contracts in NSW, Australia at Port Kembla and Newcastle with which I was concerned. In both contracts monitoring of different environmental parameters was carried out.

In Port Kembla the successful tenderer offered a cheaper alternative method of dredging which had a considerable pollution risk. The pollution monitoring programme is described in the paper but, one non technical aspect is worth mentioning here. The proposed alternative dredging method caused the local environmentalists to be very concerned about ocean pollution and particularly about pollution of nearby beautiful surfing beaches. Therefore the client and the contractor set up a vigorous public relations and press campaign to publicise the results of the monitoring and demonstrate that pollution was negligible.

Similarly at Newcastle there was considerable pollution hazard due to noise and vibrations from the rock blasting. A residential area lay within a few hundred metres of the approach channel where considerable blasting was to take place. In order to avoid delays and consequent increases in cost the client, the Maritime Services Board, and the contractor set up a careful and well advertised campaign giving information on the limited working hours for blasting noise and the measurement of vibrations to reassure the public on these matters.

In both contracts the cost of the monitoring was very small — a fraction of a percent of the project cost — but the costs of delays due to interference by environmentalist groups could be excessive.

The point I wish to emphasise is that in order to complete successfully environmentally sensitive dredging projects and avoid significant cost increases or delays one must not only carry out a monitoring programme but also use the results in a carefully thought out public exercise.

R B DAVENPORT (UK)

Referring to the need to try and reduce the commitment to dredge in order to maintain channels, I support others who have touched on this point.

It is necessary to ask,

1. What is the source of material to be dredged? Silt and water should be analysed.
2. Can the material be diverted? e.g. Silt traps.
3. Can it be minimised? By training walls, pumping or impounding at restricted times, water mixing or chemical dosing?

There may well still be a need to dredge but these points are part of the whole cycle.

The priority research item should be the causes of sedimentation.

M. VAN DEN DOEL (THE NETHERLANDS)
REPORTER GENERAL

The general opinion of the speakers had been that a public owned dredging fleet is advan-

*An Errata to this paper has been submitted to the Publisher and appears at the end of this section.

tageous provided that the equipment can be kept busy a high percentage of the time. Therefore, co-operation between ports is necessary.

Private dredging can then be used for emergencies or peaks.

This is partly different from the American/Dutch approach where strategic and emergency arguments are used to justify a publicly owned fleet.

None of the speakers has mentioned the possibility of chartering private dredgers (the private company guaranteeing a certain over capacity to be available within a specified time) on medium long-term (3 - 4 years).

In this way a port can be sure of having available enough base-load capacity without having a complete dredging fleet to support.

Capital dredging is usually carried out by private enterprise.

I note remarks made by Professor McDowell about the long term effects of dredging. Although I agree with the importance of this, I ask myself whether or not we were going beyond the "optimisation of the dredging cycle", and if we are not going beyond the field of PIANC.

My reasoning is that we do not know the long term effects of such works as the deepening of the mouth of the Rhine, or the cleaning of the Scheldt etc. If we had to wait for this knowledge to be acquired, we could not do anything. We can only learn by trial and error.

CONCLUSIONS

The economic maintenance of required depths in access channels and basins is an essential factor in port activity.

During the coming years programmed dredging and automatic data processing will be increasingly used.

However, more research is needed in the field of rapid data transmission and processing so that effective feed back is possible during the execution of the work.

Extensive research is required into the whole dredging cycle with the objective of improving its economy and reliability. This research should include:

a) Soil behaviour and the disposal of material having regard to hydraulic mechanisms;

b) the selection of equipment;

c) methods of execution of the whole cycle;

d) environmental effects;

e) long term effects of dredging and disposal.

Shared use of dredgers between ports may offer economical advantages and should be carefully considered in suitable circumstances.

There is a need for the establishment of clear criteria and an understanding of the significance of norms in the execution of dredging works and the disposal of dredged materials.

The disposal of dredged material either to open water or to the land raises important questions of the law, land-use planning, environmental protection and economics. Policies which do not have proper regard to all of these factors can create serious problems and this is an area requiring careful study.

The concept of "nautical depth" in fluid mud areas can lead to important savings in the cost of maintenance dredging.

It is recommended that PIANC consider the whole of the above as possible subjects to be remitted to PTC I/PTC II for study.

ERRATA FOR

The Miracmichi Channel Study: An Economically Optimized Dredging Plan in Section II — Volume 2, Marine Ports and Seaways, Inland and Maritime Waterways and Ports.

Page 223 ESTIMATION OF SILTATION RATES: reference to Table 5 should read Table 4a.

Page 225 Add:

Table 4a. Summary of Annual Siltation Quantity Estimates (in cubic metres per year)

Channel Sector	Nodes	Design Drafts (m)			Maintenance: Capital Ratio
		7.0	7.6	8.2	(96)
River	00-17	16 500	35 000	64 500	6.1
River Mouth	17-21	7 600	16 000	27 500	5.0
Inner Bay	21-23	33 000	60 000	95 500	3.0 - 3.5
Horse Shoe	23-24	27 700	40 000	51 000	4.9
Outer Area	24-28	46 700	77 000	114 000	10.7
Total		131 500	228 000	352 5000	5.2 - 5.4

MARITIME PORTS AND SEAWAYS

SECTION II — SUBJECT 3

Recent developments in cargo handling systems and equipment with particular reference to the design and layout of terminal facilities

Wednesday 13 May 1981

Chairman:	*N N B ORDMAN (UK)* *Noel Ordman and Associates Ltd*
Vice Chairman:	*Prof F VASCO COSTA (Portugal)* *Technical University of Lisbon*
Reporter General:	*J H W NORTHFIELD (UK)* *Chief Engineer, The Felixstowe Dock and Railway Company*
Secretary:	*P LACEY (UK)* *Ove Arup and Partners Ltd, London*
Asst. Secretary:	*Miss M-M DANEELS (Belgium)* *Secrétaire AIPCN Secrétariat Générale, Brussels*

Speakers

V J DAVIES (GB), J S BALFOUR (GB), J CHATTAWAY (GB), T KERISEL (France), M ENRIQUEZ FRANCISCO (Spain), J A SIMOEN (Belgium), D J VANDENBOSSCHE (Belgium), J F MAQUET (France), A T RUSSELL (USA), N J FERGUSON (Australia), A L MOSS-MORRIS (South Africa), R LECLERCQ (France), W H LEWIS (USA), A G F EDDIE (Australia), A J CARMICHAEL (GB), N N B ORDMAN (GB), D L POPE (GB), D JONES (GB), F VASCO COSTA (Portugal), H THOMAS (France), H K DALLY (GB), P A COX (GB)

J. H. W. NORTHFIELD (UK) REPORTER GENERAL

The Papers have been prepared by Authors from Australia, Belgium, Canada, Finland, France, Germany (F.R.), Japan, Netherlands, Spain, Sweden, United Kingdom, Union of Soviet Socialist Republics and the United States of America, and it can be seen that the views expressed are representative of a very wide international outlook. Some Papers cover the many aspects of cargo handling systems, whilst others refer to a specific trade or commodity where this may be a predominant feature of the sea borne trade of that particular country, but in most cases the Authors describe how changes in that trade have affected the design of the facility within the Port, or changes in vessel design.

Two of the Papers, those submitted by Canada and the United States of America, deal specifically with the Research and Development aspect of planning for present and future needs in port planning and management and on inland waterway systems, and how a particular problem has been investigated.

Papers have been prepared by Authors from the four corners of the Earth but the basic similarity in the problems experienced and the development of facilities to overcome these problems should be noted. That this is to be expected is not unusual since by its very nature, shipping is international and cargoes loaded in one port of the World have to be discharged in another. Therefore, compatibility at each end of the voyage is highly desirable.

The advent of unitised methods of handling cargo and, in particular the container, has meant that virtually the same type of facility has to be provided at each end of a voyage since containers are constructed to an International Standard (I.S.O). Generally, labour intensive operations are being replaced by mechanically orientated ones and this is particularly so in the industrialised nations where labour costs are very high. An increasing use of automation and programmed control is evident.

COMMENTS

1. GENERAL

Generally the ship owner sets the pace by his marine developments and terminal facilities have to be constructed to meet these requirements. It is difficult to see how this can be done otherwise. The cost of constructing facilities to handle larger ships and the cost of the larger ships themselves is very high and therefore it is necessary to ensure that a vessel spends as much of its life as possible at sea. This means that discharge and loading must take place as rapidly, and economically, as possible, and to this end efficient operation of ports is becoming increasingly important.

2. PRELIMINARY INVESTIGATION

Most of the Papers stress, and if not it is implied, that adequate research and analysis should be undertaken prior to the construction of a particular terminal or facility, and at least two of the Papers suggest, in detail, how this can be carried out.

It is recommended that this is one aspect of terminal and vessel design that could receive further attention, but at the same time such work must be based on practical data and design to give practical results.

3. COMPATIBILITY (OR STANDARDISATION)

Because of the international character of the sea borne trade, standardisation should be considered wherever possible. Standardisation may be too strong a term to use but what is suggested is a high degree of compatibility between port facilities. Without it the container 'revolution' would not have taken place, certainly not as we know it.

4. TRADE WITH DEVELOPING COUNTRIES

All Papers have been prepared by Authors from highly industrialised countries where the national wealth enables very expensive and sophisticated facilities to be considered. On the other hand, developing countries usually have far less resources available and the development of port facilities in these countries is conditioned by this fact. It is suggested that this should be borne in mind by those countries who seek to help by means of consultancy services, the supply of equipment or even the methods of trading. In offering any of these services it must be appreciated that "the coat must be cut according to the cloth".

5. RESEARCH

It is encouraging that all Papers mention these facts and point to the need to undertake adequate research in respect of traffic likely to be handled and the best way in which this operation can be carried out.

In recent years it has been evident that in certain areas of the world port facilities have been constructed, perhaps for very good national reasons, but without apparent regard for the type or volume of cargo to be handled or where that cargo will originate or where it will go.

In other words, ports have been designed without reference to cargo handling systems best suited to the traffic likely to pass through the ports.

6. STANDARDISATION

Because of the international character of shipping it is desirable – one can say essential, that shipowners, naval architects, port operators and engineers work to achieve a greater degree of compatability, or standardisation, as possible between their respective disciplines. To quote an example – we all know of the roll-on roll-off vessel that appears at a port, without any prior warning, and will not fit the bridge or shore ramp until makeshift arrangements have been carried out. The increasing trend towards unit loads, such as the container, roll-on roll-off and large bulk carriers makes consultation more and more important.

7. DEVELOPING NATIONS – AID TO

Several Authors have described facilities covering particular types of cargo handled in their own countries.

That these are appropriate to those countries cannot be denied, but when highly industrialised countries offer services to the developing nations it must be borne in mind that what is appropriate to one nation may not be suitable for a nation where industrial development is low, and the level and range of skills limited. It may not be desirable to reduce the manpower required by the installation of sophisticated equipment, or to provide facilities to give high throughput when the annual volume of cargo handled is low.

Therefore industrial nations should not seek to impose their own methods on developing nations, but should apply technology most appropriate to the situation.

8. ENERGY

The depletion of the worlds fossil fuels, on which all current economies are based, means that the remaining resources must be used as economically as possible. This is the more important until alternative types or sources of energy are developed. We have a duty to future generations not to waste these resources. Therefore research into the most economical ways of carrying cargo and loading and discharging vessels should take a high degree of priority in future design studies.

9. POLLUTION

Finally, the aspect of pollution control or protection of the environment must receive greater attention. This is discussed in a number of the Papers before you, and with the growth of industries producing dangerous products, this is very important.

The Paper by the Dutch Authors shows one possible solution to the problem, but once again continuing development on the control of the effects of pollution must continue.

PROPOSALS

Modern ports are increasingly extravagant in their use of land and we have seen this in the growth of container terminals in particular. At the same time to cope with the increased throughput of these modern terminals, it is essential that communications in the form of road, rail etc. are adequate and that there is no point in constructing a modern fast turn-round terminal if imports cannot be removed and exports received.

Although ship design and operations may set the pace, the provision of ships, ports and equipment should be considered as a single entity. More consultation must take place. By reducing his own costs the shipowner can require the provision of very expensive, and maybe unnecessary, port facilities, or port equipment. While this may be in his own interests it may not be so in the case of the community.

I believe it is the duty of all engineers to try to overcome these sectional interests and continuing consultation is one way of achieving this.

We live in a world of change and reluctantly even developing countries will have to accept that change is taking place. Therefore, they should seek to develop their facilities to meet this challenge.

SUMMARY

1. The introduction of the container and ro.ro operation ie. unit loads, and reduction in break bulk, and increase in size of vessel

has made ports constructed in the 19th Century largely redundant.

2. The introduction of heavy equipment ie. Fork Lift Truck, Straddle Carrier has brought about the need to rethink pavement design.

3. The introduction of fast and large bulk material handling facilities has introduced pollution problems that were not significant two or three decades ago.

4. The solution to these problems is compounded further by the energy crisis which has yet to be solved in the long term.

   Thus it can be seen that the solution to one problem invariably produces another and this long term research, is just as important as resolving the immediate problem.

DISCUSSION

V J DAVIES (UK)

I have read the paper from Australia by Mr. Ferguson on open sea terminals with interest because my company have recently completed a study followed by the design of a similar installation in Argentina. I would like to comment on the problem of predicting downtime due to wave action and its importance in site selection and jetty orientation, using the project in Argentina as an example.

The consultant's brief for the terminal in Argentina was to find a site and recommend a shiploading facility for the transport of limestone from a quarry in Patagonia to a new plant at San Antonio Oeste, some 580 km to the north.

Several sites were examined along this rocky and irregular coastline. Some sites had more natural protection than others but generally these would have been more expensive in terms of rock dredging and be less safe for navigation and be more restricted for expanding the port for use by larger ships. Clearly the open sea sites were only viable if the downtime due to wave action was not excessive because the cost of breakwaters would have been prohibitive.

Eventually an open sea location was chosen on a headland named Punta Alpat and this site is effectively unprotected from the east roughly around to south west.

The prevailing winds are from the west from which the site is well protected. However, south westerly winds blowing across the Gulf of St. Jorge generate waves that can be predicted, and these when combined with the observed heights of waves and swells from the east and south east give a wave rose for the Punta Alpat site.

It was assumed that ships could remain loading in waves up to 1½ metres provided they were from the head although the calculations were based on a maximum acceptable wave of 1 metre.

The jetty is orientated 20 degrees – 200 degrees north to ensure that ships may berth stemming the most frequent wave direction. This angle was also influenced by local navigation considerations.

Thus we arrived at the conclusion that, the downtime due to wave action is likely to be less than 20% for 15,000 tdw ships and this is satisfactory.

J S BALFOUR (UK)

As the representative of a port user and of an oil company involved internationally with the movement, reception and handling of oil and gas cargoes, I feel that I should state our case – as we in this industry see it – at this Congress. As responsible operators we have been and are continuing to be closely involved in developing and improving every aspect of oil and gas, and recently coal and dry bulk, cargo handling techniques and equipment.

Most of you who were present at the session on Monday morning will have heard the chairman refer to one of our "sister" oil companys as happening to have a good record in handling gas cargoes; I would like to take the opportunity of stating categorically that these things do not just happen. We have industry groups examining and working on all aspects of oil and gas handling techniques both on ship and ashore, and also in improving all aspects of ship to shore transfer or vice versa. These groups come under the umbrella of the Oil Companies International Marine Forum (OCIMF). I had the pleasure of being chairman of one of these meetings last week, here in Edinburgh, which was attended by over 40 representatives from oil companies and oil terminal operators from all over the Middle East and Europe. At these meetings we discuss our operating problems and review the progress of our work groups which, amongst other items, are preparing specifications for ships' mooring equipment, oil transfer loading arms, mooring ropes, hoses, terminal procedures and check lists, to mention just a few items.

J CHATTAWAY (UK)

I would make only a few points which all refer to financial considerations.

1. The role of the port design engineer is to design the most economic practical solution to enable the port operator to carry on his business with the least possible capital cost and running cost burden. This gives the port operator a better chance to make a profit.

2. The port operator (or his advisers) and the port design engineer (who may be the same organisation) should calculate jointly the cost of structures combined with the capital cost and running cost of handling equipment. For example, it is not necessarily better financially to use a relatively cheap fork-lift truck, requiring larger and stronger areas of paving to handle containers, instead of a more expensive machine that requires less space and a less strong (and therefore less costly) paving.

3. It has been said (in the draft conclusion issued today) that where the shipbuilders go the port operator must follow and provide

the shore facilities required — at the cost of the port operator. For example, as many members of PIANC, the Reporter General and I know only too well the immense variety of RoRo ship's ramps has caused considerable difficulties and cost to port operators. The ship operators and their ship designers may not have fully appreciated that this must add cost to the ship operators' own operations. Perhaps they will conform to the 150 recommendations for shore ramps due to be published — after some sometimes strong international discussions — in draft form in a few months' time.

4. Earlier in this session, the Chairman — in an effort to inject controversy into the discussions — referred to engineers as "devious". "Ingenious" certainly — very like the French word for "engineer" — but most of the time engineers should be straightforward in their quest to produce the most economic overall solution to any situation.

T KERISEL (FRANCE)

These reports give examples of terminals for coal freighters exceeding 150,000 tdw or container ships of 3,000 TEU.

Two comments on these expensive and sophisticated facilities:

1. Even in the industrial and supposedly affluent countries, ports need rather to adapt certain installations so as to make the maximum use of existing equipment and limit the amount of their investments. By way of example, we may quote the case of the coal installations at Rouen. Situated, like Paris, on the Seine, Rouen — 120 km from the sea — is the 4th French seaport in terms of overall tonnage. In 1980, the coal traffic at Rouen represented about 4 Mt out of a total traffic exceeding 22 Mt. This position means a saving in land transport, but the draught at Rouen is limited to 11 m. So as to maintain and develop Rouen's coal traffic, it was made clear to the French coal importers that it was in their interest to receive at Rouen not only ships of 40,000 tdw fully laden but also ships of 80,000 tdw or 120,000 tdw which had been lightened in a coastal port, Le Havre or Dunkirk, so as to bring to Rouen cargoes of 50,000 t and 70,000 respectively. The saving on land transport for the coal brought to Rouen is greater than the slight increase in maritime freight. In addition to British and Polish coal, Rouen thus succeeded in receiving in 1980 nearly 1 Mt of coal from the United States in ships of 80,000 tdw. And this required, at a very limited cost, only the adaptation of 2 existing quays by placing there cranes with greater off-wharf span and a greater draught.

2. As regards container traffic, there is still room for terminals other than terminals for integral container ships of 3,000 TEU. This is the case at Rouen, which has a substantial traffic with the developing countries of the west coast of Africa and the Indian Ocean, since more than 2 ships a day leave Rouen for those destinations. For this type of traffic, Rouen has installed a mixed terminal for integral container ships of 1,500 TEU, but which also handles conventional ships and semi-container ships. And Rouen has limited the cost of this terminal by equipping it with container gantries rather than the most sophisticated gantries. These container gantries, while having a very good output, have more limited geometrical characteristics, as well as polyvalent cranes of 25 tons which can work on the automatic spreader. We have thus reached nearly 1 Mt of containers/year and this traffic is growing by 40% annually.

These two examples of adaptation of equipment, rather than creation of large sophisticated terminals, also show that estuary ports located far inland have lost none of their chances in maritime competition.

M ENRIQUEZ FRANCISCO (SPAIN)

First I am going to refer to the eighth figure of the Spanish paper (page 499) which is wrong, because the text says that the quay is designed with an earth covered surface. The correct description is a slab with L shape and a thickness of earth of about one and a half metres. So — it is possible to excavate and to incorporate easily new facilities in the ground. Of course, it is not an original solution, but I want to emphasize the flexibility.

Secondly, the great part of the paper refers to the ro-ro traffic which is growing dramatically. It is easy to provide port facilities for this traffic without tide like the Spanish ports in the Mediterranean Sea. But this service is not without problem. In order to accelerate the manoeuvres of berthing and unberthing, because the rapidity of the dispatch of the ship is essential in this traffic, the ships use the bow thrusters (jets) and lateral propellers like a brake or like an impeller.

If the quays were not designed for such a use, for example, in the case of old facilities remodelled for ro-ro traffic, the jets cause damage.

a) On the surface of old concrete blocks.

b) On the bank which serves as foundation for the block wall.

The impact of the jets, increased by the angular effect, is so strong that it is able to remove stones of one ton weight and produce very large holes under the wall. The solution we have applied, among others, is to refill the holes with cement bags or pumping concrete and to build a slab of pumped concrete over the bank, diminishing in this case the depth of the quay.

Logically there is another solution: to forbid such a manoeuvre, but it seems that this solution is to try to solve in an administrative way a problem that must have an engineering treatment.

I wonder whether, as at the Leningrad Congress, the French and Russian papers treated the problem of ground erosion by propellers in inland navigation, there is also experience about these phenomena in your ports, solutions adopted and if there were special designs of the ro-ro facilities to prevent them.

I should be grateful for any information about this problem.

J A SIMOEN (BELGIUM)

With reference to our paper concerning the development programme for the port of Zeebrugge on the Belgian coast. I wish to give a brief supplementary explanation about the constraints which limit, on site, the possibilities of extending the port. These constraints call for a great deal of imagination and flexibility on our port in determining the internal lay-out of the port and will oblige us to be strictly selective in choosing the types of traffic to become established there.

This flexibility has already become apparent in the recent and quite favourable evolution of the port within its present limits, until such time as the major extension, now in course of execution, becomes available.

The Reporter General made special reference in his report to the subject of these constraints limiting the extension of the port of Zeebrugge, but he attributed them to the proximity of population centres. This is only partially true, and I should therefore like to add some words of explanation about these constraints. As for the inner harbour, it has not been possible to make it penetrate further south in view of the proximity of Bruges, a town of great historical value.

To the east of the feeder canals forming the limit of the inner harbour, the development plan provides for the maintenance of a green belt, given over to agriculture, which will act as a buffer zone between the port and the seaside resort of Knokke-Heist-Le Zoute.

To the west of the Baudouin canal, any extension of the port is out of the question owing to the presence of an agricultural area with a village and structures of great historical value. As for the outer harbour, a glance at the plan will show that a major extension along the coast, i.e., in the transversal direction, is impossible because of the presence of the tourist and seaside resorts of Zeebrugge-Plage to the west and Knokke-Heist-Le Zoute to the east. This is why the new western breakwater commences at a distance of only 150 m from the former mole, which means an absolute minimum for the access roads and railways. The start of the new eastern breakwater has been located just next to the built-up area of Knokke-Heist-Le Zoute, in such a way that the tourist establishments on the sea front remain untouched.

Lastly, there is the limit of the new outer harbour seawards. In other words, how was the length of extension of the new outer harbour determined?

This length of extension is the result of a thorough study in which 3 main factors were taken into consideration, i.e., the hydraulic factor, the nautical factor and the economic factor. It is the hydraulic factor which played a decisive role in the final choice of the extension length.

In the course of the study, we contemplated several lengths and forms of extension of the outer harbour. But as the outer harbour of Zeebrugge is situated at the eastern tip of the Belgian coast forming an integral part of the Scheldt estuary, the principal constraint for the seaward extension stems from the concern not to upset the hydraulic regime of this estuary and to limit the increases in current speeds caused by the narrowing of the estuary to 10% in general and to a maximum of 15% locally.

The zones, including navigable channels of an international character, in which these constraints are imposed and which will be respected after the execution of the selected extension of the outer harbour, have very precise limits.

D J VANDENBOSSCHE (BELGIUM)

The topic I will refer to is "how to place an outer port and assess its capabilities for unknown cargo handling techniques and even unknown ships". I presume that many colleague port planners and designers have to deal with this problem SII 3 (p. 403 Fig. 5). This is certainly the situation in Zeebrugge.

One has to bear in mind that the outer port extension master plan has been defined in Autumn 1977 and finally adopted by the government in June 1979. In 1985, as the outer port breakwater will be finished, only the LNG terminal in the east outer port will be operational. This means that the western outer port cannot be operational e.g., container trade, before 1990. On the other hand, from the physical constraint pointed out in the paper and by Mr; Simoen earlier it may be clear that whatever determines the seaward extension, the actual development schemes do not permit future expansion. In this respect no firm decision has been made and has to be taken about the Western harbour internal layout. The assessment of the outer port capabilities is done in an engineer's way from given physical port data, present and short term shipping prospects and comparable facilities offered by other ports in the Le Havre – Hamburg range. It is perhaps not a bright method, but a very useful one indeed, a prognosis of future development for a medium sized port like Zeebrugge only on the basis of mathematical cargo flow models is highly risk prone, due to the geographical location of the port and existing and assigned trades. In fact, the western outer harbour is well situated for transhipments where speed and high efficiency are dominating factors (for example, ro-ro and container trade) should the area protected by the western breakwater stay unreclaimed or become partly reclaimed the water surface will be fairly calm. This means that, for example, ship to ship transfer like LASH or SEABEE traffic with barges sailing up the River Scheldt is possible. If the whole area should be converted to land based cargo transhipment, a renovation of existing mole may be considered for general cargo trade or ferry terminals. Apart from the area demand, or renovation of the existing harbour infrastructure, the majority of the 405 HA in the west outer harbour are well suited to container and ro-ro trade. The main limitation is the available back-up land area. Should one dock be planned the overall terminal area per metre quay wall is approximately 700 metres squared per metre. If two docks, with the northern for specific trades, the ratio decreases to approximately 400 metres squared per metre. As stated before, it is interesting to compare these figures with other existing and future container terminals in the Le Havre – Hamburg range (p. 404 Fig. 6).

1. It would be of interest to hear from compilers of Fig. 6 whether these are the results of a detailed process plan of container handling or are resulting from a general port planning procedure and were areas offered to port clients.

2. The implementation of the outer port extension scheme is going on (p. 405 Fig. 7)

- planning and design started in September 1976.
- the work harbour and auxiliary facilities construction started from mid-January 1978 and were commissioned in 1979.
- the real "kick-off" of the harbour construction has been the start of construction of the south-east breakwater in June 1979. That peninsula is now almost finished.
- the remaining breakwater construction will start soon and will be commissioned in the Autumn of 1982.
- the western breakwater root section was started in September 1979 and can be finished to chainage 1050 metres in November of this year.
- the foundations and bottom protected works in the alignment of the remaining breakwater section have been in hand from September 1979. The north east and south west sections have been finished.

3. More information concerning the Zeebrugge Port Extension Scheme will be found in the paper and the latest issue of the PIANC bulletin (volume 3/1980).

J F MAQUET (FRANCE)

My comments are based on experience at the port of Le Havre, at the mouth of the Seine.

Two major problems arise for a modern port:

- the first, about which much has already been said, is that of space, which is a rare and valuable commodity,
- the second, of which little has been said, is that of labour, also valuable but quite often abundant.

I would give an example relating to the general cargo traffic at the port of Le Havre.

- In 1975, container traffic, at less than 200,000 TEU, was largely equivalent to the conventional traffic.
- In 1980, container traffic, at over 500,000 TEU, was more than 3 times as much as conventional traffic.

Surface requirements have been more than doubled. Labour requirements have been halved.

On the first point – space – one cannot but advise ports located in countries where there is still space to reserve large areas for the ports, but for the industrial countries and certain densely populated countries (India, Indonesia), this will be impossible.

On the second point – labour – we can reduce the impact of containerization by arranging for the dockers to perform other tasks, but this requires training.

This leads me to make two suggestions for the conclusions:

1. Research and analysis in the field of design of port equipment should pay attention to the need for facilities and processes which will make it possible to save not only energy but also space.

2. Research and analysis should deal with labour problems, which will be of two types:

- reduction in manpower employed on handling tasks
- training workers for the new facilities and activities.

A T ROSSELLI (USA)

Concerning the planning of port facilities in developing nations, I would like to tell you about an experience I had recently in India where I went to consult on the planning of a port at Mhava-Shera, a proposed new port needed to relieve congestion at the Port of Bombay.

I approached this assignment with the thought that a principal concern would be to marry the concept of modern technology with the problems of Bombay's large surplus labour force. To my surprise, I learned from meetings with high Transportation officials that they were not in the least bit interested in labour intensive techniques. They believe that they have an unusual opportunity with the new port to develop one of the most modern ports in the world. The manner in which it was put to me was "we don't want to think of this as an Indian port – rather as a modern port that happens to be in India."

The point is that all generalizations (i.e. labour in transit, cargo handling methods should be used in developing countries) have their exceptions.

A consultant can only advise and seek to persuade. In the final analysis however, the aspirations of the client will dictate the result.

N J FERGUSON (AUSTRALIA)

One aspect that could be stressed in our conclusions is that the shipping of low cost, but often high volume, raw commodities, often may not justify conventional harbour solutions.

No one denies the advantage of an in-harbour sheltered berth. But for large vessels, the cost of dredging or breakwater protection, or both, becomes prohibitively expensive, unless coupled with many trades and very large total port throughputs.

For bulk commodities, alternative solutions exist, such as going offshore. This compromise involves balancing considerable savings in capital cost against some loss of berth availability offshore. Typically for studies in N.S.W. a 200,000 DWT ship would involve say \$150 m. offshore and 3-4 years construction period, compared to \$300 - \$400 m. for inshore rock dredging and breakwater entrance, coupled with a longer construction period, say 5-6 years minimum.

Similarly, in developing countries, the economics should be carefully studied, as mentioned by our Chairman and Reporter General. Often low cost solutions are possible, using simple facilities for what are relatively low cargo throughputs. This should not prevent flexibility in a master plan to permit growth and throughput.

As an example, I would refer to the offshore island concept for handling salt off the Atlantic Brazilian coast. This was constructed during the mid 70's and is some 14 km. offshore, at the edge of the shallow continental shelf. It is fed by lighters from the shore, to prepare cargoes for ocean bulk ships.

The original idea had been to dredge a channel to the shore for a conventional berth. Not only was the dredging costly, but the channels could well have been unstable with respect to maintenance.

The alternative of the offshore island at the edge of deep water was less costly and carried the considerable social benefit of not putting the lighter trade out of business. I understand that these lighters had previously loaded the vessels in a protracted fashion by a direct shuttle service.

Two points raised by Mr. Davies.

1. Mr. Davies requested information concerning wave heights for loading bulk vessels offshore. At Punta Colorada, also on the Patagonia coast, I believe 30,000 - 50,000 DWT vessels have been successfully loaded in waves of up to 2 - 2½ m. This is a multiple orientation berth, where the vessel can be headed into the prevailing sea.

2. The remarks in my paper p. 383 regarding the dominant effect of waves on offshore piled structures, apply to large ships with water depths of 17 - 21 m. These depths involve design waves of about 15 m on the N.S.W. Australian coast.

As a final point, more use of research and co-operation is required at the engineer/mariner interface for the berthing of large vessels at offshore bulk loading or unloading berths. Often a ship can stay moored and continue to load in much higher swells at a suitably designed berth, whereas the limitation would be in actually berthing the vessel.

A L MOSS-MORRIS (SOUTH AFRICA)

Certain of the speakers have referred to the advisability of treating developing countries differently from the developed countries when considering provision of new cargo handling facilities, in developing countries. As a representative of a newly developed country I must differ most strongly with this view point. If when planning new facilities the existing under-developed condition of the country is taken as governing the type of design, the effect will be to keep that country permanently relegated to second class status. Harbour facilities are planned with a minimum twenty year life and therefore if this view is allowed to hold sway then as planners, your clients facility will be about 25 years out of date when it is commissioned. This will lead to strong resentment on the part of the client.

A more realistic attitude is that which has happened in regard to the change over to containerisation in South Africa and Singapore. Whereas container terminals were operating at the end of the sixties in many European and American ports, the change over to container terminals in South Africa took place when the next port expansions took place in the 1970's and these dedicated quays were taken into operation in 1977 and have rapidly taken over from the break bulk berths. In Singapore general cargo berths without container cranes were planned and constructed in the early nineteen seventies.

However the owner had the foresight during the course of the contract to insist on a change over to container cranes and has since been building nothing but container handling berths at an ever increasing tempo.

Do not relegate the developing countries to permanent second class status by planning and designing out of date facilities because of the apparent low labour costs prevalent today in those countries.

R LECLERCQ (FRANCE)

I should like to make a brief comment on a very general question, that of the opposition between engineers and financiers.

I feel sure that our Chairman did not wish to object to the principle of profitability calculations, but to the way in which they are often carried out. Profitability calculations are a very difficult matter when they relate to infrastructures with a long life. The first difficulty encountered is that of assessing the benefits and costs in the distant future. A second difficulty is the choice of a proper rate of discounting so as to bring the costs and benefits — expressed in constant terms — back to the original date. This rate must be in direct relation to the real rate of interest existing on the financial market. It must also be in direct relation to the rate of development of production.

In my opinion — but this is only a personal view — investments should not be eliminated *a priori* once their rate of profitability exceeds — say — 3%, provided that the benefits are not over-estimated.

The purpose of my remarks was simply to combat the idea that economic profitability calculations are useless.

W H LEWIS (USA)

1. Port planning and construction in developing countries must consider the technology of port operators which apply to other ports. The technology may be shown in its charge to the developing countries, but will eventually follow the experience in development countries.

2. The same principles should apply to the planning of port facilities in developing countries as apply to comparably sized ports in developed countries.

3. In projects being financed by international banking institutions, the consultant must satisfy the expectations of the country client and the lending bank. The country client does not have to be persuaded to consider the future requirements.

4. Endorse attempts to encourage participation by Developing countries in the affairs of PIANC. This will result in realistic consideration of their problems and views. Treat these representations as full partners in the port industry.

A G F EDDIE (AUSTRALIA)

I refer to the subject of dry-bulk cargo handling at offshore terminals in exposed sea conditions.

I endorse Mr. Ferguson's remarks that large capital cost savings are possible by constructing such terminals offshore rather than in newly constructed sheltered harbours. This is done at the expense of some loss of berth availability – the question is how much. Mr. Davies had asked what is the limiting wave height for continuance of cargo handling at an offshore berth. The question really is not one of wave height but of ship motion. We have adequate means by mathematical or physical modelling of estimating ship motion in six degrees of freedom, given the wave climate. However, we have no clear definition of how much ship motion will cause cargo handling to cease. This is especially important for unloading which is much more difficult at an offshore berth than loading. This is the real gap in our knowledge of cargo handling at offshore dry bulk terminals. and Mr. Eddie asked if this might be referred to in the recommendations.

On a different subject, I would like to mention that coal-fired ships have recently been reintroduced by some Australian operators. So far these are confined to the coal carrying trade and will experience no problems in bunkering. However, if the trend continues into other types of ships, we should perhaps be careful that in planning new terminals and cargo handling facilities that we do not preclude the possibility of the later addition of bunkering facilities for coal-fired ships.

A J CARMICHAEL (UK)

You may be interested to know the World Bank's definition of financial viability for ports. It is that the port establish tariffs for its services to ships and cargoes which will produce revenues sufficient to cover all operating and maintenance costs and depreciation, with the residual income providing a satisfactory rate of return on properly valued net fixed assets in operation.

The specified rate of return is designed to produce sufficient revenue to meet working capital and debt service requirements and to make a contribution towards the ports' capital expenditures. Normally these required returns have been in the range of 6-8%. This situation is not likely to be achieved when the first ship sails into the new facility. Losses could well be generated in the months or even years following the opening. But, on long term, financial viability can be achieved. The governing permit for development is economic rather than financial. A port may have to take an initial short-run financial loss to achieve national economic benefits. This point should be made clearly at the highest levels as national financial assistance may be required by the port in the short term. Flexible phased development of the Transport System, as a whole, is often the appropriate answer.

Lastly, I would wish to take exception to what I understood Mr. Davies to recommend, i.e., the saving of money on site borings – especially those more expensive offshore borings. In my opinion, the engineer responsible for a project must specify and insist on the number of borings and the extent of site investigation essential for the project – to accept otherwise is to invite disaster.

N N B ORDMAN (UK)

The Chairman intervened to draw attention to several implications of the recent cargo handling "revolution" in the fields of politics, economic and planning. The cost of modern port developments is so great that it generally falls to governments or municipalities to finance them. Thus, more than ever, port development is in the public sector and the subject of regional or national policy.

Modern ports require large land areas. In some countries this is increasingly creating difficulties, prompting the greater use of reclamation. The idea of the off-shore island has been extensively explored and we may expect to see it widely exploited in coming years. The road and railway approaches to ports also require a great deal of land. This "land-hunger" may create serious land-use planning problems with sensitive political implications. Their solution may require legislation and it is important that they be foreseen at the earliest possible time if they are to be successfully overcome.

The economic and financial valuation of port projects raises the question as to what is the appropriate discount rate in "discounted cash flow" calculations. The application of the "cost/benefit analysis" approach is also problematical because ports are frequently regional or national economic generators and their main justification may be in this fact. Hence the benefits accrue over a wide area outside the port; many of them are of a social nature and difficult to quantify. It is, of course, the case that port managements must apply strict financial disciplines but it is doubtful if most ports can be considered as normal "commercial" enterprises.

D L POPE (UK)

Despite container and ro-ro revolution, traffic in breakbulk general cargo will continue, particularly through small ports, and the ports of small countries, with insufficient traffic volumes to justify containerisation. Moreover, the nature of the residual breakbulk cargo is changing viz – rapid increases in unit levels – preponderance of special types of cargo unsuitable for containerisation.

Should general cargo berths be provided with quay cranes, and if so, of what capacity? Many ports lavishly equipped with quay cranes seldom use them and we find that the cranes and their rails inconveniently interrupt the free flow of apron traffic. Other ports without quay cranes find that mobile cranes are not suitable for removing heavy unit loads from ships' holds.

I suggest that the forum of PIANC, where shipowners, port operators and port planners are represented, should investigate the relative economics for providing heavy lifting equipment for unitised general cargo on the ship or the quayside.

D JONES (UK)

I believe that Port Authorities must work closely with Pilots to obtain the best possible service.

As an example, I would like to describe how an excellent pilotage service was introduced and operated at Port Talbot Harbour in the Severn Estuary, South Wales.

This British Transport Docks Board Harbour which was designed for ore carriers of 100,000 tons dead weight replaced an impounded dock which could only accommodate ships of 10,000 tons maximum size.

Before the harbour was opened in 1970 a 50,000 ton ship was chartered for a short period to give the pilots, who had no experience of handling ships bigger than 10,000 tons, practise in bringing the ship into and out of the harbour and berthing and unberthing it. When the harbour was opened for commercial business the pilots were able to handle 100,000 ton ships with no technical problems.

After some years of incident free operation the possibility of handling 200,000 ton ships part discharged to a draught of 47 feet was considered. Before a decision was taken on whether to admit these vessels which would have a displacement of about 150,000 tons, it was decided to monitor the berthing of ships in the harbour over a period of about 1 year. Equipment was installed to measure the approach velocity of berthing ships, to record it and also to display the information to the Pilots as it was being recorded.

Following this, the pilots were able to improve their berthing techniques in a way which would not have been possible without this aid.

I therefore suggest that if PIANC decides to foster an interest into the efficiency of pilotage services that the views of pilots should be obtained as to the kind of equipment which Port Authorities should instal so as to allow the best possible service to be obtained.

F VASCO COSTA (PORTUGAL)

The use of sophisticated equipment in remote locations poses acute problems of maintenance. This is specially the case when the equipment comes from different makers in different countries and spare parts and skilled personnel are difficult to obtain at short notice.

H THOMAS (FRANCE)

My remarks follow on logically from those of Professor Vasco Costa. The development of new packaging methods for goods leads to the design of more and more sophisticated equipment relying largely on automation and electronics. Likewise, the requirement that these devices should have flexibility of use also tends to make their design more complex.

It so happens that port equipment is generally subjected to severe operating conditions (meteorology, hygrometry, atmospherics, dust) which render these automatic devices vulnerable, unless extremely strict maintenance is practised. On the other hand, the technical reliability of this equipment is a basic requirement for the port users, more particularly the shipowner who is very sensitive about the turn-round of his ship and the costs when it is out of action.

My proposed recommendation therefore concerns the need for bearing in mind constantly, in the relations between port authorities and designers of equipment, this requirement of reliability of the plant in operation in harsh conditions, as well as the absolute necessity for an operating and maintenance personnel training policy that is adapted to the growing complexity of the equipment.

H K DALLY (UK)

1. I think the port planning function should be separated from equipment especially when discussing the needs of developing countries. In my view ports in developing countries should be planned on modern lines, but the equipment should not necessarily incorporate the very latest technology. In this respect I agree with the views put forward by M. Marquet and M. Thomas of the French Delegation. Electronic controls and automated equipment can be difficult to maintain by ports in developed countries such as the UK. This is because the maintenance tradesmen usually only have the skills of garage mechanics. Electronically controlled equipment does not necessarily improve performance. One UK port had electronically controlled cranes which were difficult to maintain and as a result the cranes had a poor availability record. Eventually the electronic equipment was replaced by conventional electrical controls and this resulted in improved operational performance and reduced downtime.

2. Handling performance is determined by labour relations and not advanced technology. The

British National Ports Council recently carried out a survey of container handling performance. It was found that the handling rate varied from less than 10 to 32 containers per gross hour. This was for terminals using similar equipment. The point is that motivation of the labour force and human relations are more important than having the latest technological devices.

3. Much has been said about modern ports requiring considerably greater land areas than was previously the case. The main reason for this is because of greater throughputs. In fact modern cargo handling methods make better use of land by using it more intensively. A conventional general cargo berth will process about 15,000 tons per acre per year whereas a deep sea container berth will handle 40 to 50,000 tons per acre per year. Short-sea berths with a progression of small ships arriving at regular invervals can process up to 100,000 tons per acre per year.

P A COX (UK)

I wish to refer to a matter mentioned by the Chairman at the beginning of the session but which has not been subsequently discussed. There is the acquisition or reservation of land for port facilities and land access routes. I will give three examples to illustrate the necessity for this.

Many years ago the Port of London Authority reserved land at Tilbury to allow further development of the dock facilities there, although at that time there was no specific need. This land is now being used extensively for the deeper draft container and other vessels now in service which could not be accommodated in the dock systems closer to the city centre. These latter facilities are now disused or going out of existence.

In recent years it was proposed to construct a combined port and airport at Maplin on the north side of the outer Thames River Estuary. The area did not present a problem as it was to be on reclaimed land; However the land access routes to London would have been through an extensive developed urban area. Access routes were earmarked in the preliminary plans, but I believe there would have been serious environmental problems in developing these routes if the project had been proceeded with. If this had occurred then the viability of the port and airport facility would have been in jeopardy. It is probably right to say that the requirements for major deepwater facilities which were proposed for Maplin could not have been foreseen, say 25 years ago. Changes in ship drafts and cargo handling facilities are likely not to change as much in the future as they have done in the last generation and so it should therefore be possible to avoid the type of problem which I have outlined as regards Maplin. This will however require planners to take a wide view of potential future requirements.

Foresight in reserving land was also shown by the Port of Calcutta. Many years ago land for port-development was reserved at Haldra, in the Hooghly River downstream of Calcutta. This is now being used for the new port facilities at Haldra. Without this reservation the current development would have been difficult.

D J VANDENBOSSCHE (BELGIUM)

Mr. Kerisel of the Rouen Port Authority has been stressing the aspect that even so-called "small draft" ports can normally compete in a fairly good manner. We are as consultants involved not only in the Zeebrugge Port Extension, but also in the renovation and expansion schemes in the Port of Ghent.

The existing draft of the Ghent harbour is 60,000 tdw or better approximately 13.50 m. water depth. The Port of Ghent is situated about 80 km. inland via the western Scheld Estuary and the Ghent Terneuzen ocean shipping canal. Due to the good connections by water, road and railway systems to the natural hinterland, the Port of Ghent has been able, up to now, fairly well to withstand the rush to deeper draft.

This is an introduction to an amendment I wish to formulate to the draft conclusions.

Under point 1, I would suggest to add "...... and compatibility with the cargo traffic chain as a whole". In this respect I am thinking of dry bulk cargo as coal and ore.

I thought with there only being two examples of inland situated ocean ports, it seems to be well established that the elements – other than ships and port facilities are playing an important part in the concept.

CONCLUSIONS

1. It is important that the planning and construction of ports be preceded by adequate research and project analysis.

2. These preliminary activities should have regard regard, inter alia, to:

   (i) the need for compatibility within the transportation system as a whole, and as between different ports and different countries;

   (ii) the fact that although it is desirable that port facilities in developing countries as elsewhere in the world should be planned to modern standards, there are often real problems in maintaining and making proper use of advanced plant and equipment;

   (iii) the concept of "appropriate technology";

   (iv) the need for energy economy;

   (v) environmental considerations;

   (vi) land-used policy taking into account the land needed not only for the port installations but also for landward access in the immediate and long terms;

   (vii) national or regional economic and social implications.

3. It is to be expected that ship design and operations will continue to set the pace to

which the providers of port facilities must respond. However, there is still a need for more consultation and cooperation between those responsible for the construction, navigation and management of ships on the one hand and for the planning and operating of port installations on the other.

MARITIME PORTS AND SEAWAYS

SECTION II — SUBJECT 4

Design and construction of port facilities and arrangement of quay platforms intended for heavy loads on soft ground using new techniques

Thursday 14 May 1981

Chairman:	*N N B ORDMAN (UK)* *Noel Ordman and Associates Ltd*
Vice Chairman:	*T KANHO (Japan)* *Technical Director, Bureau of Ports and Harbours, Tokyo*
Reporter General:	*G P MARTIN (UK)* *T F Burns and Partners, Hove*
Secretary:	*P LACEY (UK)* *Ove Arup and Partners Ltd, London*
Asst. Secretary:	*Miss M-M DANEELS (Belgium)* *Secrétaire AIPCN Secrétariat Générale, Brussels*

Speakers

A J JIMENEZ-SALAS (Spain), D A BARENDSEN (The Netherlands), E BARATONO (Italy), G MATTEOTTI (Italy), M LOEWY (UK), N N B ORDMAN (UK), P COUPRIE (France), F IRWIN-CHILDS (UK), J de NEKKER (The Netherlands), P G R BARLOW (UK), J L DAWSON (UK), A L MOSS-MORRIS (South Africa), H D HOEFT (FRG), J F MAQUET (France), E SERRANO (Spain), E LACKNER (FRG)

G. P. MARTIN (UK) REPORTER GENERAL

The problem of structures on soft ground was raised specifically as long ago as 1961 at the 20th Congress under Subject I of Section II, (sub-head e) but to judge from the General Report, the contributors of papers preferred to avoid this difficult subject. The Reporter General of that day drew attention to "the need for procurement of more complete sea-bed information by utilising to the full, the latest principles in soil mechanics as applied to coastal areas", and indeed his conclusion was formally adopted by the Congress.

By the time of the 21st Congress, the problem of soft ground had become worthy of a whole subject to itself (S II - 6, Ports and maritime structures built in soft ground with special reference to the need for increased depths), and 12 countries contributed interesting papers. The Reporter General of the day felt that "the construction of maritime structures in soft ground is a problem of great complexity" and that "it would be hazardous to formulate specific conclusions". Indeed the only conclusion that the Congress felt able to adopt was that "the papers and the discussion provide a useful increase in the documentation on the subject".

During the 15 years that have ensued, the subject has lain, not explicitly discussed at Congress, quietly gathering energy for a new airing at the 25th Congress 1981.

The very nature of coastlines has always meant that ports with good ground have been the exception rather than the rule, but the continuous development of world trade has obviously led to the using up of any better ground and to the situation where new ports, and particularly port extensions, have had to be founded in areas of poorer and poorer ground.

Fortunately, along with this process, technology has been developing also, and the fields of Soil Mechanics (now grown to the status of Geotechnics), Instrumentation, Computing, and Applied Mechanics have greatly expanded to help in the battle to keep building ports on ground that would have been thought impossible in earlier days.

From the papers submitted to this Congress it can be readily seen that large strides have been made in the techniques of site investigation in coastal areas. Comprehensive instrumentation and data processing for monitoring behaviour of actual structures is described by a number of the authors and the technique of Finite Element Analysis of a structure and its foundation soil has been increasingly applied. Computer techniques for slip circle analysis and earth pressures are discussed in several of the papers. Advanced techniques of mathematical analysis have been applied to the pavement and foundation soils of paved areas in ports.

Innovative techniques of construction and soil improvement are presented, ranging from precast berth wall units weighing 360 tonnes (Australia) to buoyant or semi-buoyant foundations (U.K.) and deep (under water) cement-soil stabilization (Japan) to induced seismic activity for soil consolidation (France).

TOPICS FOR DISCUSSION

Your Reporter General suggests that this most interesting and wide ranging set of papers include many subjects that warrant further discussion. It would be of assistance therefore if the authors could enlarge on the following to assist in the general discussions.

Australia. A description of the method of handling and placing the 360 tonne units would be most instructive in view of the great saving of construction time apparently achieved. It would also be interesting to hear if the untied crane rails have been fully satisfactory.

France. The reasons for selecting for trials and apparent ultimate rejection of the "sparker" technique would assist generally in discussion on seismic techniques for soil consolidation.

Germany (D.F.) An enlargement of the statement that similar tests could be applicable to systems other than dolphins would be of general advantage.

Germany (F.R.) Any information which could be given with respect to comparative costs of the quays described would add to the value of the paper.

Italy. The assertion that "during the design phase no investment gives a better reward than high technology Geotechnics" certainly warrants further discussion.

Japan. The unfortunate accidents to the monitoring instrumentation of the soil/structure seems such a common occurrence that a discussion of its causes and prevention would be productive. Any further experience with the "Deep Mixing Method" would also be of interest.

Netherlands. Further details of the modified vibro-compaction method barge in use on the huge Oosterschelde Storm Barrier project, its success and economics, would promote discussion on these techniques generally.

Poland. The explanation of the method of extracting the Penesonde would complete the description which could generate discussion on other new methods of site investigation.

Spain. The "cyclic compaction" technique used is of great interest and could, with profit, be further discussed.

U.K. A deeper look at the design and use of buoyant or semi-buoyant monoliths using diaphragm walling would be of general interest to promote discussion.

U.S.A. The study of full scale models of soft ground problems; and how they are financed, are of special interest.

U.S.S.R. The tests on large scale models showing modification of current theoretical predictions of earth pressures due to local loading are interesting and warrant further discussion.

I think you will agree that most of the authors of the papers presented have closely conformed to the subject as defined and that we have indeed been favoured with descriptions of new and interesting techniques in this field of Engineering.

I would, therefore, like to congratulate them all and to thank them for teaching me, at least, a great deal — I hope you all feel the same way and have learnt something too. Although the papers cover a wide range of projects, I understand that it is my task to attempt to find a conclusion or perhaps to define a modern trend in the solution to the problem of building structures in soft ground.

It would appear, Mr. Chairman, that we are running out of good sites on which to build harbour structures. A number of papers mentioned this fact. Perhaps it would be more accurate to state that soft ground conditions are being found wherever new structures are required. The problem is, of course, compounded because of the deeper drafts required for quays and because the loads being applied are heavier, particularly with the increase in container traffic.

May we for a moment consider the options which are open to Engineers faced with the design of a structure on a site consisting of soft soil:-

1. One would look at the possibility of transferring the loads to a lower stratum which was capable of supporting the loads. I refer, of course, to piles of some form but these become increasingly larger and more expensive as the depth increases.

2. The engineer can design the structure to be as light as possible using new materials or techniques to limit as far as possible the loads which impinge on the soft soil such as semi-floatation.

3. The engineer can attempt artificially to change the properties of the soft soil in some way to improve its load carrying capacity.

In reading the papers for the second time, it became clear to me that the tendency appears to be that the third option is being favoured; that is, changing the properties of the soil rather than designing the structure to suit the difficult conditions. Now I realise that this is an oversimplification but, to obtain a conclusion from such a wide range of ideas, must inevitably be a simplification.

Shall we, then, briefly look at some of the methods used for changing the nature of the soil which are available and have been described in the paper.

For convenience I have divided them into four groups:-

1. The Replacement Methods
2. The Stabilisation Methods
3. The Consolidation or Compaction Methods
4. The Reinforcement Methods

I am aware that in some cases it is difficult to place them accurately in these categories, but let me try.

1. The method of changing the properties of a soft soil by removing it and replacing it with good granular soil was carried out by:-

   Australia — combined with the large precast concrete cantilever wall.

   Germany (F.R.) — in conjunction with the high sheet piled walls;

   Italy — combined with a breakwater construction.

   USA — one of various proposals for the quay proposed.

2. The second group involving stabilisation of the existing soil was included in the papers from:-

   France — sand stabilised with extra fines related to a pavement foundations.

   Japan — 'Deep mixing method' — most interesting proposal for a variety of uses and could be a major contribution if it is developed further.

3. The third group involving consolidation or compaction was represented by:-

   France — Menard dynamic compaction method
   Large electric sparks at depth
   Sand drains
   Explosives

   Italy — Preloading by Caissons

   Netherlands — Sand drains
   Well pointing
   New Amphirol vehicles

   Spain — Cyclic preloading by the 'Dune method'

4. The fourth group involving soil reinforcement was included in the papers from:-

   Japan — Vibrated sand piles

   Spain — Passive piles

   USA — Stone columns

I have mentioned eight countries which have described methods which, in general, I suggest, change the nature or properties of the soil rather than consider structures which are designed specifically to suit the soft ground. I trust you would agree that there is, therefore, a tendency towards this technique.

By their nature these processes involve a detailed knowledge of the ground properties and it is to this matter I would suggest our recommendations, if any, should relate. This aspect was touched upon in our deliberations yesterday and I was most grateful to hear from Mr. Carmichael that the world bank appreciates the necessity of site investigation.

Italy in its paper indicated the importance of site investigation and noted the improvements of sampling techniques available such as "down the hole" testing, and Poland's paper was devoted entirely to a description of a new equipment for this purpose.

A thorough knowledge of the ground is essential for all maritime design work and I would suggest that no accurate site investigation is wasted. (Inaccurate results, however, can be worse than none at all, in my experience).

I hope I have not given the impression that all the papers are concerned with removal or changing of the soft soil, or that this principle is the only one applicable to use in these conditions.

The U.K. paper contained a description of a waffle slab deck which clearly reduced weight compared with a more conventional deck and reference was made to the use of diaphragm walling as a means of constructing a semi-buoyant structure.

The USA paper described various alternative designs in their quest for the cheapest solution for a quay on soft ground.

The paper from Russia dealt, perhaps, more with the heavy loading aspect of the problem than with particular respect to soft ground.

The paper from Germany (D.R.) dealt mainly with conventional piling problems.

To sum up, I suggest that the message should be that for structures in soft ground, all methods of design should be considered including both well tried and the new, and that to enable this to be done the best possible site investigation should be undertaken.

DISCUSSION

A J JIMENEZ-SALAS (SPAIN)

A lot of money is being spent in the intensive compaction of loose sand deposits which originated by natural sedimentation or by hydraulic filling. In many cases, the only aim is to avoid liquefaction in the case of an earthquake. The same result can be obtained at a fraction of the cost, by means of overconsolidation (Ishihara et al. Soils and Foundations 19:4:59-68, 1979). As is described in the Spanish Report, one practical way to perform this overconsolidation is by shifting (bulldozing) a "Travelling Dune" across the area. A procedure for estimating the quantitive effect of this operation is presented. It is based on the endochronic constitutive model of the soil (Cuellar, V. Et Al. Jour. Geot. Eng Div. ASCE 103:399-416, 1977). For a certain sand, the effect of a single pass of a 14 m. high dune is found to be four times greater than the effect of an earthquake of 6.5M.

The pass of the dune also has beneficial effects on cohesive layers which are greater than could be expected taking account of the limited time of load application. The alternative shear strains induced by the dune produce residual pore pressures, and a delayed effect of consolidation, extrusion and/or diapirism of the cohesive layers (origin of future differential settlements) can be easily avoided. This is not the case in some of the usually employed methods of intensive compaction.

D A BARENDSEN (THE NETHERLANDS)

Most of the authors have devoted their attention to soil improvement and only a few discussed the question of soil replacement.

In the port of Amsterdam where the site of a new quay was to be prepared by dredging, 15 m of very soft clay forming the banks of the backup area were removed and replaced with good sand. The aim was to increase the stability of the waterside slope which was necessary on account of the heavy surcharge expected on the adjoining site.

PIANC should be grateful to the Commission for Waterfront Structures of the German Society for Harbour Engineering for allowing the authors of the West German paper to include in their report a preview of the recommendations for soil replacement design and execution which the Commission has prepared.

A basic disadvantage of soil removal is that the bearing capacities of the original soil, however limited, is not used at all. All possible alternatives should be carefully considered. The ultimate choice will be a matter of economy, which may not be restricted to the initial cost. In many cases the time factor will be the decisive one.

Over half of the length of the Amsterdam dock the subsoil consisted of loosely packed fine sand in which there was a danger of a flow slide (liquefaction) developing. This sand was improved, instead of removed, by the use of subsoil explosions. Charges were placed in boreholes spaced at about 15 metres centres. The result of the explosions was an immediate settlement of 30 to 50 centimetres which resulted in a substantial increase in the density of the sand. The cost of this soil improvement procedure was in this case less than half the estimated cost of other subsoil improvement methods considered.

A few pictures of the quay wall construction which was built after the soil replacement referred to are shown on page 603 of the West German paper and these indicate the large dimensions of this structure.

E BARATONO (ITALY)

On page 620 of the Italian paper two graphs are shown. One represents the time settlement relationship and the other the dissipation of pore pressure with time.

The last readings of the instruments shown in the paper relate to a date in April 1980. To bring the settlement graph up to date the recorded settlement in February 1981, after completing the core to the second phase was 31 cms. in eight months. With respect to the graphs of pore pressure, graphs 1 and 8 represent typical patterns. Piezometer 1 recorded an increase in pore pressure after the completion of the initial load and this then dissipated with time, whereas Piezometer 8 recorded a steady increase in pore pressure with increase in load. Certain irregular patterns of pore pressure dissipation were influenced by external factors such as the production of gas in the mud from organic decomposition.

The settlement meters recorded a settlement of about 10 cm. at the extreme end of the berm at the end of the first phase. After the second phase only 2 cm. approximately was recorded. This shows that the load consolidated the ground without causing shear failure in the foundation.

Referring to the Reporter General's request to the Authors of the Italian paper to elaborate on "The assertion that – during the design phase no investment gives better reward than high technology Geotechnics – certainly warrants further discussion". I can affirm that an ample supply of geotechnical information is essential to the design of the overall stability of a structure and to the assessment of settlements. Foundation problems are more easily solved with the help of sophisticated research and this results in savings in construction costs.

In the case of the industrial Port of Gagliari for example the detailed geotechnical study described indicated higher bearing capacities in the clay than had been assessed previously and resulted in the works being completed in two thirds of the time. This resulted in considerable savings to the Administration on account of lower construction costs, or more accurately, from lower costs arising from escalation, than would have been the case if the project had run for the original period.

The investment cost of the above mentioned study represents about 1% of the cost of the works and the overall profit (savings) resulting from the reduction in construction time was about 6% of the overall cost of the quay.

The East Quay of the commercial port of Gagliari was to be completed in three stages with a break of 24 months to allow the ground to consolidate between the first and second stage and of 8 months between the second and third stage. During the period of the first break the records obtained from the control instruments of the rate of settlement and pore pressure measurements showed that the dissipation was completed in about half the time anticipated. The works were therefore recommenced 12 months ahead of programme.

In this case the investment in a good geotechnical investigation which cost approximately 1.5% of the cost of the works has resulted in a saving, arising from the curtailment of escalation costs, of 8% of the cost of the works.

In addition, of course, a geotechnical investigation is very desirable to ensure the safety of the works and to control their execution.

G MATTEOTTI (ITALY)

My contribution relates to the Sibari Harbour in Italy where construction began in 1969. In 1971 the northern rubble mound breakwater, which was then under construction, suddenly collapsed into the foundations.

These foundations consist mainly of a very thick layer of soft clay between elevations of -30 and -75 metres from mean sea level. Above this there is a bed of alluvial sand to -12 metres and the whole overlies a thick bed of sand and gravel. The sandy gravel bed is subjected to a very significant artesian pressure due to the interlinking of this bed with the streams running in the adjacent South Apeenine mountains. At the level of -75 metres a water head of 115 metres has been recorded which means an artesian pressure of 115-75 = 40 metres of water at that level.

This very high pressure causes water to percolate upwards through the clay and the artesian pressure decreases from 40 metres of water at -75 metres to zero at -30 metres. This percolation results in very poor values of undrained cohesion in the soft clay.

Evidently the original design did not take these facts into account and this led to the huge failure.

At this stage my colleague Professor Kerisel from Paris and I were asked by Cassa per il Bezzogiorno, an Italian Employer for public works in Southern Italy, to propose a new design.

We decided, after many preliminary investigations,

which disclosed this interesting artesian phenomenon, that the following criteria should be incorporated in the design and construction:-

1. To preload the alluvial sand with a submarine fill. The side slopes of the fill to be no steeper than 1 in 9 to avoid any punching effect into the soft clay.

2. To drain the upper part of the soft clay by means of sand drains 50 m. deep.

The purpose of the specification outlined above was to improve the soil strength.

The very deep sand drains were installed using a vibro-jetting technique both in the alluvial sand and in the soft clay. The rubble inside the tube was prevented from segregating by using an inverse circulation of water under high pressure which also prevented the filter from clogging.

At present we are waiting for a period of one year to allow the upper part of the soft clay layer to consolidate. The sand fill will be removed and floating caissons will be sunk onto a platform prepared at -11 metres. The dredging will be taken to -13 metres and from that depth to -11 metres a 2 metre thick layer of reinforced earth, reinforced with a plastic net which has a tensile strength of 50 kN/m^2, will be laid to increase the overall strength of the foundation.

The caissons will be designed to allow for the bearing pressures resulting from a 4 metre high wave and will be linked together. The final weight of the structure will be calculated so that the stress gradient from the entrance to the shore does not exceed 1 KPa per metre in any horizontal direction in accordance with the theory of Barre de Saint-Venant. This theory which was published at the end of the last century refers to the problem which arises when frictionless material is squeezed between two parallel plates.

E LOEWY (UK)

I would like to describe the situation and experiences at the Port of Belawan in NE Sumatra by courtesy of Mr. Soejono, Director of Ports and Dredging, Sumatra, and Mr. Sumardi, Chief Engineer, Port of Belawan, both of whom are attending the Congress through the initiative of the PCDC. The Port of Belawan was studied in 1974 in a Feasibility Study for the Asian Development Bank by Sir William Halcrow and Partners which forecast a traffic flow increasing by 7.3% per annum from 2.9 million tons per annum in 1975 to 5.5 million tons per annum in 1983 and to 8.9 million tons per annum in 1988 and 15.8 million tons per annum in 1998.

The older port, built in 1920, had 1180 metres of quay, known as Ujung Baru, of 8.5 m depth. Further basins built in 1960 quickly silted up and had to be modified. The 1974/1975 study recommended a First Phase of Development of 1300m of piled quay of 9.5 m depth at low water, along the outer side of the curved approach channel. This channel was 12km long, leading to the deepwater of the Malacca Straits. The Project was studied in a very sophisticated hydraulic model at the Wallingford Hydraulic Laboratory.

The project entailed extensive reclamation over 50 ha. needing 5 million m^3 of sand to depths between 2m and 17m. The sand was dredged and pumped and transported from river sources 12km away. The suboils consist of three thick beds of soft clay between 15 m and 30 m thick separated by 2m thick layers of fine sand. Along the quay line it was necessary to remove 800 000 m^3 of very soft silt up to 18m deep.

In order to minimise and accelerate settlement and consolidation of the soft subsoils which, without special attention might exceed 4 metres vertically and take several years to achieve, ground treatment and subsoil improvements of "dynamic compaction"; "surcharging"; and "vertical drains" both separately and in combination were adopted. The first one would only be effective for the sand filling and the second and third together for the rapid dissipation of pore water pressure and primary consolidation in the soft clays. Traditional sand drains were discarded because of a risk of "holding up" the adjacent soil and breaking the drainage paths from lateral displacement. New developments in plastic drains ("Castle" brand, made in Japan) which avoided such disadvantages, were used and were inserted into the soil to depths between 30 m and 45 m by new sophisticated vibrating pile-driving equipment specially developed by the Japanese contractors, Rinkai. The spacing varied between 1.7m and 3m and, to date, the Castle drains are proving quite quick and cheap to instal and quite effective in operation. A carefully controlled procedure of sand filling has been adopted in association with the vertical drainage and surcharging so that these are installed when the surcharge has reached +3m. At this level any dynamic consolidation to be done is carried out before raising the surcharge to +7m which is retained until the area is taken over by the next contractors, for roads, services, buildings, etc. 85% pore pressure dissipation in 9 months should be achieved but certain small residual secondary compression will still be expected to occur over a much longer period and this has been taken into account in the design of the structures, roads, services, etc.

I hope to be able to describe the fuller, later experiences of the project at the next congress when construction of the First Phase should be complete.

N N B ORDMAN (CHAIRMAN) (UK)

An important aspect of measures to improve or replace poor ground is that they often take a long time. This can be a significant economic consideration, per se, because "time is money". Moreover, it is frequently a matter of planning significance, particularly when large structures (including industrial plants) are to be erected within the port environs.

Some of these structures impose heavy loads on the ground. Where heavy loading is over a restricted area, they do not create a particular problem because piling can be an economical solution. However, in cases where floors or external paving over a large area are required to sustain heavy loads a serious difficulty may arise either due to significant settlement which may be expected during the operational life of the facility concerned or due to the significant delay which may otherwise occur before the land can be developed.

Problems of a similar kind may also apply to road and railway approaches.

P. COUPRIE (FRANCE)

The recent completion of a quay with diaphragm walls at the Port of Rouen shows the adaptability of the method to different conditions.

In this case the line of the completed quay lies in front of the line of the top of an embankment and the wall had to be constructed in the presence of water.

To achieve this a mound of chalk rubble was tipped onto the slope of the existing embankment. As this material was too permeable to contain the bentonite mud the mound was consolidated using cement bentonite poured in parallel trenches which improved the permeability and the bearing strength.

Following this the quay wall was constructed in the conventional manner. That is to say construction of the guide walls, trenching for the quay wall which was concreted under bentonite mud, etc.

F IRWIN-CHILDS (UK)

Although the conclusions regarding methods of improving soft soil are valuable they should not be formulated in such a way as to discourage the development of structures suitable for use in ground which cannot be, or has not been, improved.

In the ultimate these would have to include buoyant structures and there is no difficulty in providing support for very heavy loads by monoliths — as shown in Fig. 8 page 273. Fig. 9 page 274 illustrates the simplicity obtainable with in-situ rather than precast construction.

Most waterfront structures are subject to lateral loading in addition to vertical loading:

> For locks this can be resisted by internal strutting and a scheme exists for a completely buoyant lock.
>
> For quay walls both front strutting and tying back are difficult in bad ground but resistance can be provided by walls or buttresses set at right angles to the face if they are built of diaphragm walling. This is because this in-situ method of construction mobilises the inter-action with the soil in a way not achieved by precast techniques, and there are a number of major port structures in the U.K., notably at Liverpool, Redcar and Bristol which rely solely on this principle for their stability.

J de NEKKER (THE NETHERLANDS)

The Port Authority of Rotterdam is considering whether to fill old harbour basins that are no longer in use with dredged material. This would provide a dumping area for highly contaminated dredged material which arises as spoil from the maintenance dredging but would also provide a cheap source of material to fill the basins so that the land thus reclaimed could be used for residential or industrial development.

It is proposed to close the mouth of the harbour with a sand dike and then to fill the basin gradually with dredged silt allowing the silt to consolidate. Material obtained from maintenance dredging and dumped under water will require a very long time to consolidate, and horizontal or vertical drainage will be essential.

Some laboratory tests which gave good results have been completed and in the near future some full scale experiments will be put in hand. Some old drinking water basins which are no longer in use will be filled with silt from the maintenance dredging. The fill will be placed from 3 metres below to 4 metres above average water level. The following drainage systems will be investigated:

1. A sand layer on the bottom of the basin with a horizontal drainage system in this layer. Water will be pumped out.

2. Vertical strip drains combined with furrowing of the top layer

and

3. a combination of 1 and 2 above.

It is hoped that results will be available within about one and a half years.

P G R BARLOW (UK)

In amplification of the part of the U.K. paper outlining the case history of Port Keland, I explained the historical reason for the acceptance by Management of the operational inconvenience of offshore wharves with bridge approaches — i.e. the over-riding importance of minimum capital cost at the time the site was first opened up, and the later desirability of maintaining hydraulic continuity for the whole of the long line of berths comprising the North Port.

However, since writing the paper we have embarked on a technical, operational and economic study of the new Port Site at Pulau Lumut, and in this we will be carrying out a cost-benefit analysis of marginal wharves versus the present type of offshore structures with bridge approaches. We are finding if the ground at the new site is the same as at the North and South Ports, the most economical solution to the problem may well be to perpetuate the present design but with a much wider deck, wide enough to accommodate a very flat earth-retaining slope supporting contiguous reclamation. This is because the ground at this site consists of marine clays with low shear strengths right down to the bedrock level of -85 m. below datum. Even if it were economically feasible to replace the ground material down to the sandy layers at -25 m to -35 m. in which we are currently founding our piles, this would not solve the problem as the low shear strength of the material below that level would leave the new filling material, and the structure built on it, subject to slip circle failure.

J L DAWSON (UK)

I suggest there is agreement on the importance of soil investigations for engineering works on soft ground. They can be expensive. Borings should be supplemented where practicable by cheaper methods such as seismic survey and echo sounding. The surface of the London Clay on the proposed Maplin Airport/Seaport complex was determined in this way through the overlying estuarine silts and clays.

I question the suggestion made in one paper that flexible pavements are always unsatisfactory in a port environment and point out the dense stable bituminous surfacings can be produced using 'Marshal' design methods. The risk of fuel spillage does make bitumen bound materials unsatisfactory. However, in areas where this risk does not exist I suggest rolled, dry lean concrete makes a satisfactory sub-base to a well designed asphalt surface.

Piling continues to be the normal way of dealing with foundation problems on PSA (Property Services Agency) maritime sites although we have successfully used bentonite slurry replacement methods, or diaphragm walls.

Finally, I would point out that unfavourable ground conditions continue to be one of the common reasons put forward to explain cost overruns and even after the most careful preliminary investigations considerable uncertainty remains. Informed pessimism should therefore be used when assessing contingency sums for estimates.

A L MOSS-MORRIS (SOUTH AFRICA)

In response to the request by our Reporter General, I will give a few details of the methods of handling and placing the 360 ton counterfort units.

The manufacture took place in a yard of very limited extent which was only large enough to cast 4 counterfort units at a time. The three positions of the unit, namely the front wall, the base and the counterfort were all cast in the horizontal position. The face and base were rotated through ninety degrees using a large overhead gantry and were then in the correct location with respect to the horizontal counterfort form. The third stage to be cast was the counterfort and this included a short length of the face wall directly above the base.

The completed element was rotated to the vertical position using the 170 ton gantry lifting on two stiff plate girders under the counterfort. Once in the vertical position the 360 ton capacity floating crane lifted the counterfort element off its bed and transported it directly to its final position. The crane used was a luffing derrick with 48 m long boom on a 51 x 21 m barge. This barge was moored securely in position and the counterfort element held in position relative to the barge using light wire ropes running from air winches.

From this initial position the units were placed to within 50 mm of their required position and the gaps between units were maintained between 10 and 110 mm.

In regard to the Reporter General's other question, the North Quay has been in use for about 15 months and we have not been informed of any difficulties with the untied crane rails.

H D HOEFT (FRG)

The Reporter General, in his reference to the West German paper, has asked for details of costs of the different quays described. The costs of the Ore Terminal at Hansaport which is referred to in Section II pages 603 and 607 are as follows:

1. Cost of construction as shown for the complete works but excluding soil replacement — approximately	DM 30,000/ metre (in 1975)
For todays equivalent cost add 1/3rd	DM 40,000/ metre (in 1981)
2. The cost of soil replacement is difficult to establish because the quay was part of a bigger scheme, but approximate cost	DM 10,000/metre
So total cost at 1981 price level	DM 50,000-60,000/metre.

The soil replacement solution was chosen after several other designs had been considered including diaphragm walls, caissons and other prefabricated elements. Site trials using the Menard's method of soil improvement were also carried out but this method was not suitable for the prevailing conditions. All the alternative solutions were considerably more expensive which surprised us but analyses showed that this was because of the heavy superimposed ore load of 30/t m^2 and the height of the quaywall (bed to deck) of nearly 24 metres.

It was not possible to use the soil replacement method at the northern end of the quaywall as this would have endangered an existing structure. In this section the initial permissible load had to be reduced to 15 t/m^2 instead of the 30 t/m^2 required. During the early life of the structure the actual duration of each imposed load was electronically recorded for every spot and as consolidation of the subsoil took place so the permissible load was increased. The design requirement of 30 t/m^2 was reached in a period of less than 5 years.

J F MAQUET (FRANCE)

The first part of my contribution refers to the second and third conclusions proposed by the Reporter General. The accuracy to which we work our design calculations shows that our theoretical knowledge of the behvaiour of structures and soils far exceeds our practical knowledge of the way structures behave in the field where the soils are always heterogeneous and where the work is not perfectly constructed in accordance with the details of the design office. I think that in addition to the preliminary geotechnical studies it is desirable that observations and detailed measurements should be made more often on actual constructed works.

My second remark concerns a new type of quay construction used in the port of Le Havre. The current method of ground treatment often presents two drawbacks. Namely, treatment often takes a long time to complete which, as the Chairman has pointed out, leads to high costs, and the methods used are not always appropriate to the construction of an extension of an existing structure.

To overcome the problem of bad ground where large deposits of silt have been present the port of Le Havre has used the diaphragm wall technique. To accommodate large moments the quay walls are laid in a "zig-zag" form similar to sheet pile sections. The portions of the quay wall already constructed have been tied back using pretensioned cables which have been provided with good anchors in shelly sands. As there is no good ground in which to anchor tie rods the new sections of quay have been built with relieving slabs which transfer the load from the back of the wall to piles and stays.

This type of diaphragm wall technique is very useful when applied to quay construction because the works can be carried out quickly and without disturbing the adjacent quay structure or the operation on the quay. Also, in this case, the cost of this form of construction was lower than other methods.

E SERRANO (SPAIN)

I would like to say a few words to stress one aspect of the subject being considered and to describe an experience which may be intersting to some of you.

The aspect I would like to consider is time. We have all many times been involved in designing and constructing facilities on soft ground. As the Reporter General has pointed out good ground is the exception. In each case we have had to consider several alternative methods of construction from total removal of the bad ground to the use of different consolidation techniques, including carrying out extensive geotechnical investigations and providing instrumentation to monitor the actual behaviour of the ground. The optimum solution in each case is different.

However, the time factor has always been an important element in the decision and in some cases the lack of time has been the cause of selecting a more expensive consolidation technique than would otherwise have been required.

Generally the consolidation of soft ground requires a lot of time. Whether it is the time required to allow a reduction in the pore water pressure induced by preloading, even if drains are used to accelerate this process, or whether it is the time necessary for a chemical reaction to take place or the time of the operational procedures related to piling, sinking sand drains or the use of vibrofloatation.

Unfortunately, engineers are always confronted with a lack of time. Those who are responsible for building any kind of facility often take months or even years to decide to go ahead but when they have decided they want the facility, not tomorrow, but yesterday.

On the other hand we have all seen, many times, vast areas of poor ground which have been reserved for future harbour extensions or industrial development which have not been investigated until the decision to proceed with the development has been taken. In these circumstances it is often too late to take advantage of the simplest way of consolidating the ground which may often be a preloading, because of the lack of time that is available.

A possible recommendation to anyone in this position is to plan well ahead and consider the possibility of consolidating the reserved land well before the development is required, perhaps by using the technique explained by Professor Jimenez Salas (travelling dunes), with or without the help of drains. In this way one may find oneself in a better position when the development of the facility is finally required.

The experience I would like to decribe concerns a very special type of "soft soil" we often find in the rocky region of Northern Spain. This is an artificial fill of quarry run which is placed without compaction, and is very much more economical than, for example, sand fill obtained by dredging.

Ten years ago we were confronted with the problem of building a silo for storing 20,000 tons of soja in a port area where the foundations consisted of 20 m of artificial fill of this type, in which there were stones of varying size up to 1 ton. Below the fill a few metres of fine sand overlaid rock. The silo was to be built between a quay with 14 m depth of water below low water, and the other breakwater of the port of Bilbao.

In our opinion the only method of consolidating such fill was by simple preloading and as we did not have, at that time, any data to indicate the amount of settlement to expect in this sort of fill, we had to provide an amount of preload that would produce a pressure equivalent to the pressure that would result from the loaded silo, which was in the range of 22 tons/m^2. However, the quay was originally designed for only 6 ton/m^2 and so it was necessary to locate the silo further behind the quay face than we had planned.

To achieve the required preload a height of 12 m of quarry waste was used. As expected the settlement was rapid but the amount, 1.10 metres, was rather more than anticipated. After the preload was removed and the silos were built, the recorded settlements were less than 20 mm with the silo fully loaded.

Now to return to my first point, the proprietors of this silo are proposing to extend its capacity to 40,000 tons. At the time the preloading was carried out there were some temporary buildings on the area of the future extension and so it was not possible at that time, to extend the preload over this area. We advised the owner of the silo to undertake the preloading of the ground as soon as the temporary buildings were removed. The time has passed without this work being undertaken and so after 10 years we are once more confronted with the problem of consolidating the ground in a hurry.

J A JIMENEZ-SALAS (SPAIN)

At Dumai (Sumatra) the soil conditions are very similar to those at Belawan which were described by a UK colleague. At an existing refinery the tank farm is located in an area where sand drains were provided and where pre-loading was carried out. The tanks are continuing to settle and need successive re-levelling.

The cause of this seems to be the high alophane content in the clay which leads to a high percentage of secondary consolidation, which is unaffected by the presence of vertical drains.

At present a major extension of the refinery is under construction and the sand drains have been omitted so it will be very interesting to follow the future behaviour of the vertical drains at Belawan.

DR E LACKNER (FRG)

I would like to say a few words concerning the West German paper. The Reporter General has asked about the cost of the wharves which were described and I can give the costs of the first two projects described.

The cost of the Container Terminal Wharves at Bremerhaven was very high. The height from the sea bed to the deck is 26.5 m, the soil conditions were extremely poor, the water pressure and imposed loads were very high and last but not least, the cost of the chamber to absorb storm waves was very high.

The proposal for the wave chamber was prepared by Professor Dr. Hensen, full professor of the Technical University of Hanover and Director of the Franzins-Institute, also in Hanover. My duty was to incorporate the proposal into the design of the structure and indeed this was not an easy matter. On account of the size it was necessary to use prefabricated reinforced concrete units which weighed more than 600 tons.

Because of the above reasons the costs of the quaywall inclusive of the excavation of bad ground and the replacement with good sand was approximately Dm 150,000/metre or £30,000/metre.

The cost of the quaywall in the port of Brunsbuttel was only approximately Dm 75,000/ metre or £15,000/metre.

We have also had a lot of experience in the reinforcement of bad ground etc. in West Germany but we have had some bad experiences with these methods occasionally. For this reason, on a big project, where enough good sand is available within a reasonable distance, and where suitable deposit grounds exist for the excavated ground we prefer to totally replace the bad ground with good sand.

The method looks very easy but it is very important to follow certain procedures when there is a large current and very silty water. Only if these procedures are followed will the replacement be good.

It is on account of this that Recommendation R109 of the Committee for Waterfront Structures of the Society of Harbour Engineering of Hamburg was prepared. Recommendation R110 gives guidance on the correct method of calculating earth and water pressures.

The risk of encountering trouble with quaywalls designed using the above referred Recommendations is low, and the structures so designed are economical.

CONCLUSIONS

1. The papers presented to Congress were directed more towards treatment of the ground rather than the design and construction of works to suit difficult soil conditions. Nevertheless, it is also clear that there is considerable progress in the design of such structures using techniques such as diaphragm walling whereby increased interaction between soil and structure is obtainable.

2. The treatment of poor ground can range between total removal of the soft soil and replacement by better soil to sophisticated consolidation processes of the soft soil. It is recommended that all alternatives should be carefully considered so that the appropriate method is adopted.

3. The techniques normally require accurate assessment of the ground conditions and it is strongly recommended that those responsible should set aside sufficient funds to enable detailed geotechnical site investigations to be made. More attention should be given to reviewing the techniques being used, by monitoring structural behaviour in order to test the validity of these techniques and modify them if necessary.

4. It is recommended that the scope of such investigations should be carefully controlled or monitored by the engineers who are responsible for the design of the project and the soils engineers should be fully informed of the reasons for the investigation and of the soils data required.

5. It is important to appreciate that ground treatment and replacement techniques can take much time and this is an element which should be taken into consideration in any overall economic evaluation.

MARITIME PORTS AND SEAWAYS

SECTION II — SUBJECT 5

Coastal erosion caused by harbour works and corrective measures

Thursday 14 May 1981

Chairman:	*N N B ORDMAN (UK)* *Noel Ordman and Associates Ltd*
Vice Chairman:	*A F G EDDIE (Australia)* *Managing Partner, Connell Eddie and Associates, Melbourne*
Reporter General:	*Prof P. HOLMES (UK)* *Department of Civil Engineering, University of Liverpool*
Secretary:	*P LACEY (UK)* *Ove Arup and Partners Ltd, London*
Asst. Secretary:	*Miss M-M DANEELS (Belgium)* *Secrétaire AIPCN Secrétariat Générale, Brussels*

Speakers

U TOMASICCHIO (Italy), F ABACACIS (Portugal), J CASTANHO (Portugal), P P VAIDYARAMAN (India), D J VAN DEN BOSSCHE (Belgium), A ROGAN (Greece), N P CAMPBELL (South Africa), F ENRIQUEZ (Spain), P M A DE CANDT (Belgium), J L DELORME (France), R TENAUD (France), D H SWART (South Africa), D DREYFOUS-DUCAS (France), E R HEIBERG (USA), C MOUTZOURIS (Greece), W A PRICE (UK)

Prof. PATRICK HOLMES (U.K.) (REPORTER GENERAL)

It is convenient to divide a summary of this difficult problem into three sectors all of which are necessary to the prediction of coastal erosion and to the evaluation of remedial measures as follows:

1. Information and data necessary to the problem and its solution – a 'Data Base';
2. The prediction of coastal erosion and the validation of such predictions; and
3. The design of remedial measures and their efficiency.

These three sectors apply equally to all types of interference – either existing harbours, potential developments or remedial measures – to the coastal sediment transport process. All of the papers in this Section of the 25th Congress include the sections to varying degrees.

Since the problem of coastal erosion and sediment transport is of significant importance in many countries and can involve very high capital or continuous financial investment it is worthwhile considering the proposition that an international commission should be set up to bring together the considerable experience of engineers in this field.

The terms of reference of such a commission could be based upon the need to provide a state-of-the-art document on the three above. One would hope that the discussion of the papers might lead to a clearer remit for such a commission.

There is, of course, a need for further research work in this field. We are all aware that such work is very expensive and it may be that international collaboration and contribution to such work might be a way forward. There are large research programs on coastal dynamics in progress in various countries but they tend to be relatively fundamental in nature and the end product may not readily be applicable to engineering problems.

Members of the Congress might wish to give some thought to the potential for an international coastal engineering experiment at a site or sites where port development has interfered, or is about to interfere, with sediment transport.

DISCUSSION

U TOMASICCHIO (ITALY)

I agree wholeheartedly with the general report. The object of our paper was to give some examples of the interaction of harbour works built on the Italian coastline which is often a low coastline. Even though we chose a few cases we necessarily have had to deal with them in a general way indicating the causes of beach erosion and the remedies that we used in each case. That is, our exposition didn't try to give a complete picture of the Italian coastal scene but we hope it gives you enough information of our problems and the way in which we tackled them.

I simply now want to enumerate the cases dealt with in our paper and they are, in order:

1. Chiavari and Lavagna marinas and Carrara and Viareggio Harbours in the North Tyrrhenian sea.

2. The Calabrian coast from Diamante to Amantea and Cetraro harbour in the south Tyrrhenian Sea.

3. The coast from the Cape of Gargano to the river Po, and the Venetian littoral coastal zone in the central and North Adriatic Sea where there are several inlets.

If you would like more information then our bibliography at the end of our paper will help. People from overseas have the well-known poetical image of Italy plunging like a bather into the warm waters of the Mediterranean and so everyone can appreciate how important the maintenance and use of our beaches is to the economy of Italy. The coastal zone not only constitutes a large part of our country but is also important economically. The need to solve the problem of how best to manage this area has raised and still raises studies and research to lead to more adequate technical and economic answers. Working in parallel the programmes of both Ministero dei Lavari Publica and Consiglio Marimale delle Ricerche are aimed towards a solution of these problems. From an operational point of view the Ministry mentioned above recommended a triannual programme of interventions of coast defence works while the National Council for Research starts a major project called "soil preservation" which is divided into subject groups one of which concerns "littoral dynamics". Within this last project several operational units with the necessary expertise collaborate. These include Universities and also public and private organisation provided they have the necessary skills. Although perhaps the project has proceeded slowly for various reasons at the present time it is well developed and we hope it will come up with good results during the present year. This was the time originally allocated to the project. As it often happens in the research field we cannot anticipate sensational results. (Sicut Natura, Scientia rare facit saltus).

The project however succeeded in promoting studies and research in every field connected with the best use of the coastal zone and with its defence from natural causes or from the interference of man. Many groups of researchers (economists, geographers, geologists, geophysicists, engineers, meteorologists) actively collaborated.

Large field surveys for the collection of data have been started which previously were almost non-existent. At first it was necessary to refer to the more advanced work done by experts in foreign countries, particularly from the United States, but now the work is beginning to go along by itself and is providing more appropriate results to our local situations. I will not bore you with a list of the work we have done and propose to do. I wouldn't have time and neither could I because my experience is limited to engineering problems. More detailed information will be found in the text of the paper which was written from an engineering point of view.

I would like to explain that in some university hydraulic laboratories in Italy we try to establish in general the most important characteristics of sea defences and, in doing this, it would seem that the tendency is towards imitating natural systems like submerged barriers and artificial beach nourishment. It is also our objective to improve our mathematical modelling which must be both reliable and handy.

Other scientific organisations, working at the same level as the committee, are making proposals to determine the tasks and instruments for the people that must collect and register the data. In this way more adequate instrumentation will be available to the projects.

We look carefully at our field experience and its planning is the first priority within the operable research schemes that I have already told you about.

Paragraph 6 of our Paper contains a description of some of the types of sea defences we use at the moment or propose for the future. I want to stress that we have dwelt upon submerged barriers because they seem to us to have as many advantages as the well-known emerging barriers but, of course, they have their own shortcomings.

Our research continues but the results are, as yet, inconclusive. In our Paper, in the last paragraph but one, we give some considerations that illustrate the new ways we are approaching our problems in Italy. We consider the environmental aspects important and consider many aspects like landscape, pollution and social and economic consequences.

I hope I have been able to give you a better understanding of what we are doing in Italy in the coastal engineering field but I would ask you to read our paper for more details.

F ABACASCIS (PORTUGAL)

1. Human intervention in the littoral processes is also important. The alluvial control of rivers and the extraction of sand from beaches are two effects among others which must be taken into account in these sort of studies.

2. A good knowledge of basic data is essential. For example, for the moment, there is not an entirely satisfactory way to observe wave directions. This is a serious ommission taking into account the sensitivity of the evaluation of littoral drift intensity to the wave direction. Several of the papers draw attention to this fact especially the paper from the United Kingdom.

3. Regular beach surveys do not always provide data from which the net drift can be calculated. Only in very particular cases can such surveys provide reliable results but these are mainly quantitative.

4. There is a lack of knowledge about the behaviour of cohesive sediments within the littoral process. I feel quite strongly that more attention should be paid to research in this field.

I would like to say that the "future developments" mentioned in the British paper should be carefully taken into account in the preparation of the conclusions.

The report from South Africa is very interesting and my attention was drawn to the events that happened to the north of the North breakwater in Richards Bay. With respect to what occurred I would like to tell you about our experience to the south of the South jetty in the Aveiro lagoon. I must draw your attention to figures 8 and 9 of the Portuguese paper. With a net littoral drift of about a million cubic yards per year in a southerly direction the zone immediately south of the South jetty was stable up until 1972. The two jetties were constructed in 1958. We attribute this to:

a) Diffraction effects on the predominant north-westerly waves and the protection that the jetties afford from this direction.

b) The south-westerly waves happen to produce a filling of the beach to maintain it in equilibrium within an environment of an onshore-offshore transport.

c) Protection by the offshore bar which formed as a consequence of the natural bypassing of sand from north to south by the inlet.

As is described in the Portuguese paper the field of eleven groynes was constructed in 1972 to protect the shoreline in the critical area a few kilometres south of the inlet. Immediately after the construction of these groynes the zone immediately south of the southern jetty suffered severe erosion. This is attributed to the fact that the groynes intercepted temporarily the south-north littoral drift and interrupted the previous state of equilibrium that existed in the area adjacent to the South jetty.

J CASTANHO (PORTUGAL)

Our Reporter General divides the coastal defence methods into two basic categories:

1. Hard defences of the classic type (groynes, detached breakwaters, seawalls)

2. Soft defences of the beach nourishment type.

In this connection, I should like to draw your attention to two points. Firstly, from a reading of the different papers of Section II, Subject 5, I seem to have perceived an increasing tendency towards or even a preference for using soft methods (whether or not combined with hard methods); this is perhaps due to the great advantages of the soft type, more particularly the fact that it interferes very little or not at all with the coastal regime.

Secondly, several authors report on successes achieved with beach nourishment (by-passing, reclamation of dredgings, etc.) but attach very little importance to or even show a certain distrust of offshore dumping, i.e., beyond the breakers. Indeed, although in some examples the sand is not deposited on the beach, there are others where the results were very good. I think it all depends on the local conditions.

As a successful example, I should like to quote the case of the widening of Copacabana beach, in Brazil. Some 3 million m^3 of sand were deposited here with very good results, from the sea with a hopper dredger which came as close as possible to the beach (the method was combined with landward nourishment, on the foreshore). Most of the sand dumped moved towards the coast.

P P VAIDYARAMAN (INDIA)

In determining the best plans for the layout of ports (assumption of maintenance dredging etc.) it is essential to obtain as close an estimate as possible of the rate of littoral drift. Where adequate field data is available this is not normally a serious problem. However, often such information is lacking and then one has to refer to existing empirical relationships like the CERC formula which relates the wave energy to the rate of littoral drift. However, here is where due caution is called for since misuse of such empirical relationships can result in misleading figures. To illustrate the point a reference is made to the case of Vishakhapatnam, one of the major harbours on the East coast of India. Fortunately there is adequate data on the quantities of material dredged from which it is seen that the littoral drift at this location is of the order of 0.765×10^6 yd^3 per year. Using wave data the drift rate was calculated using the said formula which gave a gross drift of 3.03×10^6 yd^3 per year which is nearly four times the actual value. An examination of this discrepancy indicated that the CERC formula as originally developed is applicable to areas where the wave energy intensity is limited to 2000 ft lbs/ft per day. Obviously the extrapolation to such high rates of wave energy using the original relationship is unlikely to be satisfactory.

An analytical approach was carried out at the Central Water and Power Research Station, Poona (India) in which the alongshore currents induced by waves was calculated using the Putman-Munk-Taylor formula which was then substituted into a sediment transport equation such as the one given by Du-Buoys-Straub. This led to a gross littoral drift of 916 100 yd^3 per year which was closer to the actual dredging rate than that given by the CERC relationship. When the relationship given by Engleson is used to calculate the wave induced currents then a drift of the order of 893 000 yd^3 per year is obtained which is a closer approximation to the actual value than the other two cases I have mentioned.

Calculation using the wave energy indicated shows that for the case mentioned above the drift rate is given by the equation.

$$Q = 4.35 \ (E_a)^{1.33}$$

where Q = alongshore littoral drift in yd^3 per day

E_a = alongshore wave energy in millions of ft lbs/ft per day per ft of beach.

For the case of low intensities of energy (30 million ft lbs/ft per day) the relationship was found to be close to that given by Fairchild for the North Atlantic coast i.e. $Q = 0.55 \ (E_a)^{1.9}$.

I therefore suggest that PIANC initiate a survey of the data available at different ports in the world to establish the applicability of the particular relationship for each region. This would prove invaluable in working towards a better understanding of the complex phenomena associated with the mechanics of littoral drift.

Reference

An analytical estimation of littoral drift by C V Gole *et al* 14th International Conference on Coastal Engineering, Copenhagen, 1974. Paper no. 3.4.1.

D J VAN DEN BOSSCHE (BELGIUM)

I wish to congratulate Professor Holmes on his General Report but want to clarify a misunderstanding that might have arisen with respect to the Belgian beach restoration scheme. The reference was made to "hard" coastal defences. I would like to point out that one of the major considerations during the planning study was to decide whether or not a "hard" groyne was necessary to preserve the economic viability of the renourished "soft" beach. In fact the coastal system is attacked not only by waves but is subject to strong tidal currents. In planning the project we had to include as an alternative large undersea groynes which traversed the ebb gulley called Appelgak in order to reduce the effect of tidal currents. Its aim was to interfere with the causes of littoral transport.

An economical assessment was undertaken to define the optimum solution. The following schemes were considered:-

1. A solely soft sandy beach which would be subject to maintenance.

2. A beach protected by an underwater groyne about 1 km long which might be anticipated to require less maintenance on both the beach and the groyne.

Our conlusion was that there was no significant evidence to suggest that there was any economic advantage to either scheme. If one decides to alter the groyne construction one has to monitor the beach behaviour carefully bearing in mind that the adjacent port extension works of Zeebrugge are progressing.

Hence the beach nourishment of Kuolake Heist (Belgium) is classified as one of the longest soft coastal defence schemes undertaken up to the present time. I do not entirely agree with the General Reporter's remarks that the main criticism of groynes and similar structures necessarily lies in their expense and inflexibility. For this reason groynes should be recommended only if they are inevitable. In fact the result of our economical assessment was that the well known "step by step" approach of our predecessors applied to coastal defences is valid in general.

A. ROGAN (GREECE)

I fully agree with the General Reporter that the criteria related to cohesion are in need of definition. Also I think it is appropriate to emphasise the complexity of the interference that exists between harbour structures and the consequent coastal erosion or accretion.

The Port of Kalamata is situated on the southern coast of Peloponnisos. It is exposed to a fetch of 240 miles so that high waves can be generated. The first part of the breakwater was built during the last third of the 20th century and subsequent to 1945 this breakwater was extended by 250 metres. After 1946 extensive large-scale erosion started westwards of the port. During the period 1954 to 1979 the coast retreated by a maximum amount of approximately 90 metres into the town over a length of 1500 metres.

Simple and empirical coastal protection did not resist the wave attack. The coast to the east of the port remained unaltered and at the same time the port of Kalamata, following the trend towards containerisation, required further development because of its geographical location and needed to be extended landwards.

After the submission of the Technical chamber committee's report and the intense reaction of the local authorities, the Ministry of Public Works issued some months ago invitations to tender for the design of the continuous protection of the west coast and the land reclamation. This would cover the needs of the port for land. This case adds emphasis to yesterday's conclusions of the need to create land to cover the future requirements of port development.

N P CAMPBELL (SOUTH AFRICA)

In South Africa three of the East coast harbours have a northerly littoral drift problem with quantities ranging from just under 500 000m^3 per year at East London to 800 000m^3 at the new bulk cargo port of Richards Bay.

India seems to have much the same difficulty on the East coast and in the United States they are bypassing quantities of up to 800 000m^3 per year at some of their harbours. However, due to the heavy sea and swell conditions experienced on the South African coastline fixed or stationary bypass pumping systems have not proved successful and we have been forced to maintain a sand trap on the updrift side of the South breakwaters by using sea-going suction dredgers.

As the sand transport takes place in the surf zone it is necessary to form the sand trap within some 50 m or 150 ft from the toe of the breakwater armour. As the swell conditions are often normal to the breakwater we cannot for safety resaons trail so close to the breakwater so we have developed a combined bow pipe/side trail dredger of 4 000t hopper capacity.

In working the sand trap the dredgers drop two stern anchors on 4½ inch wire moorings and head into it at right angles to the breakwater checking the forward movement with the stern anchor winches. Within about 150 ft of the breakwater the bow anchors are dropped, the ship is set back slightly to improve the angle of the head anchors and the 4½ inch diameter bow pipe lowered through a well in the forward part of the vessel. This pipe can reach a depth of 72 ft below water level. In good weather conditions a load of 4 000t can be obtained in half an hour, but this has to be pumped ashore on the downdrift side of the harbour in a separate operation from a berth inside the harbour.

Some indication of the weather conditions under which the work is undertaken is illustrated by the fact that sand trap dredging can only be carried out on about 80 to 120 days per year. Every opportunity is therefore taken to dredge the sand trap whenever the weather permits. From the results of model studies undertaken at Durban harbour it has been established that if a sand trap were allowed to fill in and heavy south east swell conditions were to develop the entrance channel depths would be reduced from -42 to about -19 ft in about 5½ days.

When weather does not permit sand trap dredging the dredgers are able to trail the channels and turning basins in the protection of the harbours concerned.

I have been advised by the ship yards that South

Africa should modernise its dredger fleet by buying standard twin trail-pipe vessels. However, I believe that our bow pipe dredgers, over long experience dating back to the 1890's and from model studies, are the only vessels capable of keeping Richards Bay, Durban and East London open to the international sea routes and the 150 000dwt bulk carriers and third generation container ships that ply our trade.

Although our fleet of five suction dredgers, one to be launched in August, are highly sophisticated diesel electric and diesel ships, they are the only vessels of this type afloat to my knowledge and although some would consider that they are an outdated concept, I recommend their use to anyone with a problem like ours.

F ENRIQUEZ (SPAIN)

Taking into account the point (1) of the conclusions of the General Reporter, we point out the following aspects:

When the maritime engineer designs a work on the coast he must consider that due to the principle of action and reaction, nature will react sometimes immediately and frequently in an unwanted and surprising manner. For this reason the idea of a data bank as proposed by the General Reporter seems to us excellent.

There are two areas. Firstly, the area of the existing natural data which can be obtained by the direct study of the physical system, the inputs and outputs of which can be known and, secondly, the area of the data which appear after the maritime work is completed. For instance, the construction of a dam on a river which is supplying solid material into the littoral. When this happens it is necessary for the engineer to take corrective measures. It would be convenient, if possible, from the beginning to obtain all the data, which requires a co-ordination sometimes difficult to achieve.

We emphasise that it is very important to establish a methodology that we consider could be worthwhile at an international level, but applying it by taking into account (as in the case of mathematical models) the special characteristics of each place.

P M A DE CANDT (BELGIUM)

In addition to the paper called "Beach protection as part of the harbour extension at Zeebrugge, Belgium", I would like to give some complementary study-results and a first evaluation of the observation programme east of the new outer harbour at Zeebrugge, Belgium, which is now under construction.

The study was aimed at investigating the probable consequences of harbour extension works on the coastal region east of the harbour after beach restoration. The beach restoration was executed by hydraulic fill of about 8.5 million m^3 of sand which was borrowed some 20 km offshore.

One might presume that the building of an underwater groyne would result in erosion of the total coastal system east of the harbour. This is untrue, due to the fact that we only spoke about local erosion and did not mention local sedimentation caused by tidal transport near the groyne.

Even so, I would like to remind you that the groyne construction which was taken into consideration is an underwater groyne, below low-water, in order not to prevent the longshore transport. In our situation, groyne-building was intended to reduce tidal currents and consequently tidal transport rates in the trench, situated in part of the beach.

However, the Belgian authorities are not interested in the sand gain of the total coastal system, but in the locations of tidal erosion and consequently those of beach regression due to bank instability.

In figure 1 distinction is made between the situation of harbour extension alone and harbour extension plus one groyne.

The calculations show, that in the case of harbour extension above, erosion is expected along practically the entire coastline of about 8 kms.

On the contrary, in the case of harbour extension plus one groyne erosion is expected along a stretch of only 4 kms of coastline.

However, the erosion gradient is twice as much as in the case of harbour extension alone and is situated in the most frequented part of the beach by tourism.

Those calculations have led to the conclusion that groyne building should not be recommended until further observations and studies have been made of alternatives.

As we all know how speculative sediment transport calculations are, even after an extended calibration of the transport calculation formula, a detailed programme of observations has been drawn up, in order to compare the observed and calculated tendencies.

First of all we wanted a control of the tidal velocity – predictions by the physical tidal model which were accepted as the most authentic in comparison with the mathematical tidal model and the physical state model.

During the harbour extension works, tidal velocities were observed and were compared with the measured velocities in the model for the same construction phase.

It can be seen from Figure 2 that there is a rather good correspondence between model and in situ measurements, as well as for the velocities as for the directions for the given point of comparison during the construction of the eastern breakwaters.

Secondly, beach observations were taken from the air using photogrammatic techniques. These methods enable us to calculate beach erosion or sedimentation above the low-water line for any beach section at the same time.

It was observed that the beach regression with reference to the situation immediately after

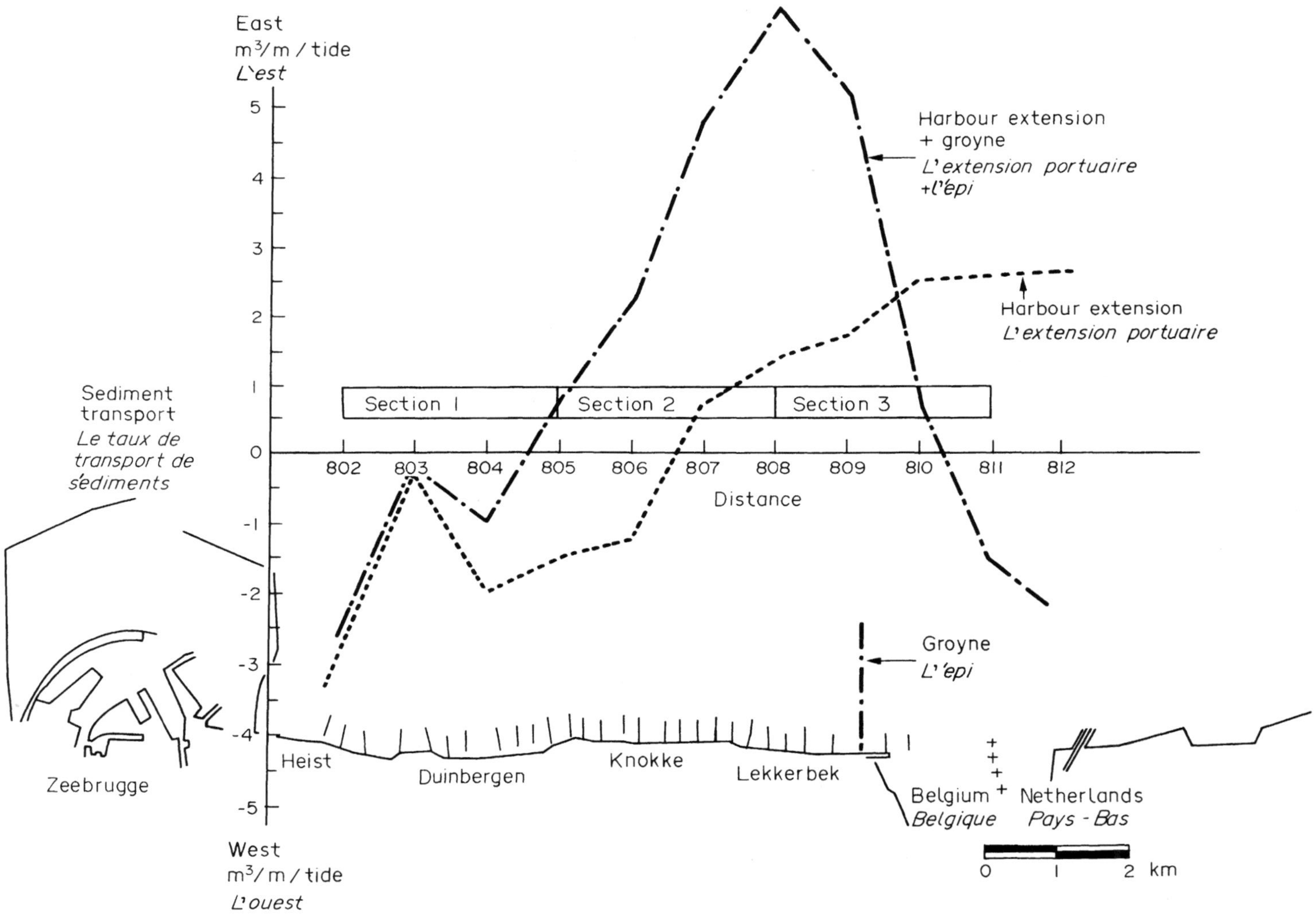

Fig. 1: Transport rates caused by tidal currents
Les taux de transport côtier le long du littoral provoqués par les courants de la marée

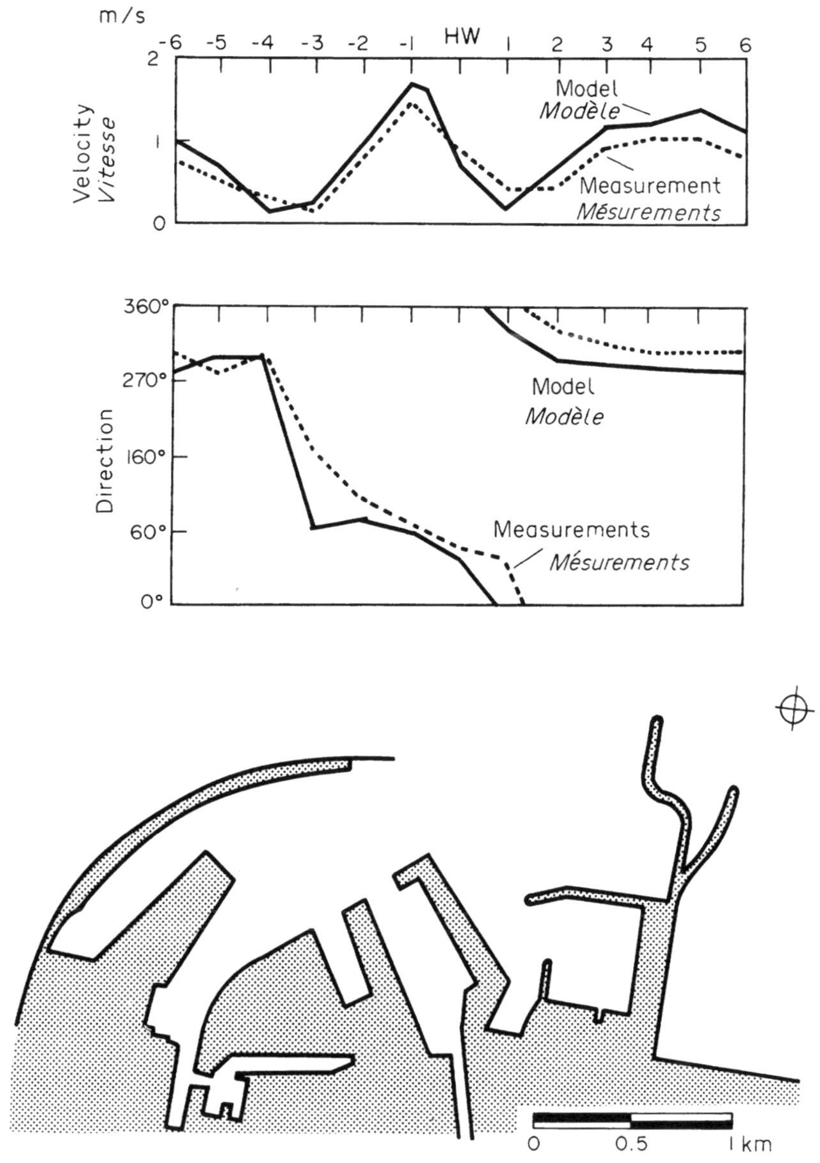

Fig. 2: **Comparison between predicted and measured tidal velocities**
La comparaison relative entre les résultats du modèle et ceux de l'observation sur le terrain pour la force des courants

beach replenishment showed that important erosion rates occurred along the entire coastline (Figure 3). The erosion rates just east of the harbour are due to harbour extension construction work proper and may not be taken into consideration.

The formulae correspond to the calculated erosion locations for the situation of harbour extension alone, although the harbour is only partially extended. Actually, a beach erosion above low-water of about 400,000 m^3 of sand has occurred since the beach restoration work.

However, most of the erosion is due to beach instability, and the eroded material contributes to the filling up of the Appelzak trench which previously was the main cause of beach regression.

Finally, I would like to show the evolution of of the trench in front of the beach.

Figure 4 locates the trench at three different time intervals:

1. The situations in 1977 before harbour extension works and beach restoration. One can see how close the trench is to the beach.

2. The situation in 1979 after beach replenishment of about 8.5 million m^3 of sand.

3. The situation one year later with only a minor harbour extension.

   The trench has migrated eastwards due to beach instabilities by which it was partially filled up with beach material.

This phenomenon was anticipated and in fact was the reason we chose a soft-coastal defence system.

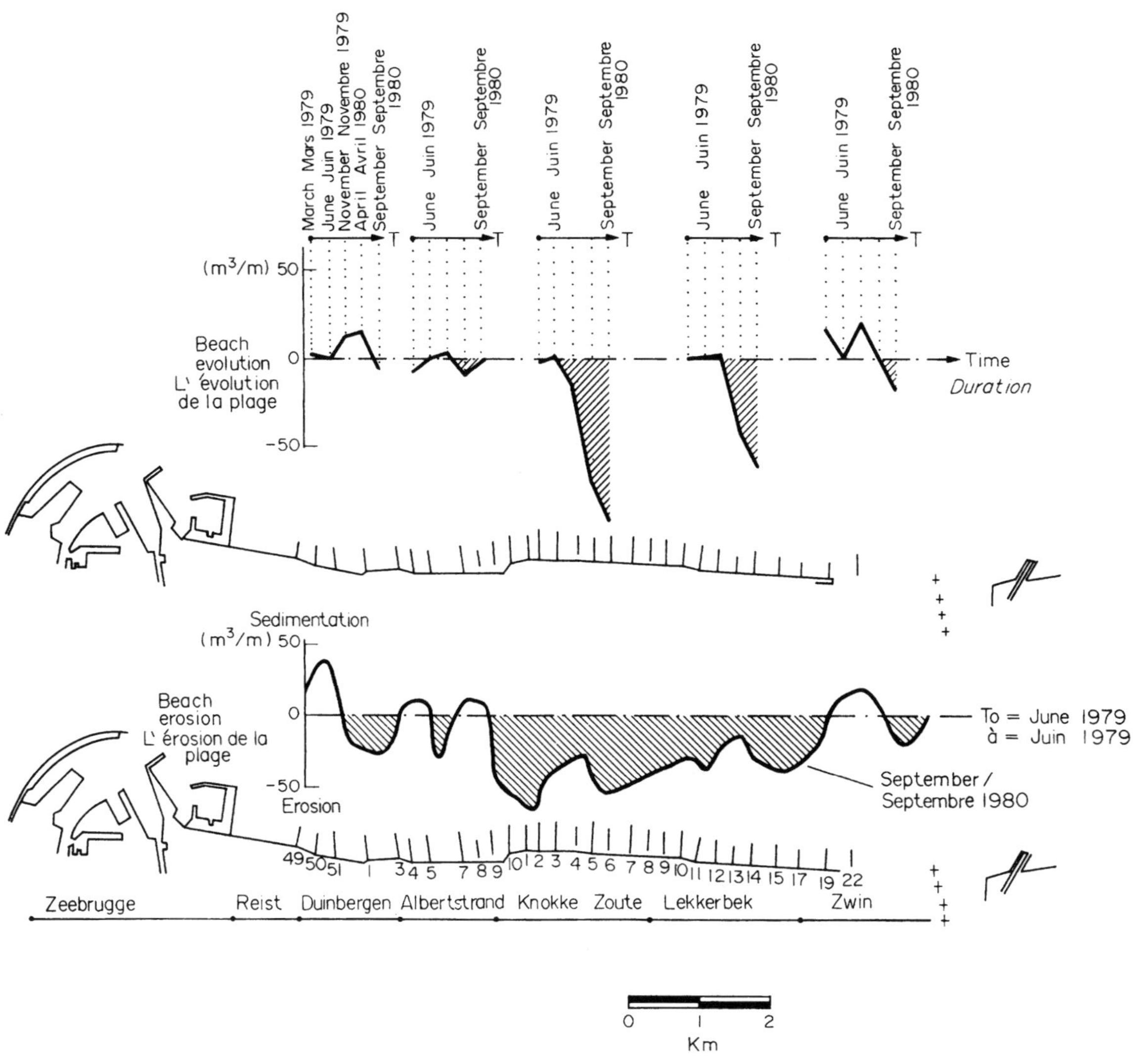

Fig. 3: Beach erosion rates along the coast
Les taux d'érosion le long de la côte

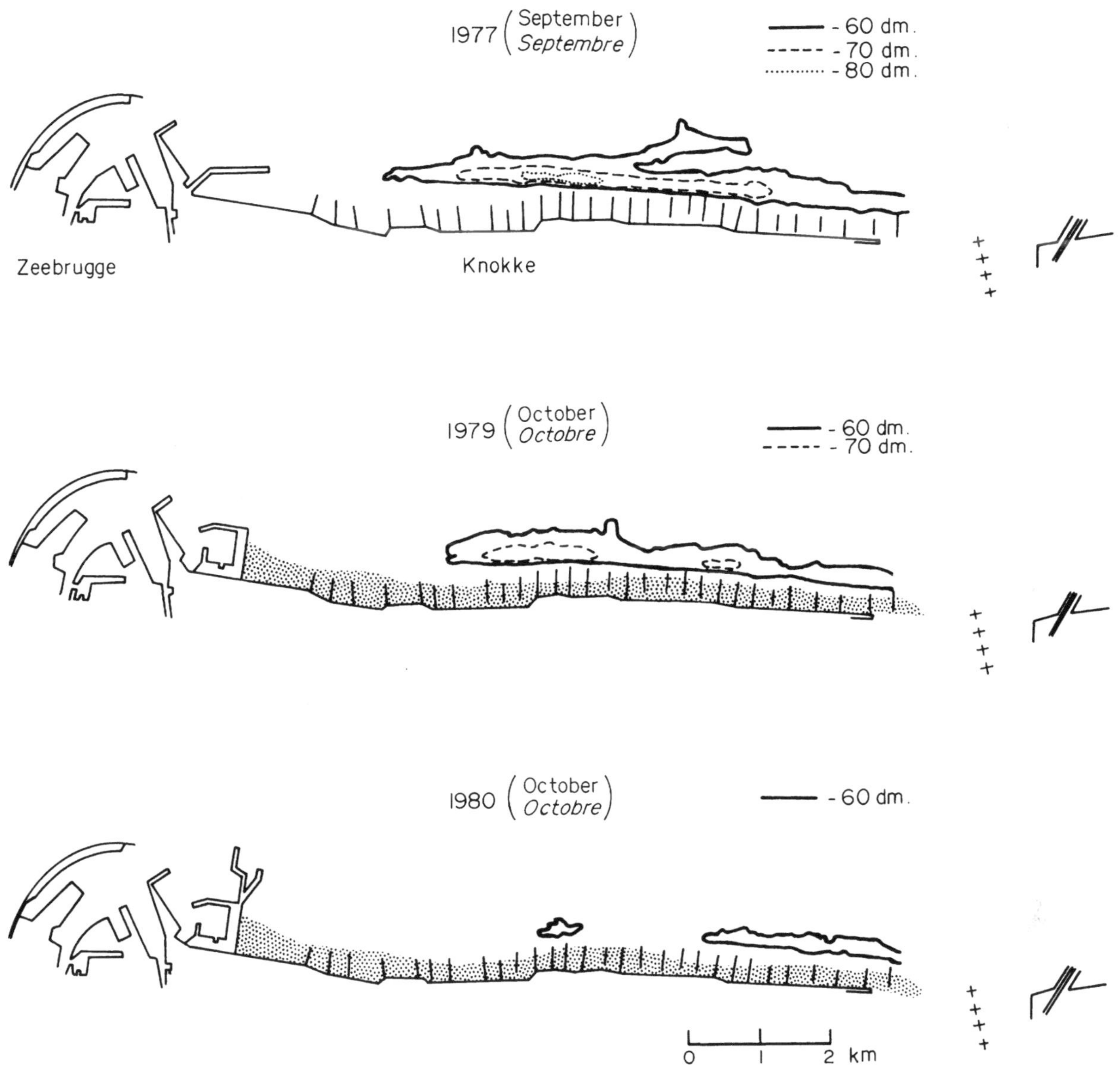

Fig. 4: Evolution of the "Appelzak" Trench
L'évolution de la tranchée "Appelzak"

In conclusion, I would like to mention that the time interval between beach restoration and the actual measurements is only 18 months – which is too short to give the proper coastal tendencies.

The measurements are repeated regularly in order to provide a long-term understanding of beach and coast dynamics. They will permit verification of the calculations which are being continued and allow the Belgium authorities to take action in good time for satisfactory coastal protection subsequent to the harbour extension.

I hope to be able to give you the final results of our studies and observations at the next PIANC Congress.

J L DELORME (FRANCE)

My purpose is to stress certain aspects of experience available in France concerning coastal defence linked to harbour works and to make two comments on points raised in the General Report.

1. In the first place, it should be recalled that the French coastline is very long (nearly

4,000 km) and extremely varied, but that the greater part of it is undergoing erosion, and in some cases very marked erosion. For instance, on the sandy Aquitaine coast, it is by no means unusual for beaches to recede more than 10 m in a year.

In this context, the increasingly intensive use of the coastline led, in 1975 or thereabouts, to a census of all these phenomena of coastal erosion. This catalogue is now being supplemented by more detailed monographs to form a comprehensive source of reference.

2. Harbour works, with their upsetting influence, interfere with the coastal sedimentary regime. More than a dozen examples are quoted in the French paper, based on recent projects most of which have been implemented or are in progress; they relate not only to small harbours for pleasure craft but also to big commercial ports and even the case of a trench dredged offshore for the extraction of materials. The latter case, studied on a sedimentological scale model, moreover shows that this trench is filled in mainly by landward erosion by the action of the swell.

   In any case, the interaction of harbour and coastline is studied systematically in France at the same time as the harbour itself; furthermore, the works cannot be engaged upon until the port's compatibility with the other uses of the coastline has been explicitly verified.

3. If erosion is serious, the coastal defence measures are complex. An example is provided by the port of Bayonne, situated on the Atlantic coast and exposed to heavy sea swells (fifty-year amplitude of the order of 12 m); the adjacent beach to the south, 4.5 km in length, was subjected to alternating and balanced transports, parallel to the shore, of 500,000 m^3 per year, and to erosion exceeding 10 m per year.

   The system installed to protect the harbour entrance and to slow down erosion of the shore comprises:-

   a) Two harbour embankments almost perpendicular to the shore, respectively 400 m and 900 m long.

   b) Seven straight groynes, one of which can be converted into a breakwater; these groynes are combined with landward supplies of coarse sands.

   c) The dumping of dredging products at sea in front of the beach in the shallows (4 to 7 m below lowest water mark). The results are promising, but have yet to be confirmed in the longer term. This method of beach nourishment is an alternative to the landward delivery methods described in several papers.

   In cases where the sedimentary nourishment deficit is great, the example of Bayonne also brings out the fact that it is not enough to provide groynes or breakwaters which act only partially, either for part of the time, owing to the tide, or for part of the sediment transports, as in the case of upper beach works.

4. I should like to make two comments prompted by the General Report presented by Mr. HOLMES.

   Firstly, I join with him in emphasizing the importance of measuring accurately the direction of the swell in stormy periods at sea, and hence far away from land-based observers.

   This parameter, difficult to define precisely, indeed proves to be altogether indispensable, even if the local wind rose does not always provide the answer.

   Secondly, there is the net displacement of sediments discussed in the General Report: this displacement is the result of alternating transports and does not constitute an adequate datum, even though it is more easily accessible. The example of Bayonne is obvious in this connection, as the net displacement there is nil, and yet the displacements parallel to the shore explain a great many of the phenomena. It is therefore necessary to make allowance for the backward and forward movements of sediments, as otherwise very serious mistakes will result.

   In conclusion, it may be said that a thorough knowledge of the site will always be essential, owing to the difficulty of sorting out the pertinent data describing complex phenomena.

R TENAUD (FRANCE)

I should like to draw attention to a problem concerning the use of groynes for coastal protection.

When the coastal transit is variable and has a well-defined direction, we know that groynes are a form of defence that is widely used and in general very effective.

When the coastal transit, while appreciable, has no well-defined resultant, it is often thought that groynes are of no use. The 3rd report by the International Waves Commission does not mention groynes as a method of defence in this case.

Coastal transit is essentially provoked by the swell, the direction of which varies within a wide sector, even though there is a prevailing direction.

When it is said that the resultant of a coastal transit is nil, this is a mean estimated for several years.

In the course of a year or even more, there may be a series of storms causing a coastal transit in the same direction. In that case, very large volumes of materials may be moved and shore erosions may occur.

Groynes are therefore not useless in such a case.

Another comment relates to the dimensions of the groynes. We think that the groynes should be as unaggressive as possible. Low, dipping groynes are less open to attack and more economical.

Tests on scale models, in the case of Bayonne, described by Mr. Delorme, have shown that such groynes were even more effective. We think that the most effective groyne is the one that is no longer visible.

D H SWART (SOUTH AFRICA)

In Section II, p. 942, it is stated in the US paper that fixed dredging plant is used at Durban. This was only the case for a short period of time about 30 years ago and was discontinued because material did not collect at the site of the jetty, which was at the root of the South breakwater.

The methods of wave direction measurement used in South Africa are:

- DOSO orbital velocity indicator.
- Clinometer, or graded telescope.
- radar imagery.
- aerial photographs at regular intervals.

For topographical changes near harbour structures there are various predictive tools:

- empirical models of longshore and onshore-offshore transport
- shoreline evolution models, as described in British, Dutch, South African papers.
- Mathematical.
- Physical models.
- Combinations of the above.

One should carefully consider the level of prediction required for each given situation.

Frequently the level of complexity required increases as the size of the structure decreases.

The accuracy of all the above-mentioned methods could be greatly improved by controlled measurements in the field (see e.g. the French and Belgium papers, also refer to U.S.A. NSTS programme and the German and Polish coastal measurement programmes).

The use of more than one different technique, even in one category, is advisable before a decision is reached.

No paper specifically mentions "beachfill design" (see Section II p. 910). The additional losses due to beachfill are for Richards Bay 5% of the net drift, for Durban however it was 40%.

By-passed material should be placed where the waves and the currents erode sand – this is not practically possible in most cases.

The characteristics of by-passed material, as opposed to native material, is also important.

Care should be taken with the design of a beachfill placement, see, for example, the USA paper.

Losses will, however, always be greater than if the correct material would have been placed ideally. The overfill required to compensate can be predicted/estimated by e.g.

KRUMBEIN/JAMES)	(use only sediment
JAMES)	characteristics and
DEAN)	neglected fill geometry)
SWART) (based on ref.13 Section II p.916)	(Uses sediment characteristics and fill geometry).

Referring to the Reporter General's conclusions, one must not overlook the summarising work done by the USA for their Shore Protection Manual.

1. a) Suggest adding "and techniques".
   b) Suggest rewording "Prediction of water and Sediment Motion and their interactions."

D DREYFOUS-DUCAS (FRANCE)

Suggestions as to how the volume of replenishment necessary to balance erosion may be reduced.

1. The permanent variation in the equilibrium gradient of beaches as a function of the characteristics of the swell tends to be overlooked. This tilt occurs from the lower foreshore in the vicinity of mark 0. Beaches are generally flatter in winter with a considerable scouring of the upper foreshore. The slope is gradually restored with the small swells in spring and summer.

2. Groynes can check or slow down lateral transports, but they cannot correct the effects of "leeward" erosion of harbour jetties. Only longitudinal works on the lower foreshore, continuous or partial, make it possible to trap the sand (Italy, Pointe de Grave).

3. The defence works, whatever they may be, must be designed so as not to disperse the sand:

- oversteep slopes of the upper facing which repel a substantial part of the incident waves and give rise to clapotis making the deposit of sand impossible.
- oversmooth slopes which do not check the water of the return wave and cause erosion of the feet of the structures.

4. There are no reports of any test of openwork harbour entrance jetties in the vicinity of foreshores making possible the lateral transport of sand and the reduction of "leeward" erosion. In a word, we must learn to observe nature and phenomena and to help rather than combat them.

E R HEIBERG (USA)

One aspect of harbour, and also beach protection that is a major problem in the United States is in eliciting public or community support for an improvement and sometimes even for maintenance. Perhaps many of you share my feeling that this subject is still an "art", and not yet a well understood "science". We are still unable to predict precisely the effects of a new structure.

We are convinced that "hard" (structural) solutions and "soft" (dredging or bypassing) should be investigated and compared to find the best solution from both a cost and environmental standpoint. Often a combined solution (jetty with by-passing) is best as compared to straight dredging forced on us by environmentalists. Sometimes, worse, we are forced to a "no project" solution which is often attractive to those who prefer man not to work on harbours and beaches.

Let me assure the Reporter General that we use by-passing willingly only where we think it is the cost effective solution, or when it is the only solution available.

It seems to me that an international effort, as suggested in the draft conclusions, can only help.

In the USA, the engineer continues to be under heavy pressure from both environmental interests and from Government officials who are reluctant to construct needed work. It will help the Army Corps of Engineers if we can point to corroborating conclusions under PIANC or another prestigious multi-national sponsor. I sense that many other members, based on the comments made, would agree with me. The USA will help carry out the recommendation if it is accepted by PIANC.

C MOUTZOURIS (GREECE)

I have a brief comment to make on the General Report.

I would like to draw attention to the fact that from the wave mechanics points of view it is not only the deep sea angle of approach which is difficult to define. It is also the angle of the breaker. ϕ_b.

Wave refraction theories do not hold in the breaker zone, especially in complicated topographies.

W A PRICE (UK)

I would like to direct my remarks to the way in which research might help to solve one of the problems associated with the design and construction of coastal harbours.

There is an increasing demand for deep water and this is why the coastal harbour is taking over from the estuarial port in many parts of the world. The change has meant that we move from an environment where the siltation in dredged channels is controlled by tidal flows, salinity variations and the like to one where waves are present. In the UK paper we have tried to give some idea of how sediment transport can be enhanced by wave action. (see Section II p. 939 Table 2).

For a 2 m wave 8 sec. period in 10 m of water the sediment transport rate will go up of the order of 14 times over what it would be in a steady current and of the order of 60 times if the wave height doubles to 4 m. Suppose we assume that the dredged channel traps most of this sediment in movement, and this is not an unreasonable assumption for deep channels, then the consequences are obvious. Dredged depths in a storm can disappear overnight and I have seen this happen. The consequence on the characteristics of dredging operations is equally dramatic. In the shelter of an estuary the siltation rates might be as indicated in Figure 1., with a dredging capacity indicated by the dotted line. With waves present the picture is quite different. (Fig. 2). The peaks represent bursts of heavy siltation. To keep the port operational requires a much larger dredger of a capacity again indicated by the dotted line. Hence better estimations of the siltation rates at a time when a coastal port is being planned are vital. Hence, I would suggest that one of the most important tasks for the researcher is to establish the effects of waves on sediment transport.

I would seriously question the dredging policy in many estuarial ports. The philosophy of taking the dumped spoil to a place from which it takes a long time to return is often very uneconomic and can be positively harmful to the natural environment. It is similar in a coastal situation. The material should be placed in such a way as to nourish beaches. Even if a large proportion returns to the dredged cut it might still be economic to dredge and dump quite close at hand. Long hauls to dumping grounds should be avoided.
There is an error in the equation on page 938 of our paper which should appear as:

$$S_{w.c.} = (S_c) \left\{ \frac{U-U_c}{U_c} \right\}^2$$

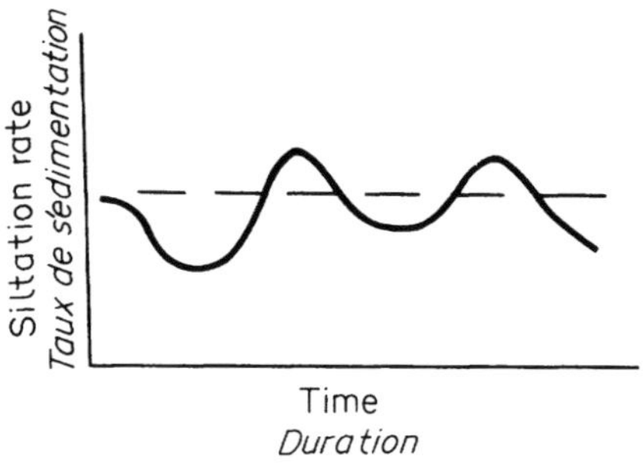

Fig. 1

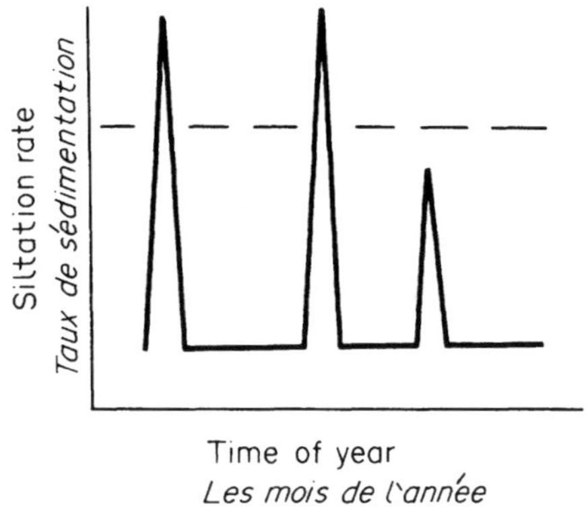

Fig. 2

CONCLUSIONS

1. The papers on Subject 5, the discussion and the Reporter General's appreciation clearly establish the need for an authoratative state-of-the-art report of international status for the use of design engineers. This document should contain the best available advice on three subjects:

   a) Information and data requirement techniques.
   b) Prediction of Sediment Motions.
   c) Remedial measures.

2. Also established is the need for enhanced international collaboration between researchers and engineers involved with coastal dynamics problems.

3. There is a need for an international exercise in the course of which an open coastal site can be thoroughly instrumented and measured with the objective of furthering the understanding of the relationship between hydrodynamics and sediment transport. It would also be of great value if this were a site where it was intended to construct an artificial intervention such as a jetty or breakwater to enable predictions to be made and monitored. Such an exercise will require governmental and probably intergovernmental support. Its results are potentially so important that it would certainly justify such support.

4. It is recommended that both PTC I and PTC II should consider what contribution PIANC can make to satisfy these needs in collaboration with other established International bodies such as I.A.H.R. and the Coastal Engineering Research Council.

PORTS ET ACCES MARITIMES

SECTION II — SUJET 1

Progrès réalisés dans la construction des navires, les aides à la navigation, les voies d'eau et les ports, l'organisation du trafic et l'exploitation des installations à terre, en tenant compte plus particulièrement de l'analyse des risques et des critères de sécurité relatifs au transport, au déchargement et à l'entreposage des gaz naturels liquéfiés et des gaz de pétrole

Lundi 11 mai 1981

Président:	*N N B ORDMAN (GB)* *Noel Ordman and Associates Ltd*
Vice Président:	*ENRIQUEZ FRANCISCO (Espagne)* *D Ing Caminos, Canales y Puertos, Madrid*
Rapporteur Général:	*G B M OLIVER (GB)* *Assistant Director, Technical Services,* *National Ports Council, London*
Secrétaire:	*P LACEY (GB)* *Ove Arup and Partners Ltd, London*
Secrétaire Adjoint:	*Mlle M-M DANEELS (Belgique)* *Secrétaire AIPCN Secrétariat Générale, Bruxelles*

All page numbers cited in these discussions refer to Maritime Ports and Seaways, Volumes 1-5, Proceedings of the XXV Congress of the Permanent International Association of Navigation Congresses (PIANC) Edinburgh 1981, ISBN 0 08 027278 9 Pergamon Press, 1981

Orateurs

A FUGLUM (Norvege), R H SMITH (Canada), V BRATIANU (Etats-Unis), W H R LAWRENCE (GB), G P KOSTYLEW (OMCI), M SUZUO DAN (Japon), J A ZWAMBORN (Afrique du Sud), A L MOSS-MORRIS (Afrique du Sud), N F MATTHEWS (AISM), L R DUMAS (France)

G. B. M. OLIVER (U.K.) RAPPORTEUR GENERAL

L'utilisation des gaz naturels et des gaz de pétrole en tant que sources d'énergie a connu un extraordinaire développement au cours des dernières années et devrait, selon les prévisions, continuer de progresser. Plusieurs rapports, parmi lesquels ceux des Pays-Bas, de la Finlande et du Japon, en attestent. En conséquence, alors qu'en 1966 on ne comptait dans le monde que 150 méthaniers, d'une capacité globale de 500.000 m3 à peu près, en 1979 il y avait en service ou en commande un peu plus de 600 de ces navires, représentant une capacité totale de 14 millions de m3. Ces chiffres montrent que la croissance du trafic s'est accompagnée d'un agrandissement de la taille moyenne des navires, qui en fait a été multipliée par sept.

Lors de la préparation du présent rapport, il a semblé opportun de se pencher sur les sujets suivants, afin d'évaluer dans quelle mesure les divers rapports y fond des apports nouveaux au niveau de la connaissance et de pouvoir ainsi déterminer les domaines sur lesquels devrait porter l'attention à l'avenir:

- les scénari de risques potentiels
- l'analyse de risques
- la conception et la construction des méthaniers
- l'histoire des transporteurs de gaz en matière de sécurité
- l'organisation du trafic
- l'implantation, la conception et l'exploitation des terminaux
- la sécurité et les actes de sabotage.

La plupart de ces sujets peuvent être considérés comme se rangeant sous l'aspect "critères de sécurité" figurant dans l'intitulé du sujet. Ceci donne une première idée de l'ampleur du domaine qu'il faut envisager si l'on veut réduire à un minimum le risque collectif associé au transport des gaz liquéfiés.

Il ressort de tous les rapports que l'organisation du trafic dans les zones encombrées est à présent acceptée en tant que contribution positive à la sécurité de la navigation, pourvu toutefois que le système choisi soit adapté aux conditions et aux exigences locales.

Si l'on ne peut contester ceci en tant que principe général, on peut cependant s'inquiéter de la tendance des divers ports et des divers pays de mettre au point leur propre système sans tenir compte des procédures et des pratiques adoptées ailleurs, alors même que normes et procédures diffèrent déjà considérablement aussi bien d'un pays à l'autre qu'au sein d'un même pays. Il peut en résulter confusion et hésitations dans le chef des capitaines et donc création de situations potentiellement dangereuses.

Bien que les rapports présentés sous ce thème n'en fassent pas mention, on ne peut oublier le travail en cours au sein de la CEE, dans le cadre de la coopération européenne dans le domaine des projets de recherche scientifique et technique (COST). Ce travail vise l'harmonisation et la rationalisation des systèmes de gestion du trafic maritime à partir de la terre et doit déboucher sur des procédures et des usages similaires dans tous les ports des pays membres de la CEE.

LES DEBATS

A FUGLUM (NORVEGE)

Le rapport norvégien en cette matière souligne deux grands problèmes liés à la sécurité de la navigation des méthaniers dans le chenal d'accès aussi bien qu'à l'intérieur du port.

Leur solution a demandé:

1. Une analyse de risque portant sur les possibilités d'accidents et l'impact de ceux-ci sur les gens et sur l'environnement;

2. un essai sur modèle physique dans une section étroite du chenal d'accès en vue d'effectuer des améliorations sur place.

M. Oliver, Rapporteur Général, a déjà mis en évidence les éléments essentiels du rapport, mais j'aimerais ajouter quelques commentaires sur certains points soulevés par le Rapport Général.

La publication des résultats de l'analyse de risque décrite dans mon rapport suscita un vif débat. La probabilité de morts d'hommes en raison d'un accident survenant à un méthanier était estimée à 1 x 10^{-7}, ce qui équivaut à peu près à la probabilité de mourir frappé par la foudre. Néanmoins, la foudre ne provoque pas d'accidents mortels partout et en beaucoup d'endroits la probabilité est quasi nulle.

Il est important de présenter les résultats d'une analyse de risque de telle sorte qu'ils soient aisément compréhensibles. Le Rapporteur Général, par ailleurs, a fait état de l'acceptation par le public de certains degrés de risque liés à différents types d'accidents.

Il n'en reste pas moins que les accidents entraînant mort d'hommes liés au transport de certains types de marchandises en vertu de réglementations officielles auraient un degré d'acceptation publique inférieur à celui d'accidents provoqués par des individus.

La fixation d'un niveau acceptable de risque avant de disposer d'éléments d'appréciation suffisants pose incontestablement problème et peut donner lieu à des décisions mal justifiées et non économiques. En tout état de cause, une sous-estimation du niveau de risque est susceptible de donner lieu à une critique publique et subséquemment à la perte de son emploi par le responsable.

Le rapport norvégien aussi bien que le Rapporteur Général ont également souligné l'importance des facteurs humains en tant que causes d'accidents, de même que celle des défaillances mécaniques affectant des navires en chenaux ou passages étroits.

Je voudrais montrer quelques diapositives illustrant le passage étroit au pont situé sur le fleuve Bravik, à un endroit où le chenal forme une courbe en S. On connaît plusieurs cas de problèmes de propulsion ayant affecté les navires dans cette région. Il a été difficile d'en établir les causes, mais l'utilisation des remorqueurs y a depuis lors été rendue obligatoire.

Il fut également décidé de réaliser des études sur le terrain et des essais sur modèles qui ont débouché sur une méthode d'amélioration du chenal qui s'est avérée économique en dépit de la nécessité de faire sauter le solide lit rocheux norvégien. Nous nous préoccupons également de créer des zones de sécurité à l'intérieur du port et de séparer des autres activités portuaires les navires transportant et manipulant des marchandises dangereuses. Le besoin de telles zones de sécurité est reconnu en Norvége comme dans d'autres pays, mais les données scientifiques disponibles sont encore insuffisantes pour fonder les décisions en ce domaine.

De maniére général, je partage les recommandations d'action ultérieure formulées par le Rapporteur Général, mais je souhaiterais que soient en outre pris en considération les éléments suivants:

1. Dans quelle mesure le degré de risque et la probabilité d'accidents sont ils déterminés par la conception et la construction des navires?

2. Dans quelle mesure les chenaux d'accès, la localisation des terminaux et la surveillance — ou le manque de surveillance — des mouvements des navires suscitent-ils des risques pour les navires?

Je souhaite concrètement que les conclusions générales quant à la poursuite des travaux tiennent compte de ce qui suit:

1. Recommandations en vue d'améliorer la conception et la construction des navires pour intégrer les contraintes externes particulières.

2. Adoption d'une norme internationale commune spécifiant le type de risque à analyser en liaison avec le transport maritime de GNL et de GPL.

3. Suggestions de directives internationales en matière de définition de niveaux normaux de risque et de leur présentation de manière clairement compréhensible par le public.

4. Etude des mesures de prévention physiques à mettre en oeuvre le long des voies d'accès en vue d'une sécurité de navigation optimale.

5. Compilation et présentation à l'échelle mondiale des règlements en matière de contrôle de trafic.

6. Recommandations portant sur les zones de sécurité et les barrières physiques à l'intérieur des ports.

Les rapports traitant de ce sujet, de même que les commentaires du Rapporteur Général, démontrent qu'il s'agit ici d'un des principaux sujets pris en charge par l'A.I.P.C.N. Je crois que la poursuite des travaux en ce domaine est absolument indispensable et je suggère que ceci soit confié au Groupe de Travail qui a déjà été créé dans le cadre de la Section II.

R H SMITH (CANADA)

En m'inspirant de l'expérience de l'Unité de Recherche sur les Accidents de la Garde côtière canadienne, je voudrais proposer les commentaires qui suivent:

1. Une présentation statistique des victimes et des accidents à bord des navires enregistrés par la Garde côtière canadienne au cours de l'année 1979 donne les résultats que voici:

Cause	% du total
Erreurs opérationnelles	38
Déficiences équipement/ouvrages	17
Environnement	15
Autres, y c. comportement du navire, aides, etc.	17
Non identifiées	13

   Cette brève synthèse confirme la conclusion préliminaire de l'auteur quant à l'importance du facteur humain dans les accidents impliquant des navires.

2. En l'absence d'enquête publique, il ne nous est pas normalement possible de déterminer la cause d'un accident identifiable: ainsi, il n'est pas possible d'incriminer le capitaine X ou le pilote Y si ceux-ci ne peuvent se

défendre légalement. Nous pouvons réaliser de bonnes études sur les grands accidents parce que dans ce cas une Enquête Prélimin-aire est complète et que nous sommes raisonnablement autorisés à avoir confiance dans le rapport d'enquête, dans la mesure où il nous est livré à titre confidentiel. L'analyse peut être présentée de manière anonyme. C'est pourquoi nous pensons que l'enquête par voie de questionnaire n'est pas adéquate.

Nous soutenons donc l'appel lancé par l'auteur en faveur de données détaillées, fiables et uniformes.

3. Le nombre de mouvements (densité/fréquence) nous pose également des problèmes, mais l'introduction du sytème VTM nous a beaucoup aidé à cet égard et son effet deviendra plus sensible encore à mesure que les programmes informatiques s'amélioreront.

4. En résumé, si les enquêtes sur les accidents ne sont pas publiques, et si donc tous les détails ne sont pas rendus disponibles et si l'organisme chargé de l'étude n'a pas accès direct aux rapports confidentiels complets, il est virtuellement impossible de réaliser une compilation complète et significative.

5. Enfin, sur la base de l'expérience canadienne, nous donnons notre appui au point (i) du projet de conclusions du Rapporteur Général, à ce stade, de suggérer en termes généraux l'addition d'une phrase: "et que chaque pays soit encouragé à prendre les mesures qui s'imposent à cet égard".

V BRATIANU (USA)

Je voudrais rendre compte brièvement de certains essais modélisés sur le comportement des grands méthaniers et faire mention ensuite d'informations disponibles sur les bras de chargement maritime, qui constituent un chaînon essentiel du système.

Le comportement des grands méthaniers à l'amar-rage est extrêmement sensible à la période des lames. Des essais sur modèles de méthaniers de 125.000 m3 ont démontré que le môle est inopérant pour de tels navires en présence de large trains de lames dont les périodes dépas-sent 10 secondes, même pour des hauteurs de lames significatives de 0,50 à 0,75 m. Il est donc important, en vue de la planification, de disposer d'un équipement adéquat et capable d'enregistrer également les lames de longue période.

Le Forum Internationa Maritime des Sociétés Pétrolières (O.C.I.M.F.) a publié un manuel d'instructions très complet sur la construction des bras de chargement maritimes.

Les bras maritimes des terminaux GPL et GNL modernes sont équipés des systèmes de libér-ation d'urgence décrits dans de nombreux rapports. Quant à savoir si ces systèmes doivent être libéres automatiquement en cas de surportée, cela mérite une étude attentive, particulièrement en cas de terminaux de dé-chargement recevant des transporteurs non spécialisés (problème de houle).

La plupart des terminaux industriels ont écarté la solution des fils électriques entre navire et môle. Pour éviter une éventuelle étincelle due aux courants parasites, les bras de charge-ment sont équipés hors bord de brides isolantes.

W H R LAWRENCE (GB)

Tout d'abord, je voudrais féliciter M. Oliver. Son rapport constitue une excellente synthèse des rapports présentés dans le cadre de ce sujet, rapports extrêmement complexes et riches en in-formations. Le résumé dense et plein d'intérêt qu'il en a fait mérite le respect.

Cependant, je voudrais intervenir sur la partie de son rapport qui traite des risques spécifiques liés aux fuites de gaz liquéfié, dans la mesure où je pense que ces risques peuvent prêter à confusion en l'absence d'explications suffisantes.

Le rapport définit une fuite majeure comme étant un épanchement d'au moins 1 000 tonnes résultant d'un accident de navigation entraînant une dé-chirure du système de rétention du navire. Cette définition d'une fuite majeure en vaut une autre. Je pense néanmoins qu'elle est erronée en matière de risques spécifiques susceptibles d'affecter la population locale (paragraphe 9). L'accent de tous les rapports présentés dans cette section est placé de diverses manières sur les conceptions et les procédures d'exploi-tation adoptées en vue d'éviter une fuite majeure. Il me semble donc qu'il conviendrait de définir les risques d'atteinte directe aux populations locales par rapport à la fuite maximale crédible au cours des opérations de chargement et de dé-chargement. Comme l'indiquent les rapports, les conceptions envisagent généralement une fuite maximale d'environ 15 m3 et même beaucoup moins dans la plupart des situations.

C'est pourquoi la définition des risques donnée au paragraphe 9 en termes d'une fuite de 1 000 tonnes prête à confusion.

Je voudrais aussi dire quelques mots de la terminologie utilisée dans le paragraphe 9. Un feu est une description émotive de ce que l'on appelle plus correctement incendie concentré.

Celui-ci est provoqué par la combustion d'un ensemble concentré de matière qui donne lieu, en raison d'un mélange relativement faible des vapeurs avec l'air, à un feu de hautes flammes lentes qui, dans le cas du propane, est également très fuligineux. Un tel incendie provoquerait certainement une radiation, mais il est clair que si la quantité impliquée est réduite et la durée de l'incendie limitée, il serait relativement aisé de se protéger de cette radiation, comme M. Oliver l'a indiqué.

Il est également fait mention de la possibilite d'explosion. A cet égard, je me permets de rappeler que les travaux expérimentaux réalisés à ce jour sur les fuites limitées démontrent que la détonation ne survient pas pour les quantités dont nous parlons et probablement pas pour des quantités supérieures. Les vitesses d'accélération des flammes mesurées sont trop faibles pour provoquer une détonation. C'est pourquoi il est trompeur de mentionner des distances par rapport au centre d'une fuite susceptible de provoquer des blessures et des dégâts. Je dois ajouter que je parle ici d'une fuite de GPL et de GNL en espace non restreint.

La dérive des nuages de vapeur enflammable a fait l'objet d'une grande quantité de recherches qui ont débouché sur des modèles mathématiques de prévision du cheminement du nuage. Celui-ci est bien entendu fonction de l'importance de la fuite. M. Oliver mentionne une distance de 10 kms, mais celle-ci suppose une fuite de quelque 25.000 m3. Pour les quantités que j'ai dites être probables, soit de l'ordre de 15 m3, la distance parcourue par le nuage avant que celui-ci ne se disperse sans dommages serait de 100 à 200 mètres.

Je voudrais saisir cette occasion pour appuyer les souhaits exprimés en faveur d'une régulation des mouvements des navires. Bien que je ne sois pas d'accord pour suivre aveuglément tout ce qui se fait ailleurs, je pense que chaque situation doit être étudiée avec soin en vue de tirer le plus grand parti possible de la protection naturelle qu'offre tout site ou port. Ceci, assorti d'un contrôle raisonnable et inspiré des situations concrètes, devrait assurer des conditions satisfaisantes de sécurité.

Enfin, je voudrais appuyer la recommandation de M. Oliver selon laquelle un domaine utile de recherche future pour l'A.I.P.C.N. pourrait être une étude visant à favoriser une meilleure compréhension des critères de localisation des terminaux maritimes destinés à la manutention des gaz liquéfiés.

G. P. KOSTYLEW (OMCI)

A l'OMCI, nous nous intéressons aux activités de l'AIPCN du fait de votre intérêt pour la "navigation" qui forme une partie très importante du travail de notre Organisation. Nos efforts tendent à augmenter de façon permanente l'efficience et la sécurité de la navigation et dans cet ordre d'idées, l'OMCI a pris des mesures effectives.

A ce stade, il convient de reprendre brièvement l'historique de l'OMCI et des faits qui ont conduit à sa formation. Lorsqu'on a discuté de l'établissement de l'OMCI en tant qu'agence spécialisée des Nations Unies s'occupant exclusivement d'affaires maritime, l'idée était de mettre au point un outil international tendant à améliorer la sécurité en mer. Il y avait à cela deux raisons principales. Tout d'abord, la navigation a toujours été une occupation dangereuse. En second lieu et du fait du caractère international de cette industrie, on s'est aperçu depuis longtemps que toute action tendant à améliorer la sécurité de la navigation serait plus efficace si elle se développait sur le plan international plutôt qu'au niveau de pays individuels agissant unilatéralement sans coordination avec les autres. Bien qu'un certain nombre d'accords internationaux importants aient déjà été adoptés, beaucoup d'Etats convinrent de la nécessité d'un organisme permanent qui pourrait coordonner et promouvoir d'autres mesures sur une base plus durable.

C'est dans cet état d'esprit que la Conférence Maritime des Nations-Unies de 1948 adopta la Convention établissant l'Organisation Maritime Consultative Intergouvernementale (OMCI) comme le premier organisme international qui se soit jamais consacré exclusivement aux affaires maritimes.

Durant la décade qui avait précédé la Convention, d'autres problèmes ayant trait à la sécurité mais pour lesquels l'approche devait être légèrement différente, avaient attiré l'attention internationale. Un des plus importants était la menace de pollution des mers par les navires et plus particulièrement de pollution par les hydrocarbures transportés par les pétroliers. Une convention internationale sur le sujet a été adoptée en 1954, quatre ans avant la fondation de l'OMCI. La responsabilité de l'administration et de l'application de la Convention a été une des premières tâches entreprises par l'OMCI dès ses débuts en janvier 1959. Donc, dès l'abord, l'amélioration de la sécurité maritime et la prévention de la pollution marine ont été les deux objectifs principaux de l'OMCI.

Permettez-moi maintenant d'évoquer brièvement la structure de l'OMCI. Ses organes principaux sont l'Assemblée et le Conseil. L'Assemblée qui est l'organe de direction suprême est formée de représentants de tous les Etats membres; elle décide du programme de travail de l'Organisation, approuve les propositions qui lui sont soumises, vote le budget auquel contribuent tous les Etats membres selon une répartition convenue et élit le Conseil de l'OMCI. L'Assemblée se réunit généralement à Londres tous les deux ans. Le Conseil est formé de représentants de 24 Etats membres élus par l'Assemblée pour deux ans; il se réunit normalement deux fois par an et constitue les instances de gouvernement de l'OMCI entre les sessions de l'Assemblée. Début mars 1981, l'OMCI comptait 120 membres et un membre-associé.

Le travail technique de l'Organisation est confié à un certain nombre de Commissions, dont les plus importantes sont le Comité de la Sécurité Maritime et le Comité de la Protection du Milieu marin. Le Comité de Sécurité Maritime a un certain nombre de sous-comités qui s'occupent de domaines tels que la navigation, les radiocommunications, les engins de sauvetage, la formation, la recherche et le sauvetage, la conception et l'équipement des navires, la prévention de l'incendie, le compartimentage, la stabilité et les lignes de charge, les navires de pêche, les conteneurs et les cargaisons, les marchandises dangereuses et les produits chimiques en vrac. Le dernièr est en même temps Sout-comité du Comité de la Protection du Milieu Marin, qui mène les activités antipollution de l'OMCI, alors que d'autres Comités sont le Comité Juridique, le Comité de la Coopération technique et le Comité de la simplification des formalités.

Pour arriver à ses objectifs, l'OMCI a, durant les vingt et une dernières années, recommandé l'adoption de 31 Conventions, et préparé un grand nombre de Codes et de Recommandations sur différents sujets ayant trait à la sécurité maritime et à la prévention de la pollution. Le premier travail concernant une Convention est généralement effectué par une Commission ou une sous-commission; un projet est établi et approuvé par une commission compé tente avant d'être soumis avec l'accord du Conseil et de l'Assemblée à une Conférence Diplomatique à laquelle sont invitées des délégations de tous les Etats membres des Nations-Unies — même les Etats qui ne seraient pas membres de l'OMCI. Les Conférences, si elles arrivent à bonne fin, adoptent un texte final qui est soumis aux Gouvernements pour ratification, adhésion ou acceptation.

Les deux objectifs primaires de l'Organisation sont l'adoption de normes de sécurité maritime aussi élevées que possible et la prévention et le contrôle de la pollution due aux navires. Le facteur qui peut le mieux contribuer à la réalisation de ces deux objectifs est la formation maritime et en conséquence, les activités de l'OMCI se sont étendues à ce domaine vital qui a joui d'une priorité absolue ces dernières années.

Le facteur humain et ses implications dans toutes les activités du domaine maritime ont nécessité la prescription de normes professionnelles minimales pour les gens de mer qui tiennent compte de la sécurité maritime. Ces normes se retrouvent dans la Convention Internationale sur le degré de formation, l'attestation et de veille des Gens de mer (1978) ("Convention on Standards of Training, Certification and Watchkeeping for Seafarers").

A cet égard, j'aimerais me référer au programme exhaustif et pragmatique mis au point par OMCI pour fournir une assistance technique aux pays en voie de développement, particulièrement dans le domaine de la formation maritime.

L'OMCI est la première agence spécialisée des Nations-Unies qui ait officiellement établi une Commission de Coopération Technique. En fait, ceci signifie que la coopération technique fait maintenant partie du travail habituel de l'OMCI et que la Commission de Coopération Technique a été mise sur le même pied et fonctionne aussi régulièrement que les Commissions de Sécurité Maritime ou de Protection de l'Environnement marin, etc. Le programme de coopération technique est axé sur les services de conseils fournis aux pays en voie de développement. Ce programme de conseils est financé en ordre principal par l'UNDP, mais certains conseillers sont financés par des gouvernements donateurs. Il existe des consultants et conseillers en matière de législation de sécurité maritime, de formation, de prévention de la pollution marine, etc. mais aussi en matière d'activités techniques portuaires.

Les consultants portuaires se sont déjà rendus dans nombre de pays en voie de développement et ont prodigué leurs avis sur les activités techniques portuaires. Certains des sujets qui ont fait l'objet de conseils sont repris ci-dessous:

1. Equipement pour la manutention des marchandises, grues, vêhicules, etc. et augmentation de la productivité par l'introduction d'équipement moderne et l'utilisation de meilleurs techniques;

2. entreposage des marchandises;

3. introduction du Code IMDG dans les règlementations portuaires;

4. amélioration des communications portuaires, de l'exploitation et de la sécurité des terminaux, de la lutte contre l'incendie et du nettoyage des nappes de pétrole;

5. aides à la navigation, systèmes de bouées, leur modernisation, leur utilisation et leur entretien;

6. conseils en ce qui concerne le développement de la main d'oeuvre technique et le planning prospectif;

7. la formation du personnel à quai dans différents domaines;

8. conseils sur l'acquisition de matériel portuaire, de remorqueurs, etc.: formation de pilotes.

Voice, Monsieur le Président, une courte description des lignes principales du travail et des compétences de l'OMCI.

M SUZUO DAN (JAPAN)

Le port d'Himaji est situé à l'ouest d'une région à forte densité de population appelée Kinki, qui compte 20 millions d'habitants. Le port est situé dans la "Setonaikai" — le mer intérieure réputée pour ses qualités esthétiques aussi bein que pour son intense activité industrielle. Son accès facile et une importante industrie de la pêche font d'Himaji un port très actif.

En 1979, nous avons présenté un plan d'importation de GNL — un combustible propre — visant à assurer nos besoins à long terme de gaz de ville et d'électricité sans détruire le magnifique environnement de la mer intérieure. Nous avons organisé des réunions avec les habitants et avec les pêcheurs sur le thème de la sécurité de l'exploitation du terminal gazier et du méthanier. Parallèlement, les autorités locales procédaient à leur propre évaluation de la sécurité et du respect de l'environnement. En fin de compte, toute le monde marqua son accord pour aller de l'avant. La construction du terminal GNL fut commencée en novembre 1976 et terminée en décembre 1978. L'exploitation du méthanier au terminal fut lancée en février 1979 et en avril 1981 53 méthaniers ont déchargé leur gaz indonésien sans aucun accident. Notre recherche et notre expérience me permettent de donner les indications suivantes sur le scénario de risque potentiel:

1. Les boules de feu proviennent essentiellement d'un échappement soudain de gaz liquéfié sous pression. Le GNL est transporté et stocké à basse température sous pression atmosphérique. En cas de fuite et d'inflammation, les possibilités de boules de feu sont très réduites. Ceci est démontré par le fait qu'aucun essai de mise à feu de GNL n' a en aucun endroit du monde, donné lieu à ces boules de feu.

2. On dit que l'explosion d'un nuage de vapeur de GNL est impossible dans des conditions normales. En cas d'explosion de, par exemple, 1 000 tonnes de gaz liquéfié, la zone de danger est supposée être d'environ 250 m.

3. Selon le rapport de la Garde côtière des Etats-Unis, une fuite instantannée de 1 000 tonnes de GNL dans la mer donnerait lieu à une zone de dispersion de gaz inflammable d'environ 1,5 km.

Je termine en concluant que le GNL est le plus sûr des combustibles propres.

J A ZWAMBORN (AFRIQUE DU SUD)

M. Oliver, notre Rapporteur Général, nous a fourni une excellente synthèse des risques inhérents à la manipulation des GPL, et ce y compris les conséquences d'accidents en mer (problèmes de trafic) liés au stockage, à la conception des transporteurs, à certains aspects de la conception (tracé) des terminaux et à d'éventuels actes de sabotage.

Il conclut que (1) une banque de données sur les accidents devrait être créée, (2) les systèmes de trafic devraient être harmonisés et (3) une meilleure compréhension des critères de localisation des terminaux gaziers est nécessaire. Nous appuyons sans réserve ces recommandations.

Bien qu'il s'agisse de toute évidence des aspects essentiels du sujet dont nous débattons aujourd'hui, je crois que le Sujet 1 va au-delà de ceux-ci. Si l'on se réfère à son intitulé, il comprend en effet "Progrés réalisés dans la construction des ... voies navigables et ports ..., avec une attention particulière pour les risques ... du transport, du déchargement du gaz naturel liquéfié et des gaz de pétrole".

A mon sens, ceci couvre <u>entre autres choses</u> les risques relatifs à l'<u>accostage</u> des navires et la possibilité de <u>talonnage</u> dans le chenal d'accès ou du port.

Les problèmes d'<u>accostage</u> sont traités dans les rapports de l'Australie (élasticité des ducs d'Albe d'accostage par rapport à celle du navire), du <u>Canada</u> (forces de résistance dans les terminaux à courants forts), du Japon (vitesses d'accostage) et de l'<u>U.R.S.S.</u> (charges à l'accostage).

Les possibilités d'<u>échouage</u> et les risques qui y sont associés sont brièvement mentionnés dans les rapports de la <u>Finlande</u> (95% des accidents survenus avec du GPL eurent lieu dans des passes étroites, pas nécessairement par mauvaise visibilité), de la <u>France</u>, de l'<u>Allemagne</u> (pied de pilote de 10% dans le Jade), de la <u>Norvège</u> et des U.S.A. (M. Bratiano vient de souligner l'importance des mouvements des navires produits par les lames).

Le rapport des Pays-Bas étudie en grand détail le dimensionnement des chenaux d'entrée et mentionne comme sources d'échouage une visibilité médiocre, des vitesses de vent élevées, des courants forts et la houle. Il précise qu'en raison du facteur de risque élevé associé au GPL, il faut prévoir un pied de pilote relativement important si l'on veut réduire le danger de toucher le fond du chenal. Je crois qu'on retient un tirant d'eau de 35% au lieu des 20% utilisés pour les autres navires. Bien que le "squat" soit également une cause d'accidents, le facteur principal des plus graves de ceux-ci est constitué par les lames de longue période (>12 s) ou la houle. Le rapport donne un exemple d'amplitude de houle maximale calculée, soit $Z_{max\ (houle)} = 1,25$ H où H est la hauteur de lame.

Le rapport de l'Afrique du Sud fournit des données enregistrées sur les mouvements verticaux des navires à Richards Bay. La profondeur du chenal d'accès de ce port est celle qui correspond au tirant d'eau maximum du plus grand navire plus <u>40%</u>, au lieu des 20% recommandés dans le Supplément au Bulletin n° 35. Cette profondeur est basée sur des tests sur modèles physiques qui ont démontré un enfoncement d'environ <u>5 m</u> pour des houles de 12 s de période et de <u>2,5 m</u> de haut en angle de 90° de travers.

Les mesures sur prototypes décrites dans le rapport comprennent déjà un enfoncement maximum <u>enregistré</u> dans le chenal d'entrée de Richards Bay de 4,5 m pour une lame significative de 3 m de haut, soit $Z_{max} = L,5\ H_s$. Ceci signifie déjà qu'une surprofondeur de 30% est nécessaire à Richards Bay, alors même que les directions de lames les plus critiques ne sont pas encore survenues au cours des périodes d'enregistrement. Il <u>semble</u> donc que la tolérance prévue de 40% n'est <u>pas</u> excessive.

Il apparaît donc que les mouvements des navires provoqués par la houle peuvent, dans certaines conditions, être beaucoup plus amples que les valeurs de calme préliminaires mentionnées dans le Supplément au Bulletin n° 35 de l'A.I.P.C.N. En raison du nombre de ports dans le monde soumis à la houle et compte tenu du fait que de nombreux détroits maritimes ont des eaux peu profondes par rapport aux tirants d'eau des grands navires actuels, y compris les transporteurs de GPL qui peuvent exiger des critères de sécurité plus sévères (Manche 24 m, Détroit de Singapour 23 m et chenaux d'accès de la Baltique 17 m), il est suggéré à la présente Assemblée d'envisager d'ajouter la recommandation qui suit à celles du Rapport Général, si, du moins, Monsieur le Président, ceci vous paraît acceptable:

"La poursuite de l'étude des mouvements verticaux des navires dûs aux lames de longue période et à la houle en fonction du risque de talonnage en mer ou en chenal."

A L MOSS-MORRIS (AFRIQUE DU SUD)

La vue d'ensemble complète donnée par le Rapporteur Général de l'analyse de risque et des critères de sécurité relatifs au transport, au déchargement et au stockage des gaz liquéfiés n'a pas fait mention d l'avantage évident de localiser les terminaux GNL et GPL à proximité de l'entrée du port. Ceci permet de séparer, aussitôt que possible, après l'entrée dans le port, les chargements dangereux du reste du trafic et ainsi de réduire les risques de collision. Il est manifestement nécessaire de placer le terminal au sein d'un site suffisamment étendu qui doit lui-même être séparé par une distance "de sécurité" des autres installations de manutention et de stockage. Je crois que ce Congrès doit s'efforcer de définir cette distance de sécurité en fonction de l'accident maximum crédible. Si le Congrès ne dispose pas des données nécessaires, je pense qu'il s'agit là d'un sujet d'étude tout à fait essentiel. L'expression "accident maximum crédible" est utilisée dans l'industrie de l'énergie nucléaire et il s'agit évidemment de l'incident à prendre en considération dans l'étude de localisation d'un terminal.

Certains pays tels que l'Australie ont la chance d'avoir une vaste côte encore non développée qui peut recevoir des installations de chargement et de stockage: deux installations GPL sont en cours de planification dans des endroits isolés, ce qui permet la séparation de la navigation en cas d'eaux limitées.

Cette situation heureuse ne se rencontre pas dans les pays industrialisés importateurs de GPL et de GNL tels que le Japon et les pays européens. Il est évident que l'acceptation par l'opinion publique des risques inhérents au transport et au stockage de grandes quantités de ces combustibles hautement volatiles serait notablement favorisée par la localisation des terminaux dans des endroits isolés. Aussi, les transporteurs se trouveraient-ils également éloignés des voies navigables étroites et encombrées. La meilleure solution à cet égard est de placer le terminal aussi près que possible de la mer, même si ceci implique la construction d'ouvrages de protection tels que les môles ou les brise-lames.

En conclusion, je répète que je crois que le Congrès devrait mettre sur pied une Commission chargée de définir des lignes directrices en matière de séparation des installations de stockage et de leurs jetées par rapport aux autres installations portuaires.

N F MATTHEWS (AISM)

Mon organisation, l'A.I.S.M., a eu l'honneur de collaborer avec l'A.I.P.C.N. dans une série de commissions et sur un ensemble de projets.

J'ai pris connaissance avec grand intérêt du Rapport Général de M. Oliver et ses projets de conclusions me semblent à la fois sages et utiles.

Mon association s'intéresse bien entendu tout particulièrement aux Aides à la Navigation et c'est pourquoi je voudrais commenter la deuxième Recommandation, relative à une "harmonisation accrue des Systèmes de Trafic Maritime".

Les participants ne savent peut-être pas clairement que dans presque tous les pays où il y a un système de trafic maritime de quelque importance, l'organisation des installations incombe au Service National des Phares.

L'exception remarquable à cette règle est le Royaume-Uni, où apparemment chaque port assure son propre service.

Ces Services de Signalisation maritime sont tous membres de l'A.I.S.M. et comme les systèmes VTS sont généralement totalement reliés aux autres Aides à la Navigation, une Conférence de l'A.I.S.M. a décidé, en novembre dernier, de créer une Commission chargée presque exactement de la même mission que celle dont M. Oliver a fait la proposition dans ses remarques introductives.

Le Bureau Exécutif de l'A.I.S.M. se réunit la semaine prochaine à Paris, avec, notamment à leur ordre du jour, l'approbation de la liste des membres de l'A.I.S.M. qui souhaitent travailler dans cette Commission ainsi que le nom du Président proposé.

La première réunion devrait donc pouvoir se tenir vers septembre/octobre de cette année. Une fois le travail terminé, nous devrions normalement soumettre ces recommandations, après leur approbation par le Bureau Exécutif, à l'adoption par nos membres, et ensuite à l'O.M.C.I., en vue d'obtenir son soutien.

Aux termes d'un accord permanent entre les Secrétaires Généraux de l'A.I.S.M., de l'A.I.P.C.N. et de l'A.I.P.H., nous nous informons de ce que nous faisons en vue d'éviter dans la mesure du possible tout double emploi non justifié. A la suite de la réunion du Bureau Exécutif de la semaine prochaine, selon cet Accord, toute l'information nécessaire sera fournie aux Secrétaires Généraux de l'A.I.P.C.N. et de l'A.I.P.H., de même que leurs organisations seront invitées à contribuer à notre travail. Nous accueillerons donc volontiers l'apport de l'A.I.P.C.N. en ce domaine, et je me réjouis que ces problèmes aient été soulevés au cours du présent Congrès.

En ce qui concerne les remarques du Cap. Lawrence, je voudrais souligner que notre intention est d'harmoniser les problèmes de procédures, de routines et d'hommes et peut-être de traiter quelque peu de la terminologie. Nous ne cherchons pas à harmoniser les infrastructures des systèmes.

Enfin, j'en terminerai avec une remarque personnelle.

Comme l'a dit M. Oliver, la C.E.E. envisage la création d'un groupe d'étude chargé de ce problème du VTS.

Travaillant à temps plein pour une organisation internationale, j'accueille avec faveur toute coopération internationale. J'ai été étroitement associé pendant plusieurs années au système des bouées de l'A.I.S.M. dont M. Oliver a parlé.

Mon expérience en ce domaine me pousse à émettre quelques réserves envers la constitution d'une approche exclusivement européenne. La navigation est vraiment internationale et je préfèrerais au départ une "approche globale" quitte ensuite à l'adapter aux conditions locales.

L R DUMAS (FRANCE)

Mr. N. Matthews de l'AISM a exprimé une partie de ce que j'avais l'intention de dire.

La semaine précédente, le symposium de Bremen a laissé apparaître un certain consensus entre ingénieurs et marins sur les services de trafic maritime.

Ces services sont à l'ordre du jour dans beaucoup d'organismes internationaux, l'I.A.P.H., l'AISM qui a créé une commission technique spécialisée, la Commission des Communautés Européennes, etc. ainsi que dans de nombreux organismes nationaux. Il faut distinguer les services portuaires où les nations appliquent généralement une réglementation nationale, avec quelques variantes selon les sites et les services concernant les eaux internationales comme le Pas-de-Calais où seule l'OMCI peut légiférer.

Il semble admis qu'une harmonisation internationale d'ensemble serait nécessaire, au plan des procédures.

La Commission technique de l'AISM semble le meilleur organe pour établir des propositions pertinentes. Cependant le sous-comité scientifique et technique COST 301 de la C.E.E. permettrait aussi de confronter les vues européennes et faciliter le travail de l'AISM.

CONCLUSIONS

Le développement du transport maritime des gaz liquéfiés est un phénomène relativement récent. L'AIPCN, par ces divers organismes, est exceptionnellement bien placée pour servir de forum international permanent, où l'expérience des nations intéressées par cette activité pourrait faire l'objet d'échanges de vues.

1. La décision de l'AIPCN de créer un Groupe de Travail pour étudier les problèmes créés par le transport maritime des matières dangereuses et leur manutention est une heureuse initiative et la Section II estime que les divers aspects du transport maritime de gaz liquifiés et de leur manutention devraient être inclus au nombre des préoccupations du Groupe de Travail. L'Association devrait promouvoir, en liaison avec d'autres organismes compétents, une meilleure connaissance des critères de choix des terminaux pour le transbordement des gaz liquifiés et permettre notamment une meilleure circulation de l'information et des opinions, entre les diverses branches de l'industrie et des organismes associés.

2. Une gestion efficace du trafic est une condition importante de la sécurité. Il convient d'encourager une harmonisation internationale des procédures du trafic maritime, qui constituerait la base de dispositions locales.

3. La définition et le rassemblement des données nécessaires pour l'analyse des risques et les évaluations relatives à la conception des navires, l'emplacement des terminaux et la conception des chenaux d'approche font déjà l'objet d'un travail considérable. L'Association elle-même devrait s'intéresser à ces travaux, par l'intermédiaire du Groupe de Travail précité, ou par tout autre moyen utile, en étant consciente de l'intérêt d'atteindre à long terme, sur le plan international, des niveaux efficaces de standardisation et d'uniformisation.

PORTS ET ACCES MARITIMES

SECTION II — SUJET 2

Optimisation économique de l'ensemble du cycle de dragage compte tenu des avantages acquis

Mardi 12 mai 1981

Président:	*N N B ORDMAN (GB)* *Noel Ordman and Associates Ltd*
Vice Président:	*E ALMAGIA (Italie)* *Chairman SIDER SpA, Rome*
Rapporteur Général:	*M VAN DEN DOEL (Pays-Bas)* *Rotterdam Port Authority*
Vice Rapporteur Général:	*H MOLENAAR (Pays-Bas)*
Secrétaire:	*P LACEY (GB)* *Ove Arup and Partners Ltd, London*
Secrétaire Adjoint:	*Mlle M-M DANEELS (Belgique)* *Secrétaire AIPCN Secrétariat Générale, Bruxelles*

Orateurs

C C CABLE (Etats-Unis), J B HERBICH (Etats-Unis), L NEDERLOF (Pays-Bas), M F C THORN (GB), D M McDOWELL (GB), A GENEVOIS (France), Y KREPS-HEYNDRIKX (Belgique), A FUGLUM (Norvege), J CHAPON (France), P SIREYJOL (France), V V DEGTYAREV (URSS), E LESPINE (France), D JONES (GB), J J C M VAN DOOREMALEN (Pays-Bas), G B M OLIVER (GB), J De KONING (Pays-Bas), A H C STIRLING (GB), R B DAVENPORT (GB)

M. VAN DEN DOEL (PAYS-BAS) RAPPORTEUR GENERAL

Le maintien des profondeurs d'eau requises dans les chenaux d'accès et dans les darses est une des tâches essentielles parmi toutes celles qui sont exécutées dans les ports du monde entier pour permettre à ceux-ci de fonctionner efficacement en tant qu'endroits où les navires chargent et déchargent leurs marchandises. Dans certains cas, c'est une tâche coûteuse mais qui, fort heureusement, peut être maîtrisée à la fois techniquement, commercialement et financièrement. C'est pourquoi l'optimisation des activités de dragage peut être considérée comme à la fois importante et réalisable. C'est ce qui ressort aussi bien du nombre que de la teneur des rapports qui ont été présentés.

Aspects soumis à la discussion.

1. Les relations coût-bénéfice dans le domaine du dragage comme instrument de décision.
2. Contrôle de processus et d'exécution et automatisation à bord des dragues en marche.
3. Programmation du dragage.
4. Voies souhaitables de recherche en matière de matériels et de méthodes de dragage.
5. Dragage et exigences nautiques.
6. Entrée des ports et tracé des chenaux en liaison avec la qualité du dragage.
7. Nature des matériaux dragués et possibilités d'évacuation.
8. Déroctage et dragage des roches.
9. Utilisation de la drague à cuiller.

LES DEBATS

C C CABLE (USA)

Je voudrais compléter le rapport des Etats-Unis par quelques indications relatives à d'autres travaux d'engraissement de plages réalisés dans l'Etat de Floride.

Le district de Jacksonville, U.S. Army Corps of Engineers, utilise depuis plusieurs années des matériaux de dragage à des fins d'engraissement de plages. Sur un chantier récent, au port de Fernandia, Floride, le dragage du projet d'aménagement du port a pu être optimisé en déposant les matériaux de dragage sur une plage fortement érodée. Les travaux de dragage étaient notamment destinés à approfondir à 40 pieds (12,2 m) le chenal d'entrée de la base stratégique pour sous-marine de Kings Bay, terminée en juin 1979. L'approfondissement de l'entrée exposée du chenal a été réalisé par la drague porteuse McFARLAND, assistée de la drague porteuse GOETHALS. Sur un total d'environ 2,3 millions de yards cubes (1,76 million m^3) enlevés par les deux dragues dans le cadre du projet d'approfondissement pour la U.S. Navy, quelque 500.000 yards cubes (382.277 m^3) de matériaux adéquats ont été déposés au moyen d'un système de pompage direct sur une plage littorale au sud du chenal d'entrée à Fernandia, Floride. La méthode de travail retenue consistait à recueillir une charge donnée de matériaux sur les barges, de les ammarrer ensuite à une barge d'amarrage située juste en-dehors du chenal à proximité de la jetée sud et de pomper les matériaux de dragage à travers une conduite partiellement immergée le long de la plage sur une distance d'environ 6000 pieds (1829 m) par rapport au début de la zone de remblayage de plage. Grâce à l'addition de deux pompes-relais à cet endroit de la plage, la zone de remblayage a pu être étendue vers le sud d'environ 7000 pieds (2134 m), soit une distance de pompage totale à partir de la drague de quelque 13.000 pieds (3962 m).

En raison de l'irrégularité de l'alignement de la plage existante, la zone de remblayage avait une largeur variable comprise entre 60 (18) et 600 pieds (183 m) calculée pour réaliser un alignement de plage relativement continu avec une hauteur de berme de + 11 pieds m.l.w. (3,4 m).

Si le dépôt des matériaux de dragage provenant des travaux d'approfondissement sur la plage érodée a entraîné un coût supérieur ($6,68/ cu yd, $8,74/ m^3) à celui de leur évacuation en mer ($2,64/ cu yd, $3,45/ m^3), les autres sources de matériaux d'engraissement de plages coûteraient encore bien plus à l'heure *actuelle* ($5,68/ cu yd, S+/ 7,43/ m^3). La décision de la direction d'utiliser cette méthode d'engraissement de plage permet la réutilisation du sable valable en même temps que l'économie de ($1,64/ cu yd, $2,15/ m^3).

Un autre projet d'engraissement de plage de très grande importance est le projet de protection contre l'érosion et l'immersion par les marées du County de Dade. Dans ce cadre, du sable a été obtenu de sources adéquates en mer et pompé sur la plage à Miami Beach, Floride.

Le projet prévoit dans une première phase le placement de 14,2 millions de yards cubes (10 millions m^3) de matériaux destinés à conconstituer une dune de plage et de protection sur une distance de 10,5 miles (16,7 km) de côte à Miami Beach.

Le programme prévoit une dune de 20 pieds (6,1 m) de large pour une élévation de 11,5 pieds (3,5 m) au-dessus du niveau de marée basse moyen. Du côté mer de la dune, une berme d'une élévation de 9 pieds (2,7 m) audessus du niveau moyen de marée basse s'étend sur 50 pieds (L5,2 m), de sorte qu'un remblai naturel descend vers la mer. La plage sera engraissée régulièrement, selon les besoins résultant des pertes d'érosion.

A l'heure actuelle, le coût estimé du projet, y compris dix ans d'engraissement de plage, s'élève à environ $56 millions, dont $31 millions seraient pris en charge par le budget fédéral.

Les matériaux nécessaires au projet proviennent d'endroits situés de 6 (1,83m) à 12.000 pieds (3,6 km) en mer. La majeure partie des travaux a été réalisée au moyen de dragues suceuses à désagrégateur d'une puissance de 7200 CV pour les désagrégateurs. Le diamètre du bec d'aspiration est de 34 inches (0,9 m) et celui des tuyaux de pompage et d'évacuation de 27 inches (0,7 m). L'ILLINOIS a déplacé des matériaux à travers une moyenne de 12.000 pieds (3,6 km) de conduite, dont 9.700 pieds (2,9 km) étaient immergés. Pour l'ALASKA, ces distances étaient respectivement de 11.000 pieds (3,3 km) et 7900 pieds (2408 m). Ces dragues étaient assistées par une station de pompage relais.

Au début des travaux, il fut constaté que des matériaux sur-dimensionnés étaient déposés sur la plage. Les contrats prévirent donc que tous les matériaux dépassant 1" (2,5 cm) de diamètre devaient être écrasés jusqu'à être ramenés à cette dimension.

Outre les possibilités d'aménagement à des fins de loisirs qu'ils offrent, ces projets d'engraissement de plages sur la côte de Floride constituent une protection contre l'immersion par les marées.

J B HERBICH (USA)

Je voudrais ajouter trois remarques relatives au dimensionnement des aires de dépôt à périmètre limité et l'assèchement des matériaux de dragage.

I. Le dimensionnement correct des aires de retenue à périmètre limité est évidemment particulièrement important, non seulement pour les dimensions des aires elles-mêmes, mais également pour la hauteur des digues nécessaires. C'est pourquoi nous avons mis au point une méthode de laboratoire permettant de déterminer le facteur d'entassement des matériaux à draguer. Ce facteur est défini comme

$$B = \frac{Vc}{Vi}$$

où Vc = volume dans la zone de dépôt

Vi = volume sur place

ou $$B = \frac{\gamma di}{\gamma dc}$$

où γdi = densité à sec sur place

γdc = densité à sec dans la zone de dépôt

ou $$B = \frac{Wc\ Gs + 100}{Wi\ Gs + 100}$$

où Wc = teneur en eau dans la zone de dépôt

Wi = teneur en eau sur place

(La dernière équation n'est valable que pour un sol en conditions de saturation).

Une procédure détaillée pour déterminer le facteur d'entassement en laboratoire est proposée dans la référence Di George III, F. P. et J. B. Herbich, "Détermination en laboratoire des facteurs d'entassement pour des matériaux côtiers à fine granulation au Texas", Texas A and M University Report Nr 218, août 1978.

PROCEDURES DE LABORATOIRE — FACTEUR D'ENTASSEMENT

Ce qui suit est une présentation chronologique étape par étape des essais en laboratoire portant sur le facteur d'entassement:

1. La cire est disposée à partir des échantillons non remués à mesure que ceux-ci sont préparés pour l'essai. L'échantillon luimême est alors façonné en une forme uniformément cylindrique au moyen d'un couteau et d'une petite équerre de menuisier.

2. L'échantillon est soigneusement mesuré au moyen d'un triangle métrique et son volume en centimètres cubes est calculé à partir de ces mesures pour être ensuite utilisé dans la détermination du facteur d'entassement.

3. Le poids de l'échantillon arrondi au décigramme est déterminé au moyen d'une balance métrique et son volume spécifique est calculé en divisant le volume de l'étape 2 par son poids.

4. L'échantillon est découpé en morceaux et mélangé à une masse homogène au moyen d'un couteau et d'une plaque de découpe de verre.

5. Dans le cas des échantillons testés en eau douce, avec 13,1 $^o/oo$ d'eau salée et avec 28,6 $^o/oo$ d'eau salée, 3 port-ons de 200 grammes sont prélevées sur l'échantillon et déposées séparément dans des coupes fermées de 1000 ml.

   Dans le cas des échantillons soumis aux essais de sédimentation avec 28,6 $^o/oo$ d'eau salée seulement, une seule portion de 200 grammes est déposée dans une coupe fermée de 1000 ml. Des portions de chaque échantillon sont alors rescellées dans de la paraffine et conservées pour les essais de limite d'Atterberg et d'analyse en tamis.

6. Le volume "sur place" de chaque échantillon de 200 grammes est obtenu en multipliant son poids par le volume spécifique calculé en 3.

7. Les portions de chaque échantillon sont alors mises à l'imprégnation dans leurs coupes respectives avec 500 ml de l'eau dans laquelle ils devront être testés. La période d'imprégnation est d'environ 24 h.

8. Après imprégnation, un mélangeur à vitesse variable et une lame spéciale à quatre branches en forme d'impulseur sont utilisés pour mélanger les particules de sol et l'eau en une boue homogène. Au cours de cette opération, on ajoute de l'eau pour amener le volume de boue jusque 975 ml. Une densité de boue de 1200 gr par litre au poids est souhaitée pour simuler la densité caractéristique des boues de dragage. L'impulseur crée un fort tourbillon dans la coupe et permet d'élever les particules de sol dans la suspension. En observant à travers les parois de la coupe, on peut aisément déterminer qu'une durée de mélange de cinq à six minutes est nécessaire pour être sûr que toutes les particules se trouvent dans la suspension.

9. La boue est alors versée dans un cylindre gradué de 1000 ml. 25 ml environ d'eau de salinité adéquate sont utilisés pour rincer des particules de sol adhérent à l'impulseur et à la coupe et les faire tomber dans le cylindre, ce qui accroit le volume au sein du cylindre jusque 1000 ml. Cette procédure permet de réduire à une quantité négligeable la perte de particules de sol au cours de l'opération de mélange.

10. La boue est alors mise à reposer pendant que les particules de sol sortent de suspension. Le niveau de l'interface entre les matières en suspension et le liquide surnageant est observé et noté une demi-heure après le début de l'essai et chaque heure ensuite jusqu'à ce que le niveau de dépôt soit réduit à 10 ml par heure au maximum. Le niveau des matières en suspension est encore noté ensuite toutes les 24 heures à partir du début de l'essai et jusqu'à ce que la quantité de dépôt soit indétectable pendant une période de 48 heures.

11. Au terme de l'essai de sédimentation pour chaque échantillon particulier, le liquide surnageant est retiré et sa salinité est déterminée à l'aide du conductimètre "Hydrolab". L'échantillon et le cylindre sont pesés ensemble et mis à sécher au four à une température de 140° F.

12. Les cylindres sont retirés du four et pesés à intervalles de 24 heures jusqu'à ce que deux passages consécutifs donnent les mêmes résultats. Compte tenu du poids de la petite quantité d'eau salée restée dans le cylindre avant placement au four, de celui du sel séché demeuré au-dessus des particules de sol après extraction du four et encore du poids du cylindre lui-même, le poids à sec de l'échantillon et la teneur en humidité des matières sédimentées sont établis. La teneur en humidité est ensuite utilisée pour calculer le facteur de vide des matières sédimentées.

Les procédures d'essai décrites sont applicables sur le terrain aux conditions suivantes:

(a) La portion de 200 gr retirée de chaque échantillon pour l'essai est représentative de la totalité de l'échantillon.

(b) L'eau de mer artificielle d'une salinité de 28,6 °/oo est une approximation raisonnable des conditions réelles.

(c) L'opération de mélange destinée à mélanger la boue est une approximation satisfaisante du processus de dragage. Le plus souvent, le mouvement toubillonnant de la boue dans la coupe entraîne la chute sur le sol de petits morceaux d'échantillon pour y constituer des boulettes d'argile d'un diamètre variant entre 1/16 et 1/4 de pouce. On n'a pas essayé de casser ces sphères et de les intégrer de force à la suspension. Ceci aurait donné lieu à des facteurs de dimensionnement plus élevés et il semble que leur constitution est un indicateur d'une simulation raisonnablement précise du processus de dragage. Les boulettes d'argile se déposent d'ailleurs immédiatement au fond lorsque la boue est versée dans le cylindre.

(d) La perte de particules de sol par adhérence à l'appareil mélangeur de laboratoire est négligeable.

(e) Les effets de compactage dus à l'introduction de retraits successifs de matières de dragage n'ont pas été simulés.

(f) Les effets de séchage en surface par déshydratation mécanique et par évaporation naturelle n'ont pas été simulés.

(g) Les effets de dépôt à long terme et de consolidation interne n'ont pas été simulés, non plus que les effets supposés de contraction résultant de ces causes tels qu'ils apparaissent dans le facteur de tassement du graphique.

II. Le deuxième point que nous voulons souligner est la nécessité de mettre à sec le site de dépôt aussi tôt que possible de sorte que le volume supplémentaire dans l'aire de retenue soit prêt à être évalués plus tard, par exemple lorsqu'il est affecté à une fin industrielle ou autre. Les méthodes de mises à sec sont décrites en détail dans le Programme de Recherche sur les Matériaux de Dragage du Centre d'Expérimentation pour les Voies Navigables du Corps of Engineers à Vicksburg, Mississippi. Plusieurs véhicules ou porteurs remorqués peuvent être utilisés pour construire des digues dans la zone de retenue afin de faciliter la mise à sec. L'un de ces véhicules est le RUC (Riverine Utility Craft).

III. Enfin, pour l'évacuation en mer, part particulièrement en eaux peu profondes, les lames et les courants peuvent entraîner une érosion assez rapide des îles construites par dragues à désagrégateurs. Une recherche en laboratoire a été menée à l'Université A and M du Texas (Référence Vyas, Y. K. et J. B. Herbich,

"Erosion of Dredged Material Islands due to Waves and Currents", Proceedings, Hydraulics in the Coastal Zone Conference, American Society of Civil Engineers, 1977) en vue d'évaluer les taux d'érosion. L'échelle réduite a été établie par comparaison d'une île à échelle réduite avec une île prototype subissant une érosion substantielle au cours d'une période de 13 ans.

L NEDERLOF (PAYS-BAS)

Je voudrais intervenir sur deux sujets dans lesquels des résultats nouveaux ont été obtenus.

Les expériences les plus récentres ont permis de tirer la conclusion que les systèmes de petites dimensions agitation/dragage pouvaient être particulièrement efficaces dans les zones caractérisées par des boues liquides. Les travaux effectués à Rotterdam nous ont en outre amenés à penser que ces instruments sont précieux dans les ports à petit budget des pays en voie de développement.

Ma deuxième remarque porte sur les concepts de "fond nautique" et de "profondeur nautique" dans les zones à matériaux de fond boueux. Normalement, on y trouve une couche supérieure d'eau chargée de sédiments en flottaison, à laquelle succède une couche de sédiments non compacts elle-même suivie par une couche de sédiments solides, dont les densités sont respectivement de 1,00 à 1,10 t/m^3, 1,10 à 1,20 t/m^3 et 1,20 à 1,35 t/m^3.

Jusqu'à ce jour, la profondeur a été mesurée au moyen d'un système sonar qui enregistre la couche supérieure du fond sédimenteux (environ 1,03 t/m^3). A Rotterdam, on utilise désormais pour étudier la densité au fond un densimètre radio-actif.

En outre, le Ministère des Travaux Publics (Rijkswaterstaat) et les autorités portuaires (Ville de Rotterdam) ont procédé à des essais sur modèles et à échelle réelle en vue d'étudier plus avant les conditions de sécurité des manoeuvres des grands navires au-dessus de fonds boueux. Un des points forts de l'étude consistait à déterminer si une zone d'eau contenant des sédiments non compacts pouvait être incluse dans le pied de pilote des navires.

Ces essais comparatifs ont donné lieu aux conclusions suivantes en ce qui concerne les navires:

- résistance accrue: la vitesse ne peut être maintenue qu'au prix d'un nombre plus élevé de révolutions des hélices;

- distance d'arrêt réduite;

- vulnérabilité réduite en ce qui concerne le déjaugeage et la déviation;

- plus grande efficacité de gouvernail en raison de la résistance supérieure.

Il s'ensuit que la présence de sédiments à faibles densités dans la marge de pied de pilote modifie le comportement des navires en mouvement sans toutefois entraîner de situations dangereuses.

Dans la région d'Amsterdam, la couche de densité 1,20 t/m^3 est, pour des raisons de sécurité, retenue comme "fond nautique": en d'autres termes, la "profondeur nautique" s'étend de la surface de l'eau jusqu'à cette couche de densité 1,20 t/m^3. Cette "profondeur nautique" inclut le tirant d'eau du navire ainsi que le pied de pilote normal pour cette région.

L'utilisation de la "profondeur nautique" pour les zones sédimenteuses permet:

- d'une part d'obtenir une meilleure définition du niveau de fond;

- d'autre part d'éviter de draguer les matériaux de fond dont les densités sont inférieures à 1,20 t/m^3 (qui contiennent 90% d'eau et 10% de matériaux solides).

De plus amples informations peuvent être trouvées dans le numéro de mai 1981 de "Dock and Harbour Authority".

M F C THORN (GB)

Mon expérience me conduit à penser que les processus constitutifs du cycle de dragage retiennent insuffisamment l'attention. Si ces processus sont mal mesurés ou compris, l'optimisation du cycle de dragage peut déboucher sur des absurdités. Je suis déçu que le rôle de la recherche en ce domaine n'a pas été davantage souligné dans les documents relatifs à cette session.

La proposition des Pays-Bas de définir la "profondeur nautique" par un critère de densité plutôt que par le retour d'un écho est un bon exemple de la manière dont un minimum de recherche fondamentale appliqué à la compréhension d'un processus peut s'avérer extrêmement productif.

Je vais donner quelques exemples des contributions possibles de la recherche scientifique et de la mesure des processus de dragage à l'optimisation et à l'accroissement de la production effective.

1. Des mesures de densité de charge sur une drague suceuse porteuse traînante ont montré comment le débordement pouvait réduire la charge de la drague et donc le rendement du cycle. Le cycle le plus productif était celui dans lequel le remplissage du chaland était effectué dans le temps le plus bref: la charge était supérieure, de même que le nombre de cycles par tour.

2. Des mesures effectuées au moyen de traceurs radioactifs afin de comparer l'efficacité des modes de dragage par déchargement sur chaland et par rejet latéral ont montré que, alors même que l'efficacité en termes de "enlèvement de matériaux/charge" était nettement supérieure dans le cas due déchargement sur chaland, le temps perdu en déplacement et en déchargement rendait deux fois plus élevé le rendement effectif dans le cas du rejet latéral.

3. Des mesures par traceurs radioactifs de la dispersion des matériaux de dragage déposés dans un lieu donné ont montré qu'une proportion très faible de ces matériaux demeurait dans la zone concernée et que plus

de 80% d'entre eux étaient totalement dispersés. Le concept du transport de déblais et de leur dépôt dans un lieu donné s'est avéré totalement erroné.

D M McDOWELL (GB)

Il fut convenu à Bruxelles que le domaine des techniques et des équipements de dragage était suffisamment couvert par exemple dans le cadre du WODCON. Le rôle de l'AIPCN y fut considéré comme plus large, dans la mesure où cette association compte parmi ses membres des ingénieurs et des directeurs de ports aussi bien que des représentants des gouvernements. Il fut donc décidé que le sujet devait couvrir l'analyse économique de l'ensemble de l'opération de dragage et inclure les aspects plus larges de l'évacuation des matériaux de dragage aussi bien que du dragage lui-même dans la mesure où évacuation peut s'avérer extrêmement coûteuse.

On peut comparer le dragage à un jeu, un jeu extrêmement sérieux pour les participants, qui peuvent néanmoins conserver un certain sens de l'humour. Au contraire de la plupart des autres jeux, celui-ci est joué par plusieurs équipes simultanément. Chaque équipe a ses propres règles, qui sont rarement connues des autres. Ces équipes sont constituées de responsables politiques, de fonctionnaires, d'entrepreneurs de dragage et de clients. A l'échelon inférieur, on trouve le chef de chantier de dragage, dont l'objectif est le même que celui de tous les autres: faire du bon travail en fonction de ses propres règles. Bien sûr, dans les faits, l'objectif de nombreux joueurs est de donner l'impression qu'ils font le travail pour lequel ils sont payés tandis que l'objectif d'autres participants est de s'assurer que les premiers réalisent effectivement le travail.

Au contraire d'autres jeux encore une fois, le coup de sifflet final ne s'adresse qu'à certains des participants; l'entrepreneur arrivera sans doute finalement à un accord et, du moins peut-on l'espérer, il sera payé. Pour la plupart des autres joueurs, le jeu se poursuit indéfiniment. Nous en avons de nombreux exemples, dont le plus ancien, à la connaissance de celui qui vous parle, est celui du canal de Manchester. Depuis plus de quatre-vingts ans, ses propriétaires sont obligés d'évacuer les déblais de dragage sur la terre ferme. Cette exigence résulte d'une loi votée pour des raisons qui semblaient bonnes à l'époque. De nos jours, cette opération est devenue de plus en plus difficile et coûteuse à mesure que s'épuisaient les terrains convenant à l'évacuation des déblais. Cependant nous ne savons toujours pas quels avantages ont pu être retirés de cette disposition légale ni même s'il est justifié de continuer indéfiniment à enlever les sédiments fins.

D'autres exemples sont fournis par le cas classique de l'évacuation à terre des déblais de dragage provenant de l'estuaire du Delaware aux Etats-Unis et, plus récemment, l'étude approfondie qui a débouché sur le dépôt à terre des matériaux enlevés de l'estuaire de la Tamise en Grande Bretagne. Après quelques décennies, quels en sont les effets à long terme? Un autre cas encore est celui du chenal de Rotterdam, dont l'approfondissement a entraîné une pénétration accrue d'eau salée, qu'il a fallu endiguer, en déposant au fond une couche de graviers résistant à l'érosion.

Des enseignements ont été tirés de tous ces cas, mais il existe des exemples contemporains, entre autres de dragage dans les deltas tropicaux dont les effets à court terme peuvent être prévus mais dont les effets à long terme ne le peuvent pas.

A GENEVOIS (FRANCE)

Comme l'y invitait le sujet, le rapport français a traité en détail 3 cas concrete et je voudrais d'abord en reprendre les résultats et enseignements essentiels.

<u>ler exemple</u>: aménagement et entretien d'un estuaire à fortes marées et sables très fins — l'estuaire de la Seine, qui mène au port de Rouen.

Parti d'un estuaire dont, jusque vers 1960, le chenal divaguait et acceptait des navires d'au plus 8000 tpl à pleine charge, une première grande étape de travaux, achevée en 1962, aura permis à elle seule de gagner 2,50 m de tirant d'eau (navires de 25.000 tpl),

- en faisant appel au calibrage par une digue Sud partiellement submersible, pour orienter l'action des courants et autodraguer le chenal,

- après des études sur modèle sédimentologique complètes et affinées grâce à la présence de données nombreuses et essais d'historique.

Une deuxième étape basée sur le même principe s'achève actuellement. Elle permettra l'accueil des 35.000 tp;, moyennant un calibrage amélioré par une digue Nord submersible et économique (avec prise en compte des problèmes d'environnement rencontrés).

Au total: gain de plus de 4 m de gain en tirant d'eau

navires 8.000 t → 35.000 tpl à pleine charge

mais <u>volume d'entretien resté du même ordre</u>: 5 millions de m3

<u>2e exemple</u>: politique d'entretien et dragage des vases en Gironde.

Le rapport fait suite à la communication présentée à Leningrad en 1977. Il montre comment, dans l'intervalle, une diminution d'environ 20% des charges d'entretien, toutes choses égales par ailleurs, a été rendue possible:

- mise en place d'un système de sondage automatisé et performant.

- meilleure connaissance des mécanismes de sédimentation des vases et de leur dragage (exploitation des données — études physicochimiques),

- passage progressif à une politique d'entretien préventif.

De ces deux exemples concrets, confortés par

d'autres, je tire la conclusion suivante:

1. le dragage d'entretien est un mal, sans doute nécessaire, mais il faut le combattre par tous moyens, revenir au dilemme "draguer ou ne pas draguer" et remettre en cause les idées reçues.

2. Un problème d'entretien, spécialement dans un estuaire, ne doit jamais être considéré comme résolu. Bien au contraire, les solutions sont toujours perfectibles.

3. Les moyens existent et sont nombreux: meilleur calibrage plutôt que dragages massifs, systèmes de positionnement et sondage, regroupement des moyens etc ... les rapports en font largement état.

4. Mais un moyen particulièrement efficace et qui ne nous parait pas toujours suffisamment utilisé, c'est de mieux connaître les données physiques du problème, les mécanismes de fonctionnement de l'estuaire: c'est bien de gagner quelque % en optimisant le cycle de dragage au sens strict de l'engin, mais il faut au préalable s'être interrogé sur le choix des zones de dépôt, sur les phénomènes de recyclage des matériaux entre ces zones et le chenal, pour faire un calcul économique complet. M. Thorn en a cité quelques exemples. Ils sont nombreux.

Chaque problème d'estuaire ou d'entretien a ses particularités, ses évolutions propres.

Pour une autorité portuaire, investir pour améliorer constamment les données et leur interprétation, travailler dans ce but simultanément avec des laboratoires d'hydraulique spécialisés, des praticiens des aménagements d'estuaire et de dragage, mais aussi faire preuve d'imagination et de flair constitue également une recommandation très importante. Elle est valable dans les pays industrialisés et dans les pays en voie de développement. C'est une source de progrès et d'économies constantes.

Y KREPS-HEYNDRIKX (BELGIQUE)

Renseignements complémentaires concernant le sujet Canal Maritime de Gand à Terneuzen — Mise en dépôt des boues dans un puits.

Les travaux suivants ont été exécutés:

1. L'écran étanche. Un examen approfondi du sous-sol a été fait. 25 essais de pénétration de profondeur de 25 à 30 m sur tout le tracé de la paroi, 3 sondages suivant la technique Ackerman jusque dans la couche d'argile — résultat: la paroi étanche est exécutée en zones de différentes profondeurs (1 m dans la couche d'argile).

L'expérience a montré que les essais géotechniques doivent être exécutés avec beaucoup de soins et en grande quantité afin de connaître avec précision les niveaux des couches étanches (argile). Sinon on pourrait laisser des zones plus ou moins perméables, ce qui nuirait au but = construire une cuve étanche.

Exécution de la paroi: murs emboués en bentonite-ciment. Résultats des essais de perméabilité sur 6 échantillons:

K = L,57 x 10^{-8} cm/sec (5 x 10^{-8} cm/sec était imposé)

Méthode: l'on fore des pieux de 3,60 m de largeur qui s'empiettent de 0,90 m. Pendant l'exécution, il y a un abaissement de la nappe phréatique.

Le mélange bentonite-ciment a été fabriqué sur place avec une capacité de 100 m3/heure.

2. Exécution du puits. Le puits a été exécuté par dragage du sable au moyen d'une drague-cutter démontable.

Quelques caractéristiques techniques:

Ø des tuyaux = 700 mm

puissance = 6000 C.V.

pression de sortie = 12 à 13 kg/cm2

vitesse dans les canalisations = 4 à 5 m/sec

concentration = L,4 t/m3 à 1,8 t/m3

production = 1 700 m3/h à 2 800 m3/h

Le sable a été transporté à une distance de 9 km. Le sable sera employé pour la construction des digues d'un réservoir d'eau potable.

3. Programme de contrôle de la qualité de l'eau de la nappe aquifère. (voir dessin) Sur 3 axes on a foré des tubes de prise d'échantillon d'eau phréatique. Des échantillons sont pris à 9 m et à 15 m de profondeur et celà aux emplacements 1, 2, 3, 4, 5 et 6.

Pour chaque emplacement:

index A: à l'intérieur de la paroi d'étanchéité

sans index: en dehors de la paroi

index B: à 50 m de la paroi d'étanchéité.

A trois emplacements on a foré des tubes dans la couche de sable se trouvant en-dessous de la couche d'argile.

Les échantillons d'eau sont analysés sur 27 paramètres.

Situation de départ = situation zéro — donc avant la mise en dépôt de la boue dans le puits.

Dans les tubes 5 à 6 on peut admettre que l'eau est potable (suivant les normes C.E.E.)

Les tubes 1, 2, 3, 4 démontrent un certain degré de pollution — probablement dû à la présence dans les environs d'un dépôt de gypse.

4. Programme de contrôle après mise en dépôt des boues de dragages:

a) contrôle des échantillons d'eau des tubes, 3 mois après la mise en dépôt, 6 mois, 9 mois et 12 mois — ensuite 2 ans et 3 ans.

b) étude par modèle de simulation:

- pour donner une estimation de la nature, de l'évolution dans le temps et la définition de la zone influençable par une pollution,

- pour donner les bases de recherche des suites d'une pollution et donner des solutions de remède dans des cas extrêmes de pollution de la nappe aquifère qui pourraient par ex. être dûs à une malformation du puits, ou un changement soudain dans le régime des eaux des environs du puits.

Les calculs se font au moyen d'un ordinateur. Un cas concret de calcul a démontré: avec une surpression de 1 m dans le puits, une perméabilité de la paroi étanche 100 fois plus grande que prévu, et une charge de 110 mg de fluorides par litre d'eau; il faut 5 années pour que les fluorides intoxiquent une zone de 10 m autour du puits. On peut également conclure que les métaux lourds resteront dans le puits.

Le modèle de simulation démontre également l'influence positive du fossé autour de la digue du puits (prend 98,5% des lignes de courant).

Entretemps les travaux de remplissage avec les boues de dragages ont commencé et le problème qui nous occupera bientôt est de trouver une méthode adéquate pour consolider la boue sur une profondeur de 18 m.

Avis de spécialistes en la matière seraient bienvenus.

A FUGLUM (NORVEGE)

Je voudrais souligner l'importance d'une planification à long terme au niveau international visant à recueillir des données prévisionnelles sur les volumes de matériaux de dragage qui seront enlevés au cours des années à venir. Ceci permettrait à l'industrie du dragage d'élaborer des plans d'investissement à long terme en fonction du nombre et des types de dragues qui devront être construites.

Je suggère que les normes actuelles d'identification et de classification des matériaux de dragage (Bulletin AIPCN 1972) soient revues et mises à jour en faisant appel à des indices chiffrés plutôt qu'à des descriptions littéraires. L'expérience a en effet montré que ces descriptions donnent lieu à des interprétations différentes dans les divers pays et peuvent conduire à des confusions quant aux types de dragues à utiliser sur tel ou tel chantier. Je mentionnerai le système de sondage par réfraction sismique tel qu'il est décrit dans mon rapport sur ce sujet en tant que méthode plus précise d'identification et de classification des matériaux de dragage.

Je voudrais enfin inciter l'industrie à mettre au point des appareils électroniques simples pour la recherche des poches d'eau profonde et peu profonde après dragage initial, appareils qui pourraient être utilisés à des fins de contôle avant le retrait des équipements de dragage des chantiers.

J CHAPON (FRANCE)

Mon intervention concerne le partage souhaitable des dragages entre le secteur public et les entreprises privées qui le Rapporteur Général a évoqué dans la remarquable synthèse qu'il a faite des intéressants rapports présentés.

Je ne prétends pas vous donner une solution universelle et d'une valeur absolue; permettes-moi d'évoquer la position française sur le problème.

Je considère pour cela le secteur public comme englobant les moyens de l'Etat et ceux des activités portuaires qui sont, en France, des activités publiques.

1. Le potential de dragage dont doit disposer le secteur public doit garantir que les ports rempliront leur mission de service public à l'égard des usagers, et pour cela seront toujours en mesure d'assurer les profondeurs des chenaux et des bassins.

   Pour cela, le secteur public doit être capable de faire face à trois catégories d'opérations — et de le faire avec ses propres moyens.

   a) Les opérations de sécurité (par exemple atterrissements subits provoqués par une crue ou une tempête): on ne fait pas un appel d'offres — on n'en a pas le temps — pour déterminer la voiture de pompiers qui doit aller éteindre l'incendie!

   b) Les opérations dont les quantités sont pratiquement impossibles à mesurer (par exemple des atterrissements dont le volume et l'emplacement fluctuent rapidement, dans le chenal d'un estuaire): même si on confie ces travaux à une entreprise, il faut règler cette dernière en fonction du temps passé — et non des quantités draguées puisqu'on sait difficilement les mesurer.

   c) Enfin aux opérations qui, du fait de la conjoncture risquent de tomber sous le coup d'un monopole du secteur privé — car, dans ce cas, la puissance publique ne peut plus contôler, ni contenir les dépenses.

2. Mais la volonté d'assurer le service public, ne saurait signifier qu'on renonce à une saine économie: la puissance publique doit se préoccuper de la rentabilité pour la collectivité.

   Il convient donc que les moyens du secteur public aient un volume tel que puisse être assuré le plein-emploi du personnel et du matériel.

   Il faut également qu'ils soient gérés avec la même rigueur que les moyens privés — notamment que leur coûts soient analysés et connus avec la même précision.

3. Cela a conduit la France à calculer le volume de ses moyens publics d'après le volume des dragages d'entretien courant des ports: les besoins au delà de l'entretien courant doivent être couverts en faisant appel au secteur privé.

   Cela ne signifie pas que les règles administratives interdisent à une drague publique de participer à des travaux d'investissement, pas plus qu'elles empêcheraient une drague privée d'être employée sur un chantier d'entretien. Il s'agit simplement d'aligner le potentiel des moyens publics sur le volume de l'entretien; mais la plus grande souplesse — et même la plus grande liberté — est laissée pour l'emploi des engins de chaque secteur sur les chantiers d'entretien ou de travaux neufs. Une structure a même été créée, permettant une meilleure utilisation combinée des dragues françaises du secteur public avec celles du secteur privé national.

P SIREYJOL (FRANCE)

J'ai été très intéressé par l'analyse à laquelle s'est livrée notre rapporteur général qui conduit à définir une politique de dragages à partir de considérations techniques d'une part et des considérations de marché d'autre part.

Ce dernier aspect des problèmes est très connu des autorités portuaires des pays développés. Il l'est moins sans doute dans les pays en voie de développement.

Dans ces pays en effet, une condition prépondérante pour pouvoir effectuer un travail de dragage important est de réunir les fonds nécessaires au paiement des travaux, ce qui suppose qu l'on y a intéressé un organisme de financement extérieur.

Lorsque cette condition a été réalisée on s'occupe de l'organisation technique de l'appel d'offres sans se préoccuper des conditions de marché. Si celles-ci sont défavorables au moment du lancement de l'appel d'offres, on peut être conduit à contracter les travaux à un prix très élevé.

Il est souhaitable que les autorités portuaires des pays en voie de développement prennent les dispositions nécessaires pour disposer à chaque instant d'une certaine aisance au point de vue financier. Etant parvenues à ce résultat, il leur est possible, en se tenant au courant du marché des dragages, ou, d'une manière plus précise, de la disponibilité des dragues qui existent dans la région, de négocier dans les meilleures conditions les travaux de dragages qui leur sont nécessaires, qu'il s'agisse de dragages d'entretien ou de travaux neufs d'importance limitée.

V V DEGTYAREV (URSS)

La flotte fluviale joue un rôle important dans le système intégré de transports de l'U.R.S.S. Dans les régions nordiques de Sibérie, les navires fluviaux sont les seuls moyens de transport de vrac.

Les possibilités de développement des voies navigables en U.R.S.S. sont grandes. On dénombre sur le vaste territoire de notre pays plus de cent mille voies fluviales totalisant environ 4 millions de kilomètres. Des études techniques et économiques ont en outre montré que plus de cinq cent mille kilomètres de voies fluviales et de lacs pouvaient être aménagés pour la navigation. A l'heure actuelle actuelle, quelque 146.000 kilomètres de voies navigables sont déjà utilisés pour le transport de marchandises et de passagers.

En raison de la croissance ininterrompue de notre économie nationale, les voies navigables artificielles sont utilisées plus intensivement d'année en année. Leurs dimensions de chenal sont accrues, qu'il s'agisse des profondeurs, des largeurs ou des rayons des courbes.

Les moyens les plus utilisés en U.R.S.S. pour accroître les dimensions de chenal navigable sur les voies fluviales dans des conditions naturelles sont le dragage et la construction d'ougrages de régulation. Les volumes de dragage d'entretien avoisinent les 50 à 60 milliers de m^3 par section de 10 km de voie fluviale navigable, mais ils peuvent atteindre 100.000 m^3 dans les voies à fond variable (Dvina septentrionale) et même 340.000 m^3 (Ob).

En raison de l'importance du volume de dragage, il est économiquement justifié d'utiliser des dragues à rendement élevé et à faible tirant d'eau. Sur les fleuves à modification de fond intensive, la réduction du temps de dragage contribue à accroître la stabilité de la voie navigable en même temps qu'à réduire le coût direct de l'opération. Dans certains cas, par exemple, lorsqu'il faut couper à travers une courbe en période de crue, le rendement élevé des dragues est un facteur décisif de l'efficacité des chantiers. Ce rendement des dragues revêt même une importance vitale dans le grand nord, où il faut enlever des volumes de dragage très substantiels au cours de la saison de navigation de 2 à 3 mois. En particulier, des dragues spéciales pouvant enlever 5.000 m^3 par heure ont été mises au point en vue du dragage des des chenaux navigables dans les embouchures des fleuves sibériens.

Les chantiers de dragage sur le réseau de navigation intérieure n'impliquent aucume interruption de la navigation, ce qui exclut l'utilisation de dragues à béquilles de travail. Les recherches effectuées, jointes à l'expérience acquise, ont conduit à la mise au point d'un certain nombre de systèmes visant à accroître l'efficacité des techniques de dragage, parmi lesquels nous citerons: dragage sur une section fluviale par "coupes successives d'amont en aval"; utilisation de têtes d'aspiration du type "dustpan" particulièrement larges permettant de réduire le sur-dragage des coupes et du même coup les volumes dragués; utilisation de systèmes d'orientation pour le positionnement automatique de la drague au cours du travail; utilisation d'embarcations auxiliaires spécialisées et équipées des systèmes et dispositifs de commandes à distance permettant le déplacement des ancres de dragage; programmation du travail de dragage sur la base de relevés permanents.

Sur les voies navigables à processus de fond intense et en particulier en cas de débit insuffisant, l'efficacité du dragage est considérablement accrue si celui-ci est réalisé conjointement à la construction d'ouvrages de régulation. En U.R.S.S., ceux-ci sont le plus souvent réalisés en terre. Cette méthode s'est avérée la plus économique dans les faits et elle permet en outre une construction totalement mécanisée.

De manière générale, le dragage et les ouvrages de régulation n'ont pas pour seul objectif d'accroître les dimensions des chenaux navigables, mais visent en outre à améliorer la sécurité de la navigation et à atténuer les effets néfastes de celle-ci sur l'environnement Sur la base de recherches entreprises de longue date, des recommandations ont été élaborées en vue de tenir compte dans la programmation des travaux de dragage de la nécessité d'éviter qui la technologie de dragage et la localisation des "canaux" immergés n'entraînent des risques sérieux pour la qualité de l'eau et les conditions écologiques des bassins.

Des méthodes de calcul analytiques ont été mises

au point pour estimer les modifications de la turbidité de l'eau entraînées par les opérations de dragage.

E LESPINE (FRANCE)

En prolongement de notre sujet, je crois que l'on peut aborder les problèmes d'optimisation qui se posent au niveau de la définition du parc des dragues nécessaires pour couvrir des besoins de dragage donnés. Je voudrais vous faire part des conditions dans lesquelles on aborde ce problème en FRANCE, dans la ligne de ce que nous disait M. Jean CHAPON.

En 1979, la Direction des ports maritimes a jugé opportun de mettre en commun tous les moyens de dragage précédemment gérés de façon presque autonome par chacun des 14 services publics responsables de l'entretien des chenaux d'accès des ports français.

Une Société de droit privé, appelée "DRAGAGES-PORTS", que j'ai la charge de diriger, a été créée à cet effet. Les 140 dragues et engins de dragage appartenant à l'Etat français lui ont été remis en pleine propriété. "DRAGAGES-PORTS" loue ses engins coque nue aux 14 Services publics qui les exploitent avec leur personnel.

Quelles sont les missions essentielles de "DRAGAGES-PORTS"?

- d'abord renouveler son matériel et mettre en place des engins peu nombreux, mais performants,
- ensuite veiller en permanence, en liaison avec ses membres, à la meilleure utilisation possible de tous les engins du parc.

Grâce à cette mise en place d'un parc d'engins de dragages au niveau de l'ensemble des ports français et à son exploitation coordonnée, nous escomptons une diminution sensible du coût des dragages d'entretien des ports français, malgré l'importance des charges d'amortissement et des charges financières résultant des investissements.

Pour réduire ces coûts, nous devons assurer le plein emploi des engins nécessaires pour les dragages d'entretien. C'est pourquoi les Services publics, maîtres d'ouvrage, peuvent confier des dragages d'approfondissement aux engins de "DRAGAGES-PORTS".

Inversement, comme nous le disait M. Jean CHAPON, si des dragages d'entretien sont trop irréguliers et ne justifient pas la mise en place par "DRAGAGES-PORTS" de moyens de dragage permanents, les ports ont toute latitude pour faire appel aux moyens d'autres entreprises privées.

Nous pouvons donc prévoir de beaux jours en France pour la coopération entre "DRAGAGES-PORTS" et les autres Sociétés de dragage françaises ou étrangères.

Autre conséquence de la création de "DRAGAGES-PORTS". La France dispose à présent d'un organisme qui regroupe en son sein toutes les compétences acquises au long des années par les spécialistes de dragage français. Voilà donc un organisme qui a vocation, en s'appuyant sur les moyens des Ports Autonomes et des Services Maritimes, et en liaison avec les autres sociétés d'ingénierie françaises, à apporter son concours aux pays étrangers,

- non seulement pour la mise au point des projets de ports comportant des travaux de dragage importants,
- mais aussi pour le suivi des chantiers de dragage.

D JONES (GB)

Je me suis rendu compte, au cours de ma carrière, que rien, plus rapidement que le dragage, ne peut transformer un port rentable en un port déficitaire.

Les recettes des ports ne sont pas acquises aisément et en ces temps de récession il est extrêmement difficile de les accroître. C'est pourquoi, les coûts doivent être sévèrement contenus et pourquoi aussi le dragage d'entretien, qui constitue généralement une charge importante, doit faire l'objet d'une étude rigoureuse. Un port déficitaire, s'il peut réduire ses coûts de dragage, a souvent la possibilité de revenir au-dessus de la ligne.

Mon autorité portuaire, le British Transport Docks Board, gère 19 ports en Grande Bretagne. Le dragage étant nécessaire dans chacun d'entre eux, l'autorité portuaire possède et dirige une flotte de dragues. Ceci ne nous empêche pas de faire régulièrement appel aux entreprises privées de dragage pour faire face à des besoins variables et incertains.

La recherche est un facteur vital en ce domaine et nous poursuivons un effort constant pour l'approfondir. Toutefois, nous vivons dans un monde imparfait. L'existence d'unités de recherche ne garantit pas leur utilisation judicieuse ni même leur utilisation tout court. Et pourtant, la sanction d'un effort de recherche insuffisant ou mal orienté peut être très lourde et nous devons nous assurer que ceux qui prennent d'importantes decisions d'investissements en sont conscients.

Je suis heureux de constater que l'honneur que plaçaient généralement les ports dans la détention d'une flotte de dragues fait place peu à peu à l'approche plus rationnelle du partage des ressources. Il fut un temps en effet où chaque port voulait absolument disposer souverainement de sa flotte de dragage, même si ceci s'avérait extrêmement coûteux. Mais les dragues vieillissent et le coût de leur remplacement est horriblement élevé.

Aussi les ports, et en particulier, ceux qui dépendent d'une même autorité, souhaitent-ils, aujourd'hui, mettre en commun leurs ressources en ce domaine et donc la charge qu'elles représentent. Les dragues — coûteuses — doivent être mises en commun.

Mais reste le problème des hommes qui manoeuvrent les dragues. En Grande Bretagne, traditionnellement, la plupart des ports possèdent leurs dragues et effectuent les travaux nécessaires pour leur propre compte. Très souvent, les conditions de travail des équipages ont été définies au temps déjà lointain des dragues à godets. Elles sont donc tout à fait inadaptées aux dragues modernes. En effet, aussi sophistiqué que soit l'équipement, le cycle de dragage ne peut être optimisé si les dragues passent une partie substantielle de leur temps amarrées à leur accostage. Une autorité portuaire qui n'est pas en mesure de négocier des accords de production avec ses propres équipages a tout intérêt à abandonner le dragage avec sa propre main d'oeuvre. En définitive, il y aura toujours un besoin du secteur privé du dragage et c'est par rapport à celui-ci d'ailleurs que les autorités portuaires devraient estimer leur propre efficacité. Il n'y a de meilleur jugement que celui du marché.

J J C M VAN DOOREMALEN (PAYS-BAS)

L'automatisation de l'équipement de dragage est devenue une nécessité absolue en raison de la nature complexe du processus de dragage et du nombre de facteurs qui interviennent dans celui-ci. Il faut être conscient de ce que la décision de mettre en place des systèmes automatisés n'est pas une opération ponctuelle. Elle implique la nécessité de disposer d'un personnel capable de faire fonctionner et d'entretenir l'équipement. En règle générale, ceci exige qu'une formation supplémentaire soit assurée pour les futurs équipages des engins. De surcroît, le propriétaire de l'équipement doit se garder de penser que l'automatisation lui permettra de recruter du personnel moins qualifié. Tout au contraire, étant donné que les processus d'automatisation impliquent toujours la fixation de maxima et de minima (limites opératoires) pour les paramètres qui interviennent et comme les conditions se modifient constamment au cours du cycle de dragage, un capitaine et un équipage de dragage expérimentés peuvent seuls fixer ces limites.

Il est important de comprendre que la qualité de l'automatisation est une fonction directe de ses signaux d'entrée. C'est pourquoi je pense quant à moi que nous devrions dans l'avenir proche nous soucier en priorité de l'amélioration de la qualité des détecteurs qui fournissent ces signaux d'entrée.

L'automatisation est rentable lorsqu'il s'agit de contrôler des processus complexes; elle n'est cependant pas exclue en cas de processus relativement simples dans la mesure où:

- un engin automatisé ne se fatigue pas: il travaille 24 heures sur 24;
- un engin automatisé est "régulieré";
- en cas d'enregistrement des résultats, il permet de rassembler des données utiles en vue de travaux de recherches futurs;
- il ne s'énerve pas.

En conclusion, je voudrais proposer que l'A.I. P.C.N. envisage de mettre au point des recommandations à l'usage des propriétaires présents et actuels de dragues automatisées complexes, en particulier afin qu'ils accordent beaucoup plus d'attention à la formation théorique et pratique de leur personnel. Je pense en effet que nous manquons actuellement de personnes capables d'assurer cette formation.

G B M OLIVER (GB)

Je voudrais me référer à la Recommandation 2 du Projet de Conclusions ainsi qu'aux remarques de M. Nederlof ce matin. Je suis convaincu que nous sommes tous conscients de la contribution à la réduction des coûts de dragage en zone de boue liquide apportée par les travaux réalisés à Rotterdam autour du concept de profondeur nautique. M. Nederlof a introduit ses commentaires par un peu de publicité sur l'importance de la Hollande pour le dragage et du dragage pour la Hollande. J'espère qu'il ne m'en voudra pas si je rétablis un peu l'équilibre des choses en faisant remarquer que l'avantage que retire actuellement Rotterdam du concept de profondeur nautique est dû en grande partie aux travaux de deux chercheurs britanniques (à savoir les Drs. Kirby et Parker de l'Institut des Sciences Océanographiques de Taunton) ainsi qu'à la conception, à la mise au point et à la fabrication en Grande-Bretagne d'un densimètre radioactif. Vous m'excuserez, Monsieur le Président, mais nous ne pouvons quand même pas tout abandonner à la Hollande!

Mais en fait si j'ai demandé la parole, c'est pour poser une question. On nous a expliqué qu'il est à présent admis à Rotterdam que de la boue d'une densité allant jusque 1.2 peut être comprise dans le pied de pilote sans effet dommageable. Il s'agit là comme je l'ai dit d'un projet considérable mais 1.2 ne représente quand même qu'un peu plus que de l'eau sale. Ma question est donc de savoir si M. Nederlof et ses collègues envisagent d'aller plus loin encore — peut-être jusqu'au stade où la quille du navire passe effectivement à travers de la boue d'une densité de 1.1 ou 1.2?

M. Jones, qui a pris la parole il y a quelques minutes, a eu l'amabilité de mentionner certains travaux réalisés il y a quelques années au sein du National Ports Council sur l'idée de mettre en commun les dragues de plusieurs ports. Cette idée a également été soulevée par d'autres orateurs. Le travail effectué a consisté en une simulation informatisée de très grande ampleur représentant la totalité de l'activité de dragage d'entretien des ports britanniques. Ces travaux ont effectivement mis en avant le très grand avantage financier qui résulterait d'une mise en commun des dragues. Je suis donc d'accord avec M. Jones pour dire que le temps est révolu où les ports individuels pouvaient être propriétaires exclusifs de leurs équipements de dragage (sauf peut-être dans quelques cas très particuliers), mais il s'agit là avant tout, sinon exclusivement, d'un problème d'organisation. C'est pourquoi le British Transport Docks Board, qui dirige — comme M. Jones l'a dit — 19 ports en Grande-Bretagne, est à même de gérer la mise en commun des dragues alors que d'autres ports en Grande-Bretagne ne font preuve que de peu ou pas d'intérêt pour l'idée. En ce domaine, les avantages vont à ceux qui sont à même de se les octroyer, mais il s'agit d'un problème d'organisation.

J de KONING (PAYS-BAS)

Je voudrais attirer votre attention sur le rapport canadien.* A la page 224, au Tableau 2, sous (b), on y lit que la tolérance moyenne de

---

*An Errata to this Section has been submitted to the Publisher and appears on page 148.

dragage est de 0,15 m pour toutes les sections de chenal. La référence (b) indique que, je cite, "la tolérance de dragage (± 0, 15 m) montre la précision avec laquelle une drague porteuse moderne peut travailler à une profondeur donnée", fin de citation.

Au Tableau 4 de la page 225, nous apprenons que la gamme de chenal couvre:

Fleuve 00 - 17	limon et limon sablonneux
Embouchure fluviale 17 - 21	limon et boue de baie
Baie intérieure 21 - 23	boue de baie
Anse 23 - 24	sable fin moyen
Zone exposée (aux lames) 24 - 28	sable fin

Je crains que nous soyons ici une nouvelle fois en présence d'une erreur très ancienne et persistante.

Les gens ont tendance à penser que la chose imprimée est le reflet de la réalité.

Une tolérance d'un pied est mentionnée dans de nombreux soumissions et contrats de dragage. Le danger de cette pratique est mis en évidence par l'exposé dont nous parlons.

Les tolérances de dragage effectives d'une drague porteuse à section remorquée de la classe moyenne seront, dans les conditions mentionnées, d'environ 0,50 à 0,75 m inférieures à la profondeur de dragage moyenne effective.

Puis-je suggérer qu'une commission soit constituée pour étudier, établir et publier une liste de tolérances de dragage. Ce pourrait être la Commission sur la "Classification des Sols à Draguer". Puis-je également proposer que ce travail soit si possible réalisé en collaboration avec l'O.M.A.D. (Organisation Mondiale des Associations de Dragage). (WODA).

A H C STIRLING (GB)

Je voudrais faire quelques remarques sur le rapport portant sur deux grands contrats de dragage, respectivement à Port Kembla, N.S.W., Australie et à Newcastle, auquel j'ai été mêlé. Les deux contrats prévoyaient la prise en considération de divers paramètres d'environnement.

A Port Kembla, le soumissionnaire qui a emporté le contrat proposait une méthode moins coûteuse de dragage qui comportait, par contre, un risque de pollution élevé. Le programme de lutte contre la pollution est décrit dans le rapport mais je pense utile de mentionner un aspect non technique. La méthode de dragage proposée conduisit les défenseurs de l'environnement locaux à se préoccuper de la pollution maritime et en particulier du risque de pollution de quelques magnifiques plages voisines où se pratique le surf. En conséquence, le client et l'entrepreneur ont lancé une campagne de relations publiques et de presse de grande envergure pour faire connaître les résultats du programme de lutte contre la pollution et démontrer que celle-ci était négligeable.

A Newcastle, le risque de pollution était dû au bruit et aux vibrations résultant du déroctage par explosifs. Une zone résidentielle était située à quelques centaines de mètres du chenal d'approche dans lequel l'utilisation des explosifs devait avoir lieu. Afin d'éviter les retards et les accroissements de coûts qui leur sont liés, le client — c'est-à-dire le Maritime Services Board — et l'entrepreneur ont entrepris une campagne soigneusement préparée et bien orchestrée pour fournir toutes les informations relatives aux fourchettes d'heures limitées pendant lesquelles les explosions auraient lieu ainsi qu'aux mesures des vibrations, de manière à donner au public tous apaisements sur ces questions.

Dans les deux contrats, le coût de ces programmes était très faible — une fraction de pourcent du coût total du projet —, alors que les coûts et retards qu'auraient entraînés d'éventuelles interventions de la part des défenseurs de l'environnement auraient pu être prohibitifs.

Ce que je veux souligner, c'est que, pour réaliser dans de bonnes conditions des projets de dragage sensibles du point de vue de l'environnement et éviter d'importantes hausses de coûts ou des retards substantiels, il ne suffit pas de mettre en oeuvre un programme de lutte contre la pollution mais il faut aussi en utiliser les résultats dans une campagne soigneusement préparée d'information du public.

R B DAVENPORT (GB)

Cette intervention se borne à souligner la nécessité de tenter de réduire les besoins de dragage d'entretien.

Elle se rallie aux autres orateurs (Néerlandais, Français — "Profondeur nautique" et murs d'entraînement) qui ont abordé ce point.

Il y est demandé,

a) Quelle est la source des matières à draguer? Les sédiments et les eaux devraient être analysés.

b) Est-il possible de dévier les matériaux? Pièges à sédiments.

c) Est-il possible de minimiser le dragage? Murs d'entraînement, pompage ou endiguements à des périodes déterminées. Trituration de l'eau ou traitement chimique?

Ces moyens n'éliminent pas nécessairement la nécessité de draguer mais font partie du cycle global.

Le premier sujet de recherche devrait devenir: "Origines de la sédimentation".

VAN DEN DOEL (PAYS-BAS) RAPPORTEUR GENERAL

Les divers orateurs se sont généralement accordés à reconnaître que la possession par les autorités publiques de leur propre flotte de dragage s'avère intéressante dans la mesure où le matériel peut être utilisé suffisamment intensément. Ceci ne peut généralement être obtenu que par le recours à une collaboration entre ports.

Dans ce cas, il est toujours possible de faire appel aux entreprises privées pour rencontrer les pointes d'activité.

Cette approche s'écarte partiellement de la philosophie américaine et néerlandaise, qui va dans le sens du contrôle public de la flotte de dragage pour des raisons d'ordre stratégique et de capacité de réponse à des cas d'urgence.

Aucun des orateurs n'a mentionné la possibilité d'accords de chartering à moyen/long terme (3 à 4 ans) avec des entreprises privées de dragage, celles-ci garantissant en permanence une capacité rendue disponible dans un délai préalablement précisé.

De cette manière, le port peut s'assurer la disponibilité d'une capacité de base suffisante sans devoir entretenir une flotte de dragage complète.

Le dragage de construction est généralement réalisé par des firmes privées.

J'ai encore réagi aux remarques du Professeur Mc Dowell sur les effets à long terme du dragage. Tout en reconnaissant leur importance, je me demandais si ceci ne dépassait pas le thème de "l'optimalisation du cycle de dragage" et donc le champ de compétence de l'AIPCN.

Bien que je ne l'aie pas dit explicitement, mon raisonnement était que nous ne connaissons pas les effets à long terme de travaux tels que l'approfondissement de l'embouchure du Rhin ou le nettoyage de l'Escaut, etc, S'il fallait attendre cette connaissance, il ne serait possible de rien faire. Je crains que l'apprentissage par essais et erreurs soit la seule possibilité à cet égard. Néanmoins, le comité de Rédaction de l'AIPCN a jugé que ce problème méritait plus ample examen. A cet égard, j'ai indiqué dans mes conclusions qu'il ressortait des rapports que l'impact sur l'environnement des travaux de dragage peut généralement être atténué ou neutralisé à un coût relativement modeste, pourvu que cet aspect soit pris en considération de manière correcte dès le stade de la planification.

CONCLUSIONS

Un entretien économique des profondeurs nécessaires dans les chenaux d'accès et les bassins constitue un élément essentiel de l'activité portuaire.

Au cours des prochaines années, la programmation des dragages et le traitement automatique des données connaîtront une utilisation croissante.

Toutefois, la transmission et le traitement rapides de l'information doivent faire l'objet de nouvelles recherches afin de pouvoir utiliser les résultats obtenus pendant l'exécution des travaux.

Une vaste action de recherche doit être entreprise portant sur l'ensemble des opérations de dragage afin d'en améliorer l'économie et la fiabilité. Cette recherche doit couvrir:

a) le comportement du sol et la mise en dépôt des produits de dragages compte tenu de l'action des forces hydrauliques;

b) le choix des équipements;

c) les méthodes d'exécution des travaux pour l'ensemble des phases du dragage;

d) l'impact sur l'environnement;

e) les conséquences à long terme du dragage et de la mise en dépôt des produits dragués.

La mise en commun de moyens de dragage par plusieurs ports peut s'avérer économiquement intéressante et devrait être sérieusement envisagée lorsque les circonstances s'y prêtent.

Il est nécessaire d'établir des règles claires et de prendre conscience de l'importance des normes pour l'exécution de travaux de dragage et la mise en dépôt des matériaux dragués.

La mise en dépôt des produits de dragage — en mer comme à terre — pose d'importants problèmes sur le plan de la loi, de l'aménagement du territoire, de la protection de l'environnement et de l'économie. Les politiques qui ne prennent pas en compte tous ces facteurs, peuvent conduire à de sérieuses difficultés: c'est un sujet qui nécessite une étude soignée.

Le concept de "profondeur de navigation" dans les fonds de vase fluide peut permettre d'appréciables économies sur les coûts des dragages d'entretien.

Il est recommandé à l'AIPCN de bien vouloir considérer l'ensemble des points précédents comme des sujets d'étude possible pour les CTP I et II.

PORTS ET ACCES MARITIMES

SECTION II — SUJET 3

Progrès récents réalisés dans les moyens et les équipements de manutention des marchandises et plus spécialement des points de vue de la conception et de la disposition des installations des terminaux

Mercredi 13 mai 1981

Président:	*N N B ORDMAN (GB)* *Noel Ordman and Associates Ltd*
Vice Président:	*Prof F VASCO COSTA (Portugal)* *Technical University of Lisbon*
Rapporteur Général:	*J H W NORTHFIELD (GB)* *Chief Engineer, The Felixstowe Dock and Railway Company*
Secrétaire:	*P LACEY (GB)* *Ove Arup and Partners Ltd, London*
Secrétaire Adjoint:	*Mlle M-M DANEELS (Belgique)* *Secrétaire AIPCN Secrétariat Générale, Bruxelles*

Orateurs

V J DAVIES (GB), J S BALFOUR (GB), J CHATTAWAY (GB), T KERISEL (France), M ENRIQUEZ FRANCISCO (Espagne), J A SIMOEN (Belgique), D J VANDENBOSSCHE (Belgique), J F MAQUET (France), A T RUSSELL (Etats-Unis), N J FERGUSON (Australie), A L MOSS-MORRIS (Afrique du Sud), R LECLERCQ (France), W H LEWIS (Etats-Unis), A G F EDDIE (Australie), A J CARMICHAEL (GB), N N B ORDMAN (GB), D L POPE (GB), D JONES (GB), F VASCO COSTA (Portugal), H THOMAS (France), H K DALLY (GB), P A COX (GB)

J. H. W. NORTHFIELD (RAPPORTEUR GENERAL)

COMMENTAIRES

Ces rapports ont été rédigés par des auteurs représentant l'Australie, la Belgique, le Canada, l'Espagne, les Etats-Unis d'Amérique, la Finlande, la France, le Japon, les Pays-Bas, la République Fédérale d'Allemagne, le Royaume-Uni, la Suède et l'Union des Républiques Socialistes Soviétiques. Les opinions exprimées reflètent donc un ensemble d'approches très largement international. Certains rapports traitent des nombreux aspects des systèmes de manutention des marchandises, d'autres se concentrent sur un circuit commercial ou une marchandise particulièrement importants pour le trafic maritime du pays concerné, mais la plupart des auteurs s'attachent à décrire la manière dont des modifications intervenues à ces divers niveaux affectent la conception des installations portuaires ou des navires.
Bien que les rapports présentés aient été rédigés par des auteurs originaires de toutes les parties du monde, on ne peut s'empêcher de remarquer la similarité des problèmes rencontrés par tous et des manières dont les installations ont été développées pour les rencontrer. Ceci n'a, du reste, rien d'extraordinaire en raison de la nature internationale par essence de la navigation et du fait que les marchandises chargées dans un port du monde doivent être déchargées dans un port situé dans une autre partie du monde. C'est d'ailleurs pourquoi la compatibilité aux deux bouts de la chaîne de transport est tellement souhaitable.

L'apparition des méthodes unitarisées de manutention des marchandises, et en particulier du conteneur implique automatiquement la similarité des installations de départ et d'arrivée, dans la mesure où une norme internationale (ISO) régit la construction des conteneurs. On note en outre de manière générale une tendance à remplacer les opérations intensives en main-d'oeuvre par une exploitation mécanisée, tendance particulièrement vive dans les pays industrialisés en raison du coût élevé de la main d'oeuvre. Une utilisation accrue de l'automatisation et des commandes programmées semble donc inévitable.

1. GENERAL

C'est généralement du côté du navire que sont initiés les progrès dans le domaine maritime, les installations des terminaux devant le plus souvent s'y adapter. On voit mal comment cet état de choses pourrait être modifié. Le coût de construction des installations capables de recevoir des navires plus grands et le coût de ces navires eux-même sont très élevés. C'est pourquoi il est important de minimiser le temps que ces navires ne passent pas en mer. Ceci implique des temps de chargement et de déchargement aussi réduits que possible et exige de plus en plus une exploitation portuaire efficace et économique.

2. RECHERCHES PRELIMINAIRES

La plupart des rapports indiquent explicitement ou implicitement l'importance d'une recherche et d'une analyse adéquates avant que toute installation de port ou de terminal soit mise en chantier et deux d'entre eux au moins précisent de manière détaillée les modalités de réalisation de ces investigations préliminaires.

Il est recommandé d'accorder à l'avenir plus d'attention à cet aspect particulier de la conception des navires et des terminaux, pourvu toutefois que ce travail soit basé sur des données concrètes et une conception réaliste, seules susceptibles d'en assurer le succès.

3. COMPATIBILITE OU NORMALISATION

En raison du caractère international du trafic maritime, la normalisation doit être envisagée chaque fois que c'est possible. Il ne doit pas toujours s'agir de normalisation à proprement parler mais il faut en tout cas recherche un degré élevé de compatibilité entre installations portuaires. Sans cette compatibilité, nous n'aurions pas connu la "révolution" des conteneurs, du moins pas dans ses modalités actuelles.

4. ECHANGES AVEC LES PAYS EN VOIE DE DEVELOPPEMENT

Tous les rapports ont été préparés par des auteurs appartenant à des pays hautement industrialisés où la richesse nationale permet d'envisager des installations très coûteuses et très sophistiquées.

Par contre, les pays en voie de développement disposent de beaucoup moins de ressources et cet état de choses pèse d'un poids très lourd sur le développement des installations portuaires de ces pays. Ceci ne devrait jamais être perdu de vue par les pays qui offrent leur assistance sous forme de services de consultance, de fourniture d'équipement ou même d'organisation des activités. Adapter les réalisations aux ressources disponibles doit être une préoccupation constante de qui veut faire oeuvre utile dans ces pays.

5. RECHERCHE

Il est encourageant que tous les rapports mentionnent ces faits et soulignent le besoin d'une recherche adéquate en matière de trafic prévisible et de la meilleure manière de le traiter.

Il est devenu évident au cours des dernières années que dans certaines régions du monde ont été construites des installations portuaires répondant sans doute à d'excellentes objectifs nationaux mais qui ne tiennent apparemment pas compte du type ou du volume du trafic attendu, ni de ses points d'origine et de destination.

En d'autres termes, des ports ont été conçus sans prendre en considération les systèmes de manutention les mieux adaptés au trafic prévisible.

6. NORMALISATION

En raison du caractère international du trafic maritime, il est souhaitable — voire essentiel — que les armements, les architectes navals, les exploitants des ports et les ingénieurs oeuvrent ensemble dans le but d'atteindre un degré de compatibilité aussi élevé que possible entre leurs disciplines respectives.

Rôle de l'A.I.P.C.N. Dans la normalisation du trafic roulier, par ex. extrémité de rampe, épais/fin, doigts. Modifications dues aux moteurs à vapeur, modifications des unités au cours des 25 dernières années. Transmission des systèmes de docks construits à la fin du 19ème siècle. Introduction des charriots automoteurs à bras élévateurs pour la manutention des conteneurs, conséquences pour la conception des plateformes, augmentation des coûts.

7. AIDE AUX PAYS EN VOIE DE DEVELOPPEMENT

Plusieurs auteurs ont décrit des installations répondant à des besoins spécifiques dans leurs propres pays.

On ne peut nier que ces installations conviennent à ces pays, mais lorsque les pays très industrialisés offrent leurs services aux pays en voie de développement, ils ne peuvent perdre de vue que ce qui convient à un pays n'est pas nécessairement adapté aux besoins d'un pays en cours de développement lent, et dont les ressources en compétences et leur variété sont limitées. Il peut ne pas être souhaitable de réduire les besoins en main d'oeuvre par l'introduction d'une technologie avancée ou de prévoir des équipements à plus haut rendement alors que le volume annuel du trafic traité reste faible.

Plus grande adéquation des installations intensives en main d'oeuvre. C'est pourquoi les pays industrialisés ne doivent pas chercher à imposer leurs propres méthodes aux pays en voie de développement, mais au contraire appliquer la technologie la mieux adaptée à chaque situation.

8. ENERGIE

J'en viens maintenant au problème de l'utilisation de l'énergie. La raréfaction des combustibles fissiles au niveau mondial, alors que toutes les économies actuelles en dépendent, appelle une utilisation aussi économique que possible des ressources existantes. L'importance en sera encore accrue jusqu'au moment où des sources et des types alternatifs d'énergie seront disponibles. Notre devoir envers les générations futures est de ne pas gaspiller ces ressources. C'est pourquoi la recherche sur des moyens plus économiques de transport des marchandises ainsi que de chargement et de déchargement des navires doit se voir reconnaître une importance tout à fait prioritaire dans les études de conception futures.

9. POLLUTION

Enfin, une attention accrue doit être accordée à lutte contre la pollution ou à la protection de l'environnement. Plusieurs des rapports qui vous ont été soumis en traitent, notamment en liaison avec le danger accru résultant de la croissance des industries produisant des substances dangereuses.

Le rapport des auteurs néerlandais décrit une solution possible du problème. Il souligne néanmoins la nécessité de poursuivre le développement des moyen de lutte contre les effets de la pollution.

BESOINS EN TERRAINS/BOULIMIQUES/SYSTEMES DEVELOPPES DE COMMUNICATION

Les ports modernes deviennent de plus en plus boulimiques dans leurs besoins en terrains, et ceci est particulièrement évident dans le développement des terminaux pour conteneurs. Parallèlement à l'accroissement de la capacité des terminaux modernes surgit le besoin de développer des moyens de communication adéquats sous forme de routes, de voies ferrées, etc. Il n'y a aucun intérêt à créer un terminal moderne de grande capacité si les importations ne peuvent être enlevées et les exportations reçues.

En conclusion, je voudrais rappeler les remarques que j'ai faites et qui sont résumées sous les points 1, 2 et 3 de la note qui vous a été remise.

Même si la conception et l'exploitation des navires peuvent mener le jeu, la mise en place des navires, des ports et des équipements doit être envisagée comme un tout indivisible. Ceci appelle un processus renforcé de consultation. En voulant réduire ses propres coûts, le propriétaire du navire peut exiger des installations portuaires peut-être inutilement coûteuses. Son propre intérêt ne va donc pas nécessairement de pair avec celui de la collectivité.

Je crois qu'il incombe aux ingénieurs d'essayer de dépasser ces intérêts fractionnels et la consultation continue peut les y aider.

CHANGEMENT

Nous vivons dans un monde en changement et même les pays en voie de developpement devront — fût-ce contre leur gré — accepter ce changement. Ils doivent donc s'efforcer de développer leurs installations pour relever ce défi.

L'introduction de la vapeur a, en son temps introduit un changement radical. Plus récemment, nous avons connu:

1. L'introduction du conteneur et du navire roulier, c'est-à-dire des charges unitaires, et la réduction du trafic vraquier, parallèle à l'accroissement des dimensions des navires. De ce fait, les ports construits au 19ème siècle ont largement perdu de leur utilité et ont dû être déplacés en aval.

2. L'introduction de l'équipement lourd, notamment charriot automoteur à bras élévateur et portique de manutention, a obligé à revoir la conception des revêtements de sol.

3. L'introduction des grandes installations de manutention rapide du vrac a accru les problèmes de pollution qui étaient encore minimes il y a seulement vingt ou trente ans.

4. La solution de ces problèmes se complique encore du fait de la crise de l'énergie dont une solution à long terme doit encore être trouvée. On voit donc que la solution à un problème donne invariablement lieu à un autre problème et cette recherche à long terme est tout aussi nécessaire que la solution du problème immédiat.

LES DEBATS

V J DAVIES (GB)

J'ai lu avec intérêt le rapport australien de M. Ferguson sur les terminaux en pleine mer. En effet, ma société a récemment mis le point final à l'étude et la conception d'une installation semblable en Argentine. Je voudrais tout d'abord soulever le problème de la prévision des temps d'inopérationalité dûs à l'action des lames ainsi qu'à l'importance de ce phénomène au niveau du choix du site et de l'orientation du brise-lames, en me référant à titre d'exemple au cas argentin.

Pour ce terminal argentin, les consultants devaient trouver un site et formuler des recommandations en vue de réaliser une installation de chargement pour le transport de calcaire à partir d'une carrière située en Patagonie vers une nouvelle usine créée à San Antonio Oeste, à quelque 580 kms au nord.

Plusieurs sites ont été étudiés le long de cette côte particulièrement rocheuse et irrégulière. Certains sites bénéficient d'une protection naturelle plus abondante que d'autres, mais se seraient généralement révélés plus coûteux en termes de dragage de roches, moins sûrs pour la navigation et plus limitatifs au niveau de l'expansion du port, en vue de son utilisation par de plus grands navires. Par ailleurs, les sites en pleine mer ne pouvaient manifestement être viables que si les temps de non opérationalité dûs à l'action des lames n'étaient pas excessifs, car autrement le coût des brise-lames auraient été prohibitif.

Finalement, un site en pleine mer situé sur un cap approché Punta Alpat, site qui est effectivement non protégé d'est en sud-ouest, a été choisi.

Les vents dominants sont des vents d'ouest, direction dans laquelle le site jouit d'une bonne protection. Cependant, les vents de sud-ouest soufflant à travers le Golfe de St Jorge, engendrent des lames qui peuvent être prévues. Ces prévisions, jointes aux hauteurs de lames et aux houles d'est et de sud-est observées, donnent une rosace des lames du site de Punta Alpat.

On a supposé que les navires pouvaient continuer à charger en présence de lames atteignant 1 1/2 mètre, pourvu qu'elles soient de bout. Cependant, les calculs ont été basés sur une lame maximum acceptable de 1 metre.

Le brise-lames est orienté de 20 à 200 degrés au nord afin de s'assurer que les navires puissent accoster contre la direction de lames la plus fréquente. Cet angle a également été choisi en fonction de considérations de navigation locale.

Nous sommes donc arrivés à la conclusion que le temps d'inopérationalité dû à l'action des lames devrait être inférieur à 20% pour des navires de 15 000 tpm et cela nous semble satisfaisant.

Il est évident que, pour les raisons indiquées par M. Ferguson, l'utilisation de navires plus grands tend à réduire les temps d'inopérationalité dûs à l'action des lames. L'installation de Punta Alpat a donc été conçue pour pouvoir recevoir des navires de 35 000 tonnes.

Le problème de la conception en présence d'une information insuffisante est un des risques inhérents à la profession d'ingénieur civil, mais il est difficile de justifier le coût élevé de trous de forage en mer dans des régions éloignées du monde dont la géologie est relativement prévisible. Malheureusement, il peut être nécessaire de recueillir la meilleure information disponible grâce à des trous de forage sur terre et de se baser sur les connaissances locales et l'inspection de plongée sous-marine pour préparer un cahier des charges susceptible, du moins peut-on l'espérer, de réduire le coût d'éventuels dommages à un niveau inférieur à celui des forages en mer.

Ma dernière remarque porte sur les commentaires que l'on trouve à la page 383 et qui sont relatifs aux ouvrages d'accostage en mer. L'affirmation selon laquelle les forces de lames inspirent la philosophie de la conception économique en mer ne s'applique qu'à un type bien précis d'ouvrages. Dans le cas du brise-lames argentin en question, le tracé sur pieux a été déterminé par les poids axiaux nécessaires pour résister aux forces d'accostage des navires. Les moments de torsion dûs à l'action des lames n'ont pas constitué un facteur critique.

Enfin, je ferai référence au projet de conclusions de cette session pour demander spécifiquement un effort plus grand d'information, de recherche ou d'étude sur les mouvements acceptables des navires de diverses dimensions aux accostages situés en pleine mer.

J S BALFOUR (GB)

En tant que représentant d'un port en exploitation et d'une société pétrolière impliqués à l'échelle internationale dans le trafic, la réception et la manutention de chargements de pétrole et de gaz, je crois devoir informer le Congrès de la manière dont nous voyons les choses. Tous, en tant qu'opérateurs responsables, nous nous sommes intéressés de très près, et nous continuons de le faire, à la mise au point et à l'amélioration de tous les aspects des techniques et de l'équipement de manutention du pétrole, du gaz et plus récemment du charbon et du vrac sec.

Ceux d'entre vous qui étaient dans cette salle lundi matin ont entendu le Président de session dire qu'une de nos sociétés pétrolières-"soeurs" semble bien s'en tirer pour la manutention des chargements de gaz.
Je voudrais saisir cette occasion pour dire fermement que ces choses-là ne se font pas toutes seules. Nous avons des groupes industriels qui étudient et élaborent tous les aspects des techniques de manutention du pétrole et du gaz tant sur les navires qu'à terre, de même que les problèmes posés par le transbordement navire-terre et vice-versa.

Ces groupes sont rassemblés sous l'égide du Forum Maritime International des Sociétés Pétrolières — O.C.I.M.F. en anglais. J'ai eu le plaisir de présider, pas plus tard que la semaine dernière, une des réunions de cette association, à laquelle participaient, ici à Edinbourg, plus de 40 représentants de sociétés pétrolières et d'exploitants de terminaux pétroliers venus des quatre coins du moyen orient et d'Europe. Nous y avons discuté nos problèmes d'exploitation et passé en revue l'avancement du travail de nos diverses commissions. Entre autres choses, celles-ci sont chargées de la préparation des normes pour les équipements d'amarrage des navires, les bras métalliques de chargement pour le transbordement du pétrole, les cables d'amarrage, les tuyaux, les procédures et les "check lists" dans les terminaux, etc.

Quoi que nous fassions à l'O.C.I.M.F. et à l'A.I.P.C.N. pour approfondir de telles questions et en dépit des facteurs de sécurité dont tiennent compte nos ingénieurs dans la conception de nos accostages, il reste un domaine qui nous cause des soucis importants et grandissants, particulièrement en Grande-Bretagne, et qui semble rester hors de contrôle.

Je voudrais dire, Monsieur le Président, combien j'ai été déçu de voir que ce problème n'était pas inclus dans vos conclusions et recommandations pour le Sujet 1 de cette Section. Or, aujourd'hui encore, il n'en est pas fait mention. Il s'agit d'inconséquences dans la manoeuvre des navires commises par les pilotes à l'arrivée et au départ de l'accostage.

Il me semble pour le moins étrange que partout les pilotes soient ou bien indépendants ou bien au service d'organismes autres que l'Autorité Portuaire et que les règlements obligent à y avoir recours, sans pour autant les rendre <u>responsables</u> ou <u>redevables</u> des conséquences de leurs actes. Si la plupart d'entre eux sont extrêmement qualifiés et diligents, encore qu'incontrôlés, il n'est pas surprenant que certains aient leurs propres "manies" et s'obstinent à manoeuvrer les navires d'une manière dont il est impossible de tenir compte dans la conception des jetées, ridiculisant de ce fait les normes détaillées de conception mentionnées ci-avant et qui devraient comprendre des recommandations opérationnelles précises et concrètes.

Je m'étonne donc qu'en ces temps de réglementation croissante et souvent d'utilité contestable, une telle lacune puisse subsister dans un domaine crucial pour la sécurité d'utilisation des installations portuaires.

J'aimerais en conséquence suggérer, Monsieur le Président, que ce Congrès recommande que l'A.I.P.C.N. prenne ma proposition en considération et qu'il ajoute, soit aux recommandations du Sujet 3 qui nous préoccupe aujourd'hui soit à celles du Sujet 1 traité auparavant le thème suivant: "ETUDE DU PROBLEME DU CONTROLE ET DE LA RESPONSABILITE DES PILOTES IMPLIQUES DANS L'ACCOSTAGE ET LE DESACCOSTAGE DES NAVIRES, ET PARTICULIEREMENT DES TRES GRANDS NAVIRES MARCHANDS ET DES METHANIERS".

J CHATTAWAY (GB)

Très rapidement, je voudrais faire quelques remarques portant toutes sur l'aspect financier:

1. Le travail de l'ingénieur chargé de la conception d'un port consiste à trouver la solution la plus économique qui permettra à l'exploitant du port de limiter autant que possible et son investissement en capital et ses frais d'exploitation, de manière à garder toutes ses chances de faire un bénéfice.

2. L'exploitant du port (ou ses conseillers) et l'ingénieur responsable de la conception (qui peut faire partie du même organisme) doivent calculer globalement le coût des ouvrages, le coût du capital et le coût d'exploitation des installations de manutention. C'est ainsi qu'il n'est pas nécessairement plus rentable d'utiliser un élévateur à fourchette relativement bon marché pour transporter des conteneurs requérant des zones pavées plus grandes et plus résistantes, plutôt qu'un engin plus cher, mais qui exige moins d'espace et une zone de dépôt moins solide (et donc moins coûteuse).

3. On a dit (dans le projet de conclusion distribué aujourd'hui) que là où vont les constructeurs de navires, doivent aller les

exploitants des ports, qui sont supposés fournir aux premiers, à leurs frais, les nouvelles installations portuaires dont ceux-ci rêvent. Par exemple, comme de nombreux membres de l'AIPCN, le Rapporteur Général et moi-même ne savons que trop que la variété infinie de rampes de navires rouliers a entraîné nombre de difficultés et de dépenses pour les exploitants des ports. Les constructeurs de navires et les propriétaires de ceux-ci ne se sont-ils pas rendu compte que cette situation entraîne des coûts supplémentaires pour eux aussi? On peut espérer cependant qu'il suivront les recommendations pour rampes de quai que l'ISO va publier sous forme de projet d'ici quelques mois, au terme de débats internationaux parfois vifs.

4. Plus tôt au cours de cette session, le Président, s'efforçant sans doute d'animer les débats – a qualifié les ingénieurs de "tortueux". "Ingénieux", sans conteste, terme si proche du mot français "ingénieur". Il n'en reste pas moins que, la plupart du temps, les ingénieurs devraient s'efforcer d'être aussi simples que possible dans la recherche des solutions les plus économiques aux problèmes qui leur sont posés.

T KERISEL (FRANCE)

Les rapports sur le Sujet 3 donnent des exemples de terminaux pour les navires charbonniers de plus de 150.000 tdw ou les navires porte-conteneurs de 3000 TEU.
Deux remarques concernant ces installations coûteuses et sophistiquées:

1. Même dans les pays industriels, supposés riches, des ports sont conduits plutôt à adapter certaines installations pour réutiliser au maximum les équipements existants et limiter le montant de leurs investissements. A titre d'exemple est cité le cas des installations charbonnières de Rouen. Rouen est le 4e port maritime français par le tonnage global, situé comme Paris, sur la Seine, à 120 km de la mer.

   Le trafic de charbon a représenté à Rouen en 1980 environ 4 Mt sur un trafic total de plus de 22 Mt. Cette position procure une économie de transport terrestre mais le tirant d'eau de Rouen est limité à 11 m. Pour maintenir et développer le trafic de charbon de Rouen, il a été démontré aux importateurs français de charbon qu'il était intéressant de recevoir à Rouen non seulement les navires de 40.000 tdw à pleine charge mais également des 80.000 tdw ou des 120.000 tdw allégés dans un port côtier, Le Havre ou Dunkerque, et amenant à Rouen respectivement des cargaisons de 50.000 t et 70.000 t. L'économie de transport terrestre pour le charbon remonté à Rouen est plus importante que l'augmentation légère de fret maritime. Rouen a ainsi réussi, en plus des charbons britanniques et polonais, à recevoir en 1980 près de 1 Mt de charbon des USA par navires de 80.000 tdw. Et ceci n'a nécessité, pour un coût très limité, que l'adaptation de 2 quais existants en y mettant en place des grues à plus grande portée hors quai et plus grand tirant d'eau.

2. La 2e remarque c'est qu'il continue pour le trafic des conteneurs à y avoir place pour des terminaux autres que les terminaux pour porte-conteneurs intégraux de 3000 TEU.

   C'est le cas de Rouen qui a un trafic important avec les pays en voie de développement de la côte occidentale d'Afrique et de l'Océan Indien puisque plus de 2 navires par jour partent de Rouen vers ces destinations. Pour ce type de trafic, Rouen a mis en place un terminal mixte pour navires porte-conteneurs intégraux de 1500 TEU mais traitant également les navires conventionnels et les navires semi-porte conteneurs.

   Et Rouen a limité le coût de ce terminal en ne l'équipant pas de portiques les plus sophistiquées mais plutôt de portiques à conteneurs qui, tout en ayant un très bon rendement, ont des caractéristiques géométriques plus limitées, ainsi que de grues polyvalentes de 25 tonnes pouvant travailler au spreader automatique.

   Nous avons ainsi atteint près de 1 Mt de conteneurs/an et ce trafic croît de 40% par an.

L'orateur projette 2 exemples d'adaptation d'équipements, plutôt que de création de grands terminaux sophistiqués, qui montrent également que les ports d'estuaire situés profondément à l'intérieur des terres conservent toutes leurs chances dans la compétition maritime.

M ENRIQUEZ FRANCISCO (ESPAGNE)

Je mentionnerai tout d'abord la figure 8 du rapport espagnol (page 499). Elle est en effet erronée, dans la mesure où le texte dit que le quai est conçu avec une surface recouverte de terre. La description correcte est celle d'une dalle en L avec une épaisseur de terre d'environ 1 1/2 mètre. De la sorte, il est possible d'excaver et d'introduire aisément dans le sol de nouvelles installations. Bien entendu, il ne s'agit pas d'une solution originale, mais je souhaitais souligner la souplesse qu'elle offre.

Ensuite, la majeure partie du rapport traite du trafic roulier, dont l'expansion est saisissante. Il est facile de créer des installations portuaires sans marées pour ce type de trafic, comme c'est le cas des ports espagnols en Méditerranée. Mais ce service comporte certains problèmes. Afin d'accélérer les manoeuvres d'accostage et de désaccostage (la rapidité de mouvement des navires est essentielle pour ce genre de trafic), les navires utilisent les propulseurs d'étrave et les hélices latérales comme freins ou comme moyen de déplacement.

Si les quais n'ont pas été conçus en fonction de cette utilisation, comme c'est le cas d'installations anciennes adaptées au trafic roulier, les jets d'eau provoquent des dégâts.

a) à la surface des anciens blocs de béton

b) sur la rive qui sert de fondation au mur de blocs.

L'impact des jets, accrû par l'effet angulaire, est si fort qu'il peut déplacer des pierres pesant une tonne et provoquer de très grands trous sous le mur. Une des solutions que nous avons appliquées a consisté à remplir les trous de sacs de ciment ou à y injecter du béton et à construire une dalle de béton pompé sur la rive, ce qui diminue la profondeur du quai.

Il existe une autre solution logique: interdire cette manoeuvre, mais cela reviendrait à tenter de résoudre en termes administratifs un problème qui doit être approché en termes de génie civil.

Je me demande si, de même qu'au Congrès de Léningrad, les rapports soviétique et français traitaient du problème de l'érosion du sol par les hélices dans le cas de la navigation intérieure, vous avez également connaissance de ce phénomène dans vos ports. Si oui, quelles sont les solutions retenues et existe-t-il des conceptions spéciales de terminaux rouliers susceptibles d'éviter ces problèmes?

Je serais reconnaissant de toute information que je pourrais recevoir à cet égard.

J A SIMOEN (BELGIQUE)

Je n'ai rien à ajouter ni à enlever de notre rapport concernant le programme de développement du port de Zeebrugge sur la côte belge. Je voudrais seulement donner un mot d'explication supplémentaire quant aux contraintes qui limitent sur le terrain les possibilités d'extension du port et qui nous acculent à faire preuve de beaucoup d'imagination et de flexibilité dans la détermination du lay-out interne du port, et qui nous obligeront à observer une sélectivité rigoureuse dans le choix des trafics qui voudront s'y établir.

Cette flexibilité s'est déjà manifestée dans l'évolution récente et assez favorable que le port a connue dans ses limites actuelles, ceci en attendant que la grande extension, aujourd'hui en exécution, soit disponible.

Monsieur le Rapporteur Général a fait une mention spéciale dans son rapport au sujet de ces contraintes qui limitent l'extension du port de Zeebrugge, mais il les a attribuées à la proximité de centres de population. Ceci n'est vrai que partiellement, et c'est pourquoi je voudrais vous donner brièvement quelques explications supplémentaires au sujet de ces contraintes (projection 1er transparent). (l'orateur projette des dia.).

Quant à l'arrière-port, il n'a pas été possible de le faire pénétrer davantage vers le sud vu la proximité de Bruges, ville de grande valeur historique.

A l'est des canaux de dérivation qui y forment la limite de l'arrière-port, le plan d'aménagement prévoit le maintien d'une zone verte à caractère agricole qui fera fonction de zone tampon entre le port et la ville balnéaire Knokke-Heist-Le Zoute.

A l'ouest du canal Baudouin, toute extension du port est interdite à cause de la présence d'une zone agricole avec village et constructions d'une grande valeur historique.

Quant à l'avant-port, un simple coup d'oeil sur le plan suffit pour constater qu'une grande extension le long de la côte, donc dans le sens transversal, est impossible vu la présence des sites touristiques et balnéaires de Zeebrugge-Plage à l'ouest et de Knokke-Heist-Le Zoute à l'est. C'est pourquoi la nouvelle digue ouest prend racine à une distance de 150 m seulement de l'ancien môle, ce qui signifie un minimum absolu pour les voies d'accès (routes et chemins de fer). La racine de la nouvelle digue est a été localisée juste à côté de la zone urbanisée de Knokke-Heist-Le Zoute, de telle façon que les établissements à caractère touristique se trouvant à front de mer, restent dégagés.

Reste finalement la limite du nouvel avant-port côté mer. En d'autres mots, comment la longueur d'extension du nouvel avant-port a été déterminée?

Cette longueur d'extension est le résultat d'une étude approfondie dans laquelle principalement 3 facteurs furent pris en considération, notamment le facteur hydraulique, le facteur nautique et le facteur économique. C'est le facteur hydraulique qui a joué le rôle déterminant dans le choix final de la longueur d'extension.

Nous avons envisagé pendant l'étude plusieurs longueurs et formes d'extension de l'avant-port. Seulement, comme l'avant-port de Zeebrugge est situé sur l'extrémité est de la côte belge qui fait partie intégrante de l'estuaire de l'Escaut, la contrainte principale de l'extension en mer réside dans le souci de ne pas perturber le régime hydraulique de cet estuaire et de limiter les augmentations des vitesses des courants, causées par le rétrécissement de l'estuaire, à 10% en général et localement à 15% maximum.
Les zones, qui comprennent des passes navigables à caractère international, dans lesquelles ces contraintes sont imposées et qui seront respectées après la réalisation de l'extension de l'avant-port retenue ont des limites bien précises.

D J VANDENBOSSCHE (BELGIQUE)

Je veux parler du sujet suivant: "comment planifier un avant-port et estimer sa capacité de manutention et les techniques appropriées, alors qu'on ignore les chargements et même les navires qu'il recevra". Je suppose que c'est un problème que connaissent bien beaucoup de collègues planificateurs et concepteurs de ports (voir fig. 5, page 403).

Dans le cas de Zeebruges, en particulier, il faut tenir compte du fait que le maître-plan d'extension de l'avant-port a été établi en automne 1977 pour n'être adopté par le gouvernement qu'en juin 1979. En 1985, lorsque les brise-lames de l'avant-port pourront être terminés, seul le terminal LNG de l'avant-port est sera opérationnel. Ceci veut dire que l'avant-port ouest ne pourra être opérationnel pour, par exemple, les conteneurs, avant 1990. En outre, en raison des contraintes physiques décrites dans le rapport et soulignées par M. Simoen, on aura compris qu'en ce qui concerne l'extension vers la mer, le plan de développement actuel interdit toute expansion future. C'est pourquoi aucune décision ferme n'a été et n'a dû être prise pour l'agencement intérieur du port ouest. L'évaluation des capacités de l'avant-port se fait à la mode des ingénieurs, à partir de certaines données physiques relatives au port, des perspectives de trafic actuel et à court terme et en tenant compte des installations comparables d'autres ports situés dans la zone qui va du Havre à Hambourg. Ce n'est peut-être pas une méthode très raffinée, mais elle est efficace. En effet, une prévision de développement pour un port moyen comme celui de Zeebruges, qui ne serait basée que sur des modèles mathématiques de flux de trafic, comporterait de nombreux risques en raison de la localisation du port ainsi que du trafic existant et escompté.

En fait, l'avant-port ouest est bien situé pour les transbordements dans lesquels rapidité et efficacité élevées sont les principales exigences (par exemple, trafic roulier et transport de conteneurs). Que la zone protégée par brise-lames ouest soit partiellement asséchée ou non, la surface de l'eau sera relativement calme. C'est dire que les transferts navire vers/dans navire du type LASH ou SEABEE avec péniches remontant l'Escaut sont possibles. Si la totalité des 405 ha sont réservés au transbordement à quai des marchandises, on peut envisager une rénovation du mole existant pour l'affecter au trafic général ou à des terminaux pour ferries.

Outre le besoin de terrain pour la rénovation de l'infrastructure actuelle du port, la plus grande partie des 405 ha situés dans l'avant-port ouest sont bien adaptés au trafic roulier ou conteneurs. La seule limitation vient du terrain de réserve disponible.

Si une darse est programmée, la surface totale de terminal par mètre de mur de quai est d'environ 700 m^2 p.m. Avec deux darses, celle du nord étant réservée au trafic spécifique, le rapport tombe à environ 400 m^2 p.m.

Comme on l'a déjà dit, il est intéressant de comparer ces données avec celles d'autres terminaux pour conteneurs existants ou programmés dans la zone Le Havre-Hambourg (fig. 6, page 404).

Conclusions

1. Il serait intéressant que des collègues dans la salle nous disent si les chiffres du Graphique 6 sont ou non le résultat d'un plan détaillé de traitement de la manutention de conteneurs, ou bien s'ils découlent de la procédure de planification portuaire d'ensemble, qui prévoyait de réserver des espaces aux clients du port.

2. La réalisation de la phase d'extension de l'avant-port se poursuit (fig. 5, page 403):

- planification et conception commencées en septembre 1976;
- la construction du port de travail et des installations auxiliaires a commencé à la mi-janvier 1978 et a été commissionné en 1979.
- le vrai "coup d'envoi" de la construction du port a été donné en juin 1979, avec le début des travaux du brise-lames sud-est. Cette péninsule est aujourd'hui pratiquement terminée;
- la construction de l'autre brise-lames LNG commencera bientôt et devrait être réceptionnée à l'automne 1982;
- les fondations du brise-lames ouest ont été commencées en septembre 1979 et doivent être terminées au chaînage de 1050 m en novembre de cette année;
- les fondations et les ouvrages de protection du fond dans l'alignement des autres sections de brise-lames sont en cours depuis septembre 1979. Les sections nord-est et sud-ouest sont terminées.

3. De plus amples informations sur le plan d'extension du port de Zeebruges peuvent être trouvées dans le rapport et dans le dernier numéro du Bulletin de l'AIPCN (Vol. III/1980, no 37).

J F MAQUET (FRANCE)

Je voudrais tout d'abord remercier le rapporteur général qui a réussi à résumer en moins de dix lignes certains rapports qui font 20 pages.

Mon intervention ne concernera donc que le projet de conclusions et mes commentaires seront tirés de l'expérience du port du Havre situé à l'embouchure de la Seine.

Pour un port moderne deux problèmes majeurs se posent:

- le premier dont on a déjà beaucoup parlé est celui de l'espace qui est un bien rare et précieux,
- le second dont en a peu parlé, celui de la main d'oeuvre qui est aussi précieux mais bien souvent abondant en quantité.

Je donnerais un exemple avec le trafic de marchandises générales du Port du Havre.

- En 1975, avec moins de 200.000 TEU, le trafic conteneurs était sensiblement équivalent au trafic conventionnel.
- En 1980, avec plus de 500.000 TEU, le trafic conteneurs est plus de 3 fois le trafic conventionnel.

Les besoins en surface sont multipliés par plus que 2. Les besoins en main d'oeuvre de manutention sont divisés par 2.

Sur le premier point — l'espace — on ne peut que conseiller aux ports qui sont dans des pays où il y a encore de l'espace, d'en réserver de larges quantités pour les ports, mais pour les pays industrialisés et certains (Inde, Indonésie) très peuplés, ce ne sera pas possible.

Sur le deuxième point — la main d'oeuvre — on peut diminuer l'impact de la conteneurisation en faisant faire d'autres tâches par les ouvriers dockers mais cela nécessite de la formation.

Cela me conduit à 2 suggestions pour les conclusions:

1. la recherche et l'analyse en matière de conception de construction des équipements

portuaires doivent se préoccuper du besoin d'installations et de procédés qui permet tront d'économiser non seulement de l'énergie mais aussi de l'espace;

2. la recherche et l'analyse doivent se préoccuper des problèmes de main d'oeuvre qui seront de deux types:
   - diminution de la main d'oeuvre de manutention;
   - formation de la main d'oeuvre pour les installations ou les activités nouvelles.

A T RUSSELL (USA)

Monsieur le Président, permettez-moi de réagir à deux de vos remarques; la première portant sur la planification d'installations portuaires pour les pays en voie de développement et l'autre sur les débats impromptus.

Mes commentaires, en effet, sont impromptus, dans le mesure où je voudrais simplement vous faire part d'une expérience qui j'ai eue récemment en Inde, où j'étais il y a un mois seulement, en tant que consultant pour la planification d'un nouveau port qui doit être implanté à Mhava-Sheva dans le but de remédier à l'engorgement du port de Bombay.

J'ai entrepris cette mission dans la conviction qu'une de mes préoccupations principales devrait être d'allier la technologie moderne et le problème de main d'oeuvre excédentaire que connaît Bombay.

A ma grande surprise, les réunions avec les hauts responsables des transports du pays m'ont appris qu'ils ne prêtaient pas la moindre attention aux techniques intensives en travail. Ils sont persuadés que ce nouveau port leur offre une occasion unique de réaliser l'un des ports les plus modernes au monde. Ceci m'a été exprimé de la manière suivante: "Nous ne voulons pas considérer ceci comme un port indien, mais plutôt comme un port moderne, même s'il se fait qu'il est situé en Inde".

Ceci veut sans doute dire que toutes les généralisations (en l'occurrence: des méthodes de manutension intensives en travail doivent être utilisées dans les pays en voie de développement) ont leurs exceptions.

Un consultant ne peut que conseiller et essayer de convaincre. En définitive, ce sont les aspirations du client qui déterminent le résultat.

N J FERGUSON (AUSTRALIE)

Un des aspects qui mériterait d'être souligné dans nos conclusions est le fait que le transport maritime de matières premières à faible coût, mais souvent en volume important, ne justifie pas, dans de nombreux cas, les solutions portuaires habituelles.

Nul ne nie les avantages des accostages protégés à l'intérieur des ports. Mais dans le cas des grands navires, le coût du dragage ou de la protection offerte par les brise-lames, et parfois des deux, devient extrêmement élevé s'il n'est pas compensé par une grande variété de trafics et un volume d'activité portuaire très important.

Il existe des solutions de remplacement pour les marchandises en vrac: par exemple, les terminaux offshore. Cette solution de compromis implique un arbitrage entre de substantielles économies du point de vue de l'investissement et une perte de disponibilité à l'accostage offshore. Ainsi, des études menées en Australie méridionale (N.S.W.) ont montré que la réception de navires de 200.000 Tpl exigerait, disons un investissement de $150 m offshore, à comparer aux $300 à $410 m que coûteraient le dragage en fond rocheux et l'accès avec brise-lames, la première solution de demandant que 3 à 4 ans pour construire les ouvrages et la deuxième au moins 5 à 6 ans.

De même, dans les pays en voie de développement, l'aspect économique des choses doit faire l'objet de la plus grande attention, comme l'ont fort opportunément rappelé notre Président et notre Rapporteur Général. Dans de nombreux cas, il y a des solutions moins chères recourant à des installations simples lorsque le taux d'activité du port est relativement faible. Ceci n'exclut en rien que le maître-plan soit suffisamment souple pour faire face à toute croissance éventuelle du trafic.

A titre d'illustration, je voudrais mentionner l'idée d'île offshore retenue pour la manutention du sel à partir de la côte atlantique brésilienne. Cette île fut construite vers le milieu des années soixante-dix et est située à quelque 14 km au large, à l'extrémité de la zone d'eau peu profonde du plateau continental. Elle est alimentée par des allèges qui y amènent les marchandises en vrac que transportent ensuite les navires de haute mer.

Au départ, l'intention avait été de draguer un chenal jusque la côte où se trouverait un accostage conventionnel. Non seulement ce dragage aurait coûté beaucoup d'argent, mais le chenal aurait sans doute exigé un entretien sérieux en raison de son instabilité.

La solution alternative d'une île en mer à la limite des eaux profondes s'est avérée moins coûteuse et a entraîné l'avantage social non négligeable de permettre la survie du secteur des allèges. Auparavant, en effet, celles-ci étaient utilisées sur une échelle limitée pour une navette directe de chargement des navires.

Deux réponses à M. Davies

1. M. Davies a demandé des informations sur les hauteurs de lames lors du chargement des navires offshore. A Punta Colorada, et je crois aussi sur la côte de Patagonie, des navires de 30 à 50.000 TPL ont pu être chargés sans problèmes avec des lames de 2 à 2½ m. Il s'agit d'un accostage à orientation variable, qui permet d'orienter le navire vers la mer dominante.

2. Les commentaires de mon intervention relatifs à l'impact prépondérant des lames sur les ouvrages offshore sur pieux s'appliquent à des grands navires avec mouillages de 17 à 21 m. Sur la côte méridionale d'Australie, ceci implique des lames déterminantes d'environ 15 m.

Pour terminer, je voudrais souligner la nécessité de poursuivre le travail (recherche et collaboration) au niveau de l'interface ingénieur/responsable de la manoeuvre pour l'accostage des grands navires vraquiers, tant aux postes de chargement que de déchargement. Très souvent, en effet, un navire peut rester à l'amarrage et continuer le chargement/déchargement en présence de houles très importantes pourvu que l'accostage soit bien conçu: le problème se pose au niveau de l'accostage lui-même.

A L MOSS-MORRIS (AFRIQUE DU SUD)

Certains des orateurs ont souhaité que soit réservé aux pays en voie de développement un traitement différent de celui des pays industrialisés au niveau de la conception des nouvelles installations de manutention des marchandises. En tant que représentant d'un nouveau pays industriel, je dois m'inscrire en faux contre cette approche. Si la situation actuellement moins avancée d'un pays est retenue comme élément déterminant de la conception de nouvelles installations, la conséquence ne peut en être que de maintenir indéfiniment ce pays dans une condition de deuxième ordre. Comme les installations portuaires sont programmées pour une durée de vie minimale de vingt ans, permettre à cette approche de prévaloir parmi les planificateurs signifie que les ouvrages auraient environ vingt-cinq ans de retard au moment où vos clients les commissionneraient. Ceux-ci ne peuvent qu'en concevoir un grand dépit.

Une attitude plus réaliste me semble être celle qui a été adoptée pour le passage à la conteneurisation en Afrique du Sud et à Singapour. Des terminaux pour conteneurs fonctionnaient à la fin des années soixante dans de nombreux ports européens et américains. Leur introduction en Afrique du Sud eut lieu dans le cadre des expansions portuaires qui suivirent dans les années soixante-dix et les quais réservés à cette fonction devinrent opérationnels en 1977 et prirent rapidement le relai des accostages pour vracs pondéreux. A Singapour, des quais pour marchandises générales sans portiques à conteneurs ont été programmés et construits au début des années dix neuf cent soixante-dix.

Néanmoins, le propriétaire avait eu, au cours des travaux, la perspicacité d'insister sur le passage aux portiques à conteneurs et depuis lors, il a construit à un rythme croissant des quais de manutention de conteneurs.

Ne reléguons donc pas les pays en voie de développement dans un statut permanent de deuxième classe en planifiant et en concevant pour eux des installations dépassées en raison des coûts salariaux apparemment bas que connaissent actuellement ces pays.

R LECLERCQ (FRANCE)

Pour répondre à une invitation du Président, je veux faire une courte intervention sur une question très générale, celle de l'opposition entre les ingénieurs et les financiers.

Je suis persuadé que notre Président n'a pas voulu s'opposer au principe des calculs de rentabilité mais à la façon dont ils sont souvent conduits. Les calculs de rentabilité économique sont très difficiles lorsqu'il s'agit d'infrastructure à longue durée de vie. Une première difficulté est d'évaluer les avantages et dépenses dans l'avenir lointain. Une deuxième est de choisir un taux d'actualisation convenable pour ramener les dépenses et les avantages — exprimés en monnaie constante — à la date d'origine. Ce taux doit être en relation directe avec le taux réel d'intérêt constaté sur le marché financier. Il doit être aussi en relation directe avec le taux de développement de la production.

A mon avis, mais ce n'est qu'un point de vue personnel, on ne devrait pas éliminer a priori des investissements dès que leur taux de rentabilité est supérieur à — mettons — 3% à condition que les avantages ne soient pas surestimés.

L'objet de mon intervention était seulement de combattre l'idée que les calculs de rentabilité économique sont sans utilité.

W H LEWIS (USA)

1. La planification et la construction des ports dans les pays en voie de développement doivent tenir compte de la technologie d'exploitation portuaire mise en oeuvre dans les autres ports. Le développement de cette technologie peut être plus lent dans les pays en voie de développement, mais en définitive, ceux-ci doivent suivre ce qui se fait dans les ports des pays industrialisés.

2. La planification des installations portuaires dans les pays en voie de développement doit être basée sur les mêmes principes que ceux qui sont retenus pour des ports de dimensions semblables dans les pays industrialisés.

3. Dans le cas de projets financés par des institutions bancaires internationales, le consultant doit rencontrer les besoins du pays client en même temps que les exigences de l'organisme financier. Il n'est pas nécessaire de convaincre le pays client d'envisager les besoins futurs.

4. Il faut soutenir les tentatives visant à encourager la participation des pays en voie de développement dans les activités de l'AIPCN. Ceci permettra de tenir compte de manière réaliste de leurs problèmes et de leurs opinions. Les représentants de ces pays doivent être traités comme partenaires à part entière au sein de l'industrie portuaire.

5. Il est suggéré d'amender le Point II du projet de conclusions en omettant la dernière phrase.

A G F EDDIE (AUSTRALIE)

M. Eddie traite du problème de la manutention de chargements secs en vrac aux terminaux offshore exposés aux conditions maritimes.

Il accepte les remarques de M. Ferguson indiquant la possibilité de réaliser des économies substantielles en coût de capital par la construction de terminaux au large plutôt que dans l'enceinte de nouveaux ports protégés. La contrepartie en est une moindre disponibilité à l'accostage et le problème est quantifier cette réduction. M. Davies a demandé quelle était la hauteur de lame maximale permettant la poursuite de la manutention des marchandises à un tel accostage situé au large. Le problème, en fait, n'est pas tant la hauteur des lames que le mouvement des navires. Les modélisations mathématiques et physiques dont nous diposons nous permettent d'estimer correctement le mouvement des navires avec six degrés de liberté en fonction des conditions des lames. Néanmoins, nous sommes encore incapables de déterminer clairement la quantité de mouvement du navire qui empêche la poursuite des opérations de transbordement. C'est particulièrement crucial pour le déchargement, qui pose beaucoup plus de problèmes que le chargement aux accostages en mer. C'est là que se situe la véritable lacune dans l'état actuel de nos connaissances relatives aux opérations de manutention de vrac sec aux terminaux situés au large. M. Eddie aimerait qu'il en soit fait mention dans les recommandations.

A un autre égard, M. Eddie fait remarquer que les navires propulsés au charbon viennent d'être remis en service par certains exploitants australiens. Jusqu'ici, ces navires ne s'occupent que de transport de charbon et n'ont donc pas de problème de plein. Cependant, si cette tendance s'étendait aux autres types de trafic, il serait sans doute utile de prévoir, dans la planification de nouveaux terminaux et installations de manutention, la possibilité d'ajouter ultérieurement des installations de charbonnage pour navires à charbon.

A J CARMICHAEL (GB)

Peut-être cela vous intéressera-t-il de connaître la définition que donne la BANQUE MONDIALE à la viabilité financière des ports. La voici: le port établit les barêmes auxquels il fait payer ses services aux navires et aux chargements de telle sorte que ceux-ci engendrent un revenu suffisant pour couvrir tous les coûts d'exploitation et d'entretien ainsi que l'amortissement du capital, tout en assurant une marge de revenu suffisante pour procurer un taux de rendement adéquat sur l'actif immobilisé net en exploitation, celui-ci étant évalué correctement.

Le taux de rendement indiqué doit permettre une marge bénéficiaire suffisante pour fournir le fonds de roulement et assurer le service de la dette et réserver une possibilité de contribution aux dépenses en capital du port. Normalement, ces taux de rendement exigés sont de l'ordre de 6 à 8%.

Il est peu probable que cette situation puisse être atteinte dès le moment où le premier navire entre dans le port: des pertes doivent être attendues dans les mois, voire les années, qui suivent l'ouverture de celui-ci. Mais, avec le temps, la viabilité financière peut être atteinte: le paramètre dominant en vue du développement est d'ordre économique et non financier. En effet, un port peut devoir encourir, à court terme et initialement, une PERTE, pour permettre des AVANTAGES économiques au niveau national. Cette considération doit être précisée clairement aux plus hauts niveaux, dans la mesure où un soutien financier national peut s'avérer nécessaire pour le port à court terme. La réponse adéquate à cette situation est souvent une programmation souple et graduelle du développement du SYSTEME DE TRANSPORT.

Enfin, je voudrais me distancer de ce qu'a dit M. Davies, notre premier orateur, si du moins je l'ai bien compris. Il a en effet recommandé d'essayer de réaliser des économies sur les forages sur les sites, particulièrement les plus coûteux, c.-à-d. les forages au large. A mon avis, l'ingénieur responsable du projet doit spécifier et insister pour que soient respectés le nombre de forages et l'ampleur de l'étude de site indispensable au projet. Accepter que l'on s'en écarte, ce serait s'exposer aux pires catastrophes.

N N B ORDMAN (GB)

Le Président, M. Noel Ordman, prend la parole pour attirer l'attention sur les implications politiques, économiques et de planification de la récente "révolution" intervenue dans le domaine de la manutention de marchandises. Le coût des développements portuaires modernes est si élevé qu'il incombe souvent aux gouvernements et aux municipalités de les financer. C'est pourquoi le développement portuaire est de plus en plus du ressort du secteur public et du domaine de la politique régionale ou nationale.

Les ports modernes exigent de grandes superficies de terrain. Dans certains pays, cela donne lieu à des difficultés croissantes qui incitent à se tourner de plus en plus vers la récupération de terrains sur la mer. Le concept d'îles au large a fait l'objet de très nombreuses études et nous pouvons nous attendre à ce qu'il soit exploité de manière intensive à l'avenir. Les accès routiers et ferroviaires du port demandent eux aussi beaucoup de terrain. Cette "voracité" pour l'utilisation du sol pourrait créer de nombreux problèmes d'aménagement du territoire, avec toutes les implications que cela comporte du point de vue politique. Un travail législatif peut s'avérer nécessaire pour les résoudre: c'est pourquoi il est important, pour que cela se fasse de manière satisfaisante, de prévoir suffisamment tôt ces problèmes.

L'évaluation économique et financière des projets portuaires soulève la question du taux d'actualisation approprié à utiliser dans le calcul du "cash flow actualisé". L'application de l'analyse par "coûts/bénéfices" pose également des problèmes dans la mesure où les ports sont fréquemment des sources de développement économique régional ou national et où celui-ci peut en fait être leur principale raison d'être. Les avantages vont à une vaste région bien au-delà du port et beaucoup de ces avantages sont de nature sociale et donc difficilement quantifiables. Ceci ne veut bien entendu pas dire que les responsables de la gestion des ports ne doivent pas s'en tenir à une stricte orthodoxie financière. Néanmoins, on peut se demander si'il est possible de considérer la plupart des ports comme des entreprises "commerciales" conventionnelles.

D L POPE (GB)

Contexte. En dépit de la révolution des conteneurs et des navires rouliers, le trafic de marchandises diverses en charges rompues se poursuit, particulièrement par l'intermédiaire de petits ports ou de ports situés dans des petits pays où le volume insuffisant du trafic ne justifie pas la conteneurisation. En outre, la nature de ces chargements résiduels de vrac pondéreux se modifie du point de vue:

- de l'accroissement rapide des charges unitaires
- de la prépondérance de types particuliers de chargements qui ne se prêtent pas à la conteneurisation.

Question. Les accostages pour marchandises diverses doivent-ils être équipés de grues de quai, et dans ce cas, quelle doit être leur capacité? De nombreux ports disposant d'un grand nombre de grues de quai ne les utilisent que rarement, alors que ces grues et leurs rails de roulement constituent un obstacle à la libre circulation sur le quai. D'autres ports, dépourvus de grues de quai, trouvent que les grues mobiles ne sont pas adéquates pour le déchargement des charges unitaires lourdes contenues dans les cales du navire.

Suggestion. L'AIPCN, où sont représentés les armateurs, les exploitants des ports et les planificateurs de ceux-ci, devrait étudier les implications économiques comparées de la mise à disposition d'un équipement de levage lourd pour charges générales unitarisées sur le navire ou à quai.

D JONES (GB)

Je ne pensais pas intervenir dans cette discussion, mais je réagis à l'invitation du Président demandant des commentaires impromptus, particulièrement en liaison avec les contributions des orateurs précédents. C'est que je souhaite venir à la rescousse des pilotes à la suite des paroles de M. John Balfour.

M. Balfour, en effet s'est plaint des services que rendent les pilotes à la navigation et a suggéré que l'AIPCN devrait inciter à une plus grande attention pour leur travail et leurs organisations.

Si je suis d'accord pour que l'AIPCN se penche sur ces problèmes, je crois que les autorités portuaires doivent collaborer étroitement avec les pilotes pour en obtenir les meilleurs services.

A titre d'illustration, je voudrais rappeler comment on a pu introduire et administrer un excellent service de pilotage à Port Talbot dans l'estuaire de la Severn, Galles du Sud.

Ce port du British Transport Docks Board, conçu pour recevoir des minéraliers de 100.000 tpl, a remplacé une darse ne pouvant recevoir que des navires de 10.000 tonnes au maximum.

Avant l'ouverture du port en 1970, un navire de 50.000 tonnes a été affrété pendant une brève période pour permettre aux pilotes, qui n'avaient aucune expérience des navires dépassant 10.000 tonnes, de se familiariser avec la manoeuvre d'assistance des navires à l'entrée et à la sortie du port ainsi qu'à l'arrivée et au départ à et de l'accostage. Au moment où le port a été ouvert au trafic commercial, les pilotes étaient à même d'assister des navires de 100.000 tonnes sans problèmes techniques.

Après quelques années d'exploitation sans aucun incident, on étudia la possibilité de recevoir des navires de 200.000 tonnes partiellement déchargés pour les amener à un tirant d'eau de 47 pieds. Avant de prendre la décision ou non d'accepter ces navires, dont le déplacement serait de 150.000 tonnes, il fut décidé de suivre l'accostage des navires dans le port pendant une période d'environ un an. On installa les instruments nécessaires pour mesurer les vitesses d'approche des navires accostants, les enregistrer et montrer ces informations à mesure qu'elles étaient enregistrées. Ceci permit aux pilotes d'améliorer leurs techniques d'accostage dans une mesure qui n'aurait pu être atteinte en-dehors de cette collaboration.

Je suggère donc que, si l'AIPCN décide d'orienter une partie de ses travaux sur l'efficacité des services de pilotage, elle s'informe auprès des pilotes quant aux types d'équipement qu'ils souhaitent voir installer par les autorités portuaires en vue de permettre l'amélioration la plus grande possible de leurs services.

F VASCO COSTA (PORTUGAL)

L'orateur fait remarquer que l'utilisation d'instruments sophistiqués en des endroits éloignés pose de graves problèmes d'entretien. Ceci est surtout vrai lorsque les appareils proviennent de différents fabricants établis dans des pays eux aussi différents et que les pièces de rechange ainsi que les techniciens compétents ne sont pas disponibles à brève échéance.

H THOMAS (FRANCE)

Mon propos sera bref, d'autant qu'il s'inscrit dans la suite logique de l'intervention de M. VASCO COSTA. Le développement des nouveaux modes de conditionnement des marchandises conduit à concevoir des équipements d'outillage de plus en plus sophistiqués faisant un large appel aux automatismes, à l'électronique. De même, l'exigence de flexibilité d'utilisation de ces engins tend également à rendre leur conception plus complexe.

Or, les équipements d'outillage portuaires sont en règle générale soumis à des conditions de service sévères (météorologie, hygrométrie, perturbations électriques dans l'atmosphère, poussières) qui rendent vulnérables ces automatismes, sauf à pratiquer une maintenance extrêmement rigoureuse. D'autre part, la fiabilité technique de ces équipements est une exigence fondamentale de l'usager du port, notamment l'armateur très sensible à la durée de son escale, et aux coûts d'immobilisation de son navire.

Ma proposition de recommandation concerne donc la nécessité dans les rapports autorités portuaires-concepteurs d'engins d'avoir en permanence à l'esprit cette exigence de fiabilité de l'engin en exploitation dans des conditions sévères et également la nécessité impérieuse d'une politique de formation du personnel — exploitation et maintenance — adaptée à la complexité croissante des équipements.

H K DALLY (GB)

1. Je pense que la fonction de planification du port doit être séparée des problèmes d'équipement dans la discussion des besoins des pays en voie de développement. Selon moi, les ports dans les pays en voie de développement doivent être conçus selon des critères modernes, tandis que l'équipement ne doit pas nécessairement toujours incorporer la technologie la plus récente. Je suis d'accord, à cet égard, avec ce qu'ont dit Messieurs Maquet et Thomas, de la délégation française. Les commandes électroniques et les équipements automatiés peuvent poser des problèmes d'entretien aux ports des pays industrialisés, tels que le Grande-Bretagne. La raison en est que le personnel d'entretien n'a généralement que la qualification de mécanicien garagiste. En outre, les équipements électroniques n'améliorent pas toujours l'efficience d'exploitation. Un port britannique s'était doté de grues commandées électroniquement qui, à cause des problèmes d'entretien qu'elles posaient, n'étaient pas suffisamment opérationnelles. Finalement, cet équipement électronique fut remplacé par des commandes électriques conventionnelles, ce qui permit d'accroître l'efficacité opérationnelle et de réduire les temps d'indisponibilité.

2. L'efficacité de la manutention est déterminée par les relations sociales plutôt que par la technologie avancée. Le Conseil National des Ports britanniques a récemment réalisé une enquête sur l'efficacité de la manutention des conteneurs. Il en ressort que le taux de manutention varie de moins de 10 à 32 conteneurs par heure brute. Ce résultat vaut pour des terminaux utilisant des équipements similaires. Il apparaît que la motivation de la main-d'oeuvre et les relations humaines sont plus importantes que le fait de disposer ou non de la dernière technologie.

3. On a beaucoup insisté sur les besoins en terrain plus élevés des ports modernes par rapport à leurs prédécesseurs. La raison en est les débits plus élevés. En réalité, les méthodes modernes de manutention des marchandises font une utilisation meilleure, parce que plus intensive, du terrain disponible. Tandis qu'un accostage conventionnel pour marchandises générales traite environ 15.000 tonnes par acre (0,4 hectare) de terrain en une année, un poste pour conteneurs en eau profonde en manutentionne 40 à 50.000 par acre et par an. Les accostages en eau peu profonde où les arrivées des petits navires sont programmées régulièrement peuvent quant à eux traiter jusque 100.000 tonnes par acre et par an.

P A COX (GB)

Je voudrais revenir à un aspect qui a été mentionné par le Président au début de cette session, mais qui n'a été repris par personne depuis. Il s'agit de l'acquisition ou de la réservation de terrains pour recevoir les installations portuaires et leurs voies terrestres d'accès. Je vais donner trois exemples qui en illustrent la nécessité.

Il y a de nombreuses années, l'Autorité du Port de Londres avait réservé du terrain à Tilbury pour y permettre l'extension des bassins de réception des navires, alors qu'à l'époque la nécessité ne s'en faisait nullement sentir. Aujourd'hui, ce terrain est utilisé très largement pour les porte-conteneurs à grand tirant d'eau et les autres navires qui ne pourraient être reçus dans les bassins proches du centre de la ville. Ces derniers sont désormais de moins en moins utilisés, voire mis hors service.

Au cours des dernières années, il a été proposé de construire un port/aéroport combine à Maplin, du côté nord de l'estuaire extérieur de la Tamise. Le terrain nécessaire à ces installations ne posait pas de problème, puisqu'il a été gagné sur l'eau. Mais les routes d'accès vers Londres auraient dû traverser une zone urbaine très développée. Ces voies d'accès avaient été repérées dans les plans préliminaires, mais je suis persuadé que de sérieux problèmes se seraient posés du côté de la protection de l'environnement si le projet avait été poursuivi. Ces problèmes auraient bien entendu constitué une menace pour la viabilité du port et de l'aéroport.

Il est sans doute juste de dire que le besoin de grands développements en eau profonde du type de ceux proposés pour Maplin n'auraient pas pu être prévus, disons, il y a vingt-cinq ans. Pourtant, l'évolution future tant des tirants d'eau que des équipements de manutention ne sera sans doute plus aussi rapide qu'elle a été au cours de la dernière génération, de sorte qu'il devrait être possible dorénavant d'éviter le genre de problèmes que je viens d'illustrer avec le cas de Maplin. Ceci exigera cependant des responsables de la planification portuaire qu'ils aient une approche extrêmement ouverte des besoins futurs potentiels.

Le Port de Calcutta a lui aussi fait preuve de perspicacité dans sa politique de réservation de terrain. En effet, il y a de nombreuses années, il a réservé du terrain en vue du développement du port à Haldia, sur le Fleuve Hooghly en aval de Calcutta. Ce terrain est à présent utilisé pour les nouvelles installations portuaires de Haldia. Sans la réservation du terrain, ce développement ne pourrait pas s'effectuer dans de bonnes conditions.

Lors de la planification de nouvelles installations portuaires, il est également nécessaire de s'assurer que les organisations commerciales associées à l'exploitation du port sont prêtes à venir s'établir sur le site de ce port. Ceci peut requérir l'intervention des pouvoirs publics. Il y a des exemples dans le monde d'installations portuaires qui ne sont pas utilisées comme elles le devraient parce que les organisations commerciales n'ont pas accepté de déplacer leurs établissements vers le nouveau port.

D J VANDENBOSSCHE (BELGIQUE)

M. Kérisel, de l'Autorité du Port de Rouen, a insisté sur le fait que même les ports "peu profonds" peuvent de nos jours se défendre de manière relativement satisfaisante face à la concurrence.

En tant que consultants, nous nous occupons non seulement de l'extension du port de Zeebruges, mais aussi de la rénovation et de l'extension du port de Gand, par exemple.

Le tirant d'eau limite de ce port est de 60.000 tpm, ou mieux, une profondeur d'eau d'environ 13,5 m. Le port de Gand est situé à quelque 80 km à l'intérieur des terres et est relié à la côte par l'estuaire de l'Escaut occidental et par le canal maritime Gand-Terneuzen. Grâce à ses bonnes liaisons par eau, par terre et par chemin de fer avec son hinterland naturel, le port de Gand a pu jusqu'à présent résister plutôt bien à la ruée vers l'eau profonde.

Je propose ces remarques comme introduction à un amendement que je voudrais apporter au projet de conclusions

Sous le point (i), je voudrais ajouter: ... "et compatibilité avec la chaîne de transport des marchandises dans son ensemble". Je pense à cet égard aux charges sèches en vrac telles que le charbon et les minerais.

Je pense que ces deux exemples de ports maritimes installés à l'intérieur des terres suffisent à montrer que des éléments autres que les navires et les installations portuaires jouent un rôle important dans le concept d'ensemble.

CONCLUSIONS

1. Il est important que la conception et la construction des ports soient précédées par des études et des analyses adéquates.

2. Ces préliminaires devraient concerner entre autres:

   (i) la nécessaire compatibilité à l'intérieur du système de transport dans son ensemble et entre différents ports et différents pays.

   (ii) le fait que, bien qu'il soit désirable que les projets d'installations portuaires soient conçus dans les pays en voie de développement comme dans le reste du monde, suivant les normes modernes, l'entretien et l'utilisation convenable d'outillages et d'installations perfectionnées posent souvent de réels problèmes.

   (iii) le concept d'une "technologie appropriée".

   (iv) la recherche d'économies d'énergie.

   (v) la prise en compte de l'environnement.

   (vi) la politique d'occupation des sols, tenant compte des surfaces nécessaires non seulement pour les installations portuaires mais aussi pour les accès terrestres, dans l'immédiat et à long terme.

   (vii) les implications économiques et sociales au plan national et régional.

3. Il faut s'attendre à ce que la conception et l'exploitation des navires continuent à imposer les conditions auxquelles devront s'adapter ceux qui aménagent les ports.

   Cependant, il est nécessaire de développer les contacts et la coopération entre ceux qui sont responsables de la construction, de la navigation et de l'exploitation des navires d'une part, ceux qui ont en charge la conception et l'exploitation des ports d'autre part.

PORTS ET ACCES MARITIMES

SECTION II — SUJET 4

Conception et construction d'installations portuaires et aménagement des terre-pleins destinés à recevoir des charges lourdes sur des terrains inconsistants en utilisant des techniques nouvelles

Jeudi 14 mai 1981

Président:	*N N B ORDMAN (GB)* *Noel Ordman and Associates Ltd*
Vice Président:	*T KANHO (Japon)* *Technical Director, Bureau of Ports and Harbours, Tokyo*
Rapporteur Général:	*G P MARTIN (GB)* *T F Burns and Partners, Hove*
Secrétaire:	*P LACEY (GB)* *Ove Arup and Partners Ltd, London*
Secrétaire Adjoint:	*Mlle M-M DANEELS (Belgique)* *Secrétaire AIPCN Secrétariat Générale, Bruxelles*

Orateurs

A J JIMENEZ-SALAS (Espagne), D A BARENDSEN (Pays-Bas), E BARATONO (Italie), G MATTEOTTI (Italie), M LOEWY (GB), N N B ORDMAN (GB), P COUPRIE (France), F IRWIN-CHILDS (GB), J de NEKKER (Pays-Bas), P G R BARLOW (GB), J L DAWSON (GB), A L MOSS-MORRIS (Australie), H D HOEFT (RFA), J F MAQUET (France), E SERRANO (Espagne), E LACKNER (RFA)

M. MARTIN (Rapporteur Général)

INTRODUCTION

Le problème des ouvrages en mauvais sol a été soulevé en tant que tel dès le XXème Congrès, en 1961 dans le cadre du Sujet 1 de la Section II (rubrique e) mais, à en juger par le rapport général, les auteurs préféraient en général éviter cet épineux sujet. Le rapporteur général attira à l'époque l'attention sur "la nécessité d'une information plus complète sur le fond marin, qui fasse appel aux principes les plus récents de la mécanique des sols et les applique aux régions côtières". Cette conclusion fut adoptée par le Congrès.

Dès le XXIème Congrès, le problème des terrains mauvais méritait de faire l'objet d'un thème à part entière (Section II 6, Ouvrages portuaires et maritimes construits en terrain mauvais, avec référence particulière à la nécessité de profondeurs accrues). Douze pays présentèrent d'intéressants rapports. Le rapporteur général souligna alors que "la construction d'ouvrages maritimes en terrain mauvais pose un problème très complexe "et qu "il serait dangereux de formuler des conclusions précises en ce domaine". Effectivement, la seule conclusion que le Congrès se sentit en mesure d'adopter fut que "les rapports et la discussion contribuent très utilement à enrichir les références en ce domaine".

Au cours des quinze années qui ont suivi, le sujet en est resté là, jamais explicitement discuté au cours des congrès, s'enrichissant tranquillement pour pouvoir être abordé à ce XXVème Congrès de 1981.

La nature-même des régions littorales explique que les ports érigés en terrain solide ont toujours été l'exception plutôt que la règle. Cependant, le problème est devenu plus aigu encore à mesure que les terrains pas trop mauvais étaient utilisés parallèlement à l'expansion des échanges mondiaux, de sorte que les nouveaux ports et particulièrement les extensions portuaires ont dû se réaliser en terrain de plus en plus mauvais.

Fort heureusement, la technologie a fait des progrès parallèles à cette évolution et des domaines tels que la mécanique des sols (qui a désormais acquis le statut de "géotechnique"), l'instrumentation, l'informatique et la mécanique appliquée ont pu de plus en plus efficacement apporter leur contribution à la bataille pour construire des ports sur des sols dont on aurait chaque fois pensé quelque temps avant qu'ils ne pouvaient être utilisés à cette fin.

Les rapports soumis au présent Congrès reflètent bien les grands progrès réalisés par les techniques d'étude de sites en région côtière. Plusieurs auteurs décrivent ainsi les appareils complexes et les traitements informatiques utilisés pour surveiller le comportement des ouvrages existants. On apprend ainsi notamment que la technique d'analyse par les éléments finis appliquée tant aux ouvrages qu'à ses fondations est de plus en plus répandue. D'autres rapports font état de l'application des techniques informatiques à l'analyse des cercles de glissement et au calcul de la poussée des terres. De même, les analyses mathématiques les plus raffinées sont appliquées aux fondations et aux revêtements des zones de terre-pleins dans les ports.

De nouvelles techniques de construction et d'amélioration des sols sont présentées, qui vont des unités de murs d'accostage préfabriquées de 360 tonnes chacune (Australie) aux fondations flottantes et semi-flottantes (R.U.) et à la stabilisation au ciment des sols en eau profonde (Japon) ainsi qu'au serrage des sols par activité sismique induite (France).

THEMES DE DISCUSSION EN SEANCE

Votre Rapporteur Général suggère que cet ensemble de rapports très intéressants et de très large portée couvre de nombreux sujets susceptibles de discussions. Il serait donc utile que leurs auteurs commentent les points suivants en guise d'introduction aux discussions générales.

Australie. une description de la méthode de manutention et de placement des éléments de 360 tonnes serait des plus instructives en raison de l'importante économie de temps qu'elle permet apparemment. Il serait également intéressant d'apprendre si les rails de grue non solidarisés ont donné pleine satisfaction.

France. Les raisons pour lesquelles la technique de "l'étincelle" a été retenue pour les essais et finalement rejetée mériteraient d'être explicitées dans le cadre de la discussion générale de l'utilisation des méthodes sismiques pour le compactage des sols.

République Démocratique d'Allemagne. Une explicitation de l'affirmation selon laquelle des essais semblables pourraient être appliqués à des systèmes autres que les ducs d'albe serait hautement appréciée.

République Fédérale d'Allemagne. Toute information qui pourrait être donnée sur les coûts comparatifs des quais décrits dans le rapport serait de nature à enrichir encore celui-ci.

Italie. L'affirmation que "au cours de la phase de conception aucun investissement n'est plus rentable qu'une étude géotechnique faisant appel à la technologie avancée" appelle de toute évidence quelques précisions.

Japon. Les accidents regrettables affectant les appareils de surveillance de l'ensemble sol/ouvrage semble survenir de manière tellement général qu'une discussion de leurs causes et de leurs modes de prévention serait certainement intéressante, de même d'ailleurs que la présentation d'autres expériences réalisées avec la "méthode de mélange en profondeur".

Pays-Bas. Des détails supplémentaires sur la barge utilisée sur l'énorme chantier de la barrière-tempête de l'Escaut oriental pour l'application d'une variante de la méthode de vibro-compaction, sur la manière dont elle a fonctionné et sur ses aspects économiques pourraient utilement susciter une discussion générale de ses techniques.

Pologne. L'explicitation de la méthode d'extraction de la pénésonde constituerait un complément d'information qui pourrait donner lieu à une discussion d'autres nouvelles méthodes d'investigation de chantier.

Espagne. La technique de "compactage cyclique" présente un grand intérêt et constitue un thème de discussion des plus fructueux.

Royaume-Uni. Un examen plus approfondi de la conception et de l'utilisation des monolithes flottants et semi-flottants avec écran d'étanchéité serait certainement générateur de plus amples discussions.

U.S.A. L'étude des modeles à échelle réelle en liaison avec les problèmes de terrain mauvais et de leurs modes de financement offre un intérêt tout particulier.

U.R.S.S. Les essais sur grands modèles qui ont donné des résultats différents des prévisions théoriques habituelles sur les poussées de terre dues aux charges locales appellent sans conteste, par leur intérêt intrinsique, de plus amples discussions.

Malgré la diversité des sujets abordés par les rapports soumis dans le cadre de ce sujet, je crois comprendre qu'il m'incombe de tenter d'en dégager une conclusion et peut être d'y identifier une tendance moderne dans le sens d'une solution au problème de la construction d'ouvrages de génie civil en terrains inconsistants.

Il semble, Monsieur le Président, que se fasse jour une pénurie de sites appropriés pour recevoir des installations portuaires. C'est en tout cas ce qui ressort de nombreux rapports. Il serait plus correct de dire que partout où de nouveaux ouvrages sont programmés, on trouve des sols meubles. Le problème se complique bien évidemment du fait des profondeurs d'eau accrues nécessaires auprès des quais et des charges supérieures que doivent recevoir ceux-ci en raison, particulièrement, de l'accroissement du trafic de conteneurs.

Penchons-nous donc un instant sur les options qui s'offrent aux ingénieurs chargés de la conception d'un ouvrage sur terrain inconsistant.

Premièrement, il conviendrait de rechercher la possibilité de transférer la charge à une strate inférieure de sol capable de supporter cette charge. Je veux parler, bien entendu, du recours à une forme ou l'autre de fondation sur pieux, encore que la taille et le coût de ceux-ci s'accroissent avec la profondeur nécessaire.

Deuxièmement, l'ingénieur peut tenter de réduire autant que possible, grâce à des matériaux et techniques modernes, le poids de son ouvrage, de manière à limiter au maximum la charge posant sur le sol meuble. On pense notamment au semi-flottage et

Troisièmement, l'ingénieur peut s'efforcer de modifier artificiellement les propriétés du sol meuble en vue d'accroître ses qualités de portance.

A la deuxième lecture, il m'est apparu clairement que la tendance qui ressort des rapports va dans le sens de la troisième option, à savoir la modification des conditions de sol plutôt que la conception de l'ouvrage en fonction de ces conditions. Je suis conscient que, disant cela, je simplifie outrancièrement les choses, mais est-ce évitable lorsque l'on tente de synthétiser une gamme d'idées aussi vaste?

Tournons-nous donc vers certaines des méthodes utilisées pour modifier les conditions de sol disponibles, et qui sont décrites dans les rapports.

Pour simplifier, je les ai réparties en quatre groupes:

1. méthodes de remplacement
2. méthodes de stabilisation
3. méthodes de consolidation ou de compactage
4. méthodes de renforcement.

Bien qu'il soit parfois difficile de s'en tenir à ces quatre catégories, je vais le tenter.

1. La méthode la plus immédiate consiste à modifier les propriétés du sol meuble en l'enlevant tout simplement et en lui substituant un bon matériau granulaire tel que

le sable. Cette méthode a été appliquée en:

Australie — en combinaison avec de grands murs en porte-à-faux.

République Fédérale d'Allemagne — en combinaison avec d'énormes murs sur palplanches.

Italie — en combinaison avec la construction d'un brise-lames.

Etats-Unis — en tant qu'une de plusieurs propositions pour le quai décrit.

2. La deuxième catégorie, impliquant la stabilisation des sols existants, est mentionnée dans les rapports de:

la France — sable stabilisé au moyen d'extra-fines en liaison avec le fondement d'une plateforme;

le Japon — "méthode de mélange en profondeur" — proposition extrêmement intéressante pour une série d'utilisations. Pourrait constituer un apport majeur si cela était développé.

3. Dans le troisième groupe, utilisant la consolidation ou le compactage, on trouve que:

- la France mentionne plusieurs techniques sophistiquées de compactage, parmi lesquelles la méthode dynamique de Ménard, qui fait appel à la chute d'une lourde masse, aux puissantes étincelles provoquées en profondeur, au freinage du sol au moyen de drains de sable, aux explosifs et aux opérations séismiques;
- l'Italie décrit le pré-chargement au moyen de caissons;
- les Pays-Bas mentionnent les drains de sable, le repérage de puits en un nouveau véhicule, l'"Amphirol", utilisé pour consolider les matériaux de dragage;
- l'Espagne décrit la méthode de préchargement cyclique, ou "méthode des dunes".

4. La catégorie du renforcement des sols est abordée comme suit:

- le Japon mentionne les pieux de sable vibré
- l'Espagne rappelle l'utilisation des pieux passifs sous les cales sèches
- les Etats-Unis envisagent les colonnes de pierre dans certaines conceptions de quais.

J'ai ainsi déjà cité huit pays qui ont décrit des méthodes visant, selon moi, à modifier la nature ou les propriétés du sol plutôt qu'à concevoir les ouvrages en fonction spécifique des sols meubles. Je serais heureux de savoir si vous partagez mon avis, selon lequel ceci reflète une tendance vers l'octroi à cette technique d'une place privilégiée.

Par leur nature, ces procédés impliquent une connaissance approfondie des propriétés des sols. C'est pourquoi je suggère que, si nous en formulons, nos recommandations portent sur cet aspect du problème. Nous en avons brièvement parlé dans nos débats d'hier (rapport 3) et j'ai été très heureux d'entendre M. Carmichael nous dire que la Banque Mondiale reconnaît l'utilité de l'étude du site.

L'importance de celle-ci a été mentionnée par l'Italie dans son rapport. Celui-ci relevait en outre une série d'améliorations apportées aux techniques d'échantillonnage telles que les essais "en profondeur". D'ailleurs, le rapport polonais était totalement consacré à la description d'un nouveau matériel conçu à cette fin.

Une connaissance approfondie du sol est essentielle pour toute conception d'ouvrage maritime. Je dirai même que nulle étude précise de sol n'est superflue. (Bien que j'aie personnellement constaté que des résultats incorrects sont plus dangereux que l'absence de toute donnée).

J'espère ne pas avoir donné l'impression que les rapports s'intéressent exclusivement à l'enlèvement ou la modification des sols, ou que cette technique est la seule qui soit utilisable dans les conditions mentionnées.

Le rapport britannique présente une plateforme de quai "gaufrée" réduisant clairement le poids par rapport aux plateformes conventionnelles et cite le rideau d'injection comme mode de construction d'un ouvrage semi-flottant.

Le rapport des Etats-Unis décrit plusieurs conceptions possibles envisagées pour trouver la solution la plus économique applicable dans le cas d'un quai sur sol meuble.

Le rapport soviétique s'intéresse sans doute davantage à l'aspect "charges lourdes" du problème qu'à la relation de celui-ci avec les sols meubles.

Quant au rapport de la République Fédérale d'Allemagne, ce sont surtout les problèmes conventionnels des constructions sur pieux qui en font l'objet.

En raison de tout ceci, je suggère que nous disions que, pour les ouvrages en sol meuble, toutes les méthodes de conception doivent être envisagées, qu'elles soient confirmées ou nouvelles, et que ceci n'est possible qu'en passant par de scrupuleuses études de site. Je recommande que les conclusions présentées à la fin de mon rapport soient adoptées par le Congrès.

LES DEBATS

J A JIMENEZ-SALAS (ESPAGNE)

On dépense beaucoup d'argent pour compacter des dépôts de sable meuble résultant de la sédimentation naturelle ou du remblayage hydraulique. Souvent, le seul objectif est d'éviter la liquéfaction en cas de tremblement de terre.

Le même résultat peut être, obtenu pour un coût sensiblement réduit, au moyen d'une surconsolidation (Ishihara et al. — Soils and Foundations 19:4:59-68, 1979). Comme il est indiqué dans le rapport espagnol, l'une des manières pratiques de réaliser cette surconsolidation consiste à pousser (au bulldozer) une "dune mobile" au travers de la zone concernée.

Une procédure quantitative pour estimer l'effet de cette opération est présentée. Elle est basée sur un modèle constitutif endochronique du sol (Cuellar, V. et al. — Jour. Geot. Eng. Div. ASCE 103:399-416, 1977). Pour un sable donné, l'effet d'un seul passage d'une dune de 14 m peut s'avérer quatre fois supérieur à l'impact d'un tremblement de terre de 6,5 m.

Le passage de la dune a en outre des effets bénéfiques sur les couches cohésives. Ces effets sont plus grands que ne permet de l'attendre le temps limité d'application de la charge. Les forces de cisaillement alternatives induites par la dune, qui provoquent des pressions interstitielles résiduelles et un effet retardé d'extrusion, de consolidation et/ou de diapirisme des couches cohésives (origine des tassements différentiels futurs), peuvent être aisément évitées. Ceci n'est pas vrai pour les méthodes usuellement employées de compactage intensif.

D A BARENDSEN (PAYS-BAS)

La plupart des auteurs se sont penchés sur les problèmes d'amélioration du sol. Peu ont parlé du remplacement du sol.

Dans le port d'Amsterdam, le long des côtés d'un nouveau dock portuaire qui devait être dragué, une argile très meuble allant jusqu'à 15 m de profondeur a été enlevée et remplacée par du bon sable. L'objectif était d'accroître la stabilité des talus latéraux en raison des surcharges importantes que devait recevoir le site voisin.

L'A.I.P.C.N. doit être reconnaissante envers la Commission des Ouvrages Maritimes de la Société Allemande du Génie portuaire d'avoir porté à la connaissance de ce Congrès, en primeur, les recommandations qu'elle a élaborées en matière de conception et d'exécution du remplacement du sol.

Un désavantage fondamental de l'enlèvement de sol est que les capacités en port du sol original, aussi limitées soient-elles, ne sont pas utilisées du tout.

Toutes les autres possibilités doivent être envisagées avec soin; le choix final se pose en termes économiques, concept qui dépasse le coût initial. Dans de nombreux cas, le facteur temps joue un rôle déterminant.

Sur plus de la moitié de la longueur du bassin d'Amsterdam, le sous-sol consistait en un sable fin peu cohérent. Il y avait danger de liquéfaction. Au lieu d'être enlevé, ce sable a été amélioré par explosions dans le sous-sol. Des charges étaient placées dans des trous forés tous les 15 m. Les explosions ont entraîné un accroissement suffisant de la densité du sable. Un tassement immédiat de 30 à 50 centimètres s'est produit. Le coût de cette méthode d'amélioration du sol n'a atteint dans ce cas que la moitié du coût estimé des autres méthodes d'amélioration du sous-sol envisagées.

Quelques illustrations sont présentées à la page 603 du rapport de la R.F.A. sur la construction du mur de quai. Elles montrent en particulier les grandes dimensions de cet ouvrage construit après enlèvement du sol.

E BARATONO (ITALIE)

A la page 620 du rapport italien vous avez pu noter deux graphiques dont l'un représente les tassements en fonction du temps et l'autre représente l'évolution de la pression interstitielle en fonction également du temps.

Les relevés des instruments dans le rapport correspondent à la date d'avril 1980.

Dans le graphique des tassements, mis à jour au mois de février 1981, après le chargement complet du talus en roches de la 2e phase, nous avons enregistré en 8 mois un tassement moyen de 31 cm.

Dans le graphique des pressions interstitielles l'évolution typique de ces pressions est représentée par l'évolution des données des tubes pièzométriques pneumatiques nos 1 et 8.

Ayant complété la charge initiale, le premier piézomètre montre une surpression qui s'épuise avec le temps.

Le tube piézométrique no 8, par contre, montre des surpressions interstitielles régulières concomitantes avec le chargement.

Certaines évolutions irrégulières des surpressions sont influencées par des facteurs extérieurs tel que, par exemple, le développement de gaz dans la vase à cause de la décomposition des éléments organiques.

Les inclinomètres ont démontré des déplacements, à l'extrême limite de la berme de la Ière phase, d'environ 10 cemtimètres et, après la 2e phase, de 2 centimètres seulement. Cela prouve que la charge a consolidé les terrains sans provoquer le cisaillement du sol.

Pour répondre au commentaire de M. le Rapporteur Général (page XXXii) que je lis textuellement: "l'affirmation que, au cours de la phase de conception, aucun investissement n'est plus rentable qu'une étude géotechnique faisant appel à la technologie avancée, appelle de toute évidence quelques précisions". — Je puis affirmer que la stabilité de l'ensemble d'un ouvrage et une distribution acceptable des tassements, nécessitent la connaissance de beaucoup de données géotechniques.

La solution des problèmes de fondation s'effectue plus facilement par des recherches sophistiquées ce qui donne lieu à une économie dans le coût de construction.

Dans le cas du port industriel de Cagliari — par exemple — une recherche géotechnique plus approfondie a indiqué des valeurs de résistance des couches d'argile supérieures aux données résultant d'explorations précédentes et les travaux ont pu être abrégés de 1/3.

Ce temps réduit s'est traduit par une économie considérable pour l'Administration, due soit à un coût inférieur des constructions, soit — ce qui est très important — à un effet moins conséquent de l'escalade des prix.

Le coût d'investissement des recherches susdites, évaluables à environ 1% du coût de la construction, a produit un bénéfice, dû au temps inférieur de la construction, d'environ 6% du coût total de la jetée.

Pour la jetée Est du port commercial de Cagliari le projet prévoyait l'exécution de l'ouvrage en 3 étapes avec des arrêtes pour la consolidation du sol de 24 mois entre la Ière et la 2e phase et de 8 mois entre la 2e et la 3e phase.

Pendant l'arrêt entre la Ière et la 2e phase de la Ière tranche des travaux (et aussi pour la 2e tranche qui a suivi la première après environ une année), les données des instruments de contrôle ont très clairement mis en évidence, à travers l'évolution des tassements et des pressions interstitielles, que les phénomènes d'affaissement s'épuisaient avant les délais prévus (env. 50%).

De cette façon, on a pu recommencer les travaux 12 mois plus tôt que les prévisions du projet.

Ainsi, dans ce cas, l'investissement dans de sérieuses recherches géotechniques, dont le coût s'est élevé à environ 1,5% de celui des travaux, a eu comme résultat de réaliser une économie de 8% sur le montant du coût de l'ouvrage, essentiellement dûe au fait d'avoir pu réduire l'inflation.

Evidemment la recherche géotechnique est aussi très utile pour la sécurité de l'ouvrage et pour le contrôle de son exécution.

G MATTEOTTI (ITALIE)

La construction du Port de Sibari (Italie) a commencé en 1964, mais il y a dix ans, le brise-lames à talus nord, en cours de construction, s'est subitement enfoncé dans le sol de fondation.

Ce sol consiste essentiellement en une très épaisse couche d'argile meuble située entre 30 et 75 m en-dessous du niveau moyen de la mer et recouvrant un lit épais de sable et de gravier. Ce lit de gravier sablonneux est le siège d'une très importante pression artésienne due à la liaison continue entre l'eau et les écoulements parcourant les Apennins méridionaux voisins.

Au niveau – 75, des manomètres ont enregistré une chute d'eau de 115 mètres, ce qui correspond à une pression artésienne de 115-75, soit 40 mètres d'eau. Cette pression élevée entraîne d'une part, une percolation verticale à travers l'argile, la pression artésienne passant de 40 m au niveau – 75 à 0 au niveau – 30; d'autre part, une tenue très mauvaise de la cohésion non drainée de l'argile meuble.

De toute évidence, la conception originale n'avait pas tenu compte de ces données et ce fut la cause de la rupture spectaculaire de l'ouvrage.

Mon collègue le Professeur Kerisel de Paris et moi-même fûmes alors approchés par la Cassa per il Mezzogiorno, un maître d'oeuvre de travaux publics italiens, en vue de formuler un nouveau projet.

Au terme des recherches préliminaires approfondies qui avaient mis à jour cet intéressant phénomène artésien, nous décidâmes d'intégrer dans la conception et dans la construction projetées les critères suivants:

1. préchargement du sable alluvial au moyen d'un remblai sous-marin de pente latérale au moins égale à 1:9 afin d'éviter tout poinçonnage dans l'argile meuble;

2. drainage de la partie supérieure de l'argile meuble au moyen de drains de sable de 50 m de long.

L'effet de ces deux mesures devait être de renforcer la résistance du sol.

Ces drains de sable très profonds furent exécutés par vibro-flottation non seulement du sable alluvial, mais aussi de l'argile meuble; le cailloutis se trouvant dans le tuyau est désagrégé et éliminé par injection en sens inverse d'eau sous pression élevée.

Nous attendons maintenant un an pour la consolidation de la partie supérieure de la couche d'argile meuble.

Ensuite, après enlèvement du remblai de sable, nous immergerons des caissons flottants pour les déposer sur une plateforme située au niveau – 11. Le dragage ira jusqu'à – 13. A partir de ce niveau et jusque – 11, une couche de 2 m de terre renforcée, consistant en un filet en plastic d'une résistance à la traction de 50 KW/m, sera mise en place afin d'accroître la résistance du sol de fondation.

Les caissons seront conçus pour tolérer la pression engendrée par une lame de 4 m de haut et seront reliés les uns aux autres. Leur poids final est calculé de telle sorte que la pente longitudinale des tensions, de l'entrée jusqu'à la côte, ne dépasse pas 1 KPa/m dans aucune direction horizontale. Ceci afin de respecter la loi établie par BARRE DE SAINT-VENANT à la fin du siècle dernier à propos des matériaux non soumis aux frictions pris en tenaille entre deux plaques parallèles.

M LOEWY (GB)

Je voudrais parler des conditions et de l'expérience du Port de Belawan, à Sumatra N.E., avec la gracieuse permission de M. Soejono, Directeur des Ports et du Dragage et de M. Sumardi, Ingénieur en Chef, Port de Belawan, tous deux présents au Congrès grâce à l'initiative de la C.P.V.D. Le Port de Belawan a été mis à l'étude en 1974, dans le cadre d'une analyse de faisabilité réalisée pour le compte de la Banque Asiatique de Développement par Sir William HALCROW and Partners. Il en résulta une prévision de croissance annuelle du trafic de 7,3% par an qui devrait porter le volume de celui-ci de 2,9 millions de tonnes en 1975 à 5,5 mtpa en 1983, 8,9 mtpa en 1988 et 15,8 mtpa en 1998.

L'ancien port, construit en 1920, avait 1180 mètres de quai et un mouillage de 8,5 m. Des bassins qui furent ajoutés en 1960 s'ensablèrent rapidement et durent être modifiés. L'étude de 1975 recommandait une première phase de développement consistant en 1300 m de quai sur pieux avec une profondeur d'eau par basses eaux de 9,5 m le long du côté extérieur du chenal d'approche incurvé. Ce chenal avait une longueur de 12 km et conduisait aux eaux profondes du Détroit de Malacca. Le projet fut étudié à l'aide d'un modèle hydraulique très élaboré au Laboratoire Hydraulique de Wallingford.

Il entraîna une récupération de terrain de plus de 50 ha impliquant le dépôt à des profondeurs allant de 2 à 17 m de 5 millions de m^3 de sable dragué en rivière à une distance de 12 kms, pompé et amené sur le chantier. Les sous-sols consistent en trois lits d'argile meuble de 15 à 30 m d'épaisseur séparés par deux épaisses couches de sable fin. Le long de la digue de quai, il fallut encore enlever 800.000 m^3 de sédiments très meubles situés jusqu'à 18 m de profondeur.

Afin de minimiser et d'accélérer le tassement et la consolidation des sous-sols meubles, qui, laissés à eux-mêmes auraient pu atteindre 4 mètres verticalement et demander plusieurs années — un traitement du sol et une amélioration du sous-sol furent réalisés au moyen du "compactage dynamique", du "surchargement" et de "drains verticaux", employés séparément aussi bien qu'en combinaison. La première procédure n'était efficace que pour le remblayage de sable, tandis que les deuxième et troisième, ensemble, devaient servir à la dissipation rapide de la pression d'eau interstitielle et à la consolidation primaire des argiles meubles. Les drains de sable traditionnels furent écartés en raison du risque de "rétention" du sol adjacent et de rupture du chemin de drainage en raison du déplacement latéral.

Les drains plus évolués, en plastic, de la marque "Castle", fabriqués au Japon, évitant ces désavantages, furent préférés et introduits dans le sol à des profondeurs allant de 30 à 45 m. Ceci fut fait au moyen d'un nouvel équipement élaboré de fichage de pieux par vibration spécialement mis au point par la société japonaise Rinkai.

L'espacement varie de 1,7 à 3 m et, à ce jour, la mise en place de ces drains s'avère rapide et peu coûteuse et leur comportement satisfaisant. Une procédure soigneusement contrôlée de remblayage de sable a été adoptée en combinaison avec le drainage vertical et le surchargement afin que l'installation soit terminée au moment où le surchargement atteignait + 3 m. A ce niveau, toute consolidation dynamique à effectuer est réalisée avant d'élever le surchargement à + 7 m, niveau qui est maintenu jusqu'à la livraison de la zone aux entrepreneurs chargés des routes, des services, des bâtiments, etc. Une dissipation de 85% de la pression interstitielle devrait être atteinte en 9 mois, sans toutefois exclure une compression secondaire résiduelle pendant une période beaucoup plus longue. Il en a été tenu compte dans la conception des ouvrages, routes, services, etc.

Je serais heureux de pouvoir décrire à l' occasion du prochain Congrès l'expérience plus complète qui sera alors acquise, la première phase de développement étant terminée.

N N B ORDMAN (GB)

Un aspect important de l'amélioration ou du remplacement de mauvais sols est le temps que demandent les opérations. L'impact économique peut en être important en soi, car "le temps, c'est de l'argent". Mais, en outre, ceci a un impact sur la planification, surtout lorsqu'il s'agit de construire des installations importantes (industrielles notamment) dans les environs du port.

Certaines de ces installations font peser des charges importantes sur le sol. Lorsque ce poids s'exerce sur une surface limitée, il n'y a pas de problème particulier, dans la mesure où les pieux peuvent constituer une solution économique. Néanmoins, dans les cas où une dalle ou un pavement externe est nécessaire sur une grande surface pour soutenir ces charges importantes, de sérieux problèmes peuvent surgir, soit qu'un tassement important doive être attendu au cours de la durée de vie opérationnelle de l'installation, soit que l'aménagement du sol entraîne un retard important.

Le même genre de problème peut se poser pour les accès routiers et ferroviaires.

M COUPRIE (FRANCE)

La réalisation récente d'un quai en parois moulées dans le sol au port de Rouen illustre l'adaptabilité de ce procédé à des conditions variées.

En effet, dans ce cas, le nouveau quai se situe en avant du haut d'un talus: c'est dire qu'il a fallu réaliser la paroi malgré la présence d'eau. Pour ce faire, un remblai en blocs de craie a été réalisé par déversement sur le talus existant. Mais un tel matériau très perméable ne pouvait contenir la boue bentonitique.

Il a fallu consolider ce remblai frais et cela a été réalisé en creux par tranchées parallèles remplies d'un coulis bentonite-ciment qui pénètre les vides du sol et durcit, améliorant l'imperméabilité et la résistance mécanique.

Après ce traitement, le quai a été réalisé suivant le procédé classique: murettes guides, creusement de la paroi sous la boue bentonitique, bétonnage, etc.

F IRWIN-CHILDS (GB)

Sans mettre en cause la validité des conclusions relatives aux méthodes d'amélioration des sols meubles, je pense qu'elles ne devraient pas être formulees de manière qui puisse décourager l'élaboration d'ouvrages susceptibles d'être érigés sur des sols qui ne peuvent pas (ou n'ont pas été) être améliorés.

En dernier ressort, ces ouvrages peuvent être flottants, et il est très simple de fournir des arguments en faveur de charges très importantes sur <u>monolithes</u>, comme indiqué à la Fig. 8, page 273. La Fig. 9, page 274, illustre néanmoins la simplicité d'une construction sur le site plutôt qu'à partir d'éléments préfabriqués.

La plupart des ouvrages maritimes sont soumis à des charges latérales qui s'ajoutent aux charges verticales:

> Dans le cas d'écluses, ce problème peut être rencontré par entretoisement interne, et il existe un projet d'écluse flottante complémentaire.
>
> Pour les murs de quai, l'entretoisement de la face aussi bien que l'étançonnement arrière sont rendus difficiles sur sols mauvais, mais

la résistance nécessaire peut être obtenue par des murs ou des contreforts placés à angle droit par rapport à la paroi, en cas d'écran d'étanchéiteé. La raison en est que cette méthode de construction sur le site mobilise l'interaction avec le sol d'une manière qui ne peut être atteinte avec des éléments préfabriqués. Il y a une série d'ouvrages portuaires en Grande-Bretagne (entre autres à Liverpool, Redcar et Bristol) dont la solidité est entièrement fondée sur ce principe.

J de NEKKER (PAYS-BAS)

L'autorité portuaire de Rotterdam envisage de remblayer avec des matériaux de dragage d'anciens bassins portuaires désaffectés.

Ceci aurait comme avantages d'une part, de fournir un endroit pour déposer les matériaux, gravement contaminés en provenance du dragage d'entretien et, d'autre part, de procurer un matériau bon marché pour remblayer les bassins portuaires désaffectés en vue de réutiliser ceux-ci en tant que zones industrielles ou résidentielles.

Le système proposé consiste à fermer l'embouchure du port au moyen d'une digue de sable, de remplir progressivement le bassin de sédiments dragués et de permettre à ceux-ci de se consolider. Les matériaux provenant du dragage d'entretien et immergés prennent beaucoup de temps pour se consolider. C'est pourquoi le drainage horizontal et vertical sera essentiel.

Au terme de quelques essais en laboratoire (qui ont donné de bons résultats), des expériences vont très prochainement être menées à l'échelle 1:1. Certains anciens bassins d'eau douce (désaffectés) vont être remplis de matériaux de dragage sur une hauteur allant de 3 m sous le niveau moyen de la mer jusque 4 m au-dessus de celui-ci. Trois systèmes de drainage seront étudiés:

1. Couche de sable sur le fond du bassin comportant un système de drainage horizontal. L'eau sera enlevée par pompage.

2. Drains sous forme de bandes verticales et sillons dans la couche supérieure.

3. Combinaison de 1 et 2.

Les résultats sont attendus dans environ 1 an et demi.

P G R BARLOW (GB)

Prolongeant la partie du rapport britannique décrivant l'histoire du cas de Port Kelang j'ai expliqué la raison historique pour laquelle les responsables ont accepté le désavantage opérationnel des môles en mer reliés par passerelles à la terre, à savoir l'importance prédominante de la minimisation de l'investissement en capital au moment où le site a été ouvert, et ensuite, le besoin d'assurer une continuité hydraulique tout au long de la longue ligne de quais du Port nord.

Cependant, depuis la rédaction du rapport, nous avons entrepris une étude technique, opérationnelle et économique du nouveau site portuaire de Pulau Lumut. Cette étude comprendra une analyse coûts-bénéfices des modèles marginaux par rapport aux types actuels d'ouvrages en mer avec accès par ponts. Nous constatons que, si le sol du nouveau site est identique à celui des ports nord et sud, la solution la plus économique pourrait bien être de maintenir la conception actuelle, mais avec un pont beaucoup plus large, assez large pour tolérer un talus de rétention des terres très plat permettant une récupération contigue de terres. La raison en est que le sol de ce site consiste jusqu'au niveau – 85 de la couche rocheuse en argiles marines à faible résistance au cisaillement. Même s'il était économiquement possible de remplacer le matériau de sol jusqu'aux couches sablonneuses situées de – 25 à – 35 m de profondeur, dans lesquelles nous fichons actuellement nos pieux, ceci ne résoudrait pas le problème, puisque la faible résistance au cisaillement du matériau situé en-dessous de ce niveau maintiendrait le danger d'éboulement suivant un cercle de glissement, du nouveau matériau de remblai et de l'ouvrage qu'il recevrait.

J L DAWSON (GB)

J'ai suggéré que nous étions d'accord sur l'importance des études de sols pour les ouvrages érigés sur sols meubles. Ces études peuvent être coûteuses. Les forages doivent, chaque fois que c'est possible, être complétés par des méthodes plus économiques telles que l'étude séismique et par sonar. La surface d'argile de Londres du complexe portuaire/aéroportuaire envisagé à Maplin avait été déterminée de cette manière à travers son épaisse couche supérieure de sédiments et d'argile.

J'ai mis en cause la suggestion formulée dans un rapport, selon laquelle les revêtements souples ne donnaient jamais satisfaction dans un environnement portuaire. J'ai fait remarquer que des revêtements hydrocarbonés denses et stables pouvaient être obtenus grâce aux méthodes de conception "Marshall", mais que c'était le risque de fuite de combustible qui posait problème avec tout revêtement à liant hydrocarboné.

J'ai indiqué qu'un béton roulé, sec et mince constituerait une base satisfaisante pour une surface en asphalte bien conçue.

J'ai dit que les pieux restaient le moyen normal de résoudre les problèmes de fondation sur les sites maritimes PSA (Property Services Agency) et que nous avions utilisé avec succès des méthodes à base de coulis de ciment à la Bentonite pour remplacer les écrans d'étanchéité.

Enfin, j'ai rappelé que de mauvaises conditions de sol demeuraient l'une des raisons les plus fréquemment avancées pour expliquer les dépassements des coûts projetés. Une large marge d'incertitude subsiste à cet égard même au terme des études préliminaires les plus approfondies. Un pessimisme informé devrait guider l'estimation des marges de sécurité nécessaires pour tenir compte de cette incertitude dans les estimations de coûts.

A L MOSS-MORRIS (AUSTRALIE)

En réponse à la demande de notre Rapporteur Général, M. G. P. Martin, j'ajoute quelques précisions relatives à la manutention et à la mise en place des unités de contrefort de 360 tonnes.

Elles ont été fabriquées dans un chantier de très petites dimensions qui ne permettait que d'en fabriquer quatre. Les trois parties du contrefort, à avoir la paroi avant, la base et le contrefort ont toutes été coulées en position horizontale. L'avant et la base ont, à l'aide de la grande grue à portique, été mises en position correcte par rapport au contrefort en position horizontale, en subissant une rotation de 90 degrés. La troisième étape du coulage est essentiellement celle du contrefort, mais comprend également une petite longueur de la paroi avant située immédiatement au-dessus de la base.

Une fois assemblée, l'unité est mise en position verticale par rotation au moyen du portique levant de 170 tonnes et placée sur les deux poutres rigides sous le contrefort. La grue flottante de 360 tonnes lève ensuite l'unité de contrefort et la transporte directement vers son emplacement final. Cette grue est une grue à volée variable dotée d'une flèche de 48 m et placée sur une barge de 51 x 21 m. Celle-ci est solidement amarrée à l'endroit approprié et l'unité de contrefort est maintenue en position par rapport à la barge au moyen de cables légers commandés par treuils à air.

Au départ de cette position initiale, les unités ont pu être placées à moins de 50 mm de leur position idéale, tout en maintenant les espaces entre les unités entre 10 et 110 mm.

Pour ce qui est de l'autre question du Rapporteur Général, le quai nord est en service depuis 15 mois et nous n'avons pas connaissance de difficultés occasionnées par les rails de grues non solidarisés.

H D HOEFT (RFA)

Dans son Rapport Général, Mr Martin avait exprimé le désir de recevoir des détails complémentaires sur les coûts des quais décrits dans le rapport de la R.F.A. En ce qui concerne le terminal minéralier du Hansaport, à Hambourg, pages 603 et 606/607, les coûts peuvent être chiffrés comme suit:

1. Coût de construction comme indiqué pour le travail terminé, mais excluant le remplacement de sol; environ — 30.000 DM/mètre (prix 1975)
   Pour obtenir le prix actuel, augmenter l'un tiers environ, soit: — ±40.000 DM/mètre courant (prix 1981)

2. Le coût du remplacement du sol est difficile à établir, p.c.q. le quai faisait partie d'un projet plus large dont coût approximatif: — 10.000 DM/mètre

   Dès lors le coût total au niveau de prix actuel serait: — 50.000 à 60.000 DM/mètre

Cette solution (remplacement de sol) a été retenue après étude approfondie d'autres conceptions y compris les murs-écrans, les caissons et autres éléments préfabriqués.

Des essais d'amélioration de sol effectués sur le terrain selon la méthode Menard ont également été effectués mais se sont révélés inadéquats dans les conditions du site. Toutes les autres solutions se sont avérées plus coûteuses, à notre propre surprise d'ailleurs. Des analyses ont démontré que ceci était dû à l'importante charge minéralière surimposée (30 T/m2) et à la hauteur du mur de quai de près de 24 m (de la base au tablier).

Il n'était pas possible d'utiliser la méthode de remplacement de sol à l'extrémité nord du mur de quai en raison des risques qu'on aurait fait courir aux ouvrages existants.

Dans cette section, la charge tolérable a dû être limitée à 15 T/m2 (au lieu des 30T/m2 souhaités). Au début de l'exploitation, la durée des charges imposées a été enregistrée électroniquement en chaque endroit et à mesure que la consolidation du sous-sol progressait, la charge tolérable fut augmentée. L'objectif des 30 T/m2 a pu être atteint dans un délai de moins de cinq ans.

J F MAQUET (FRANCE)

La première partie de mon intervention concerne les deuxième et troisième conclusions proposées par le rapporteur général.

La puissance des méthodes de calcul fait que nos connaissances sur le comportement des ouvrages et des sols sont beaucoup plus étendues sur le plan théorique que sur le plan pratique d'un sol réel toujours hétérogène et d'un ouvrage qui n'est pas parfaitement semblable à celui du bureau d'études.

Je pense donc qu'en plus des études géotechniques préliminaires, il est souhaitable que l'on fasse plus souvent des expérimentations et des mesures sur le comportement des ouvrages réels.

Ma deuxième intervention concerne un nouveau type de quai qui a été construit au port du Havre.

Les méthodes de traitement des terrains qui semblent les plus courantes aujourd'hui présentent souvent deux inconvénients.

Le premier est qu'il faut du temps pour les mettre en oeuvre et que cela coûte cher comme l'a souligné M. le Président.

Le deuxième inconvénient est que ces méthodes ne sont pas toujours appropriées pour la construction du prolongement d'un ouvrage existant.

Pour faire face à un mauvais terrain où de larges épaisseurs de silt étaient présentes, le port du Havre a utilisé la technique de la paroi moulée.

Pour reprendre des moments importants, la paroi du quai est en zigzag comme la forme de palplanches à module.

Les parties du quai déjà construites avant

étaient ancrées en arrière par des tirants précontraints qui trouvaient un bon ancrage dans les sables coquilliers.

La partie nouvelle comprend un portique qui reporte les charges arrières sur des pieux et des barettes car il n'y avait pas de bonne couche pour ancrer les tirants.

En conclusion, ce type de quai en paroi moulée est une technique très intéressante car l'ouvrage peut être construit très rapidement sans perturbation du quai voisin ni des opérations. L'ouvrage était aussi moins cher que les techniques concurrentes sur le site considéré.

E SERRANO (ESPAGNE)

Quelques mots seulement pour attirer l'attention sur un facteur qui peut avoir une influence dans le domaine étudié par cette session et pour décrire une expérience dont certains d'entre vous pourront tirer des enseignements.

Ce facteur, c'est le temps.

Comme sans doute beaucoup d'entre vous, nous avons pris part à la conception et à la construction d'installations sur sols meubles. Comme l'a dit le Rapporteur Général, les bons sols sont l'exception. Chaque fois, nous avons dû étudier plusieurs possibilités, allant du déblaiement de la totalité du sol meuble à diverses techniques de consolidation, y compris des recherches géo-techniques approfondies tant théoriques que pratiques et de collectes de données détaillées pour connaître le comportement réel. La solution optimale s'est avérée différente dans chaque cas particulier.

Pourtant, le facteur temps a toujours revêtu une importance particulière dans la prise de décision et, parfois, le manque de temps a conduit à adopter des techniques de consolidation plus coûteuses qu'il n'aurait été nécessaire dans d'autres circonstances.

La consolidation des sols meubles requiert en effet le plus souvent beaucoup de temps, parfois pour obtenir la réduction souhaitée de la pression de l'eau interstitielle induite par le préchargement, que le processus doive être accéléré ou non à l'aide de différents types de drains, ou bien pour permettre à la réaction chimique de se produire ou aux procédures opératoires de renforcer le sol meuble, que ces renforcements soient réalisés au moyen de pieux, de colonnes de sable ou de pierre, par vibroflottage, etc.

Malheureusement, nous sommes toujours confrontés, en tant qu'ingénieurs, au manque de temps. Ceux qui sont chargés de construire un ouvrage, quel qu'il soit, prennent parfois des mois (voire des années) pour décider d'aller de l'avant, mais une fois ceci fait, ils voudraient que les travaux soient terminés, comme nous le disons familièrement, non pas demain, mais hier.

En outre, nous avons de nombreuses fois vu de vastes superficies de terrain caractérisés par de très mauvaises conditions de sol, réservées en vue d'extensions futures des installations portuaires ou industrielles, qui n'on pas fait l'objet d'études ou de traitement adéquats préalables au moment où la décision est prise d'y construire un ouvrage. A ce moment, il est bien entendu trop tard pour prendre le temps de tenter de mettre en oeuvre la méthode de consolidation la plus simple qui, souvent, peut être le préchargement, tout simplement.

Une recommandation que l'on peut faire à tout qui se trouve dans cette situation est de programmer, essentiellement, les utilisations possibles du terrain réservé et de mettre en oeuvre un processus continu de préconsolidation du sol (au moyen, par exemple, de la technique décrite par le Professeur Jimenez Salas, de la dune mobile, renforcée ou non par l'un ou l'autre type de drain artificiel). Ainsi, on sera dans la position idéale au moment où l'ouvrage devra êtra construit.

L'expérience dont je voulais vous faire part a trait à un type très spécial de "sol meuble" que nous trouvons souvent dans les régions rocheuses du nord de l'Espagne.

Il s'agit d'un remblai artificiel fait de tout-venant de carrière, placé sans façons, qui s'avère de loin plus économique que, par exemple, le remblai de sable de dragage.

Il y a dix ans, nous devions construire un silo portuaire pour y stocker 20.000 tonnes de soja sur un remblai artificiel de 20 m de ce type, comportant de très petites pierres aussi bien que des blocs de plus d'une tonne.

Sous le remblai se trouvaient quelques mètres de sable et en-dessous, du rocher. Le silo devait être construit entre un quai de 14 m de profondeur sous le niveau des basses eaux et le brise-lames extérieur du Port de Bilbao.

Aucun des systèmes de consolidation, à l'exception du préchargement simple, n'était, à notre avis, applicable et nous ne disposions pas, à l'époque, des données permettant de prévoir les tassements éventuels d'un remblai de ce type, non compacté. Nous devions donc prévoir la possibilité d'obtenir une précharge similaire au supplément de pression que le silo allait entraîner, de l'ordre de 22 tonnes/m^2. Ceci nous mit devant un autre problème, car le quai avait été conçu, au départ, pour une charge de 6 tonnes/m^2. Ceci put être résolu en plaçant le silo un peu plus loin que prévu de la face du quai.

Les tassements se firent, comme prévu, très rapidement, de sorte que nous dûmes atteindre une hauteur de préchargement de 12 m avec le même type de remblai, et, avec ceci, le tassement fut de 1,10 m. Une fois retirée la charge, le silo fut construit et les tassements finaux, à pleine charge n'atteignirent pas 20 mm.

Et à présent, pour en revenir à mon point de départ, les propriétaires de ce silo veulent accroître sa capacité, pour la porter à 40.000 tonnes. Lorsqu'on a exécuté le préchargement, des bâtiments provisoires empêchaient de l'étendre jusqu'à la zone d'expansion prévue. Nous avons recommandé de le faire dès que les bâtiments provisoires seraient enlevés. Le temps a passé sans que cela ne se fasse et, aujourd'hui, dix ans après, on nous demande de nouveau de consolider le sol de toute urgence.

A JIMENEZ-SALAS (ESPAGNE)

A Dumai, Sumatra (Indonésie, les conditions de sol sont très semblables à celles qui ont été décrites par notre collègue britannique pour Belawan. Dans une raffinerie qui existe là-bas, les réservoirs sont situés dans une zone préchargée et équipée de drains de sable verticaux. Les tassements sont continuels et exigent des remises à niveau répétées des réservoirs.

La raison semble en être la teneur élevée en alophane de l'argile, ce qui entraîne un pourcentage élevé de consolidation secondaire qui échappe à l'influence des drains verticaux.

On a maintenant entamé une importante extension de la raffinerie, mais l'utilisation des drains verticaux a été rejetée. Il sera donc intéressant de suivre le comportement futur des drains verticaux à Belawan.

E LACKNER (RFA)

Je voudrais seulement ajouter quelques remarques relatives au rapport ouest-allemand. M. Martin, le Rapporteur Général du Sujet 4, s'est interrogé sur les coûts de construction de notre mur de quai. Je puis vous indiquer les coûts de nos deux premiers projets.

Les coûts du mur de quai de notre terminal-conteneurs au Port de Brême sont très élevés. Le mur de quai a une hauteur de 26,5 m du pied à la tête, les conditions de sol étaient très mauvaises, la pression de l'eau très élevée, de même que les charges de surface. Enfin, mais non moins important, le coût du sas de protection contre les lames de tempête ont été considérables.

La proposition de ce sas a été faite par le Professeur Dr. Hensen, professeur ordinaire à l'Université Technique de Hanovre et directeur de l'Institut Franzius à Hanovre.

On m'a demandé de couler cette idée en un projet, ce qui ne fut pas facile. En raison des dimensions, nous avons dû utiliser des sections de béton renforcé préfabriquées pesant plus de 600 tonnes.

Pour toutes les raisons mentionnées ci-dessus, le coût de ce mur de quai, y compris l'excavation du mauvais sol et son remplacement par du bon sable, s'est élevé à environ 150.000 DM/m ou 30.000 £/m.

Le coût du mur de quai dans le port de Brunsbuettel a été d'environ 75.000 DM/m ou de 15.000 £/m.

En République Fédérale d'Allemagne, nous avons également quelques bonnes expériences de consolidation de sol meuble, etc. Avec certaines méthodes, pourtant, les résultats ont été décevants. C'est pourquoi, pour un grand projet, nous préférons remplacer tout le sol meuble par du bon sable, assez de bon sable est disponible à une distance raisonnable et déposer ailleurs dans de bonnes conditions le sol enlevé.

Cette méthode paraît très simple, mais il est très important de suivre des règles particulières en présence de courants importants et d'eau très sédimenteuse. Ce n'est qu'ainsi qu'il est possible d'obtenir un bon remplacement. Ceci est prévu par la Recommandation R 109 du Comité sur les Ouvrages Maritimes de la Société de Génie Civil portuaire à Hambourg. Quant à la R 110, elle couvre les règles adéquates de calcul des pressions terrestres ou de l'eau.

Le risque d'être confronté à des problèmes pour les murs de quai conçus suivant les Recommandations ci-dessus, est minime; de plus, les ouvrages ainsi conçus sont économiques.

CONCLUSIONS

1. Les rapports présentés au Congrès ont privilégié le traitement des sols plutôt que la conception et la construction d'ouvrages adaptés aux terrains de mauvaises qualités.

   Il est cependant clair que des progrès considérables ont été accomplis dans la conception d'ouvrages de ce type, utilisant des techniques, telles que la paroi moulée, qui permettent d'accroître l'interaction entre le sol et l'ouvrage.

2. Le traitement des mauvais terrains peut aller de l'enlèvement du sol peu consistant et son remplacement par un sol de meilleures caractéristiques jusqu'à des processus sophistiqués de consolidation; il est recommandé d'étudier attentivement toutes les possibilités afin de choisir la méthode appropriée dans chaque cas.

3. Les techniques utilisées impliquent généralement la nécessité d'une évaluation précise des caractéristiques du terrain et il est fortement recommandé aux responsables des projets de réserver des ressources suffisantes pour permettre la réalisation de reconnaissances géotechniques détaillées sur le site considéré. Davantage d'attention devrait être accordée à un examen critique des techniques utilisées, en suivant le comportement ultérieur des ouvrages afin, d'apprécier la validité de ces techniques et de les modifier si cela paraît nécessaire.

4. Il est recommandé que les investigations relatives aux sols soient attentivement contrôlées et suivies par les ingénieurs responsables des projets et que les spécialistes des sols soient complètement informés des raisons qui motivent ces investigations ainsi que des données requises.

5. Il est important de se rendre compte que les techniques de traitement et de substitution de sol peuvent prendre beaucoup de temps: cet élément doit être pris en compte dans toute évaluation économique globale.

PORTS ET ACCES MARITIMES

SECTION II — SUJET 5

Erosion des côtes dues à des travaux portuaires
et mesures visant à y remédier

Jeudi 14 mai 1981

Président:	*N N B ORDMAN (GB)* *Noel Ordman and Associates Ltd*
Vice Président:	*A F G EDDIE (Australie)* *Managing Partner, Connell Eddie and Associates, Melbourne*
Rapporteur Général:	*Prof P HOLMES (GB)* *Department of Civil Engineering, University of Liverpool*
Secrétaire:	*P LACEY (GB)* *Ove Arup and Partners Ltd, London*
Secrétaire Adjoint:	*Mlle M-M DANEELS (Belgique)* *Secrétaire AIPCN Secrétariat Générale, Bruxelles*

Orateurs

U TOMASICCHIO (Italie), F ABACACIS (Portugal), J CASTANHO (Portugal), P P VAIDYARAMAN (Inde), D J VAN DEN BOSSCHE (Belgique), A ROGAN (Grèce), N P CAMPBELL (Afrique du Sud), F ENRIQUEZ (Espagne), P M A DE CANDT (Belgique), J L DELORME (France), R TENAUD (France), D H SWART (Afrique du Sud), D DREYFOUS-DUCAS (France), E R HEIBERG (Etats-Unis), C MOUTZOURIS (Grèce), W A PRICE (GB)

Prof. P. HOLMES (Rapporteur Général)

Une synthèse portant sur ce problème complexe peut, pour des raisons pratiques, être divisée en trois sections, dont chacune est nécessaire à la prévision de l'érosion des côtes et à l'évaluation des mesures qu'il convient de prendre pour y faire face:

1. Informations et données nécessaires à la compréhension du problème et à sa solution — banque de données.
2. Prévision de l'érosion côtière et confirmation de celle-ci.
3. Conception des mesures visant à y remédier et évaluation de leur efficacité.

Ces trois sections portent également sur tous les types d'interférences — qu'elles soient provoquées par des ports existants, des extensions envisagées de ceux-ci ou les mesures correctrices elles-mêmes — dans le processus de transport de sésiments côtiers. Tous les rapports présentés dans cette section du XXVème Congrès impliquent ces aspects à des degrés divers.

Les rapports présentés dans cette section du Congrès fournissent une information très riche relative à des situations côtières très diverses, et c'est pourquoi ils présentent un intérêt certain pour la profession.

Etant donné que le problème de l'érosion côtière et du transport littoral se pose de manière aiguë dans de nombreux pays et peut impliquer des dépenses en capital ou un financement continu très élevé, il semble opportun d'étudier la proposition qu'une Commission internationale devrait être chargée de rassembler l'expérience considérable acquise par les ingénieurs dans ce domaine. Le mandat d'une telle commission pourrait partir du besoin d'un document cohérent et à jour faisant le point de chacune des rubriques mentionnées ci-dessus. On peut espérer que la discussion des rapports fournirait à cette commission un cadre de référence plus clair.

La recherche doit bien entendu être poursuivie dans ce domaine. En raison de son coût, une collaboration internationale à cet égard constituerait peut-être une manière de progresser. De nombreux pays ont entrepris de grands programmes de recherche sur la dynamique côtière, mais ils sont le plus souvent orientés vers la recherche fondamentale, dont le résultat n'est pas toujours directement exploitable par les ingénieurs sur le terrain.

Peut-être les membres du Congrès souhaiteront-ils soupeser l'idée d'une recherche appliquée de génie civil côtier menée en collaboration au niveau international et réalisée en un endroit ou en des endroits où les développements portuaires ont affecté ou sont en passe d'affecter le transport littoral.

LES DEBATS

U TOMASICCHIO (ITALIE)

Je suis en total accord avec le Rapporteur Général. Je voudrais seulement apporter quelques éléments d'information supplémentaires.

Notre rapport n'a d'autre but que de décrire divers cas d'interaction entre ouvrages portuaires et configuration de la côte en Italie, côte qui, comme vous le savez, est souvent une côte basse. L'exposé, bien que limité à quelques cas, n'en est pas moins par nécessité de portée générale, dans la mesure où il identifie les causes de l'érosion des côtes, lorsqu'elle existe, ainsi que les mesures qui sont ou qui devraient être mises en oeuvre pour la combattre dans chaque cas particulier.

Il ne s'agit donc pas de donner une description précise de chaque situation concrète qui se présente en Italie, mais, à notre avis, du moins, de donner une idée suffisante des problèmes qui peuvent se présenter et des mesures que ceux-ci appellent.

Je voudrais seulement rappeler les situations décrites dans le rapport, à savoir, dans l'order:

- marinas de Chiavaril et de Lavagna, ports de Carrara et Viareggio, mer Tyrrhénienne du nord,
- côte de Calabre entre les ports de DIAMANTE

et ceux de AMANTEA et CETRARO, mer Tyrrhénienne du sud,

- côte du Cap Gargano jusqu'au Pô, littoral vénitien en mer Adriatique centrale et du nord, comportant plusieurs embouchures.

L'image poétique de l'Italie plongeant dans les eaux chaudes de la méditerranée n'est que trop connue à l'étranger. L'importance de la protection des côtes en Italie peut donc être perçue par tous. La surface côtière ne constitue pas seulement une part substantielle du territoire national: elle revêt une importance particulière du point de vue de l'économie nationale. Le problème que pose la meilleure gestion possible de cette partie du territoire est donc partiellement crucial. Il a suscité et continue de susciter en Italie une série d'études et de recherches visant à trouver les solutions techniquement et économiquement les plus appropriées. Parallèlement, les programmes du Ministero dei Lavori Pubblici et le Consiglio Nazionale delle Ricerche vont dans le même sens. Du point de vue opératoire, le Ministère mentionné ci-dessus a proposé un programme triennal de mesures de défense des côtes, tandis que le Conseil National de la Recherche soutient un programme précis intitulé "Préservation du sol" et qui comprend deux sous-programmes, dont l'un a trait à la "Dynamique du Littoral".

Au sein de ce programme collaborent plusieurs unités opérationnelles appartenant à des Instituts universitaires ou à des organismes privés et publics et de compétence reconnue. Si le lancement du programme a été lent pour diverses raisons (sans doute de même nature que l'évolution hésitante de la législation), la recherche a maintenant acquis sa vitesse de croisière et on peut espérer qu'elle livrera des résultats valables avant la fin de l'année en cours, terme initialement prévu pour ce programme. Comme c'est souvent le cas dans le domaine de la recherche, nous n'attendons cependant pas de résultats exceptionnels (Sicut Natura, Scientia rare facit saltus).

Ce projet a néanmoins réussi à promouvoir des études et des recherches dans tous les domaines liés à l'aménagement adéquat du territoire et à la protection de celui-ci contre les actions nocives dues aux éléments naturels autant qu'aux manipulations humaines impropres.

Plusieurs groupes de chercheurs se penchent activement sur la défense des côtes (économistes, géographes, géophysiciens, ingénieurs, météorologues). Des collectes et des traitements de données à grande échelle sur le terrain ont été organisés pour la première fois.

Dans un premier stade, il a été à la fois utile et nécessaire d'étudier les expériences étrangères les plus récentes, notamment aux Etats-Unis. Dans l'état plus avancé actuel de la recherche, ses résultats semblent plus directement représentatifs des conditions locales.

Je ne veux pas vous ennuyer avec la liste de ce qui a été fait et de ce qui n'a pas été fait. Je n'en ai pas le temps et ne pourrais de toute manière être complet, mon expérience étant limitée aux problèmes de génie civil.

Je me contenterai donc de vous dire que, dans les laboratoires d'hydraulique de certaines universités italiennes, nous nous efforçons dans les grandes lignes de déterminer les caractéristiques les plus recommandables de certains ouvrages de défense (et il semble qu'on s'oriente de plus en plus vers le choix de systèmes quasi-naturels tels que barrières immergées et alimentation artificielle des plages) et d'améliorer certains modèles mathématiques pour les rendre plus fiables et manipulables en tant que systèmes de recherche utiles et rapides.

Un certain nombre d'organismes scientifiques, de même niveau que le Comité, formulent des propositions destinées dans une deuxième étape à être intégrées dans une règlementation en vue de déterminer les missions et les moyens des organisations appelées à recueillir et à traiter les données (banques de données). Ainsi pourra-t-on mettre des instruments de plus en plus raffinés à la disposition des responsables de projets. Nous suivons également avec attention les expériences sur le terrain: leur programmation est un des premiers résultats nouveaux des systèmes opérationnels de recherche dont je vous ai parlé.

Le 6ème paragraphe du rapport propose une description des types de défense que nous utilisons ou proposons. Je voudrais indiquer une nouvelle fois que nous avons accordé beaucoup d'attention aux barrières immergées parce qu'elles semblent aussi efficaces que les barrières hors eau actuelles, sans avoir leurs désavantages. Cependant, les recherches se poursuivant, rien n'est encore définitif en ce moment.

Enfin, dans le dernier paragraphe, nous décrivons la nouvelle approche organique adoptée en Italie, en matière de défense des côtes: cette approche tient compte de tous les aspects du problème, non pas seulement de l'évolution physique, mais aussi du paysage et des composantes sociales, économiques et de salubrité publique du territoire concerné.

J'espère vous avoir donné, même rapidement, une idée concrète et compréhensible de ce qui se fait actuellement en Italie dans le domaine des travaux côtiers. Vous trouverez de plus amples détails à cet égard dans le rapport lui-même.

F ABECASIS (PORTUGAL)

Je voudrais dire tout d'abord combien j'apprécie le travail réalisé par notre Rapporteur Général, M. Holmes. Je souhaite appuyer certains points et en proposer quelques commentaires:

1. Une bonne connaissance des données de base est essentielle. En ce qui concerne la direction des lames, il n'existe, à l'heure actuelle, aucune méthode d'observation réellement satisfaisante. Il s'agit d'une lacune extrêmement grave, en raison de la très grande influence qu'exerce la direction des lames sur l'évaluation de l'intensité du cheminement littoral. Plusieurs rapports, en particulier celui de la Grande-Bretagne (p. 934), appellent avec plus ou moins de netteté l'attention sur ce problème.

2. L'impact prévisible des interventions de

l'homme dans les processus littoraux. L'évolution ultérieure du contrôle alluvionnaire des voies d'eau et les effets de l'extraction de sable sur les plages doivent être pris soigneusement en considération dans les études.

3. Il n'est pas toujours vrai que "une surveillance régulière des plages ... fournisse des renseignements sur le mouvement net". Ce n'est en fait que dans des cas très particuliers que de telles observations peuvent fournir des résultats fiables, surtout du point de vue quantitatif.

4. Il y a un manque de connaissance sur le comportement des sédiments adhérents dans les processus littoraux. Je suis intimement convaincu qu'un énorme effort de recherche doit être fait en ce domaine. Je voudrais dire tout le bien que je pense du point "Evolution future" dans la contribution britannique (p. 939). Je souhaite que ce point se voie accorder toute l'attention qu'il mérite dans la préparation des conclusions.

Deuxième partie. Je trouve la contribution sud-africaine très intéressante. En particulier, mon attention a été retenue par les phénomènes intervenus au nord du brise-lames nord de Richards Bay (p. 908). A cet égard, je voudrais soumettre le cas de ce qui s'est passé au sud de la jetée sud de la Lagune d'Aveiro. A cet effet, je vous invite à regarder les figures 8 et 9 du rapport portugais (p. 885-886). Avec un cheminement littoral net d'environ 10° m^3 par an vers le sud, la zone située immédiatement au sud de la jetée est restée stable depuis la construction des 2 jetées (1958) jusque 1972. Les raisons semblent en être:

1. Les effets de diffraction des lames nord-ouest dominantes et la protection contre celles-ci assurée par les deux jetées.

2. L'apport occasionnel dû aux lames sud-ouest, l'équilibre étant maintenu par le transport côte-large.

3. La protection contre ces mouvements assurée par la barre de la houle du large qui s'est constituée suite à la déviation naturelle du sable de nord en sud de la calanque.

Comme l'indique le rapport portugais, un champ de 11 épis fut mis en place en 1972 en vue de protéger la côte située quelques kilomètres au sud de la baie, dont la situation devenait critique. Aussitôt après la construction des épis, un violent processus érosif attaqua la zone située immédiatement au sud de la jetée sud. Ce processus érosif est attribué au fait que les épis en question interrompent le courant littoral temporaire sud-nord, bouleversant ainsi l'équilibre préexistant dans la zone adjacente à la jetée sud.

J CASTANHO (PORTUGAL)

Notre Rapporteur Général, le Professeur HOLMES, sépare les méthodes de défense côtière en deux catégories fondamentales:

- défenses "en dur" ("hard defences"), du type classique (épis, brise-lames détachés, brise-mers)

et

- défenses "souples" ("soft defences") du type alimentation artificielle ("beach nourishment").

A ce sujet, je voudrais attirer votre attention pour 2 points:

1. Le premier c'est qu'en lisant les différents rapports de la Section II, Sujet 5, je crois m'avoir aperçu qu'il existe une tendance, ou même une préférence, à employer de plus en plus les méthodes "souples" (en conjugaison ou non avec les méthodes "dures"), cela peut-être à cause des grands avantages du type "souple", notamment le fait qu'il n'interfère pas ou interfère très peu sur le régime littoral.

2. Le deuxième point c'est que plusieurs auteurs font état des succès obtenus avec alimentation sur l'estran (by-passing), refoulement de dragages, etc.), mais, par contre, on donne très peu d'importance, ou l'on se méfie même, de l'alimentation appelée "offshore dumping", c'est-à-dire au delà du déferlement.

En effet, si dans certains exemples le sable n'arrive pas à se déposer sur la plage, il y en a d'autres où les résultats ont été très bons. Je crois que tout doit dépendre des conditions locales.

Comme un exemple de succès, je voudrais vous présenter le cas de l'élargissement de la plage de Copacabana (au Brésil). Ici, on a déposé avec de très bons résultats environ 3 millions de m3 de sable, par mer, avec une drague "hopper" qui s'approcha le plus possible de la plage. (La méthode a été conjuguée avec l'alimentation par terre, sur l'estran). La plus grande du sable versé s'est dirigée vers la côte. (L'orateur montre des diapositives qui justifient ces considérations).

P P VAIDYARAMAN (INDE)

Pour déterminer les meilleures localisations et dispositions pour les ports, pour évaluer les besoins de dragage etc., il est crucial de disposer de l'estimation la plus précise possible du taux de cheminement littoral. Ceci ne pose pas de grand problème quand on dispose de données fiables recueillies sur le terrain. En l'absence de celles-ci, cependant, il est fréquemment nécessaire d'avoir recours à des relations empiriques du type de la formule C.E.R.C., qui établit une liaison entre l'énergie de la houle et le taux de cheminement littoral. Ceci appelle une extrême prudence, dans la mesure où une utilisation impropre de ces relations empiriques peut donner lieu à des chiffres erronés. A titre d'illustration, il est fait mention de l'avant-port de Visakhapatnam, l'un des grands ports de la côte est de l'Inde. On dispose heureusement dans ce cas de données de dragage fiables qui indiquent en cet endroit un taux de cheminement littoral de l'ordre de $0,765 \times 10^6$ yd^3/an. En utilisant les données des lames, le taux du cheminement fut calculé sur base de la dite formule ce qui donna un cheminement brut de $3,08 \times 10^6$ yd^3/an, soit presque 4 fois le volume réel. Une étude détaillée de ce résultat a révélé que la formule C.E.R.C., dans sa configuration originelle, est applicable aux zones où l'énergie de la houle ne dépasse pas 20 m ft ^{lb}/ft/jour, alors qu'à Visakhapatnam, cette énergie varie entre 10 et 1000 m ft ^{lb}/ft/jour. De toute évidence, l'extrapolation de la relation de base à des énergies de houle aussi élevées ne peut donner de résultats satisfaisants.

Il a été procédé au Centre de Recherche sur l'Eau et l'Energie de Poona (Inde), à une étude analytique dans le cadre de laquelle la vitesse le long des côtes induite par les lames a été calculée au moyen de la formule de Putman-Munk-Taylor, formule qui a été ensuite remplacée par une équation de transport de sédiments du type de Du-Buoys-Straub. Le taux de cheminement a ainsi été calculé. Le résultat obtenu donne un taux de cheminement brut de 916.000 yd^3/an, c'est-à-dire une meilleure approximation du volume de dragage effectif que dans le cas de la formule C.E.R.C. Lorsque la relation donnée par Eagleson est utilisée pour calculer les courants induits par les lames, le taux de cheminement estimé est de l'ordre de 893.000 yd^3/an, soit une approximation du volume effectif meilleure que dans les deux cas précédents.

Les calculs faisant appel à l'énergie des lames ont encore montré que, dans le cas qui précède, le taux de cheminement est donné par

$$Q = 4,35\ (E_a)^{1,33}$$

où Q = cheminement littoral côtier en yd^3/jour

E_a = énergie de lames le long des côtes en mio ft^{lb}/ft de plage.

Dans les cas de faible énergie (<30 mio ft^{lb}/ft/jour), la relation donne un résultat proche de celui obtenu par Fairchild pour la côte de l'Atlantique nord, à savoir:

$$Q = 0,55\ (E_a)^{1,9}$$

Il est donc proposé que l'A.I.P.C.N. entame une étude des données disponibles dans les différents ports du monde et de l'applicabilité de la relation particulière pour chaque région, ce qui revêtirait un très grand intérêt pour l'ingénieur portuaire. Ceci contribuerait ainsi à une meilleure compréhension des phénomènes complexes impliqués dans la mécanique du cheminement littoral.

<u>Référence</u>:

Une estimation analytique du Cheminement littoral, par G. V. GOLA, Z.S.T., et T. N. PAR 14ème Conférence internationale d'ingéniérie côtière, Copenhague, 1974, Rapport no 3.4.1.

D J VAN DEN BOSSCHE (BELGIQUE)

Dans cette intervention, que j'espère brève, je voudrais rectifier un malentendu dans l'excellent rapport général en ce qui concerne la contribution belge. Dans sa synthèse, le Rapporteur Général range le programme de reconstitution des plages belges dans la catégorie des défenses côtières "dures".

Il doit bien entendu s'agir d'une interprétation erronée. En effet, l'un des principaux objets de l'étude de planification a été de déterminer si un épi "dur" est nécessaire pour protéger de manière économique la plage réalimentée "douce". En fait, le système côtier n'est pas seulement attaqué par les lames, mais aussi les courants de marées forts. Dans la planification du projet, il a fallu inclure comme système alternatif de grands épis immergés traversant le goulet de jusant appelé "Appelzak" en vue de réduire les effets des courants de marées. De la sorte, le système s'attaque directement aux causes du transport littoral.

Une étude d'évaluation économique a été réalisée en vue de définir la solution économiquement optimale entre les deux options suivantes:

1. Uniquement une plage de sable douce et sujet à entretien.

2. Une plage protégée par un épi immergé long d'environ 1 km qui aurait pour effet de réduire les besoins d'entretien de la plage aussi bien que l'épi lui-même.

Il n'a pas été possible de départager les deux possibilités en termes d'optimalité économique.

Dans ces conditions, il a été décidé de modifier la construction de l'épi et d'observer attentivement le comportement de la plage, en tenant compte de la progression régulière des travaux d'extension du port voisin de Zeebruges.

Dès lors l'alimentation de plage réalisée à Knokke-Heist (Belgique) doit être considérée comme un des plus grands projets de défense douce des côtes entrepris à ce jour. Je suis tout à fait d'accord avec le Rapporteur Général lorsqu'il dit que les deux critiques majeures que l'on peut formuler à l'égard des épis et d'autres ouvrages semblables sont leur coût élevé et, ce qui est très important aussi, leur manque de souplesse. C'est pourquoi il convient de n'entreprendre la construction d'un épi que lorsque cela est tout à fait inévitable.

En réalité, le principal résultat de l'évaluation économique réalisée dans le cas décrit a été de traduire en chiffres le fait que l'approche graduelle appliquée par nos prédécesseurs en matière de protection des côtes en général garde toute sa valeur.

A ROGAN (GRECE)

Je suis tout à fait d'accord avec lui et avec d'autres auteurs pour souligner le besoin de définir les critères de cohésion. En outre, je pense qu'il convient de souligner la complexité des interférences entre ouvrages portuaires d'une part et érosion et engraissement côtiers de l'autre.

(L'orateur montre ensuite des diapositives qui donnent une vision plus précise du cas de Kalamata).

Le port de Kalamata est situé sur la côte sud du Peloponese. Il est exposé à un fetch d'une longueur de 240 miles, ce qui entraîne de hautes lames. La première partie du brise-lames a été construite au cours du premier tiers du 20ème siècle. Après 1945, le même brise-lames a été agrandi de 250 m. Après 1946, une érosion intensive et à grande échelle est apparue à l'ouest du port. Entre 1954 et 1979, la côte a reculé de jusque 90 m vers la ville, sur une longueur de 1500 m.

Une protection côtière simpliste et empirique n'a pu faire face à l'attaque des lames. La côte située à l'est du port n'a cependant pas été affectée.

Parallèlement, le port de Kalamata, suivant la tendance vers les charges unitaires et attendant une expansion en raison de sa situation géographique, doit être étendu vers l'intérieur des terres.

Suite à la présentation du rapport de la Commission de la Chambre Technique et à la vive réaction des autorités communautaires, le Ministre des Travaux Publics a lancé, il y a quelques mois, un appel d'offres pour la conception combinée de la protection de la côte ouest et de l'acquisition du terrain nécessaire à l'expansion du port.

Le cas décrit ici confirme les conclusions formulées hier quant à la nécessité de constituer le terrain destiné à répondre aux besoins à venir des ports.

N P CAMPBELL (AFRIQUE DU SUD)

Dans trois de nos ports de la côte est, en Afrique du Sud, nous avons un cheminement littoral vers le nord dont le volume varie d'un peu moins de 500.000 m^3 par an à East London et 800.000 m^3 au port vraquier de Richards Bay. L'Inde semble rencontrer un problème très semblable sur la côte est, tandis que les Etats-Unis dévient des quantités de sable allant jusque 800.000 m^3 dans certains de leurs ports.

Néanmoins, en raison de la mer forte et des conditions de houle prévalant le long de la côte sud-africaine, des systèmes de déviation par pompage fixes ou stationnaires se sont révélés inefficaces, ce qui nous a forcés à entretenir au moyen de dragues suceuses maritimes un piège à sable du côté amont des brise-lames sud des ports concernés.

Etant donné que le transport de sable s'effectue dans la zone de ressac, il est nécessaire de construire le piège à sable à une distance de 50 du pied de la carapace du brise-lames. Comme les conditions de houle sont souvent normales au brise-lames, des raisons de sécurité nous empêchent de passer avec nos dragues traînantes le long du brise-lames près des blocs de carapace. C'est pourquoi nous avons mis au point une drague combinée tuyau d'aspiration avant/drague traînante latérale d'une capacité de 4000 t de chaland.

Pour réaliser le piège à sable, les dragues jettent deux ancres arrière sur cables de 4 1/2" et se dirigeant vers le piège à sable à angle droit par rapport au brise-lames, en utilisant les treuils des ancres arrière pour contre-balancer l'inclinaison avant. A environ 150 ft du brise-lames, les ancres avant sont jetées, le bateau est retiré légèrement pour améliorer l'angle de l'ancre maîtresse et le tuyau aspirateur de proue de 4 1/2" est descendu à travers une ouverture dans la partie avant du bateau. Ce tuyau peut atteindre une profondeur de 72 ft sous le niveau de l'eau. Si les conditions atmosphériques sont bonnes, une charge de 4000 t peut être obtenue en une demi-heure, mais elle doit être pompée à terre du côté aval de l'entrée du port au cours d'une opération distincte réalisée à partir d'un accostage situé dans le port.

Pour vous donner une idée des conditions atmosphériques dans lesquelles il faut travailler, je dirai simplement que le dragage du piège à sable ne peut s'effectuer que pendant 80 à 120 jours par an. Chaque fois que le temps le permet, les opérations de dragage reprennent donc immédiatement, étant donné qu'on ne sait jamais quand les travaux pourront se poursuivre. Des études modélisées réalisées au Port de Durban ont montré que si on permettait le remplissage du piège à sable et que survenaient des conditions de mer forte avec houle SE, les profondeurs du chenal d'entrée seraient réduites de — 42 ft à environ — 19 ft en 5 1/2 jours seulement.

Lorsque le temps empêche le dragage du piège à sable, les dragues travaillent dans les chenaux et les bassins d'évitement protégés des ports concernés.

A l'heure actuelle, bien qu'il m'ait été indiqué par les chantiers navals responsables de nos nouveaux bâtiments que l'Afrique du Sud devait moderniser sa flotte de dragueurs en achetant des dragues combinées traînantes/tuyau standard, je pense que nos dragues à tuyau avant sont, sur la foi d'une longue expérience remontant aux environs de 1890 aussi bien que d'essais sur modèles, les seuls bateaux capables de maintenir Richards Bay, Durban et East London ouverts aux routes maritimes internationales ainsi qu'aux transporteurs vraquiers de 150.000 tpm et aux bateaux porte-conteneurs de la 3ème génération qui assurent notre trafic.

Bien que nos 5 dragues suceuses (dont l'une sera lancée en août prochain) soient des bateaux diesel électriques et diesel très sophistiqués, elles sont à ma connaissance les seules de ce type qui sont en service. Même si certains les considèrent comme étant dépassés, je me sens en mesure de recommander leur utilisation à tout qui est confronté à un problème semblable au nôtre.

F ENRIQUES (ESPAGNE)

Eu égard au point (1) des recommandations du Rapporteur Général et aux commentaires de celui-ci, nous souhaitons souligner les éléments suivants:

Lorsque l'ingénieur maritime conçoit un ouvrage côtier, il doit tenir compte du fait qu'en raison du principe d'action-réaction, la nature y réagira parfois immédiatement et souvent de manière indésirable et surprenante.

C'est pourquoi l'idée du Rapporteur Général de constituer une banque de données (dont nous avons présenté la méthodologie espagnole dans notre rapport) nous semble excellente. Cette banque couvre deux aspects:

- Tout d'abord, le domaine des données disponibles sur l'environnement qui peuvent être recueillies par étude directe de l'entité physiographique.

- Ensuite, le domaine des données qui deviennent disponibles après la construction et la mise en service de l'ouvrage conçu à partir du premier ensemble de données envisagé ici. Par exemple, la construction d'un barrage sur une voie d'eau peut entraîner l'apport de matériaux solides sur le littoral. Lorsque ceci se produit, c'est le moment pour l'ingénieur de prendre les mesures correctrices.

Il serait utile, si possible dès le départ, d'avoir accès à toutes les données, ce qui demande une coordination technique difficile à réaliser entre les organes techniques et politiques impliqués de diverses manières dans l'aménagement et la gestion du littoral.

Nous soulignons qu'il est crucial de définir une méthodologie qui, selon nous, pourrait être d'application au niveau international, mais selon des modalités (comme c'est le cas des modèles mathématiques) tenant compte des caractéristiques spécifiques à chaque localisation.

Nous serons heureux de voir comment le problème sur lequel nous attirons votre attention sera pris en considération dans ses conclusions.

P de CANDT (BELGIQUE)

En complément au rapport intitulé "La Protection des plages dans le cadre de l'Extension du Port de Zeebruges — Belgique", je voudrais apporter quelques autres résultats d'études et proposer une première évaluation des programmes d'observation de la zone située à l'est du nouvel avant-port de Zeebruges, Belgique, actuellement en cours de construction.

L'objectif de l'étude était de prévoir les conséquences probables des travaux d'extension du port sur la région côtière située à l'est du port après engraissement des plages.

La plage a été reconstituée par remblai hydraulique d'un total de 8,5 millions m^3 de sable puisé à 20 km au large. On peut s'attendre en effet à ce que la construction d'un épi sous-marin provoque une érosion de l'ensemble du système de protection de la côte située à l'est du port. Ce n'est pas le cas, puisque nous n'avons parlé que d'érosion locale et n'avons pas mentionné de sédimentation locale entraînée par le transport des marées à proximité de l'épi.

Malgré tout, je voudrais rappeler aux participants que l'épi envisagé est un épi sous-marin, situé sous le niveau des basses eaux, de manière à ne pas empêcher le transport littoral le long de la côte. Dans notre cas, la construction d'un épi avait pour but de réduire les courants de navires et donc les taux de transport dû aux marées dans la tranchée située en face de la plage.

Les autorités belges ne sont pas intéressées par le gain de sable dans l'ensemble du système côtier, mais bien par les localisation de l'érosion des marées et donc par les zones de régression des plages résultant de l'instabilité de celles-ci.

La Figure 1 (L'orateur montre quelques diapositives) page 182 montre les taux de transport littoral le long de la côte provoqué par les courants de marée dans la tranchée dite "Appelzak" face à la plage.

Les calculs indiquent que dans le cas de la seule extension portuaire, il faut s'attendre à une érosion sur pratiquement la totalité de la zone côtière concernée, soit 8 km.

Si l'extension du port est assortie de la construction d'un épi, au contraire, l'érosion ne devrait se produire que sur une étendue de 4 km de côte.

Néanmoins, la pente de l'érosion est deux fois plus importante que dans le cas de l'extension portuaire seule et l'érosion est concentrée dans la section la plus fréquentée de la plage.

Les calculs conduisent à la conclusion que la construction d'un épi ne doit pas être recommandée avant que de plus amples observations et études puissent dessiner d'autres possibilités.

En raison du caractère hautement spéculatif, bien connu, des calculs de transport de sédiments, même après calibration détaillée des formules de calcul du transport, un programme précis d'observation a été établi en vue de comparer les tendances observées et calculées.

Nous voulions tout d'abord un contrôle de la prévision de vitesse des marées par modèle physique des marées, méthode retenue comme étant la plus fiable en vue de la comparaison avec le modèle mathématique des marées et le modèle physique statique.

Au cours des travaux d'extension du port, on procède à des observations de la vitesse des marées, observations qui sont ensuite comparées aux vitesses calculées par le modèle pour la même phase de construction.

La Figure 2 (page 183) donne un exemple de la correspondance relativement bonne qui est obtenue entre les résultats du modèle et ceux de l'observation sur le terrain pour ce qui concerne à la fois la force des courants et leur direction.

Deuxièmement, une observation aérienne de la plage est réalisée au moyen de techniques de restitution photogrammétriques. Ces méthodes nous permettent de calculer l'érosion ou la sédimentation des plages au-dessus du niveau de basses eaux pour toute section de plage au même moment.

La Figure 3 (page 184) indique la régression de la plage par rapport à la situation suivant immédiatement la reconstitution de celle-ci. Elle révèle des taux d'érosion substantielle sur la totalité de la ligne côtière. Les taux d'érosion relevés immédiatement à l'est du port sont dus spécifiquement aux travaux d'extension de celui-ci (extraction, remblais provisoires, etc.) et doivent donc être exclus de notre examen.

La Figure 3 (page 184) illustre l'évolution de la plage en fonction du temps pour plusieurs sections de plage. Les taux d'érosion sont les plus marqués dans les sections de plage proches de Knokke-Zoute. Ces phénomènes correspondent aux localisations d'érosion calculées dans le cas de la seule extension du port, bien que celles-ci ne soient que partiellement réalisées. En fait, l'érosion de la plage au-dessus du niveau de basses eaux porte sur un volume de 400.000 m^3 de sable depuis la fin des travaux de réengraissement de la plage.

Cependant, la plus grande partie de cette érosion est due à l'instabilité de la plage et contribue au remplissage de la tranchée de l'Appelzak, qui constituait auparavant la cause majeure de la régression de la plage.

La Figure 4 (page 185) représente la tranchée à trois périodes différentes:

1. la première situation date de 1977, avant les travaux d'extension du port et de reconstitution de la plage. On voit la proximité de la tranchée par rapport à la plage;

2. la deuxième situation est celle de 1979, après une reconstitution de la plage portant sur un volume d'environ 8,5 millions de m^3 de sable;

3. enfin, on voit la situation un an après, au terme d'une extension encore minime du port.

Comme vous le constatez, la tranchée s'est déplacée vers l'est en raison de l'instabilité de la plage, ce qui a contribué à remplir partiellement la tranchée au moyen de matériaux provenant de la plage. Ce phénomène était prévu et même voulu en tant que système de protection douce des côtes.

Permettez-moi, en conclusion, d'indiquer qu'il ne s'est passé qu'un an et demi entre la reconstitution de la plage et le relevé des mesures; il s'agit bien évidemment d'une pétiode trop courte pour dégager des tendances côtières précises.

Les observations continuent de s'effectuer à intervalles réguliers afin de donner une compréhension à long terme de la dynamique des plages et des côtes. Elles doivent permettre de vérifier les calculs et de fournir ainsi aux autorités belges la possibilité de prendre en temps voulu les mesures nécessaires à une protection satisfaisante de la côte suite aux travaux d'extension du port.

J'espère être en mesure de vous faire part des résultats définitifs de nos études et de nos observations lors du prochain Congrès de l'A.I.P.C.N.

J L DELORME (FRANCE)

La présente intervention vise à souligner certains aspects de l'expérience disponible en France en matière de défense des côtes liée à des travaux portuaires, puis, pour terminer, à exprimer deux réflexions inspirées par le Rapport Général de M. HOLMES.

1. En premier lieu, il faut rappeler que les côtes françaises présentent un linéaire important (près de 4.000 km) et une grande variété, mais que la plus grande partie est en voie d'érosion, et parfois de forte érosion. Par exemple, sur la côte sableuse d'Aquitaine, des reculs de plage de plus de 10 m par an ne sont pas rares.

   Dans ce cadre, l'utilisation de plus en plus intensive du littoral a conduit, autour de 1975, à recenser l'ensemble de ces phénomènes de recul des côtes. Ce catalogue est actuellement complété par des monographies plus détaillées, qui définissent en quelque sorte un état de référence.

2. Venant perturber cette situation, les travaux portuaires interfèrent avec le régime sédimentaire côtier. Plus d'une douzaine d'exemples sont cités dans le rapport français, tirés de projets récents dont la plupart sont réalisés ou en cours; ils intéressent aussi bien de petits ports de plaisance que de grands ports de commerce, et même qu'une fosse draguée au large pour emprunts de matériaux; ce dernier cas, étudié sur modèle réduit sédimentologique, fait d'ailleurs ressortir que cette fosse se comble principalement par érosion côté terre sous l'action des houles.

   Quoiqu'il en soit, l'interaction du port et du littoral est, en France, systématiquement étudié en même temps que le port lui-même; les travaux ne peuvent d'ailleurs pas être lancés avant que la compatibilité du port avec les autres usages du littoral ai été vérifiée explicitement.

3. Si l'érosion est sévère, les dispositions de défense du littoral sont complexes. Un exemple est fourni par le port de Bayonne, situé au bord de l'Atlantique et exposé aux grandes houles du large (amplitude cinquantenaire de l'ordre de 12 m) = la plage adjacente au Sud, de 4,5 km de long, était soumise à des transports parallèles au rivage, alternatifs et équilibrés de 500.000 m^3 par an, et à une érosion de plus de 10 m par an.

   Le dispositif mis en place pour protéger l'entrée du port et ralentir l'érosion du rivage est très complet:

   - Deux digues portuaires sensiblement perpendiculaires au rivage, respectivement de 400 m et 900 m de long;

   - Sept épis droits, dont un susceptible d'être transformé en brise-lames; ces épis sont combinés avec des apports terrestres de sables grossiers;

   - Déversement des produits de dragage, par voie maritime devant la plage, dans les petits fonds (4 à 7 m sous les plus basses mers). Les résultats en sont prometteurs, mais restent à confirmer avec plus de recul. Cette méthode d'engraissement de la plage constitue une alternative aux dispositions de refoulement à terre présentées par plusieurs rapports.

   Dans le cas où le déficit d'alimentation en sédiments est sévère, l'exemple de Bayonne fait apparaître aussi qu'il est insuffisant de prévoir des épis ou brise-lames ne jouant que partiellement, soit une partie du temps, en raison de la marée, soit sur une partie des transports de sédiments, comme dans le cas d'ouvrages de haut de plage.

4. Il convient enfin de faire part de deux réflexions inspirées par le Rapport Général que M. HOLMES a présenté:

- la première consiste à souligner avec lui l'intérêt de mesurer précisément la direction des houles, en période de tempête, au large, et donc loin d'observateurs terrestre. Ce paramètre, difficile à cerner, apparaît en effet comme tout à fait indispensable, même si la rose des vents locale ne fournit pas toujours la réponse.

- la seconde vise le déplacement net de sédiments discuté par le Rapport Général: ce déplacement est la résultante de transports alternatifs, et ne constitue pas une donnée suffisante, même si elle est plus facilement accessible. L'exemple de Bayonne est manifeste à ce sujet, puisque le déplacement net y est nul, et pourtant que les déplacements parallèles au rivage expliquent une grande partie des phénomènes. Il est donc nécessaire de tenir compte des allées et retours des sédiments, sauf à se tromper très gravement.

Pour terminer, on peut indiquer qu'une bonne connaissance du site restera toujours essentielle, du fait de la difficulté de trier les données pertinentes décrivant des phénomènes complexes.

R TENAUD (FRANCE)

Je voudrais attirer l'attention sur un problème d'utilisation des épis pour la défense des côtes.

Lorsque le transit littoral est inconstant et a un sens bien défini, on sait que les épis constituent un moyen de défense très utilisé et en général très efficace.

Quand le transit littoral, tout en étant appréciable, n'a pas de résultante bien définie, on pense souvent que les épis ne sont pas utiles. Le 3e rapport de la Commission des Lames ne cite pas les épis comme moyen de défense dans ce cas.

Le transit littoral est essentiellement provoqué par la houle, dont la direction varie à l'intérieur d'un large secteur, même s'il y a une direction prédominante.

Quand on dit que la résultante d'un transit littoral est nulle, il s'agit d'une moyenne évaluée pour de nombreuses années.

Or il peut y avoir pendant une année ou même plus, des séries de tempêtes donnant un transit littoral dans le même sens.

A ce moment, il peut avoir des volumes très importants de matériaux déplacés et des érosions du rivage.

Des épis ne sont donc pas inutiles dans un tel cas.

Une autre observation concerne les dimensions des épis. Nous pensons que les épis doivent être le moins agressif possible. Des épis bas et plongeant sont moins attaqués et plus économiques.

Des essais faits sur modèle réduit, dans le cas de Bayonne, exposé par M. DELORME, ont montré que de tels épis étaient même plus efficaces. Nous pensons que l'épi le plus efficace est celui qui ne se voit plus.

D H SWART (AFRIQUE DU SUD)

A la page 942 du Rapport des Etats-Unis, on lit qu'une installation de dragage fixe est utilisée à Durban. Ceci n'a été le cas que pendant une période très brève il y a quelque 30 ans et l'expérience a été interrompue parce que les matériaux ne s'enlevaient pas à l'endroit de la jetée situé au pied du brise-lames sud.

Méthodes de mesure de direction des lames utilisées en Afrique du Sud:

- indicateur de vitesse orbitale DOSO
- indicateur de pente ou téléscope gradué
- tube-image radar
- photographies aériennes prises à intervalles réguliers.

Modifications topographiques à proximité des ouvrages portuaires

On dispose de plusieurs instruments de prévision qui vont du plus simple au plus complexe:

- modèles empiriques de transport parallèle aux côtes et de transport terre-mer
- modèles de protection des côtes, tels que décrits dans les rapports britannique, néerlandais et sud-africain
- modèles mathématiques
- modèles physiques
- combinaisons des méthodes qui précèdent.

Il faut déterminer avec soin le niveau de prévision exigé par chaque situation. Le degré de complexité varie souvent en fonction inverse de la dimension de l'ouvrage. La précision de toutes les méthodes mentionnées ci-dessus pourrait être sensiblement accrue par des mesures contrôlées sur le terrain (voir, par exemple, les rapports belge et français, ainsi que le programme NSTS des Etats-Unis et les programmes d'observation des côtes allemand et polonais). Le recours simultané à plusieurs techniques, même de la même catégorie, est recommandé avant que toute décision soit prise.

Voici quelques considérations relatives au remblayage des plages:

- Aucun rapport ne mentionne spécifiquement la "conception du remblayage des plages". Voir, cependant, p. 910. Les pertes supplémentaires dues au remblayage des plages sont pour Richards Bay de 5% du cheminement net, mais pour Durban de non moins de 40%.
- Les matériaux déviés devraient être placés là où les lames et les courants ont érodé le sable; ceci n'est pas réalisable concrètement dans la plupart des cas. Les caractéristiques des matériaux déviés, par rapport à celles du matériau originel, sont également importantes. La conception de la mise en place du matériau de remblayage doit retenir toute l'attention. Voir, par exemple le rapport des Etats-Unis.
- Les pertes seront en fait cependant toujours supérieures à ce qu'elles auraient été si le

matériau correct avait été mis en place de manière idéale. Le complément de remblayage nécessaire peut être prévu/estimé par exemple par

KRUMBEIN/JAMES JAMES DEAN	)))	(n'utilisent que les caractéristiques des sédiments et négligent la géométrie du remblayage).
SWART (basé sur Réf. 13, p. 916).	)	(utilise les caractéristiques des sédiments et la géométrie du remblayage)

Au sujet des conclusions du Rapporteur Général, je tiens à souligner qu'il ne faut pas perdre de vue le travail effectué aux USA pour leurs manuels de protection des côtes (SPM).

D DREYFOUS DUCAS (FRANCE)

4 remarques pour essayer de réduire le volume des refoulements nécessaires pour équilibrer les érosions:

1. On semble oublier la variation permanente de la pente d'équilibre des plages en fonction des caractéristiques de la houle. Ce basculement se fait à partir du bas de l'estran au voisinage de la côte 0. Les plages sont en général plus plates en hiver avec un dégraissement important du haut de l'estran. La pente se rétablit progressivement avec les petites houles du printemps et de l'été.

2. Les épis peuvent freiner ou ralentir les transports latéraux, mais ils ne peuvent pas corriger les effets de l'érosion "sous le vent" des jetées portuaires. Seuls des ouvrages longitudinaux de bas d'estran, continus ou partiels, permettent de piéger le sable (Italie, Pointe de Grave).

3. Les ouvrages de défense, quels qu'ils soient, doivent être conçus de façon à ne pas faire fuir le sable:

- pentes trop fortes du parement amont qui renvoient une fraction importante de la houle incidente et provoquent des clapotis interdisant le dépôt du sable,
- pentes trop lisses, ne freinant pas l'eau de la lame de retour et provoquant l'érosion des pieds des ouvrages.

4. Il n'est rapporté aucun essai de jetées d'entrée des ports à claire voie au voisinage des estrans permettant le transport latéral du sable et la réduction de l'érosion "sous le vent".

En résumé, il faut savoir observer la nature et les phénomènes, et les aider plutôt que les combattre.

E R HEIBERG (USA)

Un aspect de la protection des ports (et aussi des plages) qui pose des problèmes majeurs aux Etats-Unis est d'obtenir l'appui du public ou de la collectivité concernée pour réaliser une amélioration et parfois même pour assurer un entretien. Peut-être êtes-vous nombreux à partager mon sentiment qu'il s'agit ici d'un art ... et non pas encore d'une science bien comprise. Nous sommes encore incapables de prévoir avec une suffisante précision l'impact d'un nouvel ouvrage. Nous sommes convaincus que le solutions "dures" aussi bien que "douces" doivent être étudiées et comparées en vue de trouver la meilleure solution du double point de vue des coûts et de l'environnement. Il s'agit souvent d'ailleurs d'une solution mixte (jetée avec déviation), qui s'oppose au dragage pur et simple que les défenseurs de l'environnement s'efforcent de nous imposer. Je voudrais assurer le Professeur Holmes que nous n'avons recours de notre propre chef à la déviation que lorsqu'il s'agit de la solution la plus économique ou qu'elle est la seule disponible. Pire encore, nous sommes parfois contraints à une "absence de solution" jugée préférable par ceux qui souhaitent que les hommes n'interviennent pas dans les ports et sur les plages.

Il me semble que la possibilité d'améliorer cette situation passe par l'effort international suggéré dans les conclusions. Aux Etats-Unis, l'ingénieur continue d'être soumis à de fortes pressions de la part des défenseurs de l'environnement et des fonctionnaires publics qui hésitent à réaliser les travaux nécessaires. La tâche du Army Corps of Engineers sera rendue plus aisée si nous pouvons faire référence à des conclusions convergentes dans le cadre de l'A.I.P.C.N. ou d'une autre organisation internationale jouissant du même prestige. Les commentaires entendus cet après-midi me font penser que de nombreux autres membres sont d'accord avec moi.

Si le principe de cette recommandation est accepté, les Etats-Unis collaboreront à sa réalisation.

C MOUTZOURIS (GREECE)

Je voudrais brièvement faire une remarque sur le Rapport Général.

Du point de vue de la mécanique des lames, il est difficile de définir non seulement l'angle d'approche en eau profonde, mais aussi l'angle de la barre ϕ_b.

Les théories de la réfraction ne sont pas applicables dans la zone de déferlement particulièrement en présence de topographies complexes.

W A PRICE (GB)

Je souhaite faire quelques commentaires sur la manière dont la recherche pourrait contribuer à résoudre l'un des problèmes associés à la conception et la construction des ports côtiers.

L'eau profonde est de plus en plus demandée et c'est bien pourquoi le port côtier est en train de l'emporter sur le port en estuaire dans de nombreuses régions du monde. Ce glissement signifie que nous passons d'un environnement où la sédimentation dans les chenaux dragués est tempérée par les flux de marées, les variations de salinité et autres éléments semblables à une situation où nous sommes en présence de lames et de courants. Le rapport s'est efforcé de montrer comment le transport de sédiments peut être renforcé par l'action des lames (voir Tableau 2, page 939). Par exemple, le taux de transport de sédiment sera égal à 14 fois sa valeur en courant stable, pour une lame de 2 m de hauteur et de 8 secondes de période dans 10 mètres d'eau et à 60 fois pour une hauteur de lame double, soit 4 m. Si on suppose que le chenal dragué retient la majeure partie de ce sédiment en mouvement, ce qui n'est pas irraisonnable en chenal profond, les conséquences sont évidentes. Les profondeurs draguées, en cas de tempête, peuvent disparaître du jour au lendemain, ainsi que j'ai pu moi-même le constater. Les conséquences pour les caractéristiques des opérations de dragage sont tout aussi violentes. Dans le cadre protégé d'un estuaire, les taux de sédimentation seront variables mais, dans la plupart des cas, ces variations seront minimes de sorte que la capacité de dragage pourra y être assortie. La présence de lames modifie complètement la situation. Il faudra à présent concevoir les dragues de façon à ce qu'elles puissent venir à bout des bancs de sédimentation intensive se formant en cas de tempête. En général, ceci implique des dragues beaucoup plus grandes pour le même taux annuel de dragage.

Il est impératif de pouvoir disposer d'estimations plus précises des taux de sédimentation lorsqu'un port côtier est en voie d'être planifié. Soit dit entre parenthèses, la viabilité du point de vue économique d'un port côtier en eau profonde peut, dans une grande mesure, dépendre du volume des dragages qu'il nécessite. C'est pourquoi, je suggère qu'une des tâches les plus importantes qui s'offrent aux chercheurs est de déterminer l'impact des lames sur le transport de sédiments.

Je voudrais également émettre de sérieux doutes sur l'opportunité de la politique de dragage adoptée par de nombreux ports en estuaire. La philosophie qui consiste à emmener les matériaux de dragage à immerger vers un endroit duquel il faut beaucoup de temps pour revenir est souvent très peu économique et peut dans de nombreux cas entraîner des conséquences négatives pour l'environnement. C'est également vrai dans le cas d'un port côtier. Ces matériaux devraient être utilisés pour alimenter des plages. Même si une proportion importante de ceux-ci retourne vers le chantier de dragage, il pourrait demeurer économique de draguer et de rejeter à proximité. Ce qui compte, c'est le coût global de l'opération. Il faut éviter les longs transports vers les zones d'immersion.

Une erreur s'est glissée à l'impression dans l'équation de la page 938 de notre rapport. En voici la formulation exacte:

$$S_{w.c.} = (S_c) \quad \frac{U-U_c}{U_c}^{\;2}$$

Avant de finir, je tiens encore à dire que je suis, dans l'ensemble, d'accord avec le rapport général du Professeur Holmes.

CONCLUSIONS

1. Les rapports relatifs au Sujet 5, la discussion et les appréciations du Rapporteur Général établissent clairement le besoin, au plan international, d'un document de référence rassemblant, à l'intention des projeteurs, l'expérience disponible sur le sujet. Ce document devrait comporter les meilleurs avis disponibles dans trois domaines:

   a) Informations et données techniques nécessaires;

   b) prévision des mouvements sédimentaires;

   c) dispositifs correcteurs.

2. Le besoin d'une collaboration internationale plus étroite entre chercheurs et ingénieurs concernés par les problèmes de dynamique côtière, a été également mis en évidence.

3. Le besoin s'impose d'une expérience internationale au cours de laquelle une côte vierge exposée pourrait être équipée d'instruments, et faire l'objet de mesures afin d'améliorer la compréhension des relations entre l'hydrodynamique et les transports de sédiments. Il serait également intéressant que ce site ait fait l'objet d'un projet d'ouvrage, tel qu'une jetée ou un brise-lames de façon à formuler des prévisions et à les contrôler. Une telle expérience nécessitera un appui gouvernemental, et même probablement intergouvernemental. Les résultats qu'on peut en attendre sont si importants qu'un tel appui serait justifié de façon certaine.

4. La CTPI et le CTPII devraient examiner quelle contribution l'A.I.P.C.N. peut apporter pour répondre à ces besoins, en collaboration avec d'autres organismes internationaux, tels que l'Association Internationale de Recherches Hydrauliques (A.I.R.H.) et le Conseil de Recherches du Génie Civil Côtier (Coastal Engineering).

AUTHOR INDEX

Pages in this Index may be located as follows:

I/100 INLAND WATERWAYS AND PORTS (5 volumes) page 100

II/100 MARITIME PORTS AND SEAWAYS (5 volumes) page 100

SUBJECT INDEX

The following is a Subject Index for the entire 11-volume set. Pages may be located as follows:

I/100	INLAND WATERWAYS AND PORTS (5 volumes) page 100
II/100	MARITIME PORTS AND SEAWAYS (5 volumes) page 100
S100	The present volume page 100

Printed in Dunstable, United Kingdom

91342995R00159